W9-ANG-053

Dictionary of Literary Biography • Volume Thirty-three

Afro-American Fiction Writers
After 1955

Dictionary of Literary Biography • Volume Thirty-three

Afro-American Fiction Writers After 1955

Edited by
Thadious M. Davis and Trudier Harris
University of North Carolina at Chapel Hill

A Bruccoli Clark Book
Gale Research Company • Book Tower • Detroit, Michigan 48226

Munster High School
Media Center
8808 Columbia Ave.
Munster, Indiana 46321

REF
809
DICT

Advisory Board for
DICTIONARY OF LITERARY BIOGRAPHY

Louis S. Auchincloss
John Baker
D. Philip Baker
A. Walton Litz, Jr.
Peter S. Prescott
Lola L. Szladits
William Targ

Matthew J. Bruccoli and Richard Layman, *Editorial Directors*
C. E. Frazer Clark, Jr., *Managing Editor*

Manufactured by Edwards Brothers, Inc.
Ann Arbor, Michigan
Printed in the United States of America

10 9 8 7 6 5 4 3

Copyright © 1984
GALE RESEARCH COMPANY

Library of Congress Cataloging in Publication Data
Main entry under title:

Afro-American fiction writers after 1955.

(Dictionary of literary biography; v. 33)
"A Bruccoli Clark book."
Includes index.
1. American fiction—Afro-American authors—History
and criticism. 2. American fiction—20th century—History
and criticism. 3. Afro-American novelists—Biography—
Dictionaries. 4. Novelists, American—20th century
—Biography—Dictionaries. 5. American fiction—Afro-
American authors—Bio-bibliography. 6. American
fiction—20th century—Bio-bibliography. I. Davis,
Thadious M., 1944- . II. Harris, Trudier. III. Series.
PS153.N5A34   1984   813'.54'09896073   84-18724
ISBN 0-8103-1711-7

$/60. 00

For
Unareed Harris

For
Darwin T. Turner

Contents

Plan of the Series

... Almost the most prodigious asset of a country, and perhaps its most precious possession, is its native literary product—when that product is fine and noble and enduring.

Mark Twain*

The advisory board, the editors, and the publisher of the *Dictionary of Literary Biography* are joined in endorsing Mark Twain's declaration. The literature of a nation provides an inexhaustible resource of permanent worth. It is our expectation that this endeavor will make literature and its creators better understood and more accessible to students and the literate public, while satisfying the standards of teachers and scholars.

To meet these requirements, *literary biography* has been construed in terms of the author's achievement. The most important thing about a writer is his writing. Accordingly, the entries in *DLB* are career biographies, tracing the development of the author's canon and the evolution of his reputation.

The publication plan for *DLB* resulted from two years of preparation. The project was proposed to Bruccoli Clark by Frederick G. Ruffner, president of the Gale Research Company, in November 1975. After specimen entries were prepared and typeset, an advisory board was formed to refine the entry format and develop the series rationale. In meetings held during 1976, the publisher, series editors, and advisory board approved the scheme for a comprehensive biographical dictionary of persons who contributed to North American literature. Editorial work on the first volume began in January 1977, and it was published in 1978.

In order to make *DLB* more than a reference tool and to compile volumes that individually have claim to status as literary history, it was decided to organize volumes by topic or period or genre. Each of these freestanding volumes provides a biographical-bibliographical guide and overview for a particular area of literature. We are convinced that this organization—as opposed to a single alphabet method—constitutes a valuable innovation in the presentation of reference material. The volume plan necessarily requires many decisions for the

placement and treatment of authors who might properly be included in two or three volumes. In some instances a major figure will be included in separate volumes, but with different entries emphasizing the aspect of his career appropriate to each volume. Ernest Hemingway, for example, is represented in *American Writers in Paris, 1920-1939* by an entry focusing on his expatriate apprenticeship; he is also in *American Novelists, 1910-1945* with an entry surveying his entire career. Each volume includes a cumulative index of subject authors. The final *DLB* volume will be a comprehensive index to the entire series.

With volume ten in 1982 it was decided to enlarge the scope of *DLB* beyond the literature of the United States. By the end of 1983 twelve volumes treating British literature had been published, and volumes for Commonwealth and Modern European literature were in progress. The series has been further augmented by the *DLB Yearbooks* (since 1981) which update published entries and add new entries to keep the *DLB* current with contemporary activity. There have also been occasional *DLB Documentary Series* volumes which provide biographical and critical background source materials for figures whose work is judged to have particular interest for students. One of these companion volumes is entirely devoted to Tennessee Williams.

The purpose of *DLB* is not only to provide reliable information in a convenient format but also to place the figures in the larger perspective of literary history and to offer appraisals of their accomplishments by qualified scholars.

We define literature as the *intellectual commerce of a nation*: not merely as belles lettres, but as that ample and complex process by which ideas are generated, shaped, and transmitted. *DLB* entries are not limited to "creative writers" but extend to other figures who in this time and in this way influenced the mind of a people. Thus the series encompasses historians, journalists, publishers, and screenwriters. By this means readers of *DLB* may be aided to perceive literature not as cult scripture in the keeping of cultural high priests, but as at the center of a nation's life.

DLB includes the major writers appropriate to each volume and those standing in the ranks immediately behind them. Scholarly and critical counsel has been sought in deciding which minor figures to include and how full their entries should be.

*From an unpublished section of Mark Twain's autobiography, copyright © by the Mark Twain Company.

Wherever possible, useful references will be made to figures who do not warrant separate entries.

Each *DLB* volume has a volume editor responsible for planning the volume, selecting the figures for inclusion, and assigning the entries. Volume editors are also responsible for preparing, where appropriate, appendices surveying the major periodicals and literary and intellectual movements for their volumes, as well as lists of further readings. Work on the series as a whole is coordinated at the Bruccoli Clark editorial center in Columbia, South Carolina, where the editorial staff is responsible for the accuracy of the published volumes.

One feature that distinguishes *DLB* is the illustration policy—its concern with the iconography of literature. Just as an author is influenced by his surroundings, so is the reader's understanding of the author enhanced by a knowledge of his environment. Therefore *DLB* volumes include not only drawings, paintings, and photographs of authors, often depicting them at various stages in their careers, but also illustrations of their families and places where they lived. Title pages are regularly reproduced in facsimile along with dust jackets for modern authors. The dust jackets are a special feature of *DLB* because they often document better than anything else the way in which an author's work was launched in its own time. Specimens of the writers' manuscripts are included when feasible.

A supplement to *DLB*—tentatively titled *A Guide, Chronology, and Glossary for American Literature*—will outline the history of literature in North America and trace the influences that shaped it. This volume will provide a framework for the study of American literature by means of chronological tables, literary affiliation charts, glossarial entries, and concise surveys of the major movements. It has been planned to stand on its own as a vade mecum, providing a ready-reference guide to the study of American literature as well as a companion to the *DLB* volumes for American literature.

Samuel Johnson rightly decreed that "The chief glory of every people arises from its authors." The purpose of the *Dictionary of Literary Biography* is to compile literary history in the surest way available to us—by accurate and comprehensive treatment of the lives and work of those who contributed to it.

The *DLB* Advisory Board

Foreword

The mid-1950s brought changes not only to the political and social worlds of Afro-Americans in the United States but to their literary world as well. While black poets and dramatists carried immediate issues into the 1960s, black novelists carried the more introspective aspects of the times. The writers grouped in this volume reflect the trends, hopes, political aspirations, and cultural affirmations of those writers who became identified with the vocal proponents of the black aesthetic as well as those who pursued their art in quieter, less nationalistic, but equally creative ways.

From the obscurity of the 1940s, when voices such as those of Richard Wright, Chester Himes, and Ann Petry were among the few to be heard, the early 1950s gave rise to voices such as James Baldwin's and William Demby's and, through the fervor of the early days of the civil rights movement, anticipated the voices of writers such as John Oliver Killens and William Melvin Kelley in the 1960s, Ernest Gaines and Toni Morrison in the 1970s, and Leon Forrest and John Edgar Wideman in the 1980s.

The nationalistic fervor of the 1960s perhaps showed itself in less dramatic ways in the fiction than in other genres. We could look at poems by Nikki Giovanni and Haki Mahabuti (Don L. Lee) and see the typographical desire to make black poetry different in its self-imposed nationbuilding objective. While some of the writers, such as Clarence Major and Carlene Hatcher Polite, are conscious experimenters with form, many others, such as Kristin Hunter and Charles Wright, are more concerned with experimentation in approaches to their subjects. While Charles R. Johnson could produce a novel in 1982 based on the tradition of the slave narrative, and Alice Walker could produce an epistolary novel in the same year, their experiments reflect a trend in the personal pursuit of artistic achievement rather than any requirements imposed by a social or political movement.

The decade of the 1970s reflects many changes of direction in terms of style. The folk speech and culturally saturated novels of Ernest Gaines and Ellease Southerland illustrate one trend, while the conscious return to specific elements of the folk tradition, urban or rural, shown in the novels of Toni Morrison and John Edgar Wideman, illustrates another. History, both personal and communal, is also important to these writers, and it takes forms as wide-ranging as those reflected in the novels of David Bradley, Barbara Chase-Riboud, and Ishmael Reed. In contrast to their predecessors, who frequently placed more emphasis on *recording* history, these writers are more concerned with *interpreting* history.

After the 1950s, the nationalistic fervor also brought with it an increased interest in and publication of materials for and about black children. Inspired in part by the nationbuilders' concern with the future, the trend also reflected more receptive outlets for black writers of adolescent and juvenile literature. Virginia Hamilton, Kristin Hunter, and Sharon Bell Mathis are three of the more prominent among this number of writers.

In terms of less traditional literary forms for Afro-American writers, the post-1950s also saw the rise of the first regularly published black writers of science fiction, such as Octavia Butler and Samuel Delany. The most widely read and popular is Delany, who has created through several novels a world that would rival those of Anne McCaffrey and Isaac Asimov. In addition, black writers of detective fiction achieved a measure of success. One example is Donald Goines.

Ranges in genres are paralleled by ranges in talents across various genres. Some of the better-known novelists today, Alice Walker and Gayl Jones, for example, have distinguished themselves by mastering other forms as well. Both are accomplished short-fiction writers and poets; Walker has written children's books and has published a collection of essays. Though Jones and Walker follow in the footsteps of a writer like James Baldwin, who has written plays, essays, short fiction, and novels since the early 1950s, the more recent writers seem to get equal publicity for all of their forms; and they seem to be equally proficient in them.

These multitalented, multigenred writers reflect another phenomenon of the post-1950s era. Many more black women writers are getting published and are included here, and it is the women writers who seem to be setting the pace for productivity in the 1980s. Their emergence upon the scene has brought with it some distinguishing features in terms of themes and characters. Many more black women characters, for example, are protagonists in these works, and their roles are more complex than those of the mammies and matriarchs of preceding generations. The women writers seem, in addition, to be much more willing to treat subjects that have traditionally been viewed as taboo by black American writers. For example, Alice Walker has explored the subject of incest, and she has joined Ann Allen Shockley in treating lesbianism. Few other black writers prior to the 1970s were willing to confront the uproars that might be raised if they explored such topics.

Few of these writers, male or female, hold the traditional reverence for Christianity in their works. Baldwin, as the tie between the 1940s and the 1960s, is the exception in the creation of characters who still find themselves in or in reaction to the church. There are few long-suffering, forever-praying black characters in the fiction of Paule Marshall, John McCluskey, or Barry Beckham, although writers such as Leon Forrest and Ronald Fair retain a concern with the place of traditional religion in the lives of black Americans. Few matriarchs, however, are present, and the few strong women who do appear find their sources of strength from an ethic not grounded solely in Christianity.

Most of the writers are concerned with the black family, especially with black fathers and mothers and the relationships between black men and women, but there is little effort to glorify or romanticize them, as can be seen in the novels of Al Young, Rosa B. Guy, John Oliver Killens, and Joyce Carol Thomas. The writers are also concerned with the failure of personal dreams as well as the American dream, a tie they have to writers of earlier generations. John A. Williams and Sarah E. Wright are representative examples of this phenomenon. Other writers, such as Nathan C. Heard and George Cain, exhibit concerns for the drug-related horrors

that await urban blacks. Still others, for instance, Hal Bennett and Ishmael Reed, are concerned with moving beyond drug, family, and other problems to focus on self-fulfillment on whatever soil is available to their characters.

After the individual trends have been noted, perhaps a general and more major one to note is that black American novelists after the 1960s have been less aggressively concerned with black/white conflict in the United States. While they have certainly not forgotten race, their focus has been more on the interactions within the black community rather than its reaction to the white community. The emphasis is on self-reflection and self-healing. The worlds of Toni Morrison, John Edgar Wideman, and Kristin Hunter are only intermittently the worlds of black reaction to white pressures; they are more often worlds in which black people learn to depend upon each other, learn to explore their history together, and learn to live in black environments without being unduly plagued by W. E. B. Du Bois's concept of double consciousness.

Afro-American writers since the 1950s have been more productive, across a wider variety of genres, than at any other time in their history. Yet, many of the novelists included in this volume remain unknown to the majority of students and scholars of Afro-American literature. This volume is designed, therefore, to provide information that was previously unavailable as well as to encourage further research and teaching of the works of these writers.

—*Thadious M. Davis and Trudier Harris*

Acknowledgments

This book was produced by BC Research. Karen L. Rood is senior editor for the *Dictionary of Literary Biography* series. Joycelyn R. Smith was the in-house editor.

Art supervisor is Claudia Ericson. Typesetting supervisor is Laura Ingram. The production staff includes Mary Betts, Rowena Betts, Kimberly Casey, Patricia Coate, Mary Page Elliott, Lynn Felder, Kathleen M. Flanagan, Joyce Fowler, Judith K. Ingle, and Angelika Kourelis. Jean W. Ross is permissions editor. Joseph Caldwell, photography editor, did photographic copy work for the volume.

Walter W. Ross did the library research with the assistance of the staff at the Thomas Cooper Library of the University of South Carolina: Lynn Barron, Daniel Boice, Sue Collins, Michael Freeman, Gary Geer, Alexander M. Gilchrist, Jens Holley, David Lincove, Marcia Martin, Roger Mortimer, Harriet B. Oglesbee, Jean Rhyne, Karen Rissling, Paula Swope, and Ellen Tillet.

Afro-American Fiction Writers After 1955

Dictionary of Literary Biography

James Baldwin
(2 August 1924-   )

John W. Roberts
University of Pennsylvania

See also the Baldwin entries in *DLB 2, American Novelists Since World War II,* and *DLB 7, Twentieth-Century American Dramatists.*

BOOKS: *Go Tell It on the Mountain* (New York: Knopf, 1953; London: Joseph, 1954);

Notes of a Native Son (Boston: Beacon, 1955; London: Mayflower, 1958);

Giovanni's Room (New York: Dial, 1956; London: Joseph, 1957);

Nobody Knows My Name (New York: Dial, 1961; London: Joseph, 1964);

Another Country (New York: Dial, 1962; London: Joseph, 1963);

The Fire Next Time (New York: Dial, 1963; London: Joseph, 1963);

Nothing Personal, by Baldwin, with photographs by Richard Avedon (New York: Atheneum, 1964; Harmondsworth: Penguin, 1964);

Blues for Mister Charlie (New York: Dial, 1964; London: Joseph, 1965);

Going to Meet the Man (New York: Dial, 1965; London: Joseph, 1965);

The Amen Corner (New York: Dial, 1968; London: Joseph, 1969);

Tell Me How Long the Train's Been Gone (New York: Dial, 1968; London: Joseph, 1968);

A Rap on Race, by Baldwin and Margaret Mead (Philadelphia & New York: Lippincott, 1971; London: Joseph, 1971);

One Day When I Was Lost: A Scenario Based on 'The Autobiography of Malcolm X' (London: Joseph, 1972; New York: Dial, 1973);

No Name in the Street (New York: Dial, 1972; London: Joseph, 1972);

James Baldwin (photo by Layle Silbert)

A Dialogue, with Nikki Giovanni (Philadelphia & New York: Lippincott, 1973; London: Joseph, 1975);

If Beale Street Could Talk (London: Joseph, 1974; New York: Dial, 1974);

The Devil Finds Work (New York: Dial, 1976; London: Joseph, 1976);
Little Man, Little Man: A Story of Childhood, by Baldwin and Yoran Cazac (London: Joseph, 1976; New York: Dial, 1976);
Just Above My Head (New York: Dial, 1979; London: Joseph, 1979).

PLAYS: *The Amen Corner,* Washington, D.C., Howard University, 1955; New York, Ethel Barrymore Theatre, 5 April 1965;
Giovanni's Room, New York, Actors' Studio, 1957;
Blues for Mister Charlie, New York, ANTA Theatre, 23 April 1964;
A Deed from the King of Spain, New York, American Center for Stanislavski Theatre Art, 24 January 1974.

James Baldwin emerged in the 1960s as one of America's most gifted writers and one of black America's most articulate spokesmen. Although he is primarily a novelist, Baldwin has also published essays, plays, and short stories. Critics generally agree that Baldwin is at his best as an essayist, shows flashes of brilliance as a fiction writer, and is least impressive as a playwright. Baldwin's career actually began in 1946 with the publication of a book review in the *Nation*. His evolution as a writer of the first order constitutes a narrative as dramatic and compelling as his best story.

"My childhood was awful," Baldwin once said. He was born in Harlem in 1924, the son of Emma Berdis Jones, who was unmarried at the time of his birth. In 1927 when James was almost three years old, his mother married David Baldwin, a disillusioned and embittered New Orleans preacher who had recently migrated to Harlem. Although Baldwin once described his stepfather as the only man he ever hated, he has admitted on several occasions that he both loved and hated, respected and despised this man whose unabashed love he was never able to win. Nevertheless, Baldwin's ambivalent relationship with his stepfather served as a constant source of tension during his formative years and informs some of his best mature writings. David Baldwin became a model for Gabriel Grimes, a central character in *Go Tell It on the Mountain* (1953), and his death and funeral are vividly described in the essay "Notes of A Native Son."

The marriage between David Baldwin and Emma Jones produced eight children whose care fell primarily to young Jimmy Baldwin. The demands of caring for younger siblings and his stepfather's repressive religious convictions in large part shielded the boy from the harsh realities of Harlem street life during the 1930s. White racism and mistreatment, drugs, alcohol, and social and economic exploitation were real dangers endemic to the environment of the Baldwin family. The family's personal situation, of course, was complicated by the general misfortune of the Depression years. Baldwin was nevertheless able to expand his world through reading, an activity which he found compatible with his babysitting chores. Reading also became his insulation from his stepfather's frequent tirades against white racism and sin. He claims that by age thirteen he had read most of the books in the two Harlem libraries. He then began going downtown to the Forty-second Street New York Public Library where he discovered worlds removed from his own. As he cared for a succession of younger brothers and sisters, Baldwin first became acquainted with Harriet Beecher Stowe's *Uncle Tom's Cabin*, developed a passion for Charles Dickens's novels, and dreamed and discovered the path to riches with the heroes of Horatio Alger.

His passion for reading naturally led him to try his hand at writing. "For me writing was an act of love. It was an attempt—not to get the world's attention—it was an attempt to be loved. It seemed a way to save myself and to save my family. It came out of despair. And it seemed the only way to another world." His love of writing became a refuge from both the hate he believed his stepfather felt for him and the ridicule that he received in school. His superior intellectual abilities as a student and his unattractive appearance made him a natural target for the insults of other children at school. He found both support and sanctuary in the school's literary club guided by renowned poet Countee Cullen. In recognition of his writing ability, Baldwin was made editor of the *Douglass Pilot*, the school newspaper at P.S. 139.

Despite these activities, Baldwin had become convinced of his depravity by age fourteen. Everything he experienced during the summer of his fourteenth birthday, especially the changes in his own body, led him toward religious conversion. Through the influence of an older friend, Arthur Moore, and partly in defiance of his stepfather, Baldwin underwent a dramatic religious conversion and became a member of Mount Calvary of the Pentecostal Faith Church. He eventually reached the level of junior minister.

Shortly after his conversion, young Baldwin's religious devotion received a challenge. He was accepted at De Witt Clinton High School, a predominantly white school in the Bronx. For the first time he came into contact with white students his own age, many of whom were Jewish. The intellectual stimulation offered by his new environment was soured by his stepfather's insistence that he was now flirting with the enemy. In addition, the sharp contrast between the religious convictions of his fellow students and his own fundamentalist beliefs caused young Baldwin to examine his religious stance critically. Moreover, his academic and social problems at De Witt Clinton stemmed from the realization that "when the school day was over, I went back into a condition which they could not imagine, and I knew, no matter what anybody said, that the future I faced was not the future they faced."

In part, Baldwin's feelings of guilt and inadequacy severely hampered his academic performance in high school. He did not graduate with his class. He did, however, receive his diploma six months later in 1942. He also established several important and lasting friendships at De Witt Clinton. One of the most important was with Richard Avedon, with whom he shared editorial duties on the *Magpie*, the school's literary magazine. He was later to collaborate with Avedon on a picture book of America entitled *Nothing Personal* (1964).

By the time Baldwin graduated from high school, his stepfather had been forced to give up work because of his deteriorating mental condition. To help support the family, Baldwin took a job in Belle Mead, New Jersey, at the urging of another high school friend, Emile Capouya. In New Jersey Baldwin worked on the construction of the Army Quartermaster Depot. Discrimination made the entire experience a hell for him. He was fired twice and rehired after Capouya intervened on his behalf. All the while he worked, Baldwin lived frugally and sent most of his money home to his mother. By the summer of 1943, Baldwin's stepfather was near death, and his mother was about to give birth to her eighth child. After being fired a third time, James returned to Harlem, where he was coerced by an aunt into visiting his stepfather, now confined to a mental institution on Long Island. Several days before Baldwin's nineteenth birthday, his stepfather died and his mother gave birth to a baby girl whom James named Paula Maria.

Baldwin realized that the financial strain on the family following his stepfather's death could destroy his ambition of becoming a writer if he allowed it to happen. Consequently, he tried a long shot: "The long shot was simply that I would turn into a writer before my mother died and before the children were all put in jail—or became junkies or whores. I had to leave Harlem. I had to leave be-

cause I understood very well, in some part of myself, that I would never be able to fit in anywhere unless I jumped. I knew I had to jump then." He moved to Greenwich Village, where he worked at a variety of jobs and began working seriously on his first novel, which he had originally titled "Crying Holy." He changed the title to "In My Father's House" and began working diligently to complete it. He would work at his job all day, sleep three to four hours a night and write the rest of the time. It was also during this period that he first met Richard Wright. At Wright's request, Baldwin later mailed him the first sixty pages of "In My Father's House," which Wright liked enough to arrange a Eugene F. Saxton Memorial Trust Award for Baldwin. Despite his furious efforts to finish the novel, he was not able to complete it during the tenure of the fellowship. Disappointed with himself, he began reassessing himself as a writer and turned to other types of writing projects which he felt would sharpen his skills.

Success of sorts finally came in 1946 at age twenty-two when he sold his first book review (on Maxim Gorki) to the *Nation*. This review was followed by another. He also did reviews for the *New Leader* on the Negro problem. His abilities as an essayist were recognized by Robert Warshow, the editor of *Commentary*, the publication of the American Jewish Committee, who asked him to do an article on Harlem. The article, entitled "The Harlem Ghetto," dealt with black anti-Semitism. Since his high school days Baldwin had been wrestling with this question because his experiences with Jews at De Witt Clinton had not paralleled those narrated by most blacks in Harlem. Although it caused controversy in both the black and Jewish communities, the article nevertheless launched Baldwin's career as a writer. He received numerous offers to do articles for other magazines.

Following his early successes, Baldwin began work on a second novel, "Ignorant Armies," which he never completed. The novel was based on the case of Wayne Lonergin, a homosexual who was accused of killing his wife in a disagreement over extramarital affairs. Baldwin's failure to complete the novel stems from his inability to come to terms with his own sexuality at the time. "I was dealing with—it was a very halting attempt to deal with some element in myself, which I had not, at that point in my life, really come to grips with at *all*. The whole *sexual* element. . . . Well, the whole—what I was grappling with *really*, without knowing it, was the—all the implications in this society of being *bisexual*." The issue of bisexuality for Baldwin would not be explored in fiction until 1956 with the publication of *Giovanni's Room*.

Baldwin's abandonment of "Ignorant Armies" freed him to explore other subjects equally as important to his development as a writer. He worked with Theodore Pelalowski on a documentary on storefront churches. Although the documentary was never published, the project won for him a Rosenwald Foundation Fellowship. He then completed his first short story, "Previous Condition," which was published in *Commentary* in October of 1948.

"I wrote it in a white heat," Baldwin once said of "Previous Condition." The story is a thinly veiled version of Baldwin's condition in 1948. Images suggestive of torture and restraint introduce the reader to Peter, the black unemployed actor and narrator of the story. He woke up "to find the sheet was gray and twisted like a rope. I breathed like I had been running. I couldn't move for the longest while. I just lay on my back, spread eagled. . . ." The room in which Peter is living had been rented for him by his white Jewish friend, Jules, and Peter fully expects to be kicked out when discovered by the landlady. When he is evicted, Peter simply resigns himself to it despite urgings to fight back from Jules and his Irish female friend, Ida. Finally, he goes uptown seeking the comfort of familiar surroundings in a bar in Harlem. It is at this point that the reader begins to realize that Peter's dispossession has broader implications. His dispossession of his living quarters is simply a metaphor for his dispossession within American society. The whites reject him because he is black, and he, as black artist, finds himself alienated from his own people because of his sensibilities. At the bar in Harlem Peter is approached by an older woman who asks him "What's your story?" His reply: "I got no story, Ma." Peter has no story because he has no identity, a theme that will recur again and again in Baldwin's fiction.

The feelings of dispossession experienced by Peter in "Previous Condition" must have been eating away at Baldwin during this period. Although he had achieved a modicum of success as a writer, he had yet to produce a major work. His village lifestyle and experiences were also taking their toll on him. In a desperate effort to save himself, Baldwin made the decision to use his last Rosenwald Foundation Fellowship check to book passage to France. On 11 November 1948, James Baldwin left New York for Paris.

As with many other American writers, Paris did not greet Baldwin with open arms. After a brief reunion with Richard Wright, Baldwin found himself in dire financial straits. He had arrived in Paris with only about fifty dollars in his pocket. Shortly after his arrival, Baldwin found himself broke. He was locked out of his hotel room for lack of payment and forced to sell his clothes and typewriter to live. He fell ill and was nursed back to health by a Corsican woman who had taken a liking to him. He eventually ended up in jail for stealing a bedsheet, a charge of which he was innocent. Nevertheless he found respite in Paris from those pressures that had hampered his growth as a writer in the States. He discovered that even in jail he was an American first and a black man second. "I got over—and a lot beyond—the terms of—all the terms in which Americans identified me—in my own mind."

Six months after arriving in Paris, Baldwin wrote one of his best known and most influential essays, "Everybody's Protest Novel." The essay was to be Baldwin's personal emancipation proclamation from the stereotypical writings expected of black writers in America. This essay is best known, however, for its attack on protest fiction, especially that of Richard Wright. The essay traces protest fiction from Harriet Beecher Stowe's *Uncle Tom's Cabin* to Richard Wright's *Native Son*. Baldwin denounces protest fiction because it robs black men of their humanity and has the effect of reinforcing the very stereotypes that it is intended to destroy. Although Baldwin naively hoped that Wright would praise his essay, Wright felt betrayed by his younger protégé. The rift between the men was never patched up.

After outlining the principles on which future Afro-American literature should be based in "Everybody's Protest Novel," Baldwin was still laboring to finish "In My Father's House" in 1951. When he had almost decided to abandon the book, it suddenly began falling into place. He moved to a chalet owned by the parents of his friend, Lucien Happersberger. Living in virtual isolation, Baldwin completed the manuscript in three months. On 26 February 1952, he mailed the final draft to Helen Strauss of the William Morris Agency, who had agreed earlier to serve as his literary agent. Baldwin then moved back to Paris, where Ms. Strauss notified him that Knopf was interested in publishing the novel. To put added pressure on Knopf, Baldwin decided to return to New York after an absence of four years.

"In My Father's House," retitled *Go Tell It on the Mountain*, was finally published in 1953 to excellent reviews. Baldwin's ten-year struggle with his stepfather's legacy was temporarily abated, if not over. "In one sense I wrote to redeem my father," Baldwin once said of the novel. "I had to understand the forces, the experience, the life that shaped him before I could grow up myself, before I could become a writer." *Go Tell It on the Mountain* proved that James Baldwin had become a writer of enormous power and skill.

Go Tell It on the Mountain was an essential book for Baldwin. Although clearly a fictional work, it chronicles two of the most problematic aspects of his existence as a young man: a son's relationship to his stepfather and the impact of fundamentalist religion on the consciousness of a young boy. John Grimes, the fourteen-year-old protagonist of the story, grapples with the meaning of his father's cruel treatment of him and the power of a religion that gives sanction to such monstrous behavior. In reality, John Grimes is young Baldwin trying desperately to reconcile the need for a father's love with his own feelings of mistreatment, ostracism, and alienation from that father. He is young Baldwin seeking in the movies, the streets of Harlem, religion, and a silent mother the answers to questions hidden in the recesses of familial memory. And he is young Baldwin polishing his intellectual armor in hopes of using it as a weapon against the forces that would destroy him in his present environment.

The past and the present merge in *Go Tell It on the Mountain,* revealing a trail of near tragic events that lead to Harlem on this fateful day. The style of the novel is evocative of the slave spiritual tradition that "Americans are able to admire because a protective sentimentality limits their understanding of it." The novel literally reverberates with the wailing and moaning of the black folk preacher as he conjures up images of a world of danger, temptation, and wantonness. The language of the novel echoes that of the King James Bible as reshaped and reinterpreted by the black preacher to speak to a modern audience still plagued by oppression similar to that experienced by the Hebrew people of the Old Testament.

Through the use of flashbacks and a controlled internal point of view, Baldwin advances the story of John Grimes's journey from childhood to maturity. John begins his quest full of guilt over his sexual experimentations, hatred and fear of his father, confusion over the nature of the religion which leaves his parents frustrated and bitter over their lives, and the rebelliousness of his younger brother, Roy, who has his father's love. Through a series of intense images presented at the beginning of the story, Baldwin reveals the struggle of young John Grimes. Standing upon a hill in New York's Central Park, John imagines himself "like a giant who might crumble this city with his anger . . . like a tyrant who might crush this city with his heel: . . . like a long awaited conqueror at whose feet flowers would be strewn, and before whom multitudes cried, Hosanna." He compares his vision of himself as conqueror with the world's expectation that he will follow in his father's footsteps only to discover that "The way of the cross had given him [his father] a belly full of wind and bent his mother's back." Nevertheless John's own guilt over his sexual drives and his father's preachings concerning the evils of the city pervert his vision of his own possibilities of ever escaping and fulfilling his vision of himself.

The essential discoveries that John must make about himself are hidden from him in the memories of his older relatives whose stories unfold as they bring their troubles to the Lord in prayer at the Temple of the Fire Baptized. His father's sister, Florence, has spent her life attempting to wash away her blackness with bleaching creams and a false sense of respectability. She left her mother on her deathbed to come North, and she drove her husband away with her white pretensions. In essence, she has spent her life fleeing her black heritage. "It was indecent the practice of common niggers to cry aloud at the foot of the altar, tears streaming for all the world to see." Unable to make it on her own terms she has allowed her life to be consumed by hatred and guilt, and now she faces the prospect of dying alone from cancer in a furnished room, still clinging tenaciously to her hatred of her brother Gabriel who was the "apple of his mother's eye." Florence has always related her defiance of God with her hatred of her brother Gabriel. She has spent most of her life concealing a letter from his first wife which recounts his neglect of his illegitimate son and the mother, "awaiting some savage opportunity" to strike him down with it. But as the fear of damnation and isolation mounts in her, she surrenders her vow and falls on "her face on the altar."

As Baldwin says of himself in *The Fire Next Time* (1963), Gabriel struck a "bargain" with God as a young man. But what Gabriel never realizes is that their bargain hid from him the secrets of his own heart. From the moment of his conversion, he becomes blind to himself—to his sins. His major sin is that of pride; he comes to believe that he is incapable of sin. His religion protects him from a knowledge of self. Baldwin balances Gabriel's view of his purity with revelations about his past life of evasion of self. Although he is consumed by a sexual nature, Gabriel, in one sense, never surrenders to it since surrender would mean taking responsibility for another human being. In his retreat from self, Gabriel marries the "sexless Deborah," who had been raped by white men and left sterile. Even in his illicit affair with Esther, a woman full of passion and self-knowledge, he refuses to take responsibility for her or their illegitimate child. Each incident drives him deeper into religion. Finally, he marries Elizabeth, after the death of Deborah. Although he promises to treat her child as his own, he only hardens in his resolve, and John, Elizabeth's illegitimate child, serves only to remind him of his failures in the past.

Of all the characters in the novel, Elizabeth is drawn with the most sensitive hand. She, like the other major characters, is essentially blind to the true nature of her religion. She does, however, know that love is "mysteriously a freedom for the soul and spirit . . . water in the dry places," and that "Pride goeth before a fall." Her fall came when she moved to New York with Richard leaving her family behind. After Elizabeth became pregnant with his child, Richard was accused of robbery and, rather than face life in a world in which his humanity had so little value, he committed suicide. Left alone with a child to raise, she had to take a job at night cleaning floors. She saw her hope of redemption in Gabriel, whose attention to little Johnny and proposal of marriage seemed a sign of better times for her. Gabriel, however, does not live up to his promise to be a father to John, and his failure to do so becomes her cross. She discovers after her marriage to Gabriel that she has not only to protect her bastard child from the cruel white world which took his father but from his uncaring stepfather as well.

While it is clear that a knowledge of his stepfather's sin would make him seem more human to John and that a knowledge of his birth would explain Gabriel's treatment of him, if not make it understandable, Baldwin is not willing to give John this information. If he is to escape the pitfalls experienced by his older relatives, he must find his own way on terms different from those of his family. In the end, John accepts his family's way when he submits to religious ecstasy. Baldwin suggests that John is not doomed to repeat a life of failure. As Esther, the mother of Gabriel's illegitimate son, points out to Gabriel early in the novel, "[the Lord's] spirit ain't got to work in everybody the same, seems to me."

After the publication of *Go Tell It on the Mountain,* Baldwin returned to Europe, and began work on his first play, *The Amen Corner.* He was unable to complete the play and returned to New York dur-

ing the summer of 1954. His visit to New York was a productive one. From the summer of 1954 to the spring of 1955, he virtually completed *Giovanni's Room,* a second novel; *The Amen Corner,* his first play; and *Notes of a Native Son,* a book of essays. During the spring of 1955, Howard University decided to produce *The Amen Corner* under the direction of Owen Dodson. Baldwin went to Washington, rewrote many of the speeches while the play was still in the rehearsal stage, and remained for the performance. He was very pleased at the warm reception that the play received.

In *The Amen Corner* Baldwin returns to the black church, its ritual and music. Sister Margaret stands at the center of this play, a minister of enormous verbal power and magnetic leadership abilities. She demands and expects devotion and moral perfection from her parishioners. She chastises one of her members for driving a liquor truck; she shields her son, David, from the secular world; and she even advises one young woman to leave her husband and embrace God completely. Sister Margaret's leadership is being challenged at the beginning of the play because of her heavy-handed tactics coupled with the growing envy and jealousy from some members of her congregation. Her situation is being severely compromised by the return of her musician-husband, Luke. Although she has told everyone that he deserted her, he is dismayed to discover her story. From his dying bed, he gradually forces Margaret to accept the truth about herself.

As a young woman, Margaret suffered a miscarriage because she was malnourished. She blamed Luke for the loss of their child, withdrew from him, and embraced God. Luke, in search of comfort, turned to alcohol. In a desperate effort to save himself and find love, he devoted himself totally to his musical career. Before his death, Luke forces Margaret to admit that all she ever wanted was to be a good wife and mother. Ironically, her moment of revelation comes too late, since she has lost her opportunity to be a good wife and mother, and her role of minister has been taken from her. David, her son, does have an opportunity to learn from his parents' mistakes and have a more fulfilling life. He leaves the church with the intention of making his music a sacrifice to his people and not a sanctuary for himself as his father has made his music and his mother has used her religion.

The success of *The Amen Corner* must have been all the more gratifying for Baldwin in light of the difficulties that he was encountering at about the same time in finding a publisher for *Giovanni's Room,* to which publishers reacted negatively because of the novel's explicit homosexual theme. Although the details of its final acceptance are conflicting, Dial Press did sign Baldwin and accept *Giovanni's Room* in 1956. After the novel was accepted, Baldwin returned to Paris, where he put the finishing touches on it and mailed it to Ms. Strauss in April 1956. Reviews of the novel were mixed, an expected outcome given its sexual theme.

Although the story line is completely different, *Giovanni's Room* is, in one sense, a culmination of Baldwin's earlier effort, begun with "Ignorant Armies," to explore the implications of bisexuality in American society. The novel rises above its explicitly homosexual theme and explores the issue of self-acceptance and its implications for discovering one's identity. David, the protagonist of *Giovanni's Room,* wrestles with traditional Western concepts of masculinity and sexuality in an effort to come to terms with his own sexual drives. His socialization has not given him a way of conceptualizing and psychologically accepting his homosexual urges. His homosexual affair with Joey, a boyhood friend, leaves him "lonely" and wondering how "this could have happened to me, how this could have happened in me." Unable to resolve his sexual crisis, David flees into the army where he finds himself facing the same question again. Still fleeing his experience with Joey and his army experience, David finds himself in Paris.

In France, David meets Hella, a girl also in search of her identity. With her David hopes to expiate the guilt he feels over his relationship with Joey. Moreover, he sees in his proposal of marriage to Hella an opportunity to gain social respectability and a resolution to his sexual identity problem. Hella, however, is not ready for that kind of commitment and moves to Spain to think it over. Left alone in Paris, David meets Giovanni. Giovanni is to be but a brief interlude for David, but Giovanni needs more than an affair with David; he needs love. The predatory homosexual world waits to claim Giovanni and only the transcending power of David's love can save him; but David cannot save Giovanni because he cannot save himself. David's rejection of Giovanni is expressed symbolically through his growing repugnance toward Giovanni's room. "I remember that life in that room seemed to be occurring beneath the sea." David's rejection of Giovanni's love is also aided by Hella's eventual acceptance of his proposal of marriage and return to France. When Giovanni loses his job because he refuses to submit to Guillaume, his aging homosexual employer, he is unable to find comfort in David. In an effort to get his job back, Giovanni submits to Guillaume and kills him afterward. He hides from the police for a few days but is caught, tried, convicted, and sentenced to death. David tries to hide himself in Hella but cannot find respite in her. She eventually discovers him with a sailor in a bar and knows the truth of his relationship with Giovanni. She then returns to America, leaving David to face his life alone.

Artistically, *Giovanni's Room* is one of Baldwin's finest creations. The failure of the novel, or at least the one that has been most often pointed out, involves the conceptualization of David. David and homosexuality are rendered negatively, mainly because David fails to resolve his sexual conflict. In reality, Baldwin does not attempt to resolve the conflict, and if he had, the ending would necessarily have been contrived. The point that Baldwin attempts to make is that David cannot move beyond simply experiencing conflict because Western society has provided him with no other means of viewing his situation. Because Baldwin sees in the plight of the homosexual a parallel to that of the black American, his predicament, at this point in history, can only be exposed, not resolved. The homosexual, like the black American, has no place in Western society, and if he is to have a place he must make it for himself. If he allows the culture to define him, his fate is reflective of David's—confusion, disorientation, and frustration with self and society.

After the publication of *Giovanni's Room,* Baldwin was still convinced that the theme broached in the novel had not been fully developed and its potential for illuminating American racial and sexual attitudes had not been exhausted. While still in Paris, he began working on a third novel, *Another Country,* in which he would leave no room for confusion as to what he saw as the parallel. It was also during the summer of 1956 that Baldwin first established his well-publicized friendship with Norman Mailer. They found much to talk about given their inclinations toward politics. Their personalities, however, made for frequent arguments and exasperating stalemates. "Norman and I are alike in this," Baldwin observes, "that we both tend to suspect others of putting us down, and we strike before we're struck." This tendency to respond to supposed insults resulted in their now infamous fight in 1962. Baldwin and Mailer were both covering the Liston-Patterson heavyweight fight in Chicago. Mailer was representing *Esquire* and Baldwin was covering the event for *Nugget,* a less well-known magazine. Baldwin indirectly accused Mailer of being a liberal, a badge that Mailer refuses to wear since he considers himself a radical. Mailer retaliated by suggesting that Baldwin did not know the difference between a radical and a liberal.

At summer's end in 1956, Baldwin was still wrestling with *Another Country*. He decided to return to New York for inspiration. He arrived in an America on the verge of revolution. The 1954 Supreme Court decision on school desegregation had brought with it a new atmosphere of unrest among blacks. The revolution, however, was not occurring in the North; New York had not changed. Consequently, Baldwin wanted to be a part of this action, so he temporarily abandoned the novel and made his first trip to the South, a part of his own country that he had always feared. He was impressed by the courage and determination that he sensed in the people, especially the children who were bearing the brunt of the hostility of those opposed to school integration. He was fortified by the bravery and stamina of those young children who faced the storms of insults hurled at them each day and could continue knowing "that it was all to be gone through again."

By the time Baldwin returned to New York, *Giovanni's Room* had caught on with the reading

public and had been optioned as a Broadway play. Baldwin was besieged by a number of would-be Giovannis. He was not impressed with any of them until he met Engin Cezzar, a Turk. When Cezzar read the script for the Broadway production, however, he lost his enthusiasm for doing the part. He suggested that Baldwin write the play himself, which Baldwin eventually did. Although the play was never produced on Broadway, it was dramatized by the Actors Studio Workshop with Cezzar playing the lead.

Baldwin's work on the play left him with a desire to work in the theater. He apprenticed himself as a kind of playwright-in-training to director Elia Kazan. He acted as Kazan's assistant during the rehearsals of Archibald MacLeish's *J.B.* and Tennessee Williams's *Sweet Bird of Youth*. It was during this time that Baldwin began nursing an idea for a second play which he enthusiastically discussed with Kazan. He wanted to write a play based on the Emmett Till case. Till, a black youth, was killed in Mississippi in 1955. A white man was tried and acquitted of the killing. He later confessed to the murder to reporter William Bradford Huie, and

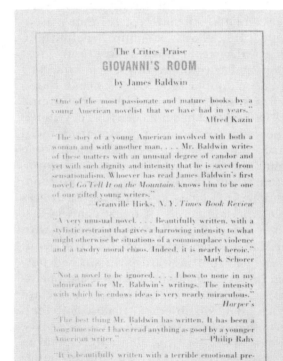

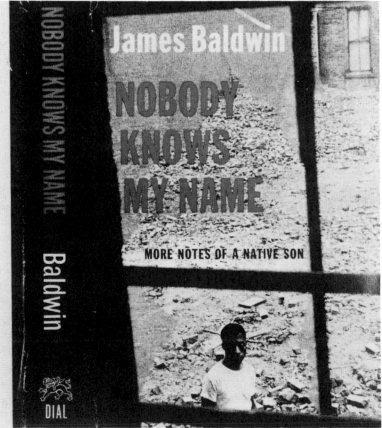

Dust jacket for Baldwin's 1961 collection of thirteen essays addressing "the question of color" and the role of the artist in "the bottomless confusion which is both public and private of the American republic"

the story was published in a national magazine. Kazan, however, frustrated Baldwin's efforts to begin work on the play by suggesting that it would make a better movie. Baldwin had no desire to write a movie script and put the idea aside.

Baldwin's flirtation with the theater was brief. He returned to France but was still unable to settle down and finish *Another Country*. He once again returned to New York, where he worked on an article for *Esquire* which eventually became "Fifth Avenue Uptown: A Letter From Harlem." The article caused a mild stir among middle-class blacks, whom it criticized. He weathered the small storm of protest and did a college speaking tour. When he was ready to resume work, he moved into the guest cottage of William Styron and his wife. Plagued by interruptions from family and friends, he dashed off to France with his youngest sister, Paula Maria. After only a couple of weeks, he left Paula Maria in Paris and flew to Istanbul, where he completed *Another Country*.

Another Country was published on 25 June 1962. Its critical reception was mixed. One *New York Times* book reviewer labeled the book "strained," and two days later in the newspaper's daily book column, the novel was hailed as "brilliantly and fiercely told." The novel for Baldwin, however, brought together satisfactorily two of the subjects that had caused him much confusion and personal anguish—race and sex.

Another Country is an ambitious novel in scope and technique. In one sense, the novel contains several stories, interrelated and interwoven, of people trying to come to terms with their identities, of which race and sex are important defining attributes. On another level, the novel deals with pain and the role of pain in allowing one to become a complete person. The first story belongs to Rufus Scott, a black jazz drummer. The source of Rufus's pain is American racism and the suffering that it has caused him. He has been so brutalized by his experiences that he can no longer separate real from imagined assaults on his humanity. For this reason, his relationship with Leona, the Southern white girl whom he attempts to exploit, is doomed from the beginning. Rufus cannot accept her love; he has been too demoralized to accept either Leona's love or himself. He finally drives her insane and commits suicide out of frustration.

Rufus's death provides the motivation for much of the action in the rest of the novel. Vivaldo, an Italian-American writer, blames himself for having failed to understand the depth of Rufus's sorrow. He attempts to make amends by having an affair with Rufus's sister, Ida. She wants to avenge the death of her brother, and she intends to do it by making a success of her singing career at all cost. Vivaldo comes to know pain when he falls in love with Ida, who deceives him by having an affair with a television producer who can help her in her career. Ida's pain is a part of her existence as a black woman who has learned to expect cruel treatment. Cass, an ex-New England debutante, and Richard Silenski suffer from the changes in their life brought about by the success of Richard's new book. They were too busy to be bothered by Rufus's problems. On one level or another, all the characters face the alienation and isolation characteristic of modern society with no way of breaking through.

Eric, a Southern white homosexual who is accepting of his life, has discovered how to keep pain from destroying him. Eric is first encountered in France, sprawled naked in his garden, attended by his lover Yves. "It was up to him to find out who he was, and it was his necessity to do this, so far as the witchdoctors of the times were concerned, alone." In Alabama where he grew up, a child of rich and uncaring parents, Eric had been left alone most of the time except for the moments he shared with the blacks. His relationships caused him "isolation" from the rest of the whites "due to the extreme unpopularity of his racial attitudes—or, rather, as far as the world in which he moved was concerned, the lack of any responsible attitudes at all." His isolation forced him into an affair with a black boy, Leroy. From this affair he learned to be a man. "For the meaning of revelation is that what is revealed is true, and must be borne."

Back in New York to pursue his acting career, Eric attempts through his affairs with Cass and Vivaldo to impart his understanding. Cass realizes that she no longer needs her affair with Eric when she makes the discovery that "everything can be borne." Vivaldo makes a similar discovery following his night with Eric. Both he and Eric realize that the love offered by their friendship is not enough to transcend pain. Vivaldo feels that kind of love only for Ida. As far as Eric is concerned the only thing left is the love of one friend for another. "So what can we really do for each other except—just love each other and be each other's witness."

The final section of the novel seems to represent a note of optimism. Eric is at the airport to meet his lover Yves. The scene explodes with light and brightness. The sun is shining and the people are dressed in bright colors, a stark contrast to the rest of the novel. Eric, who has brought sunshine to others, even if their lives are still slightly overcast, welcomes the source of his strength, Yves. Apparently, the circle of emptiness, isolation, and hatred has been broken, and "another country" of love has been created out of the chaos of the characters' lives.

In *Another Country* Baldwin explores the possibilities of the Afro-American blues tradition to deal with the chaos of twentieth-century life. The novel is literally filled with lyrics from blues songs, and the characters, in one sense, are evaluated in terms of their relationship to the blues esthetic. The blues is a form of expression which allows man to bring order to his chaotic world on a personal level and through the shared experience of the audience transforms its chaos as well. The blues is not the exclusive possession of black Americans; it is just that they have been able to use it more effectively than whites because they have a greater and more immediate sense of their suffering. And when whites are forced to recognize their suffering, they find that the world in which they have so much faith is incapable of supplying a definition for them. At this point they too can become acquainted with the power of the blues. They learn that the power to deal with suffering comes from within, and that it is suffering itself which offers the solution.

After the publication of *Another Country,* Baldwin became more heavily involved in the civil rights movement. In late 1961, he traveled south to Mississippi to visit with James Meredith, the first black to attend the University of Mississippi. On this trip, he also toured the backwoods areas of Mississippi with Medgar Evers to investigate the murder of a young black man by a white storekeeper. It was in one of the rural settings they explored that Baldwin first saw the church that he used as the setting for *Blues for Mister Charlie.* Baldwin was rapidly becoming a recognized spokesman for blacks, especially after the 1963 publication of *The Fire Next Time,* which contained two essays, "Letter From A Region of My Mind" and "My Dungeon Shook: Letter To My Nephew on the One Hundredth Anniversary of the Emancipation Proclamation." The book became a best-seller and was considered must reading for anyone enlightened to the struggles of black people.

In 1964, Baldwin completed *Blues for Mister Charlie,* his third play, and remained in New York to oversee its opening on 23 April. The play, with its complicated use of flashbacks, was difficult to stage and had a short run despite Baldwin's efforts to keep it open. The play is based in part on the Emmett Till case and, in part, on the murder that Baldwin investigated with Medgar Evers in Missis-

sippi. The play centers around Richard Henry, whose story evolves through a series of flashbacks. Richard has just returned from the North, where he enjoyed success as an entertainer before drug addiction overcame him. Back home in a small Southern town, he falls in love with Juanita, a childhood friend. Her love provides Richard with a new reason for living. He, however, refuses to acquiesce to the Southern social code of deference to whites. He subsequently provokes a dispute with a white store owner, Lyle Britten, who kills him. Britten is tried and acquitted of the murder because his wife, Jo, lies and tells the jury that Richard assaulted her. Her lie is virtually substantiated when Parnell, a supposed friend of blacks, refuses to refute it, even though he knows it to be a lie. At the end of the play, Meridian Henry, Richard's father, who has acted as a middle man between the civil rights workers in the play and whitetown, realizes that he can no longer depend on whites to help blacks achieve equality. Blacks must act for themselves.

Blues for Mister Charlie explores several issues important to Baldwin at this time. The use of nonviolent means in achieving racial equality was an issue of the day in 1964. When Meridian Henry tells Juanita that Richard's gun is under the Bible, he suggests that the moral imperative behind nonviolent action may not be strong enough to achieve the desired ends. The role of the white liberal, represented in the play by Parnell, is also held up to scrutiny. When he is placed in a position of promoting the best interests of blacks, he lies. So much for white liberalism. *Blues for Mister Charlie* was to be Baldwin's most militant statement on the civil rights question until the publication of *No Name in the Street* in 1972.

Baldwin's name and face were constantly in the public arena during the 1960s. *Nothing Personal,* a photographic essay, written with Richard Avedon, appeared in 1964. *Going to Meet the Man,* a collection of his short stories, was published in 1965. He also received several awards during this period: In 1958, he received a Ford Foundation Fellowship; he was awarded a National Conference of Christians and Jews Brotherhood Award in 1962; a George Polk Award in 1963; the Foreign Drama Critics Award in 1964; an honorary doctor of letters degree from the University of British Columbia in 1964; and he was made a member of the National Institute of Arts and Letters in that same year.

Tell Me How Long the Train's Been Gone (1968) was to be Baldwin's last novel of the 1960s. Critics were quick to point out its flaws—flat characters,

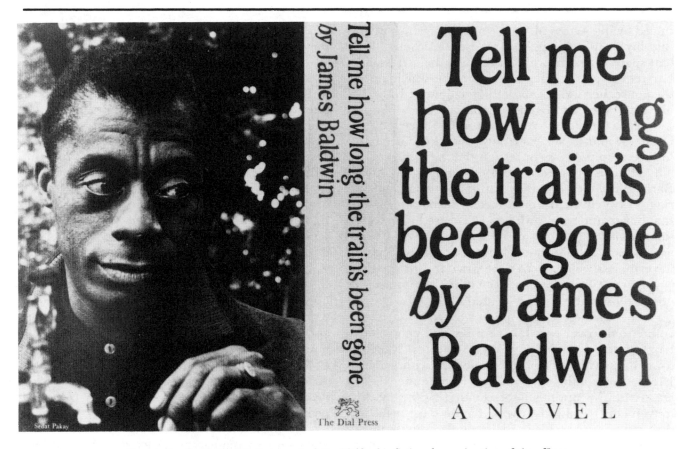

*Dust jacket for Baldwin's last novel of the 1960s, his fictional examination of the effects
celebrity has on the black artist*

vulgarity for its own sake, and polemicism. While these criticisms have some merit, the apparent flaws in the novel stem more from what Baldwin is attempting than from any lack of ability, as some critics suggested. The novel deals indirectly with the civil rights movement and the role of the black artist/celebrity in that movement. Baldwin attempts to tell the story from an internal, first-person point of view, allowing the story of Leo Proudhammer, the black actor-protagonist, to unfold through a series of flashbacks while he recuperates from a heart attack. Leo finds himself, though successful, alienated from the black community because of his newfound status and isolated within the white community because of his color. He is at a point where he must decide if he is going to play a role in the growing civil rights struggle going on around him.

As the son of parents who migrated to Harlem searching for a better life, Leo Proudhammer is witness to their poverty and disillusionment with life in the North. His decision to become an actor stems from the financial security and power within American society that the profession promised. At the beginning of the story, Leo has suffered a heart attack, and most of the story is revealed through flashbacks to his earlier life. We learn of his close relationship with his brother Caleb. Together, they experience the poverty, police mistreatment, and general exploitation found in the urban ghetto environment. Leo eventually escapes the ghetto, but Caleb, on the other hand, is first put in jail, then flees to California and into the army trying to escape white racism. He finally succumbs to religion despite an early aversion to it.

Leo is determined to be successful. His surname, Proudhammer, suggests the black worksongs and ballads which center around the black folk hero, John Henry, and his feats with the hammer. The name, in terms of the novel, indicates that Leo will work to become successful, and he does, but he will not degrade himself in the process. He remains proud. For example, when he is seen leaving the apartment of the leading lady in a play being produced by the Actors Means' Workshop, which gave him his early training, he is arrested. Although he had spent the night with Madeleine, the actress, at her request, he refuses to explain the situation to the police. Leo will not allow this incident and others like it to deter him from his goal.

As a struggling young actor Leo meets Barbara, a would-be actress from Kentucky. They fall in love despite Leo's confession that he is bisexual. The affair is doomed from the beginning because Barbara is white, and they both know what a marriage between them would mean. Barbara realizes that her relationship with Leo will cause her to forsake some of the "corny things" in life that she wants, such as "A husband, a home. . . . kids." She is nevertheless willing to pay the price for loving the wrong man. Their love for each other becomes one of the most stable aspects of Leo's life.

It is through Christopher, however, that Leo comes to discover how far from his own people he has wandered on his journey to the top. Christopher is a young black revolutionary with whom Leo becomes intimate. Through Christopher, Leo learns of the optimism of the struggling black movement. He also discovers that he must make a decision about his role in the struggle even though he knows that the outcome "would almost certainly be so violent as to blow Christopher, and me, and all of us, away." Nevertheless, "I committed myself to Christopher's possibilities." The decision to participate in the movement is in part precipitated by Leo's recollections of a visit from his brother following Caleb's conversion to Christianity. Although Leo once respected his brother above all others, he cannot accept Caleb's religion as an answer to the plight of black people. He says of his visit from Caleb that "I did not know, when Caleb walked into The Island on that far-off night, how many ways there were to die, and how few to live." The novel concludes with Leo's apparent decision to join the civil rights movement.

Tell Me How Long the Train's Been Gone reflects Baldwin's internal struggle with his role as artist/ celebrity and civil rights spokesman during the 1960s. The black celebrity has two choices: he can become a "fatcat," as Leo is labeled at one point, and withdraw into the protective shell of his success, or he can use his status as a symbol for the black community. The first situation demands no recognition of roots. But the second choice requires a conscious recognition and acceptance of roots. *Tell Me How Long the Train's Been Gone* is not so much about the making of a revolutionary as it is about the making

of a celebrity/spokesman, a problem that plagued Baldwin throughout the 1960s.

The 1970s was to be a productive decade for Baldwin. In 1971, his conversations with anthropologist Margaret Mead on world racism were published as *A Rap on Race.* Another improvised dialogue was published in 1973, this time with black poet-activist Nikki Giovanni, as simply *A Dialogue.* Two books of essays were also to appear during the 1970s: *No Name in the Street* (1972), his most militant statement to date; and *The Devil Finds Work* (1976), a history of blacks in film. *One Day When I Was Lost* (1972), a movie scenario based on Alex Haley's *Autobiography of Malcolm X,* was published but not produced because Baldwin refused to compromise with Columbia Pictures on his perceptions of Malcolm X's life. A little known fictional work, *Little Man, Little Man: A Story of Childhood,* a children's book written in black dialect and with a ghetto setting, also appeared in 1976, the year Baldwin received an honorary doctor of letters degree from Morehouse College. He also published two novels during the 1970s. *If Beale Street Could Talk,* published in 1974, became a best-seller, and *Just Above My Head* appeared in 1979.

If Beale Street Could Talk is notable for its nineteen-year-old narrator, Clementine (Tish) Rivers. She is pregnant and unmarried. Furthermore, the baby's father, Alonzo (Fonny) Hunt, is in jail for a rape he did not commit, and his prospects of getting out before the baby is born are bleak. The action of the novel revolves around the efforts of Tish and her family to get Fonny out of jail. Their efforts are frustrated by an unresponsive judicial system and Fonny's mother and sisters. Through a series of flashbacks, we learn of Tish's childhood romance with Fonny, their struggle to find happiness in a hostile world, and the difficulties with the police which lead to Fonny's arrest and conviction for raping a Puerto Rican woman.

In one sense, the antagonist in the novel is the American judicial system. Tish says at one point that "The calendars were full—it would take about a thousand years to try all the people in the American prisons, but the Americans are optimistic and still hope for time—and sympathetic or merely intelligent judges are as rare as snowstorms in the tropics." Also, it is because of the white policeman Bell, a representative of that system, that Fonny is in jail. Bell frames Fonny because he is made to look foolish when a white witness clears Fonny of blame in a street fight over Tish. Moreover, that Fonny's case is not affected when the chief witness against him, the rape victim, flees to San Juan and will probably not return, is another indication of the unfairness of the system to black people.

In a less threatening way, the Hunt women, Fonny's mother and sisters, act as obstacles to Fonny's release. They are devoutly religious. Their religion, however, simply serves as a way of achieving social respectability within the community and has nothing to do with Christian charity. When Fonny is put in jail, the Hunt women refuse to have anything to do with him because their acknowledgment of a known criminal would severely compromise their social standing, even though the criminal is son and brother. The confrontations between the Hunt women and the Rivers women are brutal and somewhat comic as the religious Hunts always come off looking absurd. The religious position, as in *Tell Me How Long the Train's Been Gone,* once again appears ineffectual and downright destructive in light of the realities of Fonny's and Tish's situation.

The novel ends on a note of uncertainty, much like the lives of the characters. In the end, Fonny is working on a piece of sculpture and the baby is heard crying in the background. Whether this is a fantasy created out of labor pains or whether Fonny is really out of jail is unclear. Given the bleakness of the story, fantasy is far more likely than reality.

The 1970s saw a much less politically active Baldwin on the whole. Primarily through his essays, he had firmly captured himself a place in the history of American letters. He also wanted to devote more time to his writing. His latest novel, *Just Above My Head,* reveals a calmer, less bitter, but more mature Baldwin. It invites comparison with and echoes some of the same themes found in one of his finest short stories, "Sonny's Blues." Both stories explore the relationship between two brothers from the older brother's point of view. Both younger brothers are musicians. Sonny is a jazz musician and Arthur Montana in *Just Above My Head* is a gospel singer. Both younger brothers through their devotion to their arts teach the older brothers something about the art of living.

Just Above My Head is told from a first-person point of view. The narrator is Hall Montana, the brother of Arthur, whose story Hall is supposed to be telling. His recollecting and telling the story of Arthur is apparently motivated in part by a dream and in part by a question from his son who had heard that Arthur was a "faggot." The story becomes Hall's attempt to redefine Arthur's life in such a way that his love of humanity overrides the

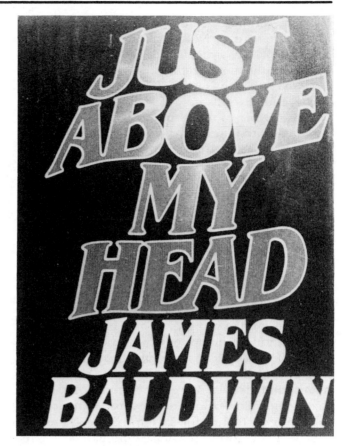

Dust jacket for Baldwin's longest novel, which, he claimed, "set him free to go someplace else"

"faggot" label. Although Hall knew of Arthur's homosexuality, he had never accepted it. The story unfolds through a series of painful recollections, a stylistic technique which Baldwin employs constantly in his fiction.

Basically, the novel has four major characters—Hall and Arthur Montana and Julia and Jimmy Miller. Julia is a child evangelist when she first meets Hall and Arthur, and Arthur makes his gospel singing debut at a service presided over by Julia. Hall is much older than Julia and Arthur, and Jimmy is the youngest. Julia is self-righteous to the point of refusing her mother any other than spiritual attention during her fatal illness. After her mother's death Julia gives up the ministry. Her brother is sent south to live with his grandmother, and Julia is forced into an incestuous relationship with her father.

Meanwhile Hall has been drafted and sent to Korea, and Arthur has begun a Southern tour with a quartet called The Trumpets of Zion. On the tour, Arthur has his first homosexual relationship with

Crunch, another member of the group. After the quartet returns to New York, Crunch has a brief affair with Julia trying to free her from her father. Eventually he too is drafted and sent to Korea leaving Julia in Arthur's care. Hall returns from Korea and eventually falls in love with Julia but is never able to get her to marry him. Arthur is eventually reunited with Jimmy at a civil rights rally in the South and they too have an affair. It is because of a fight with Jimmy that Arthur is in London, where he meets his death.

Just Above My Head is a long, complex novel, Baldwin's longest to date. It is instructive that in the novel Baldwin has finally brought together and completely resolved many of the issues raised in earlier works. In *Just Above My Head,* Baldwin presents convincingly his often muted and poorly executed conviction that suffering is the path to understanding and transcending the distances that separate us as human beings. It is only in entering fully into suffering, whether our own or another's, that we can transcend it. It is through this cathartic process that Hall comes to understand Arthur's humanity and his own. More important for Baldwin is that we not allow pain to destroy us. We must learn as Arthur did to transform it into a living art, such as the blues or gospel music. Homosexuality is revealed in the novel as simply another source of human pain, but it too can be confronted and borne. Finally, Baldwin's fight with Christianity seems to be over. In *Just Above My Head,* religion is presented from a more positive point of view. Of course, the overzealous Julia is made humble, but her situation is an individual one, and Christianity is not condemned because of her actions.

Baldwin commented following the publication of *Just Above My Head* that "what I've really been feeling is that I've come full circle. From *Go Tell It on the Mountain* to *Just Above My Head* sums up something of my experience—it's difficult to articulate—that sets me free to go someplace else." Baldwin has secured a place for himself in any literary history of America. As Fern Eckman, one of his biographers, has written: "Whatever happens, Baldwin will be remembered as the writer who forced upon the consciousness of white America the terror and the wrath of being Negro in the United States."

Interviews:
E. Auchincloss and N. Lynch, "Disturber of the Peace," *Mademoiselle* (May 1963): 174-175, 199-207;

"James Baldwin Breaks His Silence: An Interview," *Atlas,* 13 (March 1967): 47-49;

"How Can We Get the Black People To Cool It? An Interview with James Baldwin," *Esquire,* 66 (July 1968): 49-53, 116;

David Frost, "Are We On the Edge of Civil War?," in his *The Americans* (New York: Stein & Day, 1970), pp. 145-150;

Herbert R. Lottmann, "It's Hard to Be James Baldwin," *Intellectual Digest* (July 1972): 67-68;

Joe Walker, "Exclusive Interview with James Baldwin," *Muhammad Speaks,* 8 September 1973, pp. 13-14; 15 September 1973, p. 29; 29 September 1973, pp. 29-30; 6 October 1973, pp. 30-31;

"The Black Scholar Interviews James Baldwin," *Black Scholar,* 5 (December 1973-January 1974): 32-42;

Mel Watkins, "James Baldwin Writing and Talking," *New York Times Book Review,* 23 September 1979, pp. 35-36.

References:
Fern Eckman, *The Furious Passage of James Baldwin* (New York: Evans, 1966);

Kenneth Kinnamon, ed., *James Baldwin: A Collection of Critical Essays* (Englewood Cliffs, N.J.: Prentice-Hall, 1974);

Stanley Macebuh, *James Baldwin: A Critical Study* (New York: Third Press-Joseph Okpaku, 1973);

Karin Moller, *The Theme of Identity in the Essays of James Baldwin* (Göteborg, Sweden: Acta Universitatis Gotoburgensis, 1975);

Therman B. O'Daniel, ed., *James Baldwin: A Critical Evaluation* (Washington, D.C.: Howard University Press, 1977);

Louis H. Pratt, *James Baldwin* (Boston: Twayne, 1978);

Fred Standley and Nancy Standley, *James Baldwin: A Reference Guide* (Boston: G. K. Hall, 1980);

Standley and Standley, eds., *Critical Essays on James Baldwin* (Boston: G. K. Hall, 1981);

Carolyn W. Sylvander, *James Baldwin* (New York: Ungar, 1980);

William Weatherby, *Squaring Off: Mailer vs. Baldwin* (New York: Mason/Charter, 1977).

Barry Beckham

(19 March 1944-   )

Joe Weixlmann
Indiana State University

BOOKS: *My Main Mother* (New York: Walker, 1969; London & New York: Wingate, 1970); reissued as *Blues in the Night* (London: Universal-Tandem, 1974);
Runner Mack (New York: Morrow, 1972);
Double Dunk (Los Angeles: Holloway House, 1980).

PLAY: *Garvey Lives!*, Providence, R.I., Churchill House, Brown University, November 1972.

PERIODICAL PUBLICATIONS: "Listen to the Black Graduate, You Might Learn Something," *Esquire,* 72 (September 1969): 98, 196-199;
"Ladies and Gentlemen, No Salt-Water Taffy Today," *Brown Alumni Monthly,* 70 (March 1970): 20-23;
"Why It Is Right to Write," *Brown Alumni Monthly,* 78 (May-June 1978): 23-25.

Barry Beckham (photo by Layle Silbert)

Along with such writers as Cecil Brown, Ronald Fair, Carlene Hatcher Polite, Ishmael Reed, and Charles Wright, Barry Beckham has helped to change the shape and tone of contemporary Afro-American fiction. Breaking with the realistic and naturalistic modes of fiction that characterized black American writing into the 1950s and continue to predominate today, each of Beckham's books, especially his 1972 novel *Runner Mack,* is marked by stylistic innovation and the author's ability to hold the comic and the pathetic in equipoise.

Born in West Philadelphia in 1944, Beckham moved with his mother to Atlantic City, New Jersey, when he was nine. The new home would leave its imprint on the novelist's imagination. Atlantic City was, he recalls, "a strange place" in which to grow up, yet one rich in a variety of black cultures and social strata. Established jazz musicians came regularly to Atlantic City as did black entertainers, so Beckham's early exposure to the black performing arts was extensive. Moreover, although the Beckhams lived on the segregated north side of Atlantic City, the town's public-school system afforded the young Beckham an opportunity to interact with whites, who composed about sixty percent of the

student body. That he was popular enough to be voted president of his senior class suggests that he functioned well within the interracial environment of his high school. But when Beckham found himself one of only eight black freshmen entering Brown University in the fall of 1962, he could not help feeling isolated. Still Brown produced some positive effects. Under the tutelage of novelist John Hawkes, who, Beckham has observed, "gave you the impression that *all* things mattered," Beckham truly learned the importance of style in writing; and, as a senior, Beckham began his first novel, *My Main Mother.*

Following his graduation from college in 1966 and prior to his return to Brown in 1970 as a visiting lecturer in Afro-American Studies and English, Beckham spent a short time enrolled at Columbia

17

University law school, then held a variety of public relations jobs in the New York City area, including assistant editor of the *Chase Manhattan News*. These years, he maintains, were important ones. Not only did he complete *My Main Mother* (1969), but he also gained abilities and insights that were of use to him in the years ahead. His public relations positions led him to develop journalistic skills that he might not otherwise have attained, and the New York period permitted Beckham to sharpen his awareness of the social, economic, and cultural forces at work in America. Perhaps most important for those concerned with his fiction, a number of the experiences gleaned during his tenure in the business world served as source material for his second novel, *Runner Mack*. Beckham's feelings about the Western Electric Corporation, for example, found fictional outlet in his portrait of Home Manufacturing, and, while doing a journalistic piece for the *Chase Manhattan News* on dedicated employee service, he learned of a man who, like the protagonist of *Runner Mack*, reported for work despite having been struck by a motor vehicle on his way to the bank.

If book reviews alone determined writers' reputations, *My Main Mother* would have earned Beckham immediate renown. Peter Rowley, writing in the *New York Times Book Review*, found the second half of the novel so compelling that he was led to predict that Beckham could become "one of the best novelists of the decade"—and other reviewers were equally impressed. Moreover, although a film version of the novel was never made, the cinematic rights to the book were snapped up by William Castle, the producer of *Rosemary's Baby*, shortly after the novel was published.

By allowing Mitchell Mibbs to explain what induced him to slay his mother, Pearl, Beckham gains a calculated immediacy in *My Main Mother* and, simultaneously, permits his hip, highly self-conscious, late-teenaged black narrator to engage the reader's empathy. We are led to comprehend the torments that Mitchell experienced in living with an adulterous, alcoholic, self-centered mother, and we learn how she withheld her affection from Mitchell's Uncle Melvin, an older brother of Pearl's who not only provided for her when she was husbandless but virtually raised Mitchell. Beckham's first novel lacks the ideological breadth and some of the stylistic sophistication of *Runner Mack*, but it offers a credible psychological portrait of a young man betrayed.

Like *My Main Mother*, *Runner Mack* won immediate critical acclaim upon its release in the summer of 1972, making the *New York Times* annual listing of recommended books. The narrative fabric of *Runner Mack* is deeply textured. So skillfully does Beckham intertwine naturalistic scenes with daydreams, nightmares, and what the book's black protagonist, Henry Adams, at one point calls "daymares" that the reader is soon immersed in the unexpected. Beckham sees the societal multiplicity and chaos which so concerned the historical Henry Adams early in this century as having accelerated furiously in the current age.

Compared to the novel's complex texture, its plot is simplistic. Except for some flashback episodes, the tale develops linearly in two sections, the first slightly longer than the last. The initial part relates Henry's employment at Home Manufacturing Company, a brief period which dangles an illusory dream of equal opportunity in front of the protagonist, and his ill-fated, if hyperbolically rendered, tryout with the Stars, a racist major-league baseball team. Having come north from Mississippi to find a better life, Henry and his wife Beatrice instead find themselves trapped in an unbearably noisy, filthy, racist environment. But well-schooled in perseverance by his father, the naive protagonist responds enthusiastically to a draft notice and, as the book's second section opens, is at war in Alaska as a member of the armed forces. By the novel's midpoint, Beckham has utterly leveled the American Dream of success.

Runner Mack, a hip black man who raises Henry's political consciousness, is introduced in the second section of the book. Both men eventually desert the army and return to the mainland United States to help effect a revolution. But when only eight persons attend the would-be mass rally that is to precede a bombing of the White House, Mack hangs himself, and Henry, his idol dead and his wife grown deaf from the city's incessant din, bursts out of the meeting hall and into the path of an oncoming truck. Beckham wishes us to realize that the revolutionary dreams of modern-day black militants are no more likely to be realized than were the more modest dreams of those blacks who came north during the Great Migration. Moreover, the book's ending projects the reader into the vacuum created by Henry's death, whether via an onrushing truck or as a character in a novel which has no more printed pages. Rather than proposing some simpleminded solution to the ethical dilemmas caused by this country's racial prejudices and its socioeconomic plight, Beckham causes the reader of *Runner Mack* to contemplate what he or she might do to ameliorate the deplorable condition of current-day America. Stylistically and thematically

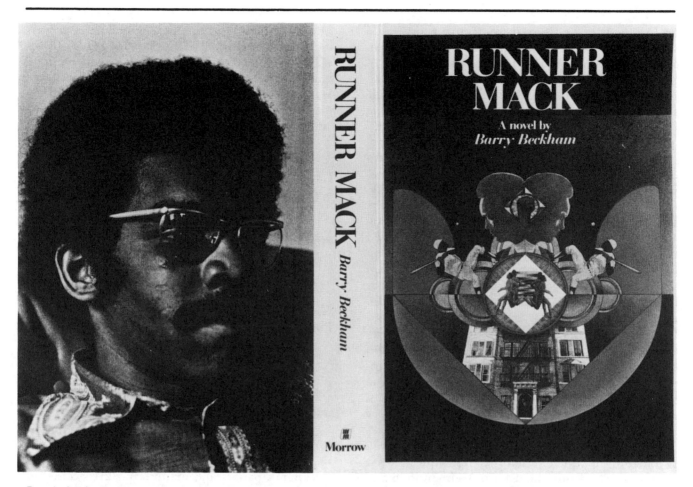

Dust jacket for Beckham's second novel, in which an ambitious black man finds social revolution as illusory as the American Dream

challenging, *Runner Mack* is a tightly wrought masterpiece which probes deeply into the American psyche.

Heartened by the reception of his second novel, his promotion to assistant professor of English at Brown in 1972, and the successful production of his play *Garvey Lives!* during the same year, Beckham, in 1974, began work on *Double Dunk,* a fictionalized biography of Harlem basketball great Earl "The Goat" Manigault. But events of the next half-dozen years were to cause Beckham to question almost all of his values, including his career as an educator and his vocation as a writer. In 1975 he was separated from his wife of almost ten years, Betty, from whom he would be divorced two years later. The experience left him so numb that he stopped writing and resigned his position at Brown.

Fortunately he was persuaded that he should remain at his alma mater and was given a sabbatical leave so that he might return to his writing. But he did so only to weather several storms with publishers and grant agencies, and then to be jarred by a

lightning bolt: the editor at Quadrangle Books who had commissioned *Double Dunk* had left the firm for Simon and Schuster, and Quadrangle was refusing to publish his now-completed manuscript. "I turned sour," he writes, recalling the period in "Why It Is Right to Write"; "I hated publishers, I hated basketball players, I hated editors, I hated writing, I hated sports." A change of heart, and fortune, took several years to effect. Beckham was promoted to associate professor and married to his current wife, Jerree, in 1979, and in 1980 he was made director of the Graduate Writing Program at Brown. His book *Double Dunk* also found a publisher, being released by Holloway House in February 1981 (although it bears the date 1980).

At least one positive effect resulted from *Double Dunk*'s rejection. In addition to adding a few new scenes before resubmitting the book, Beckham altered the narration from third- to second-person. He had known all along that Manigault was too inarticulate for first-person narration to be plausible, but it took time for him to see that the vitality and immediacy he desired to capture resided in a shift to the second person, in which Manigault becomes the "you" described and addressed.

Rather than telling the ballplayer's story as a historian might, Beckham relies on his novelistic skill to create the dialogue and action that allow the reader to understand the talents that made Manigault a brilliant athlete and the forces which reduced him to obscurity. Even as a high-school student, Manigault possessed all the classic court maneuvers, and he had the added ability to dunk, catch, and redunk the basketball in the same leap. But after fathering a bastard child, becoming a drug addict, and being jailed for drug-precipitated crimes, he no longer seemed capable of performing with the flair that might have earned him a professional career. Manigault's life has the potential for becoming a maudlin, cautionary tale about the deleterious effects of Harlem ghetto existence, but Beckham's deft handling of his subject matter elevates the text far above that level. The interjection of humor, the occasional use of surrealistic descriptions, Beckham's careful handling of tone, and the extraordinary impact of the book's second-person narration combine to make *Double Dunk* a very readable and engaging biography.

Exactly what type of writing Beckham will produce in the future remains an open question. At present, a book on the Chase Manhattan Bank, begun some years ago, remains in stasis as he considers developing a number of theatrical pieces, including a reworking of his play *Garvey Lives!*, and as he proceeds with a third novel. Perhaps Howard University Press's 1984 republication of *Runner Mack* may initiate a Beckham revival that will lift his writing out of the relative obscurity into which it has languished and into the critical mainstream, where it belongs.

Interviews:

Sanford Pinsker, "About *Runner Mack:* An Interview with Barry Beckham," *Black Images*, 3 (Autumn 1974): 35-41;

Pinsker, "A Conversation with Barry Beckham," *Studies in Black Literature*, 5 (Winter 1974): 17-20.

References:

Phyllis Rauch Klotman, *Another Man Gone: The Black Runner in Contemporary Afro-American Literature* (Port Washington, N.Y.: Kennikat Press, 1977);

Joe Weixlmann, "The Dream Turned 'Daymare': Barry Beckham's *Runner Mack*," *MELUS*, 8 (Winter 1981): 93-103.

Papers:

Beckham's papers and manuscripts are housed in Boston University's Mugar Memorial Library.

Hal Bennett

(21 April 1930-   )

Ronald Walcott
City University of New York, Kingsborough Community College

SELECTED BOOKS: *The Mexico City Poems and House on Hay* (Chicago: Obsidian Press, 1961);
A Wilderness of Vines (Garden City: Doubleday, 1966);
The Black Wine (Garden City: Doubleday, 1968);
Lord of Dark Places (New York: Norton, 1970);
Wait Until the Evening (Garden City: Doubleday, 1974);
Seventh Heaven (Garden City: Doubleday, 1976);
Insanity Runs In Our Family: Short Stories (Garden City: Doubleday, 1977).

George Harold Bennett was born in Buckingham, Virginia, and although he was reared in the North, his memories of childhood summers spent in the South are the basis of the Southern setting of his fiction. Bennett attended schools in Newark, New Jersey, became a feature writer on the *Newark Herald News* at sixteen, edited his high-school yearbook, and served in the U.S. Air Force, where he was a writer for the Public Information Division and edited a newspaper for 15,000 airmen in Korea. After his discharge, he and two others started their

Hal Bennett (Gale International Portrait Gallery)

own newspaper in Westbury, Long Island, and when that venture failed, Bennett attended Mexico City College, where he was a fellow of the Centro Mexicano de Escritores and wrote most of his first novel, which won him a fiction fellowship from the Bread Loaf Writers' Conference in 1966. He was selected most promising young writer of the year by *Playboy* magazine for his short story "Dotson Gerber Resurrected" in 1970, and he was the recipient of the Faulkner Award in 1973. As influences he cites Eudora Welty, Carson McCullers, Harper Lee, and William Faulkner for their affirmations of individuality. His work also locates him squarely within the satirical tradition articulated in Charles Chesnutt's *The Wife of His Youth,* George S. Schuyler's *Black No More,* and, especially, Wallace Thurman's *The Blacker the Berry,* with its unsparing attention to the details of social imitation and self-flagellation that, for Thurman, constituted so much of black life.

Bennett's first novel, *A Wilderness of Vines* (1966), includes a list of characters identified as light-skinned, brown-skinned, black-skinned, or white-skinned. The entire action of *A Wilderness of Vines* is set in Burnside, Virginia. Bennett's fictional

Burnside, the "burned-side" of American racial experience, is an eccentric, sad, absurd, wonderfully imagined, and scathingly satirized place, a town whose moral and psychological growth was arrested sometime during the Civil War. In Burnside, the problem is not white racism but rather a way of living and thinking founded on color hierarchies in which light-skinned blacks reign and dark-skinned blacks loathe themselves.

Burnside, used as a backdrop for much of his fiction, is important to the history that Bennett's short stories and novels amount to, a history of the post-World War I black man as he makes the journey not only from South to North and from farm to city but also from one type of bondage and bewilderment to another.

Blessed Belshazzar, Baptizer of the Beautiful Blacks, in *A Wilderness of Vines,* is "the love prophet of God" and an escaped rapist who intercedes on behalf of a woman seeking an immaculate conception. Birchie Bartley, the issue of that holy liaison, is an ugly, mad, teenage visionary who makes certain that the deaths she prophesies will come about by arranging them herself; hers is a gospel of homicidal self-hatred. Luann Archer is a half-white bringer of truth and madness, rejected by both races and driven by resentment into the unreality of drugs and fantasies of revenge; love's salvation is her ultimate truth. Preaching the beauty in madness, Charlie Hooker is the moral center of the novel. A failed soul-saver and a former Jehovah's Witness, Hooker now witnesses the country's racial insanity and prescribes a discipline of honesty, understanding, masculine effort, and self-acceptance; for him, all men are mad as a result of generations of hypocrisy; sin is the acceptance of slavery; the capacity for evil proves one's humanity, and only by showing society their insanity can blacks obtain equality. *A Wilderness of Vines* begins in the summer of 1920 and ends with the migration north of the local prostitutes at the outbreak of World War II.

The action of *The Black Wine* (1968) covers the period between July 1953 and summer 1960. Norman Eisenberg and Viola Anderson are the would-be saviors in this novel. Espousing a doctrine of nobility achieved through a regimen of agony, purpose, and self-respect, Eisenberg is attacked by rioters at the end but is saved by the gratitude and respect of his black mistress, the two thus achieving a kind of nobility. Viola Anderson has two gospels. The first is a gospel of racial triumph and self-esteem attained through the negation of murder; the second is a gospel of love and self-forgiveness and the humanness of error. She arranges "spontaneous" demonstrations, has contempt for her gullible followers, and is herself disillusioned by the North's insidious spell.

In Bennett's fiction, no one is safe and everyone is needy. Bennett's characters want to be saved, with salvation encompassing everything from esteem and love and power to a little less confusion, despair, and self-hatred. Because of the logic that persuades black children to identify themselves with "the putrid dark at the bottom of outhouses" that imprisons blacks within the myth of their sexuality and denies their humanity, and because of what it means to be "black and forever afraid," Bennett's characters search for safety and salvation with a tenacity which leads them across improbable, illusion-swept landscapes and into recesses of the mind where they content themselves with fantasies in which they are men and leaders of men, prophets and saviors, founders of religions and keepers of communal secrets, insight-blessed students of history and manipulators of dark powers. Seeking refuge in imaginary havens is the logical response of one who knows he cannot accept himself as he is or the world and its dangers as they are.

Bennett's goal "to explain what I think the Negro is and to do it in terms of fiction" has been most successfully attained in *Lord of Dark Places* and *Seventh Heaven*. *Lord of Dark Places* (1970) is an outstanding satirical novel, an experimental, assured, relentless, dazzling technical performance that offers as protagonist Joe Market, an outrageous Southern youth. Innumerable histories—familial, national, racial, religious, sexual—have conspired to make Joe Market a phallic hero; these histories record his near-apotheosis and inevitable victimization as he tries to undo legacies that simply cannot be undone.

The prologue of *Lord of Dark Places* is set in 1919, while the novel begins in 1951 with the death of Joe's mother and grandmother when the boy is twelve and living in Burnside; it ends in June 1968, shortly after the assassination of Robert F. Kennedy, with the hero's execution in Trenton, New Jersey. In the novel Bennett takes chances with his hero and with his language. Joe Market starts out as a satirical object, essentially no more than a comic foil, becomes a credible, affecting character, and ends as an Everyman who embraces the life-saving promise of madness. That Bennett is able technically to accommodate each of Market's transformations while fixing the novel's emotional center is no small feat. But it is language that distances *Lord of*

Dark Places from Bennett's other works. In its flair for the humor and undiminished joy in things physical, the novel employs a sexual vocabulary which exploits local capacities for improvisation, surprise, and lyricism. Bennett's language conveys, on the one hand, irreverence and high spirits and, on the other, pathos and the incongruous but very real vitality of an individual who has come to accept himself in terms of myths he does not in his wildest dreams suspect, far less understand. A detective story, a blues, a Bildungsroman, a black black comedy, a tragedy, and a dissertation on the histories and stereotypes that conspire to man and to unman black Americans, *Lord of Dark Places* is a turning point in Bennett's work, the first time he shows at his command the vision and verbal resources of the serious literary artist.

In *Lord of Dark Places*, Madame Eudora, Joe Market's grandmother, founds the Church of Stephen Martyr, "which taught, in a sly, abstract kind of way, that niggers ought to stay in their place and die like dogs." For Titus, her son, Christianity raises "an ideal of radical purity that can never be fully realized by black Christians," and thus, "a wide, unbridgeable gap is created between the ideas of *black* good and evil and *white* good and evil." Titus's solution is to establish a religion that makes the phallus and "the naked male black body central parts of his religious symbolism." His Church of the Naked Disciple judges a man by the things he won't do, and he saves black souls by being "as contrary to everything as I can be. When the Bible says black, I say white. When it says good, I say evil. When it says *Behold, Jehovah is a God of light,* I say, *Behold, He is the Lord of dark places; for his children gnash their teeth and cry unto Him and are not heard.*"

Grandson of Roosevelt (who was lynched and castrated) and son of Titus (who was raped and beaten to death), Joe Market nominates himself as the lord of dark places and takes his responsibilities seriously: He saves two people, one his son, from "the holocaust of life" by murdering them, taunts another into committing suicide, and sacrifices himself in the electric chair, an aspiring savior who, at the moment of death, has a vision of God.

At the start, Joe Market is a witless, self-enraptured phallic adventurer more or less convinced of his own divinity. Later, in the North, he is a man who needs dark places in which to operate; disillusioned by war and haunted by death, he is fool, prostitute, student, husband, father, veteran, murderer, detective, patriot, and cynic. At the close, he is set adrift from history and love and tries desperately, fatally, to reconnect: a guilt-driven madman dreaming an insane dream of black salvation in which he is both redeemer of his people and their redemption; slayer and slain; Christ, Father, and Holy Ghost in one; a man of supreme courage and strength—the lord of dark places answering his father's call—and a dealer in death and delusion.

Seventh Heaven (1976) is every bit as flamboyant as *Lord of Dark Places,* its language as supple and its wisdom as disturbing. *Seventh Heaven* —the community's ironic designation of a Cousinsville, New Jersey, housing project whose residents "had come from Burnside or some place like it in the South"—begins with the aftermath of the riots of the 1960s and ends with the aftermath of Watergate; along the way, the hero, Bill Kelsey, journeys to his birthplace in the South to escape ghettoes which "stifle" his freedom and "negate" his manhood, only to discover that "the true origins" of Burnside lie "in the accustomed servitude, the misery and exploitation, the familiar segregation of a Cousinsville." Somehow, Cousinsville *is* Burnside, and Burnside, we learn in *A Wilderness of Vines,* is an instance of the "larger and more malicious insanity" of the world.

Bill Kelsey, who "hates the darkness, dark things," wends his way through "ghettoes of our mind" in which black people are caricatures of themselves; the "blacker-than thou" skin game is "the Judeo-Christian concept turned around"; "the whole neo-African trend" is a "snake choking on its own tail"; white juju is actually more powerful than black juju; murderers abound, and sex is the only possible freedom, a freedom indistinguishable, however, from servitude. Impressed with his own physical beauty and virility, but aware of his aging and vulnerability, Kelsey is interested in how things begin and end and terrified that they will end for him as they ended for his father and for so many other black men—"growing old and useless" and alone. While he resents the ghetto's confinement, he knows that his "most honest, truest self" finds fulfillment in the life of the sexual slave; he is a good man but a weak one and only occasionally willing to assume responsibility for his own life. Before he is led away, at the end, "into a familiar and consoling servitude" of sex, "the magic of his own soul, corrupted by centuries of shuffling and shucking, working against him," he takes a pickax to a building and proves to himself that not even brick monsters of one's own making, not even the worst nightmares, are indestructible. He is only "half-free" at the novel's conclusion, but that is more freedom than Joe Market or most of Bennett's other characters ever know.

Complicity is part of the logic of Kelsey's life. As a teenager, he spent the two most enjoyable years of his life as the prisoner of Aunt Keziah, a juju; they were enjoyable because of "the sex, the domination, the servitude, the illusions or delusions that had made him feel like a man imprisoned on all sides by woman." In another kind of jail, he meets Bobby Bryant and knows that Bobby and he are in a "prison of innocence and childhood," that they are "paid humpers . . . living off women who wanted to be someone's mother the same way that those who were being mothered wanted to be somebody's children." Surrounded by dreaming blacks, he misses "the cool, calm presence—the undeniable authority—of some white person." And at the end, he rushes to a white woman who has proved her love for him by killing black rivals and by offering him "the familiar and consoling servitude of love."

Wait Until the Evening (1974) begins with the funerals of Kevin Brittain's brother and grandfather, in September 1944, when Brittain is eight years old. The novel ends in the fall of 1970 with Brittain, in Cousinsville, New Jersey, plotting the murder of his father in Burnside. Without solid convictions, Kevin Brittain leaves prison at the close of *Wait Until the Evening* and returns to "the monstrous edifice of time, and memory, and waiting to be free." Struck "by how little I know, how much I lie, and how desperate I generally feel," Brittain is a philosopher of sorts who understands the point of being black, which is that murder is the holiest undertaking of "people who have no other way to esteem themselves," and who puts that philosophy into action by evolving "a system of getting rid of people" who threaten or irritate him. Haunted by "the unbelievably important part" death plays in his life, he becomes obsessed with the idea of redemption and the need to sidestep tragedy, a need that makes of him a self-confessed mediocrity. When he discovers that by using holy murder to give meaning and expression to her life his grandmother has become one of "the principal players in the drama that is America," Brittain suddenly sees with "the clarity inside of shadows." From that moment he will be menace on the prowl, invisible death, the Big Nigger so feared by his surrogate parent, Cop Magee, who nonetheless arrests him for crimes he did not commit, crimes committed by his grandmother who operates in the dark, mixing her poisons, a mad, misguided, unloved woman persecuted by a husband, a former slave, who treated his family "as worse than slaves." Once upon a time, this unloved woman learned that if she could destroy her capacity for love, evil would flourish and her husband would die. Like his grandmother, Brittain comes to know that for those who own the night, history is the scent of blood in the air. In *Wait Until the Evening* Kevin Brittain and his grandmother know that only murder endows black life with both form and integrity. In *Seventh Heaven,* however, "the way" is love's sweet bondage.

The Reverend Winston Cobb, the man who is Kevin Brittain's spiritual father and Bill Kelsey's alter ego, is the only character to appear in all five of Bennett's novels. Tall, black, Northern-educated, good-looking, and shackled to a sick wife he no longer loves and must kill to become "a pure black man" fulfilling "a black man's mission," Reverend Cobb is the lord of dark places, invisible and protean, "a dreadful presence" inspiring murder and chaos. "Father, brother, friend"; Christ in the Christmas tableaux and scourge of Christianity; perfume salesman, hater of death, protector of the defenseless, castigator of the beast within; prophet who warns the races of their enslavement by hypocrisy; true democrat and emancipator who frees his people from the legacy of ignorance by having the Declaration of Independence recited on White Citizens Day, Cobb is also local historian and lunatic revolutionary who tries to burn history to the ground, apostle of love who reminds us of the violence done in love's name, and ineffective advocate of understanding, change, dignity, and mercy. Possessed by demons, Cobb is nevertheless a gifted teacher who knows that without wisdom and strength, man is destroyed.

In *A Wilderness of Vines* and *The Black Wine,* Cobb is an underpaid preacher driven by hunger to blackmail and by madness to murder. He blackmails a woman into giving him her handyman to help him run a farm recently purchased with a loan from Ida Carlisle, Burnside's petty tyrant. At Carlisle's trial for "pretending to be white," he perjures himself to make certain that Carlisle is convicted without his repaying the loan. He sets his wife on fire, flees north, meets and decides to save Viola Anderson's daughter Dolly, whom he apparently deems crippled by self-loathing. He saves her from herself and from the world by cutting her into pieces.

In *Wait Until the Evening* Brittain visits Cobb in the death house in Trenton but never quite sees Cobb in the shadows, just as earlier, sitting in the front seat of a car with him, Dolly wasn't certain that the man driving was Cobb, for in the dark, "All I saw, actually, was the figure of this black man looking at me. I think it was Winston." When Brittain proposes turning on lights, Cobb replies, "I like the dark." Cobb senses, knows, that Brittain is a fellow murderer, and the two men masturbate. The encounter with Cobb leaves Brittain "feeling like a corpse" and thinking that "somebody ought to be punished for what had been done to *me*. Why hadn't my father—somebody—taught me about the violence that men do to one another in the name of love?" He begins planning his father's death.

In *Lord of Dark Places,* Joe Market attends Cobb's execution and experiences "a certain pride at being the only colored man from Decatur who was going to see the spectacle." "After all, it wasn't every day that one nigger had the chance to see another nigger burn." The electric chair looks "like judgment seat," and Cobb, "like a tired old lizard." Cobb reminds Joe of Titus, both preachers who killed their wives. And "something inside" Joe, incipient madness, giggles. In his last words, Cobb reminds the spectators that the duty of the church is not to save sinners but to make men sin, for "it is fear of the example of Christ that causes good men to turn bad." As the current surges through his body, the lights dim and Cobb has an erection as death becomes the final dark place. As happened with Kevin Brittain and David Hunter—who, after hearing his father had murdered Dolly Anderson, went looking for people he could kill and "stuff" into his sofa—Joe leaves the site of Cobb's death "so angry and disgusted that he felt like killing somebody himself, he'd certainly kill with more mercy and dignity than" the electric chair had.

Cobb illustrates two of the guiding principles of Bennett's work: without love there is no freedom, and without history there is no hope. By escaping the bondage of love, Cobb also breaks free of the constraints of sanity and is doomed. And by becoming the lord of dark places who delivers unto murder and madness the children who gnash their teeth and cry out, Cobb seeks to transcend the suffering of history but finds that human action and its consequences take place on this plane, and from *this* plane death is the only escape. Cobb shows too that, in the face of the terrifying misery of life, survival is a matter of choosing among insanities. Nevertheless, sane or insane, Bennett's males hold truth more dear than life, and their early deaths prove at least that much.

With their alternating Southern and Northern settings, overlapping time periods, characters who appear or who are mentioned in book after book, and themes and preoccupations that are stated in one fiction but receive fuller exploration in another, Bennett's works elaborate a single story or, more accurately, cover a single territory, the landmarks and implications of which each successive fiction maps out in more and more surprising detail. Bill Kelsey is not Joe Market, but he has heard of him. Like the protagonists in Bennett's other novels, the two are brothers in spirit who wrestle with familiar problems and arrive at familiar conclusions. They are brothers who live in the same or similar places, who go on the same or similar journeys, who know many of the same people, and who are even tempted to madness by the same man. Structurally, each of Bennett's novels is a series of baptisms and falls from innocence to experience; thematically, each involves a task performed to prove masculine potential, a descent into an underworld in search of purpose and identity, and an attempt to understand the past of one's fathers. Emotionally, each is a disorienting, tragicomic excursion into and out of ghettoes of the mind, into and out of the secret, motivating depths of one's dreams and a culture's myths.

The women, however, tell a different story, a story of desperate bids for glory, of answering the call to history's main action, of being "the principal players in the drama that is America, while black men are largely ignored, or, at best, misunderstood." The women in *Lord of Dark Places* may be whores and martyrs, wives who work themselves to death and simpleminded worshippers of the black phallus, but their undeniable strength offers hope for the resurrection of the black men. In *Wait Until the Evening* Brittain's mother successfully plots her family's escape from the despotism of her father-in-law, and Grandmother Brittain is a Cobb who lives to kill another day. In *A Wilderness of Vines* Ida Carlisle single-handedly holds Burnside in thrall with her power to make blacks "uncomfortable" by reminding them of "the old days" of slavery "when they were nothing." Luann Archer rescues herself with love as does the hero's mother by freeing her repressed self. In *The Black Wine* Viola Anderson hypnotizes followers with strength of personality and sheer need, while David Hunter's mother moves rioters through force of will to find other targets. At the end of *Seventh Heaven* Maria Beñes will mother and love Kelsey and offer him "familiar and consoling servitude." And the other women in Kelsey's life will all offer him the same

Dust jacket for Bennett's fifth novel, in which Southern blacks living in a New Jersey housing project discover the true origins of their racial servitude

necessary control and guidance; they do not bow to his maleness, as he would like, but he does bow to their femaleness, to the urgency of their love, to their will to live life passionately. Without exception, the women in Kelsey's life fight over him and for him, prostitute themselves for him, kill and sometimes die for him, free him and enslave him, and make sure he knows something of love's power so that he may again become a black man—a man with "the certain hope that . . . a black woman somewhere held a sculpture of another black woman and her suckling child; and that one or possibly both of those figures represented and preserved the part of him that was sacred, soft . . . and half-free."

Strutting onstage with daggers drawn, the women are mad too, of course, mad with their juju fantasies of violence and power, their nostalgia for systems already invalidated by history, their too-ready need to confuse murder with mercy. They are as mad as the men, but Bennett's fiction allows them a vigor, a beauty, a coherence, a desire to meet life on this plane, and a capacity for growth which, with the very large exception of Joe Market, it does not allow the men. Life is no fairer to the sexes than it is to the races.

Of the stories in *Insanity Runs In Our Family* (1977), the finest are "Dotson Gerber Resurrected," "The Abominable Snowman," and "The Day My Sister Hid the Ham." "Dotson Gerber Resurrected" follows the futile efforts of a black man to return to the white community what it no longer wants, a white man he has planted in a collard patch and for whose murder he would appreciate any kind of recognition at all. Although unheralded, his act revives his wife's respect and love for him and his confidence in his ability to walk in the world as a man; but he will go to his grave, his son knows, still thinking of whites as the measure of all things. This story about rebellion and a man's need to redeem himself and the inevitability of his failure is an ironic, bittersweet example of the originality of Bennett's vision and the sureness of his craft.

"The Abominable Snowman" takes place in the Adirondacks during a racial revolution. The conflict is to the death; its unexpected source is black children; its weapons are magic and madness, and its purpose in the early stages is the elimination of the undeserving, those who have not earned the right to participate in the creation of a new world. In wanders a vacationing middle-class black couple. The woman makes no secret of her contempt for blacks in general and for her husband in particular;

her husband suffers in her estimation because he is dark-skinned and male. He is a social worker and a doctoral candidate preparing a dissertation on the revolution he thinks will be caused by "that final unacceptable insult where man's spirit must rebel or remain enslaved forever." He is proved wrong about the cause and the target: people like himself who are judged uncommitted and uncaring by the young and worthy only of execution. The story's horror unfolds gradually. That a revolution is taking place, that the husband is involved, that in dying he will fulfill his destiny, and that his crimes against race and future are greater than those of his self-hating wife do not become clear until the story's closing images. Without strain, "The Abominable Snowman" addresses generational, sexual, and racial strife, man's willful ignorance and rejection of salvation, and the need for a new mythology and symbolism. The story is a nightmare, eerie, powerful, and disturbingly logical as only the most terrifying dreams are.

In "The Day My Sister Hid the Ham," a woman gleefully emasculates her brother, who happens to be the narrator. The story concerns both her need to see her brother accept fear and irrationality as his lot in life and her pretensions to station and power as she imposes an imaginary past over the harsh circumstances of her present and envies those like her brother who choose to live in the present and in the company of men. Giving the tale its power is the care the author takes to show how the insecurities attending jealousy, race, and sexual identity play into the hands of a man's enemy as she goes about remaking him in her image. At the beginning, the narrator hears that his sister has been gossiping about his not being a man, not her kind of man. At the end, by agreeing to murder, he acquiesces in her notion of life as an act of spite and man as a wounded animal scurrying for cover, bodies of innocents in its wake.

As a revelation of complex emotions, fierce needs, disastrous choices, a brother and sister's unhealthy intimacy, and the working out of a family's doom over generations, "The Day My Sister Hid the Ham" is Bennett's "The Fall of the House of Usher." On one level of meaning, its subject is the perversions created by disappointment, betrayal, and unfocused rage, and on another, man's complicity in his own moral demise. On a third level, the story explores the peculiar nature of Bennett's craft and the limits of imagination.

At one point, the narrator, in his sister's cellar, looks at a ham she has placed in a washing machine as protection against the insects that rule her house. He places dirty clothes into the machine, turns it on and washes both clothing and ham.

> My grandmother's platter was the first casualty. As I listened to it being crunched into the machine, I felt the chains that had held me to centuries of subservience suddenly snap. I was trying to cleanse more than ham. I was trying to wash off the dirt of generations that had brought my family first from Africa, then from my grandfather's mansion to this grimy cellar.
>
> When the machine had finished its last cycle, I opened the lid and took out what was left of the ham. Most of the lean meat had separated and was spread among the damp clothes that clung like an infestation of leeches to the circumference of the tub. Most of what was left of the ham was skin and bone, and fat made even whiter by the bleach. As I lifted out the ham, I thought how white somehow always manages to survive the best efforts and the worst intentions of black men.

Horror and beauty are ingredients of Bennett's fiction. Beauty is terrible and unfathomable, Dostoevski says in *The Brothers Karamazov*, because "here the boundaries meet and all contradictions exist side by side." Roaches, cobwebs, worm-eaten beams; the electric impulse of sex; ham and clothing and detergent and bleach; the dirt of generations in a grimy cellar whose "uglier, deeper mustiness was . . . the origin of the miasma upstairs"; anger, catharsis, and escape from centuries of subservience; self-deflation and poetry; the satirist's withering gaze and his dark, dark laughter—here the contradictions exist side by side.

In Bennett's fiction, there is beauty in black people's "powerful determination not to die," in their "hallelujah of the spirit" which Bennett calls the black wine and its dance, for even as the wine kills, it makes hope possible. The dance of wine is a celebration in which "life is the dregs; love is the dance." There is beauty in the characters' "disguised defiance" and unyielding intelligence, their friendships and loyalties, their escape from certain traps and their need to take matters into their own hands, whatever the consequences. There is beauty in their bizarre, yet courageous attempts to find reasons to go on hoping and dreaming and living and in their familiarity with the ambivalence of "love's necessary and sweet bondage" and with the advice that ends *The Black Wine* that one should "love as much as you can . . . every chance you get" and forgive oneself because "nobody's perfect, not even you. . . ." There is beauty in the things that matter. The quest to redeem themselves and the world in which their children live matters. Unearthing the secrets of the past matters; so too does the power of the word be it a sermon, the Declaration of Independence, speaking in tongues, debates between friends, or the prophetic mutterings of the congenitally insane. Juju matters because it is the power of love and imagination. Truth and justice and freedom and compassion and rebellion matter. And humor matters because it may be the only sane response to the craziness which makes the world go 'round. But in the coming together of horror and beauty there is also racism, slavery, and fear; self-pity and self-loathing, guilt and hypocrisy, submission and unlived life.

"The Day My Sister Hid the Ham" also tells us about the uses to which imagination can and cannot be put. The interest of Bennett's characters in inspired perceptions and creative acts is a metaphor for the artist's ambition to fashion symbols, to transform life into art, and to surmount the problems attending the exercise of aesthetic control over his material and vision. The artist's risk-taking and discipline, his transfiguring of experience, his wedding of form to substance are, for Bennett's figures, triumphs of meaning over absurdity and audacity over unimagined possibilities.

Bennett's intention "to explain what I think the Negro is and to do it in terms of fiction" has not been translated into a commitment to naturalistic or protest fiction; instead his strategy has been to combine and in the process to subvert the conventions of several genres, including detective fiction, satire, the novels of education and manners, the picaresque epic, the tall tale, and the mythic journey of the hero to recover a sacred object (his sanity, a nation's integrity). The fiction is incisive and irreverent and as likely to skewer black hypocrisy and betrayal as white racism and delusion. But like all good satire, Bennett's work is serious, for Bennett never forgets what Ellison's hero reminds us of at the close of *Invisible Man,* namely, that the mind which has conceived a pattern of living should never lose sight of the chaos against which that pattern was conceived.

Bennett has received critical praise for his increasing maturity as a writer. Presently working on a novel in Mexico, where a man "can live like a man," Bennett will continue to explore black consciousness and reveal his "deep understanding of the complexity and difficulty of interracial communication."

References:
Hoyt W. Fuller, "Negro Writing Is Not Literature

Bag," *Black World* (November 1966): 50, 97-98;
Ronald Walcott, "The Novels of Hal Bennett, Part I: The Writer As Satirist," *Black World* (June 1974): 36, 89-97;
Walcott, "The Novels of Hal Bennett, Part II: The Writer As Magician/Priest," *Black World* (July 1974): 78-96.

David Bradley
(September 1950-   )

Valerie Smith
Princeton University

BOOKS: *South Street* (New York: Viking, 1975);
The Chaneysville Incident (New York: Harper & Row, 1981).

PERIODICAL PUBLICATIONS: "The Happiness of the Long Distance Runner," *The Village Voice* (August 1976);
"Assignment No. 4: The Business Letter," *Tracks* (Spring 1977);
"Eye Witness News," *Tracks* (Spring 1978);
"City of the Big Sleep," *Signature* (August 1979);
"Let's Just Be Friends," *Savvy* (June 1981).

David Bradley ranks among the most sophisticated literary stylists of his generation. His two novels present subtle and original perspectives on issues that traditionally have concerned significant Afro-American writers: the meaning of community, the effects of racism, the shape and substance of history. His first book, *South Street,* went out of print soon after publication and has yet to receive the attention it merits. But his award-winning second novel, *The Chaneysville Incident,* has established Bradley's reputation among major contemporary authors.

Bradley is the only son of Mrs. Harriet M. Jackson Bradley and the late Rev. D. H. Bradley, Sr. Born and raised in Bedford, Pennsylvania (farm country near the Maryland border and on the edge of the Pennsylvania soft-coal region), he attended local public schools and graduated from the Bedford Area High School in June 1968. An outstanding student, Bradley received numerous academic honors both before and upon graduation from the

University of Pennsylvania in 1972. In 1968 he was named a Benjamin Franklin Scholar, a National Achievement Scholar, and a Presidential Scholar. When he graduated summa cum laude from Pennsylvania, he was awarded a General Honors Certificate and a Thouron British-American Exchange Scholarship.

An undergraduate English and creative-writing major, Bradley felt alienated from the urban, politicized students with whom he attended college in the late 1960s and early 1970s. As he told Mel Watkins in an interview in the *New York Times Book Review,* "A lot of [the other students] had the illusion that black people had power. But I had grown up in a rural white society, and I knew damn well we had no power." He discovered an affinity with the working-class people who frequented his favorite neighborhood bar on South Street in Philadelphia. In contrast to the students, these people harbored few delusions about the nature of power and authority in this country. As he remarked to Watkins, "Their lives were terrible—they just lived with the situation and made the best of it." From the stories they told him, Bradley drew inspiration and material for his first novel, which he wrote while still in college.

South Street (1975) explores the inner life of the Philadelphia ghetto, with particular emphasis on its three social and cultural centers: Lightnin' Ed's Bar and Grill (the corner dive owned and managed by genial but formidable Leo), the Elysium Hotel (headquarters of Leroy Briggs, a bloodthirsty, womanizing numbers runner), and the Word of Life (the nondenominational, theatrical showcase

David Bradley (photo © by Thomas Victor)

of a church over which a lecherous charlatan, the Reverend Mr. J. Peter Sloan, presides). With insightful characterizations, strikingly accurate dialogue, and irreverent wit, Bradley examines the kinds of communal relationships that bind people of the street to each other.

Much of the novel focuses on Adlai Stevenson Brown, a young black poet and part-time bartender who is new to South Street. Initially he shares a luxury apartment with his upper-middle-class, Vassar-educated, English-professor girl friend named Alicia Hadley. However, material comforts and an unending round of quarrels and social obligations force a wedge between the two of them and frustrate Brown's attempts to write. To alleviate this tension and to find inspiration for his poetry, he moves to a ghetto apartment of his own.

Brown becomes something of a regular at Lightnin' Ed's when he moves to South Street; indeed, the novel appears to center on his relationship to the people he meets there. In Jake, the kind-hearted resident wino, he finds a drinking buddy and confidant, but he battles regularly with

Rayburn Wallace, an angry janitor who drinks because his wife is unfaithful. 'Nessa, a prostitute, Leroy's former girl friend, and Rayburn's sister-in-law, moves in with Brown and replaces Alicia in his affections. He helps her solve a sexual problem; in turn, she inspires him to resume his writing.

Ultimately, Brown's quest is only part of the subject of *South Street*. The novel is really about the street itself, as Bradley's energetic and shifting narrative makes clear. The stories of four other characters—Rayburn, Jack, Leroy, and Brother Fletcher (an earnest associate pastor in the Word of Life)—at different times usurp the foreground from Brown's. These frequent changes in perspective illustrate various ways in which individuals confront the turbulence of ghetto life. Furthermore, the shifts imitate the vibrancy and the multifariousness of the world the author explores.

Bradley's ability to weave the different stories together evinces his stylistic grace and energy. However, this narrative mesh is by no means his sole accomplishment in the novel. He renders physical detail with cinematic precision, as the image of a

*Dust jacket for Bradley's first novel, a cinematic view of street life
in a Philadelphia ghetto*

drunken, depressed Rayburn indicates: " [Rayburn]
lay quietly then, in the midst of a cliché: a neon light
outside the window sending red light across the
rumpled sheets of an unmade bed, blinking on and
off, on and off, like an electric pulse. Rayburn's own
blood pounded in his temples, his lungs sucked in
the heavy hot air, forcing out vomit-soured breath
which made the dust devils hiding beneath the bed,
tinted pink by the blinking light, dance drunkenly
across the floor." His ear for the cadences, idioms,
and inflections of the spoken word is unfailing:
" 'Slot-machine 'Nessa. Five balls for a dime.' That's
what they used to call me, 'fore I got smart an'
stopped givin' change, just like the subway." His
wit—broad, ironic, and unabashed—has been
compared favorably to Richard Pryor's. And his
characterizations, from Brown to the minor figures,
are generally balanced and credible.

These compelling strengths do not, unfortunately, mask the novel's two shortcomings. Brown's

relationship to 'Nessa (the hooker with a heart of
gold) is sentimentalized and provides the book with
its one false note. More significant, the novel seems
lacking in thematic unity. Bradley writes convincingly from the perspective of a range of street
people and moves smoothly from story to story. Yet
it remains unclear whether the stories are meant to
parallel or counterpoint one another. The portions
of the narrative given over to Brown, Jake, and
Brother Fletcher share a common theme: the
search for meaningful values. Leroy's and
Rayburn's stories, however, bear little relation to
this concern. Such diffuseness offers one possible
explanation for the failure of *South Street* to sustain
the popular or critical attention it deserves. But the
acclaim with which his second novel has been received may well generate a resurgence of interest in
Bradley's early work.

The Chaneysville Incident (1981), winner of the
1982 Pen/Faulkner Prize and a Book-of-the-Month
Club Alternate Selection, was over ten years in the
making. Bradley became interested in the local
legend that gives the novel its name in 1969, when
his mother, a local historian gathering facts for the
area's bicentennial, discovered thirteen unmarked
graves on the property of a Bedford County land-
owner. Mrs. Bradley's findings confirmed a regional myth: that a group of thirteen slaves, en
route to freedom on the Underground Railroad,
asked to be killed when they realized that they were
to be recaptured. Even in college, Bradley was in-
trigued with the episode, and wrote about it in an
unpublished collection of short stories.

His graduate work contributed even more to
the evolution of the novel. After Penn, he attended
the Institute for United States Studies at the University of London. He received his M.A. in area
studies, United States, from Kings College, London, in January 1974. While at Kings College,
Bradley began to study rigorously the history of
nineteenth-century America, a project he continued when he returned to the States. As he told
Mel Watkins, he soon knew that his next novel
would center on those thirteen runaway slaves and
include the fruits of his research. Finding a literary
framework to support his historical evidence
proved elusive; Bradley wrote four versions of
Chaneysville before the final draft.

The Chaneysville Incident is the story of a young
man's search for the meaning of his father's life and
death. The protagonist, a young, black, Phila-
delphia-based professor of history named John
Washington, does not know that this is what he is
after when he returns home to western Pennsyl-

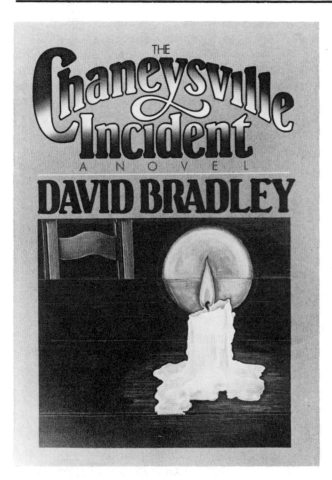

Dust jacket for Bradley's second novel, winner of the 1982 Faulkner Prize

vania to nurse (and then to bury) his ailing surrogate-father, Old Jack Crawley. But Jack's death prompts him to visit his parents' home and study Moses' (his late father's) exhaustive collection of manuscripts and journals. This research helps him to understand his father's suicide and its relation to the death of the thirteen fugitive slaves years before. Moreover, the process of describing his findings to his white psychiatrist girl friend, Judith, shows him what the true meaning of history is.

In *Chaneysville*, Bradley weaves numerous stories into his central narrative with more grace and justification than he does in *South Street*. He masters this effect here, in part, by focusing on two consummate raconteurs, Old Jack and John. Jack, a mangy shoeshiner who spent his life in an isolated cabin, was one of Moses' closest friends. He assumed responsibility for instructing John in the ways of the woods after Moses' sudden death, teaching him to drink, hunt, fish, and build a fire. Moreover, he spun for John countless yarns about his own escapades with Moses and their mutual cohort, Josh White. John's return home triggers flashbacks of his own childhood and adolescent adventures, and recalls a series of the old man's stories.

John appears to have inherited his talent for recording history from Jack, the storyteller, and from Moses, the keeper of documents, although he has difficulty reconciling his analytic and narrative abilities. In the early sections of the novel, he tends to fall into extended, pedantic stories about sociological phenomena and historical events. Indeed, Judith upbraids him for hiding his feelings by talking in lectures: "all neat and logical and precise." But John learns to transform facts imaginatively when he discovers the store of journals and manuscripts on which his father was working at the time of his death. The data Moses had accumulated means nothing to John until he can reconstruct the minds of his father and of the thirteen slaves. When he can explain what motivated the fugitives to give up their lives, he understands also his father's reason for taking his own.

Bradley unerringly captures the speech of a wide variety of characters: from Old Jack, a mine of bawdy and folk expressions, to Judith, whose irony is laced with the vernacular of her training as a psychiatrist. Again, his descriptions are precise, an accomplishment which is all the more noteworthy here since he employs such a range of narrators. For all its complexity, however, this second novel has none of the disunity that mars the first. Indeed, as Bradley himself has noted, the novel is somewhat reminiscent of a musical composition in which the different movements represent variations on a common theme. The central narrative, John's flashbacks, Jack's stories, and John's version of the Chaneysville incident all exemplify the kinds of physical and emotional cruelty that are commonplace within a racist culture. Furthermore, Bradley shows that back of each of these incidents of abuse—whether the killing of fugitives, the attempted lynching of Josh and Old Jack, or the tension between John and Judith—lies the fear of miscegenation.

During his career as a fiction writer, Bradley has worked as an editor, a professor of English, and a free-lance magazine writer. He has held editorial positions with J. B. Lippincott, Charter Books, and Ace Science Fiction. Currently assistant professor of English at Temple University in Philadelphia, he has been a visiting lecturer at the University of Pennsylvania and at San Diego State University. A frequent reviewer for the *New York Times Book Review* and the *Washington Post Book World*, he has written articles (on topics as diverse as long-distance running and long-distance relationships) for such publications as *The Village Voice, Quest/77,* and *Savvy.*

The Chaneysville Incident, acclaimed by fiction writers and by popular and scholarly writers alike, placed Bradley in the vanguard of contemporary novelists. More definitively than *South Street* does, it represents an exploration of both the uses of history in fiction and the possibilities of narrative form. Bradley is currently at work on two projects: a de-

tective novel and a book about the 1960s. The former promises to display again Bradley's skill at rendering the intricacies of a mind both analytic and speculative. With its historical focus, the latter will provide the writer with another opportunity to interpret for the present the lessons of the past.

Reference:

Mel Watkins, "Thirteen Runaway Slaves and David Bradley," *New York Times Book Review,* 19 April 1981, pp. 7, 20-21.

Cecil Brown
(3 July 1943-   )

Jean M. Bright
North Carolina A & T State University

BOOKS: *The Life and Loves of Mr. Jiveass Nigger* (New York: Farrar, Straus & Giroux, 1969);

Days Without Weather (New York: Farrar, Straus & Giroux, 1982).

PERIODICAL PUBLICATIONS:

Fiction:

"I Never Raped One Either, But I Don't Let It Bother Me," *Evergreen Review,* 16 (May 1972): 47-49;

"A Few Hypes You Should Be Hip To By Now," *Black Scholar,* 6 (June 1975): 21-29.

Nonfiction:

"The Apotheosis of the Prodigal Son," *Kenyon Review,* 30 (Fall 1968): 654-661;

"BAD WRITING, OR unclewillieandthebadpoet," *Partisan Review,* 39 (Spring 1972): 406-411;

"Interview with Tennessee Williams," *Partisan Review,* 45 (Summer 1978): 276-345;

"Blues for Blacks in Hollywood," *Mother Jones,* 6 (January 1981): 20-28.

Cecil Morris Brown is a novelist, essayist, short-story writer, university lecturer, critic, and screenwriter who is possibly best known for *The Life and Loves of Mr. Jiveass Nigger.* This satirical and outrageously comic yet deeply serious story of black survival in a corrupt society reflected the mood of both street-wise young blacks and sardonic college students of the 1960s. Confusing and boring to

some reviewers, praised by others, the novel received widespread attention.

Brown was born in Bolton, North Carolina, to Cecil and Dorothy Brown—tobacco sharecroppers. By the time he was fifteen, Cecil was sharecropping his own five-acre plot, and at the age of eighteen he entered the Agricultural and Technical State University in Greensboro. In the classroom, he and a friend named George Raleigh (the prototype, possibly, of George Washington, Brown's major fictional character) amused and delighted their classmates with irreverent, comic, and often incisive comments about the weaknesses of literary figures, critics, and textbooks which at that time totally omitted black writers. An insatiable reader, Brown was dissatisfied with what he considered the inadequate library at the school.

Brown transferred to Columbia University, where he received a B.A. in English in 1966. There he met LeRoi Jones, a drama-course lecturer whom he admired and about whom he wrote: "[Jones] taught black people how to survive . . . showed them images they could believe in . . . images that heal, soothe, and make healthy again." In 1967 Brown received an M.A. from the University of Chicago, where one of his greatest disappointments was the refusal by Saul Bellow to allow him to enroll in one of his classes.

Nineteen sixty-eight was a most important and eventful year for Brown. He had begun to write,

Cecil Brown (photo © by Jerry Bauer)

and his articles began to appear in *Negro Digest, Kenyon Review,* and *Evergreen Review.* In the summer he went to California, where he met Richard Pryor, and the two discussed the kinds of films they dreamed of making: Brown as writer and Pryor as actor. Later Brown was given second-place screenwriter credit for Pryor's film "Which Way Is Up?," and Pryor assisted Brown in having one of his plays presented at an International Film Festival in Cannes. In September of that year Brown began teaching at the University of Illinois at Chicago Circle and worked on his novel.

The Life and Loves of Mr. Jiveass Nigger was published in 1969. George Washington, the main character, is a black ex-country boy and student turned part-time confidence man who is stranded penniless in a European city. He visits an American diplomat's office for assistance, and after the two men discuss their college experiences, the diplomat offers George a job—washing windows. George declines and decides to become a gigolo catering to wealthy women in Copenhagen. He has no difficulty in pleasing his customers, but he is an inept businessman and a financial flop who shuttles back and forth between bedrooms and a tavern where he

holds forth as a literary critic. He is beaten senseless in a tavern fight, and when he regains consciousness in a hospital, he decides to find an honest way to go home again.

Brown's novel is based on the archetype of the prodigal son: A young black man, far from home, finally admits to himself that he is a fool and a prodigal destroying himself by wallowing in a moral pigsty among swinish people. The theme of an accursed society, without love or honor, is woven into this moral fable with multilevel complexity.

The ambiguity of the novel begins with the title itself: Is *Jiveass Nigger* an expression of slang humor or does it carry the undertones of racial conflict? Is the name George Washington a comic put-down of a historical figure or is it a realistic rendering of a name given to countless black male children? Again and again there are juxtapositions of characters as they see themselves and as seen by others, and sometimes this fusion of the real and the imaginary is blurred. George easily changes his name to Paul or Julius or Anthony as his imagination leads him, and no one knows the difference or cares. To himself he is Tom Jones or Joseph Andrews or the "unfortunate traveller" of Shakespeare's contemporaries or even Virginia Woolf's Orlando. To the white diplomat he is a stereotype—Sambo, boy, black menial, window washer. In the tavern George is the coffeehouse literary critic who loftily discusses Milton's *Comus* and concludes that this work "is really about the nigger marrying Miss Ann . . . very contemporary." Further, George says, he can relate to Julien Sorel and Tom Jones, to Malcolm X and Eldridge Cleaver, to the protagonists of *The Satyricon* and *The Golden Ass,* but not to Bigger (Nigger Chigger) Thomas because he cannot relate to stupidity, fear, and demoralization.

In contrast to its treatment in traditional novels of furtive and guilt-ridden adulteries, sex in Brown's novel is most often a noisy, exuberant calisthenic exercise; nowhere is there even seduction. The lovelessness and the drift toward nothingness of George's life finally cause him to recognize that he has been almost swallowed up by the futile and frantic pursuit of pleasure of his acquaintances. In his most serious moments, George is concerned with the pain of loneliness and its relationship to his fear of dying and being forgotten. He is told that he has been "busy covering up [his] loneliness with sex." As George explains to a homosexual friend, his being black and a man is what keeps his life from becoming meaningless, and

Dust jacket for Brown's first novel, which demonstrated his observation that "If you say something about sex and being a nigger then you got a best seller"

he concludes: "If you're black you don't need to get at anything. You're already there. You can live right out of your own insides." He is now ready to go home to his own people.

The reviews were mixed. One reviewer considered the novel to be a boring tale of beds and beauties. Another tried to find a satisfactory definition of the term jive. Other reviewers commented upon the influence of Joyce's *A Portrait of the Artist As a Young Man* and Ellison's *Invisible Man*.

A recurring subject of Brown's writing is the inability or unwillingness of white authors to write about blacks except as stereotypes. He was one of the critics who attacked William Styron's portrayal of black sexuality in *The Confessions of Nat Turner* (1967). In "BAD WRITING, OR unclewillieandthebadpoet" (1972), Brown stated that blacks have been exploited by white writers in this country, though whites still do not know what black people think of them. Since the time of Egyptian civilization whites have stolen from blacks, he argued, and

it is "an image of the white man's stealing from black culture" that certain white writers dislike.

In Brown's short story "I Never Raped One Either, But I Don't Let It Bother Me" (1972), the young black narrator tells of wealthy white girls who believe the myth of black male prowess to the extent that they buy their men sports cars. The narrator attributes his lack of an automobile to his reticence around wealthy white women. In a similar vein, Brown turns the outrageous tale of a suicide into humorous satire in "A Few Hypes You Should Be Hip To By Now" (1975). Tuppin, a successful comedian, considers the huge financial reward that could have been his had he chosen to use his talents to mislead gullible white liberals about the accomplishments of blacks. Some blacks are just as easily deceived, he observes, for in their homes one finds statues of black leaders made of "chitlins, ossified peas, watermelon rinds. . . ." His choice now, Tuppin concludes, is between a quick death or a long painful one of envy of rich charlatans. He tells his guest to help himself to fruit in the kitchen while he shoots himself in the living room.

In September 1969 Brown began teaching at the University of California at Berkeley, but he left after one year to venture into free-lance writing, directing, and producing his own plays. Later he taught at Merritt College in Oakland, where he organized the drama department and produced plays.

In the mid-1970s Brown began writing for Universal Studios and Warner Brothers. Although he was under contract with Warner Brothers from 1977 to 1979 and worked on several scripts, there were many things which troubled him about the television and movie industries. In "Blues for Blacks in Hollywood" (1981), Brown bluntly states that in their scramble for money, producers have found it profitable to reduce the cultural heritage of minorities to stereotypes. He quotes Baldwin as saying that the black man does not see himself as a stereotype, and he does not exist the way whites see him. Further, the reworking of an old formula to make whites feel superior to blacks by arousing their pity is to retreat back to the minstrel caricatures of Reconstruction, which were created to deal with the public's fear of black progress. Only blacks can tell their own story on the screen, he argues, and since they are not permitted to, the story is not told.

Brown's latest novel, *Days Without Weather* (1982), restates some of his earlier themes: stereotyping of blacks, betrayal by the film and television industries, and ridicule of certain critical theories. Jonah Drinkwater, the young, black,

somewhat disagreeable and unsuccessful main character of the novel, is a fledgling comedian who has vowed to use laughter as a weapon and to follow the footsteps of an uncle who was killed for laughing at a white man to his face.

Another uncle of Jonah's is a prosperous Hollywood hack who gained attention by falsely portraying his dead brother as a Christ figure, knowing that instead he was a "stand-up comic." The hack continues his prosperous way—writing to please whoever pays him—by destroying a young playwright's excellent script about the historic slave revolt of Gabriel Prosser. The rewritten script adds a borrowed Uncle Tom and Little Eva.

Brown continues to express his disenchantment with the ways of Hollywood by emphasizing Jonah's disgust with the producer who tells blacks they are "doing your race a favor" and expect to be congratulated when they discover something about black culture that is "a million years old."

Now forty-one, Brown has demonstrated in two satiric novels that he can use his outrageous sense of humor as an effective form of social protest, earning the praise of comedian Richard Pryor while pleasing social critic James Baldwin as well. There is nothing funny or titillating about the major theme of Brown's work—that a culture victimizes all its minorities if it denies a voice to any one of them—but he has not forgotten that a novelist reaches more people with his message when his books sell. "If you say something about sex and being a nigger, then you get a bestseller," Brown explained.

Octavia E. Butler
(22 June 1947-   )

Margaret Anne O'Connor
University of North Carolina at Chapel Hill

BOOKS: *Patternmaster* (Garden City: Doubleday, 1976; London: Sphere Books, 1978);
Mind of My Mind (Garden City: Doubleday, 1977; London: Sidgwick & Jackson, 1978);
Survivor (Garden City: Doubleday, 1978; London: Sidgwick & Jackson, 1978);
Kindred (Garden City: Doubleday, 1979);
Wild Seed (Garden City: Doubleday, 1980; London: Sidgwick & Jackson, 1980);

Clay's Ark (New York: St. Martin's Press, 1984).

PERIODICAL PUBLICATIONS: "Future Forum," *Future Life,* 17 (March 1980): 60;
"Lost Races of Science Fiction," *Transmission* (Summer 1980): 17-18;
"Speech Sounds," *Isaac Asimov's Science Fiction Magazine,* 7 (December 1983): 26-40.

The responsibility of the powerful to the powerless is the continuing theme of science-fiction writer Octavia E. Butler. Creating worlds of the future and visions of the past no more intrinsically humane than our own society, Butler peoples her novels with characters of seemingly limitless psychic abilities who must learn to master themselves as much as any outside force that threatens them. It is her handling of these timeless themes that has won her work virtually universal acclaim by critics and fans of science fiction and that promises to attract a wide audience among general readers as well.

Octavia Estelle Butler was born in Pasadena, California. An only child, her father died when she was still a baby, and she was reared by her mother, grandmother, and other relatives in southern California. Her own experience accounts for the positive treatment of such adoptive relationships in all of her novels. She describes herself in childhood as "a perennial 'out kid,' " shy, bookish, and taller than her classmates. Raised by strict Baptists, she wasn't permitted to dance or, later, to wear makeup. Not feeling accepted by those her own age, she was more comfortable with older people. She finds many other writers of science fiction to have been "out kids" who know how it feels not to fit in with groups. Her sympathies lie with such outsiders.

As a student at Pasadena City College and later California State at Los Angeles, she took courses in English, speech, and social sciences—history and anthropology in particular. Unable to major in creative writing, she quit formal work toward a degree but attended evening writing classes at UCLA while working in a variety of jobs, many described by the female narrator of *Kindred* (in "The Fall"). Her most useful training as a writer she attributes to work with the Writers Guild of America, West, Inc., an organization that established an "open door" program for aspiring writers in the late 1960s and early 1970s. Through this group she met writers Sid Stebel and Harlan Ellison, who provided the early criticism and encouragement she needed. It was Ellison who brought Butler to the Clarion Science Fiction Writer's Workshop in the summer of 1970, where she worked under such well-known writers of science fiction as Joanna Russ, Fritz Leiber, Kate Wilhelm, Damon Knight, and Robin Scott Wilson. The six-week session provided nuts-and-bolts advice on writing and publishing science fiction, and she sold her first two stories while a student there. After the Clarion Workshop, she continued her formal training as a science-fiction writer with classes at UCLA given by Ellison and Theodore Sturgeon. Unmarried, Butler lives in Los Angeles

Octavia E. Butler

and describes herself as "something of a hermit." Although she doesn't meet regularly with other writers while at home, she attends conventions that bring writers and fans of science fiction together. Though she and Samuel R. Delany are the only prominent black writers of science fiction today, Butler sees a growing black readership of science fiction and anticipates greater participation by blacks as writers and fans of the genre.

Five of Butler's six novels are part of the Patternist saga. Each novel deals with the descendants of Doro, a four-thousand-year-old Nubian who has survived throughout the ages by moving from one human body into another. His own survival is based on his predatory instincts, his capacity to kill not only enemies but all whose deaths can best serve the dynasty he dreams of founding. While in his many human forms he has been both male and female, young and old, and of all races, he clearly prefers the form of black male closest to his earliest Nubian identity. His long story unfolds in pieces throughout the novels, though *Mind of My Mind* (1977) and *Wild Seed* (1980) are the most direct treatments of his story. Thus an awareness of and appreciation for racial and sexual differences are at the base of the entire Patternist series; Doro is the powerful masculine hunter, progenitor of a race of superbeings gifted with physical and psychical powers that promise to take mankind to the next level of evolutionary development. Unbounded by time or space, Doro seeks both victims and progeny on two continents. His descendants carry these quests into the future and even outer space.

As different as each of the novels is in setting and plot, the basic tenets of "the Pattern" remain unchanged. The descendants of Doro have unique psionic gifts that are often too powerful for their possessors to control. In childhood Doro's far-flung progeny are "latents," gifted in telepathic or healing powers, for instance, but unable to channel their powers adequately. In adolescence, they must pass through a physically and emotionally painful process of "transition" before they become "actives" who can exercise their psionic powers effectively. Many latents never complete the transition process and die or are driven mad in the attempt. Like the patient owner of a herd of breeding stock, Doro oversees these rites of passage, with the interest of both a parent and a predator; the next body Doro might want to inhabit could well be that of the physical superman crippled by the mentally taxing process of transition. Doro kills the defective breeding stock, changing bodies with them and leaving his old, depleted self as a corpse. The family of Doro, then, forms the Pattern; he mates as often as possible within the family to produce children who share his gifts. The members of the Pattern are tied to one another and to Doro telepathically.

Though set in the far distant future, *Patternmaster* (1976) conjures up a world hauntingly reminiscent of the ancient past. Agrarian-based communities called Houses exist in what was once California as isolated outposts of a lost civilization under constant threat of attack by nomadic tribes of Clayarks. Workers in each House are virtual slaves, termed "mutes," who are totally lacking in telepathic abilities. Of all the characters in the novel, these pathetic individuals most resemble man as we know him today. The mutes serve the telepathic members of the Pattern, whose position in each House depends upon the strength and control of their telepathic gifts. Each House is headed by a Housemaster who rules through his power both to control his underlings and to protect them from the brutelike Clayarks who, lacking in mind-control abilities, rely on mechanical weaponry to destroy the Houses. The highest rung on this power ladder is occupied by the Patternmaster Rayal, and each Housemaster serves as his vassal.

The complexities of this feudal society are deftly revealed to the reader in a brief prologue to the novel which opens on a familiar domestic scene. Rayal and his "lead-wife" Jansee lie in bed discussing their two sons who are being reared in a distant sector of the kingdom. Because of their extreme sensitivity, Patternists are unable to rear their own offspring and must rely on mutes as adoptive parents for the welfare of the young. Like the incestuous Ptolemies of third-century B.C., this royal couple are brother and sister who are treated as gods by the masses. While Ptolemy II had the poet Theocritus deify his family in the popular imagination, Rayal comments that "making a religion of their [the mutes'] gratitude was their own idea." Rayal speaks as a hardened, masculine leader who sees his sons, twelve and two, as potential challengers to his position, much as he viewed the brothers he had to defeat and destroy to gain his throne in the first place. Jansee, in contrast, speaks as the eternal feminine principal; her maternal concern for the boys' welfare is hardly calmed by her husband's harsh words. The hierarchical structure of the entire society is outlined in the prologue, which ends abruptly as the Clayarks attack Rayal's House, killing Jansee and making an invalid of Rayal.

The novel proper begins as the younger son Teray reaches his majority some twenty years later and traces his education toward leadership and his inevitable confrontation with his already established older brother Coransee. Gifted as he is in telepathic powers, he learns through careful observation and the influence of a golden brown female healer named Amber that compassion is a necessary component for sustained control of the Pattern. Strength alone cannot triumph; faith in and respect for others are also vital for a Patternmaster.

Mind of My Mind introduces readers to a different era of Patternist culture, one which precedes that of *Patternmaster* by generations and provides a necessary link between that future world and our own time. Again the focus is on a family, albeit an unusual one. The time is the near future and the place is a suburb of Los Angeles—Forsyth. The dangers the characters face are not the exotic presence of the Clayarks but ones more familiar to twentieth-century American ghetto dwellers—child beating, drug addiction, prostitution, alcoholism, racism, and loneliness. In this era before the as yet unspecified catastrophe destroys the current political and social structure of the United States, Patternists are a growing but undetected minority in a society ruled by the mutes. Readers confront Doro, the progenitor of the telepathic race destined to rule the area, when he visits Rina, the mother of his daughter Mary. Rina, who has become an alcoholic and prostitute in Doro's absence, is one of the unfortunate Patternists whose telepathic gifts never reach their potential. She and many other "latents" suffer for their special gifts rather than profit through them. As the novel opens, Doro coolly demonstrates his power by assuming the body of one of Rina's customers when the man foolishly attacks him. Doro consumes the life force of his victim, changing bodies when threatened or when his current body no longer suits him. In his conversation with a terrified Rina after his kill, it becomes clear that Mary is a special offspring to Doro, one whose psionic powers promise to rival those of Doro himself. While Rina is genetically a good choice for Mary's mother, she is emotionally incapable of rearing her. Since Doro wants the best possible adoptive mother for this special child, he takes the child to Emma. While Doro is the dominant force in the novel, his longtime consort Emma is a second, almost godlike figure. Emma is a centuries-old woman whose immortality is self-generated and does not depend on the sacrifice of others. As strong in her feminine, maternal power as Doro is in his masculine aggressiveness, Emma agrees to rear Mary, her own distant offspring, as much to protect Mary from Doro as to satisfy his request of her.

Mary tells her story in the first person, with a third-person voice used for sections of the novel devoted to other characters in the story. Like *Patternmaster, Mind of My Mind* is primarily an initiation story; Mary must learn from Emma, Doro, and an assortment of other Patternists and mutes how to control her special gifts. The use of the first-person voice adds much to the description of the painful "transition" process Patternists must go through in adolescence before they reach maturity. Doro has over the years accepted the loss of many gifted offspring who are destroyed by the transition process; Mary's first act of defiance against Doro is her decision to save these lost souls through providing extra help for them through these difficult times. In one sense Mary embodies both the aggressive strength of Doro and the nurturing concern of Emma in her personality. She gathers the weblike telepathic connections of the Patternists in her own mind much as a coachman gathers the reins of his horses. Focusing their combined strength on the task of defeating Doro in a final confrontation in the novel, Mary offers a new direction to the Pattern. As in *Patternmaster,* this novel argues for the collective power of man as opposed to individual, self-interested endeavor.

Though *Survivor* (1978) is the third novel of the Patternist saga to appear, it was written first and is less polished than Butler's other works. Perhaps because of its setting on another planet, *Survivor* may be less attractive to the general reader than to the science-fiction fan. Yet even in the unfamiliar world of an alien planet, the characters deal with universal problems. Here Alanna, a young black earthling adopted by a family of white Missionaries, is taken to another planet to escape the nameless plague and genetic disease that led to the spread of the monsterlike Clayarks on earth. The Missionaries are mutes sent into interstellar space by the Patternists when this superior race on earth discovers that extreme distances are impossible for members of the Pattern to endure; the telepathic web that connects them is painfully severed by space travel. But the racial conflicts on earth between Clayarks and Patternists are present in this alien world where two warring tribes of the Kohn race, the Tehkohns and Garkohns, vie for power. The Missionaries align themselves with the Garkohns, who enslave them as they themselves are enslaved by addiction to meklah, a fruit that grows wild on the planet. Alanna, different from her adopted parents in color and in her desire to know both the Tehkohn and Garkohn cultures, is kidnapped from her Garkohn camp and forced to mate with a Tehkohn Hao, a tribal leader. Echoing the racial prejudices of our own age, the two tribes on this distant planet equate color with worth. All Kohns are capable of changing their color to indicate their emotional states. Only the most revered leaders can assume the almost sacred color of blue, however. Since both tribes know that mating with the alien Missionaries can often produce this genetic characteristic in offspring, the Missionaries are in danger of being used as breeding stock for the Kohns. Alanna grows to love her Tehkohn husband and his culture during her "captivity" and returns to the Missionaries only to make them see the dangers posed by their Garkohn allies. Dealing as it does with racial tensions, religious prejudices, and even enslavement, *Survivor* fails to resolve many of the complex issues it raises. The novel advocates power attained through the union of apparent opposites, a recognition of the positive power of differences among beings. An outsider to the Missionary, Garkohn, and Tehkohn societies, Alanna must try to understand all three, must judge her world herself.

In Butler's fourth novel, *Kindred* (1979), her only departure thus far from the Patternist series, she continues her investigation of extrahuman relationships that bind individuals together; miscege-

Munster High School
Media Center
8808 Columbia Ave.

My first memories as I came out of withdrawal were of pain, cold, hunger, and thirst. Someone gave me water—not enough. Someone lifted me and carried me to a place that was warm.

Someone tore my filthy ragged clothing from my body and washed me...the voices I heard were strange to me. They spoke in a language I could not understand. Then I remembered that I had been captured, that the speakers must be Tehkohn....

When I had slept for a time—I had no idea how long—I was awakened by people talking near me....Through the blurred screen of my own eyelashes, I could see two Tehkohn. Cold dim light came from patches of luminescence scattered on the wall behind them, and the Tehkohn themselves radiated some light—glowed softly. One was blue-green and about my size, and the other was blue. Deep blue all over and huge—larger than any of the Missionaries. He had the powerful stocky build of a hunter, but no hunter could have been as tall. And there was something about the way the native looked. I couldn't see him clearly enough to know just what, but something besides his size was bothering me, frightening me...

He knelt beside me and I tried to see his face clearly. But he had ceased to radiate light now and his deep blue was swallowed in the shadows of the room. He seemed only a shadow himself there beside me, and in spite of my fear, I reached out to touch him—to find out for certain whether or not I was dreaming....I felt the thick soft fur and the hard hand with its thick claw-like nail. The huge Tehkohn was real.

from

SURVIVOR

OCTAVIA E. BUTLER

Dust jacket for the third published novel in the Patternist saga. In order of composition, Survivor *was the first novel in the saga.*

nation is one vehicle for her themes. Butler's idea for a novel set in the era of American slavery came after she was exposed to works by black authors—particularly works about Frederick Douglass—at Pasadena City College. In *Kindred,* Dana, a black woman, celebrates her twenty-sixth birthday with her husband in 1976 only to be snatched abruptly from her home in southern California to an antebellum Maryland plantation. (Butler's research for this portion of the novel included a trip to Douglass's Maryland and a visit to Mount Vernon to see a restored plantation.) Rufus, the white son of the plantation owner, is drowning, and in his panic he discovers his ability to summon Dana across the years and the continent to help him. Despite her confusion over what has happened to her, Dana reacts almost automatically to save him. When the boy's parents turn toward her after the rescue, her own panic sends her inexplicably back to present-day California. After another such experience, Dana learns that Rufus is her "several times great

grandfather" and that he has the power to summon her when he is in extreme danger. Since he must live long enough to father a child by the slave woman Alice Greenwood in order to ensure the existence of Dana's family, Dana too is his "slave."

It is the contrasts—and perhaps even more, the similarities—between Dana's life in contemporary California and her experiences in the stratified plantation culture of the early nineteenth century that create the plot interest in this unusual novel. Alternating between two worlds, Dana and, eventually, her white husband Kevin learn what the powerlessness of the black slaves, particularly that of the women, was really like. Slowly they also come to see the situations of virtual slavery in their own technological, twentieth-century culture. Dana puts her finger on the greatest danger her husband faces in his travels back through time, one that threatens to destroy a happy contemporary marriage of mixed races and shared sex roles in the best modern tradition: "A place like this would endanger him in a way I didn't want to talk to him about. If he was stranded here for years, some part of this place would rub off on him. No large part, I knew, but if he survived here, it would be because he managed to tolerate the life here. He wouldn't have to take part in it, but he would have to keep quiet about it. . . . The place, the time would either kill him outright or mark him somehow. I didn't like either possibility." Drawing an analogy between power relationships of the early nineteenth century and the home, office, and bedroom of contemporary America, *Kindred* offers readers a chance to evaluate the racial and sexual dimensions of both cultures.

Butler's interest in cultural anthropology shows most clearly in the most sustained work to date in the Patternist series, *Wild Seed* (1980). Chinua Achebe's treatment of the Ibo people, too, is an acknowledged influence on the work. *Wild Seed* pairs the Onitsha priestess Anyanwu with the mutant Doro who might well be her own father. Like the other strong women who are part of the Patternist network, Anyanwu uses her powers of healing and—in her case—of physically transforming herself into other human and animal forms to protect herself, her children, and those she loves. Her capacity for love is both her strength and her greatest point of vulnerability. While Doro has survived for four thousand years through his ruthless destruction, first of his own parents, and then of enemies and of his own powerful offspring, Anyanwu has lived for three hundred years, watching her husbands and children grow old and die around her. Her longevity carries the curse of loneliness, of continually enduring the pain of grief. At the time she first meets Doro, she has resigned herself to a life as a hermit. She lives in the body of an old woman to protect herself from youthful longings for a man and from inspiring such feelings in the men she meets.

Doro, however, can recognize his far-flung family, even "wild seed" such as Anyanwu who were not part of his carefully structured breeding plan. Afraid of the power he possesses but attracted as well to the one man who might be the lifelong companion she could never otherwise hope to find, Anyanwu accepts him. With Doro looking on, Anyanwu achieves what Ponce de León hoped to find in the fountain of youth: "The hands were bird claws, long-fingered, withered, and bony. As he watched, they began to fill out, to grow smooth and young-looking. Her arms and shoulders began to fill out and her sagging breasts drew themselves up round and high. Her hips grew round beneath her

cloth, causing him to want to strip the cloth from her. Lastly, she touched her face and molded away her wrinkles. An old scar beneath one eye vanished. The flesh became smooth and firm, and the woman startlingly beautiful."

Anyanwu accompanies her consort Doro from the African village in which he found her to colonial America aboard a slaver. Successive sections of the novel trace the progress of Doro's dynasty from his "seed village" of Wheatley, Massachusetts, of 1690 to a Louisiana plantation in 1840. (The name of the town recalls Phillis Wheatley; it is not uncommon for Butler to allude to figures and incidents in the history of black Americans, tantalizing readers with memories of a rich past peppered with historical instances of exceptional people whose talents were as inexplicable to their times as are those of any of the descendants of Doro.) Essentially, however, *Wild Seed* is a compelling romance tracing the 150 years of struggle for love and respect between Doro and Anyanwu. The moving final pages test Doro's capacity to love, a human emotion that has atrophied in him throughout the centuries in which such feelings might have prevented the killings upon which his survival is based. *Wild Seed* is a powerful story beautifully told, and Anyanwu is the embodiment of the feminist ideal of compassionate exercise of power.

Butler's most recent novel, *Clay's Ark* (1984), deals with the catastrophe occurring between the times of *Mind of My Mind* and *Patternmaster*. She plans other historical novels covering the African and American experiences of Doro and his descendants.

Octavia E. Butler is one of the most promising new writers in America today. All six of her novels have enjoyed a favorable critical reception, and she was particularly praised for the artistry and power of her most recent works. Feminists and critics of Afro-American literature write admiringly of her handling of issues of gender and race; critics and fans of science fiction laud the fully realized worlds of the past and future which spring from her work; and general readers find that these novels by a black woman science-fiction writer present compelling stories of all-too-human beings in which questions of race, gender, and genre are background to the rich human dramas portrayed.

Interviews:
Jeffrey Elliot, "Interview with Octavia Butler,"
    Thrust: SF in Review (Summer 1979): 19-22;
Rosalie G. Harrison, "Sci Fi Visions: An Interview
    with Octavia Butler," *Equal Opportunity Forum*

Magazine, 8 (1980): 30-34.

Bibliography:

Joe Weixlmann, "An Octavia E. Butler Bibliography," *Black American Literature Forum,* 18 (1984): 88-89.

References:

Janice Bogstad, "Octavia E. Butler and Power Relationships," *Janus 4* (Winter 1978-79): 28-29;

Carolyn S. Davidson, "The Science Fiction of Octavia Butler," *Salaga* (1981): 35;

Frances Smith Foster, "Octavia Butler's Black Female Future Fiction," *Extrapolation,* 23 (Spring 1982): 37-49;

Sandra Y. Govan, "Connections, Links, and Extended Networks: Patterns in Octavia Butler's Science Fiction," *Black American Literature Forum,* 18 (1984): 82-87;

Veronica Mixon, "Futurist Woman: Octavia Butler," *Essence,* 9 (April 1979): 12-15;

Ruth Salvaggio, "Octavia Butler and the Black Science-Fiction Heroine," *Black American Literature Forum,* 18 (1984): 78-81.

George Cain
(October or November 1943-   )

Edith Blicksilver
Georgia Institute of Technology

BOOK: *Blueschild Baby* (New York: McGraw-Hill, 1971).

George M. Cain labeled himself a "scorpio"; no other precise information about his early life is available except that he was born in 1943 and grew up in Harlem, where he attended both public and private schools. He entered Iona College in New Rochelle on a basketball scholarship but left in his junior year to travel, spending time in California, Mexico, and Texas. In 1966 he returned to New York and began writing his autobiography, *Blueschild Baby* (1971), labeled by Addison Gayle in his *New York Times* review (17 January 1971) "the most important work of fiction by an Afro-American since *Native Son.*" He married in 1968 and later moved with his wife and daughter to Bedford-Stuyvesant in Brooklyn.

Cain dedicates *Blueschild Baby* to "all those who loved and helped me: mother, father, family and friends, Jo Lynne (wife) and Nataya (daughter)." He was paying tribute to a powerful support system.

Cain's book is the story of a sensitive, perceptive black man who attempts to come to terms with his own existence as a victim of both racism and drug addiction. It expresses a wide range of emotions, especially the anguish of one hooked on physically addictive drugs; it shows the difficulties of the junkie's life and the underground system that manipulates him.

The narrator is thinly disguised as George Cain himself and bears Cain's name. He has returned from prison to the Harlem drug scene. With the intensity of Dante's *Inferno,* we are guided through the labyrinth of the hard-core drug world. In one scene, Cain observes one girl, almost dead from an overdose, "loved" back to life. The life/death motif is a recurrent and unifying theme in the narration, as is the journey from the inferno through purgatory, as Cain tries to find spiritual nourishment from his devoted parents and from the loving Nandy, who nurses him through three days of withdrawal.

During these three days, Cain returns to his personal history to find the sources of his support and betrayal: the book begins like a slave narrative's account of escape, pursuit, and capture. He is another black invisible man, and he links the black situation with stressful insanity, which he equates to a Harlem inferno. "It is getting dark now and still I roam the corridors of bedlam. I need sanctuary, but there is none, and as my invisibility leaves like a cloak, I feel naked, center of all eyes, fair game for whoever first stumbles across me."

Cain's journey from his inferno through purgatory takes him through a Harlem that heaps great agony upon him in his desperate attempt to avoid destruction. Yet there are no one-dimensional villains in this piece. Black folks do not spend all of their time cursing the whites with no time for love or

George Cain (photo by Jo Lynne Cain)

hatred of each other. In the story, Cain's father and mother are admirable middle-class people who moved out of a Harlem housing project to a white community in order to try and give their talented son every educational opportunity. Scraping and sacrificing, his family had fled the housing project to New Jersey, taking him away from the security of his devoted grandmother's safe environment and the comforting network of community companions. In New Jersey, Cain had been admitted to a private school where, as one of two token blacks, he faced stressful confrontations with white teachers and snobbish students. Winning a college scholarship, with an entire community pinning its hopes on his success, he found himself splintered as a personality, trying to fulfill his parents' concept of the American dream and to achieve the athletic ambitions he shared with his friends. In many ways, he has failed them. His return journey is therefore a painful one, for he is reminded of what he once represented to the Harlem housing project residents as George Cain, the intellect, the successful basketball star, the hero of his people, the best bet to "make it."

Cain reacted with frenzied rage, desperation, drugs, and violence because he was not able to carry that much family and community weight. He became sexually aggressive and relished his athletic superiority to whites, but these exploits gave him only temporary satisfaction. As an avenger, he exploited white women, fathering a child whose mother was an Italian-American activist. "She lived in the dead yesterday of news reports or the tomorrow of reform. . . . I was amazed that she could have opinions and attitudes about everything and still hadn't fulfilled her primary function. I made her into a woman to meet my needs," brags her lover, more sexist than racist.

Yet, Cain not only exploited women; he used others and was used in turn. He matured when he realized that he had to be his own person. "Everyone but me had a piece of George Cain. Was no longer me, but a composite of all their needs and desires," he meditated after winning a close basketball game.

Gradually he stopped hating himself, the blacks who exploited their own people, and the

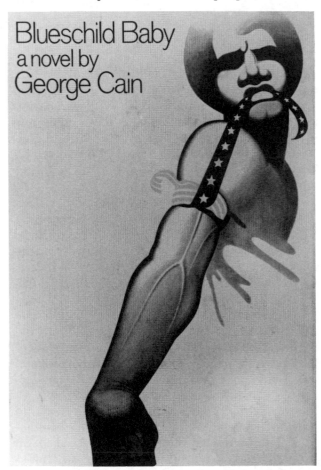

Dust jacket for Cain's autobiographical novel

whites who represented power and position. He gained pride in his ethnicity, and instead of trying to win friends among whites whom he first thought were the epitome of beauty and success, he acknowledged that "The Man can't free me. I must free myself." He realized finally that when he had exploited others and been exploited in turn, he had devalued himself.

Returning finally to his childhood sweetheart, Nandy, who patiently had waited for him during his purgatory through the white world, prison, and drugs, he reaches out to her with humility and desperation. She is his only hope to change his life. "Had been with only white women when I enjoyed the advantage of the myths each of us brought to bed. . . . Had never come to a woman naked and defenseless, just a man. Am ashamed knowing I know nothing of black women."

Cain's greatness is that he emerges as neither hero nor villain, but as a man trying not merely to endure but to survive. He must salvage first his sanity, then his life, and the reader feels this desperation as the work unfolds. Even if Cain overreacts, almost verging on sentimentality in his depiction of the idyllic loving care of Nandy as she helps her

boyhood sweetheart fight and conquer his drug addiction, the book effectively gives voice to a man crying out to be understood.

The truth of Cain's experiences and of his life is universal. He spent time on his craft and was attentive to his own heart's yearnings; the result is a voice resounding with the writer's unique version of the world.

Whether George Cain had the sustained inner strength to fulfill his gifts is unknown; he dropped out of the creative world after the early 1970s when *Blueschild Baby* was published.

References:

Houston A. Baker, Jr., *Singers of Daybreak* (Washington, D.C.: Howard University Press, 1974);

Morris Dickstein, *Gates of Eden* (New York: Basic Books, 1977);

John McCluskey, *Black World,* 2 (September 1971): 93-95;

Clarence Major, *The Dark and Feeling* (New York: Third World Press), pp. 55-56;

R. J. Meaddough, *Freedomways,* 2 (1971): 27-28; *The Yale Review,* 61 (October 1971): 121.

Barbara Chase-Riboud
(20 June 1936-   )

Marilyn Richardson
Massachusetts Institute of Technology

BOOKS: *From Memphis & Peking* (New York: Random House, 1974);

Sally Hemings (New York: Viking, 1979).

Before she became a published writer, Barbara Chase-Riboud was well established as a sculptor of international reputation. Her work in cast and polished bronze, often combined with lengths of wool, silk, and other textiles, is found in a number of major museums and in many important private collections. In the 1960s, she and her husband, French photographer Marc Riboud, traveled to the People's Republic of China. One of the first American women to visit postrevolutionary Peking, she explored the nature of her experiences there, her encounters with the Chinese and their complex history and culture, in a collection of poems, *From*

Memphis & Peking, published in 1974. Five years later, she published *Sally Hemings,* a prizewinning historical novel based on the story, long given currency in black American folk culture, that Thomas Jefferson, following his wife's death, had taken her slave half sister as his mistress and was the father of her seven children.

Born and raised in Philadelphia, Pennsylvania, Barbara Chase-Riboud was the only child of middle-class parents. Her father carried on a contracting business begun by his father. Her mother's family came from Canada, the descendants of slaves who had escaped across the border on the Underground Railroad. Chase-Riboud took degrees in fine arts at Temple University and at Yale. She studied in Rome on a John Hay Whitney Fellowship and lived for a while in London before making her

Barbara Chase-Riboud and her sons, Alexis and David (© René Burri –Magnum)

home in Paris. Married in 1961 and the mother of two sons, David and Alexis, Chase-Riboud was divorced in 1981.

Barbara Chase-Riboud has traveled widely, often with her husband, whose photographic projects frequently took him to distant regions. Her travels are a central motif in *From Memphis & Peking;* motion, change, distance, loneliness are all explored as familiar to a sensibility that thrives on artistic diversity and delights in the challenge of claiming for its own the aesthetic resources of far-flung cultures. The quest for discovery and new horizons is balanced by the earthy joys of erotic passion, sensuality, and the pleasures, great and small, of family and a shared past in which these poems are grounded. The first poems in this collection are in celebration of the rich diversity of the poet's family origins. Exotic landscapes emerge from the intense, direct, often incantatory language of poems that provide a form of autobiography of the spirit, honoring the mingled strands of her ancestry. Themes of descent into the psyche and of

return to one's origins, on a quest for mystical knowledge, are shaped by a voice full of sensual and sensory detail. There is the feel of the sun, the scent of spices, and the glare of the hot sands of the island of Zanzibar off the coast of east Africa in "Why Did We Leave Zanzibar?": "Why did we leave Zanzibar?/Sweet fragrant mango-stenched beach/Breasts pressed flat against steamed sand/ Seeping through sieve-like flesh/Carrying carats of ancestor dust/Rattling like pearls in oyster shells."

There are as well the sounds of the many musical traditions joined in her heritage, music which in all its multiplicity leads the poet/dancer to a sense of harmony and unity at the conclusion of "Come With Me": "I will play you/The calf skin/ Softly/The gourd of Africa and the/Sitar of India/The flute of the Arapaho Indians/And the bagpipes of/Scotland and Wales/. . . I will pick you up and turn you/Round/And/Lead/You/Home."

"Anna," a poem twelve pages long, divided into thirteen sections, begins with Chase-Riboud's grandmother and moves back to visions of Zanzibar and the Indian Ocean, and then forward through generations of women to her mother and herself. Incantation, the effort to conjure the past out of the strength of a powerful need to know, gives this poem a flowing urgency. A litany of names of places and people wends through the chronology of the stanzas as if one of them, Nairobi, Timbuktu, Ma Rainey, Agnes, might be the magical word that forces the mystery of those lost women's lives to yield up its meaning.

The Memphis of the book's title is in Egypt, a country Chase-Riboud first visited as a college student. She plays on the geographical ambiguity of the name, however, by interrupting "Going to Memphis," a poem in the form of a progress down a river of mystical Egyptian images, with the blues refrain, "I'm going to Memphis, I won't be back this way." Africa and black America meet as these poems become an exploration of ways to know and use the diverse elements of her personal heritage, and to move beyond it as well to the creative incorporation of other intellectual and artistic traditions. In these and in the love poems which together constitute two-thirds of the volume, as well as in the final section of poems on China, the unifying theme of the journey, both physical and spiritual, the luxuriant, sensual language with an emphasis on passions played out in the shadow of loss and death, and the almost tactile evocation of exotic settings all suggest the influence of the French poet Charles Baudelaire. Lines from his "Invitation to The Voyage" are echoed in Chase-Riboud's "I've Traveled":

"Together we've traveled/Fingers clasped in that death grip/Of sibling love/Beyond the Pale/Beyond the pale/Poppy you press again and again/Into the perfume of a wearied heart/That gleams and cracks/This dusty afternoon."

Baudelaire's "Moesta And Errabunda," with its characteristic longing for exotic pleasures and splendors, calls up as talismans of the distant and the unknown two of the lands Chase-Riboud writes of in a similar way. "Is it farther, even now," he asks of an imagined perfumed paradise, "than India or China?" The first is for her a symbol and source of the past, the second an ancient horizon suddenly, through revolution, made new and strange.

In her poems on China, the concluding portion of *From Memphis & Peking*, Barbara Chase-Riboud acknowledges a sense of being an outsider in a country long closed to Westerners: "Standing/On somebody's terrace/Feeling foreign/Gazing at a city more like a Universe Forbidden."

She also displays her extraordinary capacity to move, through the access of Chinese artistic traditions, into an articulate empathy with many facets of

The dust jacket for Chase-Riboud's first book. "Memphis" is an ancient city in Egypt.

the complex society she observes. It is that capacity which gives these poems a special significance. Shaped by the discriminating eye and deft hand of a poet who is a visual artist as well, they bring back news with which only the wisest traveler could return. The voice in these poems is vivid, graphic, and full of the language of the contrast and juxtaposition of color. Poetry, says Chase-Riboud, "is very close to a discipline both familiar and dear to me: drawing. Both are dangerous searches for perfection . . . drawing prepared me for the demands of poetry."

She chooses materials most specific to Chinese life and shapes them with an informed imagination. In "I Saw A Chinese Lady," she considers the lives of the anonymous—"I saw a small Chinese lady with bound feet in the park/ . . . Feet like an unfinished drawing running off the page/The dots of baggy trousers exclamation points"—and in "Han Shroud," the lives of the mighty—"Jade/Love's juices/Solidified/Smooth as your own flesh/I cover you drop by drop/Like emerald perfume/Running from/My favorite silver and ivory/gourd. . . ."

"Han Shroud," a double poem in the voices of a long-dead emperor and his empress, is a sensuous, moving evocation of a love so deeply shared and so powerful that it challenges Marvell's warnings about the restrictions of the grave. This motif of couples runs through Chase-Riboud's work; it appears in her sculpture, her poetry, and her fiction. In an interview with journalist and editor Susan McHenry, she describes her need to pursue this theme as both "banal and impossible, the need to join opposing forces; male/female, negative/positive, black/white."

This concern is at the heart of her skillful and controversial novel. *Sally Hemings* (1979) is, she maintains, a love story. "The whole national tragedy of slavery and miscegenation . . . of the pivotal events that led up to the Civil War—all this almost dwarfs the story of the two individuals. But there were other things as well—children and love and loyalty and a kind of grittiness they both had." In her imaginative evocation of that panorama of private and public events, Chase-Riboud lends plausibility to the story of a liaison between probably the most studied but least understood of American historical personages and the shadowy figure of the slave woman, Sally Hemings. Drawing on the findings of historian Fawn Brodie, as well as on extensive research in the products of what she came to regard as "the Jefferson industry," Chase-Riboud develops a highly intriguing meditation on sex, race, love, and power. She explores the intricacies of

A SEAVER BOOK

NEWS FROM VIKING

Barbara Chase-Riboud

talks about

Sally Hemings

The controversy over whether Thomas Jefferson fathered seven children by a beautiful slave named Sally Hemings has recently been reignited by Barbara Chase-Riboud's first novel, **SALLY HEMINGS**, to be published as A Seaver Book by The Viking Press in June. A recent front-page article about the book in *The Washington Post* said: "Several of Virginia's more prominent historians are rallying to protect the good name of Thomas Jefferson from a 177-year-old 'rumor' that refuses to die." The way Chase-Riboud sees it, many historians, especially Jefferson historians, wish there had never been a Sally Hemings. "The very idea that Sally Hemings was Jefferson's mistress for thirty-eight years," she says, "evokes violent passions and prejudices. For generations, scholars have tried to deny the existence of the liaison, devoting pages upon pages to categorical denials.

"Many great men have had socially unacceptable mistresses (Goethe and Rousseau, to name only two of Jefferson's contemporaries). Yet nowhere in their various biographies have their liaisons been described as 'vulgar' or 'defaming.' And many famous men have had illegitimate children. Tolstoy's carriage driver was his son by a serf on his estates. Yet no biographer claims that this was 'out of character.' The *real* issue in the Sally Hemings story is miscegenation.

"No other public man has ever hidden so well the passions of his private life," observes Chase-Riboud, "not only his relationship with Sally Hemings, but also with his wife and his mother. No letters or diaries or portraits exist." Although the historical evidence is sparse, Chase-Riboud asserts, "There is no doubt in my mind that the basic story of **SALLY HEMINGS** is true. If you line up all the facts one after the other, the evidence is strongly convincing."

Contact: Victoria Meyer
THE VIKING PRESS
625 Madison Avenue
New York, N.Y. 10022
(212) 755-4330

(more)

Front of a three-page publicity release for Chase-Riboud's first novel racial and sexual interaction in early American history with its attendant array of political, economic, and historical ramifications.

Sally Hemings, which may be seen as a work in the line of a continuing attempt by many black women authors to present heroines whose stories are told with a delineation of character and historical accuracy that reflect the complexity of their lives, goes far toward establishing an appropriately multifaceted context within which to consider the situation of a slave woman in post-Revolutionary War Virginia. It is not, however, a strictly "American" slave with whom Jefferson falls in love. Herself an expatriate artist as well as a keen observer of social mores, Chase-Riboud is particularly effective in depicting Hemings's European experience. It is known that in 1787 she was sent to Paris as the slave-companion of Jefferson's daughter Maria, called Polly. Away from the toil and restriction of life in Virginia, Hemings flourishes under the influence of Parisian life and culture. She displays an aptitude for the language, a ready wit, charm, and a

Dust jacket for Chase-Riboud's novel based on the possibility that Thomas Jefferson carried on a thirty-eight-year affair with his slave Sally Hemings. "There is no doubt in my mind that the basic story of Sally Hemings *is true," Chase-Riboud asserted.*

sensitive appreciation of her surroundings. As white as her young mistress and close to her in age, both her desire for education and her taste for elegance are indulged. It is to this young woman, cultured, captivating, and hauntingly reminiscent of his beloved wife, that Thomas Jefferson is inexorably drawn. It is another, less visible Sally, the one in whose submissiveness Abigail Adams recognizes a "feral self-satisfaction," the one who "has learned as a slave never to hope, never to anticipate, never to resist," who allows herself to remain in emotional and legal bondage to her lover.

The well-documented major events of Jefferson's life form the superstructure of the novel. Within that, building on Brodie's conclusions and on her own informed speculation, Chase-Riboud develops both the drama and the minutiae of a private life shared for thirty-eight years with a woman who is his lover, his companion, his victim, and his property. While Hemings is a strong, vivid presence throughout the story, the issue of her motivation is never resolved. Her youth (she was fourteen when she arrived in Paris), her early pregnancy, a longing for her family back home, all might have contributed to her decision to return to Virginia when she could have, under French law, claimed her freedom and remained in Europe. The complexity of her motivation is considered from different angles as the narrative perspective of the story shifts and revolves. There is a curious mix of independence and resignation in Sally's first-person accounts of the course of her life. She never, it appears, seriously contemplates escape or rebellion. As seen by others—by her mother, Elizabeth Hemings, by the artist John Trumbull, and by Abigail Adams—she is by turns foolish and self-indulgent, an ever-present danger to Jefferson's political ambitions, and a symbol of a profound malady at the very center of the lives of those who would presume to shape the destiny of a nation.

The reality of miscegenation in American social history is, Chase-Riboud believes, a fact that must be acknowledged and incorporated into our national consciousness if we are ever to see ourselves clearly as a nation. The genre of historical fiction has proven, in her hands, an effective means of raising this primal theme closer to the surface of our collective consciousness.

In the course of five years, Barbara Chase-Riboud published a 112-page volume of poetry and an important historical novel. *From Memphis & Peking,* though not a wide-selling book, was warmly received. *Sally Hemings* received considerably more attention, and in 1980, Chase-Riboud was awarded

Barbara Chase-Riboud (© Martine Franck – Magnum)

the Janet Heidinger Kafka Prize for Excellence in Fiction by an American Woman. According to the McHenry interview, a second volume of poetry, "Love Perfecting," has been completed, and a second novel is underway. The novel, described by Chase-Riboud as "an exploration of miscegenation on a global level," concerns a "woman of mixed race,

born in Europe during World War II. . . . Themes of religion and guilt are played out against the psychological backdrop of the Holocaust."

It is precisely the interracial and international aspects of Chase-Riboud's work that make it difficult to predict where her greatest audience will eventually be found. As with James Baldwin, her long residence abroad may compromise her credibility in the eyes of many black American readers. European audiences, on the other hand, might find much in her work to broaden their understanding of America. In 1969, Barbara Chase-Riboud was a participant in the Pan-African festival in Nigeria, an experience crucial to the development of what McHenry calls the writer's Third World Internationalism. "I found myself there," says Chase-Riboud, "with all the freedom fighters and liberation groups—the Algerians, the South Africans, the Black Panthers from America. A kind of historical current brought all these people together in a context that was not only political, but artistic." Whatever direction her work takes in the future, there will likely be at the core of her writing, as there is with her sculpture, just such a combining of the political with the artistic, the subjective with the international.

Interviews:

Judith Wilson, "Barbara Chase-Riboud: Sculpting Our History," *Essence* (December 1979): 12-13;

Susan McHenry, "Sally Hemings: A Key To Our National Identity," *Ms.* (October 1980): 35-40.

Cyrus Colter

(8 January 1910-   )

Helen R. Houston
Tennessee State University

BOOKS: *The Beach Umbrella* (Iowa City: University of Iowa Press, 1970);
The Rivers of Eros (Chicago: Swallow Press, 1972);
The Hippodrome (Chicago: Swallow Press, 1973);
Night Studies (Chicago: Swallow Press, 1980).

Cyrus Colter has often been called an old-fashioned and melodramatic writer—the latter because he believes that fiction must express feeling

and emotion, and the former because he believes a work of fiction must follow certain guidelines. As a writer, he emphasizes the fact that the black experience is multifaceted, showing a wide range of Afro-Americans, including the middle class—a dimension of black life which is underrepresented in fiction. Regardless of the strata of black society he portrays, he stresses the black man's humanity, not his color. He emphasizes the deterministic forces in society and the need for compassion, for it is only through individual relationships and commitment that mankind can reach its potential.

One of two children, Cyrus Colter was born in Noblesville, Indiana, to James Alexander Colter and Ethel Marietta Bassett Colter. His father engaged in various areas of work: insurance salesman, actor, musician, and regional director of the Central Indiana division of the NAACP, jobs which took him from Noblesville to Greensboro, Indiana, and later to Youngstown, Ohio. Cyrus Colter graduated from Rayen Academy in Youngstown and attended Youngstown College and Ohio State University. In 1936, he moved from Ohio to Chicago, Illinois, where he now resides. On arrival in Chicago, he entered the Chicago-Kent College of Law, where he graduated in 1940. On 1 January 1943, he married Imogene Mackay, a teacher, who served as his critic and catalyst until her death in 1984.

Colter's early life is marked by his legal and military career. Upon completion of his formal studies at Chicago-Kent, he practiced law and became a United States deputy collector of internal revenue. In 1942, he entered military service where he served for four years as a field artillery captain and saw combat in Europe in the Fifth Army under General Mark Clark. In 1946, he returned to civilian life and the practice of law in Chicago. In 1951, he was appointed Commerce Commissioner for the State of Illinois by Governor Adlai Stevenson, a post he held until 1973, when he went to Northwestern

Cyrus Colter and his wife, Imogene

University in Evanston, Illinois, as the Chester D. Tripp Professor of Humanities and chairman of the Department of African American Studies, a post he held until 1978. In 1977, Colter was awarded the honorary degree of Doctor of Letters by the University of Illinois, Chicago Circle. He is active in Chicago Civic groups and is a member of the Board of Trustees of the Chicago Symphony Orchestra.

In 1960, at the age of fifty, he reassessed his life's work and began an accelerated reading program that focused on Russian literature. As a result of his reading, Colter became more and more impressed with the range of characters depicted by Russian writers—especially Dostoevski, Gorki, Tolstoy, and Chekhov—and he realized the deficiency of Afro-American literature in this regard. His wife challenged him to address this problem in fiction and Colter began to write. He wrote vignettes about ghetto dwellers, the middle class, and the intelligentsia. Writing became his avocation. He spent hours on the weekend delineating on paper black characters he had encountered. After a period of vignette-making, he moved to more formally structured works.

Colter's first short story, "A Chance Meeting," was published in 1960 (the same year he began writing), in *Threshold,* a little magazine in Belfast, Ireland. In 1961, his second story, "The Lookout," was published in the *University of Kansas City Review,* now called *New Letters.* Since 1960, Colter has had over twenty-four short stories published, most of them in little magazines: *Chicago Review, Epoch, New Letters, Northwest Review, Prairie Schooner,* and *Threshold.* He has also published one short-story collection and three novels.

Colter's first book, a volume of short stories called *The Beach Umbrella* (1970), was published after his manuscript won the first Iowa School of Letters Award for Short Fiction in 1970 (chosen by Vance Bourjaily and Kurt Vonnegut). In the same year, *The Beach Umbrella* won the fiction awards of the Chicago Friends of Literature and the Society of Midland Authors. *The Beach Umbrella* contains fourteen deterministic stories, all set in Chicago. The characters are black, but their problems are universal: loneliness, guilt, sexual awakening, alienation, inability to communicate, reliance on illusions, dependence on materialism, desire for love and acceptance, and a general feeling of meaninglessness. "Blacks are human, not social integers," Colter says through descriptive words and phrases.

In "The Lookout" a young woman is scorned by her friends because she has not had their

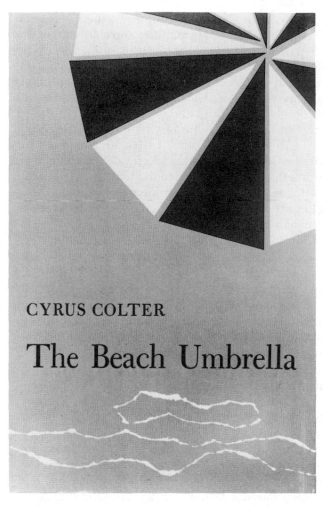

Dust jacket for Colter's first book, a volume of short stories that won the first Iowa School of Letters Award for Short Fiction

friends. However, at the end of the day, he finds he is as alone with the umbrella as he had been without it. He is alienated and isolated.

Colter's first novel, *The Rivers of Eros* (1972), is suggestive of Greek tragedy, as the title indicates. Clotilda Pilgrim, a strong, self-reliant woman, takes in sewing and operates a boardinghouse to support herself and her grandchildren. Eleven-year-old Lester seems steady and loving, and his sixteen-year-old sister Addie is a rebellious teenager bent on defying all rules. When Clotilda learns that Addie is having an affair with a married man, she is reminded of her own liaison with her brother-in-law, which resulted in the birth of Ruby, the mother of Addie and Lester. When Ruby was violently murdered, the care of her children fell to Clotilda, who becomes convinced that history is about to repeat itself as a result of her transgression. After having isolated herself in an effort to maintain her sanity, she is finally destroyed by this secret guilt she has kept locked within herself for thirty-five years.

Juxtaposed with Clotilda are the roomers. One roomer is Letitia, a middle-aged spinster who wanted to get married and have children, but who was convinced by her mother it was more fulfilling to have a job and earn money. Now she recognizes the futility of her life and is trying to find a husband. Ambrose Hammer is a scholar at work on a massive work entitled "History of the Negro Race" which will make people aware of the black man's contributions. Once this happens, the black man will be accepted into the system, he believes. Dunreith Smith and Alexis Potts, on the contrary, believe that there is no hope for the black man in this country.

In *The Rivers of Eros*, Colter shows the determining force of the past on both the individual and the group. He shows that the problems encountered by Clotilda are the result of being a part of the human condition, not solely race. In this novel, as in his short stories and later works, he underscores the multifaceted nature of the black experience and presents a broad range of black characters.

Colter's second novel, *The Hippodrome* (1973), is his most controversial work to date. Some critics call it sleazy, but Colter sees it as the most moral book he has written. To him, the novel shows how his characters have been used by fate and how tenuous our station in life is. The story is about Yaeger, a writer of religious materials. When the novel opens, he is carrying a brown bag which contains his wife's head. As he flees detection, he is offered refuge by Bea, who meets him in a cafeteria and learns of his plight. Once he is in her home, he learns she has a Hippodrome where a few black men and women

economic success. In "A Chance Meeting," when two ex-servants accidentally meet, one learns that his former employer, whom he had idealized, was an adulteress. In "Moot," a man betrayed by his wife alienates himself from society and focuses all of his love and attention on his dog. The universe does not seem to be in sympathy with the man, and he realizes, as other Colter characters do, that his life is "so damned mediocre and insignificant." The title story, "The Beach Umbrella," is an excellent example of Colter's handling of the theme of alienation and inability to communicate. Like many Colter characters, the protagonist decides that material acquisitions will insure love and compassion. He decides that he needs a beach umbrella in order to become one of the beach crowd; thus, he borrows money from his twelve-year-old son, purchases an umbrella, and goes to the beach. For a fleeting moment on the beach, he appears to have fun and

Dust jacket for Colter's first novel

perform sexual acts for a paying white audience. Bea has offered him aid because she needs another performer. Yaeger finds himself trapped; he must either participate in the Hippodrome activities or he must leave and risk detection and capture. When he is unable to make up his mind, he is forcibly ejected.

Implicit in Yaeger's thoughts and actions is the fact that he is manipulated by past events, sexual fears, guilt, accident, and chance. He feels hopeless, consumed by life's absurdity. Nothing is sure and appearances are deceiving. Yaeger decides that all he has seen in the Hippodrome is "a fantasy, a dream" and "yes! . . . yes—maybe the Hippodrome is really the house of God."

Written after several months of travel and six years of work, Colter's most recent novel, *Night Studies* (1980), won the Carl Sandburg Award. The novel covers several centuries and several locales—Paris, San Francisco, Kansas, and Chicago—in telling the stories of three main characters: Mary Dee Adkins, a middle-class Chicago black woman who studied art in Paris, falls

in love with a white Philadelphia aristocrat and finds that no matter how hard she works, she cannot now become a part of the black community; Griselda Graves, a black woman passing for white, whose heritage has been kept from her; and John Calvin, the leader of the Black People's Congress, who learned the history of his people from his father, and as a result of the discrepancy between history from the black man's point of view and the white man's point of view, ponders the question of blackness and Louis Armstrong's question in "The Prologue" to *Invisible Man,* "What did I do to be so black and blue?"

Night Studies addresses the interdependence of the races—neither can be free until the other is also free. To show the kinship of blacks and whites, Colter divides his novel into four books. Book one, "Convergence," introduces the three major characters as their lives intersect. Book two, "Chronicle," serves as the record of the black man's past told through John Calvin's dreams of the past and his ancestors. Book three, "Canticle," continues the record, introducing the discontent of black soldiers after World War I. Book four, "Crucible," presents the tests of the major characters. Questions are raised about their solutions to their various plights. An "Epilogue," in the form of a letter from John Calvin to a loyal follower, indicates the final status of the various characters.

In *Night Studies*, Colter emphasizes the suffering of the individual which, he says, results from an inability to love; he argues that it is as debilitating to ignore your history as it is to be obsessed by it; and he depicts how inextricably interwoven are the destinies of black and white people.

The failure to present the stereotypical black experience may be one of the reasons Colter is not as widely read as he deserves. However, he does have a growing audience, and his works have been translated into German, Italian, Hungarian, Danish, and Japanese. He is a writer whose straightforward, realistic style belies the density and philosophical sophistication of his writing. He has earned the respect of serious readers.

Interviews:

Robert M. Farnsworth, "Conversation with Cyrus Colter," *New Letters*, 39 (Spring 1973): 16-39;

John O'Brien, *Interviews with Black Writers* (New York: Liveright, 1973), pp. 17-33;

Robert Fogarty, "Work: Beginning to Write at Fifty: A Conversation with Cyrus Colter," *Antioch Review*, 36 (Fall 1978): 422-436;

Susan Skramstad, "Interviewing Cyrus Colter," *Story Quarterly*, 11 (1980): 65-74.

Samuel R. Delany
(1 April 1942-   )

Sandra Y. Govan
University of North Carolina at Charlotte

See also the Delany entry in *DLB 8, Twentieth-Century American Science-Fiction Writers.*

BOOKS: *The Jewels of Aptor* (New York: Ace, 1962; London: Gollancz, 1968);

Captives of the Flame (New York: Ace, 1963); revised as *Out of the Dead City* (London: Sphere, 1968);

The Towers of Toron (New York: Ace, 1964; revised edition, London: Sphere, 1968);

City of a Thousand Suns (New York: Ace, 1965; revised edition, London: Sphere, 1969);

The Ballad of Beta-2 (New York: Ace, 1965; London: Sphere, 1977);

Babel-17 (New York: Ace, 1966; London: Gollancz, 1967);

Empire Star (New York: Ace, 1966; London: Sphere, 1977);

The Einstein Intersection (New York: Ace, 1967; corrected edition, London: Gollancz, 1968);

Nova (Garden City: Doubleday, 1968; London: Gollancz, 1969);

The Fall of the Towers (New York: Ace, 1970; London: Sphere, 1971);

Driftglass (Garden City: Doubleday, 1971; London: Gollancz, 1978);

The Tides of Lust (New York: Lancer, 1973);

Dhalgren (New York: Bantam, 1975);

Triton (New York: Bantam, 1976);

The Jewel-Hinged Jaw: Notes on the Language of Science Fiction (Elizabethtown, N.Y.: Dragon, 1977);

The American Shore (Elizabethtown, N.Y.: Dragon, 1978);

Empire (New York: Berkley, 1978);

The Tales of Nevèrÿon (New York: Berkley, 1979);

Heavenly Breakfast (New York: Berkley, 1979);

Distant Stars (New York: Bantam, 1981);

Neveryóna or; The Tale of Signs and Cities (New York: Bantam, 1983).

OTHER: *Quark*, nos. 1-4, edited by Delany and Marilyn Hacker (New York: Paperback Library, 1970-1971).

Few black writers have employed popular forms—the mystery novel, the historical or gothic romance, or science fiction. Harlem Renaissance writer Rudolph Fisher has been credited with the first mystery novel by a black writer. Frank Yerby adopted the historical romance as his forte. Chester Himes wrote a series of popular detective novels set in Harlem. Each of these writers received some measure of recognition and popular success, but none of them attained the level of both popular and critical acclaim Samuel Ray "Chip" Delany has reached in the science-fiction genre. For excellence in both the novel and short story, he has captured science fiction's coveted Hugo and Nebula awards, voted him by science-fiction fans and science-fiction writers respectively. His critical writings about science fiction from the perspective of a working writer are widely respected. Samuel R. Delany is one of science fiction's preeminent authors.

The son of Samuel R. Delany, Sr., a prominent Harlem businessman and owner of Levy and Delany Funeral Associates, and Margaret Carey Boyd Delany, a licensed funeral director and a library clerk with the New York Public Library, Delany was born and raised in Harlem. The social and financial stability of his family allowed him a privileged childhood which included extended visits to the family summer home in Hopewell Junction, New York, private schools, and private summer camps. At age five, young Delany was enrolled in prestigious, private, and predominantly white Dalton Elementary School. Twice daily he made the trip from Harlem to Park Avenue in his father's chauffeur-driven black Cadillac. Delany has described the tensions of his school years in various, sometimes conflicting recollections. At times he felt himself to be "living in several worlds with rather tenuous connections between them" but seemingly without any undue stress. At other times he felt his daily journey across town to be a "virtually ballistic trip through a sociopsychological barrier of astonishingly restrained violence." His friends in Harlem were the children of maintenance men, welfare mothers, and taxicab drivers; his friends at Dalton were the children or grandchildren of television executives, New York publishers, political officials, and members of the literary establishment. The dichotomies in his daily life affected young Sam's emotional stability and his behavior; he ran away from home several times between the ages of five and seventeen, and eventually he was referred to a child-guidance center for psychotherapy because of his "deep maladjustment." Some of these same dichotomies resurfaced later in fictional guise.

Dalton was a progressive eccentric school, and Delany was successful there even though he encountered the typical problems of a bright black youth in a white setting; his childhood was "peppered and pockmarked" by incidents. He was accepted by his classmates, but his teachers, though they recognized his talents in art and verbal capability, his formidable imagination, and his manual skills, patronized him and accused him of rebel-

Samuel Delany (photo © by Sutor & Lindsay)

liousness and a lack of discipline. They failed to recognize his independence or the fact that he had to live in two different worlds. They also failed to diagnose his problems with English and spelling as dyslexia and so assigned him to remedial classwork in those areas. In his last year at Dalton, Delany was elected Most Popular Person in the Class, an honor which pleased him immensely. However, in a candid reflection on this stage of his life he notes that "Like many children who get along easily with their peers, I was an incredibly vicious and self-centered child, a liar when it suited me and a thief when I could get away with it, who, with an astonishing lack of altruism, had learned some of the advantages of being nice to people nobody else wanted to be bothered with."

In 1956 Delany graduated from Dalton and the fall of that year enrolled in Bronx High School of Science. He had begun to write while still a Dalton student and while attending summer camp. At BHSS, Delany continued to write, publishing short stories in *Dynamo,* the school magazine. In 1958-1959, he won first place for a short story and second place for an essay in the Scholastic Writing Awards contest sponsored by the W. A. Sheaffer Pen Company. Math and physics were his areas of concentration at BHSS, though he also continued his interest in music and the arts; at fourteen he wrote a complete violin concerto. Other activities included guitar practice and the study of acting and ballet. Between 1954 and 1963, Delany wrote a number of apprentice works, including *Lost Stars, Those Spared by Fire, Cycle for Toby, Afterlon, The Lovers, The Flames of the Warthog, The Assassination,* and *Voyage, Orestes.* In addition, he completed *Captives of the Flame* (1963), the first book in *The Fall of the Towers* trilogy, and had *The Jewels of Aptor* (1962) accepted as his first published science fiction. In 1960 *Seventeen* had assigned him his first essay for a major publication, but the resultant article, "The Compleat Folk Singer," did not appear until 1962, and then it was severely cut. Also in 1960, Delany received a fellowship to the Bread Loaf Writer's Conference in Vermont, where he met, among other luminaries, Robert Frost. Frost advised the young writer: "Do it your own way. Don't let anyone else tell you how to do it."

Nineteen was an auspicious age for Delany. In August 1961 he married a former Dalton classmate, the poet Marilyn Hacker. That fall he enrolled in the City College of New York but dropped out in the spring because he felt he "could not do the work" and "did not understand what was required." By his twentieth birthday, he had written his first novel. Marilyn Hacker is largely responsible for the publication of *The Jewels of Aptor.* She was working as an assistant editor at Ace Books and complaining to Delany about the poor quality of the manuscripts that were being submitted. Inspired by a series of nightmares he had recently had, he began writing with her encouragement. When the manuscript was completed, Hacker suggested he submit it to Ace editor Donald Wollheim, who liked it and bought it. Wollheim asked Delany to trim the novel by 720 lines, a painful editorial process for Delany, so that the text would fit the Ace Double format. By the time he was twenty-two, Delany had published four additional novels, including *The Fall of the Towers* trilogy and *The Ballad of Beta-2* (1965). The frenetic pace demanded by the high production needs of the science-fiction publishing trade eventually took its toll on Delany's mental health. In the summer of 1964 he suffered a nervous breakdown and had to be hospitalized and treated at Mount Sinai for general disorientation, hallucinations, and nervous exhaustion.

Delany's health problems taught him that he would have to work at a more measured pace, that he could not afford to sign the standard contracts for two and three books per year which publishers

then expected of science-fiction writers. Delany realized that if he were to write the science-fiction novels that *he* wanted to write, he would have to take more time to work on his artistry and craftsmanship. The results of his new policy were the publication of the 1967 Nebula-award-winning *Babel-17* (1966), completed after a month's excursion in Texas working on shrimp boats, and the 1968 Nebula-award-winning *The Einstein Intersection* (1967), written while Delany spent a year traveling in Europe and Turkey, occasionally earning money playing the guitar. Before going abroad, Delany began and finished his seventh published novel, *Empire Star* (1966).

As an adolescent, Delany read some of the best-known science-fiction writers: Robert Heinlein, Theodore Sturgeon, Alfred Bester, Isaac Asimov, and Ray Bradbury. Their stories and books were "more fascinating and stimulating" than anything he had ever read. The appeal of science fiction for the young Delany lay in its ability to excite "great mysterious shapes of mind" lit by "black and unholy mythic resonances" while extolling the seemingly limitless potential of technological achievements. Other literary influences ranged from Genet's plays to Camus, modern and contemporary poetry, and James Baldwin's essays. As a teenager he discovered black literature and was introduced to the poetry and prose of Paul Laurence Dunbar, Langston Hughes, Countee Cullen, Zora Hurston, Bruce Nugent, Chester Himes, James Baldwin, William Demby, and LeRoi Jones.

Delany's science fiction shows his fascination with language, myth, and the mythmaking process. As a student at Dalton he had become attuned to the differences between black Harlem speech and white Park Avenue speech. He became aware of language as an "intriguing and infinitely malleable tool." Language for Delany is the matrix of communication modes, which may be verbal or nonverbal. According to Delany, language identifies or negates the self. It is self-reflective; it shapes perceptions. *Babel-17* explores linguistic theory, and *Dhalgren* (1975), among its other accomplishments, experiments with various forms of communication. *The Einstein Intersection,* which on one level is about the creation of myth and its capacity to inform culture, is also about how myth is communicated and transformed.

Another feature of Delany's fiction is the prominent role of the artist, typically a poet or musician, who suffers some physical or psychological damage. A recurring motif frequently overlooked in Delany's fiction is his subtle emphasis on race. Black and mixed-blood characters cross the spectrum of his speculative futures, both as a testimony to a future Delany believes will change to reflect human diversity honestly and as a commentary on the racial politics of the present. Though he does not see himself as a political polemicist, Delany consciously projects a black presence into his futures because racial identity is important and his intention is to "write about worlds where being black mattered in different ways from the ways it matters now."

In his early works Delany presents possible worlds where technology has clearly gone beyond its limits; the societies that have survived are saturated in myth. The setting of *The Jewels of Aptor* is an earthlike world at a crucial stage of redevelopment. The aftermath of The Great Fire hundreds of years ago has left portions of the population mutants and made whole land masses untenable still because of lingering radiation. Geo, a poet, leads a small group of latter-day Argonauts to rescue the kidnapped High Priestess of the white goddess Argo and to restore three jewels of immense power to the control of Argo Incarnate. Iimmi, a black sailor, joins the company; he later becomes instrumental in defining for Geo the significance of the encounters the group has. *The Jewels of Aptor* presents patterns which Delany returns to in successive works: the quest theme, the artist protagonist, the destructive capability of technology, the formation and layering of myth, and the resolution of dissonance into harmony.

The Fall of the Towers trilogy (*Out of the Dead City* [1968], *The Towers of Toron* [1964], and *City of a Thousand Suns* [1965]) recounts the epic struggle of Jon Koshar, a criminal outcast, and two others to save another earthlike world, which in its distant past has experienced near-total annihilation, from invasion by the Lord of the Flames. Koshar and his friends become hosts of The Triple Being, an alien intelligence and the only force in the universe capable of combating the evil Lord of the Flames. The interwoven plot of the trilogy has all the elements of classic "space opera": a hero who struggles with himself as with the forces of evil, a clear division of good and evil, exotic aliens, space battles, and malevolent computers. The trilogy chronicles the social and cultural history of a corrupt empire; it couches the story of Toromon in mythic terms—the decline and fall of an old civilization, the rise of a new one; it employs one of Delany's favorite themes, the necessary tension between dualities, the union of opposites forging order from chaos.

The Ballad of Beta-2, like *The Einstein Intersec-tion*, is about the creation and adaptation of myth. In the former, Joneny Horatio T'wabaga, a university honors student in galactic anthropology, is assigned the task of preparing from primary sources a complete historical analysis of the ancient Earth folksong "The Ballad of Beta-2." T'wabaga's quest takes him to a derelict "generations" starship from old Earth. Here he learns the actual text of the ballad and what it signifies. The mythmaking process is one dominant theme in the novel; another is that social or intellectual rigidity and forced uniformity inevitably lead to intolerance, oppression, and stagnation. Delany handles the themes of mythmaking and shaping order from disorder more adroitly still in *The Einstein Intersection*. Humankind has inexplicably vanished from Earth; in our place a race of aliens struggles to adapt to human life and values through a welter of freely associated myths left behind—Greco-Roman, Biblical, American. Lobey, a half-man, half-beast, is a black musician whose machete makes music or kills; Lobey is also an Orpheus figure and one of the "different" ones. His quest is to find out what is killing those who are different. Kid Death, an avatar of Billy the Kid, is his antagonist. *The Einstein Intersection* is sprinkled with allusions to Jean-Paul Sartre, William Butler Yeats, Emily Dickinson, even a Pepsi slogan; at appropriate intersections, segments of the author's journal are inserted and function as part of the text, thus expanding the relationship between reality and art.

Empire Star, a short novel composed in eleven days, traces the development of Comet Jo from a "simplex" boy on a primitive outlying planet through a "complex" stage to a "multiplexual" level. Comet Jo embarks on an urgent mission with an urgent message; on his way to Empire Star he acquires a sophisticated multiplex understanding of the cyclical nature of time and history. The story, ostensibly for younger readers, is actually an allegory of the cycle of oppression, guilt, and responsibility which the enslavement of any group imposes on the free.

Babel-17, with Rydra Wong as its poet-protagonist, is also about intergalactic strife, oppression, guilt, and responsibility. Though the plot is action-filled, Delany's attention in *Babel-17* seems at first to be focused on highly innovative explorations of linguistic theory and various language systems; however, this concentration does not impede the story, rather, it adds an unexpected dimension to the tale of space intrigue and does so with verve and style. Delany argues in a provocative essay on critical method that the supposed tension between content and style is meaningless; what is important is the information carried by words, by "image-modes." This perception of the "incantatory" function of words is concretized in *Babel-17*, for the novel presents content/style/theme as one unit. *Babel-17* appears to be an enemy code. Rydra Wong, the "most famous poet in five explored galaxies," is called upon as an expert cryptographer and natural linguist to decode it for the military. Wong discovers that Babel-17 is a language, not a code. It is a separate, distinct, "analytically exact" language, capable of ensnaring those who use it by manipulating subconscious, even conscious, thought. With the aid of her friend and psychotherapist, Dr. Markus T'mwarba, Rydra is forced to break through natural and induced psychological and social barriers in order to save the Alliance from invasion. That Rydra Wong, an Asian woman, and Markus T'mwarba, an African man, are the heroic principals of this novel is a fact that few critical commentaries have noted. What the critics do note is Delany's link to French symbolist poetry through the evocation of Rimbaud and his economical yet vivid poetic imagery. Delany's appreciation of poetic compression is also evident through his selection of epigraphs; a poem by Marilyn Hacker begins each of the novel's five segments and suggests the theme developed in two sections.

Nova (1968) is the novel that completes what may be considered the first major cycle in Delany's fiction. *Nova,* too, is classic "space opera." It has interplanetary feuds, exotic beings, advanced high-tech computers, and epic battle sequences. Critic Sandra Miesel has argued that the central theme of the novel is "power—physical, social, political, economic, artistic, intellectual, and sexual." The mulatto hero, Lorq Von Ray, must locate and procure from an exploding star, a nova, the rare element Illyrion. With Illyrion in sufficient quantities the Von Ray family can contain the monopolistic drive of the rival Red-Shift Company of Draco Federation; without Illyrion, Red-Shift will stifle settlement of the outer worlds. Assisting Lorq on his mission are Katin, a frustrated novelist, and Mouse, a wandering Gypsy musician with an instrument that may delight or maim. His antagonists are Prince and Ruby Red, heirs of the Red-Shift fortunes. *Nova* is held together by a web of mythic fibers. Lorq's quest is akin to the search for the Holy Grail; his lot is that of Prometheus stealing fire. Biblical, Indian, and Celtic mythologies are also incorporated into the novel.

Following the publication of *Nova,* Delany was hailed as one of the "Renaissance men" of science fiction. Reviewer Algis Budrys said of him then: "As of this book, Samuel R. Delany is the best science fiction writer in the world." (Budrys was to recant that testimonial in a review of *Dhalgren* in 1975; he did not consider the latter science fiction or science fantasy but "quasi-fiction.")

The late 1960s was a critical period in Delany's life. His novels and stories brought him the highest honors in his field and allowed him to meet some of the genre's most distinguished writers. His personal life was a model of Bohemian flexibility. In 1967, Marilyn Hacker left New York for an extended visit to San Francisco. The couple had been sharing a back room in the New York apartment of friends. When Hacker left, Delany moved out and into the Heavenly Breakfast commune. After the move, he discovered that he had accidentally left behind an envelope full of papers, notes, letters—his "documentable" history. The loss caused a temporary writing block, and for a year he turned his attention to music for the Heavenly Breakfast rock band rather than to his writing. Some of his experiences with communal living are recorded in the book-length essay *Heavenly Breakfast: An Essay on the Winter of Love* (1979). Other versions of his experience with the commune and others in the city appear in the long, complex, controversial, ornate novel *Dhalgren*.

Dhalgren's history is almost as complex as the novel itself. Delany's initial work on the book, begun about 1968, was continually interrupted by other projects. He wrote movie reviews for *Fantasy and Science Fiction;* he wrote and directed two short films, "Tiresias" and "The Orchard"; he wrote incisive articles on the works of Roger Zelazny and Thomas Disch, two other experimental science-fiction writers. In addition he crisscrossed the country, teaching at the Clarion Writers Workshop, polishing for publication the stories of *Driftglass,* writing record and film reviews, and completing the work on his pornographic novel, *The Tides of Lust* (1973). He and Hacker coedited *Quark,* a new journal of "speculative fiction" featuring poetry, artwork, and literary criticism as well as science fiction. Four issues appeared between November 1970 and August 1971. Delany also found time in the early 1970s to enter the comic-book medium, scripting stories for *Wonder Woman* and composing a short piece for a *Green-Lantern; Green Arrow Anthology*.

In 1971, Delany's collection of short stories, *Driftglass,* was published. Each of the stories in it had appeared separately in science-fiction magazines or anthologies and each had been written as a short

Front cover for Delany's 1975 novel considered by many critics to be his most ambitious work

project, usually while Delany also worked on a longer project, his current novel. "Aye and Gomorrah . . ." appeared first in Harlan Ellison's precedent-breaking anthology, *Dangerous Visions;* it won a Nebula for best short story in 1968. Several other stories in *Driftglass* have been nominated for or have won Hugos and Nebulas: "The Star P. T." was nominated for a Hugo in 1967; "Aye and Gomorrah . . ." won a Nebula in 1968; "Driftglass" was nominated for a Hugo in 1968; "We, In Some Strange Power's Employ, Move on a Rigorous Line" was awarded a Nebula in 1968; "Time Considered as a Helix of Semi-Precious Stones" won a Nebula in 1969 and a Hugo in 1970. "The Star Pit" was dramatized for radio theater on station WBAI-FM.

In 1972, on a return trip from San Francisco to New York, forty-two pages of the *Dhalgren* manu-

script were lost. In addition, a fire at the Albert Hotel where Delany was then living almost destroyed the novel's first draft. After the fire, Delany revised the novel twice. Its massive bulk, over eight hundred pages, and its experimental structure caused the manuscript to be rejected by several publishing houses—Avon, Doubleday, Knopf, Scribners, and Simon and Schuster. Finally, in 1973, Frederik Pohl at Bantam decided to publish the novel as a special "Frederik Pohl" selection. In December of 1972 Delany had left New York to join Hacker in London. Their daughter, Iva Alyxander Hacker-Delany was born there in January 1974. While awaiting her birth Delany revised a final draft of *Dhalgren* and corrected proofs mailed to him from New York. Because of mailing problems and a printing rush, the first edition of *Dhalgren* contained nearly one hundred typographical errors when it finally appeared in 1975. (Many of these errors were repeated in subsequent printings until the Gregg Press edition in 1977.)

The setting for most of *Dhalgren* is the near future, in the decayed and violent city of Bellona. Adjacent to other typical U.S. cities, Bellona nevertheless exists in some undefined, undisclosed locale at the outer edge of the normal world. Bellona alone has suffered some nameless cataclysmic holocaust; no physical, economic, social, moral, or temporal laws apply in this wounded "autumnal city." To Bellona comes the Kid, one of Delany's psychologically damaged artist-heroes. Kid chronicles the story of Bellona's residents in his poetry; his journal contains reflections on the nature of art and the artist. *Dhalgren* examines personal and societal relationships from a variety of perspectives. Because almost everyone wears a weapon in Bellona, because scorpions on "runs" rule the streets, because violence of all kinds abounds, Bellona may appear to represent the triumph of chaos over order. Yet, Bellona has its heroes: George Harrison, a black man celebrated in the city's lore, is heroic; Reverend Amy Taylor, a black minister, adheres to her ministry heroically; the Kid too, leader of the scorpions, becomes a hero to Bellona. The artist lost, the artist finding a voice is as central to *Dhalgren* as its scenes of violence and its seeming obsession with sex. More explicit meaning is difficult to identify because ambiguity permeates Delany's text. *Dhalgren* has drawn more widely divergent critical response than any other Delany novel. Some reviewers deny that it is science fiction, while others praise it for its daring and experimental form.

In *Triton* (1976), Delany returned to the more conventional science-fiction form. First titled *Trou-*

ble on Triton, Delany began the novel late in 1973. Interplanetary war threatens between old Earth and the moon colonies of Triton and Titan. Bron Helstom is one Delany protagonist who is neither a poet, nor a musician, nor an artist of any kind. The sensitivity such endeavors require is beyond his capacity, for he is an extremely limited young man. In a work concerned with human interaction and human communication, Bron communicates little but selfish interest. Throughout the novel, despite radical changes in his physical presence, he remains an alienated and isolated individual, in Delany's words, the "epitome of the unsavory WASP."

The mid-1970s signaled change in Delany's personal life as well as his professional life. In 1975, he and Hacker separated and later divorced; they remained close friends, however, and determined that childrearing responsibilities would be shared; active parenting forced Delany to alter the amount of time and energy he could devote to his writing. Also in 1975, as a result of the correspondence he and literary critic Leslie Fiedler established about the integrity of science fiction as significant litera-

Front cover for Delany's 1983 heroic fantasy that Theodore Sturgeon called "a multilevel mandala"

"A ROCKET LAUNCH, A PHOENIX REBORN, A NEW DELANY NOVEL—THREE WONDERFUL, FIERY EVENTS!"—*Ursula K. Le Guin*

Stars in my Pocket like Grains of Sand

by Samuel R. Delany

In his first science fiction novel in eight years, Samuel R. Delany has created an epic saga of a man without a world whose celebrity on another planet sets off universe-shaking repercussions. On the following pages is an excerpt from this landmark work, to be published in hardcover by Bantam in late 1984.

Announcement appearing at the back of Neveryóna *for Delany's forthcoming novel*

ture, Delany was invited to the State University of New York at Buffalo to be Butler Professor of English. In 1977, he became a senior fellow at the Center for Twentieth Century Studies at the University of Wisconsin-Milwaukee. The same year he published a volume of critical essays on science fiction written over a ten-year period. *The Jewel-Hinged Jaw: Notes on the Language of Science Fiction* is a cogent, erudite analysis of the genre from a variety of perspectives; it includes autobiographical comment. *Empire* appeared in 1978, as did *The American Shore,* a second book of criticism. *The Tales of Nevèrÿon,* a collection of stories which falls more into the fantasy genre than science fiction, was published in 1979; *Heavenly Breakfast* appeared that same year, *Distant Stars,* an illustrated volume, appeared in 1981, and a fantasy novel, *Neveryóna or; The Tale of Signs and Cities,* was published in 1983.

Now in his settled middle period, Delany is no longer the exotic wunderkind of science fiction but its established institution. Over the years his work has developed a strong following among fans and scholars alike because it appeals on a variety of levels; with each new work he receives closer critical scrutiny, a sure sign of an ever-broadening base. Delany's new works indicate his continued interests in mining the full potential of science fiction because of the range of possibilities that the science fiction "enterprise" offers.

Interviews:
Malcolm Edwards, "An Interview with Samuel Delany," *Science Fiction Monthly,* 2 (March 1975): 10-12;
David Schweitzer, "Algol Interview: Samuel R. Delany," *Algol,* 13 (Summer 1976): 16-20;
Dennis O'Neil and Gary Groth, "An Interview with Samuel R. Delany," *Comics Journal,* 48 (Summer 1979): 37-43, 70-71.

Bibliography:
Michael W. Peplow and Robert S. Bravard, *Samuel R. Delany: A Primary and Secondary Bibliography, 1962-1979* (Boston: G. K. Hall, 1980).

References:
Sandra Miesel, "Samuel R. Delany's Use of Myth in *Nova,*" *Extrapolation,* 12 (May 1971): 86-93;
Robert Scholes and Eric S. Rabkin, *Science Fiction: History, Science, Vision* (London: Oxford University Press, 1977);
Stephen Scobie, "Different Mazes: Mythology in Samuel R. Delany's *The Einstein Intersection,*" *Riverside Quarterly,* 5 (1972): 12-18;
George Edgar Slusser, *The Delany Intersection: Samuel R. Delany Considered as a Writer of Semi-Precious Words* (San Bernardino, Cal.: Borgo Press, 1977).

Papers:
Peplow and Bravard report that several collections of Delany materials exist in the United States and Canada. Two of the most important are "The Samuel R. Delany Collection," Boston, at Boston University's Mugar Memorial Library, and "Samuel R. (Chip) Delany Papers in the Collection of Desmond K. Kay," 845 West End Avenue, New York.

William Demby
(25 December 1922-   )

Margaret Perry
Valparaiso University

BOOKS: *Beetlecreek* (New York: Rinehart, 1950);
The Catacombs (New York: Pantheon, 1965);
Love Story Black (New York: Reed, Cannon & Johnson, 1978).

PERIODICAL PUBLICATIONS: "The Geisha Girls of Ponto-cho," *Harper's,* 209 (December 1954): 41-47;
"They Surely Can't Stop Us Now," *Reporter,* 14 (5 April 1956): 18-21;
"A Walk in Tuscany," *Holiday,* 22 (December 1957): 140, 142, 144-145;
"Blueblood Cats of Rome," *Holiday,* 27 (April 1960): 203-206.

William Demby has enjoyed a distinctive literary career marked by substantial critical acclaim but a modest readership. His work does not fit tidily into a niche reserved for black writers; indeed, his writings reflect not only some aspects of black life but focus seriously upon the human conditions all people experience: Demby's literary lens focuses upon the myriad elements that illuminate character and situation in a world where moral choices create drama.

William Demby was born in Pittsburgh, Pennsylvania, to William Demby and Gertrude Hendricks Demby. His youth was spent in Clarksburg, West Virginia—a coal-mining region that served as the setting for his first book, *Beetlecreek.* Demby had five sisters and a brother. His father worked in the natural gas branch of Standard Oil Company in West Virginia.

Demby attended West Virginia State College, where he studied in a writing class offered by Margaret Walker. His schooling was interrupted by World War II; he went into the U.S. Army (the horse cavalry), where he had the experience of writing for the *Stars and Stripes* while in Italy. (He was also stationed in North Africa for a while.) It

William Demby

was while he was in the army that Demby decided finally upon writing as a career.

Demby loves music, and he recalls that his cousin, jazz alto saxophonist Benny Carter, "was the first inspiration that I had. I was definitely to become a jazz musician, a professional jazz musician." Later, while at West Virginia State College, Demby was in a jazz band, and he was unable to decide whether he wished to pursue a career in music or writing. During the war, however, Demby discovered he didn't understand the new jazz—particularly bebop: "Musicians from New York City were coming to where we were camped, giving concerts, and I tried to sit in with them but I didn't know what they were saying . . . the idiom had changed totally."

After World War II Demby returned to the United States to continue his education at Fisk University in Nashville, Tennessee. It was at Fisk that he wrote for student publications; he also illustrated and designed the college magazine. He graduated in 1947 and immediately returned to Italy, where

he studied art history at the University of Rome. Demby became an expatriate writer who, nevertheless, retained his spiritual allegiance to his native land. From the late 1940s until recent years Demby lived and worked in Italy, writing filmstrips for the Italian film industry and television. He resided in Rome with his Italian wife, Lucia Drudi, from whom he is now separated, and his son, James, who was born in Italy and still lives there. Though Demby wrote some screenplays and received credits for some commercial films, the major portion of his work was translating Italian screenplays into English. As Demby describes it: "I worked with almost everybody . . . I was really inside the Italian movie industry."

The expatriate experience helped to solidify a view of thought Demby seems to have possessed early in life. He never turned his back on realities of life in America. In fact, Demby sees himself as having never entirely left his native land: "You've been there [in Italy] for twenty years," he stated, "but you haven't changed your language, you haven't changed your personal history."

Demby's first novel, *Beetlecreek* (1950), was written in Italy, but the novel derived from "St. Joey," a short story written for Robert Hayden's class in creative writing at Fisk in 1946. In "St. Joey" a gang murders an old recluse, going beyond the gang's idea of what is normal and right: "I don't think we ever get the straight of just exactly what kind of sin it was that old Bill did, but it didn't matter too much because he was the first one and we wanted to get started. We sure felt holy."

Beetlecreek deepens the plot of this story and expands the roles of the major and minor characters. The title comes from an image in Steinbeck of a beetle run over by a car and squashed on an overheated highway: Beetlecreek is a town where human souls are crushed and trapped. In this town there is a creek full of reeds and bracken and debris—a creek that traps objects trying to flow past freely: "things became trapped in the reeds along the shore . . . in the reeds would be other objects already trapped. . . . this was Beetlecreek. . . ."

There is little question that Demby draws on his life in West Virginia in creating the setting for *Beetlecreek*. Johnny Johnson, a boy about fourteen, is sent temporarily by his sick, widowed mother to spend some time with his uncle and aunt. Johnny is a loner who is drawn to a group of boys his own age; the urge to join this gang of insensitive country boys becomes irresistible, and Johnny's initiation into the group becomes the beginning of a nightmarish life for him.

Another loner, Bill Trapp, a reclusive white man living in the black section of Beetlecreek, decides to make contact with other people after an encounter with Johnny. Bill Trapp's movement outside himself sets the stage for Johnny's horrible act that occurs at the conclusion of the novel. Bill Trapp—like old Bill in "St. Joey"—breaks the fragile social code of Beetlecreek, and Johnny, motivated by the need for acceptance, acts as an enforcer. Death and destruction are the results.

The third character, who, along with Johnny and Bill, forms this triangle of doomed desire and loneliness, is David—Johnny's uncle. Trapped in a sterile, meaningless marriage, David's search for happiness leads him away from Beetlecreek toward a relationship that will be no better than the one with his wife.

Beetlecreek has been viewed as a naturalistic novel; the deterministic ambience, the importance of Beetlecreek as a place seem to confirm this. In an interview with John O'Brien, however, Demby denies this: "The reality of the novel is not naturalistic," he said. "The movement that each of the characters makes is much more secret than any cause-and-effect relationship." But he does admit that the novel may be existential; certainly the ultimate act of each of these three persons seems to confirm this. The deeds of Johnny, Bill Trapp, and David seem to define their characters. Each character confronts the other, confronts the spiritual side of the self, and acts according to individual will. In reassessing the notion of *Beetlecreek* being an existential novel, Demby said recently: "I think that it most probably is, because black experience is itself and has been historically in this country existentialist; that is, precarious, tied to the moment, history-conscious, and history-making without possessing a constant, solid historical framework. So, in that sense, I think it is."

The critical reception of *Beetlecreek* was approving. August Derleth, in the *Chicago Sunday Tribune*, was typical: "As a first novel, 'Beetlecreek' offers something different in its situation; competently and well done, it may give readers pause to reflect that people are fundamentally very much alike, regardless of color, which is a basic truth far too many people need to learn." Demby pointedly addresses the challenges people face in life (society and the self)—white or black—and much of what the characters in *Beetlecreek* are confronted with is akin to the world of *The Catacombs*, Demby's second novel, which was published in 1965.

As the title suggests, the world of *The Catacombs* is suffused with the imagery of death and resurrection. It is also a story about blacks. Demby is a character in *The Catacombs*, along with the fictional Doris and the Count, her aristocratic lover. The setting is modern-day Rome, never far in spirit from the past. There is love, death, possible resurrection; to be sure there is alienation. Time is important. It is 1962 to 1964, and there is chaos in the world to parallel the chaos felt in the characters' hearts. Sometimes a true event of the time brings this to our attention; sometimes it is manifested by an exasperated remark, as when Doris laments, "Oh, these times!... I tell you, no kidding, the world's going to the dogs."

To show the disorder of the world, the disharmony of people in a world without a moral center, the affair of Doris and the Count is interspersed with news briefs about actual occurrences—the Algerian war, the Cuban missile crisis, a Russian spaceship launching, Marilyn Monroe's suicide. The novel is organized according to a chronology that follows the events of a day or week or month, as well as a seasonal movement, as in the supposed impregnation of Doris on Christmas ("What a Christmas I carry within my womb, what a Christmas present...."), followed by death and resurrection at Eastertime, when the Pope calls for universal peace. The cycle of life and death repeats itself; but Demby's open-ended use of time instills a hope for salvation. "Oh, I believe in a moral universe," Demby said in the O'Brien interview; and this belief provides a counterpoint to unsettling scenes that are part of the novel's composition. There is a constant reminder of the Janus-like perspective of the author as he has us look back on death and forward toward renewal. At the end of the novel this motif is repeated a final time: "Something brushes against the Count's eyes. He blinks. Drops of silver nitrate drop coldly on his closed eyelids. The newborn sees." The child Doris carries is never born, and Doris disappears in the catacombs—"Doris! Doris! Where have you gone?"—and the novel ends.

There is a sense in *The Catacombs* that Demby has written two books—one about himself and one about the times. There is history and life, past and present, within the catacombs. The author-narrator comes to terms with himself finally; Bill Demby writes that "In less than three weeks time I will be flying back to New York... I will sit at a desk in my skyscraper office, I will work to the rhythm of the Easter-Parade resurrected city." He no longer needs to be among the visible ancient ruins or the fictionalized lives of the Count and Doris. As Demby moves into the light (i.e., greater self-awareness),

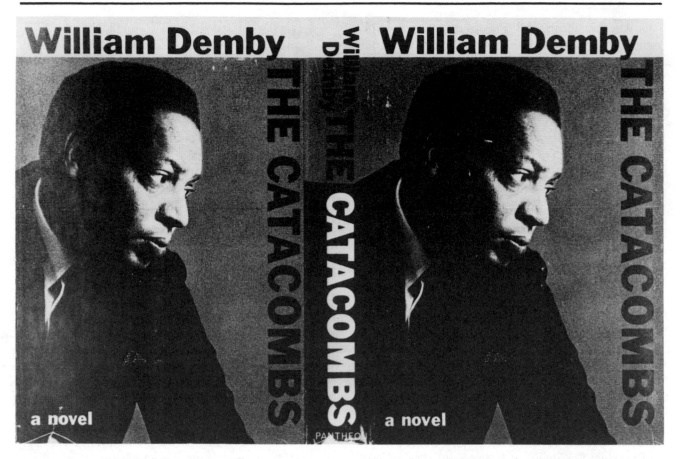

Dust jacket for Demby's second novel, in which he appears as a character arguing in favor of a moral universe

Doris gradually moves to the darkness; in the end, she is gobbled up by the dark when she is lost to the Count in the catacombs.

Critical reaction to *The Catacombs* was mixed. Peter Buitenhuir in the *New York Times* praised Demby's talents but announced his distaste for his work. Robert Bone, in an essay for *Tri-Quarterly* (reprinted as the introduction to the 1970 paperback edition of the novel), enthusiastically claims that *The Catacombs,* "which is entirely a product of the Space Age, has probed to the outer limits of contemporary consciousness."

Demby's latest novel, *Love Story Black,* published in 1978 by a firm in which Ishmael Reed is a partner, is noticeably different from his first two novels, although the male protagonist bears a striking resemblance to Demby (expatriate black novelist teaching in a New York City college). Demby has commented that there was surprise among devotees of *The Catacombs* when *Love Story Black* was published: "People who have found themselves frozen inside *The Catacombs* are a little bit upset; I guess they expect something else from me."

There is a mélange of the romantic, the humorous, the satiric, and the serious in this novel which limns life in contemporary New York City during the late 1960s. Demby said he "was interested in . . . telling a story like a medieval story . . . the kind of convoluted but simple story with a little bit of wonder and darkness to it and, at the same time, make a statement about the lives that black people have to live." And they are there—the "wonder and darkness," as the narrator seeks answers to his questions.

The story revolves around a black professor named Edwards ("approaching what for the younger members of my class, is middle age") and his efforts to piece together the life of Mona Pariss, an elderly entertainer (presumably in her 80s, but "she could pass for 50"), for a feature article in the slick black journal called *New Black Woman*. In order to get Miss Pariss to tell her story ("This is my life; the holy book of my life," she says), Edwards must disrobe completely and lie chastely beside her. From the start Edwards falls under her spell; he is bewitched by her, and the novel is transformed into a combination of fantasy and exaggeration.

Paralleling this pursuit of Mona Pariss's story is the tale of Edwards's life—as writer for the Vassar-educated editor of *New Black Woman* and as professor in the turmoil of teaching the disaffected young.

The varying levels of action and thought have made *Love Story Black* a novel that is both satire and celebration. The love story is celebration; indeed, the novel ends with happiness and triumph. Demby's sure handling of dialogue also satirically exposes the engaged, militant student who mouths revolutionary ideas while participating in the structured world of academe. And the author gently satirizes himself in the portrayal of the narrator—a black intellectual who sometimes plays false and pompous with the students in an effort to protect himself from the oral attacks of the most militant of them.

Edwards has a romance with Hortense Schiller, another Vassar-educated black woman, who aids him in the writing and research of the Pariss article. Bitten by love, Edwards is truly chivalrous, like the two knights in Chaucer's "The Knight's Tale," which he is teaching. Edwards's deep infatu-ation with Hortense causes him to abandon Mona Pariss for a brief spell, although the complexities of this relationship with her are resolved at the novel's end.

Aside from Pariss herself, Edwards's chief source of information about her life is the wino Rev. Grooms, one of Pariss's friends out of the past, the designer of her costumes, and her current neighbor. Grooms claims to be Doc—Mona Pariss's lost love who was castrated after she abandoned him. Mona Pariss and Rev. Grooms always contradict one another's stories; until the last moment of the novel, Edwards is uncertain about the truth of the information he receives from these old folks. Edwards does believe in Mona Pariss's virginity, however, which provides the romance of the novel; love and desire are ageless, Edwards learns, and Mona Pariss gives him a better definition of love than he himself—the novelist and professor—can devise.

The pursuit of Mona Pariss's history teaches Edwards more about life than he had expected. As Miss Pariss put it—"I wouldn't begin the day I was born—that's for sure—and I wouldn't begin the

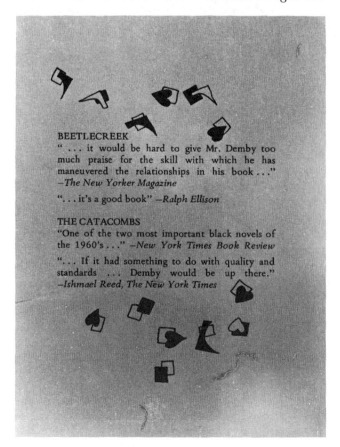

Front and back covers for Demby's experimental third novel, largely ignored by critics. "People who have found themselves frozen inside The Catacombs *are a little bit upset," Demby commented.*

day my daddy and my mother did their thing in bed either—that's not when lives begin—lives begin when you wake up out of that sleep world ghosts live in and you start to move with your own mind and not the mind of the ghost, that's when lives begin." Critics chose largely to ignore *Love Story Black,* presumably because of its nontraditional publisher.

Demby teaches at the College of Staten Island, where he has been since 1969, and lives in Sag Harbor, which he likes because of its importance in Afro-American history. Demby points out that blacks were living there since before the Revolutionary War. They traded with the Americans and British during this war, and some went to England and eventually ended up in Sierra Leone. In the cemetery at Sag Harbor there are names matching participants in the "Amistad" mutiny. Demby stresses that his devotion to this place ties him spiritually to his black heritage.

In his 1971 interview with John O'Brien, Demby mentioned a work in progress entitled "The Journal of a Black Revolutionary in Exile," which he described as a literary investigation into whether the black revolutionary "has the real possibility of starting a revolution—revolutionary activity—or whether he is just becoming aware that the breed no longer has any historical function." But the novel was aborted, for Demby found life too nearly like fiction. He has also suspended work on an autobiographical book, "Long Bearded Journey." He chooses to work at his own pace and to release a book when it's completed to his satisfaction. There is a moral center to his personal world, too.

Demby's fourth novel, as yet untitled, is still in progress as Demby explained: "I'm not satisfied with it and I'm taking new directions."

Demby feels that his novels have received fair treatment at the hands of reviewers and scholars, but he is quick to point out that critics view his work from a cultural framework different from his own. He says: "They are writing either to uphold establishment or to reinforce some ideological position. That's what critics do. It would be naive to think that they don't."

Demby feels that some of the praise he has received has been uncomprehending of his goals as a writer. He has been separated from the tradition of black literature because his novels have a universality about them. Nonetheless Demby wants to be remembered as a black novelist because "the black writer is . . . the only one who will be giving [a] voice to the experience of black people. . . . The novel is a new thing [for blacks], and so it's useless to pretend that you're in some kind of universal tradition when, in reality, you are not. You're excluded from that, and so that is always at the back of your mind as you write. You are one of the very few among the family of your people who are putting things down in this form."

Demby has a deep, private vision he wants to share with the world—in his own time, on his own terms. He is proud of his black identity. Clear-eyed and articulate, Demby continues observing the world and "the sacredly silk-threaded tapestry of lives. . . ."

References:

Robert Bone, *The Negro Novel in America,* revised edition (New Haven: Yale University Press, 1965), pp. 191-196;

Bone, "William Demby's Dance of Life," *Tri-Quarterly,* 15 (Spring 1969): 127-141;

Joseph F. Connelly, "William Demby's Fiction: The Pursuit of Muse," *Negro American Literature Forum,* 10 (Fall 1976): 100-103;

Edward Margolies, "The Expatriate as Novelist: William Demby," in his *Native Sons: A Critical Study of Twentieth-Century Black American Authors* (Philadelphia: Lippincott, 1968), pp. 173-189;

John O'Brien, ed., *Interviews With Black Writers* (New York: Liveright, 1973), pp. 34-53;

Roger Whitlow, *Black American Literature: A Critical History* (Chicago: Nelson Hall, 1973), pp. 122-125.

Papers:
The manuscript of *Beetlecreek* is at the Beinecke Library, Yale University.

Junius Edwards
(1929-   )

Australia Henderson
GMI Engineering and Management Institute

BOOK: *If We Must Die* (New York: Urbanite Publishing Company, 1961).

OTHER: "Mother Dear and Daddy," in *Beyond the Angry Black,* edited by John A. Williams (New York: Cooper Square, 1966);
"Duel with the Clock," in *The Best Short Stories by Negro Writers,* edited by Langston Hughes (Boston: Little, Brown, 1967);
"Liars Don't Qualify," in *Black Short Story Anthology,* edited by Woodie King (New York: New American Library, 1972).

Junius Edwards, who currently works for an advertising firm in New York and lives in Westchester, New York, was born in Alexandria, Louisiana, in 1929. Having studied in Chicago and at the University of Oslo in Norway, his career as a writer flourished in the late 1950s. In 1958, he won first prize in the Writer's Digest Short Story Contest for "Liars Don't Qualify"; in 1959, he received a Eugene F. Saxton Fellowship for creative writing. Since the first publication of his novel *If We Must Die* in 1961, it has been republished by Doubleday and by Howard University Press; three short stories by Edwards have also appeared. All of his published work reflects a sensitivity to the black South and the milieu of his birth.

The title of Edwards's novel is taken from a well-known poem by Claude McKay, who rallied blacks after the First World War with "If we must die, let it not be like hogs." Will Harris's death, which appears certain, forms an ironic contrast to McKay's plea, for Will is dying like an animal and is unable to communicate with his rescuer, an old man who at first assumes that Will's tongue has been cut out by the men who have beaten him and left him to die in the woods.

Set in the late 1950s, *If We Must Die* has a slight plot and minimal dramatic action. Will Harris, a Korean War veteran, decides to register to vote in an upcoming election. Refused permission to complete the application for registration, Will is fired from his job the next day. Later, he discovers that he has been blacklisted in his own town and in the

county as well. Without provocation, a group of whites attack him in a wooded area, where he is left nearly dead and tied to a tree. He manages to free himself and seek help, but his fate remains unresolved. The novel concludes with a semiconscious and perhaps dying Will being taken to a doctor. There is no resolution to the problem of black voter registration, and little suggestion that Will's act will make an impact on the community, black or white.

Will's story is clearly an extension of Will Harris in "Liars Don't Qualify." The two defeated heroes share the same characteristics: honesty, pride, and patriotism. However, the novel delineates the persecution and frustration of an ordinary black Southerner, who returns from military service with a heightened sense of himself and with dreams of a fuller life, most especially acceptance as a human being. The book-length treatment is Edwards's indictment of the South for its efforts to dehumanize and subjugate blacks. Stylistically simple in its reliance upon dialogue to forward plot, the novel effectively rejects bigotry. The rejection is strengthened by understatement; Edwards neither describes a particular Southern town nor makes obvious references to the racial identities of his characters. In effect, he implies that discrimination and oppression are widespread and entrenched in the South. At the same time, he reinforces the absurdity of treating people inhumanely because they are different.

Edwards's novel has received little critical attention. Responses range from open rejection to partial admiration. Nick Aaron Ford finds *If We Must Die* totally unacceptable; in his view, it not only deserves the "booby prize of the year" but also raises the "ugly" possibility that Doubleday may have returned "to the double standard for the publication of books by Negroes that was used in the Nineteen Twenties and Thirties. . . ." Faith Berry is more complimentary, but nevertheless feels the novel is "anachronistic" because it does not present such events as the March on Washington, which occurred simultaneously with the novel's release by Doubleday. Berry treats the book as a product of the early 1960s, without knowing that it had been completed well before 1961, the date of its first publication by a small, private press. Responding directly to the novel's content, Jean C. Bond praises the forcefulness of Edwards's portrait of a Southern town, but concludes with the hope that his style, which Bond describes as resembling a hack writer's, and his characterizations, burdened with stereotypes, would improve with his next effort.

"Liars Don't Qualify" and "Duel with the Clock" may be viewed collectively with *If We Must Die* because all three works demonstrate aspects of the problems faced by the black soldier. Edwards exhibits a sympathy for and understanding of the conflicts and obstacles the black soldier confronts. "Liars Don't Qualify," originally published in *Urbanite* magazine's June 1961 issue, contains the seeds of Edwards's novel. The story dramatizes one scene: a Korean veteran, Will Harris, attempts to register to vote in a Southern town, but after a rigorous and humiliating ordeal, he is refused the right because he is accused of lying about being a member of an organization, the Army Reserve. The obvious irony lies in the denial of civil rights to a soldier who has risked his life in war to protect the principles of democracy. Although the short story ends with Will Harris's unsuccessful effort to obtain a voter's registration application, the novel has a more developed portrayal of Will Harris, and it emphasizes his determination to stand up for his rights and his courage in facing his oppressors. However, the central scene in "Liars Don't Qualify" remains the major dramatic moment in *If We Must Die.*

Edwards treats another facet of the black soldier's experience in "Duel with the Clock," a story published in Langston Hughes's 1967 collection, *The Best Short Stories by Negro Writers.* Edwards concentrates on the soldier's personal and psychological condition, rather than on his racial treatment. He presents an eighteen-year-old soldier, James Bradley (Brad), who uses marijuana but is tempted to try heroin as an escape from army life. Brad's "duel" with time and with himself occurs when he is given an off-base pass which will expire the next morning. He is caught between using the pass so that he can alleviate his agonizing need for a "joint" and remaining in the barracks so that he cannot be linked to the death of Walker, a soldier who has just died from an overdose of heroin. Brad himself had almost tried heroin from the same bag.

Edwards's "Mother Dear and Daddy" has had greater longevity than his novel. The story's uniqueness is that it reveals the impact of the preoccupation with light skin on black children. Edwards's own youth in the multicolored society of Louisiana blacks, who frequently determined class status on the basis of skin tone, perhaps has given impetus to his story, which is told from the point of view of Jim, twelve years old and the eldest of five children. The children's parents have died, and they are facing another painful experience: separation from one another. Their mother's relatives, all "pink rose" in color, refuse to take the two boys because they are dark-skinned like their father. Jim and his eight-year-old brother, John, listen to their relatives squabble over homes for their light-skinned younger sisters. The boys recognize at once why the girls are valued and they are ignored. John becomes frantic. He looks at his hand and at his sister's. He realizes, seemingly for the first time, their difference in color. Screaming, he bolts into the room where his relatives are, jumps into the lap of one man, and begins to pummel him with his fists. Just as the man swings the back of his hand toward the boy, Jim pulls his brother away and begins comforting him by laughing. John catches Jim's mood, which also extends to the three sisters, who join them in a circle. Together, the siblings sing a song that their father had taught them, and they chant "Texas, Texas." They know that their father's father is in Texas, and that there they can continue to live together.

The point of "Mother Dear and Daddy" is that children can be more humane than their elders and have the capacity to reject demeaning traditions that rob them of their dignity. Edwards's attitude is reflected in the image of hope he ascribes to the children and in the ominous descriptions of their relatives. To Jim, their cars are "like big cats crouching, backs hunched, ready to attack." Jim's initial reaction is fear: "I wanted to turn and run away as fast as I could. I felt as if I had committed the worst crime and those faces hated me for it." Dressed in black, unsmiling and unfriendly, the relatives are not the people with whom he wants to establish family ties. By means of Jim's perspective, Edwards implies that these color-conscious individuals, who had once tried to prevent their sister from marrying a dark-skinned man, do not deserve to be inside a family circle where love, not color, dominates.

Although he won two awards in the 1950s for his writing, Junius Edwards has not subsequently received the attention accorded other black Southern writers of fiction, mainly because he has published so little. One may be inclined to view his repetitious style with impatience, yet it is moving and unrelenting. His realistic fiction is provocative, if dated, because it accurately reflects significant experiences in the lives of Afro-Americans, particularly the black soldier and veteran whose plight has been central to the post-World War II condition of blacks.

References:

Faith Berry, "Temporal Event," *Crisis,* 70 (December 1963): 364-365;

Jean C. Bond, "Death in a Southern Town," *Freedomways,* 4 (1964): 173-174;

Nick A. Ford, "The Fire Next Time? A Critical Survey of Belles Lettres by and About Negroes Published in 1963," *Pylon,* 25 (1963): 130-131.

Ronald L. Fair
(27 October 1932-   )

R. Baxter Miller
University of Tennessee

BOOKS: *Many Thousand Gone: An American Fable* (New York: Harcourt, Brace & World, 1965; London: Gollancz, 1965);

Hog Butcher (New York: Harcourt, Brace & World, 1966); republished as *Cornbread, Earl and Me* (New York: Bantam Books, 1975);

World of Nothing: Two Novellas (New York: Harper & Row, 1970);

We Can't Breathe (New York: Harper & Row, 1972);

Excerpts (London: Paul Breman, 1975);

Rufus (Stuttgart, West Germany: Peter Schlack Verlag, 1977; Detroit: Lotus Press, 1980).

SELECTED PERIODICAL PUBLICATIONS: "Excerpts from *Voices:* The Afro-Americans," *Black American Literature Forum,* 13 (Summer 1979): 93-95;

"Fellow Writers Comment on Clarence Major's Work, A Review of *All-Night Visitors,*" *Black American Literature Forum,* 13 (Summer 1979): 73;

"The Domestic," *Black American Literature Forum,* 14 (Winter 1980): 173-174;

"The Walk," *Callaloo,* 3, 1-3 (February-October 1980).

Ronald L. Fair, novelist and poet, is known for his experimental and versatile literary forms. Although he sustains the naturalistic tradition of Richard Wright by clarifying the impersonal forces that both limit and determine human life, Fair also draws upon African proverb, medieval allegory, and classical epic. Often, his prose work transcends naturalism into surrealism, the unreal world of symbolic dreams. He frequently relies upon both fable and melodrama in order to shape the political novel, as well as the urban one, into absurdist fiction. In employing humor, he manipulates voice tone and viewpoint, and he creates his characterizations with Freudian insight. Fair's skillful twists in style and wordplay embrace folk conventions such as "pretty talk." While he converts racial history into revealing metaphor, he illuminates the ritual of the rural and urban blacks who survive.

The son of Herbert and Beulah Hunt Fair, he was born in Chicago, Illinois, on 27 October 1932. He attended the public schools in that city, but left at sixteen to attend a nonaccredited school for a year. Fair began writing as a teenager because of, as he has recalled, "my anger with the life I knew and inability of anyone I knew to explain why things were the way they were." After three years in the navy (1950-1953), he attended a Chicago business college from 1953 to 1955. During the next decade (1955-1966), he served as a court reporter and stenographer while writing *Many Thousand Gone* (1965) and *Hog Butcher* (1966). Fair worked as a writer for Encyclopaedia Britannica for a year after leaving the Chicago courts. He taught at Columbia College, Chicago, during 1967-1968, and also at Northwestern University in the fall of 1968. Since his 1969-1970 appointment as a visiting fellow at Wesleyan University, Ronald L. Fair has devoted full time to his writing, and has lived mainly in Europe.

His first novel, *Many Thousand Gone: An*

Ronald Fair

American Fable, symbolically renders the historical and rural past through the story of one town, Jacobsville, Mississippi, where blacks remain in slavery until 1938. The fable of Jacobsville and its residents encompasses every element of oppression existing in the South from the 1830s to the 1960s; in particular, the sexual exploitation of black women and the lynching of black men are commonplace in Jacobsville.

Samuel Jacobs, the white founder of the town and Jacobs County, grew up in Natchez, Mississippi, where he amassed a fortune by swindling a ten-year-old girl out of her inheritance, a prosperous plantation worth $100,000. With the profit from the sale of the plantation, Jacobs establishes himself as an influential man, though one with few scruples. By 1836, he had helped drive the Chickasaw out of Mississippi and, as his reward, claimed a large tract of their land which became Jacobs County, the smallest county in the state. While raiding Chicka-

saw villages, Jacobs had captured all of the escaped slaves who had sought refuge among the Indians; these blacks provided the slave labor for Jacobs's thriving plantation. After the Civil War, Jacobs schemed with Yankee officials to isolate his county from the rest of the world, and, with fifty armed guards, he kept his former slaves in bondage. From Reconstruction to 1920, Samuel Jacobs and then his son, Sam, Jr., exercised such complete control over the blacks that they no longer remembered the Civil War or the meaning of freedom. Eventually, the physical repression and the psychological manipulation of the blacks allow for a reduction in the armed guards. After 1920 only one sheriff and three deputies are needed to prevent the blacks from rebelling or escaping.

Among the subjugated blacks of Jacobsville, there is a tradition that the firstborn child of a firstborn child will always be a pure black. The tradition is intended to preserve the race, because during the years of Jacobs County's existence, white men have raped young black girls as soon as they are of age. In the narrative present, Clay Lemkins has attempted to preserve the tradition by protecting Bessie James from assault by three white youths; for his efforts, he has to flee north in order to escape being lynched. This incident encourages Granny Jacobs, the heroine and herself a firstborn, to re-dedicate her life to preserving the purity of her granddaughter, Bertha, for Jesse Black, a young black man and the son of Sam, Jr.'s field manager. Granny is successful; however, Bertha later dies, just two months after she gives birth to a son, Little Jesse. As he returns from the funeral, Jesse, Bertha's grieving husband, kills a harassing deputy. He, like Clay, must flee north if he wishes to live. Despite the possible dangers in escaping, Jesse wants to take his infant son. Granny Jacobs, however, fears for their safety, and refuses to part with Little Jesse, though she does promise to send him to Chicago later.

Little Jesse is the hero of the novel; he is a firstborn and a pure black. When he grows into a rebellious youth and begins to antagonize whites, he is sent to his father in Chicago. In order to effect his escape, his grandmother has to stage his death and funeral, because the years have made no difference in the treatment of blacks in Jacobsville. It is Little Jesse who becomes a writer and, twenty-five years after his escape, tells the story of Jacobsville in a book. An article about Little Jesse and his hometown in *Ebony* magazine sparks an investigation by federal marshalls, who are outsmarted and jailed by Sheriff Pitch, and the other whites in the town prepare to teach the blacks a lesson as well as to maintain control over them. They soon discover that Little Jesse's writings have stirred the black community. The blacks revolt, burn down Jacobsville, and free the federal marshalls as well. Josh, the black thought to be the sheriff's pawn, not only leads the revolution but also kills Sheriff Pitch.

The plot involves several unifying elements. The first, characterization, depends too much on stereotype and stock device. While Granny Jacobs and Sheriff Pitch are well-matched opponents, the minor figures merely shed light on them. The sheriff jokes about blacks and sees humor in their oppression; he seems to be Fair's parody of a traditional American frontier hero, and true to folk tradition from which he springs, is deceptively cunning.

Most reviewers of *Many Thousand Gone* translate politics into aesthetic judgments. Sensitive to the social consequences, Martin Levin cautioned, "As if things in Mississippi aren't bad enough . . . Fair has to make it worse." Levin, who admired the simplicity of the book, observed the strange appearances and disappearances of characters, the lack of narrative consistency, and the vagueness of moral, "unless it be the impact of *Ebony* magazine." Eliot Freemont Smith, who questioned the validity of the fable in the "modern (Western) literary temperament," disliked the "ridiculous reversal of what seems the intended message." All the whites, he said, seem racist. Obviously defensive about criticism of the South, J. M. Carter wrote: "Apparently Mr. Fair does not know the difference between a fable and a bad dream. . . . Great fare for Black Muslims."

Other reviewers praised Fair's skill. Patricia MacManus remarked on the beguiling style "in a parable of cosmic scope," and the reviewer for the *Times Literary Supplement* observed that the novel was "short enough to possess an unflawed spontaneous unity, . . . a simplicity which would have been difficult to maintain at any greater length." Of all the reviewers, however, S. Shunra was possibly the most profound. Emphasizing Fair's use of stock devices, he observed the human need for myth and the law of compensation, "that suffering must have, or must be endowed with meaning. . . ."

In *Hog Butcher* Fair draws once more upon his life, especially his twelve years as a court reporter. The story tells about the life of Nathaniel ("Cornbread") Maxwell, who would probably have become a college superstar in basketball had the police not gunned him down. Although the police make a mistake in shooting the innocent Maxwell,

they cover their tracks well.

Seen first as a little kid slipping down the steps, Cornbread sneaks to the playgrounds. Later, over the years, he shows athletic prowess. The first baseman in baseball, a wide receiver in football, he also runs the 220 and the 440 in track. He is the center on the basketball team and, having received offers of scholarships from more than twenty universities, he finally chooses to attend one in Washington, D.C. There he would spare himself the burden of being the odd black; with no need to impress whites, he would accept his human worth and avoid schizophrenia. In Washington he might play basketball, run track, and even become educated. But when two policemen, the black Larry Adkins and the white John Golich, shoot him dead, the dream crumbles.

Although the narrator sympathizes with Cornbread, he identifies even more with the protagonist, ten-year-old Wilford Robinson. As Cornbread's body convulses, Wilford sees it smash into "hundreds of little pieces of glass," reflecting

Dust jacket for Fair's 1966 novel that draws on his experience as a court reporter

"no light at all on this gray day." Fearful of the police, Wilford avoids all adults as well because he realizes the tortures men impose upon each other. He remembers the advice of his teacher, Miss Carter: "If you know somebody else is tellin' a story [lie] and you don't say nothing about it well, then, that's the same as you. . . ." What Wilford first screams in the street, he repeats at the close: "They killed Cornbread and he wasn't doin' nothin'. All he was doin' was just goin' home."

Wilford's mother, Mrs. Robinson, continued the tradition into which she was born; she dropped out of school at fifteen, gave birth to Wilford, and became one more statistic on the welfare rolls. For three years, she lived with her parents, but later shares an apartment with Charlie, her boyfriend. When both he and Mr. Johnson, a local politician, want Wilford to lie about the murder of Cornbread, she resists. Even when Johnson threatens to have her deleted from the welfare rolls, she stands her ground.

Minor characters set into relief the counterplay between Sarah Robinson and her son Wilford, on the one hand, and Mr. Johnson and Charlie on the other. As the investigating officer, Patrick O'Kelly has the overtones of both tragedy and melodrama. At six-foot three, two hundred sixty pounds, he is roundheaded and blue-eyed; slightly tanned and beer-bellied, he is a poor match for Mr. Blackwell, the attorney for the dead Cornbread. Yet the philosophical and sympathetic Blackwell, who speaks with an Oxford accent, would be distanced by his very education from his client.

Larry Adkins, a black policeman for eight years, has attended night school for six of them. Perhaps he would one day return to the old neighborhood. Encouraged by his wife, Beatrice, he makes good grades and the dean's list through luck and determination. He buys a six-room house from a white who flees the city for the suburbs. When John Golich becomes his partner, he comes to resent all blacks, particularly himself, as his hope for a prospective teaching career, "the very pinnacle of his middle-class society," wanes. "He would never look back again." At the coroner's inquest, Adkins desperately believes that Wilford is "no better than the rest of the scum." From the witness stand, however, he sees Wilford as one who speaks the truth. Adkins finds the pressure unbearable; figuratively he has killed himself when he stopped defending the truth. By verifying the accidental murder, he finally provokes his own fall, but his conscience ultimately dominates. He comes to perceive Wilford as the mirror image of his younger self.

John Golich, Larry's partner, also confronts his repressed self. In a flashback, he remembers an episode from his college days. When a black freshman sexually attracted him, Golich perverted his desire for her into a racial slur. By means of an interior monologue accentuating his alienation, he associates her with the murder. Golich returns to the scene of the crime and stares through a tavern window. He examines "primitive" dancers with whom he identifies only wistfully. When his eyes fix on a girl hardly eighteen, he fantasizes sexually about her. He perceives the grace of black style, though the stereotype Little Black Sambo still haunts him. Confused and ambivalent, Golich stops to buy a black child some barbecued ribs, yet only the discursive narrator really knows what plagues him: that the political repression of the black "other" ultimately means the repression of the self.

Such narrative awareness hardly obscures flaws in *Hog Butcher*. During the coroner's inquest, the speaker shifts abruptly between Wilford's viewpoint and Blackwell's, paralleling the rough transition from dramatic to interior monologue. Elsewhere blunt conspiracy belies verisimilitude. The deputy coroner would hardly say to O'Kelly, "I'm tired of this. You guys know . . . well we'll cover for you if it's at all possible—we have to—we have to cover for each other. . . ."

Still, the story has some superior symbolic moments. In one of them, Cornbread receives the pass on the basketball court. Faking a throw to the right, he moves his head and shoulders quickly leftward. Then he springs powerfully into the air, yet turns as gracefully as a dancer. When he takes the highly arching shot, it soars above the defender's outstretched hands. Some viewers say aloud, "two points." The ten-year-olds, Wilford and Earl, jump to their feet and shout compliments. The moment reverberates with the folk tradition it draws from and lends poignance to the Messianic litany "They killed Cornbread," which echoes both the sermon form and the oral style that Fair uses to order the human as well as the social theme.

Cornbread's mother, Mrs. Hamilton, has probably the finest moment in the novel. Embodying pride and dignity at the inquest, she rises before everyone. When the deputy coroner prepares to waive the twenty-seven-dollar inquest fee—for he automatically assumes she cannot pay—she takes out a twenty and a ten, then shakes her head in protest to Blackwell who would intervene: " 'Thank you,' she said. And she walked slowly back to the first row of benches . . . the audience . . . alive with whispers about her greatness; someone in the back of the room applauded, caught himself, and stopped almost before it was noticed."

What Fair achieves transcends politics and history. Mrs. Hamilton signifies not only ethical ascent but also spiritual endurance. Her poverty intensifies her sacrifice as well as the injustice at court, and the episode authenticates the pattern in her life. She hardly bends to expediency, yet while her tears invite sympathy, she distills a communal story. Through her, Fair sustains a telling sequence of epiphanies.

Such crystallized instants escaped the reviewers. Impressed with the skillful resolution in plot, John R. Greenya observed weak dialogue and cliché; he discerned the conflict between social evil and individual good. Agreeing with him about the "tender and moving ending," Morris Renek conceded the novel was underwritten. Another reviewer in *Newsweek* remarked that at times the writing came "alive" and captured the personal horror of "life in the ghetto." Despite the limited critical response, *Hog Butcher* was made into a feature film and republished in a mass market paperback edition, *Cornbread, Earl and Me,* in 1975.

After *Hog Butcher,* Fair's rate of publication slowed. He continued to write while teaching at Columbia College in Chicago and at Northwestern University. He spent 1969 as a fellow in the center of Advanced Studies at Wesleyan University, where he completed *World of Nothing: Two Novellas* (1970). Dedicated to Sterling Brown, Fair's two novellas are experimental. In *Many Thousand Gone* Fair satirizes the romance of the Old South; in *Hog Butcher* he reveals political corruption; in *World of Nothing* he exposes religious hypocrisy. The first novella, "Jerome," focuses on a precocious child who precipitates evil.

Jerome's mother is Lula, who had been eager to escape her six siblings back home to a better life. She was sexually precocious and tormented at having frequently sinned with boys from a nearby camp. At the age of thirteen, she confesses to Father Jennings, a prideful curate who himself seduces Lula, appoints her to his staff, and uses her to advance his career. Having become his "woman," she loves him more than God. When he impregnates her the first time, she has an abortion, and he rewards her by appointing her the parish cook. Impregnated a second time, she knows Jennings will deny involvement. To tighten her hold on him, she arranges for his promotion by seducing the old rector and then exposing their affair. Lula is obsessed with having Jennings to herself, but he refuses to leave his wife and convinces himself that his

Dust jacket for Fair's experimental novellas. He described World of Nothing *as "a revolution in itself."*

and Lula's son, Jerome, is retarded.

All of the characters are counterpointed with Jerome, who has the power to elicit religious responses. When he enters public establishments, some people call him the true son of God. When he opens the poolroom door, the ceremony of it brings all games to a stop; later, a proprietor jokes that Jerome has "turned his poolroom into a church." After Jerome's appearance, violence disappears from the novella. At Episcopal mass on Sunday, Jerome sits restlessly or wanders around to watch the sun reflect on stained glass windows. Subsequently, he wonders why he senses such evil in the holy house.

Lula, however, "sees" devils above his head. Outraged that the others are obviously blind to his deception and sins, she bides her time. When she sees him at play, she takes the first step toward him; but his almost ancient visage startles her. When she frantically stabs him to death, Father Jennings extends Jerome's arms to the position of the Crucifixion. Jerome is the black Christ.

"World of Nothing," the title novella, is a rambling first-person narrative set in Chicago. The narrator describes his close association with Red Top, his Bohemian roommate; but in the process a multitude of fantastic characters appear and disappear. Red Top was born on a Southern farm, the son of a sharecropper and grandson of a slave. After a stint in the army, Red Top returned home a "modern day slave." For a time Red joined every group which promised equality and freedom. Soon, he was being investigated by federal agents for subversion, and he became reluctant to sign even a pledge card at church: "He Red Top was smart, aggressive and on the way up, good job and all, but he wanted to charge out in front of the ranks carrying the flag of the cause. And he did. When he looked around for the rest of the troops they were miles behind him and nobody was near to defend him when they pulled the flag away and cut him up in little pieces and left him for dead . . . *dead!*" The narrator uses Red Top's plight to justify his own ethic: "Buy what you want . . . beg . . . what you need." With government relief money, he moves into a dilapidated apartment. As regards writing, he says: "I don't get it published because I don't have the money to waste on stamps and all that jazz."

The structured encounters between the narrator and Red account for both themes of the novella and prompt the narrator's observations, which are sometimes insightful. The minor characters contribute to the plot precisely because they symbolically perform the folk ritual. For example, Cadillac Bill, a reformed car thief, appears in a tall tale blending humorous fantasy and surrealism. Fair characterizes Bill through blues and jazz, but he enriches the portrait through racial allegory and oral history personalized in his use of the extended family saga.

The story of the fantastic Miss Joanne Joanne contributes to the familial ritual. She appoints herself the guardian mother of little Jo-Jo, the daughter of Luhester, but the eight-day-old baby dies of inattention at a hospital. Joanne, the second wealthiest woman in the neighborhood, accepts responsibility for the baby's funeral and involves the community in it: "Red Top and I wore shirts and ties and white gloves and we rode in the big black cadillac. (I remember thinking as we drove out to the cemetery to put the little child away that it was too bad people didn't rent those big pretty cars to bring their wives and babies home from the hospital instead of always taking the ride when it's finished, when there ain't no mo!)"

Despite the allusions, the plot favors social realism and overreligious myth. For a humorous diversion, the narrator opens up yet another subplot, this one concerning Frenchy Coolbreeze, a white kid from Minnesota, who learns to play jazz and defeats Randolph Beard, an alto saxophonist, in a musical duel. Despite the difference in artistic form, Coolbreeze's playing is similar to the narrator's writing and Cadillac's oral tale: "You see there's a strange thing about stories. We've learned to never doubt . . . when it's being told because . . . you kill it—it can't be true. But if you only pretend . . . you really believe . . . you have . . . a great tale. . . ." Fair's focus throughout is on the creative imagination which sustains the humanity of his characters.

Lured finally to revivalism, Red Top and Coolbreeze depart together, both still "in search of a light." When the narrator no longer has Red for a crutch, he suspects cowardice on Red's part for leaving without telling him. Red Top writes, "Found something that gives my life meaning. . . . Hope you find it, too." But the narrator stands his ground, since courage has a price. He feels acute loneliness, as if having lost his alter ego. Red's departure, which leaves him "half dead," nearly closes the design. Only friendship saves him from suicide. Though another roommate, one more colorful than Red, reverses his mental state, his spiritual restoration ends with his need for writing: "I thought I'd better get my notebook out of the trunk and record this day because I've got the feeling that I won't be writing much longer." Yet the narrator probably will, like Red Top, "travel on," continue, and endure. His last words from his "world of nothing" are an affirmation: "here I am and here we are, brothers of our way of life."

The critical reception of the aesthetic idea, World of Nothing, was mixed. Most reviewers overlooked Fair's use of literary traditions that extend beyond Chicago, and they neglected his skillful manipulation of narrative viewpoint. They were ill-equipped to explicate the metaphors and literary conventions of black America. Paul Hogan said: "Venturesome in form and fresh in vision, Mr. Fair consolidates his position as an important artist whose work will stand as significant witness to this period of our life and literature." Freeing Fair then from the shadow of literary ancestry, he added that Fair's publisher "is comparing . . . [him] to the late Richard Wright, but . . . Fair's much more his own man. . . ." Shane Stevens proposes more inflexibly that "Jerome" fails to speak from a common humanity. Obviously at odds with "Blackness," Stevens argues for the laugh more than the scream; he recognized a tighter coherence than in *Many Thousand Gone* and *Hog Butcher*. "The power and immediacy," he stated, "come as much from its landscape as from its prose. . . . The mixture of fantasy and reality, the weaving of a modern counterpoint into an ancient fable are handled with great artfulness." In calling "Jerome" one of the best novellas for the year, he praised the depiction of the "aimless existence of the neglected, the desperate struggle of the oppressed, the hot wire emotions of the hated," all of which recall other Chicago authors—Richard Wright, Nelson Algren, and James T. Farrell. He said *World of Nothing* was a "revolution in itself."

When Fair left the United States for Finland in 1971, he anticipated brighter days. In May he had received the second highest prize from the National Institute of Letters for *World of Nothing*. His fourth book, *We Can't Breathe* (1972), became for him "the work of my lifetime, the book I've been trying to write for ten years." Though the volume won a Best Book Award from the American Library Association (1972), it demonstrated urban verisimilitude more than aesthetic coherence.

In many ways *We Can't Breathe* reveals once more the personal voice. It bears an author's note: "This is a narrative of what it was like for those of us born in the thirties. Our parents came from Mississippi, Louisiana, Tennessee, and many other southern states where the whites were perverse and inhuman in their treatment of blacks. . . . They came north, and we were the children born in the place they escaped to—Chicago." Set in Chicago during the 1930s, the work tells about five black boys—Ernie, George, Willie, Jake, and Sam—who struggle for survival and manhood. When they confront wine, drugs, street violence, and war, only Ernie wins out in the end.

Ernie's controlled narration about his family imperfectly compensates for the repetitiousness of his story. Early on he hates his father, Mr. Johnson, for drinking too much and for beating Mrs. Johnson. In defending his mother, he gets beaten himself. When Mr. Johnson invites Ernie on a trip to the amusement park, the boy declines, despite the rumors of grand rides, buttered popcorn, and sticky cotton candy. When he threatens to kill his father, Mrs. Johnson slaps Ernie wildly, almost hysterically; and both parents subsequently dis-

tance themselves from the family. Ernie still respects his politically astute Uncle Chester, who pays off the police, and his cousin Benjamin (his mirror self), who flees from white molesters. Both youngsters serve as foils for their heroic fathers, who single-handedly disperse a lynch mob by firing into its center.

The father of George Brown, one of Ernie's friends, looks Indian. Having migrated from Mississippi, Mr. Brown escapes North to Chicago to find himself equally despised and oppressed. With no employment other than coal-hiking, he has a white partner who works less but earns more money. Sometimes almost talking to himself, Brown rails continuously against the "white mind." One week before he is scheduled to quit his job to begin work in a defense plant, he is killed by a white motorist who runs him over. The tragic death undermines the romantic tone expressed earlier. Mrs. Brown has meanwhile appeared as gently submissive, yet she forces her son George to listen to her

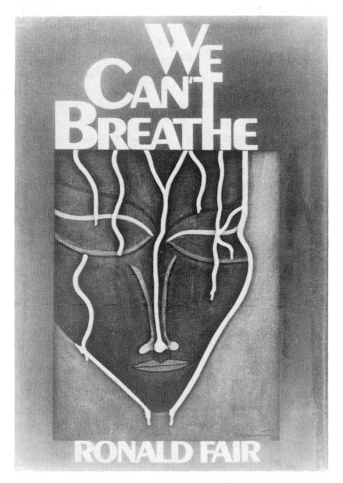

Dust jacket for Fair's 1972 "narrative of what it was like for those of us born in the thirties," as he called it

from the "magic" book, the Bible. Her faith, however, serves neither George's sister, a prostitute, nor his brother, a prisoner sentenced to two to ten years for dealing in narcotics. Fearful that George would become too militant at the coroner's inquest into his father's death, Willie keeps him high on drugs to minimize his anger. But after the judge expectedly and unjustly releases the defendant, George cuts the tires on the judge's car. When George is later killed by the police for robbing drunks, Willie is left to narrate the tale, and George's mother, Mrs. Brown, to present an apostrophe to naturalistic destiny: "We left the morgue in silence. As we stood on the elevated platform, waiting for the train, Mrs. Brown spoke in a quiet, sad voice: 'He was a good boy, Ernest . . . he just had to fight his way . . . And for all his fightin, even if he hadda lived, it wouldn'ta done no more good or changed things no mo than the shade from one cloud passin over a big oak tree stops it from growin.'"

At least two subplots weaken the metaphorical intensity and defer the narrative closure. As the mother of Jake, Ernie's fair friend, Mrs. Saunders indoctrinates her son into racial assimilation along with, indirectly, her husband, who "passes" into suicide. When the neighbors discover her subsequent plans to "pass" herself, one woman vandalizes Mrs. Saunders's stuffed furniture while another holds off the movers. Though the event is somewhat implausible, the dramatic situation forced, it encompasses Fair's unique blend of irony and humor.

Fair illuminates the narrators' minds. One appreciates his indebtedness to Richard Wright in the ambivalence of the gang fight and in the struggle for turf as well as for reputation. While Ernie beats up others to protect himself, he identifies with the grotesque; faced now constantly with his own fear, he admires Sampson, the ice-man, who signifies the imposition of mental order upon a hostile world. Whatever the probings into the individual mind, Fair emphasizes the collective one. In centering the complex of narrative techniques and subplots, the speaker functions as a human type. He is able to avoid being victimized by deterministic circumstance or by hostile gods so long as he navigates his personal hell, profits from occasional benevolence by the gods, and maintains personal heroism.

What Fair illuminates, paradoxically through modern fiction, concerns literature's own inadequacy to reform and sustain the human will. The work challenges the limits of its own structure by echoing naturalism, Shakespearean tragedy, and the black epic. Fair experiments well in narra-

tive form where the finest moments draw upon poetic devices and historical analogues. Ernie relives the child's fantasy as a man. He endows fairy tales with somberness; he measures maturation against the seasonal cycles. His tale opens with a romantic lyric. One Fourth of July he and others remain on the "Negro" side of a cyclone fence at a beach. When the police approach to maintain the racial policy, the youngsters scurry away. To restore their own self-confidence, the police humor themselves by harassing the boys. The blacks, they say, are "crazy"; but Ernie counters, "that year we showed him just how crazy we were when we tore the fence down. . . ." The literal meaning deepens into a metaphorical one, for while acts of liberation provoke serious consequences, the motivation rises above naiveté. Whatever the price, the boys knowingly rebel against the creed which confines their humanity. Nor is the excellent episode only racial allegory. Ernie structures a sequence of historical analogues which reveal individual heroism in introspection, the epiphany embracing even racial machismo. Here the gang steals:

> A scream went up and everyone in the store was so shocked that they seemed to freeze in the positions they were in and we all looked like old figures in a museum: Neanderthal man about to strike a saber-toothed tiger; the St. Valentine's Day Massacre; the idiot Custer in that famous fictitious pose with the Indians who were victorious in battle ("Hey man," a wino once said to me while looking over my shoulder at the pictures in my textbook, "looks like Custer ain't doin so hot"); the Blue and the Gray about to charge one another; the vicious, God-on-our side gas mask about to be strapped tightly into place; horses ridden by murderers.

From the early days of the Judeo-Christian era to a sad prophecy of chemical warfare, Ernie recreates the metonyms of battle, sacrifice, confrontation, martyrdom, as well as colonialism in the Americas, factionalism in the United States, and even the unspecified black arts movement, which suggests them all. Ernie's architectonic imagination literally objectifies itself into the sculpture and painting he describes, but only in the dangerous lapse from his blues song—"survival"—which ultimately repossesses him.

The well-crafted performance promotes Ernie's double identification with victory and defeat. He freely associates fairy tales clearly on his own terms: "I played all day like this in my castle, where I relived all the stories I had ever heard. I had fought off the lynch mobs. I had not bothered to climb up her hair but I had scaled the wall. I had made a king laugh. I had married a princess, but I had not been a frog in the first place. Before she kissed me I was myself. I had been black! I had never given it any thought that I had not been a frog in the first place, but had been myself. I had fought every battle the world ever fought and I had won."

Fair closes the distance between Ernie the persona and Ernie the discourser by reversing their readings of the natural world. While the youth reads the sequence of events, the story, the man reads the patterns of meaning. In the opening, the rain brings cleansing, the externalization of the relieved mind. For the young Ernie, snow blocks out the social limitations he would escape; it packs down the garbage in the alleys and levels the uneven sidewalks. Covering up the unpainted buildings, it fills the holes in the streets and yards. And, more important, it marks the ritualistic passage into manhood. He says: "When we were very young we ate the snow. Later, we washed girls' faces in it. And when we were older we rolled it up in little balls and threw them." Though in the early years the natural world seemed his ally, he must now rewin natural goodness. On a very cold day, he (the boy persona) goes to the library where he feels comfortable among books. While the temperature has been zero or below every day, the snow has already dirtied. The grit left over from the hot summer air—now stifling—has frozen solid, "covering everything with the same ugly grayness of death." At the library he sits at a table behind a radiator, slips off his shoes, and warms his toes. Near the warm floor, his socks dry out as well. With his heavy jacket and his two sweaters removed, he "soaks up" the heat and hopes to warm himself sufficiently so as to ease the walk home. Then he abruptly digresses into free association: "I read about the South and things whites had done to my people there, and I wondered why more . . . had not been written about atrocities in the North . . . a smiling face that always kept you thinking that things were going to be better." Once the means to childish joy, communal language becomes a means to confront the human cold, the brutality masking itself as politeness. Near the end, the discursive Ernie reinterprets the meaning. When the winter thaw finally comes, the temperature rises twenty and thirty degrees, seeming almost pleasant as the falling snow brightens the streets and pathways. While a new vitality emerges, Ernie confesses: "I was too old for . . . a sled now . . . too angry . . . too old to look at winter as a blessing . . .

the summer heat . . . aware of the emptiness of the faces around me and the horror that was in the minds. . . ."

Where Fair fails to achieve such eloquence, he mistakes the twofold process—experience and imaginative re-creation—for incoherently recorded autobiography. In creating Ernie's own story, Fair retells his own. Until the appearance of a helpful biography, those who would understand his life must read *We Can't Breathe.*

The critical reception of the work focused on the form, viewpoint, and history. Other emphases included the efforts in characterization and the literary sensitivity. S. L. Silverman wrote that the narrator's detachment weakened the anecdotal structure; Leonard Fleischer added that any of Ernie's friends would make a more interesting protagonist. The reader never understands, according to Fleischer, why Ernie alone "preserves a sense of self that cannot be destroyed." Fleischer also criticized the narrative structure, which allows for a larger canvas, but distracts from Ernie's own story: "Judged as a document of ghetto life, *We Can't Breathe* is detailed and informative. But Fair has chosen to write a novel, and his work must be judged as such. . . . Fair has failed to transform the deadening sameness and stultifying predictability of life in an urban slum into an experience that is imaginatively revealing." George Davis observed less craft in *We Can't Breathe* than in Fair's earlier books. *Many Thousand Gone,* according to him, was a tightly controlled and beautifully humorous story; *Hog Butcher* was a "masterful tale of human determination"; *World of Nothing* was a forceful reminder of serious conciseness. Admiring Fair's brevity, the avoidance of self-indulgence, Davis agreed that the book was truer to fact than to design. Subsequently, he made comparisons to *Native Son;* but whereas Wright's novel was the story of Bigger Thomas's suffering, *We Can't Breathe* emphasized survival. Finally, Davis viewed the book as "honest . . . full of brilliant revelation." Pamela Marshall concurred that Fair had written an "unsparing, brilliant, yet unexpectedly warm and touching book."

With some qualifications, the criticisms are valid. While Fair shows a conciseness, perhaps a weakness in development throughout the works, he displays a redundancy in the individual parts. Despite the example of *Hog Butcher,* Fair works most comfortably within seventy pages or less, yet no reviewer has noted that he probably would excel most in the writing of short stories.

Though Fair won an award for creative work from the National Endowment of Arts in 1974 and the Guggenheim Fellowship the following year, he left America when the black arts movement waned. Self-exiled in Finland, he had cut himself off from American social and political currents. Since 1975 Fair has sometimes written anachronistically, but he has enhanced his skill as a writer, having turned his attention to poetry. *Excerpts* (1975), his first volume of verse, and *Rufus* (1977), his second, rework most of the themes of his fiction.

Ronald Fair's publications in periodicals since 1979 reconfirm his artistic mission. In "Excerpts from *Voices:* The Afro-Americans," he interweaves folk dialect and epic. Sensitive to sexual brutality and racial abuse, he emphasizes the corruption of black art in the antebellum South and in the contemporary United States. Against the backdrop of the spirituals, he illuminates joy, forgiveness, and dignity.

In "The Domestic," a brief poem, he succeeds less through metrics than through the well-dramatized monologue. A friend of Mrs. Jones, the subject, tells the story to Jones's former white employees. Jones, she says, has returned South following the murder of a son and the passage of three daughters into prostitution; the domestic needed a change. Through detachment of her tale, the dramatized narrator illuminates the reverse migration. But for the speaker the possibility for return remains vicariously imagined.

"The Walk," a brilliant story, reexplores the mythic journey. During a storm, the protagonist Vernon comes home to an urban tenement. He encounters a gang molesting a girl on an elevator. His ascension in the stairwell reveals children scrubbing obscenities on the walls. Finally, he reemerges in the redemptive atmosphere of a family dinner. His world marks the double movement of epic, the descent into hell and the reascent into human communion. With masterful detachment, the narrator observes through him the rekindling of the human bond.

After almost two decades Fair has achieved the aesthetics he appreciates in the fiction of Clarence Major, who has, according to Fair, "transcended the obstructions laid before all black writers by those clamoring for more 'protest literature' . . . attacks old taboos of language and molds interlocking episodes into a singing ballad." Fair himself illustrates the diverse forms through which the achievement takes shape, more perhaps than even he concedes. The climactic decade, "the monstrous perversion . . . the '60's," which both disillusioned him and provoked his ironic detachment, persists in his creative imagination. Nearly a generation later, Fair reveals: "I'm still writing—seven books looking for a publisher, perhaps that will happen again. . . . Sorry I can't be more helpful, but I don't care to talk about many of these things . . . sorry they haven't published more of my books, but you know . . . they cut off the Black writer . . . they really cut him off."

Nonetheless, Fair's achievement endures. In the same tradition as that of Richard Wright and Gwendolyn Brooks, his life and work merit critical examination because Fair has courageously sustained exceptional literary experimentation.

Reference:

Robert E. Fleming, "The Novels of Ronald L. Fair," *CLA Journal,* 15 (June 1972): 477-487.

Leon Forrest
(8 January 1937-   )

Johnanna L. Grimes
Tennessee State University

BOOKS: *There Is a Tree More Ancient Than Eden* (New York: Random House, 1973);

The Bloodworth Orphans (New York: Random House, 1977);

Two Wings to Veil My Face (New York: Random House, 1984).

PERIODICAL PUBLICATIONS: "Oh Jeremiah of the Dreamers," *Callaloo*, 2 (May 1979): 73-80;

"Big House/Praise Shack," *Story Quarterly Magazine* (Spring 1980): 177-190.

Leon Forrest is an innovative stylist. His concern with the literary possibilities of the oral tradition places him in the company of several of his contemporaries including Toni Morrison, Albert Murray, Gayl Jones, and James Alan McPherson.

Leon Forrest was born in Chicago, Illinois, on 8 January 1937. An only child, he grew up on the South Side of Chicago, where his youth was filled with experiences that influenced his literary development. For instance, he remembers reading the Scriptures to his great-grandmother, and he says this gave him a "vivid sense of the drama in the Bible." Further he was exposed to the Roman Catholic religion on his mother's side and to the Protestant faith on his father's. Both religions figure prominently in his novels. The oral tradition, which is also an important part of the stylistic and thematic elements in the works, may also be traced to specific childhood recollections in addition to the knowledge he gained from reading. He remembers that there were numerous storytellers and liars on both sides of his family.

After graduating from Chicago's Wendell Phillips Elementary School in 1951, he was one of the few black students to attend Hyde Park High School during the years 1951-1955. His areas of academic concentration and his extracurricular interests foreshadowed the direction of his later professional development, for he divided his time between creative writing and journalism. He won several poetry and essay contests for students and served as a reporter for the school newspaper. After

high school he attended Wilson Junior College (1955-1956), Roosevelt University (1957-1958), and the University of Chicago (1959-1960). His studies at the latter were interrupted by a period in the United States Army, where he served as Public Information Specialist, which allowed him, among other duties, to write feature stories for the Third Armored Division newspaper, *Spearhead*. After his stay in the army, Forrest continued the pattern which began during his high school years. After a one-year period at the University of Chicago between 1962 and 1963, he divided his professional time during the remainder of the 1960s and early 1970s between creative writing and journalism. In 1964 he began working with the *Bulletin Booster* newspapers (community weeklies on Chicago's South Side) and was associate editor from 1967 to 1968. By 1966 he had begun writing his first novel, and two publications that year indicate his thematic focus. "Ezekiel: Notes Towards a Suicide" in *Negro Digest* foreshadows *There Is a Tree More Ancient Than Eden* in its nightmarish vision of the bread of the Eucharist being served on a switchblade. In addition, an excerpt from the novel, which would not be published until 1973, appeared in *Blackbird*, a quarterly magazine. In January 1969 Forrest began work as a reporter with *Muhammed Speaks*, the organ of the Black Muslims. He was promoted to associate editor in October 1969 and was promoted to managing editor in 1972, by which time the newspaper had a circulation of 75,000 copies per week. During the same year he was also involved with the broadcast media as investigative reporter for Hurley Green's "Issues Unlimited" on WGN-TV in Chicago. This post lasted for one year.

Nineteen seventy-three was a momentous year for Leon Forrest. In May, Random House published his first novel, *There Is a Tree More Ancient Than Eden*, for which Ralph Ellison wrote the foreword. The book was first rejected by six publishers, including Random House; however, the publishing firm decided to take a chance after a second reading. And in September he was appointed associate professor of African-American Studies at Northwestern University in Evanston,

Illinois, where he still teaches.

The effectiveness of *There Is a Tree More Ancient Than Eden* is due primarily to the author's use and transformation of elements from the oral tradition. Recurring symbols in the novel are conveyed through allusions to spiritual and secular songs. In addition, since style and character are interrelated, character may be suggested through the particular voice of the individual, and each voice has a set of symbols or phrases peculiar to it. There are two traditions which influenced Forrest's use of voices in the book—the literary and the oral. His literary predecessors include Ralph Ellison, William Faulkner, and Dylan Thomas. However, the ranges of eloquence in the Black church and on musical recordings were equally important as influences. Forrest remembers that his father used to sing in the choir at Pilgrim Baptist in Chicago and that his father was interested in spiritual singing. Further, as a child of the 1950s, he was attuned to the popularity of quartets in the black community. He recalls in particular the diversity of voices of the Ink Spots.

The themes of identity and salvation are central to the novel, which has Nathaniel Turner Witherspoon as its protagonist. The action takes place while Nathan is sitting with Aunty Breedlove in the back of a Cadillac Fleetwood as his mother's funeral cortege makes its way down the streets of South Side Chicago. This journey becomes metaphorical as Nathan probes his private pain and the collective wounds of black people.

The novel is divided into five sections beginning with "The Lives," which serves as a table of contents, of sorts, containing biographical sketches of significant characters with whom the protagonist comes into contact and historical figures who are important within the culture and with whom Nathan identifies. There are various styles evident in the biographies, the most prominent of which is the oral testimony, religious and secular, and sometimes a fusion of both. These styles are repeated in the remaining sections of the novel as Nathan confronts "The Nightmare" and "The Dream," views "The Vision," and moves toward "Wakefulness." In addition, symbols which are introduced in the first section and which have their analogues in the oral tradition are repeated, sometimes with variations, in succeeding chapters. These symbols include wings, robes, crowns, and trains, among others. The style and structure of *There Is a Tree More Ancient Than Eden*, beginning with "The Lives," are also influenced by the process of oral composition as explained by Albert B. Lord in connection with the saga singers of Yugoslavia. Forrest uses formulaic-

like lines and repeated motifs as stylistic devices to convey the sense of an orally composed narrative. The oral process is evident in the way the novel builds on the repetition of key motifs, for example, rebirth/transformation; spiritual ambivalence/loss in addition to the symbols alluded to earlier. The repeated motifs, parallel structures, and cumulative style in addition to the allusions to the spiritual tradition give to various sections of the novel a sermonizing quality.

Nathan's testimony, which begins "The Lives," reveals his inner conflicts as he journeys toward a sense of wholeness and salvation. First, he mourns for his dead mother; his sense of grief is so deep that it borders on the obsessive. This theme of the motherless child has both earthly and spiritual dimensions, for Nathan's cry is as much for spiritual salvation as it is for his earthly mother. Nathan also expresses his ambivalence toward authority and salvation, desiring and at the same time abhorring direction; he has an intense longing for redemption, yet an equally strong fear that he is too foul and hence too evil to be saved. There is also a burden of heritage which Nathan bears, for his ancestors were participants in the slave trade, and several members of the Dupont family continue their racial hatred against those with darker complexions. The burden of his racial heritage is threefold: the guilt associated with being the slaveholder, the degradation of being the enslaved, and the shame associated with his family's self-hatred. Nathan's testimony also reveals that he is suspended between two conflicting philosophies of experience: he swings between the despairing voices of his father and Jamestown on the one hand and the hopeful voice of Breedlove on the other.

The most extensive testimonies besides Nathan's are those of Jamestown and his sister, Madge Ann Fishbond. Like Nathan, Jamestown has troubles on his mind, troubles which have resulted in feelings of ambivalence, bitterness, and dislocation. In particular, he has been so damaged by the circumstances of his environment that he finds it difficult to reconcile the extreme poverty and pain which he and his family have suffered with the promises inherent in the Christian religion. Through Jamestown's biography, his personal pain and that of Nathan's are extended back through time to the Middle Passage, thus connecting their private pain to the collective wounds of black people. The link is suggested through Jamestown's recollection of his underwater struggle with an enemy. His survival causes him to question the nature of God and man. It is a question which Nathan must confront and attempt to answer before his quest for spiritual wholeness is complete. That is, what is his relationship with God in a world which in many ways, beginning with the original selling of the black man's body, denies his humanity and the humanity of others.

The author's sketch of Madge Ann Fishbond shows one of the most vital uses of the oral testimony in the novel. As Nathan listens, Madge Ann passes on to the hero a part of her personal history and that of her family, thus providing the boy and the reader with additional information concerning the struggles and disintegration of the Fishbond family. Her most touching memory is of her mother, who finally breaks under the strain of trying to hold the family together after the father has been incarcerated. Like Nathan and Jamestown, Mrs. Fishbond struggles to hold on to her faith in the face of catastrophes which confront her, mock her, and finally overwhelm her before she sends the apartment up in a final conflagration.

"The Lives" ends with an extended biographical sketch of Abraham Lincoln. Like the other sketches, this one on Lincoln reiterates several themes and foreshadows other events in the novel. Because Lincoln was the signer of the Emancipation Proclamation, his name is associated with freedom, one of the attendant themes of flight, a central motif in the book. The biography also focuses on the ambivalence of Lincoln as he tried to bring a sense of wholeness to a divided nation (paralleling Nathan's search on the personal level) and his feeling that possibly the Civil War was the price the country had to pay for the evil of exploitation. The allusion to his funeral train and to the division of his body and his memory foreshadows the significance of the train as a symbol later in the novel and the image of the lynched Christ-figure in "The Vision."

In the remaining sections of *There Is a Tree More Ancient Than Eden*, the reader is primarily inside the consciousness of the protagonist. "The Nightmare" begins with a repetition of and improvisation on several themes introduced in "The Lives." For example, Nathan believes that he is "robed in a floating tunic with strange coffin-shaped wings" which are described as being "lamblike on the outside but yellowed like an ancient scroll . . . tough and wolfish underneath. . . ." The variation in the symbolic associations with wings allows the author to convey the sense of the hero's burden of sin and spiritual darkness. In addition, the contrast in the outside and the underside of the wings suggests the ambivalence which follows the protagonist throughout his experience; that is,

what should be the proper response to the dangers confronting a pilgrim as he struggles on and upward. The contrasting nature of his wings is related as well to his relationship to Jamestown, for in spite of himself, Nathan is attracted to the wild and bitter talk of this older guide as well as to the voice of Aunty Breedy as she counsels him to keep his "hands on the plow, hold on. . . ." The opening passages of "The Nightmare" also reiterate Nathan's sense of loss and guilt through the allusions to symbols taken from the spirituals.

"The Dream," the third section, continues the hero's journey inward. Although the spiritual "Sometimes I Feel Like a Motherless Child" is not alluded to directly in this section, the theme of this song reverberates throughout Nathan's sometimes bitter confrontation with God over his mother's death. The eloquence of the folk sermon is felt in the lament for his mother. The lament builds to a rhythmic pattern which becomes chantlike. Each of the parallel sections in the chant is longer than the parallel lines in a typical sermon; however, the effect—the establishment of a rhythm—is the same.

"The Dream" contains one of the most intriguing and complex improvisations of a central symbol. In the dream, there appears a figure who seems to be a fusion of his mother, the Madonna, Breedlove, and Harriet Tubman. The figure is depicted as seated beneath a tree awaiting the arrival of death or freedom, "the pale ghost rider/serpent with a dripping red rose" who is "host, lover, cowboy." The author's treatment of the waiting woman and the serpent seems to be influenced by John's vision in Revelation of a woman with child, travailing in birth waiting to be delivered. Forrest's improvisation on this Biblical material allows him to connect Nathan's sense of loss and the Madonna's anticipation of deliverance with others who continue to wait for an uncertain freedom.

The novel's epigraph, which consists of two lines from Billie Holiday's "Strange Fruit," is the key to "The Vision." At the center of the action is a crucifixion which becomes a lynching and finally a dismemberment ritual. The ritual improvises on the themes of exploitation and destruction. After the Christ-figure is dismembered, a "band of bruised-blood angels" descends, gathers the parts of his body and places them in a sackcloth. The vision ends as the sackcloth explodes and the crucified/lynched/torn figure ascends from the sack a whole, but bruised being. On one hand, then, the phrase "strange fruit" refers to the lynched figure and those black bodies, alluded to in Holiday's song, dangling from a tree in full bloom. However, on another level, the phrase conveys the ideas of rebirth, transcendence, and strength which have been created out of the chaos and destruction.

The fifth and final section is "Wakefulness." The title would seem to suggest that the protagonist has reached the stage of salvation and freedom. However, the end of Nathan's journey is inconclusive. Although he does emerge from under the bed at Breedlove's urging, the reference to his crumbling to the floor "rising and falling and falling and rising" suggests that his quest for spiritual wholeness is a continuous process. The purpose of his quest has been to reconcile himself with his past (private and public) and to emerge with the reward—redemption (a new spiritual identity). At the end of the novel he is not still in hiding, but neither does he emerge with the total confidence needed to put his ambivalence behind him.

There Is a Tree More Ancient Than Eden was praised by most of its critics and reviewers. Critic Robert Bone called it one of the important works by a black writer to appear in the 1970s. Joel Motley said that the author "covers an impressive range of individual and collective experience . . . with artistic innovation and control." It is the style of the book that other reviewers saw as one of its strong points. Loyle Hairston, for instance, felt that the novel is "more poetry than fiction, . . . [a book] peopled with a collection of memorable characters who really come to life through the entrancing spell Leon Forrest weaves with his prose." For George Cohen, "it is not so much what Forrest says as it is his use of the tools—words, sentences, paragraphs, fragments—like an artist working in mosaic."

Following the publication of his first novel, Leon Forrest gained further recognition from the broadcast media, and his activities continued within the Chicago community as well. He made eight appearances on radio and television in connection with the publication of *There Is a Tree More Ancient Than Eden.* There was a series of papers and readings, including two lectures on creative writing, the first at Loop Junior College in Chicago in July 1973 and the second for the Chicago Urban Gateways Project in January 1974. The academic community recognized the importance of Forrest's work, for in the summer of 1975, he received a $900 grant for study and research from Northwestern University. Further, in April 1977 Boston University made a proposal for a Leon Forrest collection in the Mugar Memorial Library. During this period, Forrest was writing his second novel, *The Bloodworth Orphans.* He worked on the novel from June 1973 to September 1976.

The second novel, published in May 1977, is more expansive than the first; however, anyone familiar with *There Is a Tree More Ancient Than Eden* will recognize its links with *The Bloodworth Orphans.* First, there are several characters from the first novel who appear or are alluded to in *The Bloodworth Orphans.* Nathaniel Witherspoon, the protagonist in the first novel, is the most obvious link between the two works. However, in the second book he seems to be primarily in the position of observer and listener. The reader is aware of the unresolved tensions which are evident at the end of the first novel. Nathan is still being pulled in at least three directions—the Catholic church (represented by the presence of Father O'Keefe), the fundamentalist religion of Rachel Flowers, and the world of sensual pleasure and violence (represented by Pearlie Mae Bowers and Regal Pettibone, respectively). In addition, it is evident that his sense of motherlessness continues as he is still drawn to strong surrogate mothers. With the passing of Aunty Breedy, the role of spiritual guide is assumed by a succession of strong mother figures, including Lenore Boltwood and Rachel Flowers. The figures of Jamestown and Saltport are also present in *The Bloodworth Orphans.* The former appears in the list of characters, where it is revealed that he has come into contact with the trickster Ford, an encounter which leaves Jamestown still bitter and disillusioned. Saltport plays a slightly larger role, as Nathaniel is apparently mistaken for his former companion, now in a state of disgrace, who hides fearfully in his apartment from his Muslim enemies.

Besides the reappearance of several characters, there are elements of structure and style which are similar to *There Is a Tree More Ancient Than Eden.* As in the case of the first novel, *The Bloodworth Orphans* begins with a list of characters with accompanying biographical statements which serves as a prologue to the book. In addition, the oral testimony, secular and spiritual, plays a key role in the body of the novel. There are the secular narratives relating the lives of important characters as well as the conversion testimony and dying monologues of Rachel Flowers and her son, Carl-Rae. The eloquence of the folk preacher is represented in the style and delivery of Reverend Packwood.

The book is divided into twelve chapters with a multitude of characters and a sequence of events which is not always easy to discern. Therefore, one needs a key to the book's unity. This key seems to be the recurring thematic patterns and motifs and the classical myths which underlie these patterns.

At the center of the novel is the theme of abandonment and lost connections. The orphans of the title are Regal Pettibone, Amos-Otis Thigpen, LaDonna Scales, and Noah Grandberry, all offspring of P. F. Pourty Bloodworth, himself a foundling. It is not until the latter part of the novel that the reader learns the circumstances which have led to the abandonment of these individuals. When P. F. Bloodworth was expelled by his foster father, Arlington Bloodworth, the latter placed a curse on him. According to this curse, any offspring P. F. fathered would physically murder him just as old Bloodworth had been betrayed (in the gang rape of his daughter by all of his sons including the "nameless one," P. F.). Pourty seeks to escape this curse first by marrying the darkest woman he can find and then by attempting to avoid intercourse with her. However, in one night of drunken revelry, he sires triplets. After his wife hangs herself, P. F. gives one son to an unemployed garbage man in Memphis, telling him to drop the boy in the city garbage dump; he gives the girl to a sharecropper, ordering him to place her in a pig sty; and he gives the last child to a prostitute. She is told to get rid of the boy by any means she sees fit. Noah Grandberry, Pourty's son by Elaine Norwood, is orphaned after his mother kills Pourty and then herself.

Initially, then, one discerns motifs that are associated with Oedipus, who was abandoned by Laius after the Oracle told Laius that he would be killed by any son Jocasta bore him. The Oedipus link is continued in the novel as P. F. unknowingly kills Arlington Bloodworth and assumes the latter's position in the community. The mythical pattern of the hero being reared by foster parents away from the land of his birth is also noted in the lives of Zeus and Romulus, among others. Although the offspring of P. F. Bloodworth are the apparent orphans of the title, one realizes that their experience of abandonment and lost heritage becomes a symbol for all of the other motherless, fatherless, and leaderless individuals in the novel. This then is their link with Nathan, Rachel Flowers, Jonathan Bass, and the baby whom Nathan and Grandberry find in the middle of the gang war. This seems to suggest a continuation of the pattern of abandonment and loss for the next generation as well.

One consequence of lost connections which the book explores is the external and internal chaos which may result. The external chaos is suggested in the thread of violence which recurs throughout the novel. It is part of the Bloodworth legacy and curse, beginning perhaps with the first selling of the black man's body and in particular with the history of rape and incest which has been passed down even to LaDonna and Regal. The web of violence also encompasses the community as a whole, as the book ends in the middle of a gang war which the trickster Ford may or may not have instigated. This pattern of violence is linked with the world of myth as one discerns the Orpheus motif echoing throughout the book. It is suggested first in Regal's nightmare in which he sees himself being torn to pieces by his found siblings, a nightmare which actually foreshadows his death at the hands of vigilantes who make him the scapegoat for their misfortunes. The myth is also echoed in the fate of Abraham Dolphin, who is attacked by two youth gangs, and in the death of Carl-Rae, who is gunned in half.

A further consequence of the foundling status of the characters is that many of them search for harmony, a sense of history, and context for their lives. As a result of the questions which haunt Regal about his heritage, he has conflicting nightmares about his origins. In one dream, he has been sired by a royal father and is ultimately welcomed by him; in a contrasting dream, he is driven away by a father with a cloven hoof. LaDonna's burden of abandonment and lost connections is manifested in the sense of guilt she feels. It is her belief that her parents deserted her because they found out something vile in her personality. This sense of guilt sends her first to the Catholic church as a refuge, for it supplies her with "history, a myth, a home, . . . a sense of direction, a name, a faith." Rachel Flowers searches for the same sense of home and direction in her rather fanatical religious faith. In order to atone for the shame of her past, which involves not only abandonment but the birth of her sons, both Bloodworths, Rachel attempts to lead an existence of extreme sacrifice and submission. The extent of her spiritual fanaticism is perhaps suggested in her ludicrous attempt to baptize Nathan in a bathtub in order to save him from the Catholics. Readers familiar with Forrest's first novel are aware that Saltport believes that he has found his sense of identity and pattern in the Muslim religion.

Ultimately this search for harmony seems to result in deception and disillusionment. The primary agent of this disillusionment is W. W. W. Ford, whose name, or variations of it, recurs throughout the book. A figure from myth and folklore, Ford is a trickster who appears in many guises. There is a timelessness about his character, for it is suggested that his origins extend back to the beginning of the world, a postlapsarian world. Ford manages to catch within his web of deception and violence not only Jamestown but also LaDonna and Amos-Otis. Noah Grandberry, the fourth orphan, is the one most intricately bound to this charlatan, for it is Ford who has made him aware of his heritage. Through the trickster, Forrest seems to be making a comment on the nature of leadership. This is suggested in the links which exist between Ford and the other spiritual leaders in the book. In all instances there appears to be some element of illusion for the purpose of manipulating the masses. This is true even of Rachel Flowers, who, although not as destructive as Ford, includes theatrical devices in her performances with Regal, her foster son. The descending elevator may be an acceptable part of the religious drama. However, it unfortunately foreshadows Ford's theatrics (for instance his entombment and supposed resurrection), which are done to manipulate his followers. The book contains an equally devastating examination of the Muslim leadership as well. Saltport has been thrown out of the group for cooperating with the enemy. He has lost favor with the gods. However, the gods (in this case the Muslim leadership) are shown as beings who devise games just to entrap the unwary follower. Saltport has been fooled by an organization in which he believed and by his hero (Ford), just as Amos-Otis, LaDonna, and others are taken in by Ford in all of his various guises.

One of the reasons for disillusionment with leadership is the discrepancy between public and private morality, another key thematic pattern in the novel. This discrepancy is expressed most obviously in the protean nature of the trickster. However, it is also evident in Rachel, whose crumbling mansion houses numerous orphans, although she had deserted her own sons earlier in her effort to get deeper into the Word.

Packwood's sermon, one of the key elements influenced by the oral tradition, is handled effectively in the novel. Forrest captures the style of the folk sermon, as he does in his first novel, in Packwood's use of repetition, parallel structure, and chanting, all of which the audience responds to with great fervor. Further, Packwood's sermon is an integral part of the mythological connections in the book because of the significance with which he invests Rachel's past. His mythologizing of Rachel is in the style of Ralph Ellison's Homer Barbee in *Invisible Man,* as Rachel becomes larger than life. However, the sermon incorporates an element which is not present in the first novel: the element of humor.

Illustrating the problem which can occur when the preacher must improvise on the spot, Forrest has Packwood utter some unexpected images during his performance. For instance, he exhorts Rachel to "spit [the Devil] out, down there upon the ground" as he bops and bobs her head in his hands. The climax of the conversion scene finds Packwood up in a tree with Rachel on his back. The rather humorous episode foreshadows the ludicrous appearance of Ford up in a tree with Gay-Rail, the dancer, on his back.

The critical reaction to *The Bloodworth Orphans* was mixed. Critics generally applauded the rich characterizations in the book. Teresa Phelps in the *Chicago Tribune,* for instance, considered Forrest's "ability to create characters [the readers] can't forget" to be one of the strengths of the book. The reviewers recognized that, as in the case of *There Is a Tree More Ancient Than Eden,* style and structure are significant parts of the novel's purpose and effect. However, according to the critics, these two elements caused the greatest difficulty. Bruce Cook in the *Washington Post* noted that the book is ultimately about the language in which it is written; however, for Cook this has both positive and negative effects. This critic felt that if the book "lacks the architectonic structure of a true novel—that is, the sense of orderly development and balance—then it is because all this has been swept aside to give license to the turbulent, inspired, impassioned eloquence of his prose." The *Publishers Weekly* reviewer said that "for all its torrential eloquence, vivid characterization, and occasional infectious humor, [the novel] is a tiresomely complex story that forces the reader to search hard for its thematic structure. . . ." Phelps, on the other hand, felt that Forrest had more control over style in this second novel than in the first.

On 13 October 1978, Leon Forrest was one of four Chicago-area novelists to be awarded a gold medallion by the Chicago Public Library, and he was elected to membership in the Society of Midland Authors in February 1979; he was elected vice-president of that society in June 1980.

Leon Forrest's third novel, *Two Wings to Veil My Face,* was published in 1984. An excerpt, published as a work-in-progress, was selected the winner of the 1980 Illinois Arts Counsel Literary Award on 25 July 1980. It reveals that Forrest continues to be interested in the literary possibilities of the oral tradition and in characters whom he has introduced in his earlier works. The excerpt is a monologue by Big Momma Sweetie Reed, the estranged wife of the deceased Jericho Witherspoon, one of Nathan's guides in *There Is a Tree More Ancient*

Dust jacket for Forrest's 1984 novel, his third

Than Eden. She utters the monologue as she stands over the casket of her husband. The monologue is not a eulogy for her husband, however; rather, she uses the occasion to confront her feelings about another man in her life—I. V. Reed, her father. In addition to the imposing figure of Big Momma Sweetie Reed, there is Aunty Foisty, a powerful conjure woman who had placed a curse on I. V. before the birth of Sweetie as punishment for his duplicity.

While the talent of Leon Forrest has been recognized within academic and literary circles, he is still in search of the popular audience. One expects this to come as more readers become aware of his work, especially his ability to create complex, intriguing, and vivid characters. The reader comes away from his second novel, *The Bloodworth Orphans,* wanting to know much more about Lenore Boltwood, Carrie Trout, Lavinia Masterson, and even LaDonna Scales. There is the feeling that each character has more threads to her personality than could be contained in that one novel. Big Momma Sweetie Reed and Aunty Foisty promise to be significant additions to this list.

References:

"If He Changed My Name—An Interview with Leon Forrest with M. K. Mootry," *Massachusetts Review,* 18 (Winter 1977): 631-642;

A. Robert Lee, *Black Fiction: New Studies in the Afro-American Novel Since 1945* (New York: Barnes & Noble, 1980), pp. 245-248;

Elizabeth A. Schultz, "The Heirs of Ralph Ellison," *College Language Association Journal,* 22 (December 1978): 101-122.

Ernest J. Gaines

(15 January 1933-   )

Keith E. Byerman
University of Texas

See also the Gaines entries in *DLB 2, American Novelists Since World War II,* and *Yearbook: 1980.*

BOOKS: *Catherine Carmier* (New York: Atheneum, 1964; London: Secker & Warburg, 1966);
Of Love and Dust (New York: Dial, 1967; London: Secker & Warburg, 1968);
Bloodline (New York: Dial, 1968);
The Autobiography of Miss Jane Pittman (New York: Dial, 1971; London: Joseph, 1973);
In My Father's House (New York: Knopf, 1978; London: Prior, 1978);
A Gathering of Old Men (New York: Knopf, 1983).

Ernest J. Gaines is one of the best-known of contemporary black writers. He received popular and critical recognition for the publication and subsequent television production of *The Autobiography of Miss Jane Pittman.* His importance in this and other works is his ability to capture the experiences of the common black people of the rural South. Through dialect, setting, and characterization, he has brought to life both a region and a group of people that had been previously ignored.

Gaines was born on a plantation in Oscar, Louisiana, to Manuel and Adrienne Gaines. He grew up in rural Louisiana, and at nine years old was already digging potatoes for fifty cents a day. One of his earliest influences was his Aunt Augusteen Jefferson who, though she had no legs, was able to provide for the young child. Rather than feel self-pity for her condition, she adapted to it and found ways to do all that was necessary to see that he was fed and clothed. These two factors have influenced all of his published work. The world of the plantation, both before and after slavery, is the setting of his novels and stories. And Augusteen is the model for the recurrent figure of the aunt, a woman of strong character and religious faith whose self-sacrifice makes possible a better life for the next generation. Such characters appear in virtually all his books.

In 1948, when he was fifteen, Gaines went with his mother and stepfather to Vallejo, California, where he received a more thorough education than had been previously possible, and he began

Ernest J. Gaines (photo © by Thomas Victor)

reading extensively, especially about the South. He has said that the trouble with what he read was that it did not include the people he had known, especially blacks. Coming from a storytelling family, he began writing himself around 1950 to fill in those gaps. He found that reading Russian novelists such as Turgenev, Tolstoy, and Gogol gave him a sense of how to write about rural people. This apprenticeship period of reading and writing continued while he attended Vallejo Junior College and served for two years in the army. His first published short stories appeared in 1956 in *Transfer,* a little San Francisco magazine, while he was a student at San Francisco State College, from which he was graduated in 1957. He took advantage of a Wallace Stegner award to study in the creative writing program at Stanford University during the 1958-1959 academic year, and his serious professional writing efforts began.

His novels and short stories focus on the folkways of rural Louisiana. They capture the languages and mores of the blacks, Cajuns, and Creoles who make up the population of mythical Bayonne and the surrounding plantation country. The tales are centrally populated by the aunt figures, older, usually religious women who have seen and endured much. In the process, they have accommodated themselves to existing conditions, and they are distrustful of those who advocate change, even if that change is intended to improve conditions for blacks. Gaines's attitude toward these women is ambivalent: he admires their endurance, their strength of character, and their accumulated folk wisdom, but he also recognizes the need for change in society.

He makes it clear that reform is essential through his depictions of whites and the racist social order they have created. That order is deteriorating in most of his works, but that does not necessarily make life easier for blacks, since the way of life they found under that order is also threatened by changing economic and political conditions. Moreover, during the early and middle twentieth-century setting of the books, whites are still capable of using force to resist social change.

The challenge is issued by black men who, unlike the aunts, refuse to accept the long-standing racial relationships. Though these men come from the folk community, they reject its conservative approach and demand radical change. In some cases, their resistance is private and ineffectual, but often it is public and ultimately responsible for gains in black civil rights and education. While members of this latter group frequently die for their beliefs, they die heroes.

Catherine Carmier (1964), Gaines's first published novel, was patterned after Turgenev's *Fathers and Sons* and has as its protagonist Jackson Bradley, a young man who is returning to the plantation after several years of education. This training has alienated him from the values of the rural black community and especially his Aunt Charlotte, a very religious woman who had hoped that he would return to teach in the local school. Jackson wishes to leave but finds himself imprisoned by his inability to tell Charlotte the truth and by the rekindling of his love for Catherine. The title character is the daughter of a black Creole farmer, Raoul, who be-

lieves himself racially and socially superior to blacks and who has forbidden his daughters to have anything to do with them, including Jackson. This isolates Catherine, who nonetheless feels a deep love for her father, a man she sees as courageously resisting the Cajun takeover of all the good farmland. Though she loves Jackson, she cannot leave Raoul. Thus, both Catherine and Jackson are immobilized by the pressures of this rural community.

These twin themes of isolation and paralysis give the novel an existential quality. Characters must face an unfriendly world without guidance and must make crucial choices about their lives. Raoul, an embittered, lonely man, works his land and restricts his daughters, not out of hope for a better future but because he defines his manhood in terms of his resistance to both Cajun greed and to what he sees as black acquiescence to that greed. He takes pride in both his family history and in his own ability to work hard and productively. His increasing age and lack of a son cause him despair over the future; though doomed to ultimate failure, he continues to struggle because it is the struggle that has given his life meaning.

Aunt Charlotte seems in many ways the opposite of Raoul. She has had two sources of hope in her life: her religion and Jackson. Her religion has given her the strength to endure the difficulties of her life because she believes that there is an underlying spiritual meaning to everything that has happened. Unlike Raoul, she puts her faith in something outside herself. Her initial crisis comes when Jackson refuses to attend church services with her; she sees this as a possible judgment on her own faith and on the efficacy of her prayers. But because Jackson has returned, she has confidence that he will eventually completely reenter the community, including the church. The greater crisis occurs when he finally announces to her that he will not remain. We discover that Charlotte, like Raoul, has staked all of her hopes on a son. Her frustration is in some ways even greater because she has the son (psychologically if not biologically) and he fails to live up to her expectations. She feels so deeply betrayed that not even her religious faith can give her real relief from despair. She becomes physically ill, and even after she recovers, she cannot fully accept the meaning of the experience.

Jackson, though he intends no harm to Aunt Charlotte, cannot help but hurt her because of his own lack of faith. His experience of the outside world has led him away from what he considers the parochial values of his aunt and her community. He cannot accept an unquestioning faith in a divine order when he has both learned the value of reason and has used the reason to gain an understanding of human behavior. And though not politically active, he rejects the idea that the existing racial order is either natural or unchangeable. His problem is that he has no new values with which to replace the old ones. His reason has left him with skepticism and not with hope. The source of his despair is thus the very opposite of that of Raoul and Charlotte. The future seems closed to them because there is no one to whom they can pass on their values; to Jackson, the future is far too open because he is young but has no direction. The story is in one sense Jackson's search for a home, a place he can have faith in and still be true to his reason.

He tries to create this place through his love for Catherine, but this effort is made extremely difficult by her attachment to her father. At first, she rejects the idea that she even cares for Jackson, even though they had loved each other before he left. That separation was caused in part by Raoul's refusal to allow his daughter to have anything to do with any of the young black men. While Jackson was gone for several years, the relationship between father and daughter deepened, to the extent that her mother, Della, claimed that Catherine was more of a wife than she herself was. While no incest is implied, Raoul's attitude toward his daughter is very much that of a jealous husband. He watches over her constantly and will not allow her to develop any close ties to any other people in the community. When she falls in love with a young Creole man and bears his child, Raoul drives off the baby's father and isolates Catherine even more completely. Despite his fanatical behavior, Catherine accepts Raoul and even sees in him a kind of heroism for showing so much devotion to the land and to his family. She gladly becomes a substitute son for him, even though his actions virtually guarantee that the land will be lost to the Cajuns after his death.

Jackson disturbs this unnatural equilibrium by seeking and getting Catherine's love. But in place of Raoul's imprisoning devotion to land and family, the young man can offer escape to nowhere and nothing in particular. Catherine is torn between the desire for freedom and her love of father and the soil. Much of the book is devoted to an analysis of her fluctuating loyalties and to Jackson's uncertainties about the meaning and future of the relationship. Meanwhile the two of them continue to meet in secret, fearful of Raoul's anger. In a final confrontation, Jackson defeats Raoul in a fistfight and believes himself to have literally won Catherine. To his surprise, however, she insists that she must nurse her father back to health and that the conquerer must wait to gain his prize. Jackson's bitterness at this ironic turn is neutralized somewhat by Della's observation that he has in fact won; Catherine no longer sees her father as heroic, and her admiration has turned to pity. If the victor will be patient, he will have what he sought. Crucial to her understanding is the revelation that Raoul deliberately killed their son, Marky, the product of Della's extramarital liaison with a black man. In effect, what all the family now understands is that Jackson has exacted Marky's revenge, has in effect become the son that Raoul destroyed. Consistent with the naturalistic tone that dominates the work, the father acquires the son only by being beaten and supplanted, and the son can acquire a father and a family only by allowing himself to be imprisoned in the very life he wishes to escape. The end of the novel has Jackson waiting in the yard, "hoping that Catherine would come back outside. But she never did." The reader is left in a state of uncertainty, having to choose between Della's optimistic reading of events and Jackson's own despair. Neither possibility will bring him comfort. Either he has lost Catherine or, the deepest irony, he has succeeded in his quest, but at the price of his freedom.

Perhaps because of this ambiguity and pessimism, the book did not receive much attention when it was first published. Even with Gaines's increasing reputation, *Catherine Carmier* has been largely neglected. Those who have commented on it tend to see its pessimism as reflective of the influence of Hemingway, an influence which Gaines himself has conceded. It is considered the most despairing of his works and, perhaps for that reason, the least characteristic. While this latter point can be debated, given the tone of some later works, it is clear that *Catherine Carmier* is not entirely successful in presenting its major characters and their motivations. It is hard to understand, for example, what draws Catherine and Jackson together, given the experiences and values they have accumulated over the time of separation. Moreover, the revelation of the cause of Marky's death is unnecessarily melodramatic. On the other hand, Gaines does begin here to create a sense of the black community and its perceptions of the world around it. Shared ways of speaking, thinking, and relating to the dominant white society are shown through a number of minor characters. This element of Gaines's fiction continues to develop throughout his career; it is the very richness of this social fabric that calls into question the frustration and sterility of the major characters in this first novel.

Though *Catherine Carmier* was not a critical or financial success, Gaines steadfastly worked on his writing. Though he does not consider himself prolific, he wrote four novels (of which only *Catherine Carmier* was published) and a dozen short stories before *Of Love and Dust* brought him recognition in 1967. Some of the success of the new book can be explained by certain differences between it and his first novel. This new book deals much more directly with the black-white relationship, including miscegenation, and thus could be considered more accessible than the earlier work, which focused almost exclusively on black life. In addition, *Of Love and Dust* more clearly condemns the economic, social, and racial system of the South for the problems faced by its characters. While Gaines is not a protest novelist in the tradition of Richard Wright, his questioning of the Southern political structure certainly would strike a chord at the socially tumultuous time it was published. Finally, hope, if not optimism, is apparent at the end of this work, which clearly was not the case with *Catherine Carmier*.

Of Love and Dust is narrated by Jim Kelly, a middle-aged black man who has gained a degree of respect on the plantation where he works. He is trusted by both the owner and the overseer to do his job well. Part of that job becomes the supervising of Marcus, a young man charged with stabbing another and released into the custody of Marshall Hebert, the plantation owner. Jim is asked by Miss Julie Rand, another of Gaines's "aunt" figures and Marcus's godmother, to take care of Marcus while he is at the plantation. She believes him to be good despite his obvious bitterness, hostility, and insensitivity.

Sidney Bonbon, the white overseer on the farm, expects Jim to help break Marcus of his rebelliousness and arrogance by forcing him to labor in the fields under intolerable conditions. As a result, Marcus considers Jim a traitor to his race for cooperating with the white bosses and contemplates ways of getting even with the whites. While Jim tries to keep his promise to Miss Julie, he finds it difficult to deal with a man so unwilling to adapt to his conditions. All of the black community becomes alarmed when Marcus starts paying attention to Bonbon's black mistress, Pauline, with whom the overseer is very much in love. In fact, he cares more for her than he does for his white wife. One of the accomplishments of the novel is Gaines's presentation of the nuances of such a relationship. Everyone on the plantation, including Bonbon's wife, knows of this love, yet no one can in any way acknowledge it, not even the two children that are its products. A very careful social etiquette is followed by which everybody ignores what they all in fact know.

When Marcus is rejected by Pauline, he turns his attentions to Bonbon's wife, Louise, who desires revenge on her husband for his infidelity. The black community, represented in this instance by Aunt Margaret, is horrified by this development, not merely because of Marcus's motives, but more important because his action threatens the security of the whole community. If it is discovered that a black man is violating this most sacred of Southern taboos, then every black man is a potential target of white violence. But even though he is repeatedly warned by Jim against such behavior, Marcus's desire for self-gratification overwhelms the need for community safety.

What in fact happens is that Marcus and Louise transcend their exploitative motives and begin to love each other, much like Pauline and Bonbon. They then plot an escape with the aid of Marshall Hebert, the owner, who has his own reasons for getting back at his overseer. Hebert then betrays the lovers by arranging Bonbon's presence at the moment of their leaving. Marcus is killed; Louise goes insane; and Bonbon and Pauline flee the plantation. Jim also must leave, because Hebert realizes that he knows too much to be fully trustworthy.

In the process of telling the story, Jim comes to understand two things. One is Bonbon's statement to him that they are all victims. Race is ultimately less important than one's position in the social and economic hierarchy. Hebert and the system he has created and maintained are vastly more powerful than any of the petty manipulations of Marcus and Bonbon. The second insight Jim gains comes from observing Marcus. While Marcus's motives were primarily selfish, he still displayed a courage and spirit that deserved respect if not emulation. Jim learns that he himself has been too willing to accept his victimization. Throughout the story he has been a blues performer, singing and talking of lost loves and opportunities. He has chosen to be self-pitying and self-protective, but Marcus has taught him that risk is necessary if one is going to live in dignity. Jim acknowledges this lesson when he refuses to accept Hebert's offer of a recommendation. Though it will make his life more difficult, he realizes that his integrity requires cutting all ties to such a man. Unlike Jackson of *Catherine Carmier*, Jim Kelly has hope at the end of the novel because he has found something to believe in—himself.

By moving to a first-person narrative in *Of Love and Dust*, Gaines renders life in rural Louisiana much more effectively. Jim Kelly both speaks in the idiom of the place and time and instinctively asserts the values of the black community. Thus, a much greater immediacy is apparent here than in *Catherine Carmier*. But beyond these benefits, the first-person narration also comes closer to the ideal of the folk storyteller and thus is more appropriate than omniscient narration to the folk materials Gaines uses in his fiction. He has said that the novel was inspired by a Lightning Hopkins blues song, "Mr. Tim Moore's Farm," and clearly Gaines's method of presenting the story comes closer than his first novel to resembling black folk stories of love and trouble.

Some of Gaines's best use of folk material comes in the stories collected in *Bloodline*. Although this book came out in 1968, some of the stories were among the first of his work to be published. Three of the five, "A Long Day in November" (1958), "Just Like a Tree" (1962), and "The Sky Is Gray" (1963), preceded *Catherine Carmier*. Nonetheless, a number of factors unify the collection. The sequence is determined in part by the age of the narrator or central figure: beginning with a six-year-old in the first story, these characters get progressively older until Aunt Fe, in the last story, is on the verge of death. Further, the action of each story is confined to a single day in the area around Bayonne, Louisiana. Thematically, the stories in *Bloodline* are about the relationships between younger and older generations; more specifically, they usually deal with a son's heritage from his father. Stylistically, they are presented in the folk idiom of rural Southern blacks. Gaines displays in these stories a mastery of these speech patterns, giving them an authenticity that is seldom present in dialect writing.

The first of these folk voices, Sonny, the child narrator of "A Long Day in November," tells the story of a day of conflict between his father and his mother. At the heart of the conflict is Amy's feeling that Eddie cares more for his car than he does for his family. She leaves him, taking along Sonny, and returns to her mother's home. Unable to understand the significance of his parents' behavior, the child becomes so nervous and confused that he cannot recite his school lesson. Because of this disorientation, he replicates his father's public embarrassment by urinating on himself in front of the class.

Father and son then join in a quest for manhood. Eddie seeks advice from a variety of sources, but the only one who truly understands is the local conjure woman. He resists her demand that he burn his car, but when nothing else works, he ceremoni-ously drives the vehicle into a field and sets it afire. After this ritual sacrifice, he takes his place as the head of his family. Amy, comprehending the social importance of his role, insists that he beat her for her disrespectful actions. Though both Sonny and Eddie frown upon such mistreatment, the beating does take place and the family roles are firmly established. The happy resolution is reflected in Sonny's naive yet specific final words: "I hear the spring on Mama and Daddy's bed. I get 'way under the cover. I go to sleep little bit, but I wake up. I go to sleep some more. I hear the spring on Mama and Daddy's bed. I hear it plenty now. It's some dark under here. It's warm. I feel good 'way under here."

Gaines's selection of point of view makes it possible to see the operation of human relationships at their most basic. Sonny's innocence forces the reader out of conventional adult assumptions about what men and women expect of each other. At the same time, the concreteness of his description makes it possible to see how social rules structure private, sexual behavior.

In "The Sky Is Gray," the eight-year-old narrator also learns about social rules, in this case the rules about race relations and personal integrity. Gaines has said that this story is patterned after Eudora Welty's "A Worn Path," and the connection is clear in the journey motif and in the need for certain rituals. The difference is in the level of experience of the central character: while Welty's Phoenix Jackson has taken her journey many times, this is the initial and thus most important journey for James.

He has already had several painful episodes in his young life when his mother sought to teach him crucial lessons in survival. Because his father is in the army, she is the only one who can provide for the family. Fearing that something might also happen to her, she wants James to be able to take care of the others. Out of this necessity, she one day forces him to kill two small redbirds he has caught in a trap. When he cries that they should be set free, she beats him until he stabs them. Since the birds make very little food, James fails to understand her actions until an aunt explains that the mother wants him to learn that survival is more important than sentiment.

When he develops a toothache, an opportunity develops for him to learn another lesson in survival, this time black survival in a white-dominated, racist society. What James must become aware of is the system of rules that dictates black-white relations. His grasp of the rules is evident when he gets on the bus and immediately moves to the back, past the "White-Colored" sign, before looking for a seat. What he will acquire in Bayonne is a sense of the complexity of the system and of the means of maintaining one's dignity under such conditions.

In the dentist's office, he is presented with two different perspectives on social adaptation in a confrontation between an alienated, educated young man, much like Jackson of *Catherine Carmier,* and a black preacher who defends the principles of faith and humility. The young man rejects those principles in the name of reason and the harsh view of reality reason has given him. In frustration over this attack on his way of life, the preacher strikes the young man. The preacher acts this way not only in order to protect what is for him a relatively successful compromise with the powers that be but also because the refusal to compromise could be a threat to the entire black community. This same fear was expressed in *Of Love and Dust.* The community would be doubly threatened if its children began to admire the spokesmen of such a view, as James does here: "When I grow up I want to be just like him. I want clothes like that and I want to keep a book with me, too."

When the dentist closes for lunch without attending to James, he and his mother must walk the streets in the bitterly cold weather. Not permitted to enter any of the white-owned restaurants, they have no way of keeping warm. James now receives another lesson in survival and racial etiquette. His mother takes him into a hardware store and positions him by a hot stove. She then asks to examine an axe handle. While she looks over several, she keeps glancing at James; when she sees that he is warm, they leave without buying anything. In this way, she provides him an example of how to get the necessities of life without giving whites the satisfaction of seeing her beg.

A third lesson that is social in nature comes in an encounter between mother and son and a white couple who sincerely desire to help them. The white woman wishes to give them food, but James's mother refuses to accept it as charity. They agree that the boy must work for the food by carrying around the garbage cans. Though he believes the cans to be empty, James is prevented by the women from opening them. After the meal, James's mother wishes to buy a small amount of salt pork in the couple's tiny grocery and is offended when the owner attempts to give her a piece much larger than the quarter will buy. James's mother refuses to accept more meat than she can pay for.

This scene is important in showing the nuances of race relations. Even those people who wish to transcend racial hostilities must do so in the context of the social rules. These two women cannot face each other candidly; they must play their socially assigned roles despite their personal desires. Moreover, in the charade of the garbage cans, they conspire to teach James that the maintaining of dignity in human contacts is a fragile process. That James may have started learning this and the other lessons is indicated in the mother's last words: " 'You not a bum,' she says. 'You a man.' "

"Three Men" is much more explicit in the lessons that it teaches. The narrator, Proctor Lewis, a nineteen-year-old in jail and accused of stabbing another black man, is told the nature and meaning of his violent life by Mumford Bazille, a jailmate who has been through virtually identical experiences. At the end, Proctor must choose whether he will accept the advice of this man who has become a father figure to him. Initially, the young man seems doomed to a lifelong cycle of work-violence-imprisonment-work release, much like that of Bazille himself. Proctor has turned himself in to the sheriff because he knows that Roger Medlow, a wealthy white man, will pay to have him released in exchange for his labor in the fields. He is thus like Marcus in *Of Love and Dust* at an earlier, more malleable state of development.

But the narrator of "Three Men" must confront an issue that never came up in the novel. As Bazille explains to Proctor, he is doing exactly what the whites want by resigning himself to the cycle. By accepting work rather than imprisonment, he is in fact refusing responsibility for his actions and thus collaborating in his own emasculation. As long as black men make themselves dependent on whites by such evasions, they serve as justification for the continued oppression of the race. But to choose prison is to choose a long period of insults and beatings, perhaps even death. Thus, the choice is not an easy one.

While the narrator is mulling over Bazille's comments and tending to reject them, a fourteen-year-old black boy is thrown into the cell after being beaten. Proctor sees in this boy a young image of himself, just as in Bazille and Hattie, the homosexual, he sees alternative older images. In the process of nursing the boy's wounds, he becomes a father figure and feels compelled to assert his manhood. At the end of the story, he is passing on Bazille's advice with his own added sense of uncertainty about the outcome of his choice. But for the meaning of the story, the choice is more important than the result.

An existential theme that runs through most of Gaines's work is perhaps most clear in this story. In a world where there are no good choices and where the end cannot be known, the good man is the one who accepts responsibility and who chooses according to his deepest and truest nature. The choice becomes the key self-defining act when others control one's behavior so completely. Unlike Hemingway, whom he often takes as a model, Gaines is interested less in bold, forceful actions than in honorable, dangerous choices.

In the title story of *Bloodline*, this attitude is tested against the realities of the white world. Felix, the seventy-year-old narrator, recounts the experiences of Copper Laurent, a black ex-soldier who has returned to the plantation to claim his birthright. As the son of Walter Laurent, he is the only direct descendant of the white family who owns the land. The action of the story comprises his efforts to force his dying white uncle Frank to recognize him as a rightful heir. Frank, though he accepts the rightness of Copper's assertions, refuses to violate the rules of white supremacy that nullify his nephew's claims.

The irony of the story is that Copper is more truly a Laurent than his uncle. In comparison to Frank's weak, dissipated condition, Copper is forceful, commanding, and proud. He refuses to enter the main house through the back door; he physically overwhelms the men sent to get him; and he calls himself General. Finally, Frank must come to him if they are to talk. Such behavior indicates some madness, but that too is consistent with the reckless arrogance that is his Laurent heritage.

He does not get back the land, for Frank insists that it will be kept just the way it is, in part to take care of the blacks who have been loyal. Copper does, however, achieve recognition of his claim to a bloodline. He leaves after threatening to return with his army—all those blacks who have been disinherited from the land they earned through their work and suffering.

"Just Like a Tree" tells the story of a woman who is deeply rooted in the soil Copper wants to reclaim. The central character, Aunt Fe, has always lived on the land, but her family fears for her safety and wants to move her to the city. The move seems necessary because Emmanuel, her grandnephew, has been active in the civil rights movement; as a result, whites have started bombing black homes. The setting of the story is Fe's home the night before she is to leave. Family and friends have come for a final celebration of her life. The story is narrated by these visitors, following, as Gaines has

noted, the structure of William Faulkner's *As I Lay Dying*. Significantly, the only characters we do not hear directly from are Emmanuel and Fe herself. The effect is to give us a broadly based sense of both the public and private meanings of one of Gaines's aunts. The voices of the old and the young, male and female, black and white offer a broad and deep sense of the quality of life for which the characters in the other stories have been searching. At the end of "Just Like a Tree," we see why that quest is so crucial. In an ironic play on the spiritual from which the title is derived, Aunt Fe "will not be moved": she dies after a nightlong conversation with Aunt Lou, her lifelong friend. Her death, which seems willed, signifies that life for her is sustained by a time, place, and community that contain the richness of her experience. To leave all that is to die spiritually and, for her, physical life is nothing without the spirit.

Critics have seen *Bloodline* as a series of portraits of Southern black rural life in which the characters search for manhood. While Gaines is praised for the effectiveness of his characterizations and settings, doubts are raised about his way of defining manhood as primarily aggressive, head-oriented behavior and about the apparent lack of resolution in the stories. The latter assessment is somewhat off the mark since Gaines deliberately leaves his characters facing the future, trying to apply the lessons they have learned.

The time after the publication of *Bloodline* was devoted to the writing of what turned out to be Gaines's most effective and most popular work, *The Autobiography of Miss Jane Pittman* (1971). The novel started out as a communal biography, a fuller version of "Just Like a Tree." In writing, Gaines made the brilliant discovery of Jane's own voice, which radically changed the nature of the book. Through this point of view came both a fully rounded character and a folk history of the black experience in America from Civil War to civil rights. One hundred and eight years old when she tells the story, Jane captures the experiences of those millions of illiterate blacks who never had a chance to tell their own stories. By focusing on the particular yet typical events of a small part of Louisiana, those lives are given a concreteness and specificity not possible in more general histories. Gaines accomplishes this by showing the impact of the larger events of those one hundred years—the war, Reconstruction, segregation, the civil rights movement—on individual blacks. But the work is not simply another historical novel, for the narrator enriches the story with elements of popular culture and folk experiences. Boxing and baseball on the radio, comic strips, sermons, voodoo, and superstitions all make their way into Jane's story. What we have, in effect, is the totality of life as lived by Jane; in the process, the author reveals what it is that gives his aunt figures, including Jane, Fe, and Charlotte, their stability and dignity.

The journey motif so evident in Gaines's other works is also significant here in a variety of ways. Early in the book, a group of recently emancipated blacks set off from Southern Louisiana to find Ohio. When they stop after a day's journey, they set about renaming themselves. By doing so, they destroy the vestiges of white domination and create new, self-determining identities. That white supremacy cannot be so easily escaped is made fatally clear when the group is attacked and massacred by a band of former Confederate soldiers. The only survivors are Jane and Ned, the son of Big Laura, who led the group and died fighting. The two children continue their journey, even though they have no idea where Ohio might be. Repeatedly they meet people, both black and white, who try to dissuade them from their quest. Only when an old man shows them on a map how small a distance they have traveled and how many years it will take to get to Ohio do they decide to make their lives in Louisiana.

But the end of this trek does not mark the end of the quest for those things Ohio symbolized — equality, security, dignity. Jane becomes a steady center-point from which a series of men move toward those ideals. Ned, after being threatened for his political activity, goes off to Kansas to get an education. After several years he returns, renamed Ned Douglass, after Frederick Douglass. He opens a school, where he teaches the children both academic subjects and the principles of political democracy and equality. The white community is so disturbed that they finally have him assassinated.

During part of this period, Jane was married to Joe Pittman, a man who sought economic rather than political equality. Despite the owner's duplicitous efforts to keep him, Joe left the plantation on which he worked in order to provide a better life for his family. He worked as a horsebreaker and was willing to ride any animal, though Jane feared for his safety. Symbolically, he challenged nature out of the same impulse that led Ned to challenge the social-political order. And, like Ned, he died in pursuit of his ideals.

In both of these cases, Jane for the most part resigned herself to the deaths of those she loved. Such resignation culminated in her own religious "travels," her experience of Christian salvation. She describes the experience as a dangerous journey across a river: "I looked where He was pointing, and yes, there was a river. I turned back to Him, but He was gone. I started toward the river with the sack of bricks on my back. And briars sprung up in front of me where snakes had not been, and wide ditches and bayous with green water stood before me where they was not before."

Jane's devotion was so strong that she became the church mother, one of the spiritual guides for the community. This role did not make her self-righteous, however, for, she explains, the position was soon taken away from her when she skipped Sunday services to listen to baseball games on the radio.

The spirituality of the community is important to the development of the third strong male character, Jimmy Aaron. Out of their allegorical reading of the world, the old people see Jimmy virtually from birth as the One, a religious leader who will guide them in the future. He is to be a new Moses, reviving what they feel is a dying way of life. Because of this perception, they treat him differently by seeking to keep him pure and to prepare him for his life's special work. He tries but finds it difficult to share their religious faith.

He goes off to New Orleans for an education and later returns, now a civil rights activist. He has in fact become the One, but he seeks to lead the people into a secular rather than religious Promised Land. Consequently, he is regarded with distrust by the faithful, who see in his efforts a threat to their deeply engrained way of life and thought. Just as the community in *Of Love and Dust* feared Marcus's action, so these blacks fear that Jimmy's activities will bring the wrath of the whites down on them.

The one who does not hold this view is Jane. When Jimmy asks her to participate in his march, she questions not the rightness of his action but the effectiveness of her own: "What can I do but get in the way?" Throughout the book, she has been passive, saying repeatedly that it is not her time. But when Jimmy is killed in Bayonne, it becomes her time. At the end of the novel, she confronts Robert Samson, the owner of the plantation and symbol of the white power she has had to accommodate herself to for decades. This time is different: "Me and Robert looked at each other there a long time, then I went by him."

Though this work, like the earlier ones, leaves the character at the beginning rather than at the end of some experience, Gaines gives a much stronger sense of the character's probable success in whatever must be endured. This optimism is doubtless one reason why the book was both critically and financially successful. Consistently the work has been praised not only for its effective use of folk materials but also for its integration of political and artistic concerns.

The popularity of the book was such that a television movie was made of it. Though Stacy Keach, Jr., wrote the screenplay, Gaines was actively involved as a consultant. The production received high ratings and won praise from television critics. Because of key changes from the novel, however, the movie did stir some controversy in academic journals. The shift from a black to a white frame figure who interviews Jane, the revision of certain historical elements, and the revised ending, where Jane actually goes to Bayonne to drink from a segregated fountain, all have been cited as evidence that the producers of the film undercut the novel's message in order to make it more palatable to a largely white audience.

Gaines remained out of the controversy, preferring to return to his writing. He received a Guggenheim Fellowship in 1973-1974 to continue his work. He began a novel, "The House and the Field," which he later put aside in order to write *In My Father's House,* which was published in 1978.

This novel returns to the father-and-son theme of the earlier works. Like *Catherine Carmier,* a key character is a young man whose life is rootless and who seeks some meaning for his existence. But *In My Father's House* differs from the earlier works in its urban setting and the noncentrality of rural folk materials. The transition from rural to urban life has largely cut away such connections. Reflecting this change, the novel is set several years after the conclusion of *The Autobiography of Miss Jane Pittman.* Though the central character, Philip Martin, is a civil rights leader, the movement, like the black community, is in transition. Throughout, characters question the utility of protest and of white participation in the movement. The idealism that inspired Ned Douglass and Jimmy Aaron has dissipated.

The plot of the novel involves Martin's recognition of his illegitimate son and then his quest to find out the truth and consequences of his past life. In the beginning he is a highly respected, now rather conservative leader in the community whose reputation has been made in earlier nonviolent activism. His efforts for equality have necessarily shifted from social and political protests to less dramatic economic protests. In the process, many people, including the black middle class represented here by schoolteachers, have become indifferent and cynical. In the midst of arousing en-

thusiasm for a new demonstration, Martin is confronted with the return of his son, who calls himself Robert X. The father is so shocked by this ghost from his past that he faints when he first sees the young man. Martin's inability to justify having abandoned Robert and his mother and Robert's hostility toward his father make communication between the two impossible. Nonetheless, Martin becomes obsessed with this aspect of his past, to the neglect of his civil rights activity. He returns to the plantation where he grew up, where he loved and lived with Johanna many years before. He then goes to Baton Rouge and encounters friends of his youth, including Chippo Simon, his alter ego, who has become as dissipated as Martin would have been if he had not found religion and civil rights. In a final dramatic scene, Martin learns that his son has committed suicide. He fights with Chippo over the question of responsibility for the past and achieves a tentative reconciliation with his wife.

In some ways, *In My Father's House* is one of the most pessimistic of Gaines's books. All of the son figures are somehow misguided. Robert has been destroyed by his own hate and frustration; Billy, a young man Martin meets in Baton Rouge, has lost all contact with his father and has turned to suicidal revolutionary violence; and Jonathan, the young minister in Martin's church, refuses, in his arrogance and inexperience, to be guided by the wisdom of the past in his role as new leader. Given such characters, the future holds little promise. Moreover, the circumstances of Martin's tragedy suggest a rather strong destructive and deterministic aspect to human experience. Martin's final perception that nothing can be done about the past and that it does not necessarily bring life or enlightenment contradicts Jane Pittman's implicit assertion that history is full of meaning and that it gives vitality to the present.

This nihilistic undertone is perhaps responsible for some of the weaknesses of the book. Inadequate motivation is provided for Martin's immediate acceptance of Robert as his son and the resultant obsession with private responsibility to the neglect of social responsibility. He suddenly wants to be a father after abandoning Johanna and her children twenty years earlier. The son Martin sacrifices himself for is a flat, burned-out character whose psychological deadness is inadequately accounted for. The deterministic element gives the book a mechanical quality, with characters functioning more as opportunities for Martin to talk about fathers and sons than for effective dramatic action to take place. The resolution and hopefulness at the end seem imposed and not the natural product of the story's development.

A Gathering of Old Men (1983) returns to the rural world of Gaines's earlier fiction, but its time is closer to the present. On the Marshall plantation, the only ones left are the old blacks who have worked the land all their lives, the white Marshalls, and the Cajuns who are gradually displacing the blacks. In one sense the novel is a detective story. A Cajun work boss, Beau Boutan, has been killed in front of the cabin of Mathu, one of the blacks. Since the latter has a history of confrontations with the Boutan family, the case seems open-and-shut. But when Sheriff Mapes arrives on the scene, several black men are present with their recently fired shotguns. Moreover, Candy Marshall, in order to protect the old man who essentially raised her, claims that she is the guilty one. With an excess of suspects and the possibility of racial violence, Mapes is compelled to listen to all of their stories. Complicating the situation is the fact that the sheriff believes that none of the men except Mathu has enough courage to commit murder, and so he is baffled by this group compulsion to confess.

The emotional center of the novel is the col-

lection of stories. Each man tells of the accumulated frustrations and injustices of his life—raped daughters, jailed sons, public insults, economic exploitation—that serve as sufficient motive for murder. Though Beau Boutan is seldom the immediate cause of their anger, he clearly represents the entire white world that has deprived them of their dignity and manhood. The confessions serve as ritual purgings of all the hostility and self-hatred built up over the years. If they did not literally kill Boutan, they symbolically did so many times, and thus their confessions are psychologically true. What makes their narratives especially poignant is their previous submissiveness and even impotence; in addition to Mapes, the Cajuns, Candy, and, most important, Mathu have always assumed that they are weak and insignificant. Through their stories they face their self-hatred and enter, at least metaphorically, their manhood. The actual murderer turns out not to be Mathu, as everyone, including all the "confessors," believed, but Charlie, who for fifty years has been the weakest of them all. He has always absorbed abuse and run away from trouble, even though he is the biggest and hardest working of the blacks. When he can absorb no more,

Dust jacket for Gaines's most recent novel

177

Lou Dimes

Remembering that I was still on the job, I took out
my pen and pad and jotted down a few notes:

"Fifteen old black men with shotguns--guns probably
old as they. Five or six women old as the men. Two of the
women wear faded head rags; couple other wear aprons of
gingham that has been washed so many times the cloth has
lost all its color, too. Two or three nappy headed barefoot
children sit with the men and women. A stubborn silence
prevails.

"Framed house--your typical plantation quarters's
house--gray from sun, rain, wind, dust, sits on leaning xxxxx
cement blocks half sunken into the ground. House probably
fifty, maybe sixty, possibly seventy five-years old. Has
not seen an ounce of paint during half that time.(Note: must
ask Candy exactly age of house, also when last time painted.)
Tin roof. No loft between roof and porch, and in Summer porch
becomes an oven. Large cracks between the boards in the wall.
Originally chucked with mud; now paper and pieces of torn
cloth keep out cold in Winter, mosquitoes in Summer. Two of
the four steps leading from ground to porch missing. Weeds,
weeds, weeds. A small garden right of porch. Mustards,
turnips, cabbages, collards. Hog in backyard. Chickens

Page from the typescript for A Gathering of Old Men

94

he responds to Boutan's physical abuse by striking back in self-defense. He then tries to run, but Mathu threatens to beat him if he does. So he takes the old man's shotgun and kills the Cajun, who has come after him with his own gun. Then he runs again after begging Mathu to take the blame, which he does. But Charlie finds that something—his nascent manhood—prevents him from escaping. So he returns to accept responsibility and thus fully becomes a man, a change which is acknowledged by everyone, including the sheriff, when they call him Mr. Biggs.

Meanwhile, change is also being experienced in the Cajun community. The Boutans are planning their usual revenge on the blacks, but they come up against certain modern realities. Gil, Beau's brother, plays football at Louisiana State alongside a black running back. They are known throughout the region as Salt and Pepper. Their success as a combination has made race largely irrelevant; working together, they have the possibility of becoming All-Americans. The possibility will be destroyed for Gil if he is linked to racial violence. In other words, he has begun to measure his life by values different from those of his father and brother. His reluctance offends his father, Fix, who refuses to accept change, but at the same time the father will not act without the son. Both are frustrated, but the effect is to create a new order.

Neither father nor son can prevent the final explosion of racist violence, led by a family associate, Luke Will. He and others arrive at Marshall just as Mapes is taking Charlie away. The whites open fire, and the old black men, who have in a sense been frustrated because their confessions had so little effect, get their chance to do what they have only dreamed of. The ensuing battle blends the absurd with the heroic. Some of the blacks accidentally fire their guns through Mathu's roof, and all of them miss their targets. In the end only Charlie and Luke Will are killed. Charlie dies because he refuses to use the protection of the darkness; instead he stands at his full height and openly challenges the whites to shoot him. He kills Luke Will while being shot himself.

One of the most effective devices of the book is the variety of narrators. Developing the technique he used in "Just Like a Tree," Gaines employs white, Cajun, and black voices. He achieves thereby a range of social values as well as different perspectives on the action. Significantly, as in the earlier story, the central characters do not narrate; the words and actions of Candy, Mathu, and Charlie are reported by others. The author creates in this way a communal rather than individual story. The narrative works best when focused on the black community; the Cajun scenes lack the same rich texture, and the killing off of Charlie and Luke Will seems more related to the author's moral imperatives than to narrative necessity.

With *A Gathering of Old Men* Ernest Gaines moved back from the urban setting to what seems his natural fictional world. With the emphasis on the folk culture, he regained the hopefulness and sense of wholeness missing from *In My Father's House*. He has continued to find new possibilities in that culture, even though he has from the beginning suggested that it is dying out. What he brings out through the representation of it is not nostalgia for something gone, but rather a sense that even in its passing and with its limitations, it signifies certain enduring human values. Whether he has more tales to tell of this world remains to be seen. But whatever direction he takes in the future, Ernest Gaines has secured a permanent place for himself in black literature through his writing about the strong black identity that comes with an understanding of the folk past.

Interviews:

"An Interview: Ernest Gaines," *New Orleans Review,* 1 (1969): 331-335;

Forrest Ingram and Barbara Steinberg, "On the Verge: An Interview with Ernest J. Gaines," *New Orleans Review,* 3 (1972): 339-344;

Ruth Laney, "A Conversation with Ernest Gaines," *Southern Review,* 10 (1974): 1-14.

References:

William L. Andrews, " 'We Ain't Going Back There': The Idea of Progress in *The Autobiography of Miss Jane Pittman,*" *Black American Literature Forum,* 11 (1977): 146-149;

Jerry H. Bryant, "Ernest J. Gaines: Change, Growth, History," *Southern Review,* 10 (1974): 851-864;

Bryant, "From Death to Life: The Fiction of Ernest J. Gaines," *Iowa Review,* 3 (1972): 106-120;

J. Lee Greene, "The Pain and the Beauty: The South, the Black Writer, and Conventions of the Picaresque," in *The American South,* edited by Louis D. Rubin, Jr. (Baton Rouge: Louisiana State University Press, 1980), pp. 264-287;

Jack Hicks, *In the Singer's Temple: Prose Fictions of Barthelme, Gaines, Brautigan, Piercy, Kesey, and Kosinski* (Chapel Hill: University of North Carolina Press, 1981);

William Peden, *The American Short Story: Continuity and Change, 1940-1975* (Boston: Houghton Mifflin, 1975);

Barbara Puschmann-Nalenz, "Ernest J. Gaines: 'A Long Day in November,'" in *The Black American Short Story in the Twentieth Century: A Collection of Critical Essays,* edited by Peter Bruck (Amsterdam: B. R. Gruner, 1977), pp. 157-167;

Noel Schraufnagel, *From Apology to Protest: The Black American Novel* (De Land, Fla.: Everett/Edwards, 1973);

Frank W. Shelton, "Ambiguous Manhood in Ernest J. Gaines' Bloodline," *CLA Journal,* 19 (1975): 200-209;

Special Gaines issue, *Callaloo,* 1, no. 3 (1978).

Donald Goines
(15 December 1937-21 October 1974)

Greg Goode
University of Rochester

BOOKS: *Dopefiend, The Story of a Black Junkie* (Los Angeles: Holloway House, 1971);

Whoreson, The Story of a Ghetto Pimp (Los Angeles: Holloway House, 1972);

Black Gangster (Los Angeles: Holloway House, 1972);

Street Players (Los Angeles: Holloway House, 1973);

White Man's Justice, Black Man's Grief (Los Angeles: Holloway House, 1973);

Black Girl Lost (Los Angeles: Holloway House, 1973);

Eldorado Red (Los Angeles: Holloway House, 1974);

Swamp Man (Los Angeles: Holloway House, 1974);

Never Die Alone (Los Angeles: Holloway House, 1974);

Crime Partners, as Al C. Clark (Los Angeles: Holloway House, 1974);

Death List, as Al C. Clark (Los Angeles: Holloway House, 1974);

Daddy Cool (Los Angeles: Holloway House, 1974);

Cry Revenge!, as Al C. Clark (Los Angeles: Holloway House, 1974);

Kenyatta's Escape, as Al C. Clark (Los Angeles: Holloway House, 1974);

Kenyatta's Last Hit, as Al C. Clark (Los Angeles: Holloway House, 1975);

Inner City Hoodlum (Los Angeles: Holloway House, 1975).

Donald Goines was a popular author of fiction written for black readership. His sixteen novels all appeared as paperback originals and have never been out of print since their original publication in the early 1970s. In his five-year literary career, Goines provided perhaps the most sustained, multifaceted, realistic fictional picture ever created by one author of the lives, choices, and frustrations of underworld ghetto blacks. Almost single-handedly, Goines established the conventions and the popular momentum for a new fictional genre, which could be called ghetto realism.

Goines was born in Detroit on 15 December 1937 to Mr. and Mrs. Joseph Goines, Jr., owners of a dry-cleaning plant in that city. He attended a Catholic elementary school, where he earned good grades and was thought cooperative by his teachers. Although his father planned for Goines to take over the family cleaning business when he grew up, Goines himself wanted to be a professional baseball player. In his middle teens, however, Goines falsified his age and entered the U.S. Air Force, where he served in Japan during the Korean War. He returned to Detroit in 1955 addicted to heroin at the age of seventeen. For the next fifteen years, Goines tried a variety of illegal professions: pimp, card sharp, auto thief, armed robber, bootlegger, and all-around hustler. By the time he wrote his first novel, Goines had been arrested at least fifteen times and jailed seven times; he had spent a total of six and a half years in prison. He remained addicted to heroin from 1955 until his violent death in 1974 at the age of 36, failing to take the drug only while in jail. Goines wrote several Western novels and autobiographical short stories before he submitted anything to a publisher. He showed these writings to friends, who were encouraging but not en-

Donald Goines

thusiastic. His first published novel, written in jail, was accepted with enthusiasm by the first publisher to whom he submitted it.

Always writing about what he knew, Goines gave his characters the same illegal professions he himself had practiced. Almost all of his books are set in urban ghettos, where a dominant moral standard is seen to operate—"what goes around comes around." Goines is even known to have uttered this ghetto golden rule in conversation among friends while pronouncing judgments or predictions. The overall theme of the Goines corpus, however, seems to be that the ghetto life of the underprivileged black produces a frustrating, dangerous double-bind effect. One has only two choices, neither wholly desirable. One may settle for membership in the ghetto's depressed, poverty-stricken silent majority, or opt for dangerous ghetto stardom. Goines's characters do the latter; they become pimps, prostitutes, pushers, numbers operators, thieves, gangsters, and contract hit men. This choice extracts its price, for the characters, even those who have the reader's sympathy, lose their humanity as they gain success. Because "what goes around comes around," and because even the

novels' protagonists are forced to exploit, cheat, and kill even loved ones in order to survive, it is not uncommon that most of Goines's major characters die violent, often horrible deaths.

The violence in Goines's novels is like an uncontrollable contagious disease, affecting everyone who comes into contact with it. That is partly why the books are not cleanly plotted tales of crime or revenge, but realistic character stories in which motives are mixed, people act at the mercy of panic, frustration, and rage, and the effects of their actions are blurred by happenstance.

The novels are also ghetto cautionary tales, for Goines had a love-hate relationship with street life. Many of his novels convey not only the glamour and attraction of street life—the cars, clothes, and cash—but also its perils. The frustration, decadence, and violence of street life plagued Goines's characters and served to warn his readers. Because Goines wrote largely from his own experience in the Detroit and Watts ghettos, his publisher coined a new term for this sort of realism, calling Goines's books "Black Experience Novels" and appointing Goines the master of the form.

Goines had wanted to be a writer since the middle 1960s, and he first chose a form almost totally alien to his own ghetto experience—Western novels. His only acquaintance with this genre had been the John Wayne films he had watched in his childhood. In 1965, while in Jackson State Prison for eighteen months on a charge of illegal possession of alcohol, Goines wrote several Westerns and threw one away, presumably because his fellow inmates did not like it. In 1966 he gave the manuscript of a Western to Shirley Sailor, who later became his common-law wife. She thought it a poor piece of work but encouraged Goines to develop a talent she saw in him.

In 1969, in Jackson State Prison on another eighteen-month term, this time for larceny, Goines began to write seriously. This being his third long prison term, he decided to give up the street life and his illegal activities and become a writer. When a fellow inmate lent him a book by Iceberg Slim, the well-known pimp writer, Goines was energized. Within four weeks of reading Slim's book (most likely *Trick Baby*), Goines had written *Whoreson, The Story of a Ghetto Pimp* (1972). Goines's only first-person narration, *Whoreson* is based on his own experiences as a pimp off and on for over ten years. A fellow inmate approved of the manuscript and suggested that it be submitted to Iceberg Slim's Los Angeles publisher, Holloway House, who accepted

Whoreson enthusiastically.

Whoreson chronicles the rise and fight for survival in the Detroit ghetto of Whoreson Jones, the son of a black prostitute and an unknown white john. From age fourteen, Jones was on his own, his mother having died. By age sixteen, he was a self-supporting pimp. Much of the novel tells of Jones's skirmishes with rival pimps and the exploitation of the people closest to him in a kill-or-be-killed world. There is a univocal theme to *Whoreson*. The streets are mean, and only the mean survive there. In the ghetto, the cost of survival is a deadened capacity for love and tenderness. The rough, unpolished style of the novel helps convey the theme in a cold, brutal way.

Holloway House was so pleased with *Whoreson* that they asked Goines to submit further manuscripts. Goines was ready to comply: within a month of the publisher's notification, he submitted his second (but first to be published) novel, *Dopefiend, The Story of a Black Junkie* (1971). *Dopefiend* is the story of two black youths, Teddy and his girl friend Terry, as they descend from black middle-class respectability to the degrading agony of heroin addiction. Teddy and Terry's heroin source is the fat, cowardly, sadistic black dealer Porky. The somewhat episodic narrative details the growing number of psychological excuses, evasions, rationalizations, and sacrifices these newly addicted young people must employ in order to acquire the drug and maintain an illusion of normality in the face of their degradation.

Dopefiend is a powerful indictment of heroin addiction. Goines himself had been addicted to heroin for about fourteen years when the book was written, and the reactions and fates of the characters are similar to his own. The character of the dealer Porky represents the incarnation of all the different evils inherent in the drug. Porky is both well-drawn and despicable. Furthermore, Porky's dope house is clearly the addicts' hell. Goines's photorealistic style transforms the dope house into a gruesome cross between an operating room and a torture chamber. Although *Dopefiend* is not the most self-conscious of Goines's books which convey a message, it does contain the best-laid message. *Dopefiend* succeeds better than the other books in bringing all of its novelistic elements to bear on a message—in this case, the condemnation of heroin use.

Once out of Jackson State Prison late in 1970, Goines enjoyed advances from his publisher and the esteem of his family and friends. He began to consider himself a professional novelist. Although he had vowed to stay off the streets and discontinue his heroin habit, both the streets and the drug lured him back. In 1971 he started *Black Gangster,* his next significant novel, writing in the mornings and spending the rest of the day on the street. *Black Gangster* (1972) explores the issue of race and, in a coldly cynical and streetwise fashion, comments on the issue in a way which might not have been attempted ten years earlier. Another story of an underworld character, this novel tells of Melvin ("Prince") Walker's exit from jail and subsequent success at leading gangs in the activities of drug running, bootlegging, robbery, prostitution, and extortion. In order to provide a cover for his gang, The Rulers, Prince starts a sham revolutionary organization called the Freedom Now Liberation Movement (FNLM). Most of FNLM's black members are unaware of Prince's true purpose. Prince has a cold heart and a smooth tongue. On one hand, he articulates to the FNLM members the need for social action toward the improvement of the black man's place in society; on the other hand, he explains to The Rulers how he plans to exploit the FNLM and the Black is Beautiful ethic for the greater good of The Rulers' criminal interests. Goines created a surprising and cynical view of social justice, as well as providing another variation on the theme that ghetto prosperity and survival are inimical to a generous, openhearted ethic.

After *Black Gangster* was published, Goines and his wife, Shirley, moved to Watts in Los Angeles from Detroit in order to be closer to Holloway House. Goines also hoped to have some of his novels filmed and wanted to be close to Hollywood. He remained in Los Angeles for nearly two years and wrote his next eleven novels there before returning to Detroit.

His next significant novel, *White Man's Justice, Black Man's Grief* (1973), contains the overt and straightforward social message that America's criminal justice system exhibits gross racial inequalities. Goines had written in *Black Gangster* that justice, for the white man, means "just-*us*"; in the present novel he elaborates. The book's main character, Chester Hines, is sent to Jackson Prison for three and one-half to four years for carrying a concealed weapon. While there, he befriends Willie ("Kenyata") Brown, with whom he plans a robbery to be committed after they get out of prison. Willie gets out first, however, does this job alone, and bungles it. He kills a guard and gets caught. At his trial, Willie names Hines for having planned the job. Hines, still in prison 400 miles from the scene of the crime, is tried along with Willie and sentenced to

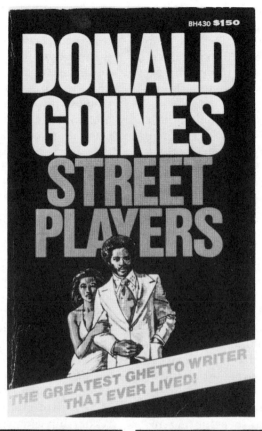

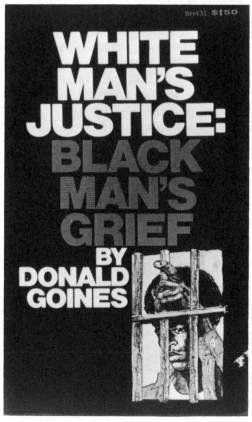

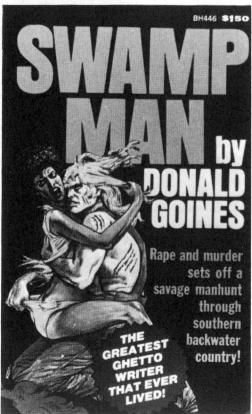

Front covers for three of Goines's sixteen novels, all published by Holloway House

life imprisonment, largely because of his color. The plot is sprinkled with anecdotes about blacks getting harsher treatment from the justice system than whites. The novel even contains an "Angry Preface" in which Goines explains the book's theme and argues that injustices in the bail-bond system should be rectified.

After publishing Goines's ninth book in little over three years, Holloway House asked him to develop a pseudonym, which he did in 1974, taking the name of a friend, Al C. Clark. Under this pseudonym, Goines wrote his next significant contribution—a four-book series featuring a black militant revolutionary character. The character's Uhuru name, Kenyatta, had already appeared with a slightly different spelling in *White Man's Justice, Black Man's Grief*. In the series, which includes *Crime Partners* (1974), *Death List* (1974), *Kenyatta's Escape* (1974), and *Kenyatta's Last Hit* (1975), Kenyatta develops from a peripheral Detroit figure with big plans and a small budget into the leader of one of the most powerful militant revolutionary forces in America. His organization swells from 50 members to 2,000, and his overall goals are to rid the ghetto of drugs and prostitution and to kill all white policemen, especially those who patrol the ghettos. In each book Kenyatta gets closer to achieving his goals; but in the final series entry, he is shot and killed just before trying to assassinate the business tycoon who is Los Angeles' main drug supplier. At the beginning of this violent series, its theme seems to have been that since the crime and poor living conditions in the ghetto are not being eradicated by the powers that be, the only alternative left for improvement is a militant, violent force from within. But Kenyatta's violent death at the end of the series, right on the point of success, implies that Goines thought that these revolutionary means must ultimately fail.

Shortly before writing *Kenyatta's Last Hit*, Goines, Shirley, and their two daughters, Donna and Camille, returned to Detroit. Goines was tired of Los Angeles. He thought it too big and sprawling, its street life lacking a center of activity; also, none of his books had been filmed, though several of his books had stimulated the interest of filmmakers. In Detroit, Goines continued writing, producing only one more book. On 21 October 1974, Goines and his wife were shot and killed in their Detroit home by two white men whose identities and motives remain unknown. Goines was shot while sitting at his typewriter. Later, the manuscript for *Inner City Hoodlum* (1975) was found on the shelf in his study.

Goines's novels are written in a rough, raw, sometimes crude style. The language is most often the speech of the streets, but sometimes it lapses into an uneasy mix of black English and standard English which is not spoken anywhere outside of Goines's novels. In almost every way, Goines's writing improved from book to book. The plotting became more complicated, the transitions smoother, the language more even and expressive, and the themes deeper. The early books, such as *Whoreson, Dopefiend,* and *Black Gangster,* resemble fictionalized versions of earlier well-known black memoirs such as *The Autobiography of Malcolm X* (1965), Piri Thomas's *Down These Mean Streets* (1967), and Iceberg Slim's *Trick Baby* (1967). Goines's later books, such as *Crime Partners* and *Never Die Alone* (1974), are less linear, with more complex plots, and less emphasis on the activities of a single character; they convey through narrative shifts and the use of irony the wider ramifications of the ghetto's moral standards and the frustrating position of its inhabitants.

Goines is the foremost example of a literary phenomenon possible no earlier than the 1970s—a successful black author of mass market fiction with a readership which is almost exclusively black. Goines has created a harsh, self-consistent fictional world and has set forth its most important aspects and concerns in a graphic, unsentimental manner. Furthermore, Goines is a prototype for the author who has achieved popular success and influence but has been almost completely ignored by reviewers, critics, and scholars. His novels have sold well over five million copies and are recommended reading at some urban New York high schools. The books enjoy strong sales on American military bases abroad. They have also been the impetus for other black authors who write in a similar vein, such as Joseph Nazel, Andrew Stonewall Jackson, Roosevelt Mallory, and James Howard Readus. Nevertheless, there has not existed even the smallest body of critical work on Goines until quite recently.

References:

Greg Goode, "From *Dopefiend* to *Kenyatta's Last Hit*: The Angry Black Crime Novels of Donald Goines," *MELUS*, 2 (Summer 1984);

Eddie Stone, *Donald Writes No More: A Biography of Donald Goines* (Los Angeles: Holloway House, 1974).

Rosa Guy

(1 September 1925-   )

Leota S. Lawrence

BOOKS: *Bird at My Window* (Philadelphia: Lippincott, 1966);

The Friends (New York: Holt, Rinehart & Winston,
1973; London: Gollancz, 1974);

Ruby (New York: Viking, 1976; London: Gollancz,
1981);

Edith Jackson (New York: Viking, 1978; London:
Gollancz, 1979);

The Disappearance (New York: Delacorte, 1979;
London: Gollancz, 1980);

Mother Crocodile (New York: Delacorte, 1981);

Mirror of Her Own (New York: Delacorte, 1981);

New Guys Around the Block (New York: Delacorte,
1983; London: Gollancz, 1983);

A Measure of Time (New York: Holt, Rinehart &
Winston, 1983).

OTHER: *Children of Longing,* edited by Guy (New
York: Holt, Rinehart & Winston, 1970).

Five of Rosa Guy's eight published novels deal
with the problems that black youths face in the
racially discriminatory and culturally impoverished
environment of Harlem. Though her novels are
usually categorized as books for young adults, she is
a compelling and courageous voice among contemporary American writers.

Rosa Guy was born in Trinidad, West Indies,
in 1925. In 1932, at the age of seven, she migrated to
the United States with her parents, Henry and Audrey Cuthbert, and her sister, Ameze. Guy says that
she came to New York, arriving in her best silk
dress, to greet the first winter of her life. "That
might account for the first horrible and long-lasting
impression I had of New York," she says. It was in
Harlem that the family made their home and where
young Rosa and her sister grew up.

Two years after the family's arrival in Harlem,
the mother died, leaving, in Guy's words, "me and
my sister with a tyrant of a father who was terrified
of raising two girls amid the corruption of big-city
life." The father rented an apartment and paid a
West Indian woman who lived next door to keep an
eye on the two girls. One week before the outbreak
of World War II, Rosa Cuthbert married Warner
Guy, a young black American whom she had met in

Rosa Guy (Gale International Portrait Gallery)

New York. It was while her husband was in the army
and after their son, Warner, Jr., was born that Rosa
Guy became involved in the American Negro
Theatre, which was then in its glory. At the end of
the war, she divided her time among night school,
the study of drama, and her job in a clothes factory.
Finally admitting how limited the field of drama was
for black women, Guy turned to writing. She attended New York University, where she studied
under Viola Brothers Shaw. In the late 1940s, Guy
became involved in the Committee for the Negro in
the Arts. She had already started writing plays and
short stories when she, John Killens, and other
young black writers got together to form the Harlem Writers Guild.

Julian Mayfield, the novelist, playwright, and
teacher, remembers meeting Rosa Guy for the first
time in 1949, in connection with the Harlem Writers

Guild. Not only was she writing plays at this time, but, according to Mayfield, she acted in some of the plays that she was writing. Mayfield recounts an incident that he says characterizes Rosa Guy. In February 1961, when Patrice Lumumba was assassinated, three young black women, all of them aspiring writers, decided to express their anger through a medium other than writing. These women were Rosa Guy, Maya Angelou, and Paule Marshall. They decided to stage a sit-in within the chambers of the Security Council of the United Nations to protest the assassination. This incident, Mayfield claims, may have changed the entire security system of the United Nations by making it more difficult for anyone to enter the premises.

In 1966, after many years of sharpening her craft, Guy successfully published her first novel, *Bird at My Window,* which is set in black Harlem. She writes about a black Harlem family that had fled the South because Big Willie, the father, had rejected the advances of a white woman who subsequently accused him of rape.

The work opens sometime after Big Willie was killed at a gambling table. Wade, the younger of his sons, is thirty-eight years old when we first meet him in the prison ward of a New York hospital, where he is in a straightjacket. Wade knows that his incarceration has something to do with his assaulting his sister, Faith, the one person he really cares about. All he can remember about the incident is that his brother, Willie Earl, somehow hurt his sister. Willie Earl, Wade's older brother, has always cared about nobody but himself, yet he is the one their mother seems to care about most. Wade considers himself a family man: his family being his mother, his sister, and his hard-drinking Uncle Dan. Mumma's inability to recognize Wade's concern and love for them all is a constant pain for him. It is a rejection that he can never reconcile.

Wade had been an exceptionally bright and sensitive child. When he was twelve years old, Professor Jones, a family friend, insisted that Wade and some other children should picket a white school to gain entrance. One of the white parents hissed in Wade's face, "We don't want you sons-of-bitches stinking up our schools. We don't go where you are. Why the hell do you want to come around us?" Then she slapped him. Unexpectedly, Wade's fear turned into anger. He grabbed the woman fully intending to kill her. It took Professor Jones as well as a police officer to pull Wade off of the woman. As a result of this incident, the twelve-year-old boy spent the night in jail. The trauma of this episode is signaled by Wade's amnesia about it.

After graduating ahead of his class, Wade launches into a life of violence. When he steals and takes money home to his mother, she never questions him. Wade kills his friend Buddy. When he joins the army, he kills a white American captain in France for calling him a "nigger" and his white girl friend, Michelle, a "whore." Emotionally crippled, Wade is twice given the opportunity to save himself. The first time is through Professor Jones, who gets Wade his first job and introduces him to Gail, a middle-class black girl. Wade is at the point of marrying her when he decides she is trapping him and taking him away from his family. The second time is when he sends all his money home during the war while he is in France. Wade's plan is that after the war he will collect his savings and return to France to start a new life with Michelle. But Mumma has spent all of Wade's money, and so this dream too is not realized.

At the end of the novel, Wade remembers how he had come to assault Faith. She had come between him and his brother when Wade was about to punch Willie Earl. Wade had found out that his brother had saved over ten thousand dollars by conspiring with Mumma to use all of Wade's savings sent home from France. With this recollection, he decides to kill Mumma, then Willie Earl, then himself. He decides that Faith should be the only one of Big Willie's "misbegotten brood" allowed to live. But Wade fluffs this plan too, for as he brings the knife down to kill his mother, his sister gets in the way. Wade knows nothing more until he finds himself sitting in the park the next day, his feet covered with blood.

Bird at My Window is an ambitious and courageous first novel. The author attempts, in the words of one critic, "to examine and explore the sociological forces behind the gradual and complete amoralization of a Black man in Harlem." Guy attempts not only to explore the racial forces that help to cripple the black man, but she also looks within the black family and shows how racism can destroy familial relationships with disastrous results. As Wade sees it, he has been twice rejected: first, by his mother and brother, and second, by the society in which he finds himself.

In this work, Guy examines the relationship between mother and children in the black family. Traditionally, the mother in the black family is a source of strength and support. Not so Mumma. As Wade sees it, having been forced on her knees years before in cotton country, Mumma never got up. When Wade is buffeted by the outside world, he looks to his family, especially his mother, for support, but he is disappointed because Mumma has accepted the role ascribed her by the white society; she accepts her inferiority and is apologetic and accepting.

At least two notable black critics found the novel lacking. Brooks Johnson in *The Negro Digest* felt that some of the dialogue was "false sounding," and Saunders Redding in the *Crisis* criticized the plot structure for not being "credible" and for lacking "conviction." However, both agreed that Guy showed promise.

In the late 1960s, Rosa Guy wanted to know "what Black youth . . . were thinking and feeling after the violent upheavals of racial riots, the civil rights marches, and the assassinations of Malcolm X and Dr. Martin Luther King, Jr." As a result she traveled throughout the United States, going into black high schools and colleges in urban and rural areas, into writers' workshops, the cotton fields, and the ghettos, seeking answers from young black people between the ages of thirteen and twenty-three. In *Children of Longing*, edited by Guy and published in 1970, Guy allows these young people to tell their own experiences in their own words, and this they do in clear, ringing tones that demand a hearing of all adults. *Children of Longing* can easily serve as a companion piece to Guy's later fiction, and if there were any doubt as to the authenticity of her themes and characters, a reading of *Children of Longing* would quickly dispel them.

From the depths of the ghettos of Harlem to the most desolate cotton patches in the heart of Mississippi, the fears, concerns, hopes, and ambitions of these young people are the same. They all want to be able to stand up and be counted. The forces working against them are also common: uncaring and sometimes vicious teachers, social welfare workers, and police officers; tired, fearful, and frustrated parents.

In the early 1970s, after the publication of *Bird at My Window* and *Children of Longing*, Guy, who was by this time separated from her husband, began traveling in the Caribbean. She lived for a time in Haiti as well as in Trinidad, studying the culture of the place of her birth and writing. Not surprisingly, then, for her second work of fiction, *The Friends* (1973), Guy decided to take her own experiences as a transplanted West Indian for the creation of her characters and her subject matter. *The Friends* is Guy's first novel for young adults and the first book in a trilogy about the Cathy and Jackson families. The Cathy family includes the insensitive, tactless father, Calvin; the beautiful, dying mother, Ramona; the pretty, eager-to-please older daugh-

ter, Ruby; and the impulsive, willful younger daughter, Phylissia, whose story this is. Harlem-born-and-bred Edith Jackson is determined to make a friend of Phylissia. Phylissia at first spurns Edith's overtures, because Edith, she thinks, is both unattractive and unkempt, though eventually the two girls strike up a kind of friendship, however tenuous on Phylissia's part. Calvin does not approve of Edith, whom he calls "a pickey-headed ragamuffin." Phylissia, who remains in conflict with her father throughout the work, is in silent agreement with him in his judgment of Edith. The tension in the novel increases when Ramona Cathy dies and Calvin is left alone to take care of his two teenaged daughters. Edith's family is motherless, too, and her family crisis comes when her father disappears, leaving Edith to take care of her sisters and brothers.

In *The Friends*, Guy again tackles a sensitive topic: the hostility and misunderstanding between Afro-Americans and Afro-West Indians. However, that conflict is not the author's only concern in this work. Again, she carefully examines family relationships and shows the need for honest and open communication among family members. *The Friends* was named by the American Library Association as "one of the Best of the Best Books published in the last fifteen years of particular interest to young people." It was also adopted as part of the English curriculum for high schools in Great Britain.

The second novel in the Jackson-Cathy trilogy was begun while Guy lived in Haiti. *Ruby* (1976) is the story of Ruby Cathy, Phylissia's older sister, after her mother's death. It deals with her total alienation and isolation from her father, her teachers, and her peers. Calvin Cathy, now a widower with two teenaged daughters, is ill at ease with his new responsibilities. Unwittingly, he becomes a tyrant to his daughters. As Calvin becomes totally involved with his restaurant and Phylissia withdraws into her books, Ruby's feelings of uselessness and loneliness increase.

Ruby's primary ambition is to love and be loved. In her loneliness, she turns to the precocious and opinionated Daphne Dupree, with whom she forms a homosexual relationship. There is conflict in the relationship when Ruby refuses to stand up to her father in spite of Daphne's encouragement. It is this same inability on Ruby's part to assert her independence that brings the friendship to a precipitous end. When Calvin arrives home just in time to stop Ruby from jumping to her death, his first reaction is typical. He begins unbuckling his belt to whip her; but then he stops and bursts into tears. When

Phylissia walks in on Calvin and Ruby's tearful embrace, she is nonplussed. Typically again, Calvin turns on Phylissia. "You—you. Always so busy. Always got that head in a book, reading, laying around the house. What's the matter with you? You ain't know you got a sister?" From this point on the family will be all right. The love has always been there; now they are learning to express and communicate it.

Like its companion volume *The Friends, Ruby* was selected as a Best Book for Young Adults by the American Library Association. However, because of the inclusion of the controversial homosexual theme, it was not adopted along with *The Friends* and *Edith Jackson,* the third work in the trilogy, for use in the school curriculum in England.

With *Edith Jackson* (1978) Guy returns to Phylissia's friend Edith and her family. Since Edith's father has deserted the family, her elder brother has been killed by the police, and her baby sister has died of malnutrition. As the novel begins, Edith and her three sisters are living together in a foster home. Edith's sole desire is to keep the family together, but her sisters have plans of their own. The child-woman, Edith, in her search for love and security, becomes pregnant. Eventually, after much soul-searching, Edith agrees with her mentor, Mrs. Bates, that she must take the responsibility for shaping her own destiny. Edith decides not to have her baby. She will take Mrs. Bates's advice and try to prepare herself to make something of her own life, for she finally realizes that until she is at ease with her own life, she cannot effectively attempt to take on the responsibility of shaping the lives of others.

Edith Jackson completes Guy's statement about the failure of the American society—the home, the school, the church, and the state—to meet the complex needs of its young people. Because of insensitivity and sometimes plain apathy on the part of adults, the lives of many young black people have been squandered.

Guy's next work, *The Disappearance* (1979), is the story of Imamu Jones, a sixteen-year-old Harlem youth who has dropped out of high school. Imamu's father was killed in Viet Nam, and his mother has since become an alcoholic. Imamu and two of his friends are holding up a neighborhood grocery store when one of them shoots and kills the owner. Imamu did not even know that the murderer had a gun. At his trial, Imamu's innocence is proved, and Ann Aimsley, a volunteer social worker, persuades the judge to make her Imamu's legal guardian. Imamu's feelings toward the middle-class Aimsleys and their West Indian family

friend, Dora Belle, are ambivalent when he first meets them. Soon after Imamu starts living with the Aimsleys, Perk, their younger daughter, disappears. The police are called, and Imamu is taken into temporary custody. When Imamu is released, he vows that he is staying on with the Aimsleys only until he solves the mystery of Perk's disappearance. Eventually, Imamu does lead the family to Perk's decomposed body buried in the basement of one of Dora Belle's houses. Dora Belle confesses to the murder, really a freak accident.

Recently Guy, whose permanent home is still in New York City, has been living periodically in Geneva, Switzerland, and doing most of her writing there. In the spring of 1980, she took time off from her writing to make a long-awaited trip to the French-speaking African nation of Senegal, where she happened upon Birago Diop's African tale of *Mother Crocodile,* which is written in French. On her return to Geneva, Guy adapted and translated this tale into her first children's picture book, *Mother Crocodile.* The book was published by Delacorte Press in the spring of 1981. This unusual story, illustrated by John Steptoe, can be read as a cautionary tale or as a symbolic retelling of the history of Africa. Either way, the lyrical warmth and grace of this remarkable book will impress young readers with the universality of human experience. Also in spring 1981, Guy successfully published another novel, *Mirror of Her Own.* This work, like the trilogy and *The Disappearance,* is concerned with the special problems of young adults and conflicts within the family. However, in this instance, the author is writing about members of a white upper-class family.

The setting of this novel is Oak Bluff, the affluent, suburban neighborhood in which Mary and Roxanne Abbot live with their parents. Their neighbors are the Drysdales, with whom the Abbots have always had a tacit rivalry. However, this is the summer that the twenty-two-year-old Roxanne and the young John Drysdale have struck up a close relationship. At the same time, seventeen-year-old Mary, shy and plain, who has grown up in her older sister's shadow, thinks herself in love with John. John's general irresponsible behavior and specifically his involvement with drugs cause Roxanne to have reservations about her relationship with him. Not so Mary. With her initiation into the use of wine and drugs, she loses all her inhibitions and becomes sexually involved with John. She soon discovers, though, that John does not love her. Finally, Roxanne is able to convince Mary that John is an unscrupulous weakling, someone who will always need a crutch, and that neither of them needs him.

In comparison to the works that make up the trilogy and *The Disappearance, Mirror of Her Own* is anticlimactic. The characters are one-dimensional and the story line is vague and improbable. Guy touches on the problems of the racially integrated neighborhood, but this theme is not sustained. Of all Guy's published works to date, *Mirror of Her Own* is the least successful. The intricacies of family relationships which the author has previously delineated with such freshness of insight seem to fall flat in this work.

In the early summer of 1981, Rosa Guy's only sister, Ameze, with whom she had maintained a close relationship, died in New York. After the funeral, the author returned to Geneva to continue work on two novels in progress. In 1983, both works, *New Guys Around the Block* and *A Measure of Time,* were published. Guy's return to the States coincided with the publication of these two literary achievements.

New Guys Around the Block, a novel for young adults, published by Delacorte Press, is a sequel to *The Disappearance.* In it we are reacquainted with Imamu Jones, now eighteen years old; his alcoholic mother; and his middle-class foster family, the Aimsleys. The "new guys" are the articulate and outgoing nineteen-year-old Olivette Larouche and his thirteen-year-old brother, Pierre. Soon after the Larouches arrive in the neighborhood, Iggy, whom we had also met in *The Disappearance,* is released from prison where he had been serving time for murder. Simultaneously, there is a spate of burglaries in the adjoining white neighborhood committed, according to the police and the media, by a "phantom burglar" who leaves no clues behind. All the black men in the neighborhood are immediate suspects. When Imamu and Olivette are picked up by the police in connection with the crimes and later released on bail, Imamu vows to find the burglar himself.

In the meantime, Gladys, a sassy teenager who is attracted to both Imamu and Olivette but spurns Iggy's advances, is found beaten into unconsciousness. Now the police have "solved" both crimes: Iggy is their phantom burglar as well as Gladys's assailant. Surrounded by dozens of armed officers, Iggy is trapped. He jumps or falls to his death. Soon after, Imamu's detective work leads him to the astounding revelation that Olivette, his new friend, is the perpetrator of both crimes. Before Imamu can decide what to do with this information, Olivette, his brother, and his mother leave town.

In *New Guys Around the Block,* Guy demonstrates as she did in *The Disappearance* that she is a skillful creator of the mystery/suspense tale. But more important is her relentless effort to focus on the realities of the urban ghettos in which black youths are trapped. The author suggests that the addicts, the alcoholics, the gamblers, the thieves who people these neighborhoods are all products of the system, of the society which programs them to live like trapped animals. Even Olivette with his brilliant mind is unable to escape the evil machinations of this environment.

A Measure of Time, published by Holt, Rinehart and Winston, is Rosa Guy's second adult novel. It is the odyssey of the indomitable Dorine Davis from an impoverished eight-year-old in Montgomery, Alabama, earning a quarter a week, to Dorine Davis (in the words of one of her lovers), "the original self-made millionaire" in Harlem by the time she is forty. The setting of the novel shifts between Harlem and Montgomery. Time is measured from the 1920s of the Harlem Renaissance and the Garvey

Dust jacket for Guy's 1983 adult novel about a black woman who leaves Alabama during the 1920s for Harlem, where she makes her way grandly

Black Nationalist Movement, the 1930s and 1940s of the Great Depression and World War II, and concludes with the first overt flutterings of the civil rights movement of the 1950s.

As with *Bird at My Window,* there is enough material here for at least two novels. There are so many subplots that the author is unable to work them all out; consequently, the reader sometimes feels cheated. However, the story is primarily Dorine Davis's and on this level it succeeds. Thus Dorine is portrayed in her myriad roles: Dorine, the child-mistress of old Master Norton down South; the small-time prostitute in Harlem, at the bidding of her lover, Sonny; the high-class booster in the major Northern cities; the convict turned preacher while serving five years in prison. Then there is Dorine Davis, the sole support of her large extended family in the South; the secret mother; the tenacious lover; the loyal friend. Tough-talking, hardheaded, bighearted Dorine Davis, the survivor, who, in her own words, cries "at the prick of a pin."

A Measure of Time is a "big book" about black life in America. Like Claude McKay's *Home to Harlem* (1928), it is a book designed to offend some blacks who are sensitive about what aspects of black life in America are made public. This work deals primarily with black people living outside the law—living high and falling hard. It is about living and dying, about black/white relationships, about man/woman relationships, about Afro-American/Afro-West Indian relationships, about family relationships. More important, it is a work about caring and loving, about the positive as well as the negative human emotions. It is about survival and hope. It is one woman's struggle and determination to rise above the limitations of her circumstances. It is a tragicomedy, an American classic. Whatever its shortcomings, *A Measure of Time* succeeds as a large slice of American realism.

One critic of this work asserts that since all the characters in *A Measure of Time* except the protagonist, Dorine Davis, are one-dimensional, Dorine's relationships with them fall flat. She concedes though that while this flaw "might prove fatal in a novel of narrower scope, in *A Measure of Time* it is merely a drawback." She faults the author too for never making clear how a self-sufficient woman like Miss Davis could have a recurring penchant for weak and manipulative men. The novel excels, she allows, "when it deals with race and racism which permeates every facet of Dorine Davis' life."

Rosa Guy is at present back in New York, which she has called home since 1932, when she, as a young child, arrived with her family on a cold, hostile winter's day. Guy, who has been a widow for many years, continues to do what she has been doing all her adult life—writing, traveling, and on occasion enjoying the company of her grown son and her two grandsons of whom she speaks with pride. Currently she is at work on the sequel of *New Guys Around the Block,* which will complete her second trilogy. Guy's reputation as a writer has long been established. Her contribution to the literature of young adults, especially that of young blacks, has been inspiring.

Reference:
Judith Wilson, "Rosa Guy: Writing With a Bold Vision," *Essence* (October 1979): 14, 20.

Virginia Hamilton
(12 March 1936-   )

Jane Ball
Wilberforce University

BOOKS: *Zeely* (New York: Macmillan, 1967);
The House of Dies Drear (New York: Macmillan, 1968);
The Time-Ago Tales of Jahdu (New York: Macmillan, 1969);
The Planet of Junior Brown (New York: Macmillan, 1971);
W. E. B. Du Bois: A Biography (New York: Crowell, 1972);
Time-Ago Lost: More Tales of Jahdu (New York: Macmillan, 1973);
Paul Robeson: The Life and Times of a Free Black Man (New York: Harper & Row, 1974);
M. C. Higgins the Great (New York: Macmillan, 1974; London: Hamilton, 1975);
Arilla Sun Down (New York: Greenwillow, 1976: London: Hamilton, 1977);
Illusion and Reality (Washington, D.C.: Library of Congress, 1976);
Justice and Her Brothers (New York: Greenwillow, 1978; London: Hamilton, 1979);
Jahdu (New York: Greenwillow, 1980);
Dustland (New York: Greenwillow, 1980; London: MacRae, 1980);
The Gathering (New York: Greenwillow, 1981);
Sweet Whispers, Brother Rush (New York: Philomel, 1982);
The Magical Adventures of Pretty Pearl (New York: Harper & Row, 1983);
Willie Bea and the Time the Martians Landed (New York: Greenwillow, 1983);
A Little Love (New York: Philomel/Putnam's, 1984).

OTHER: *The Writings of W. E. B. Du Bois,* edited by Hamilton (New York: Crowell, 1975).

PERIODICAL PUBLICATIONS: "Portrait of the Author as a Working Writer," *Elementary English,* 48 (April 1971): 237-240, 302;
"High John Has Risen Again," *Horn Book,* 51 (April 1975): 113-121.

Virginia Hamilton (photo by Cox Studios)

Drawing on her own background as a member of a rather fortunate black family living in the apparently tolerant atmosphere of a little village, Virginia Hamilton has produced a series of award-winning books about black people whose lives go beyond the typical black-white confrontations so dear to the hearts of many black writers. Writing primarily for children, she seems largely concerned with delineating black characters that foster feelings of self-worth in her young black readers and understanding in her young white readers.

Virginia Hamilton was born and raised in Yellow Springs, Ohio, home of liberal Antioch College. She is a descendent of a black man who fled slavery, made his way north to Yellow Springs, where he settled on land that remains in the family today. She is the youngest of the five children of musician Kenneth James Hamilton and Etta Belle (Perry) Hamilton.

A good student, finishing at the top of her high school class, she began writing stories at an early age. She won a scholarship to Antioch College, where she was one of very few black students. She studied creative writing there from 1952-1955, earning a B.A., and then at Ohio State University (1957-1958), still writing short stories. She left Ohio State to attend the New School for Social Research in New York City, supporting herself as a part-time cost accountant. She hoped to improve her craft, she said, "away from all the kind people who wanted to help and did help but maybe hadn't realized there came a time when help was not what was needed."

In New York, she lived in Greenwich Village, where she was geographically distant from her own people and inherently insulated from the immigrants and "intellectuals" who were her neighbors. During this period she began to be more satisfied with her writing. One of her favorite models at this time was Carson McCullers. Hamilton felt she learned from McCullers's writing "what a good sentence was."

Soon after she moved to New York, she met anthologist and poet Arnold Adoff, and they married on 19 March 1960. She and her husband traveled to Spain (where they stayed for about six months) and to Africa (North). Going to Africa had been an enduring dream of Hamilton's, and the land of dark-skinned people had "a tremendous impression" on her, she said, even though her stay was brief. The impact is apparent in her first book, *Zeely* (1967).

Hamilton credits Macmillan editor Richard Jackson with motivating her to make the momentous switch from short fiction to book-length fiction for juvenile readers. With his long-distance encouragement, she developed one of her stories into the novel *Zeely* during a six-month stay in southern France.

Zeely was a successful first book. It was chosen as an American Library Association Notable Book for 1967 and was also awarded the Nancy Block Memorial Award for promoting racial understanding. *Zeely* is the story of Elizabeth Perry, called Geeder, who with her brother goes to spend a summer on their uncle's farm. She develops a childish infatuation for Zeely Taber, daughter of a neighboring farmer. Zeely is over six and one-half feet tall and a regal young woman with an air of mystery. Geeder, completely fascinated with her, finds an uncanny resemblance between the young woman and a photograph of a Watusi queen. The child, who craves excitement in her own life, comes

to believe that Zeely is indeed a queen.

Some reviewers said that Geeder's character was not fully realized and that the encounter scene between Zeely and Geeder was anticlimactic. But most praised Hamilton's use of language, her ability to create a mood piece that has a special appeal to young girls. Her reputation as a talented writer was off to a good start.

In 1968 Hamilton's second book, *The House of Dies Drear,* was published. Reviewers again praised her writing skills, her use of language handled with poetic precision, sentences of high polish, and imaginative characters. Zena Sutherland in *Saturday Review* called it "memorable literature that gives dignity to black heritage." It is the story of a thirteen-year-old black boy who moves from his home in North Carolina to Ohio and into the house of Dies Drear, an abolitionist operating an underground railroad station in his house. The house has a past of ghosts and murders, and the sliding panels and secret tunnels all help to create an atmosphere

Dust jacket for Hamilton's first Newbery Honor Book about a neurotic, three-hundred-pound musical prodigy and his difficulties getting through the eighth grade

of mystery. This book received the Ohioana Book Award and the Edgar Allan Poe Award for best juvenile mystery.

Between 1968 and 1974 Hamilton wrote seven more books, among them a biography of W. E. B. Du Bois. This book was dedicated to her father, who had a longtime admiration for the black intellectual and his battles against discrimination and second-rate citizenship. Like all of her books, the Du Bois biography is a record of black survival against unfair odds. Implicit in the portrayal of this black man of dignity is the dignity of the black race.

A second nonfiction work was published in 1974. Her biography *Paul Robeson: The Life and Times of a Free Black Man* is about another important black man who was an enigma in this country because he did not fit the ordinary mold. Said Hamilton: "Robeson will always be a controversial figure in this country. He was the first black person that America really made a popular hero . . . , and he fell very far when the country turned on him. They misunderstood from the beginning. . . ."

Hamilton is fastidious about showing the failings of Robeson and those of Du Bois in counterpoint to their strengths and excellence. Her concern is that the truth of the black experience in all its manifestations be shown in the lives of two real black men in white America. Hamilton shows that there is much for the young black reader to admire in the lives of these two men.

The year 1974 also saw the publication of *M. C. Higgins the Great,* her sixth novel and winner of the Newbery Medal, the National Book Award, and the Boston Globe Award. Called a "brilliantly conceived and superbly written story," it tells of a relationship between the oldest son of a poor black hill family and two strangers who come into his lonely life. Coping with conflicts with his proud, difficult father, the boy goes through a growing-up phase from which he emerges more mature and ready to become a responsible adult.

There were some adverse criticisms of the book; one reviewer described it as "heavy prose," as having an "almost impenetrable" opening. Most, however, agreed with the critic who called the novel "powerful charting of growing up that is moving, poetic, and unsentimental." Black poetess Nikki Giovanni said, in a *New York Times Book Review* article, that in *M. C. Higgins* Hamilton had once again created a special world. The book, while not "an adorable book, not a lived-happily-ever-after kind of story" is still "warm, humane, and hopeful," she said, with whose characters "we can identify and for whom we care."

Dust jacket for Hamilton's 1974 novel, winner of the Newbery Medal, the National Book Award, and the Boston Globe Award

In 1975 Hamilton edited a book of Du Bois's writings. *The Writings of W. E. B. Du Bois* is a selection of "essays, articles, speeches, and excerpts from his other writings, to which she has added her own . . . introductions." She selected and annotated the pieces with discretion and wrote what she called "pithy introductions [that] convey the political atmosphere, prevailing opinions, and social conditions of the era and give perspective to each selection." Well organized and highly readable, the book makes fascinating reading for any age.

Between 1975 and 1980, she produced five more books. Three of them make up the Justice trilogy: *Justice and Her Brothers, Dustland,* and *The Gathering.* These books deal with an eleven-year-old girl, Justice, and her thirteen-year-old identical twin brothers who live in a town very much like Yellow Springs. The characters are contemporary and realistically drawn, but there are in the stories elements of extrasensory power and futurity, and the novels reveal Hamilton's interest in ecology and genetics.

Survival is an important ingredient in Hamilton's books. (Her husband calls her books survival primers.) Being a black woman in a white-male-dominated society has taught Hamilton a great deal about survival, an essential element in the story of the black experience in America. She continues her chronicle with *Sweet Whispers, Brother Rush* (1982). This story of an urban black girl with a retarded brother has elements of mystery and a rare disease as well.

While being a wife and mother requires that she devote considerable time to concomitant pursuits, Hamilton is first and foremost a writer, with a full-time dedication to her work. Always experi-

menting with new forms, new subjects, and new styles, Hamilton's active imagination seems inexhaustible in the creation of fascinating stories and characters germane to the black experience. She says, "Perhaps when I've written my last book, there will stand the whole of the black experience in white America as I see it."

References:

Marilyn Apseloff, *Virginia Hamilton/Ohio Explorer in the World of Imagination* (Columbus: The State Library of Ohio, 1979);

Donnarae MacCann and Gloria Woodard, eds., *The Black American in Books for Children: Readings in Racism* (Metuchen, N.J.: Scarecrow Press, 1972).

Nathan C. Heard
(7 November 1936-   )

Richard Yarborough
University of California, Los Angeles

BOOKS: *Howard Street* (New York: Dial, 1968);
To Reach a Dream (New York: Dial, 1972);
A Cold Fire Burning (New York: Simon & Schuster, 1974);
When Shadows Fall (Chicago: Playboy Press, 1977);
House of Slammers (New York: Macmillan, 1983; London: Collier-Macmillan, 1983).

OTHER: "Boodie the Player," in *We Be Word Sorcerers: Twenty-Five Stories by Black Americans,* edited by Sonia Sanchez (New York: Bantam, 1973), pp. 110-124.

With the publication of Richard Wright's *Native Son* in 1940, many American readers were confronted for the first time with the harsh realities of black ghetto life. Of the Afro-American urban realists who have appeared on the literary scene since Wright, Nathan C. Heard is one of the most important still publishing today. Despite the mixed popular and critical responses accorded his work, he continues to depict with stark and brutal frankness the violence, frustrations, thwarted dreams, and tragedies of black ghetto experience.

Nathan Cliff Heard was born in Newark, New Jersey, to Nathan E. and Gladys Pruitt Heard.

Raised by his mother, a blues singer, and his maternal grandmother in a cold-water flat in Newark, Heard dropped out of school at fifteen. From that point through the late 1960s, Heard spent much of his life in reform school and then in the New Jersey state prison at Trenton, where he served time for armed robbery. While he was incarcerated, Heard was an award-winning athlete and the leader of a jazz band; in addition, he began to write.

Looking back at his earliest exposure to literature, Heard recalls reading only two books in his youth—the biographies of Babe Ruth and Lou Gehrig. Even after he started reading in prison, his taste ran to time-killing, escapist fiction, including the Martian series of Edgar Rice Burroughs. Then a fellow inmate named Harold Carrington (to whom *Howard Street* is dedicated) introduced him to the works of Langston Hughes, Samuel Beckett, James Baldwin, Jean Genet, Amiri Baraka (then LeRoi Jones), Norman Mailer, and others. Heard's autobiographical description of the protagonist's growing fascination with books in *House of Slammers* reveals how this more serious fare literally changed his life: "His reading became voracious, and he turned into a happy insomniac, reading through the quiet night, sleeping in the morning, exercising

Nathan Heard (photo by Diana Bryant)

in the afternoon. . . . The thrill of learning, the exhilaration of great thoughts in books, had captured him body and soul." Heard's interest in jazz led him to writings on music and Afro-American history; discussions with black Muslim inmates led him to Malcolm X, Eric Hoffer, and Charles Silberman; and Robert Ardrey's *African Genesis* "struck him like a sledgehammer," leading him to Malinowski, Mead, and Lorenz.

After learning that the author of a particularly lurid paperback novel had received $2,000 for his work, Heard decided to try his own hand at writing professionally. Using a borrowed typewriter, he produced a manuscript he entitled "To Reach a Dream." Despite its popularity among the inmates who read it, however, Heard was unable to peddle his novel; and he began to study books on writing in order to hone his skills. By 1963, he had completed a draft of *Howard Street*.

One year after his release in 1966, Heard was arrested for parole violation and imprisoned for the last time. A young lawyer named Joel Steinberg, whom Heard's mother had asked to defend her son,

happened to read Heard's manuscript. Favorably impressed, he forwarded the novel to Dial, which published *Howard Street* in November 1968, one month before Heard was freed. New American Library soon purchased the paperback rights to the book, and *Howard Street* went through thirteen paperback printings (557,000 copies).

Having grown up within a block of Howard Street, Heard knew the brutal Newark setting of his novel firsthand. As a result, the book is marked by a verisimilitude and an immediacy which would be beyond the grasp of even the most imaginative outsider. The harsh tone of *Howard Street* is set by the opening scene of sexual exploitation (not just of the prostitute by her "john," but hers of him as well). This is a world where junkies react to the overdose death of a friend not by mourning but by eagerly seeking out the pusher responsible in order to "cop" some "boss" dope; where even Father Divine is considered a "Master Player" with a "heavy game." Survival in this world depends upon the degree to which one takes to heart the cynical ghetto adage which reverberates throughout the novel: "A man can't fool with the Golden Rule in a crowd that don't play fair."

Howard Street is primarily the story of Lonnie ("Hip") Ritchwood, a young hustler; his older sibling, Franchot, one of the few "straights" in the novel; and Gypsy Pearl, the beautiful prostitute who finds herself caught between them. However, the book is rich with many sharply etched portraits of people out to survive on the best available terms, and Heard's sensitivity to the pain and hardship which shape all of his characters' lives is the source of much of the novel's power. While he rejects easy sociological conceptions of blacks as will-less victims, Heard is also loathe either to romanticize the lives of the "streeters" or to pass moral judgment on them. On one hand, he does not condemn his characters for the strategies they adopt in their attempts to cope with life, for he knows that the distance from an awareness of one's own entrapment to self-hatred, desperation, and apathy is short indeed. On the other hand, he rarely overlooks the weaknesses and mistakes of his characters because their shortcomings are indicative of their humanity.

The flaws in Heard's novel include occasional patches of awkward diction and the coarseness of some of the humor—the seduction of a Puerto Rican man by a skillful black transvestite is especially forced. In addition, the explicit scenes of sex and brutality could easily offend the squeamish. As J. McRee Elrod notes, however, Heard "uses the sordid not to titillate but to inform." What other problems the book may have are thoroughly overshadowed by Heard's extraordinary ear for black urban folk expressions and street argot and by his ability to capture the intricate, subtle rituals and manners of the pushers, hustlers, prostitutes, addicts, straights, winos, homosexuals, pimps, cops, and gang members who people *Howard Street*.

A difficult book to ignore, *Howard Street* elicited a wide range of critical responses. At one end of the spectrum is the harsh judgment of Christopher Lehmann-Haupt, who criticized the novel's overworked plot, its "woeful climax," and "the lack of narrative vitality." At the opposite pole from his crude characterization of *Howard Street* as a "potboiler in blackface" stands Nikki Giovanni's enthusiastic declaration that Heard's novel is a "masterpiece," executed with "sheer technical skill and Black understanding." Giovanni singled out Heard's objective handling of his characters as the key to the book's success. While the majority of the critics were more moderate than Giovanni in their praise of *Howard Street*, most reviews were far closer to hers than to Lehmann-Haupt's. One writer described the novel as "stamped with the brutality of a clearly observed truth"; another called it "one of the most devastating looks at the mystique of addiction." Finally, in an article on the appearance of new Afro-American writers in the late 1960s, *Newsweek*'s Robert A. Gross noted the degree to which *Howard Street*'s "underlying themes—the search for identity and alternate values—are all integral parts of contemporary literature."

With the success of his first novel as well as the sudden florescence of black studies programs across the country, Heard soon attracted the attention of schools in search of black instructors. In September 1969, he was appointed to a one-year lectureship in creative writing at Fresno State College in California, where he won the Most Distinguished Teacher Award. Then, in September 1970, he returned to New Jersey to accept an assistant professorship at Livingston College, Rutgers University, where he taught writing and black literature for two years. Also during this time, Heard hosted a half-hour television program, entitled "New Jersey Speaks," and he completed work on his second novel.

Published in mid-1972 by Dial, *To Reach a Dream* is a major revision of one of Heard's earliest attempts at fiction. Like *Howard Street*, it opens with a shocking act of violence which immediately immerses the reader in the world of Newark's black ghetto, the world in which young Bartholomew Kedar Enos wants to make his mark. Bart's attempt to emulate the successful hustlers with their money, drugs, women, and long Cadillacs is, in part, just a search for "big fun." At a deeper level, however, his ambitions are grounded in a quest for a secure sense of his own manhood, a quest made all the more urgent by his humiliating rape while he was in prison and his girl friend's subsequent rejection of him. As Heard writes, "he became one of those who try to lump every petty triumph together into one big blast of Meaning which would insure them being Somebody."

Bart's golden opportunity arrives when he goes to work for a wealthy black widow named Sarah Hamilton, and he confidently believes that he can parlay his street savvy, good looks, and sexual prowess into the sinecure of a kept man. Bart's plans seem to be proceeding smoothly until he meets and falls in love with Querelle, the woman's college-age daughter. Trapped between his fierce desire to get ahead and his attachment to Querelle, he convinces the younger woman that they must murder her mother. One of the streeters who frequently serve as a cynical Greek chorus in Heard's fiction sums up the resolution of *To Reach a Dream* with pungent directness: "Now she [Sarah] dead, her daughter is crazy, and he all fucked up and paralyzed. The nigga was bad luck from the jump f'everybody."

In his powerful depiction of Bart, Heard effectively dramatizes the diverse ways many ghetto inhabitants struggle for self-respect, status, and fulfillment within the apparently inevitable limits of their lives. Heard's rendering of the predictable class conflicts which arise between Bart and each of his lovers is perceptive as well. Unfortunately, the portrayals of Sarah and Querelle need further development. In particular, the desperate hunger both women have for Bart's attention must be justified in more complex psychological terms.

Given the notoriety of *Howard Street*, the critical response to *To Reach a Dream* was surprisingly sparse; Mel Watkins's review in the *New York Times* is fairly representative. Calling the work "an engrossing, if not altogether satisfying, novel," Watkins lamented the contrived plot and Heard's inability to take advantage of Bart, "a memorable character who literally overwhelms other figures in the novel." After its success with *Howard Street*, New American Library published a large paperback printing (190,000) of *To Reach a Dream;* sales were disappointing, however, and it soon went out of print.

In his third book, *A Cold Fire Burning*, published in April 1974, Heard focuses on a recurrent theme in his work: the degree to which differences

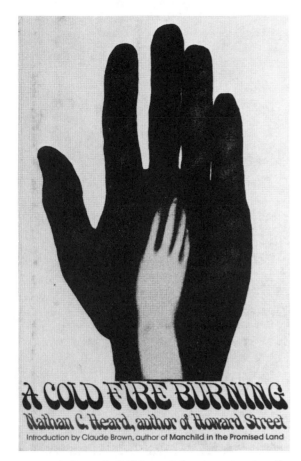

Dust jacket for Heard's 1974 novel demonstrating the effect of social class and cultural background on human relationships

in class, values, or cultural background can sabotage relationships. Presented from the first-person point of view, the novel centers on Shadow, a black man whose tremendous ambivalence toward a white social worker named Terri prevents him from satisfactorily consummating their affair. Shadow's agonizing inner struggle over his feelings for Terri involves more than just sexual impotence, however. Like Bart, Shadow has embarked upon a search for meaning, for purpose in life, and before he can take part in a healthy relationship with Terri, he must come to terms with himself as a black man. Terri's inability to accept the means through which Shadow attempts to do so insures their separation.

At its best, *A Cold Fire Burning* calls to mind Chester Himes's *If He Hollers Let Him Go,* James Baldwin's *Another Country,* Ernest Gaines's *Of Love and Dust,* and Alice Walker's *Meridian* in its frank examination of how the racial dilemma in the United States often manifests itself most powerfully and tragically through interracial sexual relationships. Shadow's decision midway through the novel

to become the leader of a local gang with nationalistic political pretensions is less convincing, however, and it is only the subsequent resumption of the conflict between Shadow and Terri that revives the book. As in the case of *To Reach a Dream,* the critical response to Heard's third novel was relatively scanty and generally lukewarm.

Published in 1977, *When Shadows Fall* contains Heard's most thorough examination of the drug scene—from the high-priced cocaine of the recording studio to the mind-numbing heroin of the projects. Unfortunately, it also represents Heard's concession to the sensationalistic conventions of popular paperback fiction, conventions he had successfully skirted in his previous books. Particularly problematic is the choice of the white singer-guitarist Joe Billy "J. B." White as a central figure in the novel (a choice urged on him, Heard recalls, by his editor).

J. B.'s disappearance over fifty pages before the end of the book suggests, however, that Heard's true interests lie elsewhere. Accordingly, *When Shadows Fall* is dominated by "Big Red," the statuesque prostitute with whom J. B. gets involved, and John Haines, the tough ex-boxer turned pot-smoking cop—two of the most striking black figures in all of Heard's fiction. What ultimately drives this fast-paced novel is the power with which Heard depicts how each of these characters attempts to "make it": in Big Red's case, by supporting J. B. so that she might profit from his imminent stardom; in Haines's, by balancing his superiors' demands for a big bust against the lucrative offer to make a movie of his life story put forward by the very target of his investigation. Particularly impressive is the care with which Heard traces Haines's painful transition from a battered idealism to the cynical acknowledgment that "men had not invented a weapon yet that they didn't use in hot pursuit of the happiness of advantage," that in this "dog-cat-dog-world" the first rule of "streetology"—look out for "number one"—is the key to not just success but survival. Moreover, the depiction of Haines as well as of the pervasive corruption and deceit among the other characters in the book suggests that underlying Heard's hard-bitten view of ghetto life is a deep cynicism regarding American society and even mankind generally: For most of the characters in Heard's fiction—black or white, rich or poor— self-interest is the principal motivating factor in their behavior.

While *When Shadows Fall* has many of the trappings of the paperback pulp thriller, it is not without merit. Both the book's publisher, Playboy Press, and its publication as a paperback original, however, reflect the degree to which interest in Heard's work had waned; and the strengths of the novel went largely unappreciated. There are no readily available reviews.

After leaving the academic world in 1972, Heard divided his time between his family responsibilities and his broadening range of creative activities. In addition to continuing his avocation as a nightclub singer, Heard acted in a number of films as well. In the late 1970s, he contributed a regular free-lance column of political commentary and vignettes of Newark life to the *New York Times,* and he served as assistant editor of "People Power," a public agency newsletter published in Newark. Then, in the fall of 1983, Macmillan published his most ambitious novel since *Howard Street, House of Slammers.*

In an interview in 1968, Heard commented, "I write of and about the things I know best, hoping to hold up a mirror that might cause one to reflect on the distortions one sees, and, perhaps to alter the worst of them." What Heard holds up for the reader in *House of Slammers* is the violent, desperate, spirit-crushing life of the men in this country's penal institutions; and to the extent that it is meant to bring about change, this novel is his most didactic. Nonetheless, it also demonstrates Heard's maturing mastery of the black urban idiom and his ability to depict the mundane details of everyday prison life with almost painful clarity. In addition, William "Beans" Butler is one of Heard's more appealing protagonists. A sharp observer of prison life and yet distanced from the other inmates by his refusal to commit himself to the social and ideological crutches they use to survive, Beans is another of Heard's characters trapped in a moral dilemma: Should he lend his support to an inmate strike or should he play it safe and not jeopardize his upcoming release? Thrust grudgingly into a leadership role, Beans finds himself caught between the disorganized, squabbling inmate groups he tries to represent on one side and, on the other, the prison officials who care more about control than rehabilitation.

House of Slammers may well be, as Heard contends, his best novel. Prepublication notices from the likes of Claude Brown, Amiri Baraka, John A. Williams, and John O. Killens were full of unqualified praise. H. Bruce Franklin, author of *Prison Literature in America,* called it "the most important novel yet published about the experience of the American prison system."

House of Slammers has also garnered some impressive reviews. While he felt that the book is

Dust jacket for Heard's book about prison life, reflecting his experiences in the New Jersey State Prison. He calls House of Slammers *his best book.*

flawed by "its lack of nuance, its stock minor characters and its tendentiousness," Mel Watkins described the novel as "a hard-hitting, arresting exposé of the horrific conditions" in American prisons. A fine novelist himself, John Wideman hailed *House of Slammers* on the front page of the *Washington Post* "Book World." In Heard's "dogged determination to illuminate the larger forces controlling an individual's fate," Wideman wrote, he has produced a powerful, effective novel which demands "that we must act upon the truth the artist brings us."

The initial printing of *House of Slammers* (described by both Heard and Macmillan as "very small") has sold out in less than a year since the book's release. Nonetheless, the publisher has evinced no plans for a second printing. Given the increasingly apathetic public response accorded the majority of novels written by Afro-Americans in the early 1980s (especially those by black males), this lack of strong publisher support virtually ensures that Heard's latest novel will not be in print long. However, Heard has survived many setbacks throughout his quite remarkable life; one more disappointment is not likely to prevent him from following through with his plans to try his hand at drama as well as to undertake an ambitious fictional look at several generations of a black Newark family.

To this point, Heard's novels have received only passing mention in the handful of critical studies of Afro-American fiction that touch upon his work at all. Perhaps *House of Slammers* will call attention to this skillful, still developing chronicler of a very real, at times disconcerting, and often overlooked side of Afro-American urban life. While Claude Brown's characterization of Heard as "the reincarnation of Richard Wright and a nightmarish William Faulkner of the American ghetto" may be extravagant, his contention that "there are very few, if any, writers in the entire country who can handle the continuously evolving dialect of blacks with Heard's accuracy and facility" is right on the mark. For this and other reasons, Nathan Heard's work deserves a serious reading.

Reference:

Noel Schraufnagel, *From Apology to Protest* (De Land, Fla.: Everett/Edwards, 1973), pp. 135-136.

Frank E. M. Hercules
(12 February 1917-)

Carol P. Marsh
Georgia State University

BOOKS: *Where the Hummingbird Flies* (New York: Harcourt, Brace & World, 1961);
I Want a Black Doll (New York & London: Simon & Schuster, 1967; London: Collins, 1967);
American Society and Black Revolution (New York & London: Harcourt Brace Jovanovich, 1972);
On Leaving Paradise (New York & London: Harcourt Brace Jovanovich, 1980).

OTHER: Untitled essay in *Voices for Life: Reflections on the Human Condition*, edited by Dom Morales (New York: Praeger, 1974), pp. 226-240.

PERIODICAL PUBLICATIONS: "An Aspect of the Negro Renaissance," *Opportunity*, 20 (1942): 305-306, 317-319;
"The Decline and Fall of Sugar Hill," *New York Herald Tribune Sunday Magazine*, 28 February 1965, pp. 6-10;
"To Live in Harlem," *National Geographic*, 151 (January 1977): 178-207.

Frank Hercules is a scholar and writer. He has served as a member of the final review panel of the National Endowment for the Humanities and a visiting scholar or writer-in-residence at Loyola and Xavier universities in New Orleans, Louisiana, in addition to being awarded, in 1977, a Rockefeller Fellowship for "distinguished scholarship in the humanities." Frank Hercules will be most remembered, however, for his finely crafted and incisive treatment of West Indian and Afro-American themes and concerns in his writings.

Hercules was born and lived until early adulthood in colonial Port of Spain and San Fernando, Trinidad, during the reign of King George V. His parents were Felix Eugene Michael and Millicent Hercules. Hercules describes his father as an "Afro-West Indian conservative goaded into a crusade, contradictory of his natural temper, by a social philosophy at fundamental odds with the inherent nature of colonialism." He recalls, further, that his father, despite his brilliant and sophisticated intellect, held a rather naive belief in the redemptive possibilities of British colonialism. This system, however, was not to reward the elder Hercules for his faith in its proclaimed ideals of justice. In spite of his outstanding contributions as a civil servant and as an educator in Trinidad, he was permanently exiled when, during a period of labor unrest, his lectures throughout the West Indies were perceived as "incitements to disorder." The official grounds for his permanent exile was that the elder Hercules had been born in Venezuela even though he had, in fact, lived most of his life in Trinidad and his parents were British subjects.

Being a member of a supportive family of substantial means, however, protected Hercules from the potentially scarring effects of this incident. Nevertheless, through his objective observations, he formed a number of negative impressions of colonialism. Indeed, he would eventually write: "The entire complex of colonial circumstances nauseated me: the arrogant white racism, the color caste system of society, the pervasive mass poverty, the decay of gifted individuals and the defeat that shrivelled their lives, forcing them to trim their beliefs, trade their principles, bend, stoop, cringe, crawl, hammered to their knees by colonialism." In revolt against "the economic misery, the social cruelty, and the political constraints counterpointed by epidemic violence and the manic relief afforded each year by Carnival," all of which was imposed by colonialism, Hercules left Trinidad for London. From 1935 to 1939 (and later in 1950-1951), he studied law at the Honourable Society of the Middle Temple of the Inns of Court. The London of that time was what Hercules terms "a place of extraordinary intellectual ferment." Flourishing thinkers and writers included Bertrand Russell, J. B. S. Haldane, Bernard Shaw, H. G. Wells, Harold Laski, John Maynard Keynes, Sidney and Beatrice Webb, Julian and Aldous Huxley. Of this group, Hercules writes that he found Haldane especially illuminating.

Hercules' objections to the inequities of colonialism, in spite of his own privileged background, touched his chosen profession of law, for his past simultaneously motivated him into and away from this area. He writes of wanting to avenge his father yet of realizing the inherent paradox embodied by the black colonial lawyer, who would in essence be forced to acquire "a class ethos essentially hostile to the interests of the oppressed." Hercules, therefore, immigrated to New York City in the 1940s and became a United States citizen in 1959.

In the United States, Hercules chose to pursue his talent as a writer. Of his choice, Hercules states, "I chose writing because of the promise it held out to me of the ultimate denial of what is vulgarly called 'success.' I decided to write: more to write on my own terms; and without the slightest concern for critics or criticism, public acceptance or rejection. Mine would be a vocation whose reward was its pursuit." As early as 1942, *Opportunity* published his article "An Aspect of the Negro Renaissance." In 1946, he married the former Dellora Howard, a

Frank Hercules (photo by Fabian Bachrach)

professional educator and one of the first black school administrators in New York City. At her wise encouragement, he abandoned his career as a businessman and cultivated his talent as a writer. Certainly, by this time Hercules had been exposed to several influences which would provide the substance of his writings. Two were his mother and aunt who, in addition to other experiences, gave rise to his deep admiration for womanhood. Yet another was his father, whose view of education was heuristic and who encouraged him early in life, like Rousseau's celebrated hero, to seek his own direction outside the traditional classroom, to become the architect of his own mentality, and to realize that thinking was his own "pilgrimage." The younger Hercules, therefore, read widely even as a child, when he also became enthralled with the possibilities of language, which, he discovered, naturally flowered into poetry. Hercules read extensively in English literature and acknowledges having been influenced by writers from the Old English, Renaissance, Neoclassical, and Romantic eras. Also of importance was his early reading of the Bible. There he observed sentence structure and the economy with which powerful effects were achieved. He also noticed the prophetic inspiration in the Old and New Testaments, from which he was, in turn, to see the importance of the social use of prophecy. This observation provided the foundation of his philosophy as a novelist, for he feels that "novelists always try to peer into the future—in this sense they are prophets."

As a writer, Hercules has experienced little or no difficulty in securing publication for his work. While his being black and, moreover, of West Indian origin presented for some potential editors the dilemma of his classification, he has had a relatively easy passage into print. He immediately found a supportive publisher in Harcourt, Brace and World, who in 1961 published his first novel, *Where the Hummingbird Flies.* Set in colonial Trinidad, this novel provides a satirical view of colonial society replete with weaknesses. In this work, Hercules explores the psychology of the colonizers and the colonized and shows through his portrayal of such characters as Mrs. Napoleon Walker and Carlo Da Silva the bizarre thinking of people who cope with degradation and oppression by, in turn, creating an elite that is based on no more than a system of color-caste. Simultaneously, Hercules shows the reader the inevitability of change through three principal characters: the brilliant Mervyn Herrick, who is at once accepting and fearful of independence; Francis Herbert, who advocates the overthrow of colonialism and who suffers as a result; and finally Dulcina, the laundress whom Hercules describes as "the archetypal West Indian . . . queenly in her instincts and majestic in her carriage . . . the very salt of the earth. Black, statuesque, imperious, proud, independent, egalitarian, beautiful in her person and stern of spirit." Dulcina, thus, symbolizes the collective positive consciousness and self-assuredness of the folk and the eventual potential of the folk to act in its own best interest. Upon its publication, *Where the Hummingbird Flies* was well received. *Newsweek* magazine judged it one of the five best first novels of the year, and a *Newsweek* reviewer wrote that the novel "manages to be vigorously wrathful at British colonialism without losing its sense of laughter." The writer also went further to praise Hercules for his comic talent and to compare the wickedness of Hercules' tone to that of Evelyn Waugh. For *Where the Hummingbird Flies,* Hercules also received the Fletcher Pratt Memorial Fellowship in Prose of the Bread Loaf Writers' Conference. Subsequently, *Where the Hummingbird Flies* was translated and published in the Federal Republic of Germany.

After the success of *Where the Hummingbird Flies,* Hercules turned his attention to concerns of Afro-American life and culture. Upon arriving in New York in the 1940s, he had gone to live in Harlem. He remained there for many years and eventually wrote two articles on Harlem. In 1965, at the request of the editor of the *New York Magazine* of the now defunct *New York Herald Tribune,* Hercules wrote an essay, "The Decline and Fall of Sugar Hill," which explores the black middle class in Harlem and which brought Hercules to the attention of the White House. Later, Hercules would be approached by the editor of *National Geographic* magazine for a contribution. That article, "To Live in Harlem," which appeared in January 1977 and was subsequently reprinted in *Reader's Digest,* reveals the author's warm personal relationship with his Harlem surroundings of several decades. As a result of this article, Hercules received the compliments of Sen. Jacob Javits, who read it into the *Congressional Record;* and the United States Information Agency secured the permission of *National Geographic* to have the article translated and circulated abroad.

Also embracing Afro-American concerns was Hercules' second novel, *I Want a Black Doll* (1967), which was published in the United States and Great Britain. According to Hercules, the novel, which deals with the theme of interracial marriage, is intended, in part, to remind blacks of their blackness. In the novel, Dr. John Lincoln, a half-black Northerner who until manhood is unaware that his father is white, marries a wealthy Southern white woman, Barbara Wakely. Ultimately, their marriage is unable to withstand the external pressures fostered by a racist society and their own insurmountable prejudices. Eventually Barbara dies of an abortion and John is shot and killed by her childhood friend and unsuccessful suitor, a white Southerner, Robert Reeve, whom John learns just before he dies is, in fact, his half brother. Peripheral to John's and Barbara's marriage is a satirical portrait of the black middle class which is preyed upon and destroyed by the racist establishment.

For the most part, *I Want a Black Doll* was not favorably received in the United States. In Great Britain and Europe, however, it was a success. A reviewer for the *Times Literary Supplement,* for example, wrote: "Mr. Hercules's greatest strength lies in his exposure of what it is like to live in a race-conscious society. He lets us see—with force—how to a Negro at any moment, any encounter may bring humiliation and how easily a white man, even with charity, may cause it. It does not follow that Mr. Hercules is impartial, with all that implies of indifference, but he does achieve a sort of passionate balance, which is far more useful." In addition, *I Want a Black Doll* was translated and chosen by book clubs in Sweden and Switzerland as their book of the month, and it was translated and published in Czechoslovakia, Holland, and West Germany. Finally, over the period of a year, it appeared in monthly installments in the German edition of *Harper's Bazaar* in Switzerland.

Hercules further pursued his involvement with Afro-American concerns in a sociohistorical work, *American Society and Black Revolution* (1972). In this work, Hercules brings a global perspective to bear on his examination of American society and the black struggle in America. He acknowledges that America is an inherently racist society and submits, even, that white America has subordinated the national interest to racism. Thus, even though America's productivity has been tremendous, it has, nevertheless, been sabotaged by the systematic exclusion of blacks from the industrial process. In this work, Hercules also considers the merits and defects of black leadership. He holds that a weakness in traditional black leadership is its essentially middle-class approach, commonly known as "operating within the system," an approach which has been ultimately rejected by the "insurgent" lower classes. Nevertheless, he sees the improvement of the black condition in America resulting from pragmatic and objective cooperation between blacks and whites. He holds, further, that the success of black Americans lies in their ability to "rise above the past and transcend the present so as to command the future." In addition, he finds it incumbent upon blacks to pursue the ideal of personal freedom. Perhaps one of the most interesting features of the book, however, is Hercules' prediction of the rise of the then governor Jimmy Carter to the presidency of the United States.

The reviewer for the *Crisis* felt that Hercules' consideration of the contributions of Booker T. Washington and W. E. B. Du Bois, based on personal acquaintances, provided "an indispensable framework in which to formulate and implement a dynamic strategy for the distant future" and praised Hercules' "pragmatism that is based on historical realities and contemporary commonsense."

Hercules' ability to put issues and concerns into a global context found further expression when, along with twenty-three other participants, he was invited to contribute an essay to *Voices for Life* (1974), an anthology of essays treating the theme of the "quality of life" in the contemporary world. Other contributors included Arnold Toynbee, Indira Gandhi, Heinrich Böll, Günter Grass, Margaret Mead, Isaac Bashevis Singer, Buckminister Fuller, Barbara Ward, Eugene Ionesco, Carlos Fuentes, and Gloria Steinem. In his essay, Hercules

puts forth the notion that, in spite of technological progress, the quality of the social and moral existence of mankind has not improved over the past two thousand years. Hercules suggests that tangible signs of success do not serve as an indicator of a high quality of life, and he postulates that "the happiness of mankind must replace the material prosperity of particular groups as a test of civilized achievement."

From purely sociological subject matter, Hercules has turned, in his most recent work, to a novel, *On Leaving Paradise* (1980). With this work, he returns to West Indian subject matter to produce what he describes as "a picaresque tale of innocence in the pastoral circumstances of a rural hamlet in southern Trinidad, West Indies, and of the ultimate invincibility of innocence when wandering abroad." He states further: "The tale is however cautionary in one at least of its aspects. The moral issue is: innocence is at its most redoubtable when fortified by commonsense." This theme is borne out in the depiction of the humorous adventures of the protagonist, Johnny de Paria, who is eventually forced to leave the Edenic surroundings of Trinidad for England, a journey which consistently tests his innocent and commonsense view of the world and his resolute virginity. The strength of the novel lies in

Dust jacket for Hercules' 1980 novel, which he describes as "a picaresque tale of innocence in the pastoral circumstances of a rural hamlet in southern Trinidad"

characterization and in Hercules' ability to capture and transmit to the reader much of the humorous Trinidadian folk experience. Nevertheless, in spite of the humor, there emerges a serious political statement; for the novel, in fact, passes judgment on the entire colonial experience. Johnny, however, has not been subdued psychologically and at the end of his adventures sits in humorous and unmalicious judgment on his former masters.

As a writer, Frank Hercules continues to maintain a valuable global perspective. In addition to having his work published in the United States and Great Britain, he has also contributed to foreign periodicals, among which are *Die Zeit* and *Geo* (Hamburg). He has also been widely interviewed both in the United States and abroad concerning his work. Since, as a true artist, he places no

stock in critical reception, he has committed himself to excellence and has chosen to communicate with a small and select audience whenever and wherever possible. Nevertheless, he continues to produce finely textured work which demonstrates his concern for the human condition. It is this concern that is manifested in the present movement of his work toward Swiftian satire which, he feels, "adapts itself more closely, accurately, and graphically to the essentials of the human condition than any other narrative form."

Reference:

Charlayne Hunter, "Living in New York: Writer Finds World in Harlem," *New York Times,* 14 July 1975, C25, C42.

Kristin Hunter
(12 September 1931-   )

Sondra O'Neale
Emory University

BOOKS: *God Bless the Child* (New York: Scribners, 1964; London: Muller, 1965);
The Landlord (New York: Scribners, 1966; London: Pan Books, 1970);
The Soul Brothers and Sister Lou (New York: Scribners, 1968; London: MacDonald, 1971);
Boss Cat (New York: Scribners, 1971);
Guests in the Promised Land (New York: Scribners, 1973);
The Survivors (New York: Scribners, 1975);
The Lakestown Rebellion (New York: Scribners, 1978);
Lou in the Limelight (New York: Scribners, 1981).

SCREENPLAY: *The Landlord*, United Artists, 1970.

TELEVISION: *Minority of One,* CBS Television, 1956.

Kristin Hunter's importance as a writer can best be measured in three areas. First, her work has heralded contemporary novels by and about black women in America. Until the 1970s, black women writers of the Harlem Renaissance, such as Jessie

Fauset, Nella Larsen, and Zora Neale Hurston, had provided the most credible explorations of black female experience. Hunter therefore stands at a pivotal point by sowing the fertile field for writers such as Toni Morrison, Toni Cade Bambara, Alice Walker, and Gayl Jones. Second, Hunter's successful series of didactic children's books have reached a neglected audience of black children and young adults and provided hopeful alternatives to the devastation of ghetto experience. Third, her portrayal of black communal life in the urban North brings out the best of black strengths and character even as she pictures socioeconomic forces that choke black development. In these portrayals, she consistently demonstrates her artistic commitment to a protest literature that will effect positive change.

Kristin Hunter was born in Philadelphia, Pennsylvania, on 12 September 1931 to George Lorenzo and Mabel Lucretia Manigault Eggleston. An only child, Kristin was named after the title character in *Kristin Lavransdatter,* by Norwegian novelist Sigrid Undset, winner of the 1928 Nobel Prize for Literature. Hunter has observed that "the name you give your children as well as the characters in your novels and stories has a lot to do with who they become."

Both of Hunter's parents were teachers. Her father was successively principal of Sumner and Whittier Elementary Schools in Philadelphia. Her mother was forced to leave her teaching job when Kristin was born; a state law forbade teachers to be mothers. Since few professional options were available to black women, the loss of a career left scars upon Mrs. Eggleston. In later years, Hunter would recall how, as a child, she was deeply affected by her mother's response to being forced out of her job.

The young Kristin attended Charles Sumner School for her elementary education and Magnolia Public School for her junior high years. She graduated from Haddon Heights High School in 1947. An avid reader from the time she was four years old, she wrote poetry and articles for school publications and for the local *Pennsylvania Gazette*. In 1946, at age fourteen, she started a teenage social column for the Philadelphia edition of the *Pittsburgh Courier* and wrote for the paper until 1952, after her graduation from college. One of her most important journalistic assignments was coverage of the annexation by the city of Camden of all-black Lawnside, New Jersey, in 1952, and of the subsequent racial disruptions there. The experience became the basis for *The Lakestown Rebellion*, Hunter's 1978 novel.

Kristin Eggleston graduated from the University of Pennsylvania with a B.S. in education in 1951 and started her first full-time job as a third grade teacher. Both her college major and the job were determined by her parents. Kristin wanted to be a writer, but her strong-willed father initially steered her in another direction. Unable to accept the compromise and adjust to the job, she quit before the year ended to accept a job as a copywriter with the Lavenson Bureau of Advertising in Philadelphia. In that same year, 1952, she again acquiesced to her father's demands and married Joseph Hunter, a journalist and writer. "For ten years," she said later, "it was a clash of who would succeed."

Writing ads by profession and short stories and dramas in her spare time, she gained enough competence to win a national competition sponsored by CBS in 1955 for her television script, *Minority of One,* and her career was launched. (*Minority of One* was based on the reintegration of an all-black Catholic School in Camden; fearing controversy, CBS revised the plot so that a French-speaking alien was admitted to an all-white school.)

Hunter's major theme is the suffering and

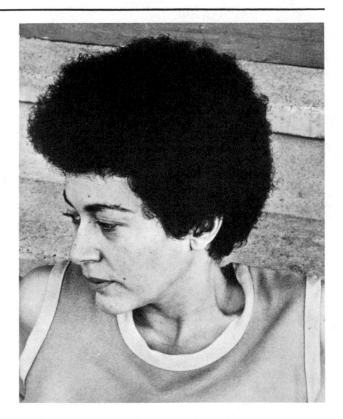

Kristin Hunter (Gale International Portrait Gallery)

deprivation of black people, usually black youth, amidst urban squalor. She aims to "unsear" the consciousnesses of middle-class blacks and appeal to sympathetic whites. In her books for children and young adults and in most of her adult novels, Hunter portrays talented young blacks who either grow up unsung and embittered or who are discovered and exploited. She is also concerned about class divisions within the black community—usually based on skin color—and how they must be erased so that the race and the children can survive. Her emphasis is on the black community and how it must survive through an innate folk ability and mother wit; seldom do whites intrude into the worlds she creates (an exception is *The Landlord*). Her commitment to having black people help themselves is reflected in the usually optimistic tones that pervade her works. Most of her plots focus upon hope and unity, in spite of the realistic obstacles that might undermine both.

God Bless the Child, published in 1964, was Hunter's first and, in many ways, best critically received book. She employs three generations of color-conscious women to show how the mulatto mother's maladjustments can fatally affect the darker-skinned child. Reared in a fatherless home by Queenie, her spineless, promiscuous mother, who becomes Rosie's adversary in order to toughen the child against a hostile world, and by an octoroon grandmother, whose synthetic love mimics the superficial relationships she observes as a faithful domestic to a wealthy family, Rosalie Fleming is determined to lift the three of them above slum existence. By combining ingenuity and an inhuman work schedule, she builds a weak financial empire as a numbers banker, a barmaid, and a fashion consultant. She succeeds in buying the house that her grandmother's white "family" had owned, only to discover that uptown termites are no less repulsive than downtown roaches. A series of additional discoveries leads to her mental breakdown and death. She finally realizes that her grandmother's hand-me-down trinkets are just as fraudulent as her love and that no one can provide the emotional or financial support needed to save her from poverty, illness, and despair. Even her effort to break the ubiquitous cycle by aborting a pregnancy does not save her from the slum existence; it leads to her death. Gutsy and street-wise, Rosalie Fleming allowed Hunter to explore in detail the invincible economic forces that prevent young black women from capitalizing on the same financial opportunities that build character and careers in aspiring nonblack Americans.

This first volume established a major theme in all of Hunter's works: impoverished slums hide many predators waiting to destroy those who attempt to escape as well as those who do not. Unlike her young adult series, *The Soul Brothers and Sister Lou* and *Lou in the Limelight,* or her domestic novel, *The Survivors,* which all have optimistic resolutions, *God Bless the Child* is the depiction of tragic reality. Tawdry criminals and bogus hustles shape Rosalie's responses to life. She is unable to sing her way out of the ghetto, as Lou did; nor does she have the opportunity to escape through some other means and return to aid homeless street waifs, as Lena Ricks of *The Survivors* did. Still, unable to surrender to poverty and despair, as her mother does, Rosalie dies in her effort to escape. Hunter's portrayal of that aspiration and its eventual demise is what makes *God Bless the Child* a critically acclaimed work. It went into a third printing within a month of the September 1964 publication date and had four additional soft-cover printings by Bantam Books in the 1970s. It also won the prestigious Philadelphia Athenaeum Award.

Hunter left the Lavenson Bureau while she was working on *God Bless the Child,* a change that paralleled many others in her life during that period. In order to secure minimal income, yet maintain the time and freedom to write, Hunter worked as a research assistant at the University of Pennsylvania School of Social Work. From 1963 to 1964 and again from 1965 to 1966, she worked as an Information Officer for the City of Philadelphia, a position she retained until her first novel had remained in print long enough for her to get an advance for the second one. Work on the novel, along with the stress of holding various jobs, perhaps contributed to the breakup of Hunter's marriage; she and Joseph were divorced late in 1962. The author recovered and later said of that period: "I was a nervous wreck, but by mid-1963, I had my life together and started writing the first text of *God Bless the Child.*"

Her first may be Hunter's most profound novel, but *The Landlord* was her most successful. Immediately after its publication in 1966, a film producer saw that the integrationist focus could be used to capitalize upon the civil rights movement. This eager reception was a marked contrast to how black readers responded to the novel; many of them thought the comic style masked the truth of the conflict presented.

In contrast to the tragic realism of *God Bless the Child, The Landlord* presents the possibilities for change in the social and physical structure of the ghetto. Elgar Enders, the white man who purchases a ragged, four-unit tenement, begins his sojourn among blacks with the intention of exacting exorbitant profits from them. He is transformed from his role of neurotic misfit by the affectionate cajoling of his earthy, vivacious tenants, who transmit humanness in terms that even he can understand. Enders brings new parks and new paint and plaster to the community. These good deeds, however, are offset by his engagement in an affair with the wife of one of his tenants—with the black man's knowledge. This element provided the controversy for the film as well as for many black readers. Enders assuages his guilt by financing a beauty salon for the woman, but the husband is pushed even further into the background; by the end of the novel, Enders has replaced him in his children's affections.

There are no black heroes in the novel to parallel Enders's transformation, and his redemption seems to be Hunter's point. Blacks have managed to sustain themselves through generations of hostility and indifference from whites. They have always accepted eccentricity within their community, as exemplified by the obese jazz singer Marge and by the homosexual "Creole" DuBois, both of whom turn to fantasies to survive. They can now use their balms to "heal" Elgar, who has been orphaned, abandoned, and tempted to suicide by all human contact except that with his ragtag black "family." This life-giving strength is black love. Elgar's financial reciprocity angered Hunter's critics, for they felt that such reciprocity seldom, if ever, happens in real life. Their skepticism was reflected in the movie version of the novel; when United Artists released the movie in 1970, Enders was transformed into an individual whose ruthless ignorance made him the white man's hero.

The witty, comic style of *The Landlord* and its positive tone of interracial resolution prompted editors at Scribners to suggest that Hunter could be an effective, persuasive writer of children's literature. Her first foray into the world of adolescent literature was the sensationally popular *The Soul Brothers and Sister Lou,* published in 1968. In 1971, she published a slim, family-oriented novelette, *Boss Cat.* Both of these works provide alternatives to the failure and self-negation sociologically perceived as pervasive in the black community. Hunter had diagrammed the need for such outlets in "Pray for Barbara's Baby," an article she wrote for *Philadelphia Magazine* and which, after reprint in *Reader's Digest,* won the 1969 Sigma Delta Chi Best Magazine Reporting Award.

The Lou series draws from the traditional one-way ticket formula for escaping the ghetto: music. Louetta Hawkins convinces her older brother, William, that he should volunteer recreational space in his print shop to keep neighborhood youths out of trouble. Then she and her friends, Ulysses McCracken, Frank Brown, David Weldon, and Jethro Jackson form a singing group. When a confrontation with agitating police ends in Jethro's death, one member of the group composes a eulogy—with the help of their high school music teacher and an old-time, homespun blues singer, "Blind" Eddie. The Soul Brothers and Sister Lou cut a record and are an overnight success.

Billed as a children's book, *The Soul Brothers and Sister Lou* has a tone of urgency that evokes the earlier works. The protagonists want to escape from the determinism of the ghetto and the traps, such as teenage pregnancy and ineffective religion, that await them there. This authentic portrayal of ethnic maturation is a key to the book's success: the first book in the series had seventeen printings, sold over a million copies, and has been translated into several foreign languages. It also won the 1968 Council on Interracial Books for Children Prize.

Following *Boss Cat,* a novelette depicting a young boy's attachment to the family cat that frightens and disgusts his mother until it effectively rids their cozy flat of mice, the prolific Hunter published a collection of children's short stories entitled *Guests in the Promised Land* (1973). Her often printed story "Debut" *(Black World, Norton Introduction to Literature, Seventeen, Directions III and IV),* about a young girl's rite of passage, is included in the collection. The lead story, "Hero's Return," shows how an older brother who has been paroled from "hard-time" prison diminishes his sibling's attraction to the same course. The final selection, the title story, is based on a plot of bitter irony and violence, which does not typify children's literature. In a scene reflecting the white-liberal condescension of the 1960s, a group of black youth are "guests" for a day in a prominent suburban country club, the veritable "promised land." The boys vent their anger in swift destruction of the premises when one of them is forbidden to play gospel hymns on the club's baby grand piano. A poignant comment gathers the common thread of the eleven-piece collection: "Because it ain't no Promised Land at all if some people are always guests and others are always members."

Guests in the Promised Land was a quiet milestone in Hunter's career. More childlike in tone than *Soul Brothers* and more exacting in realism than *Boss Cat,* the balanced aesthetic craft in *Guests* reflects adjustment and settlement in Hunter's private life. She had married journalistic photographer John I. Lattany, Sr., in 1968 and had joined the English department of the University of Pennsylvania as Adjunct Associate Professor of Creative Writing in 1972. *Guests* added to these successes when she was awarded the prestigious Chicago Tribune Book World Prize for the most outstanding juvenile literature of 1973.

The Survivors, published in 1975, echoes *The Landlord* in positing that the transcendence of class barriers can be beneficial to both giver and receiver and can provide one means of racial survival. Miss Lena Rich, a fiftyish-looking dressmaker, has a prosperous business in an inner-city neighborhood that is being repopulated by whites. She receives attention from a small, undernourished, and neglected street hustler, thirteen-year-old B. J. The two "loners" become indispensable to each other's welfare; she becomes his surrogate mother (his mother has died a few months earlier, and his father is only interested in exploiting the child for financial gain), and he instructs her in the nuances of street life. He "schools" Miss Lena about the proper taxis ("hacks") to ride in, insisting that she should only pay one dollar for a particular fare, and asserting that she does not have to tip unless she wants to. The

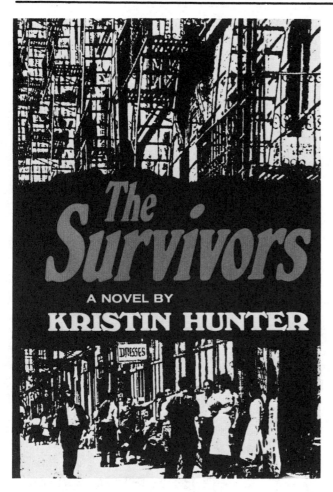

Dust jacket for Hunter's 1975 novel about the relationship between a prosperous middle-aged dressmaker and a thirteen-year-old street kid

croaching, unsympathetic white world.

The Lakestown Rebellion (1978) is aesthetically Hunter's most symbolic book. The small Lakestown community is a microcosm of the black nation. Abe Lakes, the protagonist, represents black leadership out of touch with its constituency. His desire for whiteness and his effort to rob his pale-skinned wife, Bella, of her tendency to blackness provide the backdrop against which the political rebellion takes place. It comes about because Abe has joined corrupt representatives of the state in planning a highway that will destroy most of the town and stratify what is left.

Hunter's repetitive theme of racial reconciliation culminates in *Lakestown*. Bella finally calls a halt to Abe's self-negation by drawing the line of her own identity: "I'm Bella Lakes, your black wife, not some silly white society whore. Plain old funky natural me is who you'll be getting, not a mock-up of some painted white doll. How white I happen to look has nothing to do with it. I'm a black woman inside, a real down black woman, and you're going to have to live with that." Abe and Bella represent pedestalized mulattoes who must ultimately accept total black identity.

Ikie, Abe's brother, who is a sharp contrast in terms of his black identity, articulates the spirit of Lakestown to set an example for the nation: " 'No miracle,' Ikie said. 'Just a couple of basic sociological facts you of all people should understand. One, every black person in this country is by nature an outlaw. Most of us don't dare risk overt action, because we're outnumbered, but the more we have to conform outwardly, the more we want to rebel. So, dig it: there's nothing we love better than finding sly ways of getting over on the Man. And nothing we're better at doing.' " It is no wonder that, after paying Al Young to write a review of the book, in which he favorably endorsed the political message, the *New York Times* refused to print his article.

Hunter's latest work, *Lou in the Limelight* (1981), is offered as a young adult novel billed to appeal to those millions who read *The Soul Brothers and Sister Lou* as children and teens and have grown up with the characters. The eager, spirited young girl who breathed life into the unlikely quartet is now a woman—or at least she thinks she is. That is the novel's tension: a Bildungsroman on the painful discovery of self and of a broadened horizon. While the first novel showed the boys anxious to commit petty street crimes, *Limelight* exposes the naive youngsters to vicious Mafia conspirators seeking to control and siphon profits from black entertainment. By the time they follow their sleazy manager

advice is necessary because several unemployed black men are using their own cars for taxi service in lieu of the refusal of licensed white drivers to pick up black passengers. The problem is that not all of these self-employed black brothers are honest. Only "Pops and Nelson" are acceptable, according to B. J., because they will not get Miss Lena killed, "and if they do, they got insurance to pay for it."

From this rather easy instruction, the novel moves to strengthening Miss Lena's love for B. J., in spite of the thugs, dope pushers, corrupt policemen, and small-time hoodlums he brings into her life. Miss Lena and B. J. represent the new face of survival for the ghetto; middle-classness and poverty, age and youth, relations and nonrelations must unite because the traditional black community is fading away, being swallowed alive by leviathan drugs and their uncharitable companions, and by outlandish crimes designed to benefit an en-to Las Vegas, the truant crooners are popping "uppers" and gulping "downers" to keep the pace and are reduced to depending upon a compassionate prostitute for effective counsel to fend off their avaricious predators. Terrified, they send for Aunt Jerutha Jackson (Jethro's mother), and her clever mother wit guides them to a safe port.

Hunter has made singular contributions to the development of ethnic art and social expression. She is a forerunner of those black women writers who have balanced the treatment of black feminine characterization. She has produced perhaps the most widely circulated literature that deals with the subject matter of idiom, development, and instruction of and for African-American children and young adults. She is among an exclusive club of black writers who, in the supportive atmosphere of the awakening 1960s, saw their works adapted to the cinema. As her style and form continue to develop, both in adult and in children's literature, especially in the voice of her creatively comic narrator, her studies of urban black experience will similarly continue to disclose schemes of initiation, recognition, and escape.

References:

Trudier Harris, *From Mammies to Militants: Domestics in Black American Literature* (Philadelphia: Temple University Press, 1982);

Maralyn Lois Polak, "Kristin Hunter: A Writer and a Fighter," *Philadelphia Inquirer*, 24 November 1974.

Charles R. Johnson

(23 April 1948-   )

Maryemma Graham
University of Mississippi

SELECTED BOOKS: *Black Humor* (Chicago: Johnson, 1970);
Half-Past Nation Time (Westlake Village, Cal.: Aware, 1972);
Faith and the Good Thing (New York: Viking, 1974);
Oxherding Tale (Bloomington: Indiana University Press, 1982; London: Blond & Briggs, 1983).

TELEVISION: "Charlie's Pad," PBS, 1971;
Charlie Smith and the Fritter-Tree, PBS, 1978;
For Me Myself, PBS, 1982;
A Place For Myself, PBS, 1982;
Booker, coauthored with John Allmann, PBS, 1984.

PERIODICAL PUBLICATIONS:
Fiction:
"The Education of Mingo," *Mother Jones*, 2 (August 1977): 49-53;
"Consolation," *Callaloo*, 1 (October 1978): 95-105;
"Exchange Value," *Choice*, 11/12 (Fall 1981): 63-67;
"Poppers's Disease," *Callaloo*, 5 (February 1982): 120-129;
"China," *MSS*, 2 (Winter 1982): 15-114;
"The Sorceror's Apprentice," *Callaloo*, 6 (February 1983);

"Menagerie, A Child's Fable," *Indiana Review*, 7 (Spring 1984): 26-33.
Nonfiction:
"The Primeval Mitosis: A Phenomenology of the Black Body," *Juju: Research Papers in Afro-American Studies* (Winter 1976): 48-59;
"Essay on Fiction," *Intro*, 10 (October 1979): xi-xiii;
"Philosophy and Black Fiction," *Obsidian*, 6 (Spring/Summer 1980): 55-61.

With two novels already published and two more in progress, Charles Richard Johnson has already established himself as a significant new writing talent. Despite a fair amount of commercial success, he is one of the few contemporary young Afro-American novelists whose work is not, according to one critic, trendy or opportunistic and who continues to enrich contemporary American literature with each new fictional work. Johnson was barely twenty-six, already a well-known political cartoonist and journalist, when his first novel was published. His shift in careers was not so much a change in direction as a culmination of the skills and resources he had available to him.

Both his published novels present the objec-

Charles Johnson

tive world of the Afro-American experience, but subject that world to many different levels of interpretation. Johnson's novels are fascinating, unusual, and often difficult to comprehend. He has not limited himself to one particular school or fictional mode, though it has been suggested that his versatility, as well as his thematic and structural concerns with levels of consciousness and experience, are key elements that define the "new fiction" beginning in the middle 1970s, a body of expression to which Johnson's novels undeniably belong.

Johnson's works typically explore themes essential to black American history—connections between race and sex, race and class, as well as personal relationships—themes that cut across slavery, the rural South and the urban North. His method is usually a synthesis of traditional narrative forms substantially modified. He is deliberate in tone and method.

Johnson was born in Evanston, Illinois, in 1948. He demonstrated an early talent for drawing. His father's disapproval of art as a career simply made Johnson more determined. He appealed to cartoonist and writer Lawrence Lariar, who became his teacher and mentor, and it was under Lariar's sponsorship that he launched a career as a cartoonist at seventeen.

By 1971, Johnson had completed college at

Southern Illinois University in Carbondale, where he majored in journalism, and he was beginning a second career. He created, coproduced, and hosted the PBS series "Charlie's Pad" (1971), which ran for fifty-two segments. Sometime between completing his M.A. in philosophy at Southern Illinois University in 1973 and working as a photojournalist in Chicago and Carbondale, Johnson wrote six novels, trying to merge his philosophical ideas with various forms of literary expression. His career as a novelist got a boost when he apprenticed himself to John Gardner, who was teaching creative writing at Southern Illinois University. He presented Gardner with the six completed novels and wrote a seventh one, *Faith and the Good Thing*. By the time this novel was published in 1974, Johnson was married to his classmate Joan New and enrolled in the Ph.D. program at SUNY-Stony Brook, concentrating on phenomenology and literary aesthetics.

According to Johnson, it was Gardner who helped him to draw the connection between the Afro-American historical experience and various philosophical ideas —African, Eastern, and Western—by appropriating different fictional modes. Johnson relied primarily on the oral tradition, which embraced the specific fictional devices and subgenres uniquely appropriate to his material; at the same time it permitted him the flexibility to explore different sources of information. What had appeared before to him as disparate elements were united in a conceptual design.

Faith and the Good Thing reflects Johnson's obsession with philosophy that marked this stage of his academic pursuits. Told as a folk fable whose narrator compels the reader's attention with a periodic "Listen, Children," the story centers on Faith Cross, thwarted in her pursuit of an ideal by a series of circumstances from which she is unable to escape.

The novel is essentially a physical and metaphysical journey for Faith, whose rural folk origins in Hatten County, Georgia, get redefined once she arrives in Chicago. Although her metaphysical world is sometimes muted, it is ever-present, and Johnson gives each world its own set of characters who are all in tune with a particular dimension of Faith's reality. In her metaphysical world there is a werewitch (Swamp Woman) and a mad professor; in her physical world, there are her male clients, a pretentious husband, and an estranged lover. But Faith is the only character in the novel who belongs consistently to both worlds, which she must struggle to balance as she engages in various relationships.

Faith's development from childhood innocent

to prostitute, middle-class housewife, and deserted lover ends logically in her death. Her soul returns to its source, where she symbolically changes places with the Swamp Woman. Faith's physical destruction occurs in the whorehouse, her "original" Chicago home. Her soul returns to its "original" home—the Georgia swamp—the land of her spiritual and physical birth, and now her spiritual rebirth as well.

While at times Johnson appears to be searching for the fabulous and incredible in this story, at other times he presents familiar material with a new interpretation. Clearly, Faith is searching for the meaning of her life in its most ideal form, but she is not alienated, as most twentieth-century protagonists like her would be.

Faith's physical world is so depressing that her story can have no happy ending. Her victimization and exploitation are as much a function of her innocence and economic dependency as her idealism. With her physical life destroyed, the spiritual life can proceed unencumbered.

Johnson waited eight years before publishing his second novel, *Oxherding Tale* (1982). In the meantime, he wrote television scripts for the Public Broadcasting System. In addition, he accepted a teaching position at the University of Washington (Seattle), leaving SUNY-Stony Brook without completing his dissertation. Currently he teaches creative writing and edits the *Seattle Review*. He lives in Seattle with his wife and two children.

Oxherding Tale is a modern slave narrative (which also resembles an Eastern parable). It is similar to *Faith and the Good Thing* as a novel in the oral tradition with a thematic emphasis on the movement from innocence to experience. The novel is marked by Johnson's masterful use of language, highly visual and descriptive and laden with metaphoric devices. But for all the similarities, *Oxherding Tale* is a very different sort of book from his first novel. Johnson is more conservative in his digressions into metaphysics and myth, and most of the erudite language is better placed contextually. A second difference is in the characterization. Rather than embodying different levels of consciousness in a single character, *Oxherding Tale* portrays through different characters the various ways knowledge and reality are perceived.

Andrew Hawkins, the narrator, has a familiar slave's story to tell: he was born in bondage and escaped to freedom. The natural flow of events, however, invites several interruptions due in part to the circumstances of Andrew's birth and the comic mode which characterizes the novel, as well as to

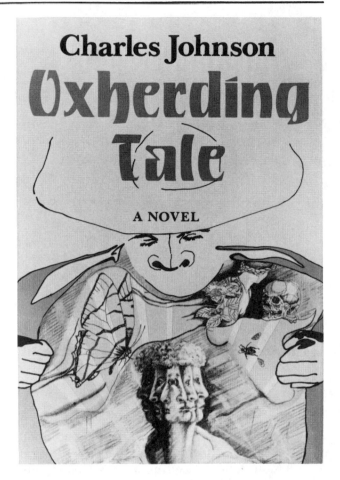

Dust jacket for Johnson's second novel, a modern version of the slave narrative

Johnson's tendency to follow a phenomenological argument. As the result of a practical joke between master and slave, Andrew is "accidentally" conceived. His mother is the mistress of the plantation and his father is a house slave turned oxherder after the "Fall" (Andrew's conception and birth). Andrew lives with his father and stepmother in the slave quarters. When Andrew turns five, he begins his education under Ezekiel, an anarchist-transcendentalist-mystic tutor.

Andrew learns everything that Ezekiel knows in the realm of abstract knowledge, and it is only with a visit from Karl Marx that Ezekiel himself is forced to question the relevance of his theoretical knowledge. Andrew, who shares the experience of Marx's visit, learns that the test of all theoretical knowledge is its application to concrete experience. Everything that happens to Andrew once he leaves the Cripplegate Plantation serves to bring practical experience and theoretical understanding together for him.

As one might guess from Johnson's philosophical approach, the unexpected is expected in this novel. There are a number of symbolic intrusions, mainly in the form of characters who are not as eccentric as Ezekiel but are equally as important to Andrew's development. None of this is distracting, however, since these intrusions are as integral to the narrative sequence as they are to Johnson's theoretical explanations. There is Flo Hatfield, from whom Andrew learns the most basic element of sensory knowledge, sex. Hatfield, a widow and owner of a highly profitable cotton plantation, trains black slaves as male concubines. Reb, a slave coffin maker on Hatfield's plantation, is the personification of experience without consciousness or feeling, a kind of stoical necessity born of slavery. Finally, there is Horace Bannon, the Soulcatcher, whose success in capturing runaway slaves is based on his ability to intuit the feelings and consciousness of his prey. Andrew's experience with each character becomes an obstacle to his real freedom. At the same time, a reversal occurs. As new levels of knowledge about each character are revealed, a redefinition of that character's relationship to Andrew and to himself occurs. Each time this happens, Andrew gets closer to freedom, until he finally arrives. Ironically, it is the Soulcatcher's reversal that grants Andrew his release. Unable to catch Reb, who escapes successfully to Chicago, the Soulcatcher confides to Andrew, "Befo, afterwards and in between didn't mean nothin to him. He had no home. No permanent home. He didn't care bout merit or evil . . . Ah couldn't entirely become the nigguh because you got to have somethin' dead or static already inside you—an image of yoself—fo' a real slave catcher to latch onto." With that the Soulcatcher fulfills a promise to himself and retires.

Oxherding Tale is the better of Johnson's two novels. It represents a refining of his fictional techniques and a more satisfying blend of reality, science, and myth. He is more skillful in drawing purposeful characters and achieves a more suitable balance between their physical, psychological, and philosophical dimensions. It is particularly significant that these characters are selected from across race, class, and sexual lines; their lives are all distinctly different, but they are united in their relationship to slave society.

Reviews of *Oxherding Tale* were generally enthusiastic, but reviewers often missed the complexity and subtlety that give the novel its power. Stanley Crouch in the *Village Voice* was an exception. He recognized the multiplicity of resources and influences for the novel, such as Frederick Douglass's autobiography, Herman Melville's *Benito Cereno,* and the *Odyssey,* and the skill with which Johnson reconstructs the slave narrative form without losing sight of the theme of the narrator's developing consciousness.

What some critics find as serious flaws in Johnson's works—the philosophical indulgences, the exploitation of the supernatural for effect, and the balance between fantasy and realism—other critics find fascinating, especially those who consider *Faith and the Good Thing* in the tradition of *Invisible Man.* Raymond Olderman, in an extensive analysis of American fiction between 1974 and 1976, placed Johnson among those writers of fiction who "can embody contact with reality, have the spiritual significance of myth and the authority of science."

Charles R. Johnson deserves more critical recognition as a novelist of ideas and as a mature craftsman. His two published novels provide ample evidence that he is a writer of achievement; moreover, he is a writer of prowess, and there is every reason to expect that he will get even better as his career progresses.

Interviews:

"Writers Should Be Able to Write Everything: Ken McCullough talks to Charles Johnson," *Coda: Poets and Writers Newsletter,* 6 (September/ October 1978): 22-25;

"Reflections on Fiction, Philosophy, and Film: An Interview with Charles Johnson," *Callaloo,* 4 (October 1978): 118-128.

References:

Stanley Crouch, "Charles Johnson, Free at Last," *Village Voice,* 28, 19 July 1983, pp. 30-31;

Arthur Davis, "Novels of the New Black Renaissance (1960-1977): A Thematic Survey," *CLA Journal,* 21 (June 1978): 457-490;

Raymond Olderman, "American Literature, 1974-1976: The People Fell to Earth," *Contemporary Literature,* 19 (Autumn 1978): 497-527;

Elizabeth Shultz, "The Heirs of Ralph Ellison," *CLA Journal,* 22 (December 1978): 101-122.

Gayl Jones

(23 November 1949-   )

Keith E. Byerman
University of Texas

BOOKS: *Corregidora* (New York: Random House, 1975);

Eva's Man (New York: Random House, 1976);

White Rat (New York: Random House, 1977);

Song for Anninho (Ann Arbor: Lotus Press, 1981).

Though not one of the best-known of contemporary black writers, Gayl Jones can claim distinction as the teller of the most intense tales. Her stories are powerful depictions of madness and violence in the lives of black people, especially women. And since she chooses to allow these women to narrate their own experiences, she effectively shows the insanity and violence from the inside, as it were. In these voices, we hear the troubles of black women in the language of the black oral tradition. The results are blues narratives that are simultaneously intense, almost gothic, psychological dramas.

Both the use of the oral tradition and the impulse to write developed out of Jones's childhood in Lexington, Kentucky. She has commented repeatedly that the speech of her characters is the speech she heard in the streets and homes of her community, which was segregated for virtually all the years she lived there. She found the language of both everyday experience and of storytelling to be rich with possibility when she began writing. Moreover, the writing of narratives was itself a part of her family heritage. Her grandmother wrote plays for church productions and Jones's mother, Lucille, began writing when she was in fifth grade and continued to do so when, as a mother, she needed ways to entertain her children. Jones herself began writing stories when she was seven or eight. In addition, some of the family history passed down in oral or written form has provided material for Jones's fiction. For example, the plot of "The Roundhouse," in which a woman takes care of a sick stranger who later anonymously pays her bills, is the story of the meeting of her grandparents.

Besides this personal and private education, she received training in the public schools of Lexington, which were segregated until she was in tenth grade. Her fifth-grade teacher, Mrs. Hodges, encouraged her writing; but, otherwise, the kinds of reading and writing done in the schools offered her little in the way of training as a writer. From Lexington, she went to Connecticut College, where she majored in English and received prizes for her poetry. From there, she undertook graduate studies in creative writing at Brown University with the guidance of William Meredith and Michael S. Harper. While still at Brown, she published her first novel. She currently teaches creative writing and Afro-American literature at the University of Michigan.

Jones creates worlds radically different from those of "normal" experience and of storytelling convention. Her tales are gothic in the sense of dealing with madness, sexuality, and violence, but they do not follow in the Edgar Allan Poe tradition of focusing on private obsession and irrationality. Though her narrators are close to if not over the boundaries of sanity, the experiences they record reveal clearly that society acts out its own obsessions, often violently. The authority of these depictions of the world is enhanced by Jones's refusal to intrude upon or judge her narrators. She remains outside the story, leaving the reader with none of the usual markers of a narrator's reliability. She gives these characters the speech of their religion, which, by locating them in time and space, makes it even more difficult to easily dismiss them; the way they speak has authenticity, which carries over to what they tell. The results are profoundly disturbing tales of repression, manipulation, and suffering.

Corregidora (1975), Jones's first novel, is what she calls "blues" narrative, in the sense that it deals with both the pains and the pleasures of human relationships. "Blues" has the further connotation that the teller of the tale gains control of her experience in the process of describing her loss of control. Like some of the author's other narrators, Ursa Corregidora manifests an increasing control over her material as she tells her story.

The title character of the book, Ursa's great-grandfather, was a Portuguese seaman who established a vast estate in Brazil with the aid of slave labor. He turned his women slaves into prostitutes,

Gayl Jones (photo © by Thomas Victor)

except for the ones he kept for himself, including Ursa's great-grandmother. He produced a daughter by this woman and later impregnated his own child. When a female child was born, the daughter escaped with the infant to the United States. All of the women, including the great-granddaughter Ursa, keep the name Corregidora as a reminder of the depredations of the slave system and of the rapacious natures of men. The story is passed from generation to generation of women, along with the admonition to "produce generations" to keep alive the tale of evil.

The need to procreate has special poignance for Ursa, since she has been rendered sterile by the violence of her first husband, Mutt. A blues singer, Ursa meets and falls in love with him at one of the small clubs where she performs. When they are married, he insists that she end her career because he is jealous of the men in the bars. Her repeated refusal infuriates him to the point that he throws her down a flight of stairs; the doctors can only save her by performing a hysterectomy. Her career, her marriage, and her ability to "produce generations"

all seem at an end. Much of the narrative occurs as flashbacks during the long period of her recovery and return to the stage. She contemplates her maternal history and her relationship with Mutt, who is as obsessed with her as she with him; despite their antagonisms, neither can escape the other. She feels guilty for her sterility, but this is complicated by her sense that her art is a form of creation. In fact, as her friend Cat points out, her suffering has enhanced the quality of her blues: "Your voice sounds a little strained, that's all. But if I hadn't heard you before I wouldn't notice anything. I'd still be moved. Maybe even moved more, because it sounded like you been through something. Before it was beautiful too, but you sound like you been through more now." Moreover, as she recalls the stories told by her grandmother and mother, she comes to understand that their hatred of men is a way of granting themselves absolute innocence and of evading their own human limitations. Thus, Ursa's mother's inability to love her husband is a function of the training in misanthropy she has received rather than a function of his inadequacies. Ursa's own second marriage fails because of coldness and hostility to Tadpole, who seeks primarily to provide and care for her.

Through this long period of recovery and contemplation, which lasts twenty years, Ursa slowly comes to a reevaluation of herself and her relationship with Mutt. She comes to see him as another victim of both history and patriarchal oppression. He is not a reincarnation of Corregidora, but a fallible human being caught in her own dilemma of desiring that which is simultaneously most pleasurable and most painful. In the final scene, Ursa joins her historical understanding to her personal experience. While performing fellatio on Mutt, she joins past and present:

> It had to be sexual, I was thinking, it had to be something sexual that Great Gram did to Corregidora. I knew it had to be sexual: "What is it a woman can do to a man that make him hate her so bad he wont to kill her one minute and keep thinking about her and can't get her out of his mind the next?" In a split second I knew what it was, in a split second of hate and love I knew what it was, and I think he might have known too. A moment of pleasure and excruciating pain at the same time, a moment of broken skin but not sexlessness, a moment just before sexlessness, a moment that stops just before sexlessness, a moment that stops before it breaks the skin: "I could kill you."

The paradoxes of human relationships become apparent in this moment: the victimizer makes himself vulnerable in the act of victimization, the liberating protest against power becomes power, passivity becomes a form of violent action, and the beloved, because of the intensity of love, becomes an object of fear and hate.

Because it acknowledges these paradoxes, *Corregidora*, despite its subject matter, does not become an ideological attack on either racism or sexism. Jones focuses on the psychological effects of history and power rather than on protests against them. Criticism of the book has generally recognized it as a primarily literary rather than political work. The only negative commentary, in fact, criticizes it for not revealing more of the historical context. It is consistently praised for its effective rendering of complex themes in a subtle and appropriate language. Even its sexual material is said to be handled with grace.

Eva's Man (1976), Jones's second novel, aroused far more controversy, and, given its subject

Dust jacket for Jones's first novel, which she describes as a blues narrative because "it deals with both the pains and the pleasures of human relationships"

matter, this was inevitable. It is much more radical than *Corregidora* in plot, theme, and narrative structure. Refusing to accept the tension of men and women, love and hate, that Ursa accepts in her last scene, Eva commits the act of sexual violence that the earlier character only contemplates. Through her obsessive narration, Eva articulates the experiences that led her to rebel against male domination in such an extreme way. But her story cannot be dismissed simply as the ravings of a psychotic woman, since the tale she tells is, in exaggerated form, the tale of all women in a male-dominated society. By pushing common events beyond their usual limits, the novel forces the reader to reconsider the "normality" of such events.

The structure of the book reinforces the effects of the narrative voice. Eva's movement through ever more intense experiences suggests a whirlpool pattern in which the speed of the narration increases through condensation of time and shortening of chapters. At the same time, repetition of key images, scenes, characters, and words creates the impression of a narrowing of perspective. At the climax, she focuses exclusively on the object she sees as the root of her condition, and she takes possession of it in an act of sexual dismemberment. At the end, at the bottom of the whirlpool, she comes to rest in a literal prison.

The novel opens at this end point, with Eva Medina Canada incarcerated in a hospital for the criminally insane. She refuses to talk to the police or the psychiatrists, but she seems to tell everything to the reader. At the same time, however, her narrative is much more closed than that of Ursa Corregidora. Eva describes events, but she never explores motives; moreover, she does not distinguish fantasy from reality. She also seems to confuse the sequence of events, making it nearly impossible to place her recollections in conventional contexts of time, space, and causality.

What is certain in her story is the malevolence of men. She tells the story of Freddy, the little neighbor boy who sexually initiates her with a dirty popsicle stick. Her husband, James, is so jealous that he will not allow a telephone in their house. Her cousin Alphonse repeatedly takes her to bars and propositions her. And Davis, the man she kills, imprisons her in his apartment. Every man sees her as an object existing only to satisfy his sexual needs.

Folk wisdom in the book reinforces this pattern. Miss Billie, who represents community attitudes, insists that men obsessively seek to dominate women and that women naturally submit to such treatment. Alphonse's relationship with his wife Jean, for example, is a blues relationship. He cannot live without her, yet she often angers him so much that he physically attacks her. Jean not only survives but seems to thrive on his assaults; her brother Otis believes that she even instigates them: "*She* starts it, Marie. Not him. She starts it and then he finishes it. She the one wonts it, though, Marie. . . . Like they were working all that blues out of them, or something." Eva's tales of women troubled by men simultaneously repulsive and attractive follow the pattern of female destiny expressed repeatedly in blues by the classic women blues singers, such as Bessie Smith and Ma Rainey.

The most tragic of Eva's stories describes the life of Queen Bee, a woman in the community who is fatally unlucky; every man she falls in love with dies shortly thereafter. Her love is somehow a deadly sting. She eventually commits suicide rather than threaten the life of her newest lover. She sym-

Dust jacket for Jones's second novel, which was controversial because of its shocking sexual violence

bolizes all the women in the book who cannot avoid their sexuality but are nonetheless blamed and punished for it. But there is another level to this pattern, implicit in the name Queen Bee. The designation suggests power, fertility, and creativity. If women, like queen bees, exist primarily as sexual objects, men, like drones, can only define themselves by service to the queen. Women in this sense have power to affirm or deny manhood.

Eva is the one who exercises this power most explicitly. She makes literal the metaphor of the queen bee by killing the drone rather than passively accepting his sexual domination. When Davis keeps her locked up, he does not allow her any amenities, including a comb to control her ever-wilder hair. She becomes, in an image made explicit in the text, a Medusa who keeps him in a perpetual state of sexual arousal. Objectification reaches its highest point; Eva is, for Davis, nothing but her sexual organs. But, like the bee, she finds in her cell the source of her strength. The phallus, as literal and figurative emblem of male power, is also the male's most vulnerable point. Eva exposes this weakness by poisoning Davis, biting off his penis, wrapping it in a silk handkerchief, and placing it back in his pants. She takes Ursa Corregidora's insight into male-female relationships to its logical extreme. This extremity is the measure of her madness.

But she goes even further by making her insane act into a moral statement. She takes responsibility for her behavior by calling the police and then waiting to be arrested. She places herself in the world of male domination, symbolized by policemen and psychiatrists, but she does so as an alternative authority, a queen bee. She refuses to talk to them, to explain or defend herself; in this sense she refuses to submit to their system of discourse, their definitions of power and womanhood. This silence, of course, only confirms them in their view of her as insane.

In another sense, though, she does speak; she tells the story. Gayl Jones provides no authorial intrusion and no questioning of Eva's point of view. We know Eva is insane, not because Jones tells us, but because the time and space distortions, the obsessions and repetitions, and the increasingly confusing and obscure references within the narrative are the linguistic markers of a psychotic personality. Unlike Ursa, Eva gains no real control over her narrative. We hear the madness in Eva's voice, but because her madness so resembles our sanity, we feel compelled to listen to her.

Critics who have listened to the voice have trouble accepting it as "merely" a literary device. On the one hand, they are bothered by Jones's refusal to repudiate Eva's vision and behavior within the text; some have even identified the values of the author with those of the character. The second criticism is related to the first; commentators have attacked Jones either for writing a diatribe against black men or for validating the stereotypes of black women as alternately promiscuous and emasculating. Only those who have taken seriously Jones's repeated assertion that she is interested in telling stories rather than making political or social statements have been able to judge the work on its literary merits.

The stories in *White Rat* (1977) continue Jones's concerns with sexuality, violence, madness, and race. With the exception of "The Roundhouse," mentioned earlier, these twelve short fictions have the dark vision of the novels. "Asylum," for example, is in some ways an abbreviated version of *Eva's Man*. The narrator is a young woman committed to a mental hospital for her irrational be-

havior. She will not allow the doctor to examine her genital area, even though she was admitted for deliberately urinating in the living room when her nephew's teacher visited their home. She explains to the reader (like Eva, she will not talk to the doctor) the reason for her behavior: "She [the teacher] just sit on her ass and fuck all day and it ain't with herself." Her madness is apparent in her obsession with acts of violation and in her graphic expression of resistance to such acts. Thus, her sense that the teacher provides a worthless education is symbolized by publicly presenting and using the family slop jar. Significantly, when the doctor tells her how he plans to return her to normal, she calls his methods "schoolwork."

More important, she views the process of mental and physical examination as rape. Whenever she is examined, she sees a "big black rubbery thing look like a snake" emerge from either her vagina or her anus. Because the story is told from her perspective, it is possible to see that she is mentally unstable, yet also understand that the experts defining her condition have turned her into an object for their psychiatric and medical manipulations. The pain and disorder she experiences are unrelieved and even aggravated by such clinical clichés as "libido concentrated on herself." The final conversation reveals the dilemma of the narrator:

"What does this word make you feel?"
"Nothing."
"You should tell me what you are thinking."
"Is that the only way I can be freed?"

If she does not speak, she will be locked up as an incorrigible; but if she does talk, she will be collaborating in her own categorization and "treatment," which will make her normal according to standards that have nothing to do with her true self. Either way, there is no freedom, no escape from this "refuge."

The same sense of frustration is apparent in the title story, "White Rat," though it deals with racial rather than sexual issues. The narrator (one of Jones's few male speakers) calls himself White Rat because he is so light-skinned that he could pass for white. His ambiguous pigmentation causes his problems since he was raised to identify with blacks but can only do so by insisting on his race in a society that has placed a curse on blackness. Carrying on the normal social functions in the Kentucky town where he lives requires that he repeatedly name himself "nigger." His use of the pejorative suggests that he has absorbed the racial values of the domi-

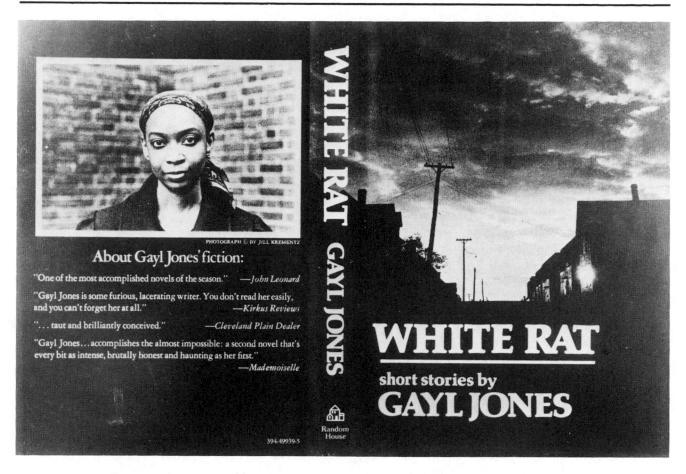

Dust jacket for Jones's 1977 collection of stories about sexuality, violence, madness, and race

nant culture. His father taught him to hate all whites, but to do so means hating those physically identical with himself. Thus, he is caught between two worlds and cannot move into either one without despising some part of himself.

He avoids psychological suicide by turning his frustration and anger outward. He becomes a hardened man who does not recognize weakness in himself and will not tolerate it in others. He constantly berates his wife Maggie for having "chickenscratch" (nappy) hair, though this is the only trait that clearly marks either of them as black. Similarly, the birth defect of his son is a source of antagonism; somebody must be at fault, and he insists that it is Maggie:

> I said there weren't nothing like that in my family ever since we been living on this earth. And they must have come from her side. And then I said cause she had more of whatever it was in her than I had in me. And then she said that brought it all out. All that

stuff I been hiding up inside me cause she said I didnt hate them hoogies [whites] like my daddy did and I just been feeling I had to live up to something he set and the onliest reason I married her was because she was the lightest and brightest nigger woman I could get and still be nigger.

As penance for his sin against his father's rule, the narrator allows his wife to run off with a darker man and then takes responsibility for her alleged pregnancy when she returns. But this gesture only substitutes one form of self-hatred for another. White Rat's problem is coming to terms with the fact that he is both black and white, as are his wife and child. At the end of the story, he is still incapable of accepting this ambivalent state of being. But his narrative, which gives full expression to his uncertainty and anguish, shows the necessity of this dialectical condition.

"The Women," a female initiation story, follows Jones's pattern of exploring the frustrations and convolutions of desire. The plot parallels the growing sexual awareness of the child-narrator Winnie with the lesbian relationships of her mother. As a little girl, she does not understand her mother's behavior, but she knows that it is condemned by the community. Her own childhood sexual experiments are also unpleasant.

The associations of sex with fear and domination are reinforced by her mother's cycles of hostility and devotion to her lovers. The women who come to stay begin as beloved, but soon, according to the mother, become "bitch's whores." This cyclical pattern contrasts with Winnie's own linear development of sexual knowledge. She gets her information primarily from other girls and generally shows indifference to boys, perhaps because of her early experience. But she makes it clear that she will never be like her mother: "I get under the covers and say, 'I ain't goin' be like my mama when I grow up. I ain't goin' be a bitch's whore.' "

Her attitude toward boys changes under the persistent attentions of her friend Garland, but her relationship with her mother still defines her behavior: "We got up and I started in my room, but changed my mind and take him into my mama's bedroom. Then I lay down on my mama's bedspread, and let him get on top of me." Heterosexual copulation in the space her mother has made homosexual suggests that Winnie defines her identity more in resistance to her mother than in terms of her own biological impulses. Ironically, her use of Garland in this way implies a self-centered manipulation much like that of men and her mother. Thus, she continues the cycle of desire and frustration.

The stories in *White Rat* reveal the same thematic concerns as Jones's longer fiction. The characters are frustrated and dehumanized by their experience of the world. They are psychological if not physical prisoners of the obsessive patterns of society. What gives poignance to the tales is the authenticity and specificity achieved through the speech of Kentucky black people. No matter how bizarre the story or how insane the character, we experience them as human beings very much in the world.

Song for Anninho (1981), a long narrative poem, addresses similar themes, but in the very different context of seventeenth-century, slaveholding Brazil. In a sense, with this story, Jones has placed in the foreground the background world of *Corregidora*. Though a poem, this book began as a novel entitled "Palmares," and it retains much of the storytelling force of fictional narrative. It is the story of the love between Anninho and his wife Almeyda, who is the narrator. They have been residents of Palmares, a settlement established by fugitive slaves, but barely escape from the Portuguese soldiers who overrun their fortress. Soon after, the two are separated when they are caught by those soldiers. When Almeyda's breasts are cut off and thrown in the river, she falls unconscious and is left for dead. In the present time of the narrative, she is being cared for by Zibatra, a "wizard-woman" and healer. She wishes to use the occult powers of Zibatra to learn the fate of Anninho, but the woman tells her: "I cannot find him for you. /It is you who must make the discovery."

The discovery can only be made through memory and imagination, for it is clear from the text that they will not be physically reunited. In the process of coming to terms with past and present, Almeyda demonstrates, as did Ursa Corregidora, the impact of history and society on the human psyche. She tells the story, for example, of a woman who, out of despair and outrage over her enslavement, did something unspecified to herself to render her body sexually inaccessible to men. More important, the existence of Palmares made the love of Anninho and Almeyda possible, but the threat of such a place to slaveholding society means that emotional ties can be severed at any moment:

> That was the question, Almeyda,
> how we could sustain our love
> at a time of cruelty.
> How we could keep loving
> at such a time. How we could
> look at each other with tenderness.
> And keep it, even with everything.
> It's hard to keep tenderness
> when things all around you are hard.

The profundity and inclusiveness of that love are made apparent throughout the narrative. The sexual, emotional, and spiritual bonds between them are all one; they transcend all the pains and uncertainties of their experience:

> I wanted to grow deep for you,
> something more than feelings,
> something of spirit,
> all of my memory and yours,
> dreams, and the whole time
> we have spent with each other,
> and beyond time;
> and even our fears,
> yes, made out of even our fears.

With this theme of transcendence, Jones moves well beyond her earliest work; though enslaved, abused, and perhaps even killed, Anninho and Almeyda are not defeated or driven mad. Desire, for the first time in Jones's writing, is a liberating rather than imprisoning quality; moreover, it serves in the poem to free the imagination and, at the end, to "make roads" which lead to the beloved. In this creativity, *Song for Anninho* moves in a new direction, but it does so within the overall blues framework of the author's previous work. Almeyda seeks to restore the experience of her love through the singing that is her narrative; in this, she is very much in the tradition of Ursa Corregidora. What this suggests is that Gayl Jones will continue to explore the possibilities of black narrative forms and to continue to produce voices that intently probe the depths of pain and love.

Interviews:

Roseann P. Bell, "Gayl Jones Takes a Look at 'Corregidora'—An Interview," in *Sturdy Black Bridges: Visions of Black Women in Literature,* edited by Roseann P. Bell and others (Garden City: Doubleday, 1979), pp. 282-287;

Michael S. Harper, "Gayl Jones: An Interview," in *Chant of Saints: A Gathering of Afro-American Literature, Art, and Scholarship,* edited by

Harper and Robert B. Stepto (Urbana: University of Illinois Press, 1979), pp. 352-375;

Charles H. Rowell, "An Interview with Gayl Jones," *Callaloo,* 5 (October 1982): 32-53;

Claudia C. Tate, "Gayl Jones," in *Black Women Writers at Work,* edited by Claudia C. Tate (New York: Continuum, 1983), pp. 89-99.

References:

Keith E. Byerman, "Black Vortex: The Gothic Structure of *Eva's Man,*" *MELUS,* 7 (Winter 1980): 93-100;

Byerman, "Intense Behaviors: The Use of the Grotesque in *Eva's Man* and *The Bluest Eye,*" *CLA Journal,* 25 (June 1982): 447-457;

Trudier Harris, "A Spiritual Journey: Gayl Jones's *Song for Anninho,*" *Callaloo,* 5 (October 1982): 105-111;

Valerie Gray Lee, "The Use of Folktalk in Novels by Black Women Writers," *CLA Journal,* 23 (March 1980): 266-272;

Claudia C. Tate, "*Corregidora:* Ursa's Blues Medley," *Black American Literature Forum,* 13 (Fall 1979): 139-141;

Jerry W. Ward, "Escape from Trublem: The Fiction of Gayl Jones," *Callaloo,* 5 (October 1982): 95-104.

William Melvin Kelley
(1 November 1937-   )

Valerie M. Babb
Georgetown University

BOOKS: *A Different Drummer* (Garden City: Doubleday, 1962; London: Hutchinson, 1963);

Dancers on the Shore (Garden City: Doubleday, 1964; London: Hutchinson, 1965);

A Drop of Patience (Garden City: Doubleday, 1965; London: Hutchinson, 1966);

dem (Garden City: Doubleday, 1967; New York: Collier Books, 1969);

Dunfords Travels Everywheres (Garden City: Doubleday, 1970).

PERIODICAL PUBLICATIONS: "If You're Woke

You Dig It," *New York Times Magazine,* 20 May 1962, pp. 45, 50;

"The Ivy League Negro," *Esquire,* 60 (August 1963): 54-56, 108-109;

"An American in Rome," *Mademoiselle,* 60 (March 1965): 202, 244-246;

"On Racism, Exploitation, and the White Liberal," *Negro Digest,* 16 (January 1967): 5-12;

"On Africa in the United States," *Negro Digest,* 17 (May 1968): 10-15.

During the course of his literary career, William Melvin Kelley, who began writing with a vision of racial coexistence, increasingly saw the impossibility of this ideal. The change in his perception and racial politics paralleled that of many black Americans during the turbulent 1960s, when the dream of the integrationist phase of the civil rights movement began to be replaced by the rage and anger of the emerging black nationalists. As Kelley became more aware of the systematic degradation of blacks throughout American history, the themes and concerns of his writing took on a more radical stance. He shifted from characters making quiet protests to regain their lost dignity to characters angrily avenging past wrongs.

Kelley's beginnings could be said to represent the culmination of the integrationist dream in America. He was born on 1 November 1937 in the Bronx, the son of editor William Kelley and Narcissa Agatha Kelley, and lived in an Italian neighborhood. The Kelleys were the only black family in the area. Kelley's schooling further reflected the hope of the races living peaceably side by side. He attended the exclusive Fieldston School, a small, predominantly white private school in New York, where he was captain of the track team, president of the student council, and, as he put it, a "golden boy." From Fieldston, Kelley went to Harvard in 1957 with plans to become a lawyer; however, in the spring term of his sophomore year, he chose to study prose fiction with John Hawkes and later with Archibald MacLeish. After these encounters, Kelley said, "I knew I would write forever."

After three and one-half years at Harvard, Kelley was failing all but his fiction course. He apparently remained untouched by his academic performance and sought solace in his ability to write. For Kelley, writing was symptomatic of an unending need to know and understand the world in which he lived. He attempted on the one hand to clarify human experience, but in another context, to define the nature of the black experience in white America. As Kelley stated: "I hope only to write fiction until I die, exploring until there is no longer anything to explore . . . the plight of Negroes as *individual human beings* in America. I want to understand it all, but do not think I will venture any answers. . . ." And yet Kelley's work does venture to give answers. In his novels, he clearly defines what it means to be black in America, and during his early phases as a writer, much of this definition was formed from his own experiences.

The cultural backdrop of white America would play a large role in the formation of the psyche of William Melvin Kelley. Kelley learned

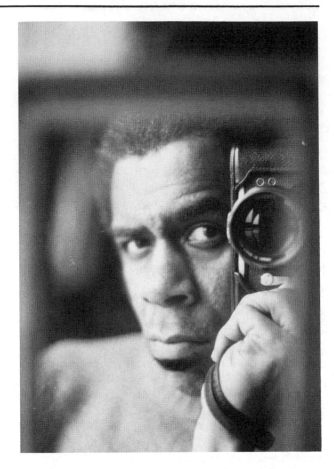

"Me In Mirror," photo by Kelley (© Eyely Foto)

early how the preconceived notions white America held of him and his people could constrain him. He recounts his experiences in childhood games where he was forced to play Tonto or the "friendly native." When, in an attempt to resist this pigeonholing, he told his friends he had a white relative, they said it was untrue because he was colored. Yet, it was true; Kelley's grandmother was white in appearance, and even more ironic, her father was the first Confederate officer killed in the Battle of Bull Run. His personal history illustrated how Kelley was caught between two worlds, and it made him realize the ambiguous position he held in American society.

Kelley would always labor against the preconceived notions of whites, because he was constantly aware of "growing up in one of the most racist countries in the world." His vision of America would act as a backdrop against which he would attempt to define himself and his role as an artist. That attempt reaped its first reward in 1960, when Kelley won the Dana Reed Prize from Harvard for the best piece of writing published in an undergraduate publication. Other awards and honors followed, making Kelley one of the foremost literary voices of the 1960s. He won the Richard and Hinda Rosenthal Award of the National Institute of Arts and Letters (1963) for *A Different Drummer* (1962), his first novel. While working on the novel in 1962, Kelley was awarded a fellowship to the Bread Loaf Writers' Conference; he also received a fellowship to the New York Writers Conference. In 1965, he became author-in-residence at the State University of New York, Geneseo. He was also awarded a grant from the John Hay Whitney Foundation, and, for a while, he taught at the New School for Social Research.

Kelley's resistance as a child to being stereotyped grew into a fierce resistance as an adult to such classifications. This defiant independence manifested itself in the focus of his writings; initially, he concentrated on his individual concerns rather than on those of his race. He felt it was time for "the individual Negro to come out from behind the shield of race." No doubt his experience at Bread Loaf helped him to feel that "each Negro must realize that his worth as a human being comes from his being unique, not a member of a race or a party or a club or group. . . . Any respect you can get is because of your humanness." In the beginning stages of his writing career, Kelley saw that to be black in America was an amalgam of many experiences, yet many white and even black leaders sought to view black consciousness as a single entity. The individual has an obligation, Kelley believed, to focus more on "what we really are: human beings, not simply members of a race."

Throughout his first novel, *A Different Drummer*—most likely begun in Hawkes's class—Kelley explores the racial situation in the mythical Willson City in a nameless Southern state. Taking its title from Thoreau, *A Different Drummer* is the story of Tucker Caliban, whose "different drummer" causes him to hear the beat of his African ancestors, who would have resisted the drudgery of his sharecropping, near-slave existence. His personal resistance eventually mirrors that of the larger black community, and his story becomes that of a man who, through the sheer force of personal will, sets in motion a powerful chain of events. Initially he buys the land he has sharecropped from David Willson; then he destroys the very land that had destroyed his forefathers. His determined, though quiet, resistance acts as a catalyst for his people.

Tucker's actions begin a mass exodus of blacks from Willson City. When the whites notice the gradual disappearance of their black population, they search for an explanation; they find it in the history of Tucker Caliban. Tucker is the great-great-grandson of an African chieftain. In the first part of the novel, the African hero leads many successful slave revolts and escapes; he attempts to kill his own baby son rather than see him sold into slavery. As the whites in the present attempt to rationalize the strange exodus, they blame Tucker's kinship to the African for his quiet destruction of the status quo. They watch helplessly as Tucker salts his land and truncates the favorite tree of his great-great-grandfather's owner; when he further burns his house and a grandfather clock symbolizing the sentimental attachments forged between the Calibans and Willsons during the days of slavery, the whites are certain that Tucker's actions can be attributed to his African heritage. What they do not see is a man, tired of being constrained by the system, who finally takes his destiny into his own hands. No longer will Tucker carry on the tradition of slavery. He symbolically severs his ties and seizes control of his own life.

Tucker's actions transcend the personal to be-

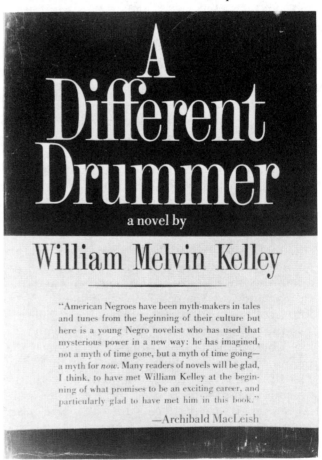

Dust jacket for Kelley's first novel, written while he was in John Hawkes's writing class at Harvard. Archibald MacLeish, who wrote the tribute on the jacket front, was a later writing teacher.

come communal inspiration in triggering similar acts by the black population of Willson City. His example illustrates that an oppressed people must free themselves and not depend upon a leader or liberal reformer to free them. Neither the enlightened whites, as represented by David Willson, nor the black leaders, as represented by Reverend Bradshaw, could lead a people to freedom. David Willson fails as a leader because he lacks the strength to stand by his own convictions; the Reverend Bradshaw changes from a dedicated progressive wanting only the betterment of the race to a manipulative "Black Jesuit" concerned with monetary gain. It is the personal decision, made by each black inhabitant of Willson City, that brings their eventual emancipation.

Critical reaction to Kelley's first novel was, on the whole, favorable. Nat Hentoff saw it as a "remarkable achievement. Written with the forceful economy and inexorable pace of a legend. . . ." Many critics noted Kelley's skill in depicting people rather than abstract representations of racial politics; it was this focus that made *A Different Drummer* the major success it was.

Although Kelley's first story, "Spring Planting," had appeared in *Accent* in 1959, a collection did not appear until 1964. *Dancers on the Shore* continued to demonstrate his development as a writer. In this collection, Kelley once again emphasizes individuality, depicting "people, not symbols or ideas disguised as people," as Nat Hentoff observed. The work lives up to Kelley's warning, stated in the preface, that for the record he is "an American writer who happens to have brown skin."

In a story such as "The Poker Party," it is the awakening of a young boy's sensibility that grips our attention. Kelley's focus in the story is on revealing the adult world through the eyes of a child, and color is only incidentally mentioned: "My father was a tall, very thin Negro. . . . My mother was a small woman and very Spanish, being half that race." The impact of the story comes from gaining a glimpse of a young boy's first realization of what grown-ups are like when their control crumbles. The lonely desperation shared by the two elderly men in "Not Exactly Lena Horne" is a human concern that touches each of us regardless of race. When a pre-law student is torn between a difficult marriage and an imposing career, and his unmarried sister faces the prospect of an unwanted baby, personal and class issues are raised by Kelley more than issues of race relations in America. In "Cry for Me," perhaps the best story in the collection, it is Wallace's personality that arrests our attention as his story completes

the tale of the exodus begun in *A Different Drummer*. The recurring theme in many of the stories is the discovery of personal identity; whether Kelley took the rising middle-class black or a member of the jazz world as a focus, his interest would lie in probing the effect that his characters' acceptance of white American values would have on the individual.

Although *Dancers on the Shore* received the *Transatlantic Review* Award (1964), critical reaction was mixed. Many felt it lacked the skill and power of *A Different Drummer,* and that while attempting to skirt the issue of race, Kelley actually became a victim of the same stereotypes he sought to destroy. While Stephen P. Ryan felt the stories in *Dancers on the Shore* could not be separated from racial themes, he said they "transcend race"; Louis Rubin, Jr., felt that the collection had an "underdeveloped surface" and that many of the stories could not go past addressing the "Negro Problem." Critics, for the most part, gave credit to Kelley for what was on the whole a well-written collection of stories, but they felt neither the technique nor the subject matter showed the promise evident in Kelley's earlier novel.

Kelley's early works mirrored the emphasis on nonviolence as an approach to righting wrongs—a view advocated by the nonviolent civil rights movement; his middle works reflect a growing dissatisfaction with the meager fruits of the movement. Perhaps memories of his experience at Harvard caused Kelley to realize that even integration had a high cost. The more blacks were incorporated into American society, the more they were separated from their own culture. Kelley's works, then, at this point in his career, show a shift in focus from exploring the workings of the individual mind to exploring how varying stimuli affect the psyche. In attempting to investigate the effect of societal influences on the personality, Kelley would simultaneously reconstruct black America's history.

In this new history, Kelley highlights the antecedents of black America. In this vision, he sees the forced transport of blacks from their native lands; he sees that, even after slavery, opportunities open to other ethnic groups were kept closed to blacks; and he sees that after six generations, the African "immigrant" was still not a part of the American mainstream. These observations and many others would represent for Kelley the ambiguous position of the black man in America. In "The Ivy League Negro," Kelley views the plight of Afro-Americans as being not so much that they are different, but that they spend so much time in "painful contemplation of that difference." What

Kelley now envisioned was freeing blacks of the negative associations whites had yoked to them and inspiring a reaffirmation by blacks of their own positive worth.

The internal realization of self-worth would become a dominant element in Kelley's ideology. As early as his stay at Harvard, Kelley felt the academic community had clouded his consciousness of being black and being proud of it. He became aware of the need for a race pride akin to American patriotism, which would stem from each black person taking pride in his personal heritage, not from a blind devotion to race. In these formative academic years, Kelley gained a growing awareness of himself as an individual separate from all groups, and this in turn made it difficult for him to be in touch with his own roots. He saw Harvard as fostering a system of aristocracy which reinforced the gulf he witnessed growing between him and his race. For Kelley, the only antidote was the discovery of his own pride, and this developmental experience shows in his next work, *A Drop of Patience.*

A Drop of Patience (1965) stresses Kelley's growing concern with the ties each man has to the system that produced him. The novel indicates the danger in not having a strong sense of one's personal worth, and it also indicates the many social influences that make for a weak self-conception. Perhaps this shift in Kelley's authorial perspective is accounted for by the fact that he wrote much of *A Drop of Patience* while he and his wife were in Rome. While there, Kelley seemed to gain a wider racial understanding as he realized that the Italians, unlike Americans, were able to acknowledge cultural differences without attaching any value judgments to them. Kelley saw the extent to which social environment affects the development not only of personal identity but also racial identity. *A Drop of Patience* is the story of a man handicapped because he is blind but also because he is black.

From sharecropping to a segregated school for the blind to the dazzle of the New York jazz world, Kelley traces the life of Ludlow Washington. A blind jazz musician (based on the aggregate experiences of musicians who fascinated Kelley at the time, such as Charlie Parker and Donald Byrd), Washington might be said to symbolize the blindness of black Americans unable to see their own value. As a child, Washington is rescued from the brutality of a special school for the blind by the no-less-brutal leader of a second-rate band. During his travels, Washington seduces and marries his landlord's daughter, but leaves wife and child and eventually has an affair with a young, white,

upper-middle-class woman. When Washington's latest lover becomes pregnant, she leaves him to return to the world in which she is more comfortable. Her desertion leaves Washington mentally deranged, and he acts out his misery by debasing himself in a minstrel routine and spending several years in and out of institutions. As the book closes, Washington's career is being resurrected by a jazz critic. He also has a new admirer to help him recover from emotional devastation. Rather than return to fame, however, he opts to return to his roots. He reasons that music comes from and can be made everywhere.

Some critics were very sympathetic to Kelley's third book. In "Only the Sound of his Music," Charles Alva Hoyt commented: "Although . . . William Melvin Kelley's *A Drop of Patience* is the direct and uncompromising story of a Negro musician who lives chiefly among Negroes, it is also something much better: the story of a man." Yet other critics were not as understanding. *Newsweek* lumped Kelley's novel in a review that also covered works by Peter Abrahams, a South African writer; H. Orlando Patterson, a Jamaican; and Roi Ottley, an American. The review considered their works in terms of a sociological rationale, and concluded: "Curiously, the non-Americans . . . have the most to offer in style, insight, and understanding. They are less self-conscious and militant than Harvard-educated William Melvin Kelley or the late Roi Ottley, both of whom write of Negro musicians whose affairs with white women break up against the shoals of the immutable 'ofay' oligarchy. . . . In America the conflict and confrontation between the races tends to obscure the flesh and blood reality of racial experience itself." It was just such interpretations that irked Kelley, and he replied that "half the reason for the Negro literary ghetto is white reviewers."

After spending a year in Rome, Kelley returned to New York in the winter of 1965 with his wife, Karen, and his daughter, Jessica. He took a post as author-in-residence at the State University of New York, Geneseo. With his return, Kelley's ideology seemed to have altered again. He began conceiving of the role of the black author in a larger sense. While he always regarded an author's first allegiance to the creation of art, he now also saw the Afro-American writer as the social and cultural conscience of Afro-American people. Kelley now felt that the black artist must use his skill to aid blacks in counteracting the values white America had given them to replace their own culture. In Kelley's opinion, the writer was also an educator who had a duty to set the thwarted history of his people aright.

As Kelley's communal consciousness grew, he began making political speeches; one of his major themes was the proliferation of the current American myth of black inferiority. Speaking at the Conference on Racism in American Education in March of 1967, Kelley expressed the radically pessimistic view that "there is no hope for American education," for it was within this system, he felt, that the institution of American racism was spread. In this speech, and others at the time, a gradually growing radicalism could be detected, one that would prompt the media to label Kelley a militant.

But Kelley's new move to the left could also be interpreted as the natural reaction of a man realizing the full extent of the injustices done to his people. Kelley saw racism as a culmination of historical lies whites forced blacks to believe; hence Kelley felt that the first step toward dispelling these lies would be a reeducation of both blacks and whites. As a remedy to this, he rewrote American history.

In Kelley's new conception of American history, he spoke of the manner in which the early Americans slew native Americans; how America took Texas and the Southwest from Mexico; and how American forces massacred Koreans and Vietnamese. Kelley felt compelled to rewrite national history because "none of the ugly facts get taught in American history." Kelley's American world became one where genocide and slavery were rationalized in the name of progress and God.

In 1967, Kelley returned to Europe, this time to France. Being in Europe for a year allowed him the objectivity to further reassess the historical relations of blacks to America. While in France Kelley met many Africans, and through this contact he began to appreciate the fact that blacks had a history which reached beyond the United States. By speaking with members of African cultures, Kelley developed a feeling of tradition, a feeling that blacks were no longer a "root-less" people in an American wasteland. Before leaving for Paris, Kelley had commented: "I want to write books that Black people can understand, books that really express African experience." Kelley gained the material for this undertaking while on his second tour of France.

Kelley's next novel, *dem* (1967), echoes the racial tensions of his world. A strongly satirical novel, *dem* is dedicated to "the Black people in (not of) America," and it enables them to have quite a bit of fun at the expense of whites. The novel reflects Kelley's vision of a need for a separatist movement

Dust jacket for Kelley's satirical 1967 novel. "Instead of writing about what American society has done to black people, I've tried to write about what American society is," he stated.

within black literature, with the black author enlightening his people to their true position in American society. As Kelley was to say of *dem,* "I've written it for black people. I've turned the white process on its head. Instead of writing about what American society has done to black people, I've tried to write about what American society is. . . . If black people read it, they can understand what America is and why it is doing what it is doing to them." The novel *dem* represents a reordering of the social history of America. Rather than having blacks as the victims, in this novel it is the whites who suffer as Kelley parodies their traditions and their values. In Kelley's satire, the disillusionment and anger many young minds of the 1960s were feeling are evident.

The story of Tam and Mitchell Pierce centers upon Tam having conceived by "superfecundation," a process by which two ova are fertilized within a short period of time by spermatozoa from separate sexual acts. What separates superfecundation from ordinary twinning is that the female has sex with different males. In the case of Tam, the men are also of two different races: one black and one white. Bored and sheltered by her upper-middle-class existence, and perhaps seeking revenge on her unfaithful husband, Tam has taken a black lover and now finds she is pregnant. Her husband, Mitchell, begins a search for the father of the black twin that leads him to Harlem. Here he is lost and cannot comprehend the language spoken by the denizens. Finally he locates—but does not know he has found—the father, Calvin Coolidge Johnson. Cooley ultimately denies his paternity by exploiting not only Tam but Mitchell as well. In Cooley, Kelley has deposited the social history of blacks, and as such departs from his usual creative technique of primarily delineating individuals. Cooley is a symbol as much as he is a character, and he represents a time when white masters forced black males to accept paternity for illegitimate mulatto offspring. Cooley, as "a long grudge-holding black man," takes a stance for all those who could not protest and avenges the black race through his act of denying Tam's child. When Mitchell finally asks, "Why me?" Cooley coolly replies, "Why my great-granddaddy?"

Kelley's sense of the growing racial polarity in the United States is evident in *dem*. The black and white twins are forever separated by virtue of their races, yet they are joined by a bond which approaches familial ties. Mitchell's inability even to understand the language of Harlem indicates just how large the gulf between the black and white worlds actually is.

The opening portion of *dem* illustrates a second concern of Kelley's at the time, the war in Vietnam. As the novel begins, Kelley reveals the story of John Godwin, a veteran of the Korean War—trained to kill in seventy different ways. His training pays off when he kills his wife and children during a domestic argument and afterwards proceeds to mow the lawn. The vignette about Godwin represents Kelley's growing disapproval of American involvement in Southeast Asia and his realization of the toll exacted from the men who went to serve their country. But it also epitomizes his attack on upper-middle-class white America. Godwin and Mitchell are both young executives; because of this kinship—and through Godwin's actions—Kelley suggests that white America is sterile in the values it pursues and is consciously, deliberately cruel.

The novel *dem* is Kelly's indictment of a society which could produce John Godwin and Mitchell Pierce, both of whom, though they seem to be aberrations, carry the values of the whole group. Kelley sends such a society its punishment in the form of Cooley and the baby he fathers. Finally, Kelley warns America that, like the baby Mitchell Pierce cannot be rid of, the racial hell America has created for blacks will return to haunt her. The book *dem* is Kelley's angry portrait of America at its worst. Overall, the critics reviewed *dem* favorably. The *New York Times Book Review* was typical of current opinion when it praised Kelley for raising vital questions concerning the makeup of our nation's psyche.

After his year in Paris, Kelley returned to the United States once again, bringing with him a new focus on the common cultural ties all descendants of Africa shared and how much of Africa was still present in black America. While in France, Kelley wrote "On Africa in the United States"; in this piece, his developing awareness of Africa's importance to black Americans is apparent. Kelley made note of blacks having a complex oral language system and how many of its remnants still remain today, as seen in the creation of the Gullah dialect and the tales of Brer Rabbit.

In studying Africa, Kelley focused most on the difference between African and European cultures, specifically that one is an oral and the other a written culture. Kelley envisioned the black author harnessing the power of his native oral tradition and using it to erect a system of communication between him and his readers. This new language would act as a barrier, excluding the enemy (whites) from the innermost feelings of blacks. Since black authors were writing of a unique cultural experience, Kelley felt they needed a language form appropriate to this experience, one that was not predominantly the tool of the white writer. An additional change took place, therefore, as Kelley molded his existing literary form to match the changes in his awareness. Each of these alterations would be evidenced in his next book, *Dunfords Travels Everywheres* (1970).

Dunfords Travels Everywheres was completed while Kelley was still living in Paris and while he still desired seeing Africa and learning more about his blackness. In the interim, while composing the novel, he also traveled to Jamaica, an experience which also reinforced his notion of a common ancestry amongst diverse black people. These cross-cultural influences coupled with Kelley's desire to create a new artistic form for the black writer and made *Dunfords Travels Everywheres* Kelley's most experimental novel.

Inspired by *Finnegans Wake* and the problem

Dust jacket for Kelley's 1970 novel inspired by James Joyce's Finnegans Wake

Joyce faced as an Irish writer within a larger English context, *Dunfords Travels Everywheres* is constructed from a language derived from Bantu, Pidgin English, and Harlem argot, among other forms of black speech. Kelley describes it as an escape from the "Langleash language" and a return to the common tongue which binds all the children of Africa. Its use represented a bold experimental step for Kelley and altered the texture of his prose.

Instead of one hero, *Dunfords Travels Everywheres* has two, Chig Dunford and Carlyle Bedlow. Through them, Kelley represents the spectrum of the black experience: the first is a "Harvard black," who relates better to whites than to blacks; and the second is a "Harlem black," who can only move within the circles of the underworld. In actuality they are aspects of the same personality, and in their creation Kelley has moved far from his initial focus of creating characters who are individuals to his present focus of creating characters who are symbolic representations of larger groups.

We follow these two characters through a world of assassinations, a world filled with covert operations of secret societies, and a world where the lower deck of a modern ocean liner holds a slave cargo. In every instance these characters of different backgrounds attempt, each in his own way, to deal with the context of the larger world around them and to discover who they are and how they might be related to each other. Through many episodes—from a narrative of the devil in Harlem to a toast of the major cold war powers—Kelley leads his characters to the answers they seek, yet neither is able to grasp them. Kelley gives ample clues; however, these clues come in the strange language of their dreams. Kelley plays an ironic linguistic trick on Chig and Carlyle, for the truth they seek is contained in the incomprehensible language of their dreams and eludes them in their waking hours. By contrast, the lies they must see through are depicted in standard English. Kelley seems to suggest that one must search through the easy lies of history, those readily available, to the greater truth of black existence. The paradox is that only in an elusive language created from the history and struggle of black people can truths about self and identity be found.

Dunfords Travels Everywheres was a complex undertaking, and while many critics credited Kelley for assuming so bold a task, most felt the language form he created and the difficulty of its reading marred the novel. At best, its formation was considered ingenious, but at worst, it was viewed to lack depth and to be a poor imitation of Joyce's language in *Finnegans Wake*. Whatever the critical reaction to *Dunfords Travels Everywheres*, it did represent Kelley's attempt to create an artistic form for the black author, one which would be more hospitable to his themes than was the written language of the white man.

After this last novel, Kelley's interests continued along a more radically political bent. He became concerned with the ideas and policies of the emerging black nationalists that had been reflected earlier in the voice of Malcolm X. Kelley continued to pursue his racial politics and to be interested in the emergence of Africa and in the revolutionary politics of the Third World.

Kelley's thematic concerns and stylistic experimentation, combined with his political convictions, make him a thoroughly contemporary author. In his personal development, we can see a chapter of our nation's history, and in his literary development, we can note some of the clearest articulations of American culture at the time. As a writer, Kelley seems to have accomplished most of his literary goals; in each of his works we find the impact of shared experience regardless of race. We also find a larger thematic message that captures our nation's character at a precise moment in time.

References:

Willie E. Abrahams, Introduction to *dem* (New York: Collier Books, 1969), pp. vii-xii;

Jervis Anderson, "Black Writing: The Other Side," *Dissent* (May-June 1968): 233-242;

"Black Power: A Discussion," *Partisan Review* (Spring 1968): 216-217;

Addison Gayle, *The Way of the New World: The Black Novel in America* (New York: Anchor, 1975), pp. 367-376;

Felicia George, "Black Woman, Black Man," *Harvard Journal of Afro-American Affairs*, 2 (1971): 1-17;

Trudier Harris, *From Mammies to Militants: Domestics in Black American Literature* (Philadelphia: Temple University Press, 1982), pp. 100-109;

Josef Jarab, "The Drop of Patience of the American Negro: W. M. Kelley's *A Different Drummer* (1959), *A Drop of Patience* (1965)," *Philologica Pragensia*, 12 (1969): 159-170;

Phyllis R. Klotman, "Examination of the Black Confidence Man in Two Black Novels: *The Man Who Cried I am* and *dem*," *American Literature*, 44 (January 1973);

Klotman, "The Passive Resistant in *A Different Drummer, Day of Absence*, and *Many Thousand Gone*," *Studies in Black Literature*, 3 (Autumn 1972): 7-12;

Klotman, "The White Bitch Archetype in Black Fiction," *Bulletin of the Midwest Modern Language Association*, 6 (Spring 1973): 96-110;

Robert L. Nadeau, "Black Jesus: A Study of Kelley's *A Different Drummer*," *Studies in Black Literature*, 2 (Summer 1971): 13-15;

Ray Newquist, *Conversations* (New York: Rand McNally, 1967);

Dudley Randall, "On the Conference Beat," *Negro Digest*, 16 (1967): 89-93;

Stanley Schatt, "You Must Go Home Again: Today's Afro-American Expatriate Writers," *Negro American Literature Forum*, 7 (Fall 1973): 80-82.

John Oliver Killens

(14 January 1916-   )

William H. Wiggins, Jr.
Indiana University

BOOKS: *Youngblood* (New York: Dial Press, 1954;
London: Bodley Head, 1956);

And Then We Heard the Thunder (New York: Knopf,
1963; London: Cape, 1964);

Black Man's Burden (New York: Trident, 1965);

'Sippi (New York: Trident, 1967);

Slaves (New York: Pyramid, 1969);

The Cotillion or One Good Bull Is Half the Herd (New
York: Trident, 1971);

*Great Gittin' Up Morning: A Biography of Denmark
Vesey* (Garden City: Doubleday, 1972);

*A Man Ain't Nothin' But a Man: The Adventures of John
Henry* (Boston: Little, Brown, 1975).

PLAYS: *Ballad of the Winter Soldiers,* Washington,
D.C., Philharmonic Hall, Lincoln Center, 28
September 1964;

Lower Than the Angels, New York, American Place
Theatre, January 1965;

Cotillion, New York, New Federal Theatre, July
1975.

SCREENPLAYS: *Odds Against Tomorrow,* Belafonte
Productions/United Artists, 1960;

Slaves, with Herbert J. Biberman, Theatre Guild,
1969.

OTHER: "God Bless America," in *American Negro
Short Stories,* edited by John Henrik Clarke
(New York: Hill & Wang, 1966), pp. 204-209;

"The Stick Up," in *The Best Short Stories by Negro
Writers: An Anthology from 1899 to the Present,*
edited by Langston Hughes (Boston: Little,
Brown, 1967), pp. 188-191;

"Rough Diamond," in *Harlem* (New York: New
American Library, 1970);

Trial Record of Denmark Vesey, edited with a foreword
by Killens (Boston: Beacon, 1970);

"The Black Writer Vis-à-Vis His Country," in *The
Black Aesthetic,* edited by Addison Gayle, Jr.
(Garden City: Doubleday, 1971), pp. 257-373;

"A White Loaf of Bread," in *To Gwen With Love: An
Anthology Dedicated to Gwendolyn Brooks,* edited
by Patricia L. Brown, Don L. Lee, and Francis
Ward (Chicago: Johnson, 1971), pp. 105-125;

John Oliver Killens (photo by Layle Silbert)

"Rappin With Myself," in *Amistad 2,* edited by John
A. Williams and Charles F. Harris (New York:
Vintage Books, 1971), pp. 97-136;

Woodie King, ed., *Black Short Story Anthology,* introduction by Killens (New York: Columbia University Press, 1972).

PERIODICAL PUBLICATIONS: "Explanation of
the Black Psyche," *New York Times Magazine,* 7
June 1964, pp. 37-38ff.;

"Black Man's Burden," *Ebony,* 20 (August 1965):
173-175;

"Hollywood in Black and White," *Nation,* 201 (20 September 1965): 157-160;

"Brotherhood of Blackness," *Negro Digest,* 15 (May 1966): 4-10;

"Speaking Out," *Saturday Evening Post,* 239 (2 July 1966): 10ff.;

"Broadway in Black and White," *African Forum,* 1 (Winter 1966): 66-70;

"The Black Writer and the Revolution," *Arts in Society,* 5 (1968): 395-399;

"Black Writers' Views on Literary Lions and Values," *Negro Digest,* 17 (January 1968): 31;

"Traveler's Guide," *Redbook,* 133 (July 1969): 55-62;

"The Artist and the Black University," *Black Scholar,* 1 (November 1969): 61-65;

"Another Time When Black Was Beautiful," *Black World,* 20 (1970): 20-36;

"Black Labor and the Black Liberation Movement," *Black Scholar,* 2 (October 1970): 33-39;

"Black Culture Generation Gap," *Black World,* 22 (August 1973): 22-33;

"Wanted: Some Black Long Distance Runners," *Black Scholar,* 5 (November 1973): 2-7;

"Image of Black Folk in American Literature," *Black Scholar,* 6 (June 1975): 45-52;

"Black Man in New China," *Black World,* 25 (November 1975): 28-42;

"Lorraine Hansberry: On Time," *Freedomways,* 19 (November 1979): 273-276.

John Oliver Killens has had a major influence on Afro-American literature. First, he has written steadily; to date he has published four novels, two children's books, a collection of essays, three plays, and two screenplays. In addition to these book-length manuscripts, Killens has published essays and short stories in such popular and scholarly periodicals as the *Saturday Evening Post, Redbook,* the *New York Times Magazine,* the *Black Scholar,* and *Black World.* He also has written a novel based on the life of Pushkin, which has not yet been published.

A second way in which Killens has influenced Afro-American literature has been through his encouragement of other Afro-American writers. He has served as writer-in-residence at Fisk University, Howard University, and Medgar Evers College in Brooklyn. Killens's interest in writers' workshops extended outside the university setting. In the late 1940s he joined John Henrik Clarke, Rosa Guy, and Walter Christmas to found the Harlem Writers Guild. At an early meeting Killens read "in a very trembly voice the first chapter of *Youngblood.*" From this shaky beginning the Guild has served as the

creative forum for a wide range of Afro-American authors: Julian Mayfield, Paule Marshall, Piri Thomas, Jean Bond, Irving Burgie, Charlie Russell, Alice Childress, Loyle Hairston, Douglas Turner Ward, Maya Angelou, Sarah Wright, Lonne Elder III, Sylvester Leaks, and Bill Ford. Loften Mitchell and Irving Burgie read a *Ballad for Bimshire* in the workshop. But perhaps the best example of the influence of the Harlem Writers Guild is that it was at one of its meetings that Ossie Davis read a rough draft of *Purlie,* the long-running Broadway musical and popular motion picture.

A third reason for Killens's literary significance can be found in his creative use of Afro-American folklore. Not since James Weldon Johnson has there been an Afro-American writer who has made as much use of traditional Afro-American themes. His four novels are replete with traditional jokes, folktales, legends, beliefs, blues, ballads, and spirituals. *'Sippi,* his third novel, is a protest novel which he based on a popular civil rights joke in which the new militant mood of Afro-Americans is summed up by the black man refusing to even "Miss" Mississippi; from now on he will simply call it 'Sippi. Killens's two children's books are based on folk materials.

Killens's leadership role among Afro-American protest writers is a fourth reason for his current prominence. Killens has fashioned his career in the protest mold of Richard Wright. For both of these writers the primary purpose of art is to attack and ultimately change society for the better. On one occasion Killens gave this version of his literary creed: "As a writer, I must believe with all my heart and soul in the ancient adage 'You shall know the truth and the truth shall set you free.' In a far deeper sense even than men of the cloth, writers must be searchers for the truth; men and women whose life's mission is to explore the truth of man's relationship to man. . . . As a writer, I must believe that most of what has already been said is a pack of lies, or, in some instances mistakes, to be more charitable to makers of the myths. It is up to the writer to create a new vision for mankind. He must be forever asking questions." And, on still another occasion, he said, "Art is life and life is art. All art is social, all art is propaganda, not withstanding all propaganda is not art. The ultimate purpose of art is to teach man about himself and his relationship with other men." Afro-American writers of a similar persuasion have been attracted to Killens. In fact, Addison Gayle, Jr., the Afro-American literary scholar, has labeled Killens "the spiritual father" of the black American novel.

Killens acknowledges Richard Wright, Langston Hughes, and Margaret Walker as his literary mentors. He admires Wright "because of the awesome . . . word power, his righteous anger, his indignation, his great success, his impact on the western world." He idolizes Hughes "because he loved Black people more than any other writer, before or after him." But it is in his discussion of Margaret Walker that Killens alludes to his conception of the proper relationship between art and propaganda: "Margaret's 'For My People' and her 'We Have Been Believers' are the most powerful and the most beautiful poems I have ever read. 'For My People' is a poetic autobiography of the African-American. In terms of Black and beautiful rhythms it taught me more than any other piece of literature. In my own writing I am always under the influence of the flowing rhythmic beauty of that poem. It is beautiful, powerful, full of healing truths that set men free; it is all this and revolutionary." In short, Killens admires these three writers because they give substance to his contention that "Art is social and political, takes a position for humanity or against. Art is functional. A Black work of art helps the liberation movement or hinders it." Furthermore, Killens senses in their writings an agreement with his own definition of the Afro-American writer's role: "The American Negro must write about himself and in so doing he writes about America—its inhumanity, brutality and violence. Even though white America has tried to forget, deny and destroy its history, the Negro cannot, he 'must face . . . [it] squarely in order to transcend it.' "

Many snatches of Killens's personal life appear in his fiction, especially his four novels. To paraphrase B. B. King, Killens has in a large measure lived the life he writes about in his books. Killens was born in Macon, Georgia, in 1916. He credits his parents with introducing him to Afro-American literature. His father made certain that his son read Langston Hughes's weekly column in the *Chicago Defender*. And his mother, who was president of the Dunbar Literary Club, taught him the intricate rhythms and tonalities of Paul Laurence Dunbar's poetry. At school he attended Negro History Week programs which featured recitations of such Afro-American poems as James Weldon Johnson's *God's Trombones*. This family and public school exposure to Afro-American literature planted the seed of his style of writing, which is based upon Afro-American folklore.

While growing up in Macon, Killens experienced several events which were later incorporated into his fiction. He and several of his classmates were arrested for engaging in an after-school fight with some white schoolboys. This experience appears in *Youngblood,* with Robby Youngblood being arrested for fighting white boys and only being released after his mother, Mrs. Laurie Lee Youngblood, has been forced to whip her son in the presence of the arresting officers. Killens's home church was the headquarters of "Operation Dixie," a Congress of Industrial Organizations (CIO) campaign to organize black and white workers in Macon. It was during this time that he heard such white advice as "stay away from that union mess. It's nothing but a whole lot of communism!" He also saw Mr. Larkin Marshall, a member of his church and local black businessman, take the heroic stance of backing the movement. Similar union organizers appear in *Youngblood, 'Sippi,* and *A Man Ain't Nothin' But a Man.*

In 1936, Killens left Macon and moved to Washington, D.C., where he took a job with the National Labor Relations Board. He held this position through 1942. Killens served in the United States Amphibian Forces in the South Pacific from 1942 to 1945. This period in his life provides the foundation for his second novel, *And Then We Heard the Thunder.* In 1946 he returned to civilian life and rejoined the NLRB. Brooklyn was now home for Killens and his family. During this postwar period Killens spent two frustrating years trying to organize black and white workers for the CIO. He philosophically recalled the experience: "For two years I was a CIO organizer. I had hopes that we could liberate the nation by joining hands with the white working class. Big mistake, but I learned from it. . . . When the labor movement didn't make it and was co-opted by the establishment, I said to myself, 'Okay, that's that.' I didn't really believe it anymore." This disenchantment with the ability of organized labor, religion, or the United States government to create an American society with "liberty and justice for all" became a more insistent theme in each of his four novels. As the civil rights movement wound down in the late 1960s, Killens spent 1967 and 1968 serving as writer-in-residence at Fisk University in Nashville, Tennessee. The events of this period serve as the foundation for *'Sippi.*

Killens's major themes evolve around social protest and cultural affirmation. All of his writings protest American racism in its social, economic, and political forms. Killens also singles out for ridicule those Afro-Americans ashamed of their color or who deny their rich African and Afro-American heritage. Philosophically, he protests against the concept of nonviolence as a means of liberating

Afro-Americans from the restrictions of American racism. Again and again Killens affirms the right of self-defense for Afro-Americans. Major cultural themes affirmed in Killens's writing include black manhood, a concept defined by the author as the ability to think and act independently of white social pressure or physical intimidation. Coming of age is another dominant theme utilized by Killens. *Youngblood*'s Robby Youngblood, *And Then We Heard the Thunder*'s Solly Saunders, *'Sippi*'s Chuck Chaney, and *The Cotillion*'s Yoruba Evelyn Lovejoy are all young Afro-Americans affected by the trauma of entering adulthood. Killens's characters do not make this transition alone; instead he places their struggle within the social context of the Afro-American family, another popular theme in Killens's novels. Thus, it is not surprising to hear Killens denounce the "Glorification by black artists of the whore, pimp and pushers." In Killens's mind these are individual Afro-Americans who have chosen life-styles at cross purposes to the Afro-American family.

Youngblood (1954), Killens's first novel, is a family saga which chronicles the struggle of the Youngbloods. The family is composed of the parents, Joe and Laurie Lee, and two adolescent children, Jennie Lee and her younger brother, Robby. It is through these four characters that Killens exposes his readers to what life was like for Afro-Americans living in the American South during the first third of this century. The novel demonstrates how these four characters band together to overcome the economic, educational, social, and religious manifestations of Jim Crow life in their hometown of Crossroads, Georgia. The question posed by Killens is: Will democracy ever come to the American South? Killens leaves the question unanswered. The novel begins with Joe Youngblood's frustration in his attempt to flee the South and find a better life in the North and ends with his death as a civil rights martyr. Other major characters include Richard Wendell Myles, Robby Youngblood's teacher, who has just moved south from Brooklyn to take his first teaching position. He is Robby's idol and provides a positive role model for the maturing Robby. The other major character is Oscar Jefferson, a poor white laborer who is befriended by Little Jim Kilgrow, an Afro-American peer who refuses to accept the subservient role that Jim Crow dictates for him.

The theme of racial brotherhood is treated in several ways by Killens. One way is found in his naming the town where the novel is set Crossroads. The Youngbloods stand at the crossroads of the

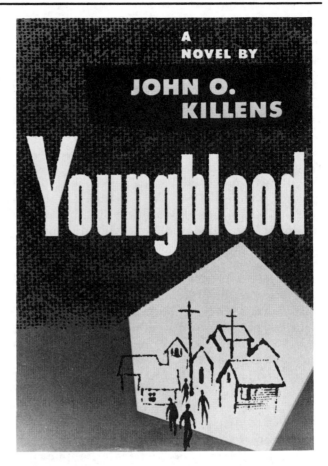

Dust jacket for Killens's first novel, the story of a Southern black family's struggles during the first third of the twentieth century

traditional Southern Jim Crow way of life and the new, Northern-based democratic way of life. They have opted to travel the new, unexplored road.

Killens's characters reflect his faith in racial brotherhood as an antidote to racism. On one occasion Richard Myles recalls how he advised his white friend Dr. Riley to redirect his missionary efforts in the direction of Southern whites: "Dr. Riley's old man was a missionary. The American Missionary Association sent him here from Vermont to teach at Talledega. And I reckon Dr. Riley considers himself dedicated to his father's work. I told him the colored didn't need any missionaries. He needed to work on those uncivilized white folks, because they were the most ignorant and unscientific and barbarous people on the face of the earth." At the end of the novel, by appealing to his colleague's basic humanity, Richard Myles prompts Dr. Riley to break the medical taboo of Southern medicine and treat the wounded Joe Youngblood at a white hospital. As Joe Youngblood's life hangs in the balance, Richard Myles argues, "You're a sensible sensitive human being, Doctor. And more than just Joe's life is at stake here. Your own integrity is on the block. You're not like that mob downtown. I know you're not. And I'm just demanding that you live up to who you really are." The white men Oscar Jefferson and his son also heed this appeal by agreeing to be tested to see if their blood types match that of the wounded Joe Youngblood. The younger Jefferson qualifies as a donor and agrees to donate blood for Joe Youngblood's transfusion.

Reflecting his National Labor Relations Board leanings, Killens believes the best hope for the future of racial brotherhood in the South lies with organized labor. Just prior to leaving the house to attempt to organize a union of hotel workers, Joe Youngblood says to his son, Robby, "I done come to realize that colored ain't gon get nowhere at all lessen they get together and stay together. Boy, if y'all be successful in forming a union in Crossroads, Georgia, and with white in it, too, y'alla be unbeatable, and y'alla go down in history just as sure as you're born." Inspired by the fatherly advice, Robby Youngblood assumes the tough task of unionizing, just as Killens himself had done for the CIO.

Youngblood abounds in black male characters who have to struggle to keep their manhood. Mr. Myles feels that Crossroads policemen "had castrated him of his manhood" when they stopped him and his future wife Miss Josephine Rollins on their walk home. A similar sense of powerlessness is experienced by Joe Youngblood each payday when he is shortchanged by the company clerk. Young Robby Youngblood is whipped by his mother because he dares to defend his sister's honor by fighting some white schoolboys. Robby has a recurring nightmare: "Robby dreamed every night the Good Lord sent . . . two mighty armies gathered in a great wide open space. Weighted down with all kinds of arms—swords, guns, knives—Everything! On one side was massed a great White army with ugly ghostlike faces, evil and leering. And on the other side the great Black army, proud and handsome and fierce and brave and everything else." This dream becomes reality later in the novel when the black men guarding the wounded Joe Youngblood engage in a brief shoot-out with the Ku Klux Klan which results in the Klan being routed: "And the white hooded figures and torch lights on the road scattered and scampered back the way they came from as the dust did fly."

Critical reception to *Youngblood* was favorable. Granville Hicks in the *New York Times* found fault with Killens's prose: "Rather crudely written, in a vernacular style that is often tiring, and at moments flatly didactic, it has the power of the author's passion." But he concluded, "The novel of social protest, which survives precariously today, justifies itself when it is as moving as 'Youngblood' and deals with so gross an evil." Although fellow black novelist Ann Petry found fault with Killens's excessive repetition of "scenes of hate-inspired violence" in her *New York Herald Tribune* review, she added, "This is a fine novel, vivid, readable. Even its minor characters . . . are as arresting as its major ones."

And Then We Heard the Thunder (1963), Killens's second novel, is an attempt at "the great American war novel." A segregated World War II amphibious unit is the setting for Killens's protest against the United States Army's Jim Crow policies. The novel's major characters include Joe "Bookworm" Taylor, the company comic; Jerry Abraham Lincoln "Scotty" Scott, the trouble-prone company cook; and Lt. Robert Samuels, a liberal Jewish officer from New York City, in many ways an extension of fair-minded white characters like *Youngblood*'s Dr. Riley and Oscar Jefferson. The novel's hero is Solly Saunders, a newly married enlisted man who dropped out of law school to take advantage of the army's Officer's Training School. As he becomes disillusioned with the army, he engages in long arguments with Lieutenant Samuels which are similar to Richard Myles's debates with Dr. Riley. The only thing that has changed is the subject: Southern racism has been replaced with the army's institutional racism.

The three major civilian characters are all lovers of Solly Saunders. First, there is Millie Belford Saunders, Solly's bride. She comes from a prominent family in Brooklyn, and her aspirations are solidly middle class. Like the author's bride, she wants her husband to earn his lieutenant's bars, leave the army after the war, and become rich and famous. Fannie Mae Branton, the young Southern schoolteacher that Solly Saunders has an affair with during boot training, is the second woman. The third woman is Celie Blake, a white Australian nurse who nurses Solly Saunders back to physical and psychological health.

Several of the major themes debated by these characters are political in nature. Solly Saunders initially perceives the war to be more than a racial conflict. During one of the company's countless bull sessions he argues, "This is not a racial war. This is a war of democracy against fascism pure and simple." But he has second thoughts by the novel's end when he is leading his men into a bloody racial conflict against white American soldiers stationed in Australia.

The black nationalist concept of self-love also emerges for the first time in Killens's fiction. After reading Richard Wright's *Twelve Million Black Voices* Solly Saunders concludes: "If I love me, I can also love the whole damn human race. Black, brown, yellow, white. Thank you, Richard." Killens will reuse this theme extensively in *'Sippi* and *The Cotillion*. Furthermore, this self-love includes an acceptance of the Afro-American's African heritage. Hence, by the novel's conclusion Solly Saunders can describe himself as a "Proud black American me, whose ancestors came from great Africa."

But once again manhood is the major theme. Like Joe Youngblood and Richard Myles in *Youngblood,* Solly Saunders and his men must fight paternalism and a psychologically castrating brand of American racism. The only difference is that in the second novel it is the United States Army and not a Southern town that instigates and sustains the racial oppression. Thus Fannie Mae Branton advises Solly: "I'll always love you . . . because you demand your dignity and manhood. Manhood is more important than money or promotion. . . . Never sacrifice your manhood—never sacrifice your manhood." And this is precisely what Solly does at the end of the novel when he joins his men and thereby forfeits a chance for Officer's Candidate School.

Reviewers of the novel tended to find fault with Killens's style while praising the book's message. P. A. Doyle's *Best Sellers* review was critical of Killens's prose: "Some of the characters are simply mouthpieces for various viewpoints. Other figures are too consciously motivated by the author. The love scenes are routine—torrid, raw, and overdone in the popular fashion. The style is often too rhetorical, too hysterical, too shrill." But, he continued: "And yet one tends to forgive most of these weaknesses because of the importance and validity of Mr. Killens's message. The author's earnestness and the obvious justice of his analysis and warning are particularly compelling and sobering." J. H. Griffin's *Saturday Review* comment on the novel also found fault with Killens's style but praised his descriptive ability, characterizations, and message: "his characters live and speak the raw language of the streets and the barracks. . . . The reader, living all the indignities of the Negro soldiers, sees clearly how it looked from the other side of the color line."

From 1954 through 1970 Killens was active in the civil rights movement. In 1955 he went to Alabama to participate in the Montgomery bus boycott and visited with Martin Luther King. In Brooklyn he worked closely with the NAACP, but he began to have serious doubts about the general appeal and effectiveness of this civil rights group as he witnessed Malcolm X's ability to draw large crowds in Harlem. By 1965 when Malcolm X, then his friend, was assassinated, Killens had fully embraced black nationalism.

Black Man's Burden (1965), a collection of political essays, demonstrates the shift in Killens's philosophy. In the series of essays on such subjects as white paternalism, black manhood, unions, sit-ins, boycotts, religion, black nationalism, Africa, nonviolence, and the right of self-defense, Killens argued that passive acceptance of racial oppression only encourages more racial violence. Killens believed that the only way blacks could break the vicious cycle of racial violence would be to respond to white violence with black violence.

Killens's third novel, *'Sippi* (1967), reflects his new militancy. The title of the novel comes from a civil rights protest joke in which a black man tells his white landlord:

> Ain't no more Mr. Charlie,
> It's just Charles from now on.
> Ain't no more Miss Ann
> It's just Ann
> And another thing,
> Ain't no more Mississippi
> Ain't no more Mississippi
> It's just plain 'Sippi from now on!

Set in the 1960s, *'Sippi* chronicles the black college student voting-rights struggle of that era. Malcolm X, Stokely Carmichael, Harry Belafonte, Paul Robeson, and Martin Luther King, Jr., are some figures Killens weaves into the fabric of this protest novel. He recounts in vivid detail the bombings, shootings, and other acts of terror and intimidation endured by the courageous students and local blacks who dare stand up and push for voter registration.

Several of Killens's major characters come from two Mississippi families, one white, the other black. The black family is composed of Jesse Chaney, a Mississippi sharecropper; his wife, Carrie Mae; and their youngest child, Charles Othello, whose name was inspired by Paul Robeson's portrayal of Shakespeare's tragic hero. The white family members are Charles James Richard Wakefield, the community father; his wife, Anne Barkley, a literary rendering of pristine Southern womanhood; and their only child, Carrie Louise, a young Southern woman who is not inhibited by her parents' sexual mores. Killens tells his story primarily

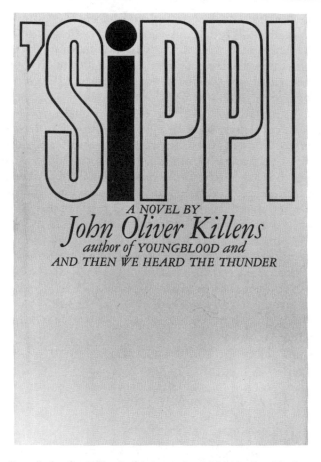

Dust jacket for Killens's third novel, which takes its title from the folk story about a stubborn black man who refuses to honor Mississippi with the title "Missis" anymore—he calls her just plain 'Sippi

through the lives of the two children caught up in the psychological and physical rigors of passing from adolescence into adulthood.

In *'Sippi* Killens makes the affluent black middle-class neighborhood of Crowning Heights (Brooklyn home of Cheryl Kingsley, Carrie Louise Wakefield's black college roommate) the intimate setting in which pertinent social, economic, and political issues are discussed. Hence, it is at a Kingsley party that Carrie Louise is rudely rebuffed by her black peers. Killens also fills this party scene with heated discussions of integration, separation, nonviolence, and self-defense. Prior to *'Sippi* Killens had placed all of his ideological discussions in Southern black settings.

Critics tended to either like or dislike *'Sippi*. There was no middle ground. An example of a favorable evaluator is John Henry Jones, who wrote in his *Freedomways* review that *Sippi* was "a poetic tapestry, richly woven with folkways speech, move-

ment, ideas, colors, smells, sounds and emotions." A cryptic example of an unfavorable reaction to the novel is *Negro Digest* reviewer Ronald Williams's assessment of *'Sippi* as being a "classically bad novel with plodding events which lead nowhere." Killens himself does not rank *'Sippi* as highly as his first two novels.

Killens's fourth novel, *The Cotillion or One Good Bull Is Half the Herd* (1971), is a literary dozens. Through hyperbole and cutting social and political commentary, Killens's novel becomes a biting didactic piece of Afro-American literature written in the tradition of verbal contests known as the dozens to many Afro-Americans. The object of the game is to unsettle one's verbal opponent with exaggerated statements of personal insult. This is precisely the plot of this novel. It begins peacefully enough with an orderly world. The Femmes Fatales, an exclusive black women's club of Crowning Heights in Brooklyn, are planning one of their annual Cotillion balls in which the cream of Brooklyn's "Negro Society" is presented in a series of social events completely devoid of Afro-American culture. But by novel's end Killens has reduced this sedate group of society matrons to a confused and disorganized group of babbling black women who have been verbally stripped of their thin veneer of white middle-class values and exposed for what they truly are: comically tragic Afro-Americans who are out of touch with their cultural heritage.

As in his first novel, Killens's primary characters—with one exception—come from one Afro-American family, the Lovejoys. First is Matthew "Matt" Lovejoy, the father, who migrated to Harlem from Georgia during the 1920s. A redcap who enjoys such cultural experiences as spending a Saturday afternoon in the neighborhood barbershop listening to the jokes and the philosophizing of customers and friends, he addresses the common values of the community. He is married to Daphne Doreen Braithwaite Lovejoy, an immigrant from Christ Church in Barbados. She has little or no appreciation for her husband's cultural tastes and has devoted herself to rearing their child in a way that excludes any reference to Afro-American culture. Caught in the middle is their eighteen-year-old daughter, Yoruba Evelyn Lovejoy. She is confronted with decisions of college, love, and culture. Yoruba's childhood sweetheart, Ernest Walter Billings, is the other major character; he returns from the Vietnamese War with a new name, Ben Ali Lumumba, and a new profession, writing. Killens makes him the cultural adviser to Mrs. Lovejoy.

All of Killens's themes are directed toward his

Dust jacket for Killens's fourth novel, about black class divisions written specifically for a black audience

Afro-American class division is the major theme in this novel. Killens approaches the problem by describing the community life in two of New York City's black communities: Harlem and Crowning Heights. Life in the latter community is culturally sterile, a point that Killens alludes to with his description of Mrs. Prissy Patterson's plastic-covered furniture and the Femmes Fatales' expensive wigs. This plastic-covered furniture is cold and painful to sit on, and the wigs will not grow. Life in Harlem is portrayed by the author in a much more positive light. "Matt" Lovejoy looks forward to his weekly snooze in the barber's comfortable leather chair, from which he can catch all of the customers signifying, joking, and philosophizing; and the Afro hairstyles sported by the majority of these Harlemites were fashioned from real, growing hair into a style that symbolizes black pride instead of white middle-class values.

Killens's message is clear and simple: black people must first unite with each other if they are ever going to be truly liberated. Black African, West Indian, black nationalist, black bourgeois, and the black masses must turn their collective backs on Western civilization's decaying culture and return to mother Africa for strength and cultural direction. Killens's climax paints this message in broad literary strokes when Lumumba leads the Lovejoys and several other Afro-Americans out of the Cotillion ballroom.

Reviewers for the *New Yorker* and the *Atlantic Monthly* were critical of the novel's prose and plot. The *New Yorker* reviewer wrote: "From its promising start as a portrait of the Harlem scene in its non-statistical variety and vitality, the novel degenerates into a mean-spirited, mechanically bawdy, and scarcely relevant satire upon a group of brown ladies whose quaint cotillion is shattered by a dashiki." Phoebe Adams reverses this critique in her *Atlantic Monthly* review: "If characters and author were white, this social comedy about the debutante racket would be as trite as a Doris Day movie. Since the characters are black and the black author is a wily blend of clown and porcupine, the moribund plot bounces merrily back to life." Leonard Fleischer in a *Saturday Review* article describes Killens's prose as being "often buoyantly evocative and musical" and "at times genuinely funny. . . ." J. R. Frakes's assessment in the *New York Times Book Review* is even more laudatory: "[*The Cotillion*] is clearly not what timid traditionalists have agreed to call a novel. . . . Everything in [it] is triple life-size, every action. . . . The whole laughing, howling, bursting career of the book zooms like a caricature-missile

Afro-American readers. The grand dream of *Youngblood*'s racial brotherhood is redefined here in terms of the various world communities of black people. Once Lumumba puts on shades and walks down a busy street, he draws mistaken praise from blacks, in much the same way that various segments of the Harlem community mistake the identity of the college student in Ralph Ellison's *Invisible Man*. His skillful dancing of the "high life" causes West Africans to claim him as one of their own. His colorful dashiki and easy grace in executing the nationalist's handshake cause him to be admired by such nationalist groups as the Black Beautiful Bad Mother Fuckahs (BBBMF). His uncommon good looks and full Afro hairstyle make him a favorite of the black bourgeois debutantes, who are participating in the Cotillion. His urbane conversation and glowing references to Barbados endear him to Mrs. Lovejoy, the West Indian.

toward the biggest Everlasting Yea. . . . Yea to 'the real world,' the black nation, Afro-natural hairdos, dashikis, Negritude. When the missile detonates, much more than whitey is demolished: cotton patches, bourgeois aspirations, black intraracial caste snobbery [and] hustlers of black nationalism. . . . Every stop is pulled all the way out. . . . Let's say it again—'The Cotillion' is not a 'novel.' And who cares?"

Killens's latest works are directed toward younger readers. *Great Gittin' Up Morning*, a biographical novel based upon the life of Denmark Vesey, the free black man who led the Charleston, South Carolina, revolt of 1822, was published in 1972. Three years later, Killens published *A Man Ain't Nothin' But a Man* (1975), which is the author's fictional account of the life and times of John Henry, the Afro-American ballad hero. Killens returns to three of his major themes in these two works. The importance of armed resistance in the black liberation movement is restated in his Vesey novel: "Denmark Vesey, Gabriel Prosser, Nat Turner, and John Brown all believed that blood would have to flow before Black men would be liberated. History has not proven them mistaken." Racial brotherhood and the need for a union are dominant themes in Killens's study of John Henry. Killens gives this folk hero two interracial companions in George Lang Lee, a Chinese worker, and Big Ben Lawson, a poor Southern white laborer; and, he places this prayer for labor in the mouth of John Henry: "Help me, Lord, in what I'm trying to do this morning. Help my wife to understand me. I'm trying to show the world that man is your greatest creation, man and woman. The onliest things you ever made on this earth in your own precious image. I'm trying to say, Jehovah, that man made the machine and he must control it, else it's gon get outa control and roll right over him, and when that happens, man's days on this blessed earth gon be numbered." However, these last two novels do not measure up to Killens's first four works. Both novels are top-heavy with their messages of social protest. As a result, their narrative flow, plot development, and character development suffer.

John Oliver Killens remains a dominant figure in Afro-American literature; and as vice-president of the Black Academy of Arts and Letters and a member of the executive board of the National Center of Afro-American Artists, he continues to encourage his peers and fledgling authors to write. But, more than that, he continues to comment on the quality of black life in America through his writings, with an eye toward changing it for the better. For as he once wrote, "Every time I set down to the typewriter, with every line I put on the paper, I am out to change the world, to capture reality, to melt it down and forge it into something entirely different." It is this zeal and literary skill that make John Oliver Killens a major Afro-American writer.

References:

Abner Berry, "Crossroads, Georgia," *Masses & Mainstream,* 7 (September 1954): 16-19;

Addison Gayle, Jr., *The Way of the World: The Black Novel in America* (Garden City: Anchor Press/Doubleday, 1975), pp. 261-277;

Horst Ihde, "Black Writer's Burden: Remarks on John Oliver Killens," *Zeitschrift für Anglistik und Amerikanistik,* 16 (January 1968): 117-137;

Phyllis R. Klotman, "The White Bitch Archetype in Contemporary Black Fiction," *Bulletin of the Midwest Modern Language Association,* 6 (Spring 1973): 96-110;

William H. Wiggins, Jr., "Black Folktales in the Novels of John O. Killens," *Black Scholar,* 3 (November 1971): 50-58;

Wiggins, "The Structure and Dynamics of Folklore in the Novel Form: The Case of John O. Killens," *Keystone Folklore Quarterly,* 17 (1972): 92-118.

Clarence Major

(31 December 1936-   )

Joe Weixlmann
Indiana State University

BOOKS: *The Fires that Burn in Heaven* (Chicago, 1954);

Love Poems of a Black Man (Omaha, Nebr.: Coercion Press, 1965);

Human Juices (Omaha, Nebr.: Coercion Press, 1966);

All-Night Visitors (New York: Olympia Press, 1969);

Dictionary of Afro-American Slang (New York: International Publishers, 1970); republished as *Black Slang: A Dictionary of Afro-American Talk* (London: Routledge & Kegan Paul, 1971);

Swallow the Lake (Middletown, Conn.: Wesleyan University Press, 1970);

Private Line (London: Paul Breman, 1971);

Symptoms & Madness (New York: Corinth Books, 1971);

The Cotton Club (Detroit: Broadside Press, 1972);

NO (New York: Emerson Hall, 1973);

The Dark and Feeling: Black American Writers and Their Work (New York: Third Press, 1974);

The Syncopated Cakewalk (New York: Barlenmir House, 1974);

Reflex and Bone Structure (New York: Fiction Collective, 1975);

Emergency Exit (New York: Fiction Collective, 1979).

OTHER: *Writers Workshop Anthology*, edited by Major (New York: Harlem Education Project, 1967);

Man Is a Child, edited by Major (New York: Macomb's Junior High School, 1968);

The New Black Poetry, edited by Major (New York: International Publishers, 1969; London: Central Books, 1969).

Clarence Major (photo by Layle Silbert)

Although Clarence Major is best known for his fiction, he has succeeded in a wide variety of linguistic undertakings. Poet, novelist, essayist, anthologist, editor, and lexicographer—Major has proved to be one of Afro-America's most versatile literary figures. In two of his most recently published novels, *Reflex and Bone Structure* (1975) and *Emergency Exit* (1979), he has pioneered a new direction for black American fiction, expressing his psychological, racial, and social concerns within a metafictional framework that leads his readers to explore, with him, the very nature of fictive discourse.

Major was born in Atlanta, Georgia, in 1936, but following his parents' divorce while Major was still a child, he and a younger sister moved to Chicago with their mother. The children did, however, maintain an enriching Southern connection by returning for summer visits to the homes of their father, their grandmothers, and various other relatives. By his mid-teens, Major had become so enchanted by Impressionist art, especially the paintings of Van Gogh, that he was driven by the thought of setting up a studio in Paris and establishing himself as "a *very* great artist." But a brief stint at the Art

153

Institute of Chicago, when Major was seventeen, convinced him that he had neither the conceptual nor the rendering skills possessed by many others at the Institute; and he began to reconsider the likelihood of his artistic aspirations achieving fruition. Although he has, to this day, not turned away from the visual arts (as the paintings interspersed with the written text of *Emergency Exit* indicate), Major began, shortly after his Art Institute experience, to succumb to a new enchantress. Having a few years earlier begun to explore the literary worlds of Raymond Radiguet, Arthur Rimbaud, and other French novelists and poets, Major, in his mid-to-late teens, started reading more deliberately and, in time, began to think of himself as a writer. Among black authors, Chester Himes, and especially Richard Wright and Willard Motley, also came to Major's attention early, but they had a less overt impact on the young Major's craft than did the European authors who fired his imagination.

Before joining the air force in 1955, Major had published *The Fires that Burn in Heaven* (1954), a twelve-page pamphlet containing what he now regards as "very, very bad poetry," but he was to produce enough poems and short stories of some quality during his two years in the military that his self-confidence in his writing ability increased. After spending some time in Omaha, Nebraska, where he was employed as a steelworker immediately following his air force discharge in 1957, Major returned to Chicago, where he continued to hone his poetic skills, started writing novels, and, in 1958, began editing and publishing the *Coercion Review,* a venture which was to continue through 1961 and bring him into contact with William Carlos Williams, Allen Ginsberg, Robert Creeley, and other writers of note. Relocating in Omaha once more in 1964, following the dissolution of his first of three unsuccessful marriages, Major soon established links with the local writers' community, and under the Coercion Press imprint, he brought out his *Love Poems of a Black Man* in 1965 and *Human Juices* a year later. Although both of these volumes of poems were printed on a mimeograph machine and distributed in editions of several hundred copies, mostly to friends, the majority of the work is mature and reappeared in 1970 in *Swallow the Lake,* Major's first important collection of verse, completed in 1967. By 1966, then, Major was a bona fide author, and so it comes as no surprise that the year found him moving to New York City, the writers' mecca.

The cluster of authors who composed the Umbra Workshop—including Tom Dent, David Henderson, Calvin Hernton, Ishmael Reed, and A. S. M. Touré—were in their last days as a unit when Major arrived in New York and settled on the Lower East Side. Not a joiner, Major attended some of the Umbra meetings and became immersed in the black literary scene in New York, but he did not become a member of Umbra or any other group.

The year 1967 marks Major's entry into the field of education. His membership on the faculty of the New Lincoln School led to his editing a *Writers Workshop Anthology* in 1967, the same year in which he completed an unpublished, sixty-five-page report on the race riots in Detroit and Milwaukee entitled "Gasoline and Shit." Other teaching positions followed: at Macomb's Junior High School in New York, where, in 1968, he edited a second anthology of student work, *Man Is a Child;* and at Brooklyn College, where he taught through the spring of 1969 and again in the early 1970s. Throughout his teaching career, which includes substantial stays at Sarah Lawrence College, Howard University, the University of Washington, and, since 1977, his membership on the faculty of the University of Colorado, where he is currently professor of English, Major has taken the education of his students very seriously, finding it a means both of personal growth and "of being involved in a useful way in the world."

But however important teaching was and is to Major, it was not the only thing occupying his time in the late 1960s. During that time he was readying *Swallow the Lake* for publication; serving as associate editor for the *Journal of Black Poetry;* completing his first published novel, *All-Night Visitors;* and, at the instigation of his associate Walter Lowenfels, compiling his *New Black Poetry* anthology.

The circumstances underlying the publication of *All-Night Visitors* (1969) by Maurice Girodias's Olympia Press are interesting, if rather sad. Girodias, who had been bold enough to publish the work of Henry Miller, Jean Genet, William S. Burroughs, J. P. Donleavy, Chester Himes, and others, expressed great enthusiasm for the quality of Major's novel and offered the author an advance on it, which Major accepted, only to learn that Olympia planned to cut his manuscript by about one-half—leaving in all of the sexual scenes and eliminating many of the passages which developed the characters' motivations. Having recently come to the realization that his fiction would be more powerful if he were to break with the realistic and naturalistic modes of writing and if he were to eradicate the distinction which he had been making between fiction and poetry, Major attempted to respond to Girodias's editing by rewriting the novel while on a visit to Mexico in 1968. But Girodias's position remained substantially unaltered, and Major was forced to live with most of the excisions or return his advance and find a new publisher. Wanting to have a published novel and needing the money, he allowed the book to go to press. The experience was extremely disillusioning.

Although the printed text of *All-Night Visitors* is a butchered version of Major's novel, it makes for compelling reading. Whether locked in the spell of the book's first-person, present-tense narration or immersed in the public and private nightmares that arise from the protagonist's past, the reader is riveted to the life of Eli Bolton, orphan, college dropout, veteran of the Vietnam conflict—and sexual voyager. Were the novel no more than surface-deep, its startlingly surreal episodes would command attention. But there are psychological and mythic dimensions beneath the book's surface luster which make *All-Night Visitors* an important first novel.

As Bolton—at times with clinical detachment, at times with intellectual curiosity, at times with emotional intensity, but never with true personal commitment—probes various female inlets, white and black, several of the central themes in Major's fiction are introduced: the mystery and otherness of women; the psychosexual nature of taboos; and the problems inherent in establishing meaningful self-identity in a chaotic, polymorphous, and bigoted universe. These issues receive more intellectually and stylistically sophisticated treatment in *Reflex and Bone Structure* and *Emergency Exit*, but the sheer intensity of Bolton's struggles to understand himself and the world he inhabits is unexcelled in Major's more recent fiction. Although Bolton's final self-assessment—that, chiefly by virtue of a single humanitarian act, he "had become firmly a man"—strains credibility, the protagonist's odyssey is deeply involving.

Released the same year as *All-Night Visitors*, Major's anthology *The New Black Poetry* provided a fitting outlet for the editorial experience he had gained as publisher of the *Coercion Review* while, at the same time, permitting him to draw on the personal contacts he had developed as a resident of New York's Lower East Side. Containing representative work by seventy-six young Afro-American poets, *The New Black Poetry* evidences Major's penchant to shun the doctrinaire. The poems of Amiri Baraka, Nikki Giovanni, and Sonia Sanchez keep company with those of Bob Kaufman, Ishmael Reed, and Al Young. And if the rhetoric of Major's introduction to the volume at times approaches the Black Aesthetic stance he had assumed in composing his famous "Black Criteria" essay for the Spring 1967 issue of the *Journal of Black Poetry*, his less political impulses become evident when he states his primary reason for including a poem in the anthology: "the artistic quality of the work."

Perhaps unavoidably, the anthology drew some criticism. Because the publisher, International Publishers, was both white-run and avowedly Communist, there were those in black literary circles who refused to support the project. And things became somewhat more thorny for Major when, after he had finished gathering materials for inclusion in the Summer-Fall 1969 issue of the *Journal of Black Poetry*, which he was to have been solely responsible for editing, he was told by regular editor Joe Goncalves that the issue contained too few militant poems as well as what Goncalves felt was an objectionable interview with Ishmael Reed. Major, who had served as associate editor of the journal since 1967, would not relent. When the issue appeared, some poems of Goncalves's choosing were included, and appended to the Reed interview was a harsh editorial assault. Feeling misrepresented and having had his commitment to a multidimensional black art implicitly, if not explicitly, assailed, Major resigned from the magazine's staff. In retrospect, the painful irony engendered by these closely juxtaposed incidents provides a somber commentary on the turbulence of the late 1960s: editorial freedom came to Major via an ostensibly doctrinaire white publisher, whereas a nominally liberated black publisher tampered with the work of one of his close colleagues.

The negative repercussions of the events of 1968 and 1969 were more than compensated for by the boost Major's reputation received from the publication of the powerful *All-Night Visitors* and *The New Black Poetry*, which became a highly respected anthology. Major's 1970 books—*Swallow the Lake*, a poetry collection, and his *Dictionary of Afro-American Slang*—served to solidify his position as a writer of prominence.

Swallow the Lake, the first of Major's books of poems to enjoy wide distribution, is also his most extensively reviewed poetry collection, perhaps due to its having been issued under the respected Wesleyan University Press imprint. Ranging from relatively conventional portraits such as "My Child" and "The Doll Believers" to formally intricate literary experiments like "Self World" and "—for IMM," *Swallow the Lake* covers an expanse of stylistic ground. The book's themes, similarly, range broadly from concerns with male-female relationships, treated most powerfully in "The Design," to the Vietnam conflict to race and music and philosophy. The collection's title poem, a stinging study in alienation, is the book's jewel.

Although Major's *Dictionary of Afro-American Slang* is in no way exhaustive, it remains today a serviceable reference volume. And the book's introduction declares, straightforwardly, Major's affirmative attitude toward black speech, which he sees, on the one hand, as having evolved from an overt Afro-American rejection of the dominant culture's racist values and, on the other hand, as having made a dramatic impact on the language of white America. Major's decision to have International Publishers do the book should not be understood as a political statement any more than the firm's doing *The New Black Poetry* was expressive of his political beliefs. International, quite simply, was amenable to publishing the *Dictionary*, and having the book in print was, for Major, a more important concern than were the criticisms of those would-be naysayers who had, shortly before, called for a boycott of the anthology. That the *Dictionary* has gone through three American printings and has been released, with a slightly altered title, by the distinguished British publishers Routledge and Kegan Paul suggests that Major's decision was sound.

Acceptance continued to follow Major's work in the early 1970s. London publisher Paul Breman brought out Major's *Private Line* as the fifteenth volume in his Heritage poetry series in 1971, the same year in which Major's *Symptoms & Madness* was released by Corinth Books, who had published volumes by black poets Amiri Baraka, Tom Weatherly, and Al Young, as well as such white luminaries as John Ashbery, Frank O'Hara, Charles Olson, and Louis Zukovsky. And, in 1972, the Broadside Press issued Major's third volume of poetry in two years, *The Cotton Club*.

The poems in *Private Line*, like the book itself, are brief. Race and male-female relationships provide the book's thematic focal points, but there is also a clear antimedia thrust (especially in "Jive reporter" and "Don't send me no more interviewers"), which projects some of the negative aspects of one's becoming well-known. The poetic forms in *Symptoms & Madness* are far more varied and, on the whole, far more interesting than those in *Private Line*. Lengthy poems appear with some regularity, most notably "The Comic Moneypowerdream," a potent assault on "the broken promise / land" that is America. Many personal verses also

inhabit the book, the main source for them being Major's 1968 trip to Mexico. And, finally, there are poems such as "Overbreak" which probe important questions of philosophy and aesthetics in a highly sophisticated manner. Throughout *Symptoms & Madness* Major fixes his iconoclastic gaze on the oppressive social conventions and institutions in contemporary America. The more compact, restrained verses that comprise *The Cotton Club* are less forceful, although their treatment of early twentieth-century New York City is not without interest.

When, in February 1972, Major headed for northwestern Connecticut to give some poetry readings, he could not have anticipated what would ensue. "Poems or Porn," "Dirty Poetry," "Parents Asked to Stand Up!"—these local newspaper headlines are representative of the reaction the readings touched off. To be sure, the poet had his defenders, but the experience was not a pleasant one. There was, however, one extremely positive outcome of the incident: his considered assessment of the reactions to his readings, "On Censorship: An Open Letter to June Jordan," was published in the July-August 1973 issue of the *American Poetry Review*, and the essay was well enough received that Major was offered a regular column with the *Review*. Eleven more of his "open letters" appeared between 1973 and 1976, among them pieces on Ralph Ellison, Willard Motley, and Jean Toomer. Although Major eventually tired of the column, feeling that he was no longer able to devote sufficient time to it, the experience served to extend the public's awareness of Major and his work.

There were, of course, other ways in which Major's reputation was developing during the *American Poetry Review* column years. His second novel, *NO*, was published in 1973. A critical book, *The Dark and Feeling: Black American Writers and Their Work*, and a new poetry collection, *The Syncopated Cakewalk*, appeared a year later. And his 1975 novel, *Reflex and Bone Structure*, became one of the early offerings of the newly formed Fiction Collective, of which Major was a charter member.

Perhaps because *NO* was published by a small black firm, or perhaps because it is extraordinarily nonlinear in its plotting, or perhaps for both of these reasons, the novel did less to promote Major's career than had *All-Night Visitors*. Only two real reviews of *NO*, one in the *New York Times Book Review* and the other in *Black Creation*, appeared, and although both were positive, the book was never properly launched.

Nearly every formal aspect of *NO* reinforces

the chaos that tears at the spirit of the book's protagonist, Moses Westby: the narrative point of view shifts; past and present intertwine; characters' identities merge; and the printed page is manipulated through such devices as the use of indentation, irregular spacing within and between lines, italics, capitalization, a variety of type fonts, and hand-drawn words and emblems. Feeling imprisoned by the conditions of his upbringing as a black man in the South, as well as by his marriage to a wife whom he is incapable of satisfying sexually, and sensing himself walled-in in a more cosmic and sinister sense, Westby experiences an existence which might best be described as a waking nightmare. Images of blood and death, human excrement, sexual organs and paraphernalia, and racism inundate the protagonist, whose personal identity is so fragmented that his concept of an integrated self is wholly absent. Escaping to Latin America with his wife Oni provides no cure for his condition, though the trip ultimately leads him to wander, self-destructively, into a bullring, where he touches and then is leveled by a "bleeding and sweating and half dead" bull, with whom Westby must establish contact despite his knowing the animal to be life-threatening. At least in some measure liberated by the confrontation, which he survives, Westby returns alone to America at the novel's end.

"I do not want to be *this way*," says Westby (or is it Major?) early in the book; "it is these words themselves that separate us, that swipe our spirits and weigh us down like cement around the waistline of an underworld victim dropped into monstrous night water." *NO* is not, in any traditional sense of the term, a realistic novel, and Westby can only be *mis*understood as a realistic character. Rather, his situation is emblematic of the human condition generally and, in a more restrictive sense, of the plight of the writer, who, to borrow from Major's poem "Overbreak," is committed to "consume an essence/to define an ultimate dimness/in a district of some god or nothing real." Major wishes his reader to understand that mankind's, and especially the writer's, basic defining tool, language, is not a construct by which one can communicate all of the *actual*, individual feelings, imaginings, and sensations which may be important to human existence (although language does—fortunately, in the writer's case—allow its user to create an *alternative*, fictive reality). Moreover, it is hard for individuals to completely grasp their own identities, to know truly who they are, since social taboos engendered by racism, Christianity, and Freudianism—to mention but three of the restrictive forces for which Major

has particular loathing—constantly prevent people from developing and acting upon their own authentic and authentifying conceptualizations. *NO* is not Major's finest novel, but it treats important issues in a provocative manner.

Major's nonfictional writing is showcased in *The Dark and Feeling*, which combines seven previously unpublished pieces with twelve reprinted ones (most of them written for *Essence* or Walt Shepperd's *Nickel Review*). Students of Major's work are likely to find the opening and closing sections of *The Dark and Feeling* more useful than part two of the collection, which contains reviews of six books from the late 1960s and early 1970s, and part three, which consists of biocritical sketches of six modern black authors. The essays in part one chart Major's development as a writer and aesthetician, discuss the problems that confront the black novelist in America, and examine "the explosion of black poetry" in the 1960s. And part four contains three useful interviews with Major, his widely anthologized "Black Criteria" essay, and the first of the "open letters" he wrote for the *American Poetry Review*. The value of *The Dark and Feeling* does not reside in its detailed analyses of other writers' work, which are notably absent, but in the clues it offers those desirous of understanding the intellectual underpinnings of Major's fiction and poetry.

Stylistically, Major's other 1974 book, *The Syncopated Cakewalk*, departs from his consciously "difficult" poetry collections of the 1960s and early 1970s. Whereas comprehension of many of the poems in *Swallow the Lake*, *Private Line*, and *Symptoms & Madness* mandates several readings, the selections in *The Syncopated Cakewalk* offer the reader immediate gratification. This is not to say that they lack sophistication—the metalinguistic poems "Words Into Words Won't Go," "Read The Signs," "Doodle," and "Take This Girl," for instance, are extraordinarily clever— but the appeal of most of the poems in the collection is not dependent upon formal pyrotechnics. Also noteworthy are the poems' diversity of subject matter. Male-female relationships continue to be the poet's focus in *The Syncopated Cakewalk*, but many other subjects command Major's attention: an old car, a dying bullfighter, an eighteenth-century native American, and black music and folklore. Of particular interest are the book's title poem, a wonderful mythic-folkloric riff; "American Setup," the poem which touched off the obscenity charges which were leveled against Major in Connecticut; and "Funeral," which earned the poet a Pushcart Prize in 1976.

Facing F.

This was the right house all right it was shaped like a large F. FRankie had given me directions years ago when before I was born. I had only to follow without failure with faith avoiding fakirs falcons false prophets all the instructions leading to and away from the ultimate mystery.

There was a man sitting on the bottom step.

If he weren't sitting on the sixth step facing me that way I might be able to start this--as a story. As it stands. Wire-clippers in right hand. Huge, thick arms with big bright brown thick hands dangling from their ends. Fingers like fat, massive worns. A dull twinkle in the eye. The afro is sculptured, so sculptured it seem looks like a cap placed on his fat head. The top lip lifted in a cynical F-like twist to the right. A slight F-like droop to the bottom. A firm big foot placed on the leaves along the walkway where it meets the step.

Frankly he is listening too closely to me to ever be part of the real life going on behind him: a woman painting the banisters; two other women on the porch talking and smiling to and smiling and at to each other. One holding a cat. The other wearing a brown trenchcoat, her black face a sharp bright contrast with it. Girl behind her with a room sweeping the planks.

broom

The man on the step says, "Can I help you?"

"I'm looking for Frankie. Does Frankie live here?"

Without answering me he pointed to the left. I assumed that he was directing me to the house next door. I looked in the direction his arm and finger suggested. There was were three tall buildings with bright glass windows, skyscrapers and in the foreground four or five old red brick abandoned three story buildings without window glass. White window ledges. Black tar roofing. Was They were surrounded by tall brown weeds and short diseased trees. A group of

Page from the revised typescript for "Facing F"

Scholars agree, however, that it was with the publication of *Reflex and Bone Structure* in 1975 that Major's writing truly matured. Like Ishmael Reed, who has made conscious, innovative use of a variety of pop-cultural genres in his fiction, Major utilizes the detective novel as his point of departure in *Reflex and Bone Structure* —a departure which proves particularly intriguing. In *Reflex*, not only is the motive behind the slayings of Cora and her lover Dale never disclosed, uncovering it is never really an issue. And while the reader eventually learns that the narrator "killed" them, he did so only in his role as narrator, as the controller of the book's events: "Dale gives Cora a hand. At the edge of the desert they step into a city. They step into a house. It explodes. It is a [literary] device. I am responsible. I set the device." Thus, the story of the book's process or construction intermingles with and, in certain important ways, supersedes the story of the characters the novel describes. That Dale, the narrator, and the free-spirited Canada slide in and out of bed with Cora and otherwise interact with one another involves the reader at one level, just as the mystery surrounding Dale's and Cora's deaths does; but it is the metafictional aspect of *Reflex* which carries the book's intellectual weight.

What Major sets out to investigate in *Reflex and Bone Structure* is nothing less than the nature of reality. Whereas the central premise underlying the so-called "realistic" school of American writing, of which the detective novel, along with the preponderance of black fiction, is so much a part, is that fiction directly mirrors life, *Reflex* makes explicit what *All-Night Visitors* and *NO* hint at: that fiction cannot and therefore should not endeavor to capture life's realities in an undistorted, mirror-image manner. On the contrary, fiction creates its own reality, one which has no absolutely direct reference to events outside itself; literature is necessarily bound to the phenomenal world only by its status as an artifact within that world (namely, that thing which we call a book, or a performance) and by virtue of its being an extension of an author whose imaginative act brought the work into existence.

The appearance of what may, here, seem to be philosophical posturing vanishes once one explores the implications of the concept. What is implicit in Major's metafictional insight is a statement of the need to question sternly all received "truths." Major wants his reader to recognize that the concept of literary realism which allowed fictional detectives like Sherlock Holmes to assemble all of the clues in a case and, from them, reason back to the one absolute, objectively verifiable solution to a mystery can,

today, be shown to be invalid. Modern physics (not to mention experience) has shown ours to be a multivalent world, in which investigation is more likely to widen the number of possible alternatives than it is to ferret out a single, unassailable answer. And ours is also a world in which blacks and members of other historically oppressed minority groups must develop their own definitions of truth rather than permit themselves to be seduced by the subjective assessments others have attempted to institutionalize as irrefutable facts. Ultimately, then, reality can only be said to reside within the self.

It is easy to imagine that the radical nature of the insights offered by *Reflex and Bone Structure*, coupled with the radically avant-garde nature of the fictional vehicle Major developed to express these thoughts, would have led commercial publishers to view the novel as a risk. So it is not surprising that in 1974 Major chose to join with other established novelists whose artistic integrity had been threatened by editorial tampering to form the Fiction Collective, which, in conjunction with New York-based publisher George Braziller, would distribute members' books free from editorial restraints. *Reflex and Bone Structure*, along with Major's 1979 novel, *Emergency Exit*, surely benefited from the arrangement. Major's recent novels have been much more widely reviewed than were his first two; and, due largely to his association with the Collective, most of whose members are white, his fiction has, for the first time, become known and analyzed outside of a distinctly black literary context.

A measure of academic stability and respectability that he had not previously known came to Major in the late 1970s. After spending ten years in a variety of low-level teaching positions, chiefly in the New York City and then Washington, D.C., areas, Major joined the University of Colorado faculty as associate professor of English in 1977. Having recognized as early as 1968 that his literary accomplishments would carry some weight within the academic community, but not enough to secure him a stable academic post, Major began putting to pragmatic use his lifelong habit of literary and artistic study, eventually earning a Ph.D. from Union Graduate School in Ohio as the 1970s came to a close. His academic achievements, combined with his authorship of more than a dozen books, led to his promotion to full professor in 1981.

Dedicated "to the people whose stories do not hold together," *Emergency Exit* amplifies the concerns and techniques developed in *Reflex and Bone Structure*. In a highly episodic, digressive, and self-conscious manner, *Emergency Exit* describes life for the Ingram family in the town of Inlet, Connecticut, which, in an attempt "to restore moral sanity and honor and dignity to at least this small part of the world," has passed a statute requiring "all males (over the age of 21)...to lift from the ground...all females (over the age of 18) and carry such females through, beyond, out of, ... doorways, entrance-ways, exits, across, beyond, thresholds, of all build-ings, dwellings, public and private." As the nar-rator, a salesman for Superior Pussy, Inc., wryly observes, Inlet has purity, cleanliness, proper con-duct, and racism "deep in the psyche."

Major's characteristically pejorative attitude toward societal taboos provides the glue which binds together the assemblage of episodes, epi-graphs, paintings, lists, visual and linguistic col-lages, schedules, catalogues, double-column pas-sages, questions, concrete (and other) poems, charts, and the like which, together, constitute the text of *Emergency Exit*. Although the book's charac-ters talk back to the narrator and at times usurp his role, they are, for the most part, consciously two-dimensional—upon occasion losing even their nominal identities and being referred to simply as "he"/"she" or "one"/"two." Even more than in *Re-flex,* Major in *Emergency Exit* is intent on emphasiz-ing fiction's status as fiction as well as the subjective nature of reality and what commonly passes for truth. "The world is not an orderly place easily defined by a cozy myth," Jim Ingram tells his son Oscar.

Not only has Major's concern for the welfare of what is often referred to as postmodern literature (but which he prefers simply to call "serious" writ-ing) led him to write works that adhere to a truly innovative aesthetic and to become associated with the Fiction Collective, but he has also demonstrated his commitment by editing half of the first issue and all of the second issue of the *American Book Review*. Begun by fellow Collectivist and University of Col-orado colleague Ronald Sukenick to pay heed to those works often overlooked in or given short shrift by the mass media, the *Review* has, since De-cember 1977, been active in promoting the books of small and university presses as well as works by minority writers and others often ignored in the conglomerative reviewing outlets.

A Fulbright lectureship at the University of Nice in 1981-1982 took Major and his wife Pamela to France. There he was one of the featured speak-ers at Maurice Couturier's important conference "Representation and Performance in Postmodern Literature." The recently published French trans-lation of *Reflex and Bone Structure* has made his fic-

tion far more widely known abroad than had the Italian and German renderings of *All-Night Visitors* a decade earlier. A book of Major's poems, "The Other Side of the Wall," was accepted for publica-tion by the Black Scholar Press in 1981, but it still has not appeared in print. As Major attempts to find a publisher for two additional book manuscripts—"Dot," a fictionalized biography of actress Dorothy Dandridge, and "My Amputations," a novel—he continues to work on a new novel, "Folksong."

Prolific, yet a careful craftsperson, Clarence Major is developing into one of the most important black writers in current-day America. *Black Ameri-can Literature Forum* devoted a special issue to his writing in 1979, and his recent novels have caused a stir among those presently engaged in assessing the direction of American fiction in the 1970s and 1980s. While Major's reputation as an "experimen-tal" writer has led some socially minded black critics to withhold support from his work, his literary fu-ture looks very bright indeed.

Interviews:
John O'Brien, "Clarence Major," in *Interviews with Black Writers* (New York: Liveright, 1973), pp. 125-139;

Clarence Major, "Self Interview: On Craft," in *The Dark and Feeling: Black American Writers and Their Work* (New York: Third Press, 1974), pp. 125-131;

Jerome Klinkowitz, "Clarence Major: An Interview with a Post-Contemporary Author," *Black American Literature Forum,* 12 (1978): 32-37;

Doug Bolling, "Reality, Fiction and Criticism: An Interview/Essay by Clarence Major," *Par Rap-port,* 2, no. 1 (1979): 67-73;

Nancy Bunge, "An Interview with Clarence Major," *San Francisco Review of Books,* 7, no. 3 (1982): 7, 8, 38.

Bibliography:
Joe Weixlmann and Clarence Major, "Toward a Primary Bibliography of Clarence Major," *Black American Literature Forum,* 13 (1979): 70-72.

References:
Doug Bolling, "A Reading of Clarence Major's Short Fiction," *Black American Literature Forum,* 13 (1979): 51-56;

Larry D. Bradfield, "Beyond Mimetic Exhaustion: The *Reflex and Bone Structure* Experiment," *Black American Literature Forum,* 17 (1983): 120-123;

Jerome Klinkowitz, "Chapter Eight: Clarence Major," in *The Life of Fiction* (Urbana: University of Illinois Press, 1977), pp. 95-103;

Klinkowitz, "Notes on a Novel-in-Progress: Clarence Major's *Emergency Exit*," *Black American Literature Forum*, 13 (1979): 46-50;

Nathaniel Mackey, "To Define an Ultimate Dimness: Deconstruction in Clarence Major's

Poems," *Black American Literature Forum*, 13 (1979): 61-68;

Larry McCaffery and Sinda Gregory, "Major's *Reflex and Bone Structure* and the Anti-Detective Tradition," *Black American Literature Forum*, 13 (1979): 39-45;

Joe Weixlmann, "Clarence Major: A Checklist of Criticism," *Obsidian*, 4, no. 2 (1978): 101-113;

Paule Marshall
(9 April 1929-   )

Barbara T. Christian
University of California, Berkeley

BOOKS: *Brown Girl, Brownstones* (New York: Random House, 1959);

Soul Clap Hands and Sing (New York: Atheneum, 1961);

The Chosen Place, the Timeless People (New York: Harcourt, Brace & World, 1969);

Praisesong for the Widow (New York: Putnam's, 1983);

Reena and Other Stories (Old Westbury, N.Y.: Feminist Press, 1983).

OTHER: "Reena," in *American Negro Short Stories*, edited by John H. Clarke (New York: Hill & Wang, 1966), pp. 264-282;

"Some Get Wasted," in *Harlem U.S.A.*, edited by John Henrik Clarke (Berlin: Seven Seas, 1974).

PERIODICAL PUBLICATIONS: "The Negro Woman in American Literature," *Freedomways*, 6 (Winter 1966): 21-25;

"To Da-duh, In Memoriam," *New World Magazine* (1967);

"Shaping the World of My Art," *New Letters*, 40 (October 1973): 97-112.

Paule Marshall explores the multidimensional experiences of West Indian-Americans in finely crafted fiction that has, since 1950, deepened in complexity and meaning. Her three novels form a unique contribution to Afro-American literature because they capture in a lyrical, powerful language a culturally distinct and expansive world. Her work, just as she has claimed, "stands as testimony to the

rich legacy of language and culture" passed on in "the wordshop of the kitchen" by the women in her immigrant community.

Born in Brooklyn to Samuel and Ada Burke, who emigrated from Barbados shortly after World War I, Marshall grew up in a culture with firm roots in the Caribbean. Precisely because of the interaction between Barbadian and American culture in her community, she developed at an impressionable age a sense of ritual, of shapes and forms of culture; moreover, she acquired an appreciation for the Caribbean, especially Barbados, which she visited for the first time when she was nine years old.

Although Marshall's earliest writings were poems expressing the beauty of Barbados, her first novel, *Brown Girl, Brownstones*, established her as a relentless analyst of character. Published in 1959, it ushered in a new period of female characters in Afro-American literature. Focused on the development of an intelligent, complex woman, *Brown Girl, Brownstones* is similar to Zora Neale Hurston's lyrical novel *Their Eyes Were Watching God* (1937) and Gwendolyn Brooks's exquisite novella *Maud Martha* (1953) in its presentation of a black woman's search for identity within a specific black community, rather than in reaction to a hostile white society. All three works acknowledge the existence of a rich black culture, and their heroines both affirm and challenge their communities' definitions of woman. Paule Marshall, however, extends the analysis of black female characters by portraying the development of her heroine, Selina Boyce, in terms of the relationship between her mother, Silla, and her father, Deighton. In *Brown Girl, Brownstones*, marital and parental relationships are affected by Barbadian-American immigrant culture, which in turn is influenced by the hostile, materialistic world of white America.

Marshall's novel is also similar to Hurston's and Brooks's in that it, too, seems to be a literary anomaly, not at all in tune with the published works of its period. As a result, it might seem to be a brilliant tour de force, but scarcely an indication of its time. Yet when one looks at the entire tradition of black women's novels, *Brown Girl,* along with *Their Eyes Were Watching God* and *Maud Martha,* indicates a point at which a leap was made, a point at which the humanity of the black woman somehow surfaced despite the deeply etched stereotypes of her that were maintained by a racist society.

Marshall's novel at the end of the 1950s shared certain elements with James Baldwin's psychological probings of that decade and with LeRoi Jones's early political poetry of the 1960s, for in her first novel Marshall attacked, head-on, sexual and racial stereotypes, from the mammies and Uncle Toms of the early twentieth century to the Amos n' Andys and Sapphires of the 1940s to Moynihan's black matriarchs and weak black boys of the 1950s. Moreover, in its emphasis on the integrity of women and their role in the black community, *Brown Girl* prefigured the major theme of black women's fiction in the 1970s.

A conspicuous element of Caribbean culture is its oral traditions. In Marshall's essay "Shaping the World of My Art" as well as Alexis de Veaux's interview with her in *Essence,* she talks about how she was influenced by the Barbadian women she knew as a child. Though not educated in a formal way, they were "talking women" who used language as an art and for whom that art was an integral part of life. Like Silla and her friends in *Brown Girl, Brownstones,* these women gathered ritualistically around the kitchen table invoking images, creating character, dissecting life with words. Marshall comments on their impact on her: "I was always so intimidated as a little girl by the awesome verbal powers of these women. That might be one of the reasons I started writing. To see if, on paper, I couldn't have some of that power." *Brown Girl, Brownstones* abounds with such verbal power as when Silla succinctly characterizes her husband, Deighton, as "one man [who] don know his own mind. He's always looking for something big and praying hard not to find it."

These "talking women" left Barbados to improve themselves, and most of them worked outside their homes, often "cleaning house" to "buy house." Marshall recalls that they "transformed humiliating

Paule Marshall (photo © by Thomas Victor)

experiences into creative ones." Their dual experience of a feudal existence in Barbados coupled with the racism they found in America made politics central to their lives, a motif that is an undercurrent in *Brown Girl, Brownstones.* Their lives as they knew it ran counter to the norm of woman upheld in America, for these Barbadian-American women could be neither passive nor cuddled creatures. But neither were they powerful matriarchs. To a large extent they desired the norm even as they had little access to it. What Marshall so deftly captures in *Brown Girl, Brownstones* is the complexity of women such as she knew in her childhood. In the finely drawn character Silla Boyce, she portrays the relationship between these women's sense of their own power and their vulnerability.

In her first novel, Marshall not only cracks the stereotype of the black matriarch, but she also penetrates the worn image of the ne'er-do-well black man with her portrayal of Deighton Boyce. In showing the conflict between sex roles in America

Dust jacket for Marshall's first novel, begun while she was attending Hunter College

and Deighton's imaginative personality, she questions the values of the Barbadian-American community, so afraid of poverty that it takes on exclusively the material values of America. For Deighton, unlike his wife, Silla, life is more than acquiring things; he would have to sacrifice much of himself to succeed in the United States and to meet Silla's expectations. He clings to a dream of returning to Barbados, where he owns a piece of land. His conflict with his wife stems from his refusal to sell his property, which for him is his heritage, in order to purchase a brownstone in New York.

But the novel is neither Silla's nor Deighton's. It is primarily about their daughter, Selina, who in sorting out the complexity of her mother's and father's characters, takes an essential step toward understanding herself, her culture, and the wider society with which she must contend. Family crises mark Selina's coming of age, but they do not rob her of her capacity for love and compassion. Although the novel is very much about the development of a brown girl into a woman, Marshall insists in her portrayal of Selina that at the core of every culture is the relationship between women and men, and that

societal definitions of what is male and female help to create and destroy the developing individual self.

Paule Marshall began *Brown Girl, Brownstones,* her autobiographical novel, while attending Hunter College in 1955 and working for a small black magazine called *Our World,* which had hired her as a researcher soon after she received her B.A. from Brooklyn College in 1953. Even though she was a Phi Beta Kappa, she was also the only woman on the staff of *Our World* and felt, she later said, as if "the men were waiting for me to fall." She eventually became a writer for the magazine and traveled to Brazil and the Caribbean on assignments. She worked on her first novel after work, yet she initially had no intention of becoming a novelist. Nonetheless, she poured out *Brown Girl, Brownstones* in what she calls her most exhilarating writing experience. Marshall left *Our World* in 1956, nearly three years before the publication of her novel, which she completed in Barbados after her marriage in 1957 to Kenneth E. Marshall. Since that time she has pursued a career as a writer of fiction.

Despite fine reviews, *Brown Girl, Brownstones* was a commercial failure, a commentary perhaps on the times. Marshall's subject matter, the development of a brown girl into a woman within the rituals and mores of a black culture, had yet to be seen as important. Used for a time as a book for juveniles, just as later Toni Morrison's *The Bluest Eye* would be, *Brown Girl, Brownstones* has a complexity of language and psychology that makes it a book for adult readers. Fortunately, contemporary readers, such as Mary Helen Washington and Dorothy Denniston, now recognize it as a Bildungsroman of a black woman, which has as much human and literary value as other novels of development.

The publication of *Brown Girl, Brownstones* was important not only to the tradition of black women's novels; it was also Paule Marshall's initiation into writing as a vocation. Writing it changed Marshall's life, for after its publication, she saw herself as *having to be* a writer of fiction, whether or not she was commercially successful. As she has often commented, in writing *Brown Girl, Brownstones,* she was learning how to write and finding her own personal mode of expression. The creation of character within the space of a physical and cultural context, a technique which relates individual personal development to a collective history, was the distinguishing characteristic of *Brown Girl, Brownstones,* a technique Marshall explores even further in her next work, *Soul Clap Hands and Sing* (1961), completed under a Guggenheim Fellowship (1960).

This work is not a novel, per se, but a collection of novellas, entitled "Barbados," "Brooklyn," "British Guiana," and "Brazil." The titles of the individual pieces immediately indicate how critical physical, cultural, and historical contexts are to Marshall. Marshall's juxtaposition of these various contexts suggests a relationship among them which she explores and shapes into a greater whole. In this collection, she emphasizes the African presence in the "New World," from the urban North and rural South of the U.S., through rural Barbados in the Caribbean, to the British colony of Guiana on the mainland of South America, and finally to Rio de Janeiro, an urban center in South America. Though the historical and cultural context of these different places are dissimilar, black people provide the focus. They mix and mingle with other peoples—the British, American Jews, Chinese, Portuguese, Germans—and produce new cultural amalgams. Their past and present are finally rooted in the culture of Africa, as well as in their common experiences of enslavement and colonization. *Soul Clap Hands and Sing* moves then from the primarily American environment of *Brown Girl, Brownstones* to a larger Caribbean and South American perspective. Increasingly from this point in her work, the Caribbean would give Marshall the manageable and inclusive landscape she needed for her fictional work.

Yet even as Marshall explores distinguishing characteristics of specific cultural contexts in *Soul Clap Hands and Sing,* she reiterates the commonality among all of them. The collection shares a common theme, as its title suggests. Taken from Yeats's famous poem "Sailing to Byzantium," Marshall's title is a signal to the reader that her four novellas are based on the eternal intrinsic quality of spiritual values, as opposed to transient material ones, an idea that becomes increasingly compelling when the beauty of flesh falls away; as Yeats states, "an aged man is but a paltry thing / a tattered coat upon a stick unless / soul clap hands and sing."

At the core of the collection is the theme of the aged man who finally understands the dire results of having refused to affirm some lasting values. Marshall's old men have based their lives on wealth or fame, cynicism or indifference, but their personal choices are all inextricably linked to the social order within which each individual character moves. Marshall specifically explores how the personal past of each of her old men is gravely influenced by the history of oppression his people have experienced. In "Barbados" the old man, Watford, has spent his entire life making money in the U.S. so that he could return to Barbados and live like the British colonials who once oppressed him. The memory of his early life has conditioned all his perceptions: "But because of their whiteness and wealth he had not dared to hate them. Instead his rancor, like a boomerang had rebounded, glancing past him to strike all the dark ones like himself. . . ." Desperately afraid of becoming like those dark ones, which in fact is who he is, Mr. Watford "had permitted nothing to sight which could have affected him." But confronted by a young girl whom he desires and whom he finds dancing in abandon with a young man in his coconut grove, Watford learns that he is a "nasty pissy old man," and for the first time "gazed mutely upon the waste and pretense which had spanned his years."

In contrast, the old mulatto Gerald Motley in "British Guiana" knows he has missed his opportunity to live. As a young man, he had shown much talent, had moved away from his upper-middle-class roots, and attempted to organize a strike among Guyanese workers. In order to set him back on the right path, he is offered a job which would return him to his proper class, one which bases its existence on the imitation of a dying British order.

Appropriately, the moment at which Motley can believe in himself takes place within the jungle interior, which is as characteristic of Guyana as the coconut groves are of Barbados. Motley is prevented from further penetrating the jungle and himself by his Negro-Chinese girl friend Sybil. His consciousness of his betrayal of himself, and Sybil's role in it, shapes his life. From then on, he bases his life on a cynicism that shuts out any possibility of growth.

Although these novellas are focused on men, all four protagonists discover the waste in their lives through their relationships with women. In two of the stories, "British Guiana" and "Brazil," the women are part of the men's past and a mirror reflection of their distorted values. In the other two stories, "Barbados" and "Brooklyn," they are young women whom the men meet in their old age, whose fresh eyes penetrate their facade of wealth or stature. Both "Barbados" and "Brooklyn" have been reissued in *Reena and Other Stories* (1983), a collection emphasizing Marshall's female characters. In *Soul Clap Hands and Sing,* as in *Brown Girl, Brownstones,* the relationship between woman and man is central to the understanding of both the major characters and the social order.

In one of the few essays she has published about her art, Marshall distinguishes *Soul Clap Hands and Sing* from *Brown Girl, Brownstones* by stating that in her second book she was consciously reaching for a political theme, while in her first novel she portrayed a rejection of American values in individual terms. *Soul Clap Hands and Sing,* then, though not as well known as *Brown Girl, Brownstones,* is a significant turning point for Marshall, not only because it is the first time she uses a New World framework as opposed to a setting primarily in the U.S. but also because she identifies political themes as central to her fiction.

Soul Clap Hands and Sing was written after Paule Marshall had just had a baby, her only child, Eran-Keith, to whom she dedicates the book. She reveals that despite her husband's objections, she got help to stay with her son and went off to a friend's apartment every day to work on her new book. Even today, the woman writer who is a mother must often write against the backdrop of continuous interruption. At least, in the last ten years, essays such as Tillie Olsen's *Silences* and Alice Walker's "In Search of Our Mothers' Gardens" propelled into the public forum discussion about the relationship between woman's artistic creativity and the creativity of her womb. But in 1960 such discussion was hardly occurring, and the individual

woman writer had to rely on the strength of her own belief that her need to express herself was as important as the society's demands on mothers. Writing *Soul Clap Hands and Sing* was, as well, a test of Marshall's determination to be a writer.

Eight years elapsed between the publication of *Soul Clap Hands and Sing* and Marshall's second novel, *The Chosen Place, the Timeless People* (1969), originally entitled "Ceremonies of the Guest House" in manuscript form. While she was working on this novel, Marshall was divorced. She received a Richard and Hinda Rosenthal Foundation Award (1962), a Ford Foundation Grant for Poets and Fiction Writers (1964-1965), and a National Endowment for the Arts Fellowship (1967-1968). She published three short stories: "Reena" (1962), "To Da-duh, In Memoriam" (1967), and "Some Get Wasted" (1968). "Reena" and "To Da-duh" are collected in *Reena and Other Stories.* Each of these stories represents a stage of Marshall's work in which she attempted to refine the depth of character analysis in her first novel while enlarging the scope of social analysis that would be the distinguishing characteristic of her second.

"Reena" is the work of Marshall's that is most often anthologized, probably because it is a short piece which uses many of the distinctive characteristics of her best known work, *Brown Girl, Brownstones.* Like that novel, "Reena" portrays the development of a West Indian-American woman. But while *Brown Girl, Brownstones* is primarily about Selina Boyce's journey through adolescence, "Reena" is told from the point of view of the middle-aged woman that Selina might have become. It is one of the first pieces of Afro-American literature to delve into the complex choices confronting the contemporary, educated black woman. Through the character of Reena, the narrator in the story presents the peculiar contradictions such a woman encounters: the illusory freedom of college, the immersion into left-wing politics that both helps to shape her yet finally does not deal with her problems, the frustrations of an interracial relationship, the restrictions of a black middle-class marriage.

Reena's story is told during a distinctive ritual of her culture, a wake for her Aunt Vi. Reena's assessment of her life is juxtaposed to and conditioned by her maternal history, as represented by women like her aunt. Thus, Reena's sense of herself as a displaced person and her desire to take her children to see Africa are measured against the lives of women like Aunt Vi who "cleaned house" to "buy house," but never got to enjoy the comfort of a home when they could finally afford one. The character "Reena" is also a foreshadowing of Merle Kimbona, the central character of *The Chosen Place, the Timeless People,* because both are middle-aged black women who feel fragmented by their experience as oppressed people in the West, and yet who retain some measure of their own vitality.

Just as Reena could be an older Selina Boyce, the nine-year-old girl in "To Da-duh, In Memoriam" could be her younger sister. The autobiographical story depicts a young Barbadian-American girl's visit to Barbados to see her grandmother, her Da-duh. As such it uses the New World framework of *Soul Clap Hands and Sing.* Like that collection, the focus in this story is on the collapsing of the past and the present into a moment of recognition. In "To Da-duh, In Memoriam," however, that past and present are represented by the land of Barbados and the technology of America which together link this story to the old country versus New York conflict of *Brown Girl, Brownstones.* The child and the grandmother develop a strong bond based on competition; one tries to prove to the other that her home is superior. Da-duh shows the young child the wonders of her village, the fruit, the flowers, the canes, while the child tells her about the marvels of New York, the radios, the cars, the electric lights. The competition continues with each gaining respect for the other, but one day Da-duh shows her grandchild her greatest wonder, an "incredibly tall palm tree which appeared to be touching the blue dome of the sky." In response, the child describes the Empire State Building and completely demolishes her grandmother, who from that time on appeared "thinner and suddenly undescribably old." When Da-duh dies the day that airplanes fly for the first time over her village, her gods and her sense of reality have been totally undercut. The past and the present are interdependent in the story; neither has precedence over the other, nor can the conflict between nature and technology be easily resolved. The story ends:

> She died and I lived, but always to this day even, within the shadow of her death. For a brief period, after I was grown, I went to live alone, like one doing penance in a loft above a noisy factory in downtown New York and there painted seas of sugar cane and huge swirling Van Gogh suns and palm trees striding like brightly plumed Watusse across a tropical landscape, while the thunderous tread of the machines downstairs jarred the floor beneath my easel, mocking my efforts.

Like Reena, Da-duh seems to be Marshall's sketch of a more fully developed character in *The Chosen Place, the Timeless People.* Neither Leesy, the character in that novel, nor Da-duh can understand the magnetism of American glamour and technology that seduces their grandchildren.

The third of Marshall's short stories, "Some Get Wasted," at first glance seems completely different from the rest of her work. It is a story about Hezzy, a black boy who is trying to prove his manhood to the Noble Knights, the Brooklyn gang to which he wants to belong. As such it is an initiation rite. The story takes place within Hezzy's head as he runs from the Crowns, the rival gang which ritualistically fights the Noble Knights on Massacre Hill every Memorial Day. Many Afro-American writers, including Ralph Ellison, Richard Wright, and James Baldwin, have used street gangs as an element in their work. Marshall's point of view on this subject, though, is linked to the rest of her work because she focuses on one definition of manhood left to those males who are unwanted in the society.

For Hezzy, who could be a second-generation West Indian-American, Boy Scouts and war veterans marching to the blare of "America . . . America" have nothing to do with him. Yet he needs to belong, must belong to some country or some brotherhood that is a ritualistic expression of his racial life and that is also opposed to the Boy Scouts of that other world. Hezzy yearns to be a man like Turner, who got a bullet crease on his forehead on another Memorial Day and is seen as a hero by his peers. For them, manhood is tinged by rage and arrogance, both rooted in the will to be recognized: "Yeah, that's right, Hezzy. Read about me in the news next week, you dumb squares." But Hezzy gets wasted, ironically by his own people, who mistake him for one of the Crowns in an initiation rite that moves to nowhere. Yet, even as he dies, Hezzy holds onto the idea of his people, who are his only measure of himself. In his desire to be a hero among his peers, to exhibit his threatened masculinity in a dangerous and glamorous way, Hezzy is linked to Vere, another character in *The Chosen Place, the Timeless People.* He, too, sees masculinity as rooted in the concept of glory; he, too, is destroyed by that desire.

In its analysis of characters who are inseparable from their particular culture, and in its insistence on the intersections of the past and present, *The Chosen Place, the Timeless People* is a culmination of her earlier work. Marshall moves from a localized setting in which she focuses primarily on one character or one family; instead she portrays the entire sociocultural fabric of Bournehills, a prototypical Caribbean island. Her scope is considerably larger than that of her previous works, yet the people of this novel are psychologically related to the Boyces of *Brown Girl, Brownstones;* to Mr. Watford and Gerald Motley of *Soul Clap Hands and Sing;* to Reena, Da-duh, and Hezzy of the short stories. *The Chosen Place, the Timeless People,* in its characters, themes, and techniques, is so consistent with *Brown Girl, Brownstones* or "To Da-duh, In Memoriam" that it creates a coherent universe of Marshall's work. Marshall has matured as a writer, but her vision has not changed dramatically; rather her emphasis moves from the way the world affects an individual psyche to how many psyches create a world.

Marshall achieves an enlarged scope without losing the intensity of character by means of the philosophical concepts of *The Chosen Place, the Timeless People.* Its plot is a familiar story in the underdeveloped world. It consists of the interrelationship between the team members of a philanthropic agency, the Center for Applied Social Research, and the underdeveloped society of Bournehills. The members of this agency believe that they have come to help Bournehills enter the twentieth century. They discover that half-measures cannot right the wrongs that have been and continue to be inflicted on the people. The novel turns on its epigraph, a saying from the Tiv of West Africa: "Once a great wrong has been done, it never dies. People speak the words of peace, but their hearts do not forgive. Generations perform ceremonies of reconciliation but there is no end." The theme is that of the complex series of interactions between the oppressed and their oppressors; its truth is that half-measures cannot substantively change those interactions. Finally, the novel portrays history as an active, creative, and moral process composed by human beings. According to Marshall, individuals and whole cultures decide upon the moral nature of an act, a series of acts, a history. Marshall summarizes the central idea of *The Chosen Place, the Timeless People* in one of her essays: "After struggling for sometime, I was finally able in my most recent novel to bring together what I consider to be the two themes most central to my work: the importance of truly confronting the past, both in personal and historical terms and the necessity of reversing the present order."

The title of the novel, as well as the names of its four parts—"Heirs and Descendants," "Bournehills," "Carnival," and "Whitsun"—are indicators of its composition. Marshall constructs the society of Bournehills by using what she considers to be the most important elements of any society—the contours of individual human beings as they form and are formed by their land and their culture, and the relationship between the past and present of a specific community as manifested in its concept of time and by its rituals. Largeness of scope does not result in tedious analysis because readers come to empathize with individual members of the society. Nevertheless, the novel is not individualistic in its approach, for Marshall's careful presentation of rituals and mores, rooted in a common history, demonstrates the inevitable influence of society on specific individuals. Because her major characters represent all aspects of the Western world, black and white, male and female, Jew and Anglo-Saxon, upper, middle, and working classes, natives and outsiders, Marshall creates a microcosm representative not only of Bournehills but also of other "underdeveloped" societies in the Third World, held captive both psychologically and economically by the metropolises of the West, yet somehow possessing their own visions of possibility. Because the personal pasts of the various characters intersect and sometimes conflict with the rituals of Carnival and Whitsun, which are embodiments of Bournehills's time and pointers to its own specific vision of the future, Marshall is able to show the necessity for and the complexity of struggling to reverse the present order.

Pivotal to the possibility of change in the novel is Merle Kimbona, the Bournehills woman who has studied in London, married an African, relinquished their child to him, and returned to her native land, wounded and fragmented. Merle is the cohesive force in the novel. She is identified with Bournehills, that abandoned land which refuses half-measures of change but which can effect revolutionary change only if it insists on creating its own history. In struggling to confront her own painful past, Merle grows toward confronting the equally painful history of her people and finally to the point where she must act to reverse *her* present order. Implicit in her development is Marshall's assertion that Bournehills must undergo a similar process. Personal and social change are inextricably linked; in a creative tension of reciprocity, one is virtually impossible without the other. Marshall calls Merle her "most passionate and political" heroine, "A Third World revolutionary spirit," and she adds, "I love her."

Marshall's presentation of a black woman as a major actor in the social, political, and cultural issues of her society can be compared to Alice Walker's title character in her novel *Meridian,* published seven years after *The Chosen Place, the Timeless People*. Both Merle and Meridian are new literary characters in Afro-American women's novels who are presented as complex women struggling to understand themselves as black and female. In seeking their own identity, they find they must pursue substantive social transformation. They are female literary characters of a social and political depth seldom seen in either Afro- or European American literature. In developing a character such as Merle Kimbona within a graphic analysis of her particular society, Marshall has announced the major theme of Afro-American women's fiction of the 1970s in which black women are finally being presented both as complex, developing persons and active participants in the sociopolitical world.

Like her first two works, *The Chosen Place, the Timeless People* received excellent reviews but was not a commercial success. Because Marshall is committed to writing fiction rather than to teaching, public performance, or magazine writing, she has had difficulty supporting herself. As a result, she has had to rely primarily on grants from institutions such as the National Endowment for the Arts and the Ford Foundation. The financial difficulties of being a writer in America, particularly for a black female novelist, have had an impact on her ability to concentrate on her work with the intensity that it deserves. Nonetheless, perhaps because of Marshall's unwavering commitment to writing and her resistance to commerciality, her work is becoming better known. As Afro-American and feminist thought advances, the depth of her work is more and more appreciated. For years *Brown Girl, Brownstones* was out of print, almost impossible to find, but in 1981 it was republished by the Feminist Press.

Since the publication of her second novel, Marshall has remarried (1970), and lives in both New York City and the West Indies with her husband, Nourry Menard, in what she calls an "open and innovative marriage" that allows her the time and freedom to work. During the 1970s she worked on her fourth book, *Praisesong for the Widow* (1983), which has as a theme one of her persistent concerns. In an interview in *Essence* magazine, she says it is about "the materialism of this country, how it often spells the death of love and feeling and how we, as Black People, must fend it off." The novel centers on a middle-class, middle-aged black woman, Avey Johnson, who has bought into the materialistic values of America but who experiences a rupture in her consciousness precipitated by a persistent dream about a childhood memory. Years before on

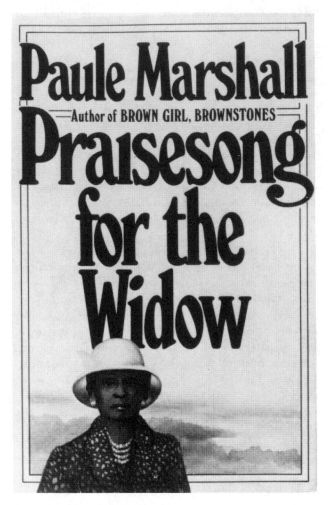

Dust jacket for Marshall's 1983 novel about the spiritual regeneration of a sixty-two-year-old widow who is reawakened to the Caribbean culture she had forsaken in New York

her annual visit to the South, her now-dead Southern aunt used to take her to a place called Ibo Landing, where slaves were said to have walked across the water back to Africa. The dream of her aunt and of the place takes hold of her consciousness in so profound a way that the past and present unite. As in Marshall's earlier work, myth and history, place and consciousness intersect; the woman struggles to become fully human. In this novel, however, the emphasis is on the relationship between class, race, and culture, concerns which other Afro-American women writers, most recently Toni Morrison, are also exploring.

Avey Johnson, a recent widow with grown children, goes on a cruise to the West Indies, partly at the urging of Sis and Annawilda, two of her three daughters, who thought that the trip would take her mind off her dead husband, Jerome. Avey's youngest daughter, Marion, objects to her mother's going on "some meaningless cruise with a bunch of white folks"; she believes that Avey should be imaginative and independent "and go off on [her] own somewhere. Learn something." Neither Marion nor Avey herself would have been able to predict that the cruise would begin the greatest independent journey of Avey's life. It precipitates Avey's decision to travel to the island Carriacou, where she explores her own past and rediscovers her identity as "Avatara," the name her great-aunt Cuney had insisted she use as a child. "Avey, short for Avatara," finds her roots as a member of the Arada people of Carriacou; her discovery prompts her plan for selling her house in North White Plains and moving to her girlhood home in Tatem for at least part of the year, so that she, like her aunt before her, could instill in her grandchildren the history and truths of their people and their past.

Twenty years after the publication of *Brown Girl, Brownstones,* Marshall continues to explore the relationship between personal growth and societal change, between the history of black peoples and their future, between their language and their lives. Having won the 1984 Before Columbus American Book Award, *Praisesong for the Widow* may be her most successful and acclaimed novel, yet its appearance reiterates that Marshall is solely a writer of fiction with special qualities rooted in the African and Caribbean tradition of storytelling. Marshall is devoted to a particular vision of the novel: "I realize that it is fashionable now to dismiss the traditional novel as something of an anachronism, but to me it is still a vital form. Not only does it allow for the kind of full-blown, richly detailed writing that I love (I want the reader to see the people and places about which I am writing), but it permits me to operate on many levels and to explore both the inner state of my characters as well as the worlds beyond them."

It is this aesthetic that permeates the work of Paule Marshall from *Brown Girl, Brownstones* through *Soul Clap Hands and Sing,* the short stories, *The Chosen Place, the Timeless People,* and her recent novel, *Praisesong for the Widow.* At the heart of her work is the love of people, their speech, gestures, and thought which she expresses in her skillful and often tender characterizations. Underlying her aesthetic is a faith in the ability of human beings to transcend themselves, to change their condition, that is at the core of much Afro-American literature. Paule Marshall's contribution to that tradition is not only her ability to render complex women characters within the context of equally complex

societies but also her creation of worlds in which the necessity of actively confronting one's personal and historical past is the foundation for a genuine revolutionary process.

References:

Kimberly Benston, "Architectural Imagery and Unity in Marshall's *Brown Girl, Brownstones,*" *Negro American Literature Forum,* 9 (Fall 1975): 67-70;

Jean Corey Bond, "Allegorical Novel by Talented Storyteller," *Freedomways* (First Quarter 1970): 76-78;

Edward Braithwaite, "Rehabilitation," *Critical Quarterly,* 13 (Summer 1971): 175-183;

Braithwaite, "West Indian History and Society in the Art of Paule Marshall's Novel," *Journal of Black Studies,* 1 (December 1970): 225-238;

Lloyd W. Brown, "The Rhythms of Power in Paule Marshall's Fiction," *Novel,* 7 (Winter 1974): 159-167;

Philip Butcher, "The Younger Novelist and the Urban Negro," *CLA Journal,* 4 (March 1961): 196-203;

Barbara Christian, "Ritualistic Process and the Structure of *Praisesong for the Widow,*" *Callaloo # 18,* 6 (Spring-Summer 1983): 74-84;

Christian, "Sculpture and Space: The Interdependency of Chaucer and Culture in the Novels of Paule Marshall," in her *Black Women Novelists* (Westport, Conn.: Greenwood Press, 1980), pp. 80-136;

Eugenia Collier, "The Closing of the Circle: Movement from Division to Wholeness in Paule Marshall's Fiction," *Black Women Writers, 1950-1980,* edited by Mari Evans (New York: Doubleday, 1984), pp. 295-315;

Dorothy Denniston, "Early Short Fiction by Paule Marshall," *Callaloo # 18,* 6 (Spring-Summer 1983): 31-45;

Alexis De Veaux, "Paule Marshall—In Celebration of Our Triumphs," *Essence,* 11 (May 1980): 96, 98, 123-134;

Trudier Harris, "No Outlet for the Blues," *Callaloo, # 18,* 6 (Spring-Summer 1983): 57-67;

Leela Kapai, "Dominant Themes and Techniques in Paule Marshall's Fiction," *CLA Journal,* 16 (September 1972): 49-59;

Marcia Keiza, "Themes and Style in the Works of Paule Marshall," *Negro American Literature Forum,* 9 (Fall 1975): 67-76;

John McCluskey, Jr., "And Called Every Generation Blessed: Theme Setting and Ritual in the Works of Paule Marshall," *Black Women Writ-*

ers, *1950-1980,* edited by Mari Evans (New York: Doubleday, 1984), pp. 316-334;

Peter Nazaruh, "Paule Marshall's Timeless People," *New Letters,* 40 (Autumn 1973): 116-131;

Deborah Schneider, "A Search for Selfhood: Paule Marshall's *Brown Girl, Brownstones,*" in *The Afro-American Novel Since 1960,* edited by Peter Bruck and Wolfgang Karrer (Amsterdam: B. R. Grüner, 1982), pp. 53-72;

Joseph T. Skerrett, Jr., "Paule Marshall and the Crisis of the Middle Years," *Callaloo # 18,* 6 (Spring-Summer 1983): 68-73;

Winifred Stoelting, "Time Past and Time Present: The Search for Viable Links in *The Chosen Place, the Timeless People,*" *CLA Journal,* 16 (September 1972): 60-71;

Marilyn Nelson Waniek, "Paltry Things: Immigrants and Marginal Men," *Callaloo # 18,* 6 (Spring-Summer 1983): 46-56;

Mary Helen Washington, "Afterword," *Brown Girl, Brownstones* (Old Westbury, N.Y.: Feminist Press, 1981), pp. 311-324;

Washington, "Black Women Image Makers," *Black World,* 23 (August 1974): 10-18.

Sharon Bell Mathis

(26 February 1937-   )

Frances Smith Foster
San Diego State University

BOOKS: *Brooklyn Story* (New York: Hill & Wang, 1970);

Sidewalk Story (New York: Viking, 1971);

Teacup Full of Roses (New York: Viking, 1972);

Ray Charles (New York: Crowell, 1973);

Listen for the Fig Tree (New York: Viking, 1973);

The Hundred Penny Box (New York: Viking, 1975);

Cartwheels (New York: Scholastic, 1977).

Sharon Bell Mathis writes first of all for black children, hoping, she says, that "Black children will leave my books with a feeling that I know they *live.*" In line with that purpose Mathis published her first book,*Brooklyn Story* (1970), as part of the Challenger Book series, a series dedicated to the promulgation of stories "written with special sensitivity to the needs of the black or the Spanish speaking communities of the United States." Her second book, *Sidewalk Story* (1971), won the Council on Interracial Books for Children Prize, and her third book, *Teacup Full of Roses* (1972), picked up awards from the *New York Times* and the American Library Association. Since then Mathis has won practically every major prize offered for writers of children's literature.

Though Mathis is a children's writer, there is nothing childish or elementary about her style, content, or vision. A reviewer's comment about Mathis's 1976 Newbery Honor book, *The Hundred Penny Box* (1975), applies to any of her books: "What

is so fine about the book is that it does not set out in that kind, condescending, nervous way to acquaint its young readers with the concepts. . . . It is a quiet work of art, not an educational project." Sharon Bell Mathis writes honestly and respectfully about black people coming to terms with themselves and with those whom they love.

Mathis was born in Atlantic City, New Jersey, grew up in the Bedford-Stuyvesant area of Brooklyn, and attended the New York parochial schools. As a child she was an avid reader and recalls particularly the impressions of Richard Wright's *Black Boy,* Willard Motley's *Knock on Any Door,* and Betty Smith's *A Tree Grows in Brooklyn.* One of four children born to Alice Mary Frazier Bell and John Willie Bell, Sharon Mathis saw her first real play when her father took her to see Tennessee Williams's *The Rose Tattoo.* Her mother protested that the girl was much too young for that kind of drama and promptly took her to a performance of *Hamlet.* Exposure to such a range of literary works influenced the poems and stories and play that she wrote while a student at St. Michael's Academy, yet Mathis consciously decided not to be a writer. "I was told that black writers could not really make a living, not even as journalists. Frank Yerby and Richard Wright were superstars. I could not see my work in their class and so limited my dreams and followed a more traditional course," she says.

That traditional course was to graduate from

Morgan State College in 1958 with a B.A. in sociology and to marry Leroy Franklin Mathis. The couple moved to Washington, D.C., where Mrs. Mathis worked briefly as an interviewer at Children's Hospital and then began teaching elementary school. She has three daughters: Sherrie, Stacy, and Stephanie, and in 1975 completed an M.S. in Library Science from Catholic University of America. Currently Mathis is in her twenty-third year of teaching and has one grandson, Thomas Kevin Allen II.

But somewhere along the way Sharon Mathis began to deviate from the traditional course. In 1968 she published a short story in *Tan Confessions*. She joined the Washington, D.C., Black Writers Workshop in 1969 and founded the children's literature division. In 1970, writers Tom Feelings and John Oliver Killens chose *Sidewalk Story* for the Council on Interracial Books Award. She won a fellowship to the Bread Loaf Writers' Conference in Vermont and acquired a literary agent. She became a professional writer.

When Mathis wrote *Brooklyn Story,* she was teaching junior high school. It was natural then that she should choose to write a high-interest, low-level vocabulary story for children such as those she taught every day. Moreover, the recent assassination of Martin Luther King, Jr., had changed the design of the civil rights movement and severely distressed the black community. She felt a strong need to reaffirm for black children their individual and collective strengths and responsibilities.

In *Brooklyn Story* teenagers Vi and Eddie Keeler have contrasting reactions to the impending visit of their mother, Della. Vi is ecstatic; Eddie is incensed. Believing his mother abandoned them as infants, Eddie refuses reconciliation. Vi tries to protect Della from Eddie's anger but must also struggle with her own jealousy about Della's preoccupation with the prodigal son. When Eddie is accidentally shot during the confusion that accompanied the assassination of Dr. King, each member of the family must plumb the depths of personal and communal grief to learn the power of their love. Vi finds the strength to ask the central question of her mother, "Why didn't you want me and Eddie?" The answers are complex and painful, but as each member recognizes his responsibilities, the family begins to knit itself together. "The design was tender. And strong. And forever."

On one hand, *Brooklyn Story* is a domestic tale with which many children can identify. It examines individual and emotional responses to love and to death. It explores the familial responsibilities and relationships, and it affirms the healing power of love. At the same time the historical moment and its effect on the Johnson family and their community make *Brooklyn Story* a larger, very positive statement.

Sidewalk Story is written for a younger audience. Nine-year-old Lilly Etta Allen discovers that her best friend's family is being dispossessed and no one seems willing to stop it. She disobeys her mother, braves a thunderstorm, and risks the real gold earrings promised for her tenth birthday in order to help her friend. In so doing she not only learns about the indifference of institutions and the frustration and loneliness of defiance but also about the personal pleasure and possible success for those who assume risks and responsibilities for the good of others. Although the child defies her mother and succeeds where adults fail, Mathis does not present those adults as uncaring or ineffectual, nor does she advocate willful rebellion. Lilly Etta's heroism has a happy ending, but both Lilly Etta and the readers become more aware of the real limitations upon one's impulses to help and of the fact that happy endings are not usual for such sidewalk stories. What Mathis demonstrates is the truth of the folk adage "Nothing beats a try but a failure."

When writing *Teacup Full of Roses,* Sharon Bell Mathis was teaching math in a special education program at Charles Hart Junior High School and teaching the writing of children's literature for the Black Writers Workshop. The book, she says, is "another salute to Black kids." Its epigram quotes Nikki Giovanni: "i wanna say just gotta say something bout those beautiful beautiful beautiful outasight black men." The protagonist is seventeen-year-old Joe Matthew. His two brothers are twenty-four-year-old Paul, his mother's favorite son, an artist, and a junkie; and fifteen-year-old Davey, exceptionally talented athletically and scholastically, idealistic and definitely not street-wise.

The mother ignores Joe's and Davey's struggles as she tries to insure the health and safety of Paul, seemingly her most vulnerable child. A disabled father and a great-aunt of dubious mental health complete the family and contribute to the tension by their weaknesses, their visions, and their attempts to help. Finally, there is Ellie, Joe's girl friend, whose absolute devotion both strengthens and hinders Joe as he tries to believe the stories he invents about a better future for them all. There are disappointments, deceits, and death in the story, yet once again Joe and his experiences affirm the existence of "A real black love place."

From 1972-1973 Mathis was writer-in-residence at Howard University where she taught

*Dust jacket for Mathis's 1972 novel written while she was a high-school math teacher. She called the book
"another salute to Black kids."*

classes in creative writing and in contemporary black literature. She was also writing a biography of Ray Charles. Says Mathis, "the triumphs of Ray Charles are the triumphs of all black people—a story of great will, of great strength, and a profound sense of survival." For this work she researched extensively the education and experiences of blind people, and *Ray Charles* (1973) not only won the Coretta Scott King Award but provided the idea for her next novel, *Listen for the Fig Tree* (1973).

Muffin lost her sight when she was ten, and she lost her father, who was murdered, when she was fifteen. From these tragedies she has realized her own strength and courage, but her mother, Leola, has maintained only a perilous hold on her sanity, has lost her health, and has become an alcoholic. As Christmas and the first anniversary of her father's death approach, Muffin's energies are torn between her preparation for Kwanzaa (a black Christmas celebration), which she sees as the affirmation of her father's legacy, and the increasing

destructiveness of her mother's grief. Neighbors and friends try to protect, support, and help Muffin reconcile these conflicts and define her priorities. From the black salesperson who refuses to exploit the mentally incompetent Leola to the mute, elderly Mr. Thomas who is savagely beaten as he fends off Muffin's would-be rapist, *Listen for the Fig Tree* is peopled with caring individuals. But Muffin must, as Mr. Dale tells her, "Listen for your growing up time" and understand the necessity for self-respect and self-determination, which is firmly grounded in shared love.

A Caldecott Honor Book, *The Hundred Penny Box* (1975) presents a contemporary version of the extended family and the consequential complexities therein. Aunt Dew has now come to live with her orphaned nephew John whom she reared, his wife Ruth, and his son Mike. Despite Ruth's best efforts, Dew does not adjust to the situation; she will not even remember Ruth's name. Instead, Aunt Dew sometimes confuses Mike with the young John and prefers to remain closeted in the bedroom among the clutter of her remaining possessions, rocking and singing "Precious Lord." Ruth's solution is to get rid of Dew's "stuff" and force her forward into a "new life." Mike, however, senses the importance of history and continuity not only for the individual but also for the descendants. The conflict eventually focuses upon the preservation of a big box containing 100 pennies, one for each year of Aunt Dew's life. Ruth determines to substitute a small rosewood box to hold the pennies, but Mike knows that Aunt Dew's box is her life. Neatly combining themes of old age, senility, family history, and self-identity, Mathis does not resolve the conflict, but Mike listens to Aunt Dew "sing her long song," and therein lies the promise.

In *Cartwheels* (1977), three girls are trying to change something in their lives, and for each one the key is winning the gymnastic competition. Zettie wants the fifty-dollar prize in order to buy a ticket back to South Carolina and her loved ones there. She is lonely and cramped in the tiny basement apartment in a big city. This dream is clouded when Zettie's mother invites a friend, who has just lost her job, and her niece Fawn to live with them. Fawn proves to be selfish and inconsiderate and upon discovering Zettie's secret includes herself in Zettie's plans. Finally, the leader of the neighborhood girls who have harassed and threatened Zettie in the past, Thomasina, also has secret plans for the prize money – she wants to buy her baby brother a winter coat. As Zettie interacts with these girls, she must reevaluate her priorities. To complicate matters further, Fawn disappears on the day of the contest and at the competition a new girl shows up with a fantastic, crowd-pleasing act. Though only one girl wins the fifty dollars, each wins respect for herself and for her place in the community.

Dale Carlson of the *New York Times Book Review* claims Mathis's talent is best demonstrated in her characterizations and descriptions of delicate relationships. Writing for *Black World*, Eloise Greenfield agrees that Mathis writes of "real people" and identifies her talent as being rooted in "a profound knowledge of people and an infinite love and respect for Black children." *Ebony* writer Carole A. Parkes proclaims her "one of the most articulate, active campaigners for black children's rights."

Mathis has dedicated each of her books to specific relatives and friends because "they gave me all I ever needed to create by themselves being creative. They taught me strength by being strong." But she draws the epigrams, literary references, details, and basic story plots from the rich mosaic of black life, and she leaves no doubt that each book is actually dedicated to the entire black community. Words of male African poet and political leader Léopold Sédar Senghor and of female Afro-American poets Nikki Giovanni and June Jordan join snatches of black gospel songs and Bible verses to form the context of her novels.

Sharon Bell Mathis writes books about people and their everyday concerns, about relationships between families, neighbors, and friends, and about the sources and manifestations of the strong, unyielding love that grows and flourishes through the storms and sunshine of black life. There are no Nancy Drews or Encyclopedia Browns, no Horatio Algers, Tom Sawyers, or Superfudges in blackface, no fairy-tale endings, and above all no Dick and Jane neighborhoods. Her youthful protagonists become familiar with the traumas of disability, aging, and death. They encounter the problems engendered by drug addiction, alcoholism, and mental illness. They know fear and frustration, the harshness of poverty, urban stress, and urban migration, but they also know the saving power and the many manifestations of love. Like Zettie in *Cartwheels,* when it is their time to fly, they are ready, and as they leap into the air, they hear those who love them say, "Fly up there, if you want to. We won't let you fall." Their flights, like Zettie's, may be confined to urban basement apartments, but they do fly.

Presently, Sharon Bell Mathis edits the "Ebony Jrs. Speak!" column in *Ebony Jr.,* and she is writing two books, "Sammy's Baby" and "Carrotsticks and Marshmallows."

Julian Mayfield

(6 June 1928-)

Estelle W. Taylor
Howard University

BOOKS: *The Hit* (New York: Vanguard, 1957; London: M. Joseph, 1959);

The Long Night (New York: Vanguard, 1958; London: M. Joseph, 1960);

The Grand Parade (New York: Vanguard, 1961; London: M. Joseph, 1961); republished as *Nowhere Street* (New York: Paperback Library, 1963).

PLAY: *Fount of the Nation,* Baltimore, The Arena Players, Inc., Community Theatre, 17 February 1978.

SCREENPLAYS: *Uptight,* with Ruby Dee and Jules Dassin, Paramount, 1968;

Children of Anger, Irving Jacoby Associates, New York, 1971;

The Long Night, with Woodie King, based on the novel by Mayfield, Woodie King-St. Claire Bourne Production Company, 1976.

FILMSTRIPS: "The History of the Black Man in the United States" (Pleasantville, N.Y.: Educational Audio Visual, 1969);

"The Odyssey of W. E. B. DuBois" (Jamaica,N.Y.: Buckingham Enterprises, 1970).

OTHER: "Into the Mainstream and Oblivion," in *The American Negro Writer and His Roots* (New York: American Society of African Culture, 1960), pp. 29-34;

The World without the Bomb: the Papers of the Accra Assembly, edited by Mayfield (Ghana: Ghana Government Press, 1963);

Ten Times Black, edited with contributions by Mayfield (New York: Bantam Books, 1972).

PERIODICAL PUBLICATIONS: "Numbers Writer: A Portrait," *Nation,* 190 (14 May 1960): 424-425;

"Challenge to Negro Leadership," *Commentary,* 31 (April 1961): 297-305;

"The Cuban Challenge," *Freedomways,* 1 (Summer 1961): 185-189;

"Love Affair with the United States," *New Republic,* 165 (7 August 1961): 25;

"And Then Came Baldwin," *Freedomways,* 3 (Spring 1963): 143-155;

"Tale of Two Novelists," *Negro Digest,* 14 (June 1965): 70-72;

"Black Writer's Views on Literary Lions and Values," *Negro Digest,* 17 (January 1968): 16;

"Legitimacy of Black Revolution," *Nation,* 206 (22 April 1968): 541-543;

"New Mainstream," *Nation,* 204 (13 May 1968): 638;

"Crisis or Crusade? An Article-Review of Harold Cruse's *Crisis of the Negro Intellectual,*" *Negro Digest,* 17 (June 1968): 10-24;

"The Negro Writer and the Stickup," *Boston University Journal,* 1 (Winter 1969): 11-16;

"Black on Black: A Political Love Story," *Black World,* 21 (February 1972): 54-71;

"Lorraine Hansberry: A Woman for All Seasons," *Freedomways,* 19 (Fourth Quarter 1979): 263-268;

"The Great Disturber of the Peace: Was DuBois a Progenitor of Negritude?," *Sagala* (Summer 1980): 23-31.

Julian Mayfield, since 1978 a writer-in-residence in the Department of English at Howard University, has had a varied, colorful, and unusual career as novelist, playwright, critical essayist, university teacher, Broadway and Hollywood actor, journalist, and adviser to the leaders of two Third-World governments, the late Kwame Nkrumah of Ghana and Prime Minister Forbes Burnham of Guyana. This variety of experience has enabled him—almost compelled him—for more than thirty years to articulate and interpret the black experience through an interesting array of media. Though he has changed the literary milieu and even the philosophical reach and direction that his first published works took, his literary reputation is still firmly based on his first two novels, *The Hit* (1957) and *The Long Night* (1958), in both of which he admits that he "tried to create a melody rather than a symphony." In these works he became a significant part of a literary tradition, one of a long line of writers who used Harlem as the vantage point from which to write about the black condition and the black experience. Thus, he is generally

Julian Mayfield as Tank in Uptight, *the film he cowrote based on Liam O'Flaherty's* The Informer

labeled a transitional protest writer, whose Harlem lies somewhere between the decadent and tragic ghetto of Paul Laurence Dunbar's *The Sport of Gods* (1902) and Ann Petry's *The Street* (1946), the haven of Rudolph Fisher's "City of Refuge" (1925) and the paradise of Carl Van Vechten's *Nigger Heaven* (1926).

Julian Mayfield was born in Greer, South Carolina, on 6 June 1928; but he is considered a native of Washington, D.C., his parents, Hudson and Annie Mae Prince Mayfield, having moved there when he was five years old from a South Carolina village bearing the name of Needmore. After graduating from Dunbar High School in the capital at the age of eighteen, he joined the peacetime army and was assigned duty in the Pacific. Upon his return to civilian life he attended Lincoln University in Pennsylvania but left before graduating in order to attempt to earn his way in New York City. In the early days Mayfield was always busy trying to make ends meet: he washed dishes, drove a cab, painted houses, did spot radio announcements, and in the early 1950s he wrote articles for a variety of newspapers, including the short-lived, left-wing black newspaper *Freedom,* a member of whose board was the black singer-actor

Paul Robeson. At the paper he came into contact with a coterie of other writers: John O. Killens, Lorraine Hansberry, Langston Hughes, Ruby Dee, John Henrik Clarke. For the first time, he says, he became an intimate part of the circle of the black intellectual left, who stirred his social consciousness and left him "reeling" with their fiercely charged discussions and exchange of ideas about racial injustice and oppression, about "new concepts in ideology, philosophy, and aesthetics." Between 1949 and 1954 he was also active in the New York theater, on and off Broadway. Off Broadway he appeared in the Harlem production of *A Medal for Willie* and downtown in a revival of John Wexler's *They Shall Not Die,* a protest play about the plight of the Scottsboro boys. Mayfield recalls that when groups of white youths opposed to the message of outrage expressed through this play attempted to curtail its performance by attacking the actors, the audience provided them safe escort out of the hostile neighborhood. In an interview with Harriet Scarupa, published in the April 1979 issue of *New Directions,* the Howard University magazine, Mayfield confesses that this kind of incident "was a hell of an exciting thing to be a part of then. I was in good health and felt that I could whip anybody. And I didn't want to miss anything." During this period Mayfield also appeared in an off-Broadway production of his own play *417,* the number around which the action in his first novel, *The Hit,* revolves. On Broadway he created the juvenile lead role of Absalom in *Lost in the Stars,* the successful Kurt Weill-Maxwell Anderson musical.

In 1954 Mayfield married Ana Livia Cordero, a physician; they have two children, Rafael Ariel and Emiliano Kwesi. That year the Mayfields moved to Puerto Rico, where he helped to set up the island's first English-language radio station on which he served as newscaster. Two years later he helped to establish and began working for the Puerto Rico *World Journal* under the supervision of William Dorvillier, the Pulitzer Prize-winning editor.

During his sojourn in Puerto Rico, Mayfield completed his first novel. The action of *The Hit* revolves around the lives of frustration of the Cooley family—twenty-six-year-old James Lee Cooley and his parents, Hubert and Gertrude. Hard-working though they are, they are the victims of poverty and oppression that deepen in the Harlem ghetto in which they are trapped. Though fifty-year-old Hubert has been a proprietor of two grocery stores, a pool hall, and a dry-cleaning shop, he has fallen on bad times and is a disgruntled, embittered janitor in a Harlem apartment house. His only hope now is that God will redeem Himself by letting him hit the numbers big. Thus, Hubert feels justified in "borrowing" from the household expenses to maintain his numbers habit. Hubert plays seven dollars on 417 and hits, but does not collect because the numbers man fails to pay off. Hubert Cooley's dream turns into a nightmare, and he is left a defeated, hopeless, broken "old" man.

The plot of *The Hit* is simple; its characters are treated sympathetically, yet realistically. They are, says Mayfield, "the types of people I really knew." Gertrude, though the stabilizing force of the black family, is abused, unappreciated, and resented by her husband, who has lost his hope and his real manhood. In his attempt to boost his ego and self-esteem, he turns to Sister Clarisse for the understanding and sweetness he claims his wife has lost. At twenty-six James Lee sees himself as a reflection of his parents' despair and, thus, hesitates to marry his girl friend for fear of repeating his parents' failure.

The Hit, a transitional Harlem novel, represents Mayfield's experience almost exclusively with black life. In it, as Arthur Davis points out in *From the Dark Tower*, "There is no Black-Power politics, no militancy, no black nationalism, no I-hate-honky fanaticism. The Harlem of 1957 had not yet become the torn and savage city of the sixties and seventies." Mayfield states that in his first novels, "despite the terrible things happening around me, Harlem was 'romantic' and I saw what I wanted to see, more of the beauty of black life than the ugliness of black life at that time."

When Mayfield returned to New York in 1958, the civil rights movement was beginning to heat up; views concerning race relationships and the plight of the black man everywhere were becoming more radical. Mayfield notes that his own point of view concerning the racial situation had changed and that he had become more concerned with taking the "romance" out of his work and putting in the "stark black and white."

In *The Long Night* (1958), Mayfield's Harlem shows signs of decay. Through his ten-year-old main character, Steely, he depicts, as he had done in *The Hit*, the variety of ways in which working-class blacks and those dependent upon them are systematically victimized by poverty and oppression, but the Harlem of Steely is much uglier than the Harlem of James Lee Cooley. Steely's father, Paul Brown, drops out of law school, leaves home, and becomes a doorway bum. Unlike Hubert Cooley, however, before being overwhelmed and defeated

by the system, he has tried to instill in his young son a sense of race pride, a knowledge of who he is, the importance of black role models, and of manliness.

The simple plot of *The Long Night* revolves also around the numbers game. Mae Brown, Steely's mother, sends Steely to collect her hit of twenty-seven dollars, admonishing him, half-seriously and half-jokingly, not to return home without the money. Steely collects the money, but it is taken from him by members of his own gang. The efforts he makes to raise the money resemble, on the one hand, the efforts of Everyman to find someone to accompany him to the grave and, on the other hand, a bittersweet comedy of errors. Mr. Lichstein, for whom Steely does odd jobs, refuses to help in any way. His friend Sugar Boy donates a dollar and dismisses him. The purse Steely snatches contains only two dollars; the bicycle he steals is stolen from him; and the drunk he rolls turns out to be his own father. The ending of this novel implies that Brown, his son Steely, and Mae Brown will be reunited—an ending that some critics assessed as unsatisfactory, unrealistic, and contrived.

Though *The Long Night*, like *The Hit*, is an excellent example of protest writing prior to the 1960s and 1970s as well as an excellent portrayal of the child of the ghetto, it anticipates a more militant stance on the part of blacks, as well as on the part of its author. For Paul Brown, the American dream is dead. After all, he is "not so sure," he says, that he wants to "be a full-fledged American." Both *The Hit* and *The Long Night* present skillfully the concerns of the author with the black family and the disintegrating and debilitating effect that the social, political, and economic climate of America can have on that unit.

Three years after the publication of *The Long Night*, Mayfield attempted a more ambitious literary project, *The Grand Parade* (1961), reprinted as *Nowhere Street* by Warner Paperback Library. Prior to the writing of his third novel Mayfield's politics had changed dramatically. He had become deeply involved in and touched by not only the civil rights movement in the United States but also by movements for freedom from oppression throughout the world. In the United States he had become a regular member of what he calls the Paul Robeson "entourage marching around with him under the pretext he needed our protection"; he was an admirer and friend of Malcolm X, whom he met in Ghana and with whom he traveled to Egypt; he had met W. E. B. Du Bois and was with him when he died. He participated in long, challenging debates and discussions with his activist-writer friends concerning African unification and the relationship between a strong Africa and a strong Afro-America. In 1959 he took an active part in the First Conference of Negro Writers, called by the American Society for African Culture in New York, where he presented a paper, "Into the Mainstream and Oblivion," reprinted in *The American Negro Writer and His Roots* (1960). In this extremely significant paper Mayfield called for a separation of the Negro writer from the so-called mainstream. Following it could lead only to oblivion for blacks since the mainstreamers had isolated themselves from the "great questions facing the peoples of the world." The Negro writer's "salvation lies," he declared, "in escaping the narrow national orbit—artistic, cultural, and political—and soaring into the space of more universal experience." In 1960, after the Castro revolution, he went to Cuba with black leftists Harold Cruse, LeRoi Jones (Imamu Baraka), and Robert Williams. It was during this time that he met Nicolas Guillen, whom Mayfield remembers as "the giant poet, who, long before the revolution, had heaped scorn and revulsion on the racial and political hypocrisies of Cuban society."

The Grand Parade, then, came out of a different orientation and may be regarded as an effort on Mayfield's part to expand the boundaries of his art. However, according to Davis, "It seems . . . that he lost some of his authority ('to give a picture of the ghetto that is poetically convincing') when he abandoned the simple vignette of black city life for the ambitious type of delineation in *The Grand Parade*."

The novel concerns itself with some of the major issues of the day: corrupt politics and politicians, antagonism between the races, and segregation in the public schools. The action takes place in Gainesboro, a "nowhere" city located between the North and the South. Its array of characters include Mayor Douglas Taylor, an idealistic white politician, who is killed by a white supremacist as he defies an angry mob and tries to integrate a predominantly white public school; Randolph Banks, an unscrupulous black politician whose brother is a member of the Communist party; Patty Speed, a beautiful but bad black gang leader; a gang of blacks accused of raping a white prostitute; and other low-life characters. "Whatever else he tried to do," says Davis of this novel, "he certainly attempted to show the oneness of American life, the interaction of black and white in the crooked politics of an American community"; but "in spite of the author's attitude toward the mainstream, *The Grand Parade* tries very hard to be a successful mainstream effort."

During this period of his life, Mayfield seemed to be always on the move in a restless, almost obsessive quest for involvement in any social movement and, indeed, any revolution that could effect social and political justice and equality for his oppressed brothers everywhere. Because of his close association with Robert Williams, the racial leader in Monroe, North Carolina, who had been accused of kidnapping a white couple during a racial confrontation, Mayfield, the object of an F.B.I. search, fled to Canada, then to England, and finally to Ghana in 1961, where he lived until 1966, shortly before President Nkrumah was deposed. During those years he wrote regularly for newspapers and the radio, served as speech writer and political assistant to Nkrumah, and was founding editor of the *African Review*, an international monthly published in Accra and concerned with economic and political affairs. In his capacity as chief documentalist for the Accra Assembly, Mayfield authored and edited in 1963 *The World without the Bomb: the Papers of the Accra Assembly*, a report of the disarmament conference of nongovernmental scientists and other scholars and intellectuals called by the government of Ghana in June 1962. He was in Spain trying to complete a book when Nkrumah, one of his heroes, was overthrown by the army in 1966. Looking back, Mayfield says that he was not surprised that the coup occurred. "It was as if you'd been watching someone you knew die of cancer over a long period of time and finally one day he is dead."

In 1966 Mayfield lived in Spain, and after moving to England for a year, he returned to the United States in 1968 as a fellow of the Society for the Humanities at Cornell University, where he conducted a seminar in race relations. It was during 1968, according to Mayfield, that he "got the screenwriting bug" while collaborating with Ruby Dee and Jules Dassin on the Paramount motion picture production *Uptight,* in which he played the leading role of Tank, a character who atones with his life for his betrayal of fellow members of a black militant organization. Mayfield received rave reviews for his performance in this picture. *Ebony* magazine declared that he had set "an entirely new image of a black leading man. He is . . . in a word . . . Every-nigger." The *Hollywood Citizen-News* stated that the "Picture's . . . outstanding aspect is a monumental film debut by Julian Mayfield whose splendid playing is more internal eruption than performing. He is excellent." Harry MacArthur wrote in the *Washington Evening Star* "Julian Mayfield may discover he is an actor in spite of himself. He prefers to think of himself as a writer (he has three novels to his credit), but if he gets an Academy Award nomination . . . it shouldn't come as a surprise." Despite his success as an actor, he was not "stage struck."

From 1968-1970 Mayfield was again actively involved in a university setting, this time as lecturer in the Albert Schweitzer Program in the Humanities at New York University, but in 1970-1971 he returned to Cornell University as the first Distinguished Visiting W. E. B. Du Bois Fellow in the African Studies and Research Program. During this stint he edited *Ten Times Black,* a collection of ten short stories on the black experience, published by Bantam Books in 1972. This book includes the works of such figures as Evan K. Walker, Hank Gay, Sam Greenlee, Nikki Giovanni, Maya Angelou, Sandra Drake, Rosa Guy, Barbara Woods, Clarence Major, as well as Mayfield's long short story "Black on Black: A Political Love Story." The two blacks in the story are an American singer and an African politician of an unidentified country. The intrigue and danger involve the greedy, ambitious, scheming politicians who surround the president: "Ambitious big fish in small puddles are easy to recognize," said Mayfield in a *New Directions* interview. "There is a certain kind of glaze over their eyes, a way of pushing out their chests, an unconscious strut in their walk."

From 1971-1974 the restless Mayfield was again in search of a cause, this time in Guyana, South America, a place that fascinated him "because it is the only country in the Western hemisphere completely controlled by blacks." During his stay in Guyana he served, first, as adviser to the minister of information and, then, as senior special political assistant to Prime Minister Forbes Burnham. Resigning in 1974, Mayfield returned to lecture at the University of Maryland (College Park) for two years before becoming a senior Fulbright-Hays fellow teaching in West Germany. During this period, under the auspices of the United States Information Service and local universities, Mayfield lectured in Vienna, Berlin, Copenhagen, Tunis, and Ankara. In 1977-1978 he was back in the United States serving as lecturer in Black Culture and American Literature at the University of Maryland.

The life and work of Julian Mayfield represent an inextricable merger of art and politics. In a *Washington Post* interview he described his philosophy of writing: "I look at writing as another form of struggle. This doesn't mean that everything has to be out and out propaganda. But certainly everything has a message." During the 1960s Mayfield strongly stressed his belief "that all writing is political. Or if it is not, it ought to be." Recently he has refined that position: "all writing reflects the political view—or lack of political view—that a writer has. But I am certainly not asking young Black writers to dedicate themselves to solving the racial problems of America through their writing."

Julian Mayfield seems at peace in his present post at Howard University. He has several projects in mind: a memoir about black Americans who lived in Ghana between 1960-1966 and a book about some of his heroes, people he has known: W. E. B. Du Bois, Paul Robeson, Malcolm X, Kwame Nkrumah.

Interviews:

Holly I. West, "The Goal of Julian Mayfield: Fusing Art and Politics," *Washington Post,* 7 July 1975, B1, B3;

Harriet J. Scarupa, "Eyewitness of Power," *New Directions* (April 1979): 12-15.

References:

Arthur P. Davis, *From the Dark Tower: Afro American Writers, 1900-1960* (Washington, D.C.: Howard University Press, 1981), pp. 198-203;

Shirley Graham, "Review of *The Grand Parade,*" *Freedomways,* 1 (Summer 1961): 218-223;

Review of *The Grand Parade, Interracial Review,* 35 (May 1962): 127;

"Uptight," *Ebony,* 24 (November 1968): 46-48.

John A. McCluskey, Jr.

(25 October 1944-)

Frank E. Moorer
University of Iowa

BOOKS: *Look What They Done to My Song* (New York: Random House, 1974);
Mr. America's Last Season Blues (Baton Rouge & London: Louisiana State University Press, 1983).

OTHER: *Blacks in History,* volume 2, edited by McCluskey (Cleveland, Ohio: New Day Press, 1975);
Stories from Black History: Nine Stories, edited by McCluskey, 5 volumes (Cleveland, Ohio: New Day Press, 1975).

John A. McCluskey, Jr., was born to John A. and Helen Harris McCluskey in Middletown, Ohio; his father was a truck driver. Middletown, an industrial town in southern Ohio, attracted a large number of Southern blacks before and during World War II to work in its factories. As a result, stories about black life in the South were plentiful as McCluskey was growing up. In high school, he was active in sports, especially football and track. In spite of his interest in athletics, McCluskey was a good student in academic subjects. Upon graduating from high school, he won a scholarship to Harvard University, where he also played football. He studied social relations at Harvard, receiving a B.A. cum laude in 1966, and took his first courses in creative writing there. After Harvard he went to Stanford University to study creative writing. He earned his M.A. in 1972. It was at Stanford that he began his first novel, which he did not complete until after he was living in Cleveland, Ohio, in 1973.

McCluskey is also a teacher. He has taught English at Miles College in Birmingham, Alabama, and humanities at Valparaiso University in Valparaiso, Indiana. From 1969 to 1977, he taught Afro-American and American Studies at Case Western Reserve University. Since June of 1977, he has been an associate professor of Afro-American Studies at Indiana University, Bloomington, Indiana. McCluskey says the writers who have been an inspiration for him are Richard Wright, Jean Toomer, Ralph Ellison, and Gabriel García Márquez. McCluskey has written: "As a writer, my commitment is to that level of creative excellence so

ably demonstrated by Afro-Americans as diverse as Ralph Ellison, Romare Bearden, and Miles Davis. Hoping to avoid any fashionable ambiguity and pedantry, I want my fiction and essays to heighten the appreciation of the complexities of Afro-American literature and life." In all of his creative work, McCluskey presents the complexity of black life.

McCluskey's major work, *Look What They Done to My Song* (1974), is a novel about a young black musician who wants to preach a message of love with his music. Mack, the main character in the novel, moves from Santa Fe across the country to Boston trying to find a place where he can play his music. In a real sense, Mack is an evangelist with a horn spreading a message of love and understanding. He wants to carry on Malcolm X's message about the need for human beings to know and understand each other.

On his pilgrimage to self-understanding, Mack stops in several places. He stays for a while in Columbus, Ohio, before moving to Cape Cod and finally to Boston. At each stop along the way, Mack meets people who enlarge his world. In Columbus, he falls in love with a young woman named Sassie Mae, who does not understand Mack or his search for something beyond material comforts. He leaves Columbus and travels to Cape Cod, where he lives with an old couple from Alabama, Dupree and Reba Sledge, who welcome him into their home. They share their food and wisdom, and they also put Mack in touch with a vital part of the black experience. Because they are in touch with themselves and their Southern past, the Sledges are not anxious about the world around them. They give Mack love without demanding anything in return. All they want is that he remain true to himself.

On Cape Cod Mack meets Michelle, a young black woman who refuses to accept her black heritage. Rather she identifies herself as Portuguese. At least for a while Mack falls in love with her, but like others she does not understand his search. He also meets Ubangi, who has left the South under duress. Ubangi believes that the world is a hustle, and he loses a great deal of time trying to find the right kind of hustle for himself, without much success. When one of his schemes goes awry, Ubangi and Mack are forced to flee to Boston.

It is in Boston that Mack meets Novella Turner, a woman who understands him and his need for his music. Novella introduces Mack to Reverend Fuller, an old-time Southern preacher who blends his traditional message with advice on how to live in the contemporary world. Like the Sledges, Reverend Fuller helps Mack understand the black Southern experience. Reverend Fuller wants Mack to bring a new message to his church with his music. On the occasion of Reverend Fuller's last sermon, Mack and his friends bring a new song to the church—a song that speaks to all. Finally Mack has found a place for his music: the church. Mack's musical message will even change winos: "The man pauses to set an empty bottle beneath a bench and no one has bothered to frown because our clap-happy rap-happy selves have been burned too cleanly by song." The author suggests that music, which has been nurtured in the church, is the soul of the black experience. Thus it is not an accident that Mack's horn leads him to Crumbly Rock Baptist Church, which becomes New Breed Baptist Church, where he will bring all people together with his music. "Church is after all any place the spirit roams free and burns us clean enough to touch, to love." Mack has found his home and place. He will spread and preach his message of love and understanding in the New Breed Baptist Church.

McCluskey has published a number of well-received short stories. As in his novels, McCluskey presents a variety of characters in his stories. He believes that black life presents the writer with a diversity of subject matter which the writer should be aware of. The first published story, "Nairobi Night" (*Black World*, January 1973), presents two small-time criminals, Hawk Perkins and Cecil B., who plan to rob a furniture store owned by blacks. They are foiled in their efforts by black nationalists who view themselves as community police protecting community property.

"John Henry's Home" (*Iowa Review*, Spring 1975), centers on John Henry, who has just returned from the Viet Nam war feeling alienated from his community. The small town no longer holds any attraction for him because life seems dull compared to the excitement of the army. Certainly he does not want to spend the remainder of his life in the town working in the local steel mill. Instead of going to work, John Henry begins to sell drugs, marijuana at first and then hard drugs. Even when he decides to take a job in the mill, he supplies drugs to the workers and some managers. He is forced to leave town when an irate father whose son has died of an overdose threatens to kill him. So John Henry leaves for a larger town that will provide him more customers. In the story McCluskey is obviously concerned about the problem of drugs in the black community, but he does not preach a sermon on the evils of drugs. Rather it is through the actions of the characters that the reader is made aware of the deadly nature of John Henry's services to the community—especially to the young.

"Winter Tell Tale" (*Seattle Review*, Spring 1978) is narrated by Delano, who with his friend Pop runs a crooked card game at the local bus station. Delano is a family man who has been laid off from his regular job, and he needs the card game to support his family. During a slack period in the game, Delano and R. V., a character who is about to leave town, tell tales in order to pass the time. R. V.'s story is about a fellow who has been unfaithful to his wife. The wife finds out and demands that he leave immediately, but not before she cuts his clothes to threads. When R. V. goes up to get on the bus, Delano notices his coat has been cut almost to rags, and it is at that moment he realizes that R. V.'s tale was about himself.

"What Happened to Red Garland?" (*Choice*, 1980) centers on a Korean War veteran who learns to cope with his problems through the music of Red Garland, a jazz piano player. For Thurman, Red Garland can roll with the punches. Red has "the light touch. He sounds like a bird tripping over those keys." Red Garland gives Thurman the courage to pick up the pieces of his life after being rejected by a woman he loved.

The long story "Forty In the Shade" (*Obsidian*, Spring 1978) was selected as a 1979-1980 Pushcart Prize story. It was part of a novel in progress—since published as *Mr. America's Last Season Blues*—but it is complete as a short story. The main character, Roscoe, is celebrating his fortieth birthday, and as he relaxes to enjoy the gifts from his three sons, he tells them the history of the family. The story of the family has been told many times before, and each time Roscoe and his sons relive the experience of Caesar Americus, who escaped from slavery in Georgia and made it to Ohio. In Ohio Caesar established his family. The boys are proud of old Caesar, their great-great-grandfather who outwitted his slave master, slave catchers, and other hostile forces to achieve his freedom. It is this proud tradition of struggle and survival that the father, Roscoe, wants his sons to carry on after his death. Roscoe functions as an oral historian; he wants his children to know

Dust jacket for McCluskey's second novel, the story of an athlete struggling to make a comeback in both his personal and professional lives

the story so well that they will be able to tell it to their children. This story, like all of McCluskey's stories, treats the black experience as any other human one.

Published in 1983, *Mr. America's Last Season Blues* is a blues novel, full of expectations, melancholy, common sense, and humor. Once the hero of the black community in Union City, Roscoe Americus, Jr., a has-been tackle for Ohio State and rookie with the Cleveland Browns until he was released after a knee injury, is haunted by the black community's constant reminders of what he used to be and by his father's ghost which asks Roscoe if he still has the "fighting spirit."

Roscoe's dreams focus on not only a physical comeback but also an emotional one. He tries to revive his image in the black community by playing football with the local semipro team; but after reinjuring his knee, he realizes he is an old man playing at a young man's game. Not only does he hope to save his marriage and bring his brothers and sister together for a long-overdue reunion but also attempts yet fails to help his lover's son, found guilty of a crime which he did not commit. By trying to be all things to all people in the black community, Roscoe seems intent on regaining for the blacks in Union City a sense of identity, unity, and purpose.

McCluskey's work reveals a strong awareness of history and an equally strong feeling for black cultural traditions. For McCluskey the Afro-American cultural experience has been a heroic one—one that has nurtured the individual and the group. The black religious experience and the oral tradition are all used very effectively in his fiction. McCluskey has the talent to become one of our major writers.

Louise Meriwether

(8 May 1923-   )

Rita B. Dandridge

Norfolk State University

BOOKS: *Daddy Was a Number Runner* (Englewood Cliffs, N.J.: Prentice-Hall, 1970; London: Hodder & Stoughton, 1972);

The Freedom Ship of Robert Smalls (Englewood Cliffs, N.J.: Prentice-Hall, 1971);

The Heart Man: Dr. Daniel Hale Williams (Englewood Cliffs, N.J.: Prentice-Hall, 1972);

Don't Ride the Bus on Monday: The Rosa Parks Story (Englewood Cliffs, N.J.: Prentice-Hall, 1973).

OTHER: "That Girl from Creektown," *Black Review No. 2,* edited by Mel Watkins (New York: Morrow, 1972), pp. 79-92.

SELECTED PERIODICAL PUBLICATIONS:

Fiction:

"Daddy Was a Number Runner," *Antioch Review,* 27 (Fall 1967): 325-337;

"A Happening in Barbados," *Antioch Review,* 28 (Spring 1968): 43-52;

"The Thick End Is for Whipping," *Negro Digest,* 28 (November 1968): 55-62.

Nonfiction:

"James Baldwin: The Fiery Voice of the Negro Revolt," *Negro Digest,* 12 (August 1963): 3-7;

"No Race Pride," *Bronze America,* 1 (June 1964): 6-9;

"The Negro: Half a Man in a White World," *Negro Digest,* 14 (October 1965): 4-13;

"The New Face of Negro History," *Frontier,* 16 (October 1965): 5-7;

"The Black Family in Crisis: Teenage Pregnancy," *Essence* (April 1984): 94-96, 144, 147, 151.

Louise Meriwether (photo by Bert Andrews)

A writer of essays, short stories, a novel, and juvenile biographies, Louise Meriwether is regarded as a minor author, eclipsed by her more prolific contemporaries. The infrequent appearance of her name in journals of literary criticism and book-length studies on black American literature is regrettable, for she is a socially conscious activist-author of meticulous craftsmanship. Exposing the insidiousness of racism and the capriciousness of sexism, she shares a great deal with her contemporaries: like them she writes about the prejudices and preoccupations of her time. Her distinction is that her feeling is not invented but personal. Her firsthand experiences with America's inequities lend themselves to plausible characters, lifelike dialogue, accurate details, and metaphorically significant settings. Her fiction shows considerable narrative skill; her nonfiction is direct and forceful.

Louise Meriwether was born in Haverstraw, New York, to Marion Lloyd Jenkins and Julia Jenkins. She is the third of five children and the only daughter of parents who made the northern trek from South Carolina via Philadelphia to New York in search of a better life. A bricklayer in Haverstraw, her father moved the family to Brooklyn, where, trapped by the Depression, he became a number runner. Meriwether lived in Harlem during her adolescence and writes "times were hard and my parents were on welfare." She attended P.S. 81, was graduated from Central Commercial High School in downtown Manhattan, and received a B.A. in English from New York University. Marrying Angelo Meriwether, a graduate student at Columbia University, she moved with her husband to the Midwest, where he found a teaching position, and subsequently to Los Angeles in the 1950s. Her first marriage ended in divorce, and so did her second to Earl Howe. Never wanting to do anything except write, she limited herself to three years on any job she secured. In Los Angeles, she worked as a legal secretary, a real estate salesperson, a reporter for the *Los Angeles Sentinel,* and as the first black story analyst for Universal Studios. In 1965, she received a master's degree in journalism from the University of California at Los Angeles. One of her graduate theses, rewritten and published in the October 1965 issue of *Negro Digest* as "The Negro: Half a Man in a White World," is a militant rendering of the mistreatment of blacks in America and documents her early preoccupation with this subject.

In the early 1960s, Meriwether appeared in print when she published book reviews for the *Los Angeles Times* and *Los Angeles Sentinel* and articles on black Americans in predominantly black journals. Her identity, however, was often obscured. At times, her name was inadvertently misspelled Merriweather; at other times, she deliberately signed her manuscripts L. M. Meriwether as a foil for editors who, she believed, at that time were insensitive to female writers. Admitting that she has "always had a budding romance with history," Meriwether generally wrote articles about blacks who overcame great odds to achieve success: Matthew Henson, Leontyne Price, Grace Bumbry, and attorney Audrey Boswell. In these early pieces, the theme of triumph over defeat contrasts with the struggle and defeat found in her fiction. Nevertheless, penetrating research, vivid character portrayal, and historical perspective are common to all her writings.

Meriwether turned to fiction in the late 1960s. Contacting Budd Schulberg, organizer of the Watts Writers' Workshop, she served as a staff member of that project and contributed to the *Antioch Review* when the group was invited in 1967 to do so. She viewed the opportunity to publish in the *Antioch Review* as a means of getting doors opened to book publishers who searched literary quarterlies for prospective novelists. Her short story "Daddy Was a Number Runner " was published in the fall 1967 Watts Workshop issue of the *Antioch Review;* a sec-

ond short story, "A Happening in Barbados," appeared in the spring 1968 issue of the *Antioch Review.*

"A Happening in Barbados" evolved from a 1967 trip that Meriwether took to Trinidad, Barbados, and Jamaica with her mother and a West Indian friend, Muriel Alleyne, with whom she grew up. It relates the bitterness that a middle-class black Harlem woman vacationing in Barbados has toward white women who befriend black men. Agitated by the infidelity of her husband, whom she has divorced, and the scarcity of eligible black men, the unnamed middle-aged narrator uses a lonely white woman as a scapegoat for her anger. She terminates publicly a relationship with a young Barbadian whom she admires and overtly woos away from a white woman an ugly Barbadian man whom she despises. Meriwether sketches a plausible black woman spitefully reacting to a historical fact and myth: the fact is that there is a dwindling supply of eligible black males, and the myth is that the white woman is capable of luring any man that she wants. Reading this short story in the *Antioch Review,* Bill Gross, an editor with Prentice-Hall, admired its veracity and boldness and requested chapters from Meriwether's novel in progress, *Daddy Was a Number Runner.* When the novel was completed, Meriwether forwarded the manuscript to Prentice-Hall, and it was published.

Approximately five years went into the writing of *Daddy Was a Number Runner.* At one point, Meriwether ceased working on her novel for nine months "in order to do battle with Hollywood director Norman Jewison and Twentieth Century-Fox producer David L. Wolper, the latter of whom bought the film rights of William Styron's *The Confessions of Nat Turner* (1967) for $600,000." Considering Styron's book an outrage because it completely emasculated Nat Turner and distorted historical truths, Meriwether and Vantile Whitfield, founder of Performing Arts Society of Los Angeles, formed an activist group called the Black Anti-Defamation Association to oppose basing the movie on Styron's book. They received a tremendous assist from actor Ossie Davis, Imamu Baraka, and other individuals, and support from the Los Angeles NAACP, Urban League, Karenga's US, the Black Panther Party, black student unions, and churches who circulated and signed petitions. Meriwether found a sympathizer in historian John Henrik Clarke, who subsequently edited and published a group of essays entitled *William Styron's Nat Turner: Ten Black Writers Respond* (1968). She gained the attention of Martin Luther King, who was assassi-

"This book should be sent to the White House, and to our earnest Attorney General, and to everyone in this country able to read. . . . Because she has so truthfully conveyed what the world looks like from a black girl's point of view, Louise Meriwether has told everyone . . . what it means to be a black man or woman in this country. . . . It is a considerable achievement. . . ."
—James Baldwin
From the FOREWORD

James E. Hinton

"We have heard from such strong black writers as Claude Brown, James Baldwin and Malcolm X of the struggle to achieve manhood in the embattled enclave of Harlem. Now it is time to hear what the struggle toward a proud black womanhood is all about. From Louise Meriwether you get it right on, with a controlled anger that adds a welcome new name to the unfolding list of black artists who are both challenging and enriching our troubled country."
—Budd Schulberg, founder of the Watts Writers' Workshop

13-197103-4

Louise Meriwether

daddy was a number runner

A NOVEL BY **LOUISE MERIWETHER**
with a foreword by **James Baldwin**

daddy was a number runner

Prentice Hall

Dust jacket for Meriwether's highly acclaimed first novel about one year in the life of a twelve-year-old girl in Harlem during the Depression

nated before he could endorse her cause; a copy of Styron's book was found among his personal possessions. The outcome of these efforts is that the motion picture was never made. Styron publicly complained that Hollywood had capitulated to a group of militants "who are basically resentful that a white man wrote about their hero rather than a black man."

Daddy Was a Number Runner (1970) details a year in the life of twelve-year-old Francie Coffin in Harlem during the Great Depression. As Francie approaches womanhood, she witnesses the total disintegration of her family as each member compensates for his economic insecurity and the negative view whites have of blacks. Her father, James, unable to provide for the family, runs off with another woman; her elder brother James, Jr., becomes a pimp; her precocious younger brother Sterling drops out of school to take a menial job; her once proud mother, Henrietta, begs the welfare worker for more money to feed her hungry children. Francie realizes life has little to offer her and that she, too, will eventually go her separate way and contribute to the disintegration of the family unit. She comments to her friend Sukie about the options in life: "Either you was a whore like China Doll or you worked in a laundry or you did day's work or ran poker games or had a baby every year." Simply cursing life at the novel's end, Francie has far less to expect from life than her white literary counterpart, Francie Nolan, the adolescent protagonist in Betty Smith's novel *A Tree Grows in Brooklyn* (1943).

Although *Daddy Was a Number Runner* is not an autobiographical novel, there are parallels between Meriwether's early life and that of Francie. Both were the only daughter and third child of a number runner and a domestic worker, both moved with their families from Brooklyn to Harlem, both attended P.S. 81 and grew up as adolescents on welfare, and both lived in the Harlem neighborhood of Fifth Avenue between 116th and 119th streets during the Depression. The similarities are helpful to the extent that they reveal what the author found valuable in her life for the purposes of her novel.

Moreover, these parallels, combined with the first-person point of view, strengthen the novel's sense of reality and historical importance. Few black writers living in Harlem during the Depression have documented the effects of this economic debacle on black Harlem families; and no one, except Meriwether, has rendered in fiction the pain it brought to a young black girl in Harlem. Meriwether transforms raw life into art by coloring her characters and adding circumstances to illuminate the disintegration motif. The destruction of this black family is appropriately symbolized in the family name, Coffin.

The first novel to come out of the Watts Writers' Workshop, *Daddy Was a Number Runner* underwent extensive revisions before its publication. The novel was originally titled "Yoruba's Children," but it was later changed to *Daddy Was a Number Runner* because to Meriwether the original name had begun to sound stereotypical, too much like Aunt Jemima and Mamba's Daughters. Liking the sound of the word "Yorubas," the name of a Nigerian tribe whose existence was unknown to her until she read W. E. B. Du Bois's *Black Folk: Then and Now* (1939), Meriwether reserved the name "Yoruba's Children" for the subtitle of Part Two of the novel which comprises chapters eight to thirteen. Part One, consisting of the first seven chapters, is subtitled "Daddy Was a Number Runner" and was originally published as short stories under different names. The short story "Daddy Was a Number Runner" was extended and became chapters one to six of the finished novel. "The Thick End Is for Whipping," originally appearing in the November 1968 *Negro Digest,* was revised and became chapter seven of the novel. The novel has gone through twelve printings with hardcover sales totaling 19,826; as of December 1980, paperback sales came to 350,646. Although there are several covers for the editions, Meriwether's favorite is the portrait of a black girl with the tenements of Harlem superimposed on her head. Meriwether purchased this photograph for thirty-five dollars at an art exhibit.

When *Daddy Was a Number Runner* was released, it generated favorable critical responses. Ruth Bauerle's reviews for *Saturday Review* noted Meriwether's "skill as a writer" and mentioned that such "considerable talent . . . produces a hopeful book." Paule Marshall wrote "the novel's greatest achievement lies in the strong sense of black life that it conveys. . . . It celebrates the positive values of the black experience: the tenderness and love that often underlie the abrasive surface of relationships . . . ; the humor that has long been an important part of

the survival kit, and the heroism of ordinary folk." Helen King observed the novel's timeliness and opined that Francie is the "prototype of thousands of black children in America who must live day by day with overwhelming despair and hopelessness." Considerable praise came from James Baldwin, whose comments in the novel's foreword were so beautiful that Meriwether wept when she read them: after recommending that the novel "be sent to the White House," Baldwin notes that Meriwether "has achieved an assessment in a deliberately minor key, or a major tragedy." Based on the reception of *Daddy Was a Number Runner,* Meriwether received two grants in 1973 to continue her writing: one from the National Foundation of the Arts in Washington, D.C., and the other from the Creative Arts Service Program, an auxiliary of the New York State Council of the Arts.

After the publication of *Daddy Was a Number Runner* in 1970, Meriwether returned to New York and began to write biographies of famous blacks for elementary school readers. Realizing that "the deliberate omission of blacks from American history has been damaging to children of both races" because "it reinforces in one the feeling of inferiority and in the other a myth of superiority," Meriwether wrote and published a thin book a year for the next three years. Replete with photographs, each book consists of approximately thirty pages and recounts the daring feats of blacks to achieve success and recognition as individuals in American history. The books were favorably received by critics in such journals as *Milwaukee Journal, Kirkus Review,* and *Library Journal* and appear in many cities on recommended reading lists for beginning readers.

The Freedom Ship of Robert Smalls (1971) was the first of the three books published by Prentice-Hall. It is a biographical account of Robert Smalls, who was born a slave in Beaufort, South Carolina, achieved freedom, and later returned with his family to Beaufort, where he was elected to Congress and served five consecutive terms. The most interesting episode in this book is Smalls's hijacking of the *Planter,* a Confederate gunboat, on 16 May 1862. Wearing the captain's hat, Smalls successfully steered the ship upstream past three Confederate forts and reached the ships of the Union fleet where he, his wife and two children, and twelve other slaves became free.

The Heart Man: Dr. Daniel Hale Williams (1972) traces the struggles and success of the famed heart surgeon Daniel Hale Williams, born to free parents in Hollidaysburg, Pennsylvania, on 18 January 1856. The book is a stunning example of the perseverance of a black physician despite obstacles of racism. Unable to practice in hospitals, Dr. Williams began his work in an orphans home and, with donations from sympathizers, opened Provident Hospital in Chicago in 1891, America's first hospital to train black nurses and the first to admit white and black patients. Although he achieved fame as the first doctor to perform a heart operation successfully, he was unable to join the white professional societies that allowed him to read his papers on his successful operations. He traveled throughout the United States setting up programs for black nurses and doctors. When he died on 4 August 1931, he was known as the father of black hospitals.

The following year, Meriwether published *Don't Ride the Bus on Monday: The Rosa Parks Story* (1973). The setting is Alabama; the central character is Rosa Parks, a middle-aged black woman who precipitated the 1955 Montgomery bus boycott when she was jailed for refusing to give up her bus seat to a white man on 1 December 1955. Owing to her heroic stand, the boycott lasted 381 days, and the Supreme Court eventually outlawed segregation on buses and trains in the South. The dramatic illustrations of David Scott Brown complement Meriwether's honest story of a proud black woman who had known segregation since childhood in Pine Level, Alabama, where the school she attended closed three months earlier than the white school so that black children could work in the fields.

Since her return to New York, Meriwether has written one short story, "That Girl from Creektown." The story was written at the request of Mel Watkins who included it in his anthology *Black Review No. 2* (1972). "That Girl from Creektown" evolved from Meriwether's CORE activities in Bogalusa, Louisiana, in the summer of 1965, when she "toted guns for the Deacons who maintained a twenty-four-hour patrol to secure black folks from the forays of the Ku Klux Klan." The story unfolds in racially tense Creektown, Mississippi, where the Elders stake out a twenty-four-hour vigil for the Klan who threaten to burn down the town in retaliation for the Elders' bailing out of jail a black man who has publicly attacked a white man. Against this background of strained racial relations in 1964, eighteen-year-old Lonnie Lyttle, volunteer worker for the Elders and a recent high school graduate, is introduced. Unable to obtain a decent job in the town's segregated rubber plant and cast aside by her boyfriend Daniel, who has married the daughter of

a high school principal, she questions her worth as a black female. Lonnie refuses to work as a white woman's maid, but she engages in sexual relations with Daniel for money to better her condition in New Orleans. The numerous characters populating this story are necessary distractions manifesting the chaotic everyday existence of a poor Southern black woman whose relationships with members of her own race are as discomforting as those with prejudiced whites.

Shortly after the publication of "That Girl from Creektown," Meriwether's activist proclivities again swept her away from creative writing. Distressed by black Americans allowing themselves to be wooed by South Africa into breaking the Organization of African Unity (OAU) boycott and going there as entertainers, she and John Henrik Clarke formed a committee known as Black Concern. They gathered information and circulated a pamphlet, *Black Americans Stay Out of South Africa,* detailing the gross inequities against blacks, coloreds, and Asians in South Africa under apartheid. Meriwether spoke on radio and at the United Nations and received support of the Committee against Apartheid there. Members of Black Concern were successful in getting Muhammad Ali to cancel a boxing match in Johannesburg.

More than ten years have passed since Meriwether's last published book, but she has continued her writing activities. She has written an unpublished novel with a Los Angeles setting and has completed the research for a historical novel about the Civil War and Reconstruction. She has joined the Harlem Writers Guild and has become intimate friends with writers Maya Angelou, Rosa Guy, and Paule Marshall, all of whom have developed a support system which to Meriwether "has become life sustaining." She taught the fiction workshop at the Frederick Douglass Creative Arts Center in New York for several years, and she is currently teaching writing courses at Sarah Lawrence College.

References:

Rita B. Dandridge, "From Economic Insecurity to Disintegration: A Study of Character in Louise Meriwether's *Daddy Was a Number Runner,*" *Negro American Literature Forum,* 9 (Fall 1975): 82-85;

Noel Schraufnagel, *From Apology to Protest: The Black American Novel* (De Land, Fla.: Everett/ Edwards, 1973), pp. 134-135.

Toni Morrison

(18 February 1931-   )

Susan L. Blake
Lafayette College

See also the Morrison entries in *DLB 6: American Novelists Since World War II, Second Series,* and *DLB Yearbook: 1981.*

BOOKS: *The Bluest Eye* (New York: Holt, Rinehart & Winston, 1970; London: Chatto & Windus, 1979);

Sula (New York: Knopf, 1973; London: Allen Lane, 1974);

Song of Solomon (New York: Knopf, 1977; London: Chatto & Windus, 1978);

Tar Baby (New York: Knopf, 1981; London: Chatto & Windus, 1981).

OTHER: *The Black Book,* compiled by Middleton Harris, edited by Morrison (New York: Random House, 1974).

PERIODICAL PUBLICATIONS: "What the Black Woman Thinks About Women's Lib," *New York Times Magazine,* 22 August 1971, pp. 14-15, 63-64, 66;

"Cooking Out," *New York Times Book Review,* 10 June 1973, pp. 4, 16;

"Behind the Making of the Black Book," *Black World,* 23 (February 1974): 86-90;

"Rediscovering Black History," *New York Times Magazine,* 11 August 1974, pp. 14, 16, 18, 20, 22, 24;

"Reading," *Mademoiselle,* 81 (May 1975): 14;

"Slow Walk of Trees (as Grandmother Would Say) Hopeless (as Grandfather Would Say)," *New York Times Magazine,* 4 July 1976, pp. 104, 150, 152, 160, 162, 164.

Toni Morrison (photo by Layle Silbert)

When her picture appeared on the cover of *Newsweek* in 1981 and her fourth novel, *Tar Baby,* was on the year's best-seller list, Toni Morrison was an anomaly in two respects: she is a black writer who has achieved national prominence and popularity, and she is a popular writer who is taken seriously. She is taken seriously by teachers of literature, who teach her works in genre as well as Afro-American literature courses; by feminists, who point to *The Bluest Eye* as a rare depiction of the onset of puberty in girls and to *Sula* as a rare exploration of friendship between women; and by black readers, who cite the accuracy, honesty, and constructiveness of Morrison's portrayal of black life.

Morrison is also a teacher; she has taught Afro-American literature and creative writing for the last decade at SUNY/Purchase, Yale University, and, most recently, Bard College. And she is one of the few novelists who is also an editor. As senior editor at Random House, she has brought into print, among other works, the autobiographies of Muhammad Ali and Angela Davis and fiction by Toni Cade Bambara, Henry Dumas, and Gayl Jones (whose *Corregidora,* she wrote, "lit up the dark past of slave women with klieg lights" and reduced her to "a hungry reader and not a professional one"). Her purpose as an editor reflects her purpose as a writer: "I look very hard for black fiction because I want to participate in developing a canon of black work. We've had the first rush of black entertainment, where blacks were writing for whites, and whites were encouraging this kind of self-flagellation. Now we can get down to the craft of writing, where black people are talking to black people."

Born Chloe Anthony Wofford, Toni Morrison grew up in the Depression in Lorain, Ohio, the second of four children of strong-minded, self-reliant parents. Her father, George Wofford, a shipyard welder, worked three jobs simultaneously for most of seventeen years and was proud enough of his workmanship that he wrote his name in the side of the ship whenever he welded a perfect seam. Her mother, Ramah Willis Wofford, sang in the church choir, reasoned with the bill collectors, and, when the family was on relief and received bug-ridden meal, wrote a long letter to Franklin D. Roosevelt. Her parents disagreed, Morrison recalls, about "whether it was possible for white people to improve." Her father thought not. Thus, "distrusting every word and every gesture of every white man on earth, [he] assumed that the white man who crept up the stairs one afternoon had come to molest his daughters and threw him down the stairs and then our tricycle after him." Her mother, on the other hand, believed in white people's possibilities. But both acted from the assumption that "black people were the humans of the globe," and both "had serious doubts about the quality and existence of white humanity." Thus they believed and taught their children that "all succor and aid came from themselves and their neighborhood."

The neighborhood of the imagination, however, stretched from Jane Austen's Mansfield Park to the supernatural. Her parents told her ghost stories. Her grandmother used a dream book to play the numbers. When she entered the first grade, Chloe was the only child in the class who knew how to read. As an adolescent, she read avidly—the great Russian novels, *Madame Bovary*, Jane Austen. "Those books were not written for a little black girl in Lorain, Ohio," Morrison says, "but they were so magnificently done that I got them anyway—they spoke directly to me out of their own specificity. I wasn't thinking of writing then—I wanted to be a dancer like Maria Tallchief—but when I wrote my first novel years later, I wanted to capture that same specificity about the nature and feeling of the culture *I* grew up in."

After graduating with honors from Lorain High School, Chloe Wofford went to Howard University, where she majored in English and minored in classics and changed her name to Toni—because people had trouble pronouncing Chloe. Howard was a disappointment: "It was about getting married, buying clothes and going to parties. It was also about being cool, loving Sarah Vaughan (who only moved her hand a little when she sang) and MJQ [the Modern Jazz Quartet]." In reaction to this sterility, she immersed herself in the Howard University Players and, in the summers, traveled with a student-faculty repertory troupe that took plays on tour in the South. Traveling in the South was a revelation to her, as she made it to the character Milkman later in *Song of Solomon*. It illustrated the stories of her grandparents, who had migrated north from Greenville, Alabama, in 1912—archetypal stories of lost land, trumped-up debt, the sharecropping trap, and surreptitious flight—and provided a geographical and historical focus for the sense of cultural identity her parents had instilled in her.

Chloe Wofford's early influences and experiences are clearly reflected not only in the texture but also in the themes and forms of Toni Morrison's fiction. Each of Morrison's novels presents a dialectic of values, alternative ways of being black, or female, or human. A basic disparity the novels explore is the one her parents took for granted—the difference between black humanity and white cultural values. This opposition produces the negative theme of the seduction and betrayal of black people by white culture—the destruction of Pecola Breedlove, for example, by her own, her mother's, and her community's absorption of white standards of beauty—and the positive theme of the quest for cultural identity, rendered metaphorically by southward travel, which enables Milkman, as well as Son in *Tar Baby*, not only to survive but to triumph.

As her father was an exacting workman, Morrison is an exacting stylist who continues to revise, she says, even after her books are bound. Her deft evocation of place and culture reflects the specificity she admired in the nineteenth-century classics, but she fits it into a mythic or fabulistic context that reflects her education in black folklore and the family habit of storytelling. "Quiet as it's kept" begins the narration of *The Bluest Eye*, and the reader senses that what follows is not a slice of life but a story, with all of a story's indifference to distinctions among various kinds of truth.

Morrison began to write after she returned to Howard in 1957 as an instructor in English. She had earned a master's degree in English at Cornell in 1955 (her thesis was on the theme of suicide in the works of William Faulkner and Virginia Woolf), taught for two years at Texas Southern University, and, at Howard, met and married Harold Morrison, a Jamaican architect. The marriage was trying and remains a subject of sensitivity; although she has explained its difficulties in part as the result of cultural differences, she refuses to disclose its date. In it, she says, she felt bankrupt: "It was as though I had nothing left but my imagination. I had no will, no judgment, no perspective, no power, no authority, no self—just this brutal sense of irony, melancholy and a trembling respect for words." When she had run out of "old junk" from high school to take to the writers' group she had joined, she dashed off a story about "a little black girl who wanted blue eyes," which became the kernel of her first novel.

She developed the story into a novel several years later in Syracuse. In 1964, after her divorce, she had returned with her two small sons—Harold Ford and Slade Kevin—to her parents' home in Lorain and, a year and a half later, found an editing job with a textbook subsidiary of Random House in Syracuse. Alone, in a strange place, restricted by small children, she worked on the novel in the evenings after the children were asleep. She sent an unfinished version to an editor, who encouraged her to finish it. In 1970, Holt, Rinehart and Winston published *The Bluest Eye,* the story of three young girls at the threshold of maturity in Lorain, Ohio—two who survive the assault of a racist world, and one who doesn't.

The Bluest Eye is a novel of initiation, a microscopic examination of that point where sexual experience, racial experience, and self-image intersect. The plot of the novel is simple: Pecola Breedlove, eleven, who considers herself ugly and thinks blue eyes would make her beautiful, is raped by her father, bears a child that dies, and retreats into madness, believing that her eyes are not simply blue but the bluest of all. What happens, however, is not the point, but *why*. And the interest of the novel lies not in the *why* itself, which is common psychological knowledge, but in how Morrison constructs it.

Pecola is a victim, whose story is also the story of her family and her culture. Much of the novel is composed of the stories of other characters who violate Pecola in one way or another as a reaction to ways in which they themselves have been violated: Geraldine, a fastidious black woman to whom Pecola represents the degradation she's been flee-ing all her life; Soaphead Church, a West Indian "spiritualist" who feeds Pecola's delusions out of his own disgust at blackness; and most centrally, Pecola's parents. Her mother, Pauline, neglects her family and storefront apartment, devoting herself to her white employers, whose clean, well-stocked house and pretty little daughter are the closest she can come to the white culture's ideals of beauty and love which she has absorbed from the movies. In one memorable scene, she abuses and denies Pecola, who has accidentally spilled a hot berry cobbler on "her" spotless floor, while soothing the little white girl who doesn't even know who Pecola is. Pauline's ideals of beauty and love have also led her to reject her husband, Cholly, who himself had been abandoned by his mother in infancy and repudiated by his father in adolescence. Cholly cannot provide the money to feed Pauline's illusions and drinks to assuage his frustration at the failure of his own quest for love and freedom. When he rapes Pecola, he is acting out of a combination of revulsion against the accusation he reads in her pathetic posture and tenderness aroused by its suggestion of Pauline when he first met her.

Pecola's madness is the manifestation of her belief that she can attain love only by being someone she is not—someone white. The characters who push her to it are, like her mother, acting on, or, like her father, reacting against, the same belief. Thus the ironically named Breedlove family—which includes symbolically all those in the community who contribute to Pecola's destruction—breeds not love but self-hatred. The novel's individual narratives develop the network of interrelationships inherent in the verb *to breed*.

The narrative structure of *The Bluest Eye* conveys the tension between Morrison's negative and positive themes. Pecola's story is a parody of the general fairy tale that she and her mother believe in. The chapters about the Breedlove family are headed by excerpts from the Dick-and-Jane basic readers, their white-picket-fence complacency emphasizing the grotesqueness of the Breedlove family life. The final scene, in which Pecola demands assurance from her mirror image that she has the bluest eyes of all, casts Pecola, the innocent victim, in the role of the wicked queen. The subverted fairy tale, however, is set within an etiological tale narrated by Pecola's schoolmate Claudia MacTeer, which purports to explain how there came to be no marigolds in the fall of 1941, but more significantly explains how Claudia and her sister Frieda have grown up successfully in a perilous world. Present events are seen from Claudia's nine-year-old point of view. Stories of past and distant events are told by an omniscient narrator who seems to be both Claudia grown up and, since she states opinions implicit in the structure of the novel, the author. Thus the novel sets the Breedlove family against, on the one hand, the white "ideal" family of the basic readers and, on the other, the strong, supportive MacTeers (who closely resemble the Woffords).

If the white ideal is destructive to the Breedloves, it is flat in comparison to the MacTeers. Claudia's memories of sagging brown stockings and Black Draught, bronchitis and burnt turnips, her mother's singing and fussing, detail a rich and secure family life, punctuated with pain, but suffused in "love, thick and dark as Alaga syrup." In a scene that parallels the one in Pauline Breedlove's white-folks' kitchen, Mrs. MacTeer is firm with her daughters and firm with the white neighbor girl who has come to tattle. In a scene that parallels the rape of Pecola, Mr. MacTeer throws out the roomer who has fondled Frieda and then (like George Wofford) throws the children's tricycle at his head. The MacTeers raise daughters who, "guiltless and without vanity," love themselves and know, at some level, that the popularity of Maureen Peal, the well-dressed and self-satisfied mulatto newcomer at school, is not their fault or even hers: "The *Thing* to fear was the *Thing* that made *her* beautiful, and not us." The difference in character between Claudia and Pecola is illustrated in Claudia's frustration with her friend: "She seemed to fold into herself, like a pleated wing. Her pain antagonized me. I wanted to open her up, crisp her edges, ram a stick down that hunched and curving spine, force her to stand erect and spit the misery out on the streets. But she held it where it could lap up into her eyes."

Frieda and Claudia lose their innocence in the course of the novel, through Pecola's experiences as well as their own. But for them the loss, like their childhood pain, is "productive and fructifying" because they have a firm foundation from which to deal with it. The metaphoric style and fabulistic form of the narrative are themselves evidence of the narrator's ability to control experience and make it productive. In another sense, however, Pecola's pathos is a component of Claudia's strength: "We honed our egos on her, padded our characters with her frailty, and yawned in the fantasy of our strength." The recognition of complicity in the fate of Pecola makes *The Bluest Eye* a complex rather than complacent fable.

The Bluest Eye received moderate though appreciative critical notice. Whether for praise or blame, most reviewers singled out the same charac-

teristics of Morrison's writing—qualities they have continued to remark upon in her subsequent novels: the impact of her vision of black life, her poetic prose, and her construction of a narrative out of discrete scenes and stories. John Leonard, in the *New York Times,* praised "a prose so precise, so faithful to speech and so charged with pain and wonder that the novel becomes poetry." Frankel Haskell, in the *New York Times Book Review,* on the other hand, complained of "fuzziness born of flights of poetic imagery" and lack of focus as "the narratives branch out to assorted portraits and events." Leonard identified the book's subject as "institutionalized waste . . . [of] children [who] suffocate under mountains of merchandised lies." Liz Gant, in *Black World,* identified a more specific theme: "an aspect of the Black experience that many of us would rather forget, our hatred of ourselves." To Ruby Dee, in *Freedomways,* who agreed that the novel was "not . . . a story really, but a series of . . . impressions," the important thing was that they were "painfully accurate impressions" that made the reader "ache for remedy."

By the time *The Bluest Eye* was published, Morrison had moved to an editorial position at Random House in New York. In the early 1970s she began to be sought after, by the *New York Times* especially, as a commentator on black life and books about it. In 1971 and 1972, she reviewed twenty-eight books for the *Times Book Review* and wrote on "What the Black Woman Thinks About Women's Lib" for the *Times Magazine.* Although the novel she had recently published and the one she was then writing, *Sula,* deal with attitudes that govern women's identity and relationships, Morrison concluded that as long as women's lib is concerned with attitudes it is irrelevant to black women; when it focuses on equal pay for equal work it will be of more interest.

Morrison's vision of moral ambiguity is developed further in *Sula,* published in December 1973. Peopled with bizarre characters and punctuated with violent deaths, *Sula* has perplexed many readers. Shadrack, a shell-shocked World War I veteran, founds— and twenty years later the whole community observes—National Suicide Day. Eva Peace, Sula's grandmother, a one-legged woman who reputedly laid her leg across a train track to collect the insurance money to feed her children, sets fire to her junkie son Plum and hurls herself from her third-floor window in a vain effort to save her daughter Hannah, who has caught fire while canning in the yard. Sula herself lets a little boy named Chicken Little slip from her hands into the river, and never tells; takes, and then casually

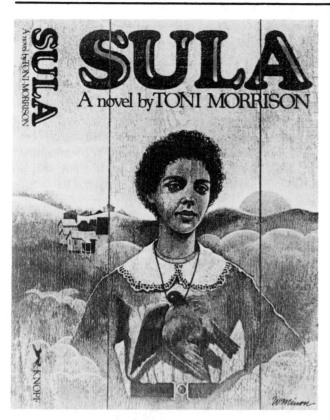

Dust jacket for Morrison's second novel, about a woman who is, in Morrison's words, "a classic type of evil force"

discards, her best friend's husband; and puts her grandmother into a wretched old folks' home. Worse, the reader never knows quite what to think of these characters and events: whether to applaud Eva's self-sacrifice or deplore her tyranny, whether to admire Sula's freedom or condemn her heartlessness.

The neighborhood in which the story is set is called the Bottom, though it is up in the hills. The narrator explains its origin as a "nigger joke": a white farmer who had promised freedom and a piece of bottom land to his slave but did not want to part with rich valley land tricked the slave into believing that "bottom land" was in the hills—"the bottom of heaven." By the narrator's present, however, when the valley farms have been developed into a hot, dusty town while the hills remain cool and shady, the white folks have changed their minds. So buildings have been leveled and trees uprooted for the Medallion City Golf Course. The Bottom has become the suburbs and the multiple ironies of its naming and history signal the shifting relationships of value throughout the novel.

The novel focuses on the relationship between Sula Peace and Nel Wright (both ironically named),

childhood friends who grow apart when Nel marries and Sula leaves home. Morrison's original intention in *Sula* "was to do something with good and evil." Nel, a more complex literary descendant of Geraldine in *The Bluest Eye,* is the conventionally good woman. Sula, in Morrison's words, is "a classic type of evil force." But there are ways in which Nel is also wrong and in which Sula is a force for good. Nel is standing by when Chicken Little slips into the river and is the first to think of escaping blame. Like Eva, Nel is possessive of the people she nurtures. Her possessiveness and her husband's immaturity are as much responsible for Jude's desertion as Sula's casual affair with him is. Sula is neither possessive nor competitive; "she simply [helps] others define themselves." "Their conviction of Sula's evil" makes the townspeople their best selves; they begin to "cherish their husbands and wives, protect their children, repair their homes and in general band together against the devil in their midst."

Ultimately, the alternatives embodied in Nel and Sula are not good and evil, but constraint and freedom. Sula and Nel are both trying to forge their own identities as black women: "Because each had discovered . . . that they were neither white nor male, and that all freedom and triumph was forbidden to them, they had set about creating something else to be." Neither is completely successful. At ten, on her return from a trip to New Orleans with her mother for her great-grandmother's funeral, Nel discovers "I'm me. I'm not their daughter. I'm not Nel. I'm me. Me." The discovery gives her the strength to cultivate a friend as different and disapproved of as Sula. But Nel becomes Jude's wife, her children's mother, and a member of the community who not only follows but endorses the community's conventions. Sula, on the other hand, leaves everything in her quest for freedom: leaves Medallion, repudiates what others consider responsibility, discards what others value. She wanders perpetually in search of something she never finds; she has "no center, no speck around which to grow." Yet when Nel, as responsible church woman, visits senile Eva Peace in an old folks' home twenty-four years after Sula's death, she is shocked into realizing her identity with the girl who let Chicken Little go and the woman who took her husband: " 'All that time, all that time, I thought I was missing Jude. . . . O Lord, Sula,' she cried, 'girl, girl, girlgirlgirl.' " Sula and Nel are in fact parts of one whole character, fragmented by the pressures put on the people of the Bottom by a world of topsy-turvy values.

Sula embodies what Shadrack's Suicide Day commemorates: the unknown and uncontrollable in Nel's life and everyone else's—death, natural disaster, even their own rage at their manipulation by the white world. Her repudiation is evidence that the structures with which people contain these forces are only structures. Like the unfinished tunnel begun in 1927—the deferred dream of commerce with towns across the river and employment for black men—they are subject to collapse on the heads of those who build them (or in the case of the tunnel, ironically, wish to build them). Morrison playfully completes the characterization of Sula as the representative of another world when she follows her into the afterlife: " 'Well, I'll be damned,' she thought, 'it didn't even hurt. Wait'll I tell Nel.' " This comic moment in a fundamentally tragic story attests, too, to the ordinariness, the immanence, of the other world and to the inseparability of what seem to be opposite modes of perception.

Offered as an alternate selection by the Book-of-the-Month Club, excerpted in *Redbook*, and nominated for the 1975 National Book Award in fiction, *Sula* brought Toni Morrison national recognition as a writer. While its poetic prose drew from reviewers the same kinds of positive and negative responses that *The Bluest Eye* had, *Sula* elicited more commentary, most of it favorable, on the reality of its surreal portrayal of black life. Barbara Smith in *Freedomways* focused on the novel's faithfulness to the felt experience of black women. Although Addison Gayle's "Blueprint for Black Criticism" in *First World* offered *Sula* as an example of negative stereotyping of black characters by black authors, both Jerry Bryant in the *Nation* and Roseann P. Bell in *Obsidian* remarked on the "originality" and "three-dimensional humanity" of the characters. Bryant considered the unsettling implications of this originality: "There is something ominous in the chilling detachment with which [writers like Toni Morrison, Ed Bullins, and Alice Walker] view their characters. It is not that their viewpoint is amoral—we are asked for judgment. It's that the characters we judge lie so far outside the guidelines by which we have always made our judgments." Odette C. Martin in *First World* also acknowledged ambiguity in the novel's value judgments and concluded that *Sula* was a "polemic against the destructiveness [for Blacks] of an unreasonable and unreasoning sense of powerlessness." Sarah Blackburn was virtually alone in her view, expressed in the *New York Times Book Review*, that "in spite of its richness and its thorough originality," *Sula* lacked "the stinging immediacy, the urgency, of [Morrison's] non-fiction." Her review brought letters of protest from Alice Walker and

Clarence Major and a sharp response from Morrison herself: "She's talking about my life. It has a stinging immediacy for me."

One of Morrison's foremost concerns is the immediate relevance of black history. In essays for the *New York Times Book Review* on summer pleasures and in the bicentennial issue of the *New York Times Magazine* on the situation of black Americans—"Slow Walk of Trees (as Grandmother Would Say) Hopeless (as Grandfather Would Say)"—Morrison focused on the relationships among black history, her family's history, and her own sense of identity. In February 1974, two months after the publication of *Sula*, Random House published *The Black Book*, which, though her name appears nowhere on it, was Toni Morrison's idea and very much her project. Composed of newspaper clippings, photographs, songs, advertisements, patent office records, recipes, rent-party jingles, and other memorabilia from the collections of Middleton Harris and others, *The Black Book* is a scrapbook, such as we would have, says Bill Cosby in the introduction, if "a three-hundred-year-old black man had decided, oh, say, when he was about ten, to keep a record of what it was like for himself and his people in these United States." As she explained in two articles that served as birth announcements for the book, Morrison conceived it as a way to recognize the history made by "the anonymous men and women who speak in conventional histories only through their leaders" and to rescue it from the faddism of mass culture and the "mysticism" of the Black Power movement. "Being older than a lot of people," she said in *Black World*, "I remember when soul food was called supper." That was a time, she added in the *New York Times Magazine*, "when we knew who we were." For Morrison, black history is the core of black identity: not in "forging new myths" but in "re-discovering the old ones" lies the clue not only to "the way we really were" but to "the way we really are."

This view of history is at the center of Morrison's third novel, *Song of Solomon* (1977), the story of Milkman Dead's quest for identity. Milkman finds himself—discovers his own courage, endurance, and capacity for love and joy; grows up, in short—when he discovers his connection with his ancestors. The reader of Morrison's personal essays realizes that the novel itself acknowledges the author's connection with her ancestors; the names Solomon and Sing and Milkman's grandfather's lost farm are parts of Morrison's family history.

Morrison had said that compiling *The Black Book* was like living through black history again.

This is what Milkman has to do to solve the riddles that lead him to his great-grandfather Solomon. As he travels southward from his Michigan home, he moves back through the generations in his family history. In Danville, Pennsylvania, he discovers his grandfather; in Shalimar, Virginia, his great-grandfather. To make sense of the clues he finds in each location, he must put himself imaginatively into the lives of his forebears, but to find the clues, and even to survive in these strange places, he must first put himself into the minds of the people he meets. It is, of course, the *process* of discovery, the geographical and imaginative journey out of self, that transforms the selfish and immature Milkman: the connection with his ancestors that he discovers is the connection with his contemporaries that he has learned to acknowledge.

Like *Sula* and *The Bluest Eye*, *Song of Solomon* dramatizes dialectical approaches to the challenges of black life. The principal character pairs are represented by Milkman's father, Macon, and his aunt, Pilate, and by Milkman himself and his friend Guitar. Macon Dead, the richest black man in a Michigan town, represents material progress achieved at the expense of human beings. He advises his son to follow his own example when he says, "Own things. And let the things you own own other things. Then you'll own yourself and other people, too." His sister Pilate, on the other hand, to whom "progress was a word that meant walking a little farther on down the road," represents folk and family consciousness, which she demonstrates by listening to her father's ghost and befriending Macon's wife and son. Milkman's progress on his quest for identity is progress from his father's values to Pilate's; he sets out looking for gold, ends up looking for family.

A variant of this dichotomy is dramatized in the relationship between Milkman and Guitar, who represent respectively self-centeredness and racial consciousness. But Guitar and Milkman move in opposite directions, and the definitions and values of these terms shift as the novel progresses. At first Guitar's racial consciousness is associated with Pilate and her humane values. Later, it is contrasted favorably with Milkman's utter selfishness, illustrated in his callous reaction to the murder of Emmett Till. Eventually, however, his racial consciousness leads Guitar to violate the humane values it first fostered. He joins the Seven Days, a vigilante group that kills whites, any whites, in retaliation for the murder of blacks, just as blacks have historically paid indiscriminately for alleged crimes against whites; by the end of the novel, he is the one ob-

Dust jacket for Morrison's third novel, winner of the National Book Critics Circle Award for fiction

sessed with gold, and his ability to kill whites has developed into the determination to kill his "brother" Milkman, whose own development has by this time led him to a healthy and productive self-awareness.

The fabulistic qualities of Morrison's earlier novels are organized in *Song of Solomon* by the general pattern of the fairy-tale quest and the specific structure of an Afro-American folktale (reported in the Georgia Writers' Project book *Drums and Shadows,* to which Morrison has clearly referred) about a group of African-born slaves who rose up from the plantation and flew back home to Africa. Milkman's quest parallels that of the traditional fairy-tale hero, who finds his treasure with the help of magical guides who appear once he learns to share his crust with a dwarf or make love to a crone. It also metaphorically reenacts the legendary flight of his great-grandfather Solomon (or Shalimar) based on that of the Africans in the folktale. Discovery of his ancestor's triumph enables Milkman at the end of the novel to leap toward Guitar and potential death himself, for it has given him his life: "Now he knew what Shalimar knew: If you surrendered to the air, you could *ride* it."

But just as Milkman's discovery of his relationship with his ancestors is actually a result of his acknowledgment of his relationship with his contemporaries, so is his surrender to the air a symbolic repetition of the journey by plane and bus and car that has brought him into the history of his family and his people (indistinguishable terms in the novel) and thus into knowledge of himself as it has carried him southward. Thus Milkman's quest focuses the tension the novel has maintained throughout between fantasy and realism.

Song of Solomon was reviewed favorably on the front page of the *New York Times Book Review* and offered as a main selection of the Book-of-the-Month Club—the first novel by a black writer to be so distinguished since Richard Wright's *Native Son* in 1940. Most reviewers responded to the relationship between realism and fantasy in the novel. Expecting realism, Diane Johnson in the *New York Review of Books* asked, "Are blacks really like this?," and Norma Rogers, in *Freedomways,* called the novel "a mockery of Afro-American life." Recognizing the interpenetration of realism and fantasy, and expressing what has become a theme in Morrison criticism, John Leonard in the *New York Times* compared the novel to Gabriel García Márquez's *One Hundred Years of Solitude:* "It builds out of history and language and myth, to music. . . . The first two-thirds of 'Song of Solomon' are merely wonderful. The last 100 pages is a triumph." Inevitably, *Song of Solomon* was compared with Morrison's earlier novels. Reynolds Price in the *New York Times Book Review* said, "Here the depths of her younger work are still evident, but now they thrust outward, into wider fields, for longer intervals, encompassing many more lives." Both Claudia Tate in *CLA Journal* and Margo Jefferson in *Newsweek,* however, found *Song* less magical and less interesting than the earlier novels. The novel's selection by the Book-of-the-Month Club reminded Jefferson "of an Academy Award denied an actress for her best performance and given several years later for a lesser one. *Song of Solomon* is flashier and more accessible than its predecessors. It is also less striking and less original."

Song of Solomon made Toni Morrison a major American writer. It became a paperback best-seller (the rights having been sold for a reported $315,000), with 570,000 copies in print in 1979. In 1978, the novel won the fiction award of the National Book Critics' Circle; Morrison received an American Academy and Institute of Arts and Letters Award and was featured in the PBS series "Writers in America." In 1980, Morrison was appointed by President Carter to the National Council on the Arts and, in 1981, she was elected to the American Academy and Institute of Arts and Letters. The publication of her fourth novel, *Tar Baby,* in March 1981 was heralded by a cover story in *Newsweek.*

The fabulistic qualities of Morrison's earlier novels are accentuated in *Tar Baby,* which might be described as an allegory of colonialism based on the tale of the Rabbit and the Tar Baby. The Rabbit in *Tar Baby* is an engaging primitive named William Green and called Son. Son has been on the run eight years since killing his adulterous wife. The tar baby is Jadine, a Sorbonne-educated model, the niece of Sydney and Ondine Childs, black butler and cook to the retired white candy manufacturer Valerian Street, who has paid for her education. The setting is Valerian's estate, l'Arbe de la Croix, on Isle des Chevaliers, a tiny French West Indian island named

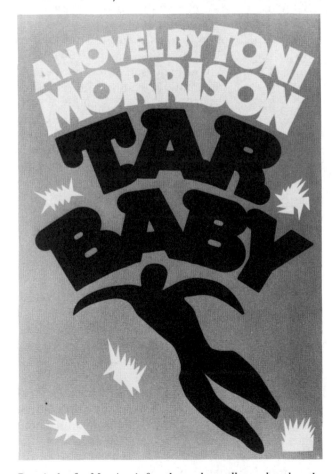

Dust jacket for Morrison's fourth novel, an allegory based on the tale of the rabbit and the tar baby

for the blind African horsemen, imported as slaves but never enslaved, believed still to be riding the hills.

The novel's characters represent various stages in the relationship between colonizer and colonized. Imperial Valerian, sole authority on his estate, represents the power of the colonizer; his wife Margaret, a former beauty queen from Maine who can neither cook nor mother competently, represents dependence and vulnerability. Gideon and Thérèse, islanders who do the yard work and laundry, represent the natives who refuse to be colonized; the fact that they are called "Yardman" and "Mary" by everyone on the estate except Son reflects the indifference of the colonizer to the identity of the native and the degree to which the colonized—Sydney, Ondine, Jadine—accept this violation of their identity. Sydney and Ondine, "Phil-a-delphia Negro[es] mentioned in the book of the very same name" (*The Philadelphia Negro*, W. E. B. Du Bois, 1899), proudly claim an identity shaped by their relationship to the colonizer but distinct from his. Jadine occupies the ambivalent position of being almost but not quite a member of the colonizer's family.

Theft is a motif in the novel, as it is in the colonial relationship. A Christmas-dinner confrontation precipitated by Thérèse and Gideon's theft of some imported apples brings out the political significance of the relationships among the characters. The consequences of the confrontation provide a dramatic commentary on the consequences of colonialism: the realization of Margaret's child abuse and his own ignorance of it makes Valerian crumble and leads to the takeover of his household by Sydney and Ondine and of his greenhouse by the jungle.

In the context of this microcosm of colonialism, the love affair between Son and Jadine is a tug-of-war between opposing attitudes toward colonialism, opposing ways of being black. Jadine considers Valerian's support her liberation; Son considers her acceptance of it prostitution. While Jadine is trying to rescue Son from naive romanticism and backwardness, he is trying to rescue her from Valerian, "meaning *them,* the aliens, the people who in a mere three hundred years had killed a world millions of years old." He thinks she is trying to subject him to domination by these aliens; she thinks he is trying to subject her to domination by the women in her nightmares who thrust out their breasts at her, accusing her of not being a woman and threatening her with the shackles of biology. Neither Son nor Jadine listens to the fine

speeches Morrison gives the other; when the sexual passion between them cools, they return to their symbolic homes—Jadine to Paris; Son, guided by the half-blind Thérèse, to the wild side of the Isle des Chevaliers.

Son faces no internal conflict; he is attracted to Jadine sexually but not emotionally or intellectually. Although, at the end of the novel, he returns to the Isle des Chevaliers to look for her, he is easily diverted when Thérèse puts him off the boat on the wrong side of the island. For Jadine, however, Son represents a part of herself—her sexuality, her capacity for human relationships—that she has long repressed because it has seemed to conflict with her individuality. Her failed affair with Son is a failed attempt to integrate the parts of her personality. Although Morrison gives Jadine a genuine conflict, she is ultimately unsympathetic toward her. At the end of the novel, as Son runs into the jungle "lickety-split" like the Rabbit to join the blind horsemen, the trees step back "as if to make the way easier for a certain kind of man." Meanwhile, Jadine, on the plane to Paris, devotes her attention to the baby sealskin coat—on the seat beside her like a companion—that symbolizes her relationship with a white man in Paris whom she does not love and that has substituted throughout the novel for the sexual and familial relationships she avoids. The dedication of the novel to five women, including Morrison's mother and grandmother—"all of whom knew their true and ancient properties"—is an implied rebuke to Jadine, who does not know hers.

The conflict between the life and humanism of black culture and the deadness and materialism of white culture, dramatized in the relationship between Son and Jadine, is repeated in the setting, on which Morrison lavishes the rich writing that has become her hallmark. The principal settings are the Isle des Chevaliers and New York City. The island is characterized by anthropomorphic flora and fauna: not only do the trees step back for Son, but clouds confer, a river is brokenhearted, and emperor butterflies gossip with angel trumpets. New York, on the other hand, is characterized by brand names, commercial establishments, and code: the Red Apple, Chemical Bank, Suggs, Mikell's, Bergdorf, Hickey Freeman, RVR, the M2. New York, where Jadine feels at home, is also contrasted with Eloe, Son's hometown, where buildings—few, scattered, shabby—are inconsequential, but human relationships are given substance by names, probingly personal conversation, and traditional mores. The two poles of setting come together on the Isle des

Chevaliers, where the vigor and passion of bougainvillea and soldier ants mock the "sane, refined mauve" of the hydrangeas Valerian raises under filtered light in his air-conditioned greenhouse. As Son returns to the jungle in the end, so l'Arbe de la Croix reverts to jungle. Setting symbolically supports action.

Published in March, *Tar Baby* appeared on the *New York Times* best-seller list by 19 April and remained on or near it for four months. Meanwhile, it received tightrope-walking reviews, which judged it "serious," "provocative," "ambitious," and "intelligent" despite stereotyped characters, a surfeit of talk, a fantasy-land setting, authorial intrusion, and stylistic excesses. Brina Caplan pulled together threads in commentaries by John Irving, Darryl Pinckney, Wilfrid Sheed, Webster Schott, Maureen Howard, and Rosellen Brown when she wrote in the *Nation:* "Here, the small black communities that nourish her mythology are peripheral, displaced by locations that represent the dominant culture: a Caribbean island retreat and New York City. Instead of folk-speech, she gives us speeches; rather than experiencing a heritage, her characters discuss it; rather than expressing communal possibility, they quarrel over the value of racial identity. *Tar Baby* is, in effect, a novel of ideas set in the white world." The most negative evaluation of *Tar Baby*'s success as a novel of ideas is represented by Pinckney, who, in the *New York Review of Books,* called the ideas confused and the style convoluted. The most positive is represented by Howard, who, in the *New Republic,* acknowledged "pleasure . . . in construing this moving and intricate plot, a pleasure I associate with the best kind of reading." Irving began his review on the front page of the *New York Times Book Review* by stating, "Our best and most ambitious writers indulge their vices as freely as their virtues," and concluded: "Thomas Hardy, full of his own instructions to damaged mankind, would have loved this book."

Morrison's indulgence of literary vices as well as virtues in *Tar Baby* throws into relief the characteristic themes and techniques of her fiction. *Tar Baby* integrates the several conflicts of the first three novels. The conflict between Jadine and Son reflects that between individual identity and black identity dominating *The Bluest Eye* and that between material and family values represented by Macon and Pilate in *Song of Solomon;* the related conflict Jadine herself faces between independence and womanliness recalls the conflict between Sula and Nel. *Tar Baby* makes it clear that all of these conflicts are aspects of the general conflict between personal

freedom and interpersonal involvement. All of Morrison's major characters long to be free of the restrictions they associate with black identity, family loyalty, and community expectations. They associate freedom with white culture, material gain, and travel. Their stories demonstrate, however, that personal freedom is possible only through human relationships: Pecola is imprisoned by her desire to escape black identity; Claudia's freedom is made possible by her secure and often restricting ties to family and neighborhood, as well as her connection with Pecola. Sula, who leaves the community, and Nel, who submits to it, are incomplete without each other. Milkman frees himself by accepting his obligations to family. And Son, "the man who prized fraternity," is perpetually free, while Jadine, who protects her independence, returns to the life she knows is a trap.

"The community" in Morrison's work is defined by personal rather than political relationships; it is made up of family and neighbors. If one is black, one's community is likely to be black, but blackness does not define it. "My tendency is to focus on neighborhoods and communities," she told Robert Stepto. "And the community, the black community—I don't like to use that term because it came to mean something much different in the sixties and seventies, as though we had to forge one—but it had seemed to me that it was always there, only we called it the 'neighborhood.'" Morrison's comment on the 1960s concept of "black community" is dramatized in the ultimate destructiveness of Guitar and the Seven Days in *Song of Solomon.* In some ways the scope of Morrison's fiction has broadened with each novel. The setting has widened from the small Midwestern town that Morrison herself grew up in to an interregional, and then an international, nexus of locations. The challenges of characterization have increased as the focus has widened from girls to women, to men as well as women, then to whites as well as blacks. The scope of relationships that Morrison is concerned with, however, has actually narrowed. Pecola and Claudia have to define themselves in the face of the white world, as its values are impressed upon them by family and neighbors; Sula and Nel face the expectations of the town; Milkman works out his relationship to his family, present and past; and for Jadine, all the other conflicts are subsumed in the very personal conflict between self and sexuality.

The absence of moral ambiguity in *Tar Baby* emphasizes the fact that, while all of Morrison's novels recommend values for living, the first three recognize moral complexity: the portrayal of characters in *The Bluest Eye* from different perspectives, the parity and incompleteness of Sula and Nel, the shifting evaluations of Milkman and Guitar—these and other slippery elements in the stories suggest that the way to act on constant values depends on time, place, and point of view. They keep the moralism in bounds. In the first three novels, too, the characters themselves discover the relationship between freedom and community—as, for example, when Nel cries "girl, girl, girlgirlgirl" on Sula's grave. In *Tar Baby,* however, no one comes to a comparable insight. And so the moral of the story is imposed from without, not released from within. In Brina Caplan's words, "If, in *Tar Baby,* [Morrison] presses her audience to redefine their thinking, she has elsewhere shown herself capable of forcing them, against the grain of experience, to redefine themselves."

The frank indulgence of fantasy in *Tar Baby* calls attention to the technique that has forced readers of Morrison's earlier works to redefine—or at least reorient—themselves: the fusion of fantasy and realism. The community in *Sula* is simultaneously small-town and bizarre. The endings of *Song of Solomon* and *The Bluest Eye*—as Milkman flies and Pecola talks to her mirror—are both symbolic and credible. In *Tar Baby,* the recognizable and the fantastic are as widely separated as the New York of Mikell's and the M2 is from a made-up island of ambulatory trees and sentient rivers, and the conclusion, Son's entry into the mythic world of the blind horsemen, is merely symbolic.

The tension between myth and reality is what makes Morrison's pervasive symbolism work. The credibility of Milkman's leap and Pecola's madness brings to life the metaphoric bases of these novels—makes *Song of Solomon* a recreation of the legend of the flying Africans, *The Bluest Eye* an antifairy tale. The folktale basis of *Tar Baby,* however, remains simply an analogy. One of the clearest uses of symbolism in Morrison's fiction is in naming. Names like First Corinthians, Pilate, and Dead attract attention to their meanings by their peculiarity and produce delight by their multiple applications to their bearers; but they win acceptance because they have been given in historically realistic circumstances (the practice of selecting names blind from the Bible, a Freedmen's Bureau official's carelessness) and because naming itself is historically symbolic in Afro-American culture. The fact that symbolic meaning is located in names is realistic because it is located there in real life. The realistic basis gives the symbolism its power.

The most obvious indulgence of fantasy in *Tar Baby,* authorial intrusion into the consciousness of butterflies and brooks, carries to extreme another characteristic of Morrison's fiction, the presence of the storyteller. Openings like "Quiet as it's kept"; an ironic tone toward the characters; obvious delight in the striking image; and the construction of the novel from discrete segments, whose shifts in perspective emphasize the author's omniscience—these characteristics, in addition to outright authorial moralizing, reveal the storyteller and remind the reader that he is hearing a story, not entering into another world.

Authorial presence, fantasy, and moral purpose make Morrison's novels fabulistic. The tension between these qualities and specificity keeps the novels from being simply fables. If *Tar Baby* is an indication of the direction of Morrison's fiction, she is moving away from the novel toward the simpler view of reality and more symbolic technique of the fable.

Toni Morrison not only recognizes but claims the characteristics of her writing that critics have identified, and she attributes both her themes and her techniques to her role and heritage as a black writer. She considers herself a teacher who writes what she calls village literature for "peasants" who have migrated to the city and face a conflict "between old values of the tribes and new urban values." She wants her books to do for blacks "what the music used to do": "clarify the roles that have become obscured . . . identify those things in the past that are useful and those that are not; and . . . give nourishment." More specifically, she says, she writes about love—"how people relate to one another and miss it or hang on to it"—and "how to survive *whole.*" Surviving whole depends upon love; Morrison sees the violence in her fiction as the distortion of love, the consequence of "love that isn't fructified, is held in, not expressed." She explores the failure of human relationships, such as the friendship between Nel and Sula, as a "way of saying to the reader, *don't let it happen!*"

Morrison is probably not surprised that critics consider *Tar Baby* a novel of ideas, for she starts, she says, with an idea and then finds a character who can express it. She is aware that pursuing her goals can mean "verging on sentimentality," and she admits that she likes "to fret the cliché, which is a cliché because the experience expressed in it is important."

Although she dislikes being called a "poetic" writer, when asked what she thinks distinguishes her fiction, she replies, "The language, only the language." Morrison sees language as an expression of black experience, a means of revelation, and a force to unify her work. Language "is the thing that black people love so much—the saying of words, holding them on the tongue, experimenting with them, playing with them. It's a love, a passion. Its function is like a preacher's: to make you stand up out of your seat, make you lose yourself and hear yourself." She relies on metaphor to "pull out" economically what the reader already knows in order to "remove cataracts" and "let people know where their power is." Repeatedly in interviews, she stresses that "the language must not sweat," "the seams must not show." She composes, unsurprisingly, by scenes and relies on the language to bind them into a polished whole. Although Morrison herself does not make this connection, her technique of stitching together pieces so that the seams don't show is consistent with her thematic goal of showing people who face fragmentation by conflicting values how to survive whole.

In her *Newsweek* review of *Song of Solomon*, Margo Jefferson wrote, "A Toni Morrison novel generally resembles a beautifully patterned quilt. One begins by admiring the intricacies of each square and ends surprised and delighted by the way the disparate fragments combine to form the grand design of the whole." Storytelling, like quiltmaking, is a folk art; a Morrison novel, like a quilt, is both pieced and highly patterned; and within the pattern of both quilt and novel there is room for whimsical juxtaposition, asymmetrical embellishment, and odd bits of one's own past.

Despite bizarre characters, deadpan violence, and the blending of realism and fantasy, Toni Morrison is an old-fashioned writer. She complains that "most contemporary books" are "not *about* anything"; her own are about self-knowledge and human relations within the family and the neighborhood. They teach the lesson Chloe Wofford's parents taught: that "all succor and aid came from themselves and their neighborhood." They celebrate what Morrison has called "the old verities"—excellence, integrity, dignity, love— "that made being black and alive in this country the most dynamic existence imaginable."

Interviews:

Mel Watkins, "Talk with Toni Morrison," *New York Times Book Review*, 11 September 1977, pp. 48, 50;

Robert B. Stepto, " 'Intimate Things in Place': A Conversation with Toni Morrison," *Massachusetts Review*, 18 (Autumn 1977): 473-489;

Jane Bakerman, "The Seams Can't Show: An Interview with Toni Morrison," *Black American Literature Forum*, 12 (Summer 1978): 56-60;

Bettye J. Parker, "Complexity: Toni Morrison's Women—An Interview Essay," in *Sturdy Black Bridges: Visions of Black Women in Literature*, edited by Roseann P. Bell, et al. (Garden City: Doubleday, 1979), pp. 251-257;

Thomas LeClair, " 'The Language Must Not Sweat,' " *New Republic*, 184 (21 March 1981): 25-29;

Claudia Tate, "Toni Morrison," in *Black Women Writers at Work*, edited by Tate (New York: Continuum, 1983), pp. 117-131.

References:

Joan Bischoff, "The Novels of Toni Morrison: Studies in Thwarted Sensitivity," *Studies in Black Literature*, 6 (1976): 21-23;

Susan L. Blake, "Folklore and Community in *Song of Solomon*," *MELUS*, 7 (Fall 1980): 77-82;

Brina Caplan, "A Fierce Conflict of Colors," *Nation*, 232 (2 May 1981): 529-535;

Barbara Christian, *Black Women Novelists: The Development of a Tradition, 1892-1976* (Westport, Conn.: Greenwood, 1980);

Jacqueline de Weever, "The Inverted World of Toni Morrison's *The Bluest Eye* and *Sula*," *CLA Journal*, 22 (June 1979): 402-414;

Karen de Witt, "Song of Solomon," *Washington Post*, 30 September 1977, C1, C3;

Colette Dowling, "The Song of Toni Morrison," *New York Times Magazine*, 20 May 1979, pp. 40-42, 48, 52, 54, 56, 58;

Robert Fikes, Jr., "Echoes from Small Town Ohio: A Toni Morrison Bibliography," *Obsidian*, 5 (Spring/Summer 1979): 142-148;

A. Leslie Harris, "Myth as Structure in Toni Morrison's *Song of Solomon*," *MELUS*, 7 (Fall 1980): 69-76;

Maureen Howard, "A Novel of Exile and Home," *New Republic*, 184 (21 March 1981): 29-30, 32;

Phyllis R. Klotman, "Dick-and-Jane and the Shirley Temple Sensibility in *The Bluest Eye*," *Black American Literature Forum*, 13 (Winter 1979): 123-125;

Barbara Lounsberry and Grace Ann Hovet, "Principles of Perception in Toni Morrison's *Sula*," *Black American Literature Forum*, 13 (Winter 1979): 126-129;

Odette C. Martin, "Sula," *First World*, 1 (Winter 1977): 34-44;

Cathleen Medwick, "Toni Morrison: A Great

American Author, a Spirit of Love and Rage . . . ," *Vogue,* 171 (April 1981): 288-289, 330-332;

Adam David Miller, "Breedlove, Peace and the Dead: Some Observations on the World of Toni Morrison," *Black Scholar,* 9 (March 1978): 47-50;

Chikwenye Okonjo Ogunyemi, "Order and Disorder in Toni Morrison's *The Bluest Eye,*" *Critique: Studies in Modern Fiction,* 19 (1977): 112-120;

Ogunyemi, "*Sula:* 'A Nigger Joke,' " *Black American Literature Forum,* 13 (Winter 1979): 130-133;

Robert G. O'Meally, " 'Tar Baby, She Don' Say Nothin',' " *Callaloo,* 4, 1-3 (October-February 1981);

Philip M. Royster, "The Bluest Eye," *First World,* 1 (Winter 1977): 34-44;

Royster, "Milkman's Flying: The Scapegoat Transcended in Toni Morrison's *Song of Solomon,*" *CLA Journal,* 24 (June 1981): 419-440;

Sandra Satterwhite, "The Full Days of a Novelist," *New York Post,* 26 January 1974, p. 35;

Wilfrid Sheed, "Improbable Assignment," *Atlantic,* 247 (April 1981): 119-120;

Jean Strouse, "Toni Morrison's Black Magic," *Newsweek,* 97 (30 March 1981): 52-57.

Walter Dean Myers
(12 August 1937-   )

Carmen Subryan
Howard University

BOOKS: *Where Does the Day Go?* (New York: Parents' Magazine Press, 1969);

The Dancers (New York: Parents' Magazine Press, 1972);

The Dragon Takes a Wife (Indianapolis: Bobbs-Merrill, 1972);

Fly, Jimmy, Fly (New York: Putnam's, 1974);

Fast Sam, Cool Clyde, and Stuff (New York: Viking, 1975);

The World of Work. A Guide to Choosing a Career (Indianapolis: Bobbs-Merrill, 1975);

Social Welfare (New York: Franklin Watts, 1976);

Brainstorm (New York: Triumph Books, 1977);

Mojo and the Russians (New York: Viking, 1977);

It Ain't All for Nothin' (New York: Viking, 1978);

The Young Landlords (New York: Viking, 1979);

The Black Pearl and the Ghost or One Mystery After Another (New York: Viking, 1980);

The Golden Serpent (New York: Viking, 1980; London: MacRea, 1981);

Hoops (New York: Delacorte, 1981);

The Legend of Tarik (New York: Viking, 1981);

Won't Know 'Til I Get There (New York: Viking, 1981);

The Nicholas Factor (New York: Viking, 1983);

Tales of a Dead King (New York: Morrow, 1983).

PERIODICAL PUBLICATION: "The Black Experience in Children's Books: One Step Forward, Two Steps Back," *Interracial Books for Children Bulletin,* 10, no. 6 (1979): 14-15.

Although Walter Dean Myers has published articles and short stories in the *Liberator, Black World,* and *Black Arts South,* his primary achievement is the juvenile books in which he attempts to touch the lives of black children. In 1969 Myers began writing children's books after realizing that the materials available "did not deliver images upon which Black children could build and expand their own worlds." Noting the resistance to his initial efforts in his article "The Black Experience in Children's Books: One Step Forward, Two Steps Back," Myers declared that "the time was soon coming when all children's literature would be truly humanistic." At the time of that article, 1979, there were fewer books for black children being published than during the late 1960s. Myers has persisted in his attempt to provide for black children good literature, which he defines as "literature that includes them and the way they live" and that "celebrates their life and their person. It upholds and gives special place to their humanity."

In response to the need for good children's literature for and about blacks, Myers has published to date more than fifteen picture books and novels for young adults. His stories deal mainly with the tragedies and triumphs of growing up in a difficult environment.

Walter Myers was born on 12 August 1937 in Martinsburg, West Virginia, where he lived until he moved with his family to New York. A graduate of the City College of New York, Myers also attended the Writers' Workshop sponsored by John O. Killens in New York. He was employed as a senior trade book editor for the Bobbs-Merrill Publishing Company in New York. In 1977 he took up writing on a full-time basis.

In his first children's book, *Where Does the Day Go?* (1969), illustrated by Leo Carty, a group of children from several ethnic backgrounds and a sensitive black father discuss their ideas about where the day goes. *The Dancers* (1972), Myers's second children's work, is a simple tale about Michael, a black boy, whose fascination with ballet leads to a cultural exchange between blacks and whites. Published in 1972, Myers's first fairy tale, *The Dragon Takes a Wife*, chronicles the misadventures of Harry, a dragon living in Lyraland, who, aided by Mabel Mae (a contemporary black fairy whom he later marries), overcomes a knight. *Fly, Jimmy, Fly* (1974), Myers's fourth children's book, tells of Jimmy who yearns to fly like the birds circling high above the cluttered maze of the city. Although discouraged by his mother, Jimmy persists, until he learns to fly in his imagination.

Other children's picture books include *Brainstorm* (1977), a science-fiction tale, and *The Black Pearl and the Ghost* (1980) and *The Golden Serpent* (1980), both set in the mysterious East. *The Black Pearl and the Ghost* consists of two mystery stories—one concerning Dr. Aramy and Mr. Uppley, spoofs of Sherlock Holmes and Dr. Watson, who solve the mystery of a stolen pearl, and the other concerning Mr. Dibble, a ghost chaser, who rids Lord Bleek's manor of a troublesome spirit. *The Golden Serpent* tells of Pundabi, a wise man, who is summoned by the king to solve a mystery and tells the king that he has lost his Golden Serpent. While searching for it, the king views the poverty and degradation in his kingdom and returns in disgust to his palace; Pundabi doubts that the king will ever find the serpent, which symbolizes goodness and compassion.

In 1975 Myers published the first in a series of novels for young adults. *Fast Sam, Cool Clyde, and Stuff*, set in the neighborhood of 116th Street in

Walter Dean Myers

New York City, tells of a group of preteen youths growing up in an adverse environment, yet making the most of their situation. They confront the types of problems facing most black ghetto youths: they are arrested mistakenly three times during the course of the story; a father dies; another deserts his family; and an acquaintance who turns to drugs is fatally shot. Because of the bonding which occurs among the members of the group, the reader realizes that each individual's potential for survival has increased.

This novel proved to be Myers's springboard into young adult literature. In his *School Library Journal* review, John F. Caviston commented that the novel is "alternately funny, sad, and sentimental, but it is always very natural and appealing." *Booklist* described the narrative as "engrossing and infused with dramatic impact," and *Horn Book* asserted that the novel has not only "the flavor of a Harlem *Tom Sawyer* or *Penrod*" but also "the merit of being swift in narrative and natural and vivid in dialogue."

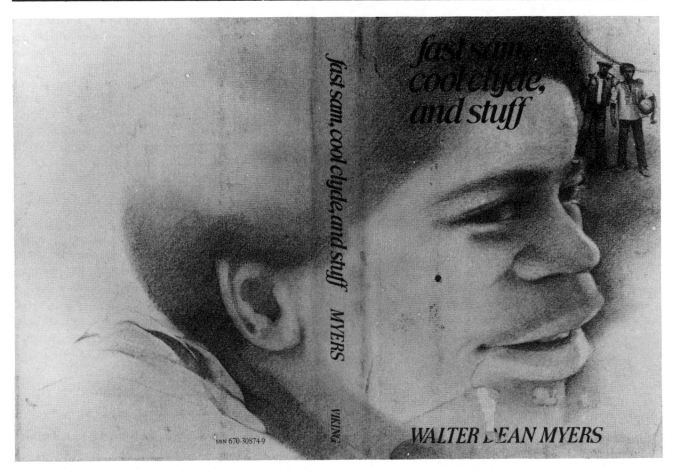

Dust jacket for the first of Myers's novels for young adults, the story of three Harlem boys and the problems they face

Published in 1977, *Mojo and the Russians*, Myers's second young adult novel, is an extremely witty book in which a group of youths institutes "Operation Brother Bad" designed to save Dean, a group member, from the wrath of Drusilla, the Mojo woman Dean had accidentally knocked down while riding his bicycle. They are also intent on discovering the reason for the presence of some Russians who appear in their neighborhood. Their adventures depict the learning experiences of most youths growing up in a big city where negative influences abound. Asserting that the author had again written a winner, the reviewer for the *School Library Journal* assessed Myers as having "a good ear for dialogue and a real flair for handling funny situations."

Myers's third novel has more serious implications than *Mojo and the Russians. It Ain't All for Nothin'* (1978) tells of Tippy, a boy whose life reaches the crossroads from which he can travel in one of two directions. He can choose the values of his father which would not improve his situation, or he can uphold the values of his God-fearing grandmother with whom he had lived before her illness. After experiencing life with his father and becoming a participant in petty crimes, Tippy decides to reject his father's world and to live with Mr. Roland, a man who befriended him in his moment of need. A poignant, sad book, *It Ain't All for Nothin'* reflects much of the pain and anguish of ghetto life. At the end of the novel, Tippy turns his father in to the police. Jane Pennington praised the novel in *Interracial Books for Children Bulletin* as a "devastating book . . . one which needs to be written. . . . Not only does it delineate the sufferings of this youngster, it also details the caring and support offered to him by members of the community."

One year after the publication of *It Ain't All for Nothin'*, Myers published *The Young Landlords*, a novel which focuses once again on the intensity of ghetto living. A group of young people one summer form the Action Group designed to improve the community. One of its first objectives is to clean up "The Joint," a dilapidated apartment building on their block. When the group confronts Mr. Harley, the owner of the building, he transfers his ownership to them and they become landlords. The group quickly discovers the meaning of responsibility and the tremendous difficulties of managing a ghetto apartment building.

Hoops (1981), Myers's next novel, focuses on Lonnie Jackson, a recent high school graduate, whose life lacks direction until he gets an opportunity to play in a basketball tournament. Lonnie and his team are coached by Cal, an ex-professional player who had once fixed games for gamblers. Down and out, Cal sees an opportunity not only to prevent some youths who deserve a chance from making his mistakes but also to have revenge against the element that had robbed him of his self-esteem. Cal outwits a gambler but is murdered by him. Lonnie, who watches Cal die, learns that nothing is worth losing one's soul over.

In 1981, Myers also published his only young adult novel set in Africa. *The Legend of Tarik* tells of a young African boy who witnesses the cruel slaughter of his entire family by the dreaded El Muerte. Wounded in the onslaught, Tarik is rescued by two wise old men who had suffered at the hands of El Muerte. They train him in the arts of combat and self-discipline. Tarik kills El Muerte after a tremendous battle; but, tired of killing, he seeks peace in his homeland. Hazel Rochman wrote in *School Library Journal* that Myers shows that "the heroic quest is also an arduous search for self knowledge and identity." Also published in 1981, *Won't Know 'Til I Get There* explores Stephen Perry's struggle with himself after his parents adopt a child and the process through which he learns to appreciate senior citizens.

Published in 1983, *The Nicholas Factor* chronicles the adventures of Gerald McQuillen, a bright, young college student, who is recruited to infiltrate the Crusade Society, an elite group of students seemingly bent on saving the world. The group, which seems harmless enough initially, gets completely out of hand when its members meet in Peru to work with the Indians there. After several Indians are left dead and dying and an African member of the Crusaders is murdered, Gerald barely escapes to tell the story.

In addition to his novels, Myers has written two nonfictional works for young people, *The World of Work. A Guide to Choosing a Career* (1975) and *Social Welfare* (1976), which examines the welfare system and suggests alternatives to it.

Whether he is writing about the ghettos of

New York, the remote countries of Africa, or social institutions, Myers captures the essence of the developing experiences of youth. His tone can be funny or serious, but his concern for young people is clearly demonstrated in the basic themes of each work. He is concerned with the development of youths, and his message is always the same: young people must face the reality of growing up and must persevere, knowing that they can succeed despite any odds they face. Furthermore, this positive message enables youths to discover what is important in life and to reject influences which could destroy them.

Walter Dean Myers is recognized as one of the premier writers of books for young black people. In 1969 *Where Does the Day Go?* received the Council on Interracial Books for Children Award for minority authors, and three of his novels for young adults—*Fast Sam, Cool Clyde, and Stuff; It Ain't All for Nothin'*; and *The Young Landlords*—have been selected as American Library Association notable books. In 1980 Myers received the Coretta Scott King Award for *The Young Landlords*. During the course of his career, Myers's focus has shifted from children's picture books to novels for young adults. This shift is an important one, for by appealing to the consciousness of young adults, Myers is touching perhaps the most important element of our society. Myers's books demonstrate that writers can not only challenge the minds of black youths but also emphasize the black experience in a nonracist way that benefits all young readers. As Myers states, "If you choose to deal with my children then you must deal with them as whole people, and that means dealing with their blackness as well as their intellect."

References:

John Caviston, review of *Fast Sam, Cool Clyde, and Stuff, School Library Journal,* 21 (March 1975): 108;

Jane Pennington, review of *It Ain't All for Nothin', Interracial Books for Children Bulletin,* 10, no. 4 (1979): 18;

Review of *Fast Sam, Cool Clyde, and Stuff, Booklist,* 71 (February 1975): 620;

Review of *Fast Sam, Cool Clyde, and Stuff, Horn Book,* 51 (August 1975): 388-389;

Hazel Rochman, review of *The Legend of Tarik, School Library Journal,* 27 (May 1981): 76;

Robert Unsworth, review of *Mojo and the Russians, School Library Journal,* 24 (November 1977): 74.

Gordon Parks
(30 November 1912-   )

Jane Ball
Wilberforce University

BOOKS: *Flash Photography* (New York, 1947);
Camera Portraits: The Techniques and Principles of Documentary Portraiture (New York: Franklin Watts, 1948);
The Learning Tree (New York: Harper & Row, 1963; London: Hodder & Stoughton, 1964);
A Choice of Weapons (New York: Harper & Row, 1966);
Gordon Parks: A Poet and His Camera (New York: Viking, 1968; London: Deutsch, 1968);
Gordon Parks: Whispers of Intimate Things (New York: Viking, 1971);
Born Black (Philadelphia: Lippincott, 1971);
Moments Without Proper Names (New York: Viking, 1975; London: Secker & Warburg, 1975);
Flavio (New York: Norton, 1978);
To Smile in Autumn, A Memoir (New York: Norton, 1979);
Shannon (New York: Little, Brown, 1981).

SCREENPLAY: *The Learning Tree,* Warner Bros., 1968.

PERIODICAL PUBLICATION: "Brotherhood" [A Speech], *Crisis* (October 1972): 274-275.

Gordon Parks (Gale International Portrait Gallery)

Gordon Parks is a photographer, journalist, and film director who has written books that in their way celebrate the black family, black strength, and the determination of blacks to survive. Also a composer and poet, he is a versatile man who has tried and succeeded at many kinds of artistic endeavors because, as he said upon receipt of the Spingarn Medal in 1972, he was "a Black boy who wanted to be somebody." That most of his published work is either autobiographical or intensely personal in mood and intent attests to the fact that he strove to be a success and by any standards achieved it.

He was the youngest of fifteen children, born 30 November 1912 on a farm in Fort Scott, Kansas, to Sarah Ross Parks and Andrew Jackson Parks. After his mother's death when he was sixteen, Parks was sent to St. Paul, Minnesota, to live with a married sister. Unable to get along with his brother-in-

law, he was put out on his own and forced to fend for himself. Having a strong determination to survive and succeed, he dropped out of high school and worked at various jobs, including playing piano in a brothel, playing semipro basketball, serving as a hotel busboy, and touring with the otherwise all-white Larry Duncan band. He got stranded in New York while with the Duncan band and, at twenty-one, joined the Civilian Conservation Corps (CCC) in 1933. He married Sally Alvis while in the CCC and returned to Minneapolis in 1934. They had three children, Gordon, Jr., Toni, and David. While working as a railroad porter and bar car waiter, he became interested in photography and bought his first camera. He taught himself camera techniques by shooting pictures in the poor black community.

After his photographic skill improved and his work became known, he moved to Chicago, where the opportunities for earning a living at photography were greater. He continued to record the life of the ordinary black people, and a series of ghetto photographs won him a Julius Rosenwald fellowship in 1941. In 1942 he moved to Washington, D.C., to work under Roy Stryker at the Farm Security Administration. While in Washington, he did the reading he had not had the opportunity to do before and learned about "writing to the point." He became a correspondent for the Office of War Information, but his chance to go overseas as a combat photographer was aborted because of what he felt was a bigoted decision. Disgusted, he left the OWI and moved to Harlem.

He became a part of a documentary-making team for Standard Oil of New Jersey between 1944 and 1948. In 1946, he wrote his first book, *Flash Photography* (1947). He spent so much time and effort revising "every second sentence" in a meticulous fashion that it was necessary to defer his publisher's deadline every week. He swore this would be his last book, adopting the motto "Leave writing to the writers." He went on to do a free-lance story on a Harlem gang leader named Red Jackson which was published in *Life*. This began a long association with the magazine; in 1948 he became a *Life* staff photographer. During 1949-1951 he lived in Paris where, he said, "I could have lived . . . relatively free of prejudice all my life . . . but I couldn't. I had to be in the [civil rights] fight." He personally knew the men who were involved in the struggle: Martin Luther King, Jr., Eldridge Cleaver, members of the Black Panthers, and others. He felt as they did that American society held him inferior because he was black, and he had "a constant inner rebellion against the failure that [he] felt white America held for [him]." However, his involvement with the civil rights movement tended more to be that of reporter of what was happening than of a militant. He justified his reluctance to join the Black Panthers (when invited to do so by Cleaver) by saying he'd lose his objectivity; he'd reduce the size of the audience he wrote for; and at fifty-seven his outlook was different from that of young black men. But though he would not join the Black Panthers, he said, "I will continue to fight also, but on my terms."

During the 1950s Parks did numerous assignments for *Life*, including pictorial reports on crime in America, segregation in the South, the Black Muslims, the Black Panthers, and civil rights leaders. He also did a spread on a twelve-year-old Brazilian slum child named Flavio (which he fol-

lowed up in 1978 with a book), and he illustrated his favorite lines of poetry with his photographs. He became involved in film and television production during the 1950s. Parks was divorced in 1961 and married Elizabeth Campbell in 1962; they had one child, Leslie, and were divorced in 1973.

In 1963 he published his first fictional work, *The Learning Tree,* written in little more than a year. He was later to explain this reversal of his earlier decision not to write another book: "I became a writer and a musician when I was living in Paris in 1950 and working full time for *Life.* I found there was so much feeling inside me from my childhood that I needed more than photography to get it out. I wanted to write poetry, music and fiction. . . ." *The Learning Tree* is the story of a Negro family in a small Kansas town during the 1920s. The youngest son, Newt Winger, is the focal point, and his adolescent problems of sex, first love, manliness tested, and death of loved ones are treated with compassion and gentleness.

Nat Hentoff said the book "is more for boys than for adults. . . . Parks writes in a sinewy though not at all distinctive style." Still, he continued, the book is "an honest, craftsmanlike sketch of a boyhood obviously similar to his own. . . . *The Learning Tree* should be placed on high school reading lists. . . . White youngsters have much to learn from this . . . and Negro boys will be able to identify much more strongly and hopefully with Newt Winger's story than they can with many books about alien American experiences which they are now required to read." Another reviewer, Louise Giles, said the book was written not with resentment "but rather with rueful reminiscence, even humor. It is an unassuming and thoroughly conventional book, but it has freshness, sincerity, and charm."

The Learning Tree seems written to be a commercial success: it has sex and violence, tender familial love, human dignity, vengeance, and tragedy. It begins with the "de-flowering" of young Newt by an older, more experienced girl as they huddle against a cyclone. It ends with the death of Newt's mother and the breakup of the family as Newt is sent away from the old homestead to live "up North" with an aunt. In between, Whitney Balliett noted, there is "an accumulation of brutal murders, dismemberments, fist fights, automobile accidents, beatings, cyclones, and blood, blood, blood."

On one level, it is the story of a particular Negro family who manages to maintain its dignity and self-respect as citizens and decent human beings in a border Southern town. On another, it is a symbolic tale of the black man's struggle against

GORDON PARKS

THE LEARNING TREE

"This is a notable fictional study of a Negro family and a Negro child in a Kansas town in the 1920's. The Kansas locale, which Mr. Parks describes so well, is important simply because it is not the deep South nor the so-called emancipated North. It is a 'frontier of democracy' where the Negroes have certain inalienable rights (if they are willing to fight for them), but in which, too, there is a mysterious and ominous color-line across which the small hero knows he cannot pass. That is the dramatic milieu of *The Learning Tree* and what makes this novel of particular interest. Mr. Parks has given us the whole picture—the town life, the Negro family through whom the town is viewed, the young hero and his friends—in an admirable chronicle which is honest, remarkably balanced and mature, and often very entertaining, despite the inevitable tensions and tragedies which are implicit in the novel's theme. A fine story."

—MAXWELL GEISMAR, noted critic and literary historian; author of *American Moderns*, *Writers in Crisis*, and other studies of modern American fiction

Dust jacket for Park's best-selling first novel, designated by the publisher "A Harper Find," meaning that "the cooperation of booksellers is enlisted to see that the book gets the attention it merits"

social, economic, and natural forces, sometimes winning, sometimes losing. The Winger family is like the majority of America's black families, who are like the majority of families everywhere: working hard to survive, to provide a better life for their children, and to keep the family together until the children can go out into the world. Because the family is portrayed as a normal American family whose blackness is a natural circumstance and therefore not a source of continual pain and degradation, the book contributes greatly to a positive view of black people. For once a black family is not full of misfits, malcontents, deviates, loveless killers, or psychopaths. The Wingers, though poor and unable to find work that can lift them above borderline poverty, are normal human beings who love, care, and tolerate human flaws in themselves and others, and whose place in the community is solid because they are good, respectable people. The book is not great literature, but it provides a view of black family life that had not been shown before in a commercially successful fictional work. Parks was

given the opportunity to produce and direct the film adaptation of *The Learning Tree* in 1968, the first black man to achieve this distinction. He also wrote the musical score for the film.

The year 1966 marked the publication of *A Choice of Weapons*, an autobiography that begins with his mother's death when he was sixteen and ends in 1944 when he went to Harlem. J. J. O'Conner wrote: It gives "an intellectual understanding of what it means to be destitute frequently and, in addition, to be kicked in the face nearly every day for some thirty or forty years simply because one happens to be a Negro. . . . The Parks story is appalling, ugly, horrible. It has a matter-of-fact sadness, interspersed with volcanic anger."

A Choice of Weapons reveals the autobiographical elements that were fictionalized in *The Learning Tree*. But the autobiographical work has greater impact because Parks documents his life with no embellishments beyond those any writer would use for style and readability. The dashed hopes and hard-won victories are presented in a forthright manner. Saunders Redding wrote of *Choice* that it "is not the overwrought, introspective and gut-wrenched jeremiad of a martyr to racial bigotry and hatred. It is, rather, a perceptive narrative of one man's struggle to realize the values (defined as democratic and especially American) he has been taught to respect."

Between 1966 and 1975, Parks's creative output was impressive. He had a show of his photographs in New York, with one of his own concertos supplying the background music. Viking published a collection of his photographs and poems in *A Poet and His Camera* (1968); and *Whispers of Intimate Things* (1971), another book of photographs and poetry, was published in 1971 by Viking. *Born Black,* a collection of articles, also came out in 1971. It has Parks's observations on such black figures as Malcolm X, Martin Luther King, Jr., Huey Newton, Stokely Carmichael, Eldridge Cleaver, and Muhammad Ali; the Black Muslims and a black family in Harlem are also treated. During 1971-1973 Parks directed three commercially successful films for M-G-M Studios: *Shaft, Shaft's Big Score,* and *The Super Cops.* He was awarded the Spingarn Medal

by the NAACP in 1972 and received several honorary degrees.

By 1975 Parks was sixty-three, professionally active, and married to his third wife, editor Genevieve Young. He was also working on another film, *Leadbelly,* and showing twenty-five years of his photographic career in a major retrospective exhibition in New York City. A slender man of medium height, "rich tobacco brown" complexion, and a large mustache, he had a New York apartment overlooking the East River from the United Nations Plaza comfortably furnished with a grand piano and Braque and Chagall prints and paintings on the walls. By this time in his life, he was saying of his photography that it "used to pay for my indulgences in poetry, in writing, music, whatever. Now the other things pay for the luxury of sort of doodling around in photography."

In 1975 he published another book of photographs, *Moments Without Proper Names,* which contains "pictures of black suffering and of response to suffering." Parks said of the book: "The first part . . . says more of what I want to say, what I felt was necessary to say. The back part . . . is the beauty

Dust jacket for Parks's 1971 collection of essays and photographs, many of which first appeared in Life *magazine*

GORDON PARKS — renowned photographer, critically acclaimed poet, successful film producer *(Shaft)*, best-selling author *(The Learning Tree)*, and now triumphant novelist.

SHANNON

A panoramic novel of romance, vengeance and tragedy...

Spans a period from the earliest rumblings of the War To End All Wars to the hectic abandon of the Jazz Age . . .

Around two love stories — one tempestuous and heady, the other tender and tragic — move the powerful social forces of the age:
- the growing strife between emerging labor unions and rich industrialists
- the tensions and conflicts between the privileged and the poor
- the powerful influence of the Catholic Church in New York's Irish community

A rich saga of passion and destiny played out from the sweatshops of New York City's garment district to the stylish mansions of high society . . .

- National author publicity
- Major national advertising
- National cooperative advertising
- More to come

ISBN: 0-316-69249-2
August, $14.95
Little, Brown and Company

Front and back covers of reviewers' bound galleys for Parks's 1981 novel

part. It is simply what it is—the beautiful moments."

In 1979 another autobiographical volume entitled *To Smile in Autumn, A Memoir* was published. It opens in 1944 when Parks's photography had begun appearing in the Conde Nast and Luce magazines. It ends in 1978 when Parks had done everything he had wanted to do. It combines passages from his poems, journals, and letters with recollections of wives, children, lovers, and career assignments. The birth of his children, the dissolution of three marriages, his oldest son's accidental death are all part of his "triumph of achievement" and momentary defeats. His brushes with the rich and famous—Gloria Vanderbilt, Dwight Eisenhower, Winston Churchill, King Farouk—all demonstrate the urbanity and sophistication of this Renaissance man in a "gracious self-portrait."

Parks's most recent novel is *Shannon* (1981), his first attempt at adult fiction. Set in New York during a twenty-year period beginning in 1903, *Shannon* tells the story of the O'Farrell family and their tragedy-ridden rise to prominence. Shannon Sullivan marries Kevin O'Farrell over her wealthy father's objections, and as Kevin turns a small tool company into a lucrative engineering firm, he and Shannon endure the opposition of her father, the death of their daughter, labor problems during World War I, Shannon's mental breakdown, and Kevin's unfaithfulness. Noting that the novel lacks credibility at times, *Publishers Weekly* nonetheless praised Parks for evoking realistically the turbulence of the early years of the century.

Gordon Parks, the first black to do many things—to work for *Life* magazine and *Vogue,* at OWI and FSA—is a man who wanted to make his mark in the world. He wanted to be somebody, and with that in mind he tried his hand at many things. His impressive photojournalistic essays and memorable photographs will undoubtedly ensure his reputation in the annals of black American artistic achievement. His book *The Learning Tree* remains memorable in its warm and wholesome view of black family life. Much of his other writing makes worthwhile reading as a record of one black man's achievement in the face of nearly insurmountable odds.

References:

C. Gerald Fraser, "Gordon Parks: An Artist Remi-

nisces," *New York Times*, 3 December 1975, p. 36;

Terry Harnan, *Gordon Parks: Black Photographer and Film Maker* (Champaign, Ill.: Garrard, 1972);

Nat Hentoff, review of *The Learning Tree, New York Herald Tribune*, 25 August 1963, p. 6;

Hilton Kramer, "Art: Empathy of Gordon Parks," *New York Times*, 4 October 1975, p. 19;

"Reporter with a Camera," *Ebony* (July 1946): 24-29;

Midge Turk, *Gordon Parks* (New York: Crowell, 1971).

Robert Deane Pharr
(5 July 1916-   )

Richard Yarborough
University of California, Los Angeles

BOOKS: *The Book of Numbers* (Garden City: Doubleday, 1969; London: Calder & Boyars, 1970);

S. R. O. (Garden City: Doubleday, 1971);

The Soul Murder Case (New York: Avon/Equinox, 1975);

Giveadamn Brown (Garden City: Doubleday, 1978).

OTHER: "The Numbers Writer," *New York*, 2 (22 September 1969): 30-33; republished in *New Black Voices,* edited by Abraham Chapman (New York: New American Library, 1972), pp. 60-69.

The civil rights movement of the 1960s inspired in many white Americans a desire to learn more about black society and culture, about what Du Bois termed life "within the Veil." In response to popular demand, American publishing companies aggressively sought out and presented the works of black writers. Rarely if ever before in U.S. history had Afro-American authors found the mainstream literary establishment so receptive to their autobiographies, poetry, and fiction. Among the major beneficiaries of this cultural awakening were not only promising young novelists like John Wideman, Ishmael Reed, Alice Walker, Ernest J.

Gaines, and Carlene H. Polite but also writers from an earlier generation who, through lack of encouragement, opportunity, or inclination, had not previously broken into print. One notable member of this latter group is Robert Deane Pharr.

Pharr's journey to literary notoriety has followed an unusual and circuitous route—as one reviewer commented, he "has been up and down, and here and there." He was born on 5 July 1916 in Richmond, Virginia, to John Benjamin and Lucie Deane Pharr, a minister and a schoolteacher, respectively. Raised in New Haven, Connecticut, Pharr returned south in 1933, when he attended St. Paul's Normal and Industrial School in Lawrence, Virginia. He spent part of the following year at Lincoln University in Pennsylvania and then enrolled in Virginia Union University in Richmond, where he earned his B.A. degree in 1939.

Pharr's earliest reading included the Bobbsey Twins, Tom Swift, Dick Prescott, and Horatio Alger. In an interview in 1968, Pharr judged this conventional childhood fare with a harshly critical eye: "[I]t was the worst reading regime that a black child could live. It totally unprepared me for the life I had to live...." The first serious novel Pharr recalls encountering was Sinclair Lewis's *Babbitt,* which shaped not only his dedication to literature

Robert Deane Pharr (Gale International Portrait Gallery)

but also his goals as a writer. The book "set me on fire," Pharr states. "Mr. Lewis let me look through windows and peek around corners at the white man as he really lived. I began to understand. And by the time I was 17 I had already made up my mind to do as Mr. Lewis had done. Only I would let white people look at the black man as he lives when the white man is not looking or listening."

Pharr pursued his writing interests at Virginia Union, where he served as the feature editor of the school paper. Later, while doing postbaccalaureate work at Fisk, he attracted the attention of John M. Ross, a Yale-trained instructor in Dramatics and English. At Ross's urging, Pharr tried his hand at playwriting, and he captured the top prize in a nationwide contest. His creative writing career was interrupted before it was fairly begun, however, by a three-year stay in a sanatorium for tuberculosis and a subsequent bout with alcoholism. Then, upon entering the job market in the late 1940s, Pharr discovered that his medical history, to say nothing of his race, effectively barred him from many employment opportunities. As a result, he began working at hotels and resorts, and two decades passed before his first novel appeared.

When Doubleday published *The Book of Numbers* in January 1969, much was made of the fact that the author was a hitherto unknown black waiter. Pharr has expressed irritation at the critical attention paid to his employment instead of to his art ("It's things like that that tend to drive a black writer up the wall"). Nonetheless, the circumstances surrounding the publication of *Numbers* reveal not only the experiences upon which Pharr draws to create his fiction but also, in Abraham Chapman's words, "the difficulties Black Americans with literary talent have so frequently found in attaining publication and conditions to devote time to writing."

Pharr was employed at the Columbia University Faculty Club at the time he finished *The Book of Numbers*. Uncertain how to handle his manuscript after a rejection by Grove Press, he was advised by a friend in the graduate program at Columbia to give it to Lewis Leary, chairman of the English department. Favorably impressed, Leary passed it on to J. R. Humphreys, the head of the Columbia writing program, who, in turn, took it to Doubleday. Two years later, Pharr had a contract, and *The Book of Numbers* was in print.

Most simply put, Pharr's first novel chronicles the meteoric rise and inevitable fall of David Greene, the young numbers king in the black ward of a small Southern city. Pharr, however, ambitiously aims for more than a mere tale of the criminal underworld. In his depiction of the black sporting life, he gives us vividly rendered characters who represent a large cross section of Afro-America in the 1930s. Among the most striking are Blueboy Harris, the garrulous black hustler who teaches his partner, Dave, the ways of the world; Althea "Pigmeat" Goines, the attractive, savvy waitress who becomes Dave's "official hostess"; Professor Blake and Dr. White, two faculty members from the nearby black college; Kelly Simms, the smart-mouthed, cynical young chemistry student who wins Greene's love; and Delilah Mazique, the dark-skinned, Gullah-speaking beauty who finally takes over the business. That these characters interact in a world almost totally devoid of whites immerses the reader even more deeply in the life of this richly diverse black community.

As directly as any contemporary novel, *The Book of Numbers* confronts one of the most painful questions surrounding the Afro-American experience: How can ambitious, intelligent, energetic blacks—"the cream of the crop," Pharr calls them—achieve the capitalist American Dream when the conventional roads to power and financial

Dust jacket for Pharr's widely acclaimed first novel, designed to give whites an insider's view of black life. Pharr was inspired by Sinclair Lewis's Babbitt, *which, he felt, "let me look through windows and peek around corners at the white man as he really lived."*

security are unjustly closed to them? In discussing his first book, Pharr posits one answer to this dilemma: "In order for there to be black wealth in that novel, there had to be law breaking. As long as black people could not break out of the economic ghetto into a world of free enterprise, they had to commit crime." Thus, Pharr's dissection of the complex social and economic ramifications of the numbers operation Greene and Blueboy mastermind reflects his attempt to depict as accurately as possible the realities of black urban existence in the mid-1930s. And at a broader level, this entrepreneurial saga is an engrossing and insightful examination of the pursuit of success, American-style.

What finally solidifies the achievement of this novel, what makes it something special indeed, is Pharr's inspired manipulation of the figurative potential of the numbers as, in one critic's phrase, "a metaphor for belief." From the book's Biblical title to the frequent reference to specific numbers which "come up" each day, Pharr skillfully exploits the suggestive links between the illegal lottery and des-

tiny: numbers become, he writes, "the Ward's merciless and impersonal God." Underlying this recognition of the randomness of life is a deeply tragic view of man's fate, a view grounded in the angry realization that even tremendous wealth cannot protect blacks from the irrational cruelty of the white world. Racism then comes to embody the inevitability of doom, the awareness of which pervades this novel even more thoroughly than it does Paul Laurence Dunbar's *The Sport of the Gods.* "Each and every Negro knows that he was born to be castrated," Pharr writes in *Numbers.* "And there is no need for him to seek out his moment under the knife. It comes faster than death and is the ultimate. There is no afterlife."

The Book of Numbers appeared at the height of interest in Afro-American literature, and it received generally favorable reviews from publications as diverse as *Spectator, Freedomways, Life,* and the London *Times Literary Supplement.* In his enthusiasm, Webster Schott declared, "A work such as this comes once in a generation. . . . If there is to be another chance for the Great American Novel as the Black American Novel, enter *The Book of Numbers* in the competition." However, even Schott was forced to admit that "Pharr's novel bleeds with flaws," including excessive length, melodrama, occasionally awkward prose, and a didacticism which subverts many of his otherwise excellent characterizations. Loyle Hairston complained, "[N]ever have I encountered characters in fiction who were such chatterboxes." He also argued that Pharr's female figures "are cast strictly from what can only be described as a male chauvinist conception of 'women.' " While Hairston somewhat overstated the case, this contention is particularly relevant with regard to Pharr's handling of Kelly Simms, a character so uniquely fascinating that we want her portrayal to be more consistently believable than it is.

In citing the considerable strengths of *The Book of Numbers,* nearly every reviewer singled out Pharr's "marvelous ear for dialogue and dialects" and his convincing depiction of the black ward. In addition, even Pharr's harshest critics had to agree that most of his structural and stylistic errors "are simply overwhelmed by his absolute belief in his characters and his total love for them." As Christopher Lehmann-Haupt observed, "He will not be credited with having advanced the frontiers of fiction by any degree, but he has written an unusually good book—a gnarled old oak tree of a book, rich and grainy in texture, sprawling and complex in configuration, a curiously friendly book to get lost in." Oddly enough, while praising *Numbers,* some critics suggested that the book's success derives from Pharr's supposed lack of literary sophistication. The use of phrases like "his crude art" smacks of a critical primitivism which has often tinged the evaluation of Afro-American artists. Such arguments, however, are unfair to this powerful, ambitious novel. As the reviewer in *Time* concluded, "Ultimately, the sense of pain and loss conveyed by the book is profound"; Pharr deserves full credit for his accomplishment.

The response of American readers to *The Book of Numbers* was warm. The novel went through two hardback printings of 7,000 and 3,500 copies each and sold over 6,000 copies before going out of print in January 1971. In June 1970, Avon published a paperback edition, which went through three printings totaling almost 300,000 copies. Three years later, Avco Embassy released a film version of the novel, produced and directed by Raymond St. Jacques.

Published by Doubleday in October 1971,

Pharr's massive second book, *S. R. O.,* centers on the life of Sid Bailey, a middle-aged, college-educated black waiter and admitted "part-time alcoholic" who moves into the Logan, a Harlem s. r. o. (single-room-occupancy) hotel. In comparison to the motley crew of addicts, lesbians, welfare recipients, winos, prostitutes, and pushers whom he meets there, Sid is, in his own words, "a chump," "an out-and-out pussy," and "a square"; and much of this book details his initiation into the Logan's way of life. Particularly instructive for Sid are his often painful and usually disconcerting interactions with characters like Sinman (alias James Ronald Person), the embittered white Juilliard student turned drug dealer and resident philosopher; the interracial lesbian couple, Joey and Jinny; Sharlee, the mysterious Dutch-Javanese-Iranian fallen angel who moves Sid to literal adoration; and Blind Charlie, whose sightlessness belies a boisterous and often vicious physical strength which makes him the hotel's enforcer.

Bailey eventually sheds some of his straight ways—even to the point of overseeing a harem of prostitute-addicts who move in with him. Becoming an accepted member of the Logan family will not save Sid, however, for most of the inhabitants are, as he describes them, "mindless, ambitionless and essentially homeless." Rather, the keys to his ultimate survival are love and self-expression. The former is in short supply in the Logan, which Ginsburg, the white manager, calls "a house of people without a God"; but Sid finds it with Gloria Bascomb, a beautiful ex-addict. The latter Sid achieves through the redemptive act of literary creation. Buttressed by his relationship with Gloria and by his writing, Sid becomes strong enough to break out of the accelerating cycle of violence, death, and madness which engulfs the inhabitants of the Logan. Charlie's closing words—"Now you walking, boy. Keep on, boy. Keep right on. . . ."—acknowledge Sid's transcendence of the fear and spiritual inertia which had prevented his growth.

More undisciplined and indulgent than Pharr's first book, *S. R. O.* is marred by several crippling problems. The first is the sheer length of the novel—569 pages. Not long after beginning the book, one is moved to second Sid's exasperated yell: "Don't the people in this goddam hotel do anything besides fuck and fight, drink wine and take dope?" Then, there is the overly large cast of characters, which quickly becomes unwieldy and, at times, confusing. Finally, while the novel is full of pain, loss, cruelty, and tragedy, the comic, almost slapstick, effects for which Pharr occasionally strives undercut the inherent seriousness of many scenes. This problem affects a number of the characterizations as well, for Pharr works with such flashy colors and broad strokes that intricacies of motivation and subtle psychological shadings are often lost.

Ultimately, several aspects of Pharr's narrative strategy prevent these flaws from completely capsizing the book. The first is the inclusion of six sections in which we shift out of Sid's mind and into the third-person point of view. Remnants of an earlier draft written entirely in the third person, these interchapters—or "insights," as Pharr calls them—are more straightforward in diction, flatter in tone, and more conventional in exposition than the remaining twenty-eight chapters; consequently, they serve as a counterpoint to Sid's narrative. Further, they present a number of important characters free of the limitations of Sid's perceptions.

The second key to *S. R. O.*'s effectiveness is the power with which Pharr conveys the agonized desperation of the protagonist, Sid Bailey. At its best, *S. R. O.* is an alternately humorous and harrowing picaresque novel about a man desperately in search of a foundation, a rock upon which he might rest as he confronts a lifetime of failure, frustration, and emptiness. On the one hand, Sid is certainly a self-dramatizing, melodramatic, repetitious, and contradictory narrator. On the other, in his brutal, self-revelatory frankness, Sid consistently involves the reader in his searing inner struggles, which entail depression, bouts of dipsomania, and a nervous breakdown before he begins to find himself.

Finally, as the most autobiographical of Pharr's novels, *S. R. O.* is a particularly significant text in his canon. Like Sid, Pharr was a waiter who lived in an s. r. o. hotel. In addition, both men graduated from Virginia Union, won playwriting contests in college, lost manuscripts of their novels about black numbers bankers, and were subsequently convinced by psychiatrists that they could reconstruct their books entirely from memory. The most revealing parallel between author and protagonist, however, concerns their dedication to writing. Sid works on his novel, which he terms "My Woman," not because he wants to, but because he has to; and Pharr himself admits, "I think a guy writes just because he has to write, to get it off his chest. . . ." For both men, writing appears to be a nearly compulsive act of self-expression. Further, Sid's question about his role as an author—"Wasn't a realistic writer supposed to descend into the very pits of all that was not quite normal so that he could

inform his readers?"—suggests at least one of Pharr's goals in his second book.

While one reviewer counted *S. R. O.* among "the best novels of the year," this judgment was a decidedly minority opinion, as critics generally found that the book did not fulfill the expectations aroused by *Numbers*. Predictably, the most common complaint involved the book's length. *S. R. O.* is, Jan Carew observed, "an endless conversation with Fate, with the Furies that pursue the damned of the earth—and with the author. And a conversation as long and as tortuous as this, even with its skillfully wrought cadences, is bound to pall, as this one certainly does toward the end of the novel." The consensus of critical opinion agreed with the reviewer in *Booklist* who described *S. R. O.* as "a profane, penetrating, but not wholly successful novel. . . ." Pharr himself concedes that it is his worst book. Selling only about 3,200 copies, *S. R. O.* went out of print in September 1973.

Several years before Avon published *The Soul Murder Case* as a paperback original in 1975, Pharr described his third novel as "All you ever wanted to know about sex and drugs but were afraid to ask a Black Man." Thus, it is not surprising that Pharr's third novel contains his most explicit treatment of sexuality. It is also his most controlled and consistently successful creation after *The Book of Numbers*.

Bobby Dee, a former singing star turned literary agent; Candice Brown, the blues vocalist who asks Bobby to publish her poems; Marion, her beautiful teenage daughter, whom Bobby helps to kick a heroin habit; and Viena, Bobby's fellow ex-addict and lover, are the major actors in this drama, and they all bear the livid scars of addiction, whether on their arms or in their minds. However, this story of love, madness, desire, pain, and death belongs primarily to the narrator, Bobby Dee. While he does not face a personal dilemma as extreme as Sid's in *S. R. O.*, both men are trapped by their pasts; and they are living lives essentially bereft of meaning. Just as *S. R. O.* is the story of Sid's resurrection, *The Soul Murder Case* follows Bobby as he gradually comes to acknowledge and then to outgrow the fear which has prevented him from confronting reality directly. As one critic puts it, *The Soul Murder Case* is "the naked exposure of the 'soul' of Soul."

The key to the success of this novel lies in Pharr's use of the confiding, self-consciously hip voice of Bobby to present the action. Unfortunately, the loquacious, knowing protagonist offers little resistance to Pharr's didactic tendencies. Consequently, Bobby lectures the reader about white-black sexual relations, the music industry, and drugs; his particular pet peeve is the government's refusal to acknowledge the efficacy of a black doctor's revolutionary drug rehabilitation program. Nonetheless, the shorter length of this novel, its small cast of characters, and the vigor of the narrative voice lend *The Soul Murder Case* a dramatic tension Pharr's other fiction too often lacks.

As frequently occurs with novels which are never published in hardback, *The Soul Murder Case* received little notice. The *New York Times* published a short review of Pharr's novel, but the writer quickly dismissed the book as "a finger-exercise by the author . . . that displays only a smidgen of his formidable talent." The reviewer in *Publishers Weekly* was even harsher: "This is to realistic fiction just about what the black exploitation flick is to films. . . . [I]f anyone is victimized it's the reader." Otherwise, Pharr's third novel was generally and unjustly ignored by critics and readers alike; it had but one printing of about 11,000 copies. Fortunately, in the face of this waning interest, Pharr

received grants from the Rockefeller Foundation, the New York State Council on the Arts, and other funding agencies. With this support, he was able to complete *Giveadamn Brown*, his fourth book.

Published by Doubleday in 1978, Pharr's fourth novel relates the experiences of Lawrence "Giveadamn" Brown, a twenty-six-year-old black man who moves from Florida to Harlem. Soon after his arrival in the North, Giveadamn's familial relationship with the legendary crime boss Harry Brown is revealed and he becomes an unwilling celebrity. When a near-fatal accident hospitalizes the older man, Giveadamn attempts to protect Harry's empire from the avaricious clutches of as grotesque a group of enemies as has likely been assembled.

Giveadamn Brown opens as a promising tale of the education of an innocent. As the plot thickens, however, the novel becomes a relatively uninspired, albeit unusual, thriller—complete with exploding trucks; crosstown, tire-squealing auto chases; and an ingenious con game involving a heroin manufacturing device. Further, Giveadamn's sudden

PHOTO BY ALEX GOTFRYD

ROBERT DEANE PHARR

Dust jacket for Pharr's 1978 novel about a twenty-six-year-old Southerner who comes to Harlem and gets involved in organized crime

display of street smarts as he helps outwit Harry's competitors undercuts his early portrayal as something of a naif. On the positive side, Pharr's handling of many of the minor characters is successful, and those portions of the novel which cover familiar Pharr territory—in particular, the effects of drug addiction—are genuinely moving as well. Nonetheless, the book's strengths are simply not sufficient to overcome its serious flaws.

Garrett Epps wrote the most favorable and thorough review of *Giveadamn Brown*. Praising Pharr's "knowing, surrealistically honest vision of life in Harlem," he compared the novel to Dashiell Hammett's *Red Harvest* and Robert Stone's *Dog Soldiers*. Epps was forced to admit, however, that "the mixed result is an intermittently compelling, oddly believable fever-dream of sex, money, and death." He even speculated that this "violent caper novel" was designed "with one eye on the black-movie-rights market." The writer in the *New Yorker* stated the case most fairly: "The plot is too contrived to be convincing, but the tough, emotion-laden dialogue and the scores of scarred lives the author describes ring absolutely true."

Like the works of a number of other Afro-American writers who began publishing in the 1960s, Pharr's books have suffered from general critical neglect. This fate is particularly unfortunate in the case of *The Book of Numbers,* which is, as Roger Whitlow contends, "the best novel of black urban 'sporting life' in black American literature—it surpasses even McKay's famous *Home to Harlem.*" In addition, Pharr's fiction stands out from that of many of his black male peers because of his concern with Afro-American women, a concern that borders on obsession. Admittedly, the protagonists of his novels are all male; moreover, his portrayal of women occasionally approaches the stereotypical. Nevertheless, over the course of his four novels, women increasingly come to dominate Pharr's fiction—so much so that most of the action in *Giveadamn Brown* is determined by female characters as ruthless, aggressive, clever, and adventuresome as any of the males, if not more so.

Recent critics have gradually begun to pay greater attention to Afro-American fiction of the past two decades. A particularly noteworthy example is Graham Clarke's essay "Beyond Realism: Recent Black Fiction and the Language of 'The Real Thing,'" in which he briefly examines, among other novels, Pharr's first three books. In particular, he focuses upon the most consistent strength in Pharr's work—his skill at capturing black speech. Referring to the fiction of Pharr and Hal Bennett, Clarke argues, "In them the imperatives of style and language exist in that contradictory mix which LeRoi Jones found to be so central to Harlem's particular nature: an 'existential joyousness' surrounded by 'every crippling vice.' It is a language of survival which insists on staying alive, but on its own terms and with its own integrity." In addition, Clarke's perceptive analysis of Pharr's language in *S. R. O.* provides access into a demanding, often frustrating novel which dulls the blades of most conventional critical tools.

In persisting in his early resolution to write, Robert Deane Pharr produced a novel, *The Book of Numbers,* which would alone merit his being accorded a high place among contemporary American authors. Although flawed, his other three novels further substantiate the seriousness and intensity of his artistic vision. Both a persistent social critic and a perceptive student of the human condition, Pharr is committed to depicting the inevitable and often unpredictable tragedies of life. However, if only through the sheer, relentless energy of his language, his fiction consistently carries the existential message that while life is often a hell, it can not only be survived but lived to the fullest. Chapters in an ongoing tale of physical and psychological endurance, Pharr's novels testify to the strength and resilience of the human spirit.

References:

Graham Clarke, "Beyond Realism: Recent Black Fiction and the Language of 'The Real Thing,'" in *Black Fiction,* edited by A. Robert Lee (New York: Barnes & Noble, 1980), pp. 204-221;

John O'Brien and Raman K. Singh, "Interview with Robert Deane Pharr," *Negro American Literature Forum,* 8 (Fall 1974): 244-246;

Noel Schraufnagel, *From Apology to Protest* (De Land, Fla.: Everett/Edwards, 1973), pp. 166-168;

Roger Whitlow, *Black American Literature* (Chicago: Nelson-Hall, 1973; revised, 1976), pp. 165-167.

Carlene Hatcher Polite

(28 August 1932-)

Hammett Worthington-Smith
Albright College

BOOKS: *Les Flagellents,* translated by Pierre Alien (Paris: Christian Bourgois Editeur, 1966); republished as *The Flagellants* (New York: Farrar, Straus & Giroux, 1967);

Sister X and The Victims of Foul Play (New York: Farrar, Straus & Giroux, 1975).

Experimental writer Carlene Hatcher Polite reflects her political and artistic concerns in a unique fictional style that has helped to establish the innovative modes popularized by Ishmael Reed. Her first novel, *The Flagellants,* published in English in 1967, ushered in an era in which Afro-American fiction moved beyond the conventions of realism. Marked by a mastery of language and a love of rhetoric, especially that of black cultural revolution, Polite's work evidences her struggle with fictional forms and reflects her doubts about the traditional novel as a medium for her art. Yet, she has written almost exclusively in the novel form. Both *The Flagellants* and *Sister X and The Victims of Foul Play* (1975) exhibit her special talent for stylistic innovations used to break out of the constraints of naturalistic plot and character development. Her two novels have earned Polite a place among contemporary Afro-American literary experimentators, particularly Charles Wright, William Melvin Kelley, Ronald Fair, and Reed. That she is the only woman among this group is not surprising because, comparable to her male counterparts and unlike the majority of black women writers, Polite has had a multifaceted life as a Greenwich Village bohemian, professional dancer, teacher of dance and yoga, political organizer, civil rights activist, expatriate writer, and college professor.

Born in Detroit to John and Lillian (Cook) Hatcher, international representatives of UAW-CIO, she attended Detroit public schools before going to Sarah Lawrence College in New York. Her stay at Sarah Lawrence, however, was brief; she chose instead to enter the Martha Graham School of Contemporary Dance and pursue a career as a professional dancer. Polite performed on stage with the Concert Dance Theatre of New York City (1955-1959) and the Detroit Equity Theatre and Van-

Carlene Polite (photo © by Jerry Bauer)

guard Playhouse (1960-1962). She has appeared as a specialty dancer in *The King and I, The Boy Friend,* and *Dark of the Moon.* Polite associates dance with her Greenwich Village period: "I lived among the beats, got involved with Zen and breath control. But Martha Graham was a philosophy all by herself, and she was my principal influence at the time." Polite has been a guest instructor in the Martha Graham technique of modern dance at the Detroit YWCA (1960-1962) and visiting instructor at Wayne State University.

Polite called the early 1960s her "freedom fighter days." She subordinated her career as a dancer to political activism for civil rights: in 1962

215

she was elected to the Michigan State Central Committee of the Democratic party; she served on the Detroit Council for Human Rights and participated in the June 1963 Walk to Freedom and the November 1963 Freedom Now Rally, the latter a protest against the Birmingham church bombing. In 1963 she organized the Northern Negro Leadership Conference; she was active in the NAACP throughout this period.

After the Detroit Council for Human Rights closed in 1964, Polite moved to Paris, where editor Dominique de Roux saw a sample of her writing and encouraged her to attempt a novel. The result two years later was *Les Flagellents* (1966), published in French by Christian Bourgois, a new publishing house which selected the novel as its first book. The auspicious beginning of her career as a writer encouraged Polite to remain in France until 1971, even though in 1967 the New York publishing company Farrar, Straus and Giroux brought out the English version that established her reputation as a novelist.

The Flagellants emphasizes the communication of ideas in lyrical, expressive prose more so than it does other aspects of fiction. As a result, the novel has a bare minimum of plot and an impressionistic handling of character. The themes are forwarded by verbal exchanges between Ideal, a young black woman with strong roots in the South, and Jimson, an aspiring poet with a sense of black history. The two meet in Greenwich Village, fall in love, and attempt to create a meaningful life together; however, they are thwarted in their efforts because neither can move beyond the limited roles granted to black men and women in a racially oppressive society. Both Jimson and Ideal are cerebral, meditative products of the 1960s, the period in which their story takes place. The novel consists of a series of stream-of-consciousness paragraphs rendering Ideal's and Jimson's internal realities which have been shaped by the condition of their black forebears. Once Ideal has revealed her innermost thoughts, a paragraph or two follows with Jimson's subconscious coming to the foreground to offer a telepathic rebuttal or counterpoint. Throughout this exchange, each literally flagellates the other as they seek not only to experience and understand love but also to define an individual and a cultural identity. Ideal and Jimson are compelled to strip from each other "layer after layer of rationalization and myth," both of which have been detrimental to blacks.

A loosely constructed prologue recalling "the Bottom," the South of Ideal's girlhood, introduces

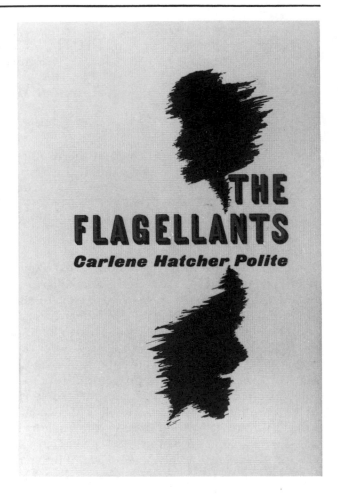

Dust jacket for the American edition of Polite's first novel, hailed as the herald of a new period in black fiction

the ideological tensions dominating the novel and the relationship between Jimson and Ideal: dream and fact; past and future; reason and emotion; religious faith and existential despair; slavery and freedom; equality and domination. The suggestive initial sequence portrays Ideal as a frightened girl standing on a brass bed and being asked to dance to the music of a blues guitar. Led away by her great-grandmother, a former slave, Ideal receives the advice: "Always walk tall. Never bow down to anything or anyone, unless, of course you feel like bowing. . . ." Her great-grandmother's lessons in black survival, presented during a phantasmagoric pilgrimage through the Bottom, stress the presence of God recognized in personal suffering and the necessity of individual strength in facing the future, both of which are geared particularly toward the survival of the black female.

Ideal attempts to incorporate her great-grandmother's messages into her relationship with

Jimson; however, she vacillates between supporting him in his endeavors and attacking him for his failures. In the process, she reveals her vulnerability, though she is so assertive and strong-willed that she is accused of being domineering and of perpetuating the stereotype of the black matriarch.

Jimson is unwilling to accept domination in the relationship, despite his initial failure to provide financial support for Ideal. He allows the image of black male servitude to incapacitate him because he fears losing his manhood and becoming like his ancestors, particularly Papa Boo, who sacrificed his integrity as a man "to be rewarded with a paltry token from the great white father." Lacking motivation, but determined to salvage his self-esteem, Jimson moves through a variety of jobs, including one in an art library where Rheba, a white librarian, falls in love with him; he rejects her advances and leaves the job, but subsequently becomes suicidal and indifferent to Ideal's attempts to help. When he finally takes a job with Bureaucratique, an agency similar to the United Nations, he urges Ideal to become a homemaker, a role for which she is temperamentally unsuited. Their verbal lacerations culminate with Jimson's affair with another woman and Ideal's decision to leave him.

The conclusion is bleak and the vision is unrelenting; nevertheless, Polite has stated that her aim in writing *The Flagellants* was the "transformation of people." Reviewers, in fact, hailed Polite as an innovative writer, one especially forceful in her reexamination of black male and female roles. Whereas Herbert Lottman praised the novel as "The Theater of Cruelty in book form" and, Roger Ebert called it "a book which makes one wish the author had not told so truthfully of a hopeless human agony," Stanley Kaufmann viewed the work as the herald of a new period in the history of fiction by black Americans. Nora Sayre pointed out that the experimental work is more essay than novel; nonetheless, she liked Polite's work because it is not bound in a racial tradition.

In 1971, Polite returned to the United States where she took a position as associate professor of English at the State University of New York, Buffalo. There she resumed her association with the NAACP, and after working with black student groups, she chaired the American Studies department. During this period she was at work on three more books.

In 1975, Polite's second novel, *Sister X and The Victims of Foul Play*, was published. It carries her tendency to develop characters and themes by means of extended monologues and speeches even farther than did *The Flagellants*. The story of the dead Sister X Arista Prolo, a black exotic dancer who worked in Paris, is told in the dialect of the streets and in the rhythms of jazz by the only two speaking characters in the novel, Abyssinia, Sister X's former costume designer, and Willis B. Black (Black Will), her former lover. All of the characters are expatriates from the United States living on the fringes of the chic artistic world in Paris. The two speakers meet in Abyssinia's rundown apartment where she recounts Sister X's experiences as "a dancer, an exotic dancer, a tiptop tappin' past master of the art of 'interpretive' terpsichore." Abyssinia and Black Will render Sister X's story and in the process pass on their observations about life from their own black cultural perspective:

> Abyssinia asked that dumb doctor (who professed to know his business when it came to knowing the colored conditions in the colonies), "After cigarettes and cancer, which C will college boys think up as our Nation's Number One killer?" Now y'all know, good 'n well, that white man was not about ready to throw all his years of "specialized" training into the ether and condescend to stand up there in that Hotel of God, and stoop to dignify some crazy colored woman by arguing with her about the fatal complications of carcinogens. Well, let me tell you, Abyssinia couldn't have cared less. She read that M.D. all the way from ADC, straight through to D & C, and then wound up by telling him that the next dread C'll be one of several things.

The dialogue between the sassy Abyssinia and the ex-con Black Will takes place, for the greater part, over a breakfast of grits, which becomes their tangible link to their heritage as black Americans. It is a prolonged breakfast interrupted by telephone calls, marked by frequent flashbacks, and interspersed with the music of the blues. Black Will is a listener. When he speaks, it is to get the rambling, self-absorbed Abyssinia back to the Sister X story or to have her comment further upon one of her philosophical tangents that are often embedded in folklore. "Nothing about [Abyssinia] looked alive any more," and she believes that she lives in a "Dead World." Obsessed with witchcraft and the supernatural, Abyssinia has a tendency to mix reality with her dreams, yet she anchors the novel in the folklore and folk traditions of blacks while she expounds on the current situation of black victimization. Abyssinia may be not only the main character of the novel but also the primary inspiration for its creation.

Sister X, however, is the central focus. She is linked to Abyssinia and Black Will as a black victim of foul play, racial preconceptions, and discrimination. Although a French medical officer reports the cause of her death as cancer, he misses the irony in his finding. Because of the narrative perspective on Sister X, the reader knows what the doctor does not: Sister X's death is the result of a cancerous society which victimizes individuals and groups, particularly blacks in this novel, and literally kills their aspirations and dreams.

Sister X's personal situation is both tragic and heroic. An artistic holdover from costumed dance shows made famous by Josephine Baker, she refuses to become either a belly dancer or a go-go girl, and she will not appear onstage without a modicum of clothing. After she is discharged as the star of the dance attraction at the Jack of Diamonds Supper Club, she returns to receive her final pay. Before going to the paymaster, she makes the rounds of the dressing rooms and becomes involved in a show taking place onstage, where she has an altercation with her replacement. When Sister X mysteriously falls from the stage, she is taken to a hospital where she dies.

Less widely reviewed than *The Flagellants, Sister X and The Victims of Foul Play* received qualified praise from critics writing in the *New Yorker* and *New York Times Book Review*, who acknowledged its inventiveness and force, but lamented its plastic characters and political abstractions. The *New Yorker* reviewer observed that "a lot can be forgiven in an energetic and fearless writer," while Frederick Busch in the *Times* conceded his admiration for Polite's "considerable talent," but concluded that her repetitious "grim rhetoric" made him "tired and impatient." In reviewing the book for *Essence,* a magazine marketed for black women, Jessica Harris decided that "Polite fulfills the promise she demonstrated in her first novel" and is "a word magician" who develops "a riveting ring of truth about the three main characters." Harris, like the writer for the *New Yorker,* found the dialogue and "jazz-writing" fascinating reading comparable to "Plato['s] dialogues filtered through Miles Davis' trumpet."

Although Carlene Hatcher Polite has not published a novel since *Sister X,* she continues to work on two other books. The particular subjects of these works have not been revealed, but they are almost certain to reflect Polite's diverse experiences in the United States and in France, and to do so in the tough, hard-edged, poetic prose that characterizes her fictional experiments in her two published novels.

References:

Roger Ebert, "First Novels by Young Negroes," *American Scholar* (Autumn 1967): 682-686;

Herbert R. Lottman, "Authors and Editors," *Publishers Weekly* (12 June 1967): 20-21;

Noel Schraufnagel, *From Apology to Protest: The Black American Novel* (De Land, Fla.: Everett/ Edwards, 1973), pp. 129-130.

Ishmael Reed
(22 February 1938-   )

Henry Louis Gates
Yale University

BOOKS: *The Free-Lance Pallbearers* (Garden City: Doubleday, 1967; London: MacGibbon & Kee, 1968);

Yellow Back Radio Broke-Down (Garden City: Doubleday, 1969; London: Allison & Busby, 1971);

Catechism of D Neoamerican HooDoo Church: Poems (London: Paul Breman, 1970);

Mumbo Jumbo (Garden City: Doubleday, 1972);

Conjure: Selected Poems, 1963-1970 (Amherst: University of Massachusetts Press, 1972);

Chattanooga: Poems (New York: Random House, 1973);

The Last Days of Louisiana Red (New York: Random House, 1974);

Flight to Canada (New York: Random House, 1976);

A Secretary to the Spirits: Poems (New York: NOK, 1977);

Shrovetide in Old New Orleans: Essays (Garden City: Doubleday, 1978);

The Terrible Twos (New York: St. Martin's/Marek, 1982);

God Made Alaska for the Indians: Selected Essays (New York: Garland, 1982).

OTHER: *The Rise, Fall, and . . . ? of Adam Clayton Powell,* by Reed, as Emmett Coleman, and others (New York: Bee-Line, 1967);

19 Necromancers from Now, edited by Reed (Garden City: Doubleday, 1970);

Yardbird Lives!, edited by Reed and Al Young (New York: Grove, 1978);

Calafia: The California Poetry, edited by Reed (Berkeley, Cal.: Y'bird, 1979).

PERIODICAL PUBLICATION: "The Writer as Seer: Ishmael Reed on Ishmael Reed," *Black World,* 23 (June 1974): 20-34.

"The most revolutionary black novelist who has appeared in print thus far," wrote Nick Aaron Ford as early as 1971, "is Ishmael Reed." Nick Aaron Ford, one of the elder statesmen of Afro-American literary criticism, could make this bold judgment of Reed's place in the black canon after Reed had published only his first two experimental

Ishmael Reed (photo © by Thomas Victor)

novels, *The Free-Lance Pallbearers* (1967) and *Yellow Back Radio Broke-Down* (1969). With the publication of what several scholars consider the two most sustained works in Reed's oeuvre, *Mumbo Jumbo* (1972) and *Flight to Canada* (1976), Ford's startling claim would seem much less hyperbolic. Ishmael Reed, author of six novels, four books of poems, two collections of essays, and editor and publisher of several anthologies, stands at age forty-six as one of the cardinal figures in the Afro-American literary tradition.

Reed's place in the tradition is, however, both unique and somewhat ironic. For Reed has chosen

219

to establish his presence as an artist not by repeating and revising the great black texts in that tradition, rather by challenging the formal conventions that these texts share through the always fragile arts of satire and parody. As the semiotician Robert Scholes has claimed, "whoever called him Ishmael picked the right name. His hand is against every man's—and every woman's, too. . . . He is a black Juvenal."

Reed, named after a second cousin, does indeed bear more than a passing familiarity with Juvenal, the great Roman satirist. Like Juvenal's extant sixteen *Satires,* Reed's texts consist of strident attacks on the vices, excesses, and foibles of contemporary American middle- and upper-class mores. Situated in a recognizable historical past (the Harlem Renaissance in *Mumbo Jumbo;* the antebellum plantation in *Flight to Canada*; the mythical Western never-never land in *Yellow Back Radio Broke-Down*; or the fantastic futuristic kingdom of "Harry Sam" in *The Free-Lance Pallbearers* and, in a more contemporary setting, *The Terrible Twos,* 1982), Reed's works show that his fictional concerns are not directed at his contemporaries but at his antecedents and his heirs. This, of course, is the traditional apologia of the satirist, only one sign of how "traditional" this clever iconoclast truly is.

Despite the author's claims, however, it is patently obvious that Reed sees the historical present as an extension of the past, yesterday's evils now grown full-blossom into today's nightmares. Even his futuristic antithetical universes are only reflections of the present, as he analyzes it in its complexities, logically extended. Reed's satires consist of an ironic wit, a sometimes bitter hatred of economic exploitation—of both victims of that process, the exploited and the exploiter—and a narrow, if consistent, optimism for the determined souls who transcend their immediate environment and penetrate illusions by daring acts of will.

Yet, it would be a profound mistake to imagine Reed primarily as a social reformer. While ostensibly concerned with racism, sexism, and economic exploitation, a careful reading of Reed's works argues forcefully that his prime target for parody is none other than literary convention itself.

Reed's use of so-called "sub-cultural" literary forms—such as the Western, modes of film narration, and the detective novel—are not merely novel devices of telling stories. Rather, they engage other, inherited strategies of narration which become as much a part of a people's "experience," narrated in literature, as does the very content of that experience itself. As the Loop Garoo Kid (*Yellow Back Radio Broke-Down*) puts the matter of the conventions of the novel, "No one says a novel has to be one thing. It can be anything it wants to be, a vaudeville show, the six o'clock news, the mumblings of wild men saddled by demons."

So, while it is fitting to recall Byron's characterization of the satirist as one who will "publish right or wrong:/Fools are [his] theme, let satire be [his] song," it is perhaps even more fitting to recall Northrup Frye's contention that parody is "often a sign that certain vogues in handling conventions are getting worn out." Reed has set as a task for himself nothing less than a sustained engagement of the fictions of Ralph Ellison, Richard Wright, and James Baldwin, among other Afro-American canonical writers. As he has said of his writing, "I try to do what has never been done before." While Reed's satire derives in part from the works of Rudolph Fisher, George Schuyler, and Wallace Thurman, he has no true predecessor or counterpart in the black tradition.

Ishmael Scott Reed was born in Chattanooga, Tennessee, on 22 February 1938, the son of Henry Lenoir, a fundraiser for the YMCA, and Thelma Coleman, a homemaker and saleslady. Later in the thirties Reed's mother married Bennie Stephen Reed, an auto worker. Reed has four brothers in his father's family and two brothers and one sister in his stepfather's family.

In 1942, Reed moved with his mother to Buffalo, New York, where his mother found employment in various wartime industries. Reed lived in Buffalo for twenty years, where he attended public schools. Reed performed unevenly ("I served time," he has put it), first at Buffalo Technical High School between 1952 and 1954, then at East High School, where he graduated in 1956.

Reed began his college education as an evening student at the University of Buffalo's night school division, Millard Fillmore College, supporting himself as a clerk in the Buffalo public library system during the day. As would the slaves he depicts in his fifth novel, *Flight to Canada,* Reed wrote his way out of the second-class status of night school into the standard bachelor of arts curriculum of the University of Buffalo. His satirical short story "Something Pure," which depicts the Second Coming of Jesus as an advertising agent whose unorthodox sales strategy earns him ridicule, scorn, and certain exile, alerted an English professor to his extraordinary gifts of storytelling and parody and secured for him perhaps his first positively reinforcing experience in academe. Reed would find such positive reactions from academic critics to be elusive in the next two decades, both in terms of reviews of his literary works and gaining tenure in an English department.

While a student at the university between 1956 and 1960, Reed was influenced by several professors in Buffalo's superb department of American Studies, especially Lyle Glazer, Terrence Hawkes, in the English department, and George Trager and Henry Lee Smith, two linguists who helped him to understand the potential of the Afro-American vernacular as a mode of literary discourse. Both influences—a classical "canonical" training in the Western tradition and a subtle and brilliant understanding of the resonance of the several dictions and "dialects" of contemporary "hyphenated-Americans"—would merge into a unique and individual blend even in Reed's earliest poems and fictions.

Reed withdrew from the university in 1960 because of a dire shortage of funds and a "wide gap between social classes" and took residence in "Buffalo's notorious Talbert Mall Project" in order to define himself against the artificial social and class distinctions that he associated with American university education. Life in the lower-class black housing project, Reed's version of Orwell's encounters described in *Down and Out in Paris and London*, was "a horrible experience," he recalls, because of his growing awareness of systemic poverty cycles over which no one individual, no matter how honestly committed or well-intentioned, had control. These daily living experiences led directly to a period of intense political activism during the latter stages of the civil rights movement and the initiatory phase of the black power movement. "A time of political activism," Reed recalls, "was followed by one of cynicism."

Reed continued to live in Buffalo between 1960 and 1962. As have so many creative writers, Reed began his professional career with a newspaper, serving as a staff correspondent with the *Empire Star Weekly*. During the summer of 1961, Reed and the editor of the *Star* served as cohosts of a radio program for station WVFO. The program, "Buffalo Community Roundtable," was controversial from its inception because of its innovative format and pioneering presentation of political opinions and personalities even further to the left than civil rights advocates. The radio station cancelled the program after Reed interviewed Malcolm X, then the most visible leader of the black nationalist movement, the Nation of Islam. Reed's relish for exercising freedom of speech and his determination to penetrate illusions and bourgeois ideology,

amply in evidence in his earliest journalistic endeavors, have remained central aspects of his career for well over two decades.

During his residence in Buffalo, Reed married Priscilla Rose in September 1960. In 1962, their daughter, Timothy Brett Reed, was born. In 1963, Reed and his wife separated. (They were divorced in 1970.) He also acted in a number of plays, including Edward Albee's *The Death of Bessie Smith*, Tennessee Williams's *Camino Real*, Lorraine Hansberry's *A Raisin in the Sun*, and Jean Anouilh's *Antigone*.

In 1962, Reed moved from Buffalo to New York City, where he lived until 1967. Reed was an active and prominent participant in several cultural organizations during his residence in New York in a period which witnessed the culmination of the civil rights movement, the assassinations of John F. Kennedy and Malcolm X, the birth of the black arts and black power movements, as well as various radical "underground" integrated political-cultural organizations. During this seminal period in American letters, Reed served as editor in chief of *Advance*, a Newark, New Jersey, weekly. It was the "dummy" for the initial number of *Advance*, which Reed commissioned his friend, the painter Walter Bowart, to prepare, which Bowart says inspired him to found the *East Village Other*, the first of the nonconventional newspapers to achieve a national circulation. Reed helped to plan the shape and scope of the *Other* and even named it after Carl Jung's well-known concept of "Otherness." Reed also was a major participant in the Umbra Workshop, a black writers' group that, Reed believes, "began the inflourescence of 'Black Poetry' as well as many other recent Afro-American styles of writing." Reed's New York period was crucial in his evolution as an artist, marked by separation from his first wife, an emerging national identity among black and white writers, organization of the 1965 American Festival of Negro Art, and the writing, in 1965 and 1966, of his first novel, *The Free-Lance Pallbearers*, published a year later to a remarkable critical reception.

Reed left New York in 1967 to assume residence in Berkeley, California. Since 1967, he has taught at the University of California, Berkeley (where in 1977 he was denied tenure but where he continues to teach), at the University of Washington, Seattle (1969), the State University of New York, Buffalo (1975), and more recently at Yale (1979) and Dartmouth (1980). In 1971, along with Steve Cannon and Al Young, Reed founded the Yardbird Publishing Company; in 1973, he started the Reed, Cannon, and Johnson Communications

Company; and in 1976, with Victor H. Cruz he established the Before Columbus Foundation. Each of these publishing endeavors is intended to expand our ideas of exactly what texts and which authors make up the canon of a truly "American" literature, a national literature that is Chicano and Chinese, Yiddish and Native American, Anglo-Saxon and Afro-American, multicolored and multivocal. In this capacity as publisher, Reed and his associates have served to direct international attention to the multiplicity of textual voices that unite to create a multifarious literature that is comparative and American.

In 1970, Reed married Carla Blank, a modern dancer. They live in Oakland, California, with their daughter, Tennessee Reed, age seven.

Ishmael Reed is perhaps the most widely reviewed Afro-American male author since Ralph Ellison. Along with Amiri Baraka, he is also the most controversial. Whereas Baraka's controversy arises from the successive political ideologies he has adopted and abandoned in a two-decade metamorphosis, Reed's source of controversy is his penchant to parody even our most sacred and shared beliefs. Reed's critics would remind him of another great satirist's warning of the dangers inherent in the art: that "satire is a sort of glass," as Jonathan Swift wrote, "wherein beholders do generally discover everybody's face but their own."

Critics tend to subsume Reed's reputation most often under the vague and often derogatory euphemism of "satirist," as if that genre relegated his stature as an artist to some nebulous corner of the absurd, allowing him to be "explained away" or dismissed summarily. But Reed's form of satire and parody is formal or "critical" parody, an attack on ways of seeing or representing content, perhaps because a concern with realism, "naturalism" in fiction, characterized nearly the whole of black fiction until Ralph Ellison published *Invisible Man*, a novel descended directly from Herman Melville's *Confidence Man*. Indeed, it remains the sine qua non of the literary heirs of Richard Wright, specifically for those whose works assume Wright's *Native Son* as their silent second text. Of Ellison's direct descendants, among whom are Leon Forrest, Ernest Gaines, James Alan McPherson, Toni Morrison, and Alice Walker, perhaps no one has mounted as concerted an attack on naturalism as has Ellison's energetic and mischievous stepchild, Ishmael Reed.

Ishmael Reed's novels consistently manage to consolidate disparate, seemingly unrelated characteristics of black written and unwritten formal expression, and thereby to redefine for us the very possibilities of the novel as a literary form. His novels are almost essays on the art of black fiction-making. His use of satire is no accident. Thematically, as in *Mumbo Jumbo,* he seems determined to force us to rediscover the still largely untold role of blacks as creators of American culture or as word sorcerers who maintain a secret culture which, from time to time, pervades all of American life. Formally, as in *Flight to Canada,* by taking imaginative liberties not only with plot, structure, and point of view but also with Newtonian notions of time and space, he is as effective in drawing attention to the craft of writing as Richard Pryor is in outlining the formal patterns of the black sermon in his "Book of Wonder" parody and as Stevie Wonder is in satirizing the vapidity of so much of "classical" Western music when he sets the words of "Village Ghetto Land" to the form of the concerto. This sort of satire by Pryor, Wonder, and Reed is the subtlest and most profound of all—the parody of forms. As with science fiction, it uncannily reveals perhaps more about the ordering of the myths we live by than does even the most painstakingly "exact" photographic reproduction. Theirs is an art based on the tension of dissonance—on the power of art to "say" more than it states—as opposed to an art where normative judgment turns on a "likeness" to the world we experience every day.

A close reading of Reed's works suggests strongly his concerns with the received form of the novel, with the precise rhetorical shape of the Afro-American literary tradition, and with the relation that the Afro-American tradition bears to the Western tradition. Reed's concerns, as exemplified in his narrative forms, seem to be twofold: (1) the relation his own art bears to his black literary precursors, including Zora Neale Hurston, Wright, Ellison, and James Baldwin; and (2) the process of willing-into-being a rhetorical structure, a literary language, replete with its own figures and tropes, but one that allows the black writer to posit a structure of feeling that simultaneously critiques both the metaphysical presuppositions inherent in Western ideas and forms of writing and the metaphysical system in which the "blackness" of the writer and his experience have been valorized as a "natural" absence. In six demanding novels, Reed has criticized, through signifying, what he perceives to be the conventional structures of feeling that he has received from the Afro-American tradition. He has proceeded almost as if the sheer process of the analysis can clear a narrative space for the next generation of writers as decidedly as Ellison's narrative response to Wright and naturalism cleared a space for

Leon Forrest, Toni Morrison, Alice Walker, James Alan McPherson, and especially for Reed himself.

By undertaking the difficult and subtle art of pastiche, Reed criticizes the Afro-American idealism of a transcendent black subject, integral and whole, self-sufficient, and plentiful, the "always already" black signified, available for literary representation in received Western forms. Reed's fictions argue that the so-called black experience cannot be thought of as static—and it is the signifiers of the Afro-American tradition with whom Reed is concerned.

Reed's first novel lends credence to this sort of reading and also serves to create a set of general expectations for reading the rest of his works. *The Free-Lance Pallbearers* (1967) is, above all else, a parody of the confessional mode which is the fundamental, undergirding convention of Afro-American narrative, received, elaborated upon, and transmitted in a chartable heritage from Briton Hammon's captivity narrative of 1760, through the antebellum slave narratives, to black autobiography, and into black fiction, especially the fictions of Hurston, Wright, Baldwin, and Ellison. The narrative of Reed's Bukka Doopeyduk is a pastiche of the classic black narrative of the questing protagonist's "journey into the heart of whiteness"; but it parodies that narrative form by turning it inside out, exposing the character of the originals and thereby defining their formulaic closures and disclosures. Doopeyduk's tale ends with his own crucifixion; as the narrator of his own story, therefore, Doopeyduk articulates, literally from among the dead, an irony implicit in all confessional and autobiographical modes, in which any author is forced by definition to imagine him or herself to be dead. More specifically, Reed signifies upon *Black Boy* and *Go Tell It on the Mountain* in a foregrounded critique which can be read as an epigraph to the novel: "read growing up in soulsville first of three installments—or what it means to be a backstage darky." Reed foregrounds the "scat-singing voice" that introduces the novel against the "other" voice of Doopeyduk, whose "second" voice narrates the novel's plot. Here, Reed parodies both Hurston's use of free indirect discourse in *Their Eyes Were Watching God* and Ellison's use in *Invisible Man* of the foregrounded voices in the prologue and epilogue that frame his nameless protagonist's picaresque account of his own narrative. In his second novel, *Yellow Back Radio Broke-Down*, Reed more fully, and successfully, critiques both realism and modernism. The exchange between Bo Shmo and the Loop Garoo Kid is telling:

It was Bo Shmo and the neo-social realist gang. They rode to this spot from their hideout in the hills. Bo Shmo leaned in his saddle and scowled at Loop, whom he considered a deliberate attempt to be obscure. A buffoon an outsider and frequenter of sideshows. . . .
The trouble with you Loop is that you're too abstract, the part time autocrat monarchist and guru finally said. Crazy dada nigger that's what you are. You are given to fantasy and are off in matters of detail. Far out esoteric bullshit is where you're at. Why in those suffering books that I write about my old neighborhood and how hard it was every gumdrop machine is in place while your work is a blur and a doodle. I'll bet you can't create the difference between a German and a red-skin.
What's your beef with me Bo Shmo, what if I write circuses? No one says a novel has to be one thing. It can be anything it wants to be, a vaudeville show, the six o'clock news, the mumblings of wild men saddled by demons. All art must be for the end of liberating the masses. A landscape is only good when it shows the oppressor hanging from a tree.
Right on! Right, on, Bo, the henchmen chorused. Did you receive that in a vision or was it revealed to you?

At several points in his first two novels, then, Reed deliberately reflects upon the history of the black tradition's debate over the nature and purpose of art.

Reed's third novel, *Mumbo Jumbo* (1972), is a novel about writing itself—not only in the figurative sense of the postmodern, self-reflexive text but also in a literal sense: "So Jes Grew is seeking its words. Its text. For what good is a liturgy without a text?" *Mumbo Jumbo* is both a book about texts and a book of texts, a composite narrative composed of subtexts, pretexts, posttexts, and narratives within narratives. It is both a definition of Afro-American culture and its deflation. "The Big Lie concerning Afro-American culture," the dust jacket states, "is that it lacks a tradition." The "Big Truth" of the novel, on the other hand, is that this very tradition is as rife with hardened convention and presupposition as is the rest of the Western tradition. Even this cryptic riddle of Jes Grew and its text parodies Ellison: *Invisible Man*'s plot is set in motion with a riddle, while the themes of the relation between words and texts echo a key passage from Ellison's short story "And Hickman Arrives": "Good. Don't talk like I talk; talk like I *say*. Words are your business, boy. Not just *the* Word. Words are everything. The key to the Rock, the answer to the Question."

Reed's signifying on tradition begins with his book's title. "Mumbo Jumbo" is the received and ethnocentric Western designation for the rituals of black religions as well as for all black languages themselves. A vulgarized Western "translation" of a Swahili phrase, *mambo, jambo,* "mumbo jumbo," according to *Webster's Third New International Dictionary,* connotes "language that is unnecessarily involved and difficult to understand: GIBBERISH." The *Oxford English Dictionary* cites its etymology as "of unknown origin," illustrating the significance of Reed's title and the phenomenon of Jes Grew, which recalls the myth of Topsy in *Uncle Tom's Cabin* who, with no antecedents, "jes' grew"—a phrase with which James Weldon Johnson characterizes the creative process of black sacred music. *Mumbo Jumbo,* then, signifies upon Western etymology, abusive Western practices of deflation through misnaming, and Johnson's specious, albeit persistent, designation of black creativity as anonymous.

But there is even more parody in this title. Whereas Ellison tropes the myth of presence in Wright's titles of *Native Son* and *Black Boy* through his title of *Invisible Man,* Reed parodies all three titles by employing as his title the English-language parody of black language itself. Although the etymology of "mumbo jumbo" has been problematic for Western lexicographers, any Swahili speaker knows that the phrase derives from the common greeting *jambo* and its plural *mambo,* which loosely translated mean "What's happening?" Reed is also echoing and signifying upon Vachel Lindsay's ironic poem "The Congo," which so (fatally) influenced the Harlem Renaissance poets, as Charles T. Davis has shown. From its title on, *Mumbo Jumbo* serves as a critique of black and Western literary forms and conventions and of the complex relations between the two.

On the book's cover, which Reed designed (with Allen Weinberg), repeated and reversed images of a crouching, sensuous Josephine Baker are superimposed upon a rose. Counterposed to this image is a medallion depicting a horse with two riders. These signs, the rose and the medallion, adumbrate the two central oppositions of the novel's complicated plot. The rose and the double image of Baker together form a cryptic *vé vé.* A *vé vé* is a key sign in Haitian *Vaudou,* a sign drawn on the ground with sand, cornmeal, flour, and coffee to represent the *loas.* The *loas* are the deities comprising the pantheon of *Vaudou* gods. The rose is a sign of Erzulie, goddess of love, as are the images of

Baker, who became the French goddess of love in the late 1920s, in the Parisian version of the Jazz Age. The doubled image, as if mirrored, is meant to suggest the divine crossroads where human beings meet their fate. At its center presides the *loa* Legba (Esu), guardian of the divine crossroads, messenger of the gods, the figure representing the interpreter and interpretation itself. Legba is master of that mystical barrier separating the divine from the profane world. This complex yet cryptic *vé vé* is meant both to placate Legba himself and to summon his attention and integrity in a double act of criticism and interpretation: that of Reed in the process of his representation of the tradition, to be found between the covers of the book, and of the critic's interpretation of Reed's view of the black tradition.

Located outside of the *vé vé,* as counterpoint, placed almost off the cover itself, is the medallion, the sign of the Knights Templar, representing the heart of the Western tradition. The *vé vé* and the medallion represent two distinct warring forces, two mutually exclusive modes of reading. Already we are in the realm of doubled doubles—not binaries. ("Doubled doubles" are central figures in Yoruba mythology, as is Esu.) Not only are two distinct and conflicting metaphysical systems represented and invoked, but Reed's cover also serves as an overture to the critique of dualism and binary opposition which gives a major thrust to the text of *Mumbo Jumbo.* Reed parodies this dualism, which he thinks is exemplified in Ellison's *Invisible Man,* not just in *Mumbo Jumbo* but also in another text, in his poem "Dualism: ralph ellison's invisible man."

This critique of dualism is implicit in *Mumbo Jumbo's* central speaking character, PaPa LaBas. "Speaking" has emphasis here because the novel's central character, of course, is Jes Grew itself, which never speaks and is never seen in its "abstract essence," only in discrete manifestations, or "outbreaks." Jes Grew is the supraforce which sets the text of *Mumbo Jumbo* in motion, as Jes Grew and Reed seek their texts, as all characters and events define themselves against this omnipresent, compelling force. Jes Grew, here, is a clever and subtle parody of similar forces invoked in the black novel of naturalism, most notably in Wright's *Native Son.*

Unlike Jes Grew, PaPa LaBas does indeed speak. He is the chief detective in hard-and-fast pursuit of both Jes Grew and its Text. PaPa LaBas's name is a conflation of two of the several names of Esu, the Pan-African trickster. Called "Papa Legba" as his Haitian honorific and invoked through the phrase "eh là-bas" in New Orleans jazz recordings of the 1920s and 1930s, PaPa LaBas is the Afro-

American trickster figure from black sacred tradition. His surname, of course, is French for "over there," and his presence unites "over there" (Africa) with "right here." He is indeed the messenger of the gods, the divine Pan-African interpreter, pursuing, in the language of the text, "The Work," which is not only *Vaudou* but also the very work (and play) of art itself. PaPa LaBas is the figure of the critic, in search of the text, decoding its telltale signs in the process. Even the four syllables of his name recall *Mumbo Jumbo*'s play of doubles. Chief sign reader, LaBas also in a sense is a sign himself. Indeed, PaPa LaBas's incessant and ingenious search for the Text of Jes Grew, culminating as it does in his recitation and revision of the myth of Thoth's gift of writing to civilization, constitutes an argument against the prioritizing in black discourse of what Reed elsewhere terms "the so-called oral tradition" in favor of the supremacy of the written text. It is a brief for the permanence of the written text, for the need of criticism, for which LaBas's myth of origins also accounts ("Guides were initiated into the Book of Thoth, the 1st anthology written by the 1st choreographer").

The prose of *Mumbo Jumbo* can be explained as a textbook, complete with illustrations, footnotes, and a bibliography. A prologue, an epilogue, and an appended "Partial Bibliography" frame the text itself, again in a parody of Ellison's framing devices in *Invisible Man*. (Reed supplements Ellison's epilogue with the bibliography, parodying the device both by its repeated presence and by the subsequent asymmetry of *Mumbo Jumbo*.) This documentary scheme of notes, illustrations, and bibliography parodies the documentary conventions of black realism and naturalism, as does Reed's recurrent use of lists and catalogs. These "separate" items Reed fails to separate with any sort of punctuation, thereby directing attention to their presence as literary conventions rather than as sources of information, particularly about the "black experience." Reed's text also includes dictionary definitions, epigraphs, epigrams, anagrams, photoduplicated type from other texts, newspaper clips and headlines, signs (such as those that hang on doors), invitations to parties, telegrams, "Situation Reports," which come "from the 8-tubed Radio," yin-yang symbols, quotations from other texts, poems, cartoons, drawings of mythic beasts, handbills, photographs, book-jacket copy, charts and graphs, playing cards, a representation of a Greek vase, and a four-page handwritten letter, among even other items. Just as our word "satire" derives from *satura*, "hash," so Reed's form of satire is a version of "gumbo," a parody of form itself.

Here Reed parodies and underscores our notions of intertextuality, present in all texts. *Mumbo Jumbo* is the great black intertext, replete with intratexts referring to one another within the text of *Mumbo Jumbo* and also referring outside of themselves to all those other named texts, as well as to those texts unnamed but invoked through concealed reference, repetition, and reversal. The "Partial Bibliography" is Reed's most brilliant stroke, since its unconcealed presence (along with the text's other undigested texts) parodies both the scholar's appeal to authority and all studied attempts to conceal literary antecedents and influence. All texts, claims *Mumbo Jumbo,* are intertexts, full of intratexts. Our notions of originality, Reed's critique suggests, are more related to convention and material relationships than to some supposedly transcendent truth. Reed lays bare that mode of concealment and the illusion of unity which characterize modernist texts. Coming as it does after the epilogue, Reed's "Partial Bibliography" is an implicit parody of Ellison's ideas of craft and technique in the novel and suggests an image of Ellison's nameless protagonist, buried in his well-lighted hole, eating vanilla ice cream smothered by sloe gin, making annotations for his sequel to *Invisible Man.* The device, moreover, mimics the fictions of documentation and history which claim to order the ways societies live. The presence of the bibliography also recalls Ellison's remarks about the complex relationship between the "writer's experience" and the writer's experiences with books.

Reed's parodic use of intertextuality demonstrates that *Mumbo Jumbo* is a postmodern text. But what is its parody of the Jazz Age and the Harlem Renaissance about, and for whom do the characters stand? Reed's novel is situated in the 1920s because, as the text explains, the Harlem Renaissance was the first full-scale, patronized attempt to capture the essence of Jes Grew in discrete literary texts. Jes Grew had made its first appearance in the 1890s, when "the Dance" swept the country. Indeed, James Weldon Johnson appropriated the phrase 'jes' grew' to refer to the composition of the musical texts of Ragtime, which depended upon signifying riffs to transform black secular, and often vulgar, songs into formal, repeatable compositions. Ellison makes essentially the same statement about the 1890s by suggesting that signifying is implicit in the common designation of this music as "Ethiopian Airs." Ellison's pun could well serve as still another signified upon which *Mumbo Jumbo* signifies. The power of Jes Grew was allowed to disappear in the 1890s, Reed argues, because it found no literary texts to contain, define, interpret, and thereby will it to subsequent black cultures.

Although the Harlem Renaissance did succeed in the creation of numerous texts of art and criticism, most critics agree that it failed to find its voice, which lay muffled beneath the dead weight of Romantic convention, which most black writers seemed not to question but to adopt eagerly. This is essentially the same critique rendered by Wallace Thurman in his *Infants of the Spring* (1932), a satirical novel about the Harlem Renaissance, written by one of its most thoughtful literary critics. Few of Reed's characters stand for historical personages; most are figures for types. Hinckle Von Vampton, however, suggests Carl Van Vechten; but his first name, from the German *hinken* ("to limp"), could suggest the German engraver Hermann Knackfuss, whose name translates as "a person with a clubfoot." Abdul Sufi Hamid recalls a host of Black Muslims, most notably Duse Mohamed Ali, editor of the *African Times and Orient Review,* as well as Elijah Muhammad's shadowy mentor, W. D. Fard. The key figures in the action of the plot, however, are the Atonist Path and its military wing, the Wallflower Order, on one hand, and the Neo-HooDoo detectives, headed by PaPa LaBas, and its "military" wing, the *Mu'tafikah,* on the other. "Wallflower Order" is a two-term pun on "Ivy League," while *Mu'tafikah* puns on a twelve-letter word which signifies chaos. Also, "mu" is the twelfth letter of the Greek alphabet, suggesting "the dozens," which forms a subdivision of the black ritual of signifying; the *Mu'tafikah* play the dozens on Western art museums. The painter Knackfuss created a heliogravure from Wilhelm II's allegorical drawing of the European authority to go to war against the Chinese. This heliogravure, *Volker Europas, wahrt eure heiligsten Guter* (People of Europe, protect that which is most holy to you), was completed in 1895. It appears in *Mumbo Jumbo* as part of a chapter in which members of the Wallflower Order plot against the *Mu'tafikah.* The pun on "Knackfuss" and *hinken* is wonderfully consistent with Reed's multiple puns on the "Wallflower Order" and "atonist."

The meaning of "Atonist" multiplies here. "One who atones" is an Atonist; a follower of Aton, (Pharaoh) Akhnaton's Supreme Being who "reappears" as Jehovah, is an Atonist; but also one who lacks physiological tone, especially of a contractile organ, is an Atonist. On a wall at Atonist headquarters are the Order's symbols: *the Flaming Disc, the #1 and the creed—Look at them! Just look at them! throwing their hips this way, that way while I, my muscles, stone, the marrow of my spine, plaster, my back supported by decorated paper, stand here as goofy as a Dumb Dora. Lord, if I can't dance, no one shall.*" The Atonists and the Jes Grew Carriers ("J. G. C.s") reenact allegorically a primal, recurring battle between the forces of light and the forces of darkness, between forces of the Left Hand and forces of the Right Hand, between the descendants of Set and the descendants of Osiris, all symbolized in Knackfuss's heliogravure.

We learn of this war in *Mumbo Jumbo*'s marvelous parody of the scene of recognition so fundamental to the structure of detective fiction, which occurs in the library of a black-owned villa at Irvington-on-Hudson, called Villa Lewaro, "an anagram," the text tells us, "upon the Hostess' name, by famed tenor Enrico Caruso." Actually, "Lewaro" is an anagram for "we oral." This recognition scene in which PaPa LaBas and his sidekick, Black Herman, arrest Hinckle Von Vampton and his sidekick, Hubert "Safecracker" Gould, parodies its counterpart in the detective novel by its exaggerated frame. When forced to explain the charges against Von Vampton and Gould, LaBas replies, "Well if you must know, it all began 1000s of years ago in Egypt, according to a high up member in the Haitian aristocracy." He then proceeds to narrate, before an assembled company of hundreds, the myth of Set and Osiris and its key subtext, the myth of the introduction of writing in Egypt by the god Thoth. The parody involved here is the length of the recapitulation of facts—of the decoded signs—which LaBas narrates in a thirty-one-page chapter, the longest in the book. The myth, of course, recapitulates the action of the novel up to this point of the narrative but by an allegorical representation through mythic discourse. By fits and turns, we realize that Von Vampton and the Wallflower Order are the descendants of Set, by way of the story of Moses and Jethro and the birth of the Knights Templar in 1118 A.D.. Von Vampton, we learn, was the Templar librarian, who found the sacred Book of Thoth ("the 1st anthology written by the 1st choreographer"), which is Jes Grew's sacred Text. In the twentieth century, Von Vampton subdivided the Book of Thoth into fourteen sections, just as Set had dismembered his brother Osiris's body into fourteen segments. He anonymously mailed the fourteen sections of the anthology to fourteen black people, who are manipulated into mailing its parts to each other in a repeating circle, in the manner of a "chain book." Abdul Sufi Hamid, one of those fourteen who we learn are unwitting Jes Grew Carriers, calls in the other thirteen chapters of the anthology, reassembles the Text, and even translates the Book of Thoth from the hieroglyphics. Sensing its restored Text, Jes Grew surfaces in New Orleans, as it had in the 1890s with the birth of Ragtime, and heads toward New York. Ignorant of the existence or nature of Jes Grew and of the true nature of the sacred Text, Abdul destroys the Book, and then, when he refuses to reveal its location, is murdered by the Wallflower Order. LaBas, Von Vampton's archenemy, master of HooDoo, devout follower of Jes Grew ("PaPa LaBas carries Jes Grew in him like most other folk carry genes"), chief decoder of signs, recapitulates this complex story in elaborate detail to the assembled guests at Villa Lewaro, thereby repeating through the recited myth the figures of *Mumbo Jumbo*'s own plot, functioning as what Reed calls "the shimmering Etheric Double of the 1920s. The thing that gives it its summary." Despite numerous murders and even the arrests of Von Vampton and Gould and their repatriation to Haiti for trial by the *loas* of *Vaudou,* neither the mystery of the nature of Jes Grew nor the identity of its Text is ever resolved. The epilogue presents PaPa LaBas in the 1960s, delivering his annual lecture to a college audience on the Harlem Renaissance and its unconsummated Jes Grew passion.

But just as we can define orders of multiple substitution and signification for Reed's types and caricatures, as is true of allegory generally (e.g., Von Vampton/Van Vechten, *hinken*/Knackfuss), so too can we find many levels of meaning which could provide a closure to the text. The first decade of readers of *Mumbo Jumbo* have attempted, with great energy, to find one-to-one correlations, decoding its allegorical structure by finding analogues between, for example, the Harlem Renaissance and the black arts movement. As interesting as such parallel universes are, however, *Mumbo Jumbo*'s status as a rhetorical structure, as a mode of narration, and the relation of this mode of narration to a critique of traditional notions of closure in interpretation is more germane. Reed's most subtle achievement in *Mumbo Jumbo* is to parody the notions of closure implicit in the key texts of the Afro-American canon. *Mumbo Jumbo*, in contrast to that canon, is a novel that figures and glorifies indeterminacy. In this sense, *Mumbo Jumbo* stands as a profound critique and elaboration upon the convention of closure, and its metaphysical implications, in the black novel. In its stead, Reed posits the notion of aesthetic play: the play of the tradition, the play on the tradition, the sheer play of indeterminacy itself.

Flight to Canada (1976) is Uncle Robin's slave narrative, written by Raven Quickskill—"the first one of [Arthur] Swille's slaves to read, the first to write, and the first to run away." The novel turns on the relationship between the demonic and decadent slaveholder Arthur Swille and three or four absolute "types" of slaves which sociologists have invented for convenience's sake. In addition to Raven Quickskill, the popular slave poet, there is Cato the Graffado ("So loyal he volunteered for slavery. . . . The slaves voted him All-Slavery"); Stray Leechfield, who exploits his exotic blackness to satisfy the fantasies of a repressed Calvinistic culture; Mammy Baracuda, a parody of Henry Bibb's unfaithful wife; but most of all Uncle Robin who, unlike his amanuensis, never left Swille's plantation: " 'Robin, what you heard about his place up North.' Arthur Swille asks his loyal servant. 'I think they call it Canada?' 'Canada,' Uncle Robin replies, 'I do admit I have heard about the place from time to time, Mr. Swille, but I loves it here so much that . . . that I would never think of leaving here. . . . Most assuredly, Mr. Swille, this is my Canada. You'd better believe it.' "

Oddly enough, it is the relationship between slaveholder and his loyal slave which is drawn most compellingly in Reed's novel. Though we are meant to laugh at Arthur Swille, there lurks in his character a masterful depiction not of mere evil but of the hubris demanded to defy the natural order. For Swille is a man deranged by his own nether side. " 'Nigger fever,' he had railed. 'Niggers do something to you. I've seen white people act strange under their influence. First, you dream about niggers, little niggers mostly; little niggers, sitting eating watermelons, grinning at you. Then you start dreaming about big niggers. Big, big niggers. Big, big niggers walking all over you, then you got niggers all over you, then they got you. . . . As long as they're in this country, this country is under their spell.' " But not only is Swille pursued by his own demonic nature, he seeks to merge with it, to consummate his reverence for it. As death approaches him in the form of the ghost of his dead sister, with whose corpse he had been engaged in a deeply satisfying necrophilic liaison, the nature of Swille's true evil becomes vividly clear: his is the transgression of human limits and the construction of a nightmare world to justify that transgression.

And Uncle Robin? What of Uncle Robin after the sudden and tragic demise of his beloved master Swille? Uncle Robin rewrites Swille's will and inherits the great Virginia mansion of his master. Moreover, he rejects Harriet Beecher Stowe's subsequent attempts to buy his story and then sends to Canada for Raven Quickskill.

As much as about any good-evil dichotomy,

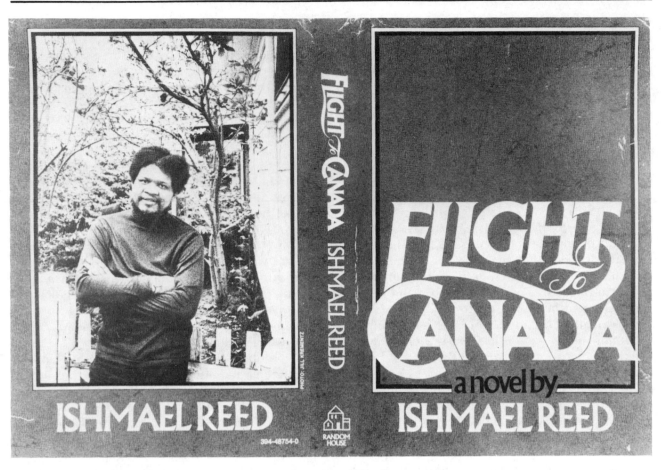

Dust jacket for Reed's 1976 novel, in which a loyal slave rewrites his master's will and inherits the plantation

Ishmael Reed is writing subtly about what Robert Stepto calls "authorial control"—the possession of one's own story, be that our collective history or even one's very own autobiography. He wants to wrestle the text away from those who would control it—be they Harriet Stowe, the well-intentioned abolitionists who "authenticated" the slave narratives, or even Clio, the Muse of history. "Why isn't Edgar Allan Poe recognized as the principal biographer of that strange war?," asks the narrator. "Fiction you say? Where does fact begin and fiction leave off? Why does the perfectly rational, in its own time, often sound like mumbo-jumbo?" Or: "Strange, history. Complicated, too. It will be a mystery, history. New disclosures are as bizarre as the most bizarre history."

Ishmael Reed's *Flight to Canada* is a major work, perhaps Reed's most "intelligent" novel. One senses here a sort of ending for this aspect of his earlier fiction: for the search for The Word, which Reed began in *Mumbo Jumbo,* has realized itself finally in the successful search for the Text—the text that at all points comments upon itself. As Arthur Swille says in a disarmingly perceptive aside on the uses of black literacy:

Look, Lincoln, one of them kinks, 40s, wiped me out when he left here. That venerable mahogany took all my guns, slaughtered my livestock and shot the overseer right between the eyes. And the worst betrayal of all was Raven Quickskill, my trusted bookkeeper. Fooled around with my books, so that every time I'd buy a new slave he'd destroy the invoices and I'd have no record of purchase; he was also writing passes and forging freedom papers. We gave him Literacy, the most powerful thing in the pre-technological pre-post-rational age—and what does he do with it? Uses it like that old Voodoo—that old stuff the slaves mumble about, Fetishism and grisly rites, only he doesn't need anything but a pen he had shaped out of cock feathers and chicken claws. Oh, they are bad sables, Mr. Lincoln. They are bad, bad sables. Not one of them with the charm and good breeding of Ms. Phillis Wheatley, who wrote a poem for the beloved founder of this country, George Washington.

One must concur with Derek Walcott's assessment of Ishmael Reed. "He alters our notion of what is possible. His importance to our use and understanding of language will not be obvious for many years."

Shrovetide in Old New Orleans (1978) is a motley collection of articles and essays, written between 1972 and 1977, in which Reed discusses what he calls "the multi-cultural" influences on his own fiction, pays homage to the black artists to whom he feels indebted, and shares in detail the often bitter controversies that he seems too adept at generating. Even more important, he reveals at length the nature of *Vaudou* (voodoo or hoodoo, as it is known popularly) and traces the patterns it assumes in his own work. It is this attention to *Vaudou,* the key metaphorical system that threads its way through all of his work, that gives this collection its unity.

Throughout, in disarmingly revealing asides,

he seems concerned to put to rest his image of the artist as an embattled man. "Writing has made me a better man. It has put me in contact with those fleeting moments which prove the existence of the soul." Even more, he seems intent on using various methods of exposition in the essays to "show that I know the difference between an essay and a work of fiction." If the matter were an open question, it remains so no longer, for in these pieces Reed uses Mencken's techniques of wry irony and a biting wit to draw a self-portrait that is alternately humorous and polemical, but at all times perceptive, honest, and human.

Reed's concerns are those of an artist. In a long interview with the satirist and essayist George S. Schuyler, as well as in two insightful critical essays on the novels of Chester Himes and on Wright's *Native Son,* Reed takes his stand against what he calls "social realism" as defined by those who "feel that life has to be a heavy Russian Doestoevskian din of intense pain, as some critics . . . require black writers to believe." His art and his critical judgments are committed, he repeats throughout, "toward overcoming the consciousness barrier erected by an al-

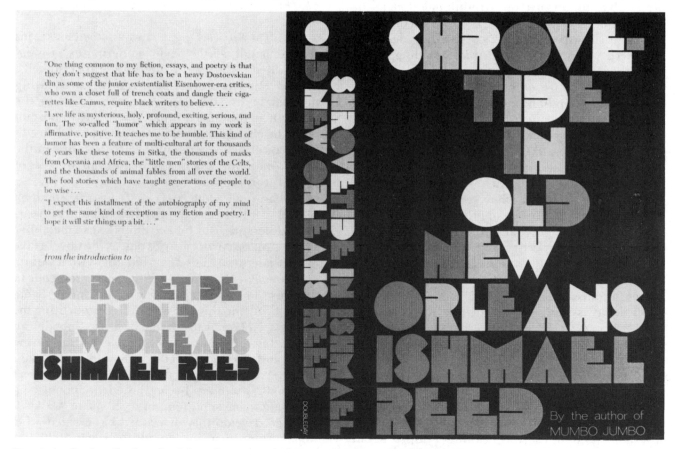

Dust jacket for the collection of articles and essays in which Reed states that writing has put him "in contact with those fleeting moments which prove the existence of the soul"

liance of Eastern-based black pseudo-nationalists and white mundanists who in the 1960s sought to dominate Afro-American intellectual thought with their social realist position papers." What he values most in all forms of human cultural expression is an art that manages to contain the triumph of even the absurdly human over the demonic forces of despair. "At least," he concludes his essay on Himes, "he doesn't sabotage his product by packaging it in poison." Even more adamantly, Reed opposes those who would reduce the complexity of the human experience to mere cant or to gross generalization, as he states rather eloquently in a moving tribute to Walter Lowenfels.

Within his three long essays on *Vaudou*, finally, Ishmael Reed not only describes in vivid detail the form and function of this metaphysical system that syncretized various African and European religions but he also demonstrates just how this system of thought has become his metaphor for the black man and the essential philosophical framework for his fiction. By deriving his symbols, physical laws, and ethical values from this still largely misunderstood system of signs, Reed reveals implicitly the arbitrary biases that undergird our traditional notions of order, ethics, and aesthetics. He contends that his is "an art form with its own laws," one that demands "the necessary scholarship" for its decoding, which more than any other reason explains the often bitter and generally confused critical reviews he receives. But Reed has taught us more about the penetration of appearances and about the remarkably persistent strength of black culture than has anyone since Ellison. Reed's essays, like his fiction, are "songs turning back onto themselves," at all points urging a more encompassing concept of reality than a merely Western one. Toward what goal? Reed answers, "The goal of racial understanding" that will come "through cultural revolution, the way most profound revolutions occur: A man enters the city on the back of an ass; his autobiography becomes the empire's best seller." With these essays, Reed reinforces his importance to modern writing by making explicit the assumptions implicit in his fictions.

It is so easy to forget that Ishmael Reed, complex artist that he is, tells a good story. One tends to be surprised by just how funny, and erotic, Reed can be "simply" by naming for us the deeper structures, myths, and presuppositions by which we, and contemporary American society, order our lives. "Simply" is emphasized because, as any would-be storyteller knows, there is nothing "simple" about telling a tale that is both humorous and riveting, on one hand, yet which simultaneously teaches its au-

dience a lesson, in the curious manner that parables and allegories can do.

If forced to compare Ishmael Reed with another artist, in another genre, the choice might be Richard Pryor. Reed, like Pryor, names things for us, like any great orator or preacher does: he fingers for us, out loud, both that which we often do not even admit to ourselves—the private emotions—as well as those economic and racial relations by which this society seeks to regulate our lives, the invisible network within which we are bound and regulated, and which few will admit exists. Ishmael Reed, like Richard Pryor, has the prophet's gift of vision—that special sort of insight that Stevie Wonder calls "inner vision." Reed, like Pryor and Wonder, tells us not only who we are, and where we as a society are, but *why*.

The Terrible Twos (1982) is the first of this prolific novelist's works in which he engages in an analysis—a critique through satire—of the nature and functioning of both our political and economic systems. Of all of Reed's works *The Terrible Twos* is the first of his satires to speculate about the economic state of the nation as a whole, although *The Free-Lance Pallbearers* satirizes the political order.

In *The Terrible Twos,* as always, Reed makes his readers laugh, all the while rendering exact judgments. Reed is "a good read," as literary critics like to say. His stature as an inventive and daring novelist lends such credence and force to the strength of his satires that, given this important thematic change of direction, it is clear that Reed's voice could well emerge in the 1980s as one of the black community's most salient and subtle voices of social reform.

The book's title derives from the common phrase that describes the psychic state of two-year-old toddlers and which Reed employs as a metaphor for an America two centuries old; as the novel's fake Santa Claus says: "Two years old, that's what we are, emotionally—America, always wanting someone to hand us some ice cream, always complaining, Santa didn't bring me this and why didn't Santa bring me that. . . . Nobody can reason with us. Nobody can tell us anything. Millions of people are staggering about and passing out in the snow and we say that's tough. We say too bad to the children who don't have milk. I weep as I read these letters poor children sent to me at my temporary home in Alaska."

To develop this idea, Reed has created a fictional America in the decade between 1980 and 1990, in which a small newly rich California elite, inextricably tied to oil money, run the White House:

"The fortieth President wears $3,000 worth of clothes including an $800 overcoat from I. Magnin. He is warm and well-fed. His friends come from Bel Air, California, where the average house sells for $800,000 and people pay $600 for a shirt and $350 for a tie and an alligator handbag goes for $1,500. His friends are warm and surfeited. During his inaugural, 50,000 hot-air balloons are set afloat. Stomach-warming Kentucky bourbon and tails are back in the White House, a Time magazine columnist rejoices." This elite of new money, however, frightens that of the traditional Eastern "establishment," old money: "Eastern circles, however, are cautious. Beer Money, car dealership money, supermarket money, and drugstore money surround the President. Eastern money has never heard of this money. This money from Sacramento and Orange County where the men wear $450 Lucchese boots. Money is as tight as Scrooge. Retailers talk of a credit squeeze, and during this season of blizzards, this cold, nasty season, the newspapers devote much advertising to quartz heaters. Millions in the United States are without heat and fires that devastate entire families occur in the wintry cities of the northeast. The President is satiated and sanguine. He dines with Brooke Astor. He is warm, eating, well-fed, smiling-smiling, well-scarfed, bundled-up and waving." And what does all this mean to the country?:

> Ebenezer Scrooge towers above the Washington skyline, rubbing his hands and greedily peering over his spectacles. He shows up at the inaugural in charcoal-gray stroller, dove-gray vest, gray-striped trousers, pleated-front shirt, and four-in-hand tie. Hail First Actor, and Ms. Actorperson on your thronelike blue winged chairs, and your opulent Republican dinners, and your tailors, and your fashion designers flown in from Paris and Beverly Hills and New York, and your full-page color coverage in Women's Wear Daily.
>
> How did the Buffalo Evening News put it? "The Wild West is Back in the Saddle Again." In the west, he campaigned as a cowboy; in the south, the crowd wept and rebel-yelled at the sight of First Actor in a Confederate uniform. Miss Nancy's beautiful white people, in the Red Room, darkies in tails passing out sour mash left and right. Thank you, Miss Nancy, said Charlie Pride.

If all of this sounds perilously familiar, it is supposed to. Creatively fusing together several ingre-

dients, like a good chicken gumbo, including the Macy's Thanksgiving Parade, the hagiography of the traditional model for Santa Claus, Saint Nicholas, Charles Dickens's *A Christmas Carol*, Dante's *Inferno,* the novels of social realism, and Rastafarian-*Vaudou* symbolism, Reed has written a novel about tiny groups of people who seek to turn a profit at the expense of blacks, Indians, and the vast poor, whose numbers in this book make even ours tiny by comparison. Even Christmas comes under the monopoly of Oswald Zumwalt's North Pole Development Corporation in Alaska, which controls all rights to the one true Santa Claus, a failed actor from the soaps.

Reed's characters include President Dean Clift, a former model-become-President because he is manipulable by Big Oil; Nance Saturday, black and sexy sleuth on the trail of the real Santa; and Jamaica Queens, sensual reporter who penetrates the inner sanctum of the Nicolaites (they who would restore St. Nicholas to the church) only to discover Black Peter, everyone's favorite hoodoo-man and wizard. The shades of Eisenhower, Truman, and Nelson Rockefeller which President Clift encounters in his Dickensian descent into the American Hell are all tortured eternally for their political crimes: Truman for Hiroshima ("Japanese faces, burnt, twisted, and peeling, with no eyeballs"), Rockefeller for the slaughter at Attica.

But if this sounds too moribund, this extract of a conversation among Bob Krantz, the TV executive who really runs the country; a beer-king from the West; and a powerful jackleg evangelical preacher gives a fair idea of how Reed develops his themes humorously:

> "How's business? the Admiral asked the Reverend. "Pretty good," the Reverend responded. "Opened a few more mail-order colleges last week. Prayed for the sick, and warned the wicked. Krantz, you're doing a good job," Reverend Jones said. The Admiral nodded.
> "I owe it all to you. You, the Admiral, and the King of Beer. I guess I'd still be working for Babylonian intervention, Reverend Jones."
> "That wasn't me, that was the Lord, son. The Lord's advice is worth more than ours. Never forget that, son." "I don't," said Bob Krantz. "I speak to the Lord day and night." "Good boy," the Admiral said.
> "Stay on your knees. That's the best position for running the state."

The Terrible Twos seems to have ended Reed's

sometimes problematic relationship with reviewers, most of whom seemed delighted with Reed's parody of the Republican administration of Ronald Reagan and with the country's unabashed commercialism in its bicentennial celebration. Whether Reed will retain this concern with economic relationships or whether he will abandon satire for even more daring experimental literary forms remains to be seen. Regardless of the directions his subsequent work assumes, however, Ishmael Reed, like his biblical namesake, will be recalled at least in part for his self-willed expulsion from the literary tradition that he parodies, for his fierce political and literary individuality, and for his skill as an archer of satire. Despite the large tasks that Reed has set for his project as a writer, he achieved the most difficult goal of all—the registering of a literary voice at once black and American, yet always uniquely his own.

Interviews:

Fred Beauford, "A Conversation with Ishmael Reed," *Black Creation*, 4 (1973): 12-15;

John O'Brien, "Ishmael Reed," in his *Interviews with Black Writers* (New York: Liveright, 1973), pp. 165-183;

O'Brien, "Ishmael Reed," in *The New Fiction: Interviews with Innovative American Writers*, edited by Joe David Bellamy (Urbana: University of Illinois Press, 1974), pp. 130-141;

Cameron Northouse, "Ishmael Reed," *Conversations with Writers II* (Detroit: Gale, 1978), pp. 212-254.

References:

Michel Fabre, "Postmodern Rhetoric in Ishmael Reed's *Yellow Back Radio Broke-Down*," in *The Afro-American Novel Since 1960*, edited by Peter Bruck and Wolfgang Karrer (Amsterdam: B. R. Grüner, 1982), pp. 167-188;

Nick Aaron Ford, "A Note on Ishmael Reed: Revolutionary Novelist," *Studies in the Novel*, 3 (1971): 216-218;

H. L. Gates, Jr., "The 'Blackness of Blackness': A Critique of the Sign and the Signifying Monkey," *Critical Inquiry*, 9 (June 1983): 685-723;

John O'Brien, "Ishmael Reed," in *The New Fiction*, edited by Joe David Bellamy (Urbana: University of Illinois, 1974), pp. 130-142;

Neil Schmitz, "Neo-HooDoo: The Experimental Fiction of Ishmael Reed," *Twentieth Century Literature*, 20 (April 1974): 126-140.

Ann Allen Shockley
(21 June 1927-)

Helen R. Houston
Tennessee State University

BOOKS: *A Handbook for the Administration of Special Black Collections* (Nashville: Fisk University Library, 1970);

Living Black American Authors: A Biographical Directory, by Shockley and Sue P. Chandler (New York: Bowker, 1973);

Loving Her (Indianapolis: Bobbs-Merrill, 1974);

The Black and White of It (Weatherby Lake, Mo.: Naiad Press, 1980);

Say Jesus and Come to Me (New York: Avon, 1982).

OTHER: *A Handbook of Black Librarianship,* compiled and edited by Shockley and E. J. Josey (Littleton, Colo.: Libraries Unlimited, 1977).

PERIODICAL PUBLICATIONS:

Fiction:

"Abraham and the Spirit," *Negro Digest*, 8 (July 1950): 85-91;

"The Picture Prize," *Negro Digest*, 11 (October 1962): 53-60;

"A Far Off Sound," *Umbra*, 2 (December 1963): 11-17;

"The Funeral," *Phylon*, 28 (Spring 1967): 95-101;

"The President," *Freedomways*, 10 (Fourth Quarter 1970): 343-349;

"Crying For Her Man," *Liberator*, 11 (January-February 1971): 14-17;

"Is She Relevant?" *Black World*, 20 (January 1971): 58-65;

"Her Own Thing," *Black America,* 2 (August 1972):
58-61, 54;

"Ah: The Young Black Poet," *New Letters,* 41
(Winter 1974): 45-60;

"The More Things Change," *Essence,* 8 (October
1977): 78-79, 93-94, 97-99;

"A Case of Telemania," *Azalea,* 1 (Fall 1978): 1-5;

"Women in a Southern Time," *Feminary,* 11 (1982):
45-56.

Nonfiction:

"Does the Negro College Library Need a Special
Negro Collection?," *Library Journal,* 86 (1 June
1961): 2049-2050;

"The Negro Woman in Retrospect: Blueprint for
the Future," *Negro History Bulletin,* 24 (December 1965): 55-56, 62;

"Tell It Like It Is: A New Criteria for Children's
Books in Black and White," *Southeastern Libraries,* 30 (Spring 1970): 30-33;

"Pauline Elizabeth Hopkins: A Biographical Excursion into Obscurity," *Phylon,* 33 (Spring 1972):
22-26;

"American Anti-Slavery Literature: An Overview—1693-1859," *Negro History Bulletin,* 37
(April/May 1974): 232-235;

"Black Women Discuss Today's Problems: Men,
Families, Society," with Veronica E. Tucker,
Southern Voices, 1 (August/September 1974):
16-19;

"The New Black Feminists," *Northwest Journal of
African and Black American Studies,* 2 (Winter
1974): 1-5;

"Black Publishers and Black Librarians: A Necessary Union," *Black World,* 26 (March 1975):
38-44;

"Joseph S. Cotter, Sr.: Biographical Sketch of a
Black Louisville Bard," *College Language Association Journal,* 18 (March 1975): 327-340;

"Oral History: A Research Tool for Black History,"
Negro History Bulletin, 41 (January/February
1978): 787-789;

"The Black Lesbian in American Literature," *Conditions: Five,* 11 (Autumn 1979): 133-142;

"The Salsa Soul Sisters," *Off Our Backs,* 11
(November 1979): 13;

"Black Lesbian Biography: Lifting the Veil," *Other
Black Woman,* 1 (1982): 5-9.

Newspaper staff writer and columnist, fiction
and nonfiction writer, teacher, librarian, lecturer,
consultant, Ann Allen Shockley is a versatile
thematic contemporary writer. Like most contemporary fiction authors, she focuses upon current
themes—racism, sexism, homophobia—to en-

Ann Allen Shockley

courage readers to accept life experiences as they
really are, without condemnation based on moral
codes that have emanated from the minds of people
with narrow vision. In nonfiction, her literary efforts are adjunct to her work as a librarian.

Ann Allen Shockley was born in Louisville,
Kentucky, on 21 June 1927. Her parents, Henry
and Bessie Lucas Allen, were both social workers.
They surrounded their daughter with books of all
types and encouraged her to read them as well as
those in the library. Thus, her escape into the book
world became a source of pleasure and influence
approved by the adults she admired. When she was
in the eighth grade, her English teacher, Harriet La
Forrest, with whom she still corresponds and shares
her literary achievements, pointed out to her that
she had something worth saying to the reading
public and the imagination and the talent to put it
into print. With this approval, Shockley turned to
writing. She became the editor of her junior high
school newspaper.

Today, Shockley says of herself: "Writing is
like a compulsion to me. It is something I *have* to do.
I am always working on something; I never let up."
Without time to write, without secretarial help,
without modern equipment, she "squeezes" writing
into a tight working schedule and types her manuscripts on a manual typewriter.

As an undergraduate at Fisk University, she
served as fiction writer of the *Fisk Herald,* which

published her short stories and articles. At the end of her freshman year, she took a summer job as staff writer for the *Louisville Defender,* where she wrote news articles, feature articles, a teenage column, a short story a week, and doubled as social columnist. In her senior year, she had a short story published in the *Afro-American* newspaper. Several more of her short stories have since been published.

After receiving the B.A. (1948) from Fisk University and the M.S.L.S. (1959) from Case Western Reserve University, Shockley continued writing for newspapers and periodicals. She was a free-lance writer for newspapers in Delaware and Maryland and for several Afro-American periodicals and columnist for the *Federalsburg Times* and the *Bridgeville News.* In addition to writing for newspapers and periodicals, she substituted in the public schools of Delaware and Maryland and worked as a librarian. In 1969, she returned to her alma mater to work in the Special Negro Collection of the university library. Today, she is associate librarian for Special Collections and university archivist, but she still finds time to serve as consultant, lecturer, teacher, and writer.

Shockley's nonfiction efforts are adjuncts to her work as librarian and archivist. They are utilitarian. After many inquiries about the "who's and what's" of black writers, she perceived the need for her book *Living Black American Authors: A Biographical Directory* (1973), which she coauthored with Sue P. Chandler. In 1977, E. J. Josey, chief of the Bureau of Specialists, Library Services, New York, invited Shockley to compile *A Handbook of Black Librarianship,* which was nominated for the 1978 Ralph R. Shaw Award for Outstanding Contributions to Library Literature. The book presents information on the names of black libraries, the location and description of black library collections, how to select and establish a black collection, education for blacks in library science, early library organizations, and best-sellers of black authors. Specifically, the book is "designed to provide reference information on the relationship of Afro-Americans to various libraries." Each of her nonfiction books is a "first" of its kind. Each is popular in the intellectual milieu. In some places, the *Handbook* is a textbook supplement.

Shockley's fiction has not attained the popularity of her nonfiction. According to Shockley, the lack of acceptance can be attributed to the subject matter, which is avant-garde, and the immediate wants of mainstream publishers. Some of her works have become best-sellers for some publishers who are established but not mainstream.

Shockley's philosophy of life and of craft penetrates her fiction. She sees her characters through the description of herself as a black feminist and social-conscious writer disturbed by injustices, biases, and uncharitable human relationships. These become the bases for her themes: racism, sexism, homophobia, which she handles objectively through her conscious use of words. In the development of these themes, Shockley imaginatively weaves bits and pieces of her own thoughts and experiences as well as conversations and observations from reading and listening into realistic fiction. In this development, Shockley says: "Words are extremely important. They are like notes to music, which make the song, and colors to painting, which produce the picture. Words set the tone to a story, give meaning, nuances, color, form, movement, and imagination to the mind's eye of the reader." Shockley's fiction expresses this concern with words.

Before writing her first novel, Shockley had published more than sixteen short stories protesting racism within the society. These stories appeared in the leading black magazines, including *Black World, Umbra,* and *Freedomways,* and in several newspapers.

Her first novel, *Loving Her* (1974), opened a new vista in Afro-American literature. It is the first black novel to deal candidly with interracial lesbian love, where the protagonist—a black singer with a child and ex-husband—is in love with a wealthy white writer. In the novel, Shockley shows Renay growing into an awareness of her own sexuality and coming to grips not only with her own relationships but also with those of people she has known. As Shockley addresses Renay's personal growth, she addresses the issues of unhappy, abusive, heterosexual relationships along with societal attitudes toward lesbians and black/white relationships; and she introduces the oft-discussed issue of what is to be done with the child whose parent is a lesbian. In working through her relationship with Terry (her lover), Denise (her daughter), and Jerome Lee (her ex-husband), Renay takes the reader through a process which ultimately allows her to accept her lesbianism, her true self. At the same time, Shockley presents a cross section of society and its views about the couple's relationship—those who are repulsed by the race question, those who are repulsed by the sex question, and even those who have arrived at the same end Renay has, but who have because of time or location chosen to remain covert with their preference. The most tolerant and accepting of the relationship are the

Dust jacket for Shockley's first novel, the story of a miscegenational lesbian affair

homosexuals and the older women, never the "normal" men. The most intolerant of the relationship, not because of race but because of lesbianism, is the black community.

The Black and White of It (1980), which was nominated for the American Library Association Task Force 1980 Book Award, is a collection of ten short stories which explore the problems confronting the lesbian, especially the black woman. Again this represents another "first" in Afro-American literature. It is the first collection of short stories about lesbians written by an Afro-American woman. The stories are about women who have achieved professionally as writers, singers, politicians, managers, teachers, and so on, but who still suffer because they are lesbians.

In the short stories, the women have a constant struggle with whether to deny or accept their sexuality. In "Play It, But Don't Say It," Congresswoman Mattie Beatrice Brown's lover says, "You play it: you might as well *say* it," and Brown responds with, "They may *think* it, but they don't *know*." Or as in

"Holly Craft Isn't Gay," a successful singer decides she needs to get pregnant, for "straight people [are] hung up on women having babies" and no one will think she is gay. As Myrtle in a later work says, "In the black community, it's always more horrendous when admitted." Also presented is the societal attitude toward lesbianism: the slurs, the cruelties, the ignoring. The parent in "Home to Meet the Folks" says when she finds out about her daughter, "I wish you hadn't told me—!" Throughout the short stories and the novels, the attitude of the black community is shown to be almost totally negative. The lesbian in the black community is shown to be doing more playing and less saying, for her sexual preference only adds to the many problems confronting her.

At the same time Shockley presents the problems facing these women, she presents some very strong, supportive, and loving relationships. The women who both play it and say it and who have accepted themselves are achievers and appear to be emotionally healthy and concerned about others. In "A Birthday Remembered," the surviving half of a white lesbian relationship reminisces about the past and the child she and her lover raised; the child, unashamed, comes home to introduce her boyfriend to her "aunt"; when she leaves, the survivor decides that she and her lover did a good job raising her. These short stories, though often painful, underscore also the fact that race becomes an overriding consideration in these black-white relationships; as Lettie in the short story "A Meeting of the Sapphic Daughters" says, "White lesbians and black lesbians are white and black people first, instilled with personal backgrounds of distrust and hostilities."

Shockley continues to be ahead of her times and yet a part of tradition. Just as her nonfiction has been utilitarian, created to aid research and to retain black history, her fiction has been designed to fill the void of subjects not touched or explored and to continue to urge institutions to bring their practice in line with their theories. In 1982, Shockley's novel *Say Jesus and Come to Me* was published. This is the story of Rev. Myrtle Black, a black, female evangelist and charismatic leader, and Travis Lee, a singer. These women's lives converge in Nashville, Tennessee, where the majority of the novel takes place. Reverend Black has recognized and accepted her lesbianism and sees no reason not to use her position, as do men, to pursue fleeting intimate relationships. Travis Lee is still trying to find who she is but comes to know, accept, and revel in her lesbianism. In the novel, Shockley presents the subjects of the homophobia of the church and the black community and the conservatism of Southern black and white women on feminist issues and sexism. Intrepid, she tackles subjects which are not often discussed and/or criticized, including the church, the minister (especially the female minister), the pimp-prostitute relationship, the pomp of black funerals, the racism in various women's groups, and varying levels of love. Thus the nature of her subject matter often borders on the risqué or taboo and is often avant-garde. Yet, she stands with other black writers when she demands that the church, and by extension America, be a place of *"Free-e-edom and Ac-ceptance."*

Throughout Ann Allen Shockley's novels and short stories, lesbian women struggle for self-fulfillment. They are productive members of society being thwarted, scarred, and annihilated by the racism, sexism, and homophobia of the society.

As a result of her subject matter, her fiction is ignored by critics, especially black ones. This is not to say that there have not been some black critics who have objectively viewed her works. Alice Walker, Rita Dandridge, and Nellie McKay have dealt fairly with her works, but this dearth of black criticism underscores the homophobia which is rampant in the black community, according to Shockley. She has been more widely reviewed in white publications by white critics. This narrowness of vision deprives the reading public of a writer who gives another aspect of life and who, in doing this, is very much a part of the times and a part of a long tradition in Afro-American literature.

Herbert Alfred Simmons
(29 March 1930-   )

Australia Henderson
GMI Engineering and Management Institute

BOOKS: *Corner Boy* (Boston: Houghton Mifflin, 1957; London: Methuen, 1958);
Man Walking on Eggshells (Boston: Houghton Mifflin, 1962; London: Methuen, 1962).

It may be said that Herbert Simmons, a native of St. Louis, wrote *Corner Boy* and *Man Walking on Eggshells* not only to create memorable characters but also to recreate the St. Louis of his mind. The jazz, joy, nostalgia, and pain in these works are as much a part of the city as those who live in it. In *Corner Boy,* the characters are the city; they manifest its hope, magic, corruption, and failure. In *Man Walking on Eggshells,* the city is the muse of the black musician. Simmons's literary photography provides graphic details of time and place: the dress, language, walk, music, and life-style of black youth of the 1940s and 1950s. Such details alternate with panoramic shots of the city within a city—the Afro-American microcosm which exists, tries to survive, and is controlled by an indifferent macrocosm of whites.

Simmons was born on 29 March 1930, the son of Alex and Almeda Henderson Simmons. He attended Lincoln University and received a B.A. from Washington University, St. Louis, in 1958. In 1959, he attended the Writer's Workshop at the University of Iowa. He edited *Spliv,* a literary magazine, and created a show, "Portraits in Rhythm."

Simmons's novels present the culture, folkways, and urban problems of black protagonists; he shows that despite the richness and variety of black city life, economic, social, and racial forces can destroy the weak as well as the strong. Simmons's somber portraits in both his novels are relieved only by his respect for black music and black musicians. The inclusion of lyrics, famous musicians, and song titles is characteristic of his fiction. Most of his figures are able to transcend the violence, poverty, and uncertainty of their lives through music. The corner boys and their girl friends revel in their hand-clapping accompaniment to the band music at the Paradise Club. In the nightclub scenes, musicians "talk" to each other on their instruments during jazz performances, trading and challenging each other in improvised riffs. Sections of *Man Walking on Eggshells* are divided by lines from blues lyrics, which parallel the sections in mood or theme. In both novels the language, style, and recurring motif are that of the jazz/blues poet who, as he composes the stories of black youths, explains the impact of the city on their lives.

In Simmons's first novel, *Corner Boy* (1957), for which he won a Houghton Mifflin Literary Fellowship, varied aspects of St. Louis street life are explored through the experiences of Jake Adams, the protagonist, and his friends Scar, Spider, and Red. Each youth survives by manipulating the system. Jake sells drugs; Scar and Spider are gamblers who make payoffs so they can use trick dice. The plot is episodic. When Jake ends his relationship with Maxine, a dancer, and begins to see Armenta, a high-school coed, his life changes. Monk, the white underworld boss for whom Jake pushes drugs, accepts Jake's reason for going to college to be with Armenta, but insists that Jake continue to push drugs. Jake agrees because he realizes that his business allows him to survive in style: he has fashionable clothes, a decent apartment, and a new Dynaflow Buick. Armenta's father dislikes Jake because he does not fit his image of a middle-class black man. He sends Armenta to school in New York, and Jake drops out of college. Jake continues to sell drugs but is haunted by memories of Armenta. He begins to talk casually to Georgia Garveli, a white

friend whose family still remains in the neighborhood. While on a ride in his new car, Jake and Georgia are in an accident, and Georgia is killed. The publicity about "interracial lovers" is coupled with the prosecutor's effort to convict Jake on rape of a white woman and on selling the drugs found in the car. Through Jake, the prosecutor also hopes to destroy Monk's drug ring. In danger of being arrested, Monk leaves the city, giving his lawyer the responsibility of defending Jake. Jake is convicted and receives a seven-year prison term. In prison, he vows to return to city life.

It is not a contradiction that Jake wants to return to a city which spawned him but also punished him, for one of Simmons's themes is the interrelationship between the corner boy and the city. The code by which Jake and his friends live is survival and self-definition. Both codes are fashioned from the merciless indifference of the city. Jake develops a psychological toughness. He refuses to consider the immorality of selling drugs to those who might be destroyed by them. While he pities Red's addiction and knows that Scar's drug dependence is worsening, he does not let his feelings interfere with his goal of living well from drug

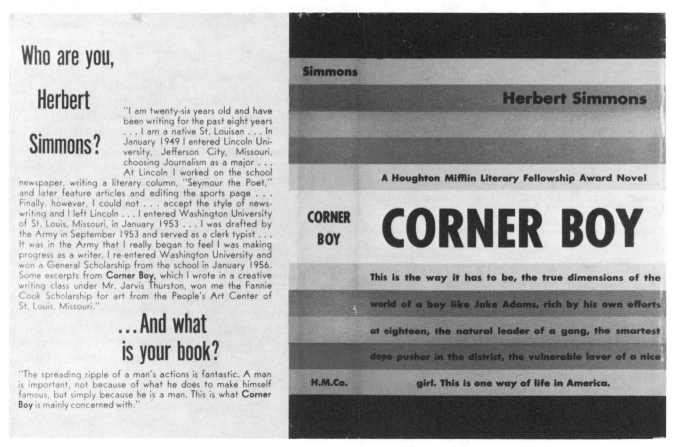

Dust jacket for Simmons's first novel, for which he won a Houghton Mifflin Literary Fellowship

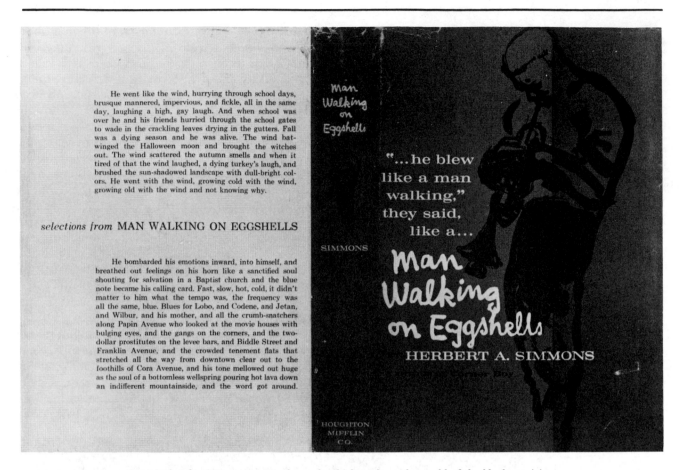

He went like the wind, hurrying through school days, brusque mannered, impervious, and fickle, all in the same day, laughing a high, gay laugh. And when school was over he and his friends hurried through the school gates to wade in the crackling leaves drying in the gutters. Fall was a dying season and he was alive. The wind batwinged the Halloween moon and brought the witches out. The wind scattered the autumn smells and when it tired of that the wind laughed, a dying turkey's laugh, and brushed the sun-shadowed landscape with dull-bright colors. He went with the wind, growing cold with the wind, growing old with the wind and not knowing why.

selections from MAN WALKING ON EGGSHELLS

He bombarded his emotions inward, into himself, and breathed out feelings on his horn like a sanctified soul shouting for salvation in a Baptist church and the blue note became his calling card. Fast, slow, hot, cold, it didn't matter to him what the tempo was, the frequency was all the same, blue. Blues for Lobo, and Codene, and Jetan, and Wilbur, and his mother, and all the crumb-snatchers along Papin Avenue who looked at the movie houses with bulging eyes, and the gangs on the corners, and the two-dollar prostitutes on the levee bars, and Biddle Street and Franklin Avenue, and the crowded tenement flats that stretched all the way from downtown clear out to the foothills of Cora Avenue, and his tone mellowed out huge as the soul of a bottomless wellspring pouring hot lava down an indifferent mountainside, and the word got around.

"...he blew like a man walking," they said, like a...

Man Walking on Eggshells

HERBERT A. SIMMONS

HOUGHTON MIFFLIN CO.

Dust jacket for Simmons's second novel, which explores the world of the black musician

profits. The women, clothes, cars, and money are Jake's substitutes for powerlessness. He accepts the fact that his blackness limits him to menial jobs and a marginal existence or to illegal jobs and the good life. He does not see life as it ought to be, but as it is. Hence, while he is in jail, the city will live in Jake's imagination, unchanged from its corruption and filth. It is this very nature of the city which he believes will allow him to return to the good life.

Family ties are overshadowed by the lure of city streets in *Corner Boy,* but in *Man Walking on Eggshells* (1962), Simmons reverses this idea, almost as if the time between the two novels allowed him to develop a more varied view of life in St. Louis. Instead, he suggests that family support and love are, perhaps, the few means by which a corner boy can achieve his dreams. As in his first novel, Simmons continues to regard the city as a grotesque wonder, but his belief that no one can emerge whole from its distorted clasp has disappeared. *Man Walking on Eggshells* is a Bildungsroman about Raymond Douglas and his family, his experiences as a corner boy and his triumph as a musician.

Raymond's grandfather and uncle have a greater influence on him than his father. From them he learns the joy of playing the trumpet. In grade school, Raymond joins a gang of his corner-boy peers, is later involved in a gang rumble, and becomes a target of the police. But music draws him away from the gangs. He attends college, continues to play the trumpet, and finally becomes part of a group of radical musicians espousing the philosophy of change of the 1960s. Seeking independence, Raymond breaks with the group to travel and perform on his own.

The extended family has no role in *Corner Boy,* but in this novel it provides Raymond with a family tradition and sense of identity and self-worth, directing him through the "eggshells" of growing into manhood when his parents cannot. Banny, Raymond's grandmother, fits the image of the "ancestor," who provides the link to family history and spiritual regeneration, according to Toni Morrison in "City Limits, Village Values." The wonderful, mysterious stories about the past fill Raymond and his sister with excitement and awe of the black heroes whom Banny claims are family ancestors. His wise and randy grandfather, Argustus, influences Raymond to accept the fact that he must follow his own beliefs about music and life and not be swayed by the militant philosophy of the corner-boy revolutionaries.

Above all, Simmons explores the world of the black musician in his presentation of Raymond's life. Simmons suggests that the experiences of Raymond, his uncle, and grandfather are the wellspring of their music. As if to emphasize the chaos, uncertainty, and tragedy of the musician's life, Simmons begins the novel by describing a violent storm and the funeral of Florence Mills (a famous black singer), both of which are concurrent with Raymond's birth. The grandfather's struggle as a musician is made more poignant by the mystery of his wife's death. Argustus never learns the true circumstances of his wife's death, but feels the impact of it through his daughter, who hates musicians because she blames him for her mother's death. While Argustus was away performing, his seven-year-old daughter had watched in horror while her mother was raped and murdered by white men during the East St. Louis riot of 1919. Raymond's talent reflects his pain over his mother's unexplained hatred for musicians and her eventual death and the death of his wife Jetan. His growth and independence as a musician are directly related to his ability to cope with his misfortune.

There is a timelessness about Simmons's portrait of the city in his two novels. The language and dress of the corner boy may have changed, but his values and life-style—his ability to make his own order out of the subterranean disorder of the city—remain the same. The city continues to be the cultural mecca of the black musician, who fashions his music from the personal and collective urban experience. Such music is still a distillation of the joy and pain expressed in the art of someone like Raymond Douglas. Herbert Simmons's portrait of city life is both a celebration of and a dirge for the black urban experience.

References:

Toni Morrison, "City Limits, Village Values," in *Literature and the Urban Experience*, edited by Michael C. Joyce and Ann C. Watts (New Brunswick, N.J.: Rutgers University Press, 1981);

Review of *Corner Boy, Jet* (25 February 1960): 4-5;

Noel Schraufnagel, *From Apology to Protest: The Black American Novel* (De Land, Fla.: Everett/Edwards, 1973).

Ellease Southerland
(18 June 1943-)

Mary Hughes Brookhart
University of North Carolina at Chapel Hill

BOOKS: *The Magic Sun Spins* (London: Paul Breman, 1975);

Let the Lion Eat Straw (New York: Scribners, 1979; London: Dent, 1980).

OTHER: "The Influence of Voodoo on the Fiction of Zora Neale Hurston," in *Sturdy Black Bridges*, edited by Roseann P. Bell, Bettye J. Parker, and Beverly Guy-Sheftall (Garden City: Doubleday, 1979), pp. 172-183.

PERIODICAL PUBLICATIONS:
Fiction:
"Soldiers," *Black World*, 22 (June 1973): 54-56;

"Beck-Junior and The Good Shepherd," *Massachusetts Review*, 15 (Autumn 1974): 719-732.
Nonfiction:
"Seventeen Days in Nigeria," *Black World*, 21 (January 1972): 29-41;

"Zora Neale Hurston," *Black World*, 23 (August 1974): 20-30;

"Zora Neale Hurston," *Encore American & Worldwide News*, 7 (19 June 1978): 38-39.
Poetry:
"Rerun," *Black World*, 20 (March 1971): 3;

"Shells," *Journal of Black Poetry*, 1 (Fall, Winter 1971): 67-68;

"The Retelling," *Poet Lore*, 67 (Summer 1972): 145-146;

"Ibo Man," *Présence Africaine,* 91 (Third Quarterly
    1974): 56;
"Seconds," *Présence Africaine,* 93 (First Quarterly
    1975): 73;
"The Red Bridge," *Black World,* 24 (September
    1975): 57.

Ellease Southerland received the Gwendolyn
Brooks Award for Poetry in 1971 for her poem
"Warlock." Her first book, *The Magic Sun Spins,* a
collection of new and previously published poetry,
appeared in 1975. However, not until 1979 with the
publication of her first novel, *Let the Lion Eat Straw,*
did Ellease Southerland reach a wide audience. As
one of her first editors, Hoyt W. Fuller, wrote after
the novel appeared: "Well, we should have known.
The strength was always there, as much inherent in
the vision as in the talent. Ellease Southerland . . .
has triumphed . . . all the beauty is there. Muted,
unstrained, honest, clear. Her achievement . . . reduces a burden we bear for all those talented writers
who would be truly free." And with both the popular and critical acclaim for *Let the Lion Eat Straw* and
more fiction and poetry on its way, it looks as if
Ellease Southerland is only just beginning to be
heard.

Southerland comes from a large family interested in reading and writing and sharing with
each other what they care deeply about; she feels
that under such circumstances her love for literature was inevitable. Born in 1943 in Brooklyn, she is
the third of Ellease Dozier and Monroe Penrose
Southerland's fifteen children. Her father's church,
primarily a family church with occasional attendance by neighbors and friends, provided an important forum for creativity. In addition to musical
sessions—she played the trumpet and piano—the
family had regular sessions of physical exercise.
The neighborhood was rough; and, Southerland
says, her father wanted to make sure his children
were strong and fit. Ellease was always pleased when
her mother kindly interrupted her participation in
the family push-ups by asking that she come help
out in the kitchen. Nevertheless, she liked exercise,
shared the family enthusiasm for track and field,
played handball, and was very good at volleyball.

It was while listening to her father's youngest
brother recite a poem about another uncle's death
that the ten-year-old Ellease resolved to be a poet.
Within months of writing her first poem, one about
a turkey which her fifth grade teacher thought too
good to have been written by a child, she became
poetry editor of her elementary school newspaper.
She was later editor of her high school's magazine

Ellease Southerland (photo by Jack M. Harris)

and continued at Queens College on the staff of the
literary magazine, receiving while at Queens the
John Golden Award for Fiction. In her father's
church, she established the fourth Sunday of each
month as "Poetry Sunday." "On those occasions,"
she says, "I systematically explained the elements of
poetry and during that hour encouraged everyone
from my brother who was three or four to my uncle
in his fifties, to make a contribution to the afternoon."

Even in her prose, Southerland remains close
to poetry. Perhaps because of her exacting requirements for herself as well as the deeply personal
nature of much of her writing to date, she has not
published a great quantity. What Southerland has
written is meticulously distilled. Although it may
seem as accessible as conversation and as immediate
as a sense impression, her poetry and fiction are also
dense with motifs, allusions, and symbols. Her love
for Yeats's "Sailing to Byzantium" prompted her to
discover her own folklore, to go back and reread the
Bible, and from there further back, to the study of
Egyptology. Her work reflects her familiarity with
the Bible, with ancient Egyptian mythology and
philosophy, with African history and lore, and with
present-day African cultures. Many of her works,
most notably *Let the Lion Eat Straw,* come directly

from her own family experiences. With what seems a natural inclination to be positive, Southerland faces her personal grief and the pains of others—for example, her mother's death; the ravages of war; racial injustice; madness plaguing members of her own family—and finds what heals, endures, or rises above the loss. Her vision is ultimately affirmative, not an easy affirmation and, therefore, all the more trustworthy.

In 1965, just after Ellease had graduated from Queens and with most of her twelve younger brothers and sisters still at home, her mother—still young herself—died of cancer. This eldest daughter, who was named after her mother and who was her mother's close friend and confidante, felt the impact of her mother's death profoundly. The poem "That Love Survives" confesses the darkness of those years at the same time that it affirms Southerland's recovery:

> Now, I think of you
> with calm joy,
> without fear that changed imagination
> into a stair of shadows,
> all the gray-sad afternoons,
> and I myself a shadow of the afternoon.
> Four years
> death was so wet against my electric nerves.
>
> Memory now, a delicate fern,
> grows in the silence
> of the years. And love survives.

Another poem "Shells," published in 1971, portrays her mother in the hospital just before she dies in all the apparent humiliation and violation that the disease itself and the necessarily mechanical attempts to arrest it can heap upon her; yet, as Southerland has since expressed it, the poem reveals that "life as we know it is external, the shell. A person can be dying and yet be, in the most important sense, intact."

After her mother's death, Southerland became a caseworker for the city of New York, a job she held from 1966 to 1972 in order to supplement her family's income. Several of the poems in *The Magic Sun Spins,* including "That Love Survives," were written during this period. The poems tend to be short; the subjects varied; many reveal Southerland's energy and enthusiasm about life in spite of the weighing concerns of the period. The book's title comes from the controlling image of "Black Is," a poem that celebrates being black; it begins, "The magic sun spins/from its black predecessor," and ends,

> And the magic sun is beautiful.
> Beautiful
> because
> Black is.

In the short poem "Ellease" she celebrates herself, here "a collection of moments," capable of realizing within herself the experiences of ages and of continents. In the midst of the passion of the prizewinning "Warlock" comes the gently comic:

> Through the dark he smiles at me
> from four faces, with four expressions.
> It's
> so confusing.
> Ellease, he says. You're not realistic.

With a close friend in the Vietnamese war and with nine brothers of her own, Southerland wrote several poems as well as the story "Soldiers" depicting some effects of war. Her poem "Vallejo" challenges the "woolen prose" of "professional country boys" who justify such a destruction of life and spirit. "Two Fishing Villages"—"a bridgeless blues," "this silent, disconnected blues"—decries the ravages of war on villagers in an unidentified land.

Some pieces Southerland explicitly locates in Africa. In 1971, she wrote an account for *Black World* of the first of what would be many trips to Nigeria. Presented as a diary, the article draws the reader into her experience of the trip—her naiveté, her excitement, and her fun, at the same time that it reveals her knowledge of Nigeria and her long anticipation of just such a journey. Then in such poems as "Blue Clay" and "Nigerian Rain" Southerland expresses her profound sense of arrival and fulfillment. "Nigerian Rain" concludes:

> Time. Water.
>   Black music
> rushes over clay prints.
> Red prints.
> After all these years, someone
> recognizes me.
> Sistah!
> Sistah!
> My black body is braced against the rain.
> Water pounds down the hills of Ibadan.

Nigeria here is home, just as it would be for the others in her family, for they all were raised feeling the natural association between Afro-Americans and Africa.

In 1972, Southerland began "officially" the
dual career that in retrospect had been there all
along—teaching and writing. She explains: "I
wanted to bring my writing to a head. I had published a few poems and a few short stories, but I
needed more time to write. I felt that attending
Columbia's School of the Arts would announce to
family and friends that I was officially writing and
so would earn for me the needed space and time.
But it didn't happen quite that way. I did get a
chance to study African American Literature, and
the professor did ask the question 'Do you teach, or
plan to teach' after I had given a report on Zora
Neale Hurston. And when I answered no, he said
emphatically, 'Oh, you'll have to teach.' " Recalling
the monthly "Poetry Sunday" of her family's church
services, she realized that she already had a good
deal of practice: "So, I felt very much at home at the
front of the classroom. . . ." She has been teaching
the literature of African peoples of Africa, the
Caribbean, and the United States ever since—at
Columbia from 1972 to 1976 in the Community
Education Exchange Program, at Manhattan
Community College in the Department of Ethnic
Studies from 1973 to 1980, and since 1975 in the
English department of Pace University. Among
those authors having the greatest influence on her,
she thinks particularly of her early readings of *Jane
Eyre* and, since, William Butler Yeats, Ousmane
Sembene, Paule Marshall, Amiri Baraka, and V. S.
Naipaul, whose *House for Mr. Biswas* affected her
structuring of *Let the Lion Eat Straw*. The first of
three essays she has published on Zora Neale
Hurston appeared while she was a student at Co-
lumbia.

However, it was a short story published in the
Massachusetts Review that same year, 1974, that
marked Ellease Southerland's public commitment
to *Let the Lion Eat Straw* and that drew the attention
of her future editor at Scribners. Originally to be
part of *Let the Lion Eat Straw*, "Beck-Junior and The
Good Shepherd" relates one of the tens of stories
that might be told about the author's large, loving,
but emotionally troubled family. Beck Torch is Ellease's own sister; the Torches here and in the novel
are the Southerlands.

Southerland had planned to write a novel
about her mother for some time before her death in
1965; in fact, she explains, her mother had
"sketched a lion and child in pencil as a possible
cover design," and adds, "her quiet and respectful
confidence that I would complete the work was
important in sustaining me." She says that the novel
was "five years plus in the writing, and in many

Dust jacket for Southerland's autobiographical first novel

moments, painful writing." When she began the
writing, she told Jacqueline Trescott of the
Washington Post, the story looked so bleak, her
mother's life so burdened, that she had to go back
and start with her life as a child to find some joy.
The completed novel affirms the fact that Southerland did find joy, again and again, side by side with
the pain and finally much closer to the core of her
mother's experience.

The story begins in a tiny rural community of
North Carolina, where the child Abeba lives with
old Mamma Habblesham. It ends less than two
hundred pages and about forty years later in New
York with the same old beloved midwife, long since
dead, ushering Abeba out of life, looking at Abeba's
family—her husband, Daniel Torch; her fifteen
children; her mother, Angela Williams Lavoi-
sier—and saying as she used to say to the little
girl Abeba, "ever so quietly, 'Hush your mouth.' "

By choosing incidents that engage the reader
with their brilliance, their poignancy, or their

humor, Southerland tells the story with remarkable succinctness and clarity. There is no sense of foreboding; each scene, instead, seems an unfolding, with Abeba always at the center fully perceiving the moment and receptive to all that has gone before so that past scenes retain their importance. For example, the tune, "Hey-bob-a-ree-bob, She's my baby," which the young Abeba heard the boys singing on the street, comes back to the woman Abeba in joyous moments. Just after Abeba had given birth to her first child, he appeared a gray, "limp body dripping blood"; then, she watched the midwife breathe into his mouth: "Color shot through the tiny body and he cried until the whole earth was bright green. He was the sun that soaked up pain." The passage, brilliantly conveying the elation that rises above the pain, ends, "Her baby, Hey bop!"

Southerland infuses the biographical with the figurative. There are numerous literal correspondences. Her father, like Daniel, comes from Florida; her mother, from North Carolina. The number of children, the birth order, the extended family, the family church are the same in fact and fiction. The Southerlands themselves, like Abeba and Daniel Torch in the novel, start a bakery successful enough to allow them to move their large family from Brooklyn to a spacious house in a quiet neighborhood in Queens. Nevertheless, Southerland has transformed her story into art. The names she chooses for the characters in the novel suggest something of the process of shaping and expanding meaning that goes on in every aspect of the book. She explains some of her names: "Abeba is named for an Ethiopian flower because she has a beauty that is fragile, a beauty which seems to be the metaphor for this life. She married a man whose last name is Torch, partially to symbolize the fire of creative ideas and partially to symbolize the fires of madness. Our family has been and still is plagued by brilliant minds on fire, and so this image throughout the book." The oldest daughter is named Kora: "The 'kora' (or 'cora') is a West African instrument used to accompany the telling of a story. It was my hidden way to identify the story teller present." She has given most of the children African names, just as her parents gave the younger brothers and sisters to whom she dedicates the novel. The circumstances of that dedication are touching: "I stopped by my father's house to see them one stormy afternoon, and found them huddled in a circle. When I asked what they were doing, they explained that every time the thunder sounds, they hug. It seemed to me a metaphor for their lives, deprived of a mother at so early an age, and clinging together."

The title and fuller inscription preceding the text come from Isaiah's prophecy of a world of peace. The lion is Daniel's own susceptibility to madness, which in times of stress can overcome him and the family he loves. Daniel actually plays the biblical Daniel in a play that Abeba created for the neighborhood; while it is great fun for everyone, it also heals. Southerland calls it "a mirror scene for Daniel. Daniel plays Daniel. His madness is spelled out: 'Physician heal thyself.' " The lion is also Abeba's mother, always around, always disapproving of Daniel and fiercely and sometimes vindictively trying to control the life of the daughter she "borned." Yet, the lion is also marvelous, beautiful in its strength and energy, and it is their ability to live with this lion that makes the Torches' lives intensely charged and capable of greatness.

Under Abeba's quiet direction and the storyteller Southerland's own vision, Isaiah's prophecy is fulfilled through a magnificent Easter celebration. Southerland locates this climactic scene in the same immense church she used to attend with her grandmother when her grandmother had weekend custody of the six-year-old Ellease and her sister. The ceremonies were spectacular: there were four choirs with her grandmother a dynamic member of one; at Easter there would be one thousand ushers all dressed in white. In the novel, the whole Torch family comes back to First Baptist for the Easter service. All but the youngest, who sits with his grandmother, are a part of the pageantry. After the children's entrance (some of them are young adults now), with the brilliance of their African prints, their drums and horns, cymbals and triangles, Abeba accompanies Daniel on the piano, just as she had more than twenty-five years before when he first came there and poured out his grief for his dead brother. He speaks to the congregation and it responds, remembering his sorrow on that day: "And I don't feel so lonesome anymore." This day the family has transformed its own griefs and antagonisms, the sorrows and the deaths of its people, into peace and magnificence; and as the artists the Torches are, they bring all the congregation with them: Closing with the song Daniel sang so many years ago, "the blackest pure bass dropped lower and lower (couldn't hear nobody pray) until the whole Easter church slipped into the low-dark voice and cried out."

With its publication in May of 1979, *Let the Lion Eat Straw* received immediate critical and popular attention. The nearly one hundred reviewers were overwhelmingly positive, proclaiming the strengths of the novel's themes and the beauty of its craftsmanship. It was voted a "Best Book for Young Adults 1979" by the Young Adult Services Division of the American Library Association, which chooses those books having a "proven or potential appeal and worth to young adults," ages twelve to eighteen. In its first two years *Let the Lion Eat Straw* appeared in four editions, with the softcover edition going through three printings in a year and a half. In 1981 the president of the New American Library reported booksellers were reordering about four hundred and fifty copies of the Signet edition per month, a sign that people were reading it and telling their friends. On this basis alone, he projected that their Signet edition would become a backlist item, selling about five thousand copies a year. In the meantime *Let the Lion Eat Straw* is becoming more widely read in high school and university classes as instructors discover the book and adopt it for their courses.

In spite of many demands on her time, Ellease Southerland appears serene, taking pleasure in most aspects of her life and deeply gratified by the responses to her work. She likes to embroider, bakes excellently, sews some, and plays the piano for relaxation. She is proud of a rug with an Egyptian design that took her four years to make. Still true to her father's regimen for his children, she exercises an hour every day. She routinely gets up as early as 5:00 for some quiet hours of writing before her day "officially" begins. Living alone in Jamaica, New York, on Long Island, Southerland stays close to her family. Her father and her two youngest brothers live in the family home in Queens; when any one of the family must be absent from a family gathering, the rest of them are keenly aware of that absence. Southerland's friendships have become increasingly literary since those early days Hoyt Fuller

recalled: "We did not know her. We knew no one who knew her. There she was . . . writing the way we thought the 'new Black writers' should be writing, and there was no one, no group, no institution, to encourage her, . . . to sustain her."

Currently, Southerland is working on a second novel and a volume of poetry. There is a story waiting to be written about her grandmother, the Angela of *Let the Lion Eat Straw,* who for all the impositions on her daughter has "spread her wings" beneficently over the grandchildren. Southerland states that her next novel will take place for the most part in New York but will include several scenes in Nigeria, since it involves friendship between New Yorkers and Nigerians studying in New York. "The rug I made is in that story," she adds. Southerland projects that her poems will become more narrative as she learns more stories. Whatever the subject or the format, one can expect an excellent body of literature to emerge from this still young author whose skill and talent, whose passion for beauty and clarity and the honesty of emotions, and whose good humor and rich perceptions of experience from ancient Egyptian and Judeo-Christian to modern African and Afro-American all serve to inform her work.

References:

Hoyt W. Fuller, Angela Jackson, and James C. Kilgore, "Two Views: Let the Lion Eat Straw," *First World,* 2, no. 3 (1979): 49-52;

Leslie Hanscom, "Black People Bigger than their Hardships," *News Day* [Long Island], 20 May 1979;

Jacqueline Trescott, "*Let the Lion Eat Straw.* Let the Author Win Glory," *Washington Post,* 6 August 1979, B1 and B11.

Joyce Carol Thomas

(25 May 1938-)

Charles P. Toombs
Purdue University

BOOKS: *Bittersweet* (San Jose, Cal.: Firesign Press, 1973);
Crystal Breezes (Berkeley, Cal.: Firesign Press, 1974);
Blessing (Berkeley, Cal.: Jocato Press, 1975);
Black Child (New York: Zamani Productions, 1981);
Inside the Rainbow (Palo Alto, Cal.: Zikawuna Press, 1982);
Marked by Fire (New York: Avon, 1982);
Bright Shadow (New York: Avon, 1983).

PLAYS: *A Song in the Sky,* San Francisco, Montgomery Theater, summer 1976;
Look! What a Wonder!, Berkeley, Cal., Berkeley Community Theater, September 1976;
Magnolia, San Francisco, Old San Francisco Opera House, summer 1977;
Ambrosia, San Francisco, Little Fox Theater, summer 1978.

Until the publication of *Marked by Fire* in 1982, Joyce Carol Thomas, longtime San Francisco Bay area literary figure, was known primarily as a poet and the writer-producer of four plays. As a poet she is often praised for her seriousness of theme, thoroughness of treatment, faithful rendering of the black and human experience, and authentic persona. In her best poems she is able to record the histories of ordinary people. Although her accomplishments in poetry are many, it is with fiction that she has achieved national critical attention. With the publication of *Marked by Fire* and *Bright Shadow* (in 1983), Thomas moved to the forefront of serious black women writers. She joins the ranks of Maya Angelou, Toni Cade Bambara, Toni Morrison, Gloria Naylor, and Alice Walker in introducing a group of characters heretofore unknown in American literature; for in the hands of white and some black male writers, black female characters have never been authentically portrayed, defined, developed, or understood.

Born in Ponca City, Oklahoma, where both *Marked by Fire* and *Bright Shadow* take place, Thomas was the fifth child in a family of nine. Like the characters in *Marked by Fire,* Thomas picked cotton for most of her early years. By the age of eight she could pick a hundred pounds of cotton a day. Reflecting on her youth, Thomas says: "One of the things we used to do every fall was to pick cotton, and that involved going to live with other families. The Lightsey family—I used their name in the novel *Marked by Fire*—had twelve children, and we looked forward to living with the Lightseys at harvest time. It was a time to play and spend the night with your best friend. Even though we missed the first part of school because of the necessity of work, we made up for it by telling stories. I suppose we were poor. I *know* we were poor, but there was the joy of being with other children your own age, and telling and hearing stories." This early fascination with storytelling encouraged Thomas to read; and by the time her family migrated to California to pick tomatoes, when she was ten, she had become an avid reader. The fruits of this writer-to-be were sown in her early childhood experiences of storytelling and creative work and play.

As an adult in San Francisco, Thomas worked as a telephone operator during the day and took a full load of night classes, while raising four children. She eventually received a B.A. in Spanish from San Jose University and in 1967 a master's in Education from Stanford University. She is the recipient of the prestigious Danforth Graduate Fellowship at the University of California at Berkeley, the Before Columbus American Book Award (for *Marked by Fire*), and the Djerassi Fellowship for Creative Artists at Stanford. Her work has appeared in many periodicals and anthologies including *Black Scholar, American Poetry Review, Giant Talk, Yardbird Reader, Drum Voices,* and *Calafia.* She has lectured at several universities in this country and has presented addresses on poetry and writing in Nigeria and Haiti. She formerly was editor of the West Coast black women's magazine *Ambrosia.* As an educator she has been assistant professor of black studies at California State University and visiting associate professor of English at Purdue University. Currently she writes full-time in Berkeley, California, where she resides.

Thomas's early poetic efforts are contained in three slim volumes, *Bittersweet* (1973), *Crystal Breezes*

(1974), and *Blessing* (1975), published by small presses and somewhat difficult to locate. In 1982 *Inside the Rainbow,* which contains most of the poems from the earlier volumes along with new poems, was published. In her poetry Thomas refuses to make simple, general statements regarding her subject matter. Instead she presents real portraits of specific families, recreates Afro-American rituals, and establishes a "once" communion with such natural objects as raindrops, fireflies, and the red dirt of Oklahoma cornfields to frame her themes. In her poems, human behavior is passionate and convincing. She does not pretend to sing new songs or travel to new lands; rather, with a new voice, new images, new accents, pitch, and command of the lyrical line, she sings universal songs of human experience. Her poetry is a celebration, an affirmation of the human spirit.

Thomas's poetic vision is large and expansive. If a single statement can be made regarding thematic concerns in her poetry it must be that she creates, for the most part, affirmative songs, seeing

even in some of life's most vicious atrocities some new fruit for the continuation of the human species. Her poems deal with birth, death, sorrow, mystery, loneliness, nature, individuality, hope, artistic creation, love, the black experience, black women, mothers, children, romance, African and Afro-American rituals, suffering, survival, racism, oppression, history, the black church, God, and the spirit.

In the volume of poems *Inside the Rainbow,* the reader can taste these subjects and themes. Thomas uses words sparsely, reserving the richest words and images to develop her ideas. For example, in "Where is the Black Community?" Thomas enunciates the theme that the black community is everywhere:

> Holding down the corner
> Where Third Street meets B
> And sitting in the second pew
> At Double Rock Baptist Church
> ....
> At Bob's Barber Shop
> Busting jokes about the man
> ....
> Scrubbing chitlin grease
> Off a kitchen stove eye
> ....
> Plowing cotton
> In a Mississippi dawn
> ....
> And arranging four kids
> In a twin-sized bed....

Thomas's lyrics soar in "Quilting Bee," where she describes a bit of often disregarded black experience:

> Why I used to straddle baby
> Brother on my hip and
> Run from the gray pack dogs
> Somebody be frying fat back and
> Potatoes on a ground stove fire
> I sat my skinny self
> Down on a crocus sack pallet
> And dined
> Never once forgot to feed the baby....

In "Quilting Bee" Thomas gently reminds the reader of the suffering and hard work black people often experience, and like the scraps of rags that hands work and rework into the finished quilt, "It's amazing how you can/Make beauty from scraps." This affirmation can be seen in other poems in *Inside the Rainbow,* such as "To a Chicano," where the poet demands that more must be done than

Dust jacket for Thomas's first book, a volume of poems

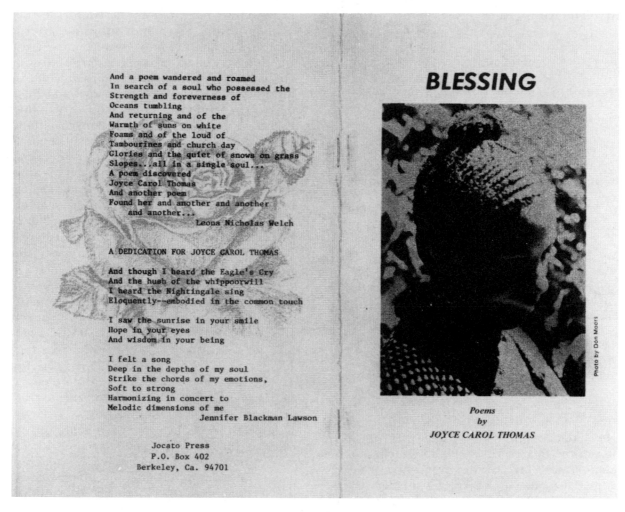

And a poem wandered and roamed
In search of a soul who possessed the
Strength and foreverness of
Oceans tumbling
And returning and of the
Warmth of suns on white
Foams and of the loud of
Tambourines and church day
Glories and the quiet of snows on grass
Slopes...all in a single soul...
A poem discovered
Joyce Carol Thomas
And another poem
Found her and another and another
         and another...
                    Leona Nicholas Welch

A DEDICATION FOR JOYCE CAROL THOMAS

And though I heard the Eagle's Cry
And the hush of the whippoorwill
I heard the Nightingale sing
Eloquently--embodied in the common touch

I saw the sunrise in your smile
Hope in your eyes
And wisdom in your being

I felt a song
Deep in the depths of my soul
Strike the chords of my emotions,
Soft to strong
Harmonizing in concert to
Melodic dimensions of me
                    Jennifer Blackman Lawson

Jocato Press
P.O. Box 402
Berkeley, Ca. 94701

BLESSING

*Poems
by
JOYCE CAROL THOMAS*

Cover for Thomas's 1975 collection of poems

merely crying at life's injustices:

> But I swear by his baby's
> Cries
> And the way he looked
> When the fireman slowly
> Treading the ladder
> Finally brought him
> Down
> All charred and curled
> Up in the blanket
> Beyond
> What he looked like
> When his mother last
> Rocked him to sleep
> I swear by the gone
> Black sparkling eyes
> I swear by the gone
> Dimpled chubby hands
> We must do more than
> Cry.

As Thomas poetically reconstructs America's history of racism, oppression, and human suffering, she also, often with subdued anger, reminds the reader that life must be better than it has been, must be "No broken backs/No missing chords," for

> There's a rainbow in my bedroom
> Red fish swim beneath my bed
> And on the arc of the curved bow
> As against a pillow
> I place my head
> And say . . .
> Feed my soul
> And water well this spirit!

While inspiration that flows through Thomas's poetry is hopeful, it is never too farfetched; it is etched in the reality of a woman who has known pain and suffering, joy and love, failure and success. It is a spirit of possibilities which she affirms in her poetry. Thomas is able to say:

> I always search for the sun
> Even when it's storming
> I turn my face
> Toward where the sun would be
> Reach way up high
> And switch on the light.

Her poetry, then, is a record of the possibilities of being a particular human being: black, woman, poet. In "Ambrosia," a poem dedicated to black women, Thomas sings:

> You are the girls in an exquisite painting
> . . . .
> You sing sparrows out of trees
> . . . .
> You are the traveler warming the world with peace
> Carrying culture in your belly and
> Caravans of bones carved on the bottoms of your feet
> . . . .
> You are cry. You are laughter. You are the guitar
>   twang
> . . . .
> You smile in spite of this strange place. . . .

In the small booklet of poetry *Black Child* (1981), Thomas continues her ability to find affirmation in the face of adversity; she celebrates the wonder of our children when she is confronted with their tragic loss during the Atlanta murders. In the foreword to *Black Child*, Thomas writes that "we can pay no greater tribute to those remaining than this: that we recommit our lives to the salvation of our youth." The opening poem of the fifteen poignant poems in *Black Child*, illustrated by Tom Feelings, reminds parents that black children carry an additional burden as they forage through life:

> My mother says I am
> Still honey in sassafras tea
> My father calls me the
> Brown sugar of his days
> Yet they warn
> There are those who
> Have brewed a
> Bitter potion for
> Children kissed long by the sun
> Therefore I approach
> The cup slowly
> But first I ask
> Who has set this table.

The poems in *Black Child* celebrate with beautiful, vivid, haunting images Thomas's dedication to the

future of the black race in this country.

Children, as theme, subject matter, and character, figure prominently in Thomas's writing. In her first venture into fiction, the award-winning and critically successful *Marked by Fire* (1982), children are central to the novel's plot and thematic development. *Marked by Fire* is the story of the first twenty years of Abyssinia Jackson, including her birth in 1951 in the cotton fields outside Ponca City, Oklahoma, her violent rape at age ten, and her emergence at the end of the novel as a young woman willing to make her contribution to her community as folk doctor and leader. The title of the novel refers to a scar Abby receives on her cheek by a spark from a fire in the cotton field where she is born, with several Ponca City women assisting in her birth. Because of her physical mark, the townspeople believe she is spiritually marked, too. Mother Barker, the folk doctor and mentor to Abby, tells Abby toward the end of the novel that she was marked for "unbearable pain and unspeakable joy." Until her rape, Abby is a free-spirited, happy, special child. All of the Ponca City women help to raise her. She has a beautiful singing voice, and she is an excellent student who likes to read and tell stories. After being raped by an elder in her church, she loses her voice, returning this gift to God, and questions her faith in the God her community and church have given her. She tells her best friend Lily Norene that after the rape she "felt dirty. Dirtier than playing in mud. The kind of dirt you can't ever wash off. . . . But the worst part was I felt like I was being spit on by God." Patience, Abby's mother, Mother Barker, Sadonia and Serena, Abby's aunts, Lily Norene and Trembling Sally, a deranged, witchlike woman, are important characters who help Abby reconstruct her life and discover the path to womanhood.

Several themes provide direction for *Marked by Fire*. The importance of community as theme is developed early in the novel. It begins with Abby's birth, when the women stop picking cotton to attend Patience and the birth of her child. This community continues throughout the novel as Thomas reveals the everyday lives of these Ponca City residents. For example, most of the women "parent" Abby, offering various perspectives on what it takes to survive as a black female. This community is also evident by the help the townspeople give each other after the big tornado destroys much of the town or when the river floods and forces some residents to move in with each other until the waters recede. Mother Barker, the folk doctor, perhaps personifies the theme of community as she saunters from family to

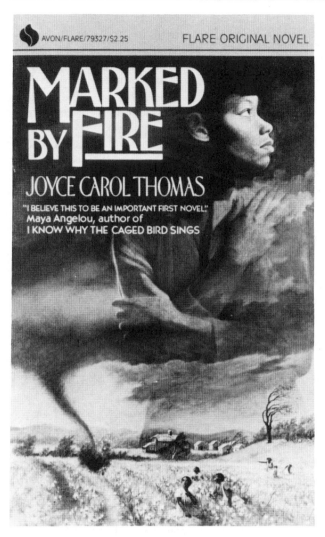

Front cover for Thomas's 1982 novel about Abyssinia, a character marked at birth by a spark from a brush fire in the cotton field where she was born

family providing basic health care, folk remedies, and a listening ear. At the end of the novel, Abby carries on this tradition of helping those in need as she becomes Mother Barker's successor. The folk language, folk stories, and small-town rituals help to show the importance of human community.

Marked by Fire is also a celebration of black womanhood, showing the full circle these women travel, from their births to their deaths. Within this circle, Thomas paints a realistic yet hopeful picture of the struggles, half-starts, and triumphs these women face. During the novel, Thomas renders, primarily through Abby, Patience, Mother Barker, Trembling Sally, and Lily, the human strength that is necessary to achieve some of life's little rewards. The reader is exposed, in a lyrical way, to the

hardships and glory of birth, the difficulty and joy of maintaining male-female relationships, the physical endurance it takes to keep a house, and such horrors as rape and wife beating. Thomas paints her canvas with portraits of these black women, young and old, leaning on each other, providing one another with social and emotional networks that make it possible for these characters to lead full lives. The reader sees, feels, and understands some of the worst and best times of these Ponca City women.

As Abby is developed, another theme emerges in *Marked by Fire:* the theme of knowing. Abby reads a great deal, pays much attention to the folktales that pervade her community, and explores her environment on her own. As a child she realizes there is a part of living unexplainable by science and books and traditional religion. After her father abandons her and after her rape, Abby comes to realize that the process of knowing is difficult and fraught with constant pitfalls. The theme of knowing is also important in *Bright Shadow.*

The critical reception of *Marked by Fire* has been marked by superlatives. The novel was named an Outstanding Book of the Year by the *New York Times* and best book by the Young Adult Services Division of the American Library Association; it also won The American Book Award in the paperback category of children's fiction in 1983. Maya Angelou, Alice Childress, Geraldine Wilson, and Susan C. Griffith have praised *Marked by Fire* for its faithful depiction of the experiences of a small-town young woman, for its memorable characters, for its poetic language, for its simplicity of style, and for its affirmation of the human spirit. Most reviewers and critics have found the novel's weaknesses—a slow-paced narrative line, its mythical overtones, its abrupt ending—minor flaws when compared to the novel's strengths. Both *Marked by Fire* and *Bright Shadow* are required reading in several high schools and universities across the country.

Bright Shadow (1983), the first sequel to *Marked by Fire,* although ostensibly a love story, quickly develops the theme of knowing as one of its major features. Abby is now a woman of twenty, independent in her thinking, attending college studying to become a doctor, and taking deliberate steps to find out who she is and what she wants. She soon discovers what she wants in the person of Carl Lee Jefferson, even though her father disapproves of him. Her father's objections to Carl Lee become insignificant after the gruesome murder of Abby's Aunt Serena. Carl Lee helps Abby to find the light when faced with the dark shadows of her aunt's death.

Abby's ability to deal with her aunt's tragic murder while she is just beginning to understand what it means to be in love is one of the themes that direct this novel. Though it is indicated by the novel's title, the theme is announced more clearly in a dream Abby has where her aunt appears and states: "We are all taken from the same source: pain and beauty. One is the chrysalis that gives to the other some gift that even in death creates a new dimension in life."

The critical attention that *Marked by Fire* received prepared readers for *Bright Shadow,* a novel that presents a story full of complex characters and situations, that explores a young woman's heart, and that creates events that strike the common notes of human experience. In 1984 *Bright Shadow* was

named a best book by the Young Adult Services Division of the American Library Association.

Joyce Carol Thomas plans four more novels in the "Abyssinia Series." In addition to writing fiction, she will continue to compose poetry. It is perhaps because Thomas was a poet first that her fiction moves the reader so. Her poetry and fiction celebrate the human experience in multifarious ways. She is able to do what great writers have always been able to do: tell a good story. Her stories beautifully tell us what it means to be a black female during the latter half of the twentieth century. She recreates, from her memories, fully fleshed characters and situations. American letters needs innovative writers like Joyce Carol Thomas.

Henry Van Dyke

(3 October 1928-)

Edward G. McGehee

BOOKS: *Ladies of the Rachmaninoff Eyes* (New York: Farrar, Straus & Giroux, 1965; London: Bodley Head, 1965);
Blood of Strawberries (New York: Farrar, Straus & Giroux, 1968);
Dead Piano (New York: Farrar, Straus & Giroux, 1971).

From the opening pages of his first novel, Henry Van Dyke has shown that he is a masterful novelist, an "original" artist with his own voice, his own style, his "language couched in wit and eloquence." One critic has stated that Van Dyke "has refined the genius inherent" in his earlier novels. He demands of himself that he "write well with clarity while conveying complex ideas and maintaining a colloquial feel." For some readers he might not be militant enough, but Van Dyke does not believe that a novel should be a tract, a sermon in disguise. He has a remarkable ear for dialogue, the apt phrase—whether the speaker is erudite, a snob and social climber, a con-artist, an English lord, or a ghetto black. In his three novels he has produced memorable characters, both blacks and whites, some formally educated and others street-wise; in well-constructed scenes, he has revealed many facets of the human comedy, cutting "back cleanly

through race antagonisms, religious differences, superficial moralities and other page-one causes to people themselves." While he entertains and amuses his readers, Van Dyke also makes them look anew at the world around them. He persuasively makes his readers empathize with a diverse group of characters, "marvelously fleshed out," no matter how grotesque, brutish, or lovable they might be. Beneath all of the "bright laughter," his novels are also, by purpose, both "sad and serious."

The eldest child and only son of Bessie Chandler and Henry Lewis Van Dyke, Henry Van Dyke was born on 3 October 1928 in his maternal grandmother's house in Allegan, Michigan. When Henry was four, his father received an appointment to teach chemistry at Alabama State Teachers College in Montgomery, Alabama. Living near the campus, Henry attended the training school connected with the college; although his mother more often than not taught on the college level, she also taught her own son when he was in the fourth grade. During the summers, in the depth of the Depression, when his father returned to Ann Arbor to complete work toward his Ph.D., the family also went along. Michigan, rather than Alabama, always remained home. After completing the ninth grade in the segregated school in Montgomery, Van Dyke returned to live

Henry Van Dyke (Gale International Portrait Gallery)

with relatives in Michigan and attended high schools in Kalamazoo and Lansing. From an early age he showed an avid interest in literature and music; much against his father's wish that his son become a physician, Van Dyke originally thought that he wanted to become a concert pianist. In 1949, when he joined the army, he now admits that "I didn't know who I was or what I was." While stationed in occupied Germany, attached to an army band and working as a typist, he eventually realized that his major interest was in writing. As an undergraduate at the University of Michigan, he majored in journalism and minored in English literature. Graduating in 1953, he decided to work toward an M.A. in journalism (1955). It was while he was a student that he received his first major recognition—the Avery Hopwood Award for Fiction. Unlike Oliver, the narrator of his first published novels and the protégé of two wealthy white families, Van Dyke faced financial struggles as a student and worked as an orderly in the University Hospital. The first years after graduation were rather irregular and trying times. For a short period he worked as a reporter for the *Pittsburgh Courier*. From 1956 until 1958 he served as a scientific editor at the Engineering Research Institute, a part of the

University of Michigan. In 1958 Van Dyke made a major change in his life and moved to Manhattan. Turned down for jobs because of his black face, in spite of his credentials, for a time he eked out a living by doing hackwork—writing true confession stories. Eventually he did get a regular job, and until 1967 he worked on the editorial staff of Basic Books. Writing by longhand in the evenings, he would on "one or two nights a week and on weekends" bring his manuscripts to the office and type them there. Farrar, Straus and Giroux accepted one of those novels, *Ladies of the Rachmaninoff Eyes* (1965), for publication.

As a result of a talk that he gave at Kent State University, he was asked if he would consider becoming Writer-in-Residence. He would, but only if it could be for one term a year; he needed to have most of his time free for writing. Starting in the fall of 1969, he has continued in that position. In addition, he has taught at Fairleigh Dickinson University and at Manhattan Community College. For several years he has lectured once a year at the School of Journalism at the University of Michigan. Van Dyke has taken on other duties and has received awards. In 1968 he held a fellowship at the Bread Loaf Writers' Conference. He received a Guggenheim Award for fiction in 1971. In 1971 and 1979, he served as one of the judges of fiction for the Avery Hopwood Award. For six years he served as a consultant in fiction for the Suffield (Connecticut) Writers' Conference. In 1974 he received an award for fiction from the National Academy of Arts and Letters. Starting in 1980, he has served on the staff of Midwestern (Canton, Ohio) Writers' Conference. Some of his shorter works of fiction have appeared in the *Transatlantic Review, Generation,* and the *Antioch Review*—which published "Du Côté de Chez Britz," later included in *The O. Henry Prize Stories, 1979.*

Mrs. Etta Klein, a Jewish widow, and Aunt Harriet Gibbs, her black companion, are the two *Ladies of the Rachmaninoff Eyes*. Their love-hate relationship which has been an ongoing affair for at least thirty years is narrated by Aunt Harriet's nephew, Oliver Eugene Gibbs; this precocious "almost" seventeen-year-old not only tells what happened that summer at the Klein estate some distance out from Allegan, but he is involved in much of the action and the emotions. Jerome Klein, Etta's son, married to Patricia Jo, née Walker, runs the family's successful factory in Kalamazoo; but he suffers. His mother continues to love her other son, Sargeant, dead some five years, more than him; and Jerome is jealous of Oliver, his mother having made

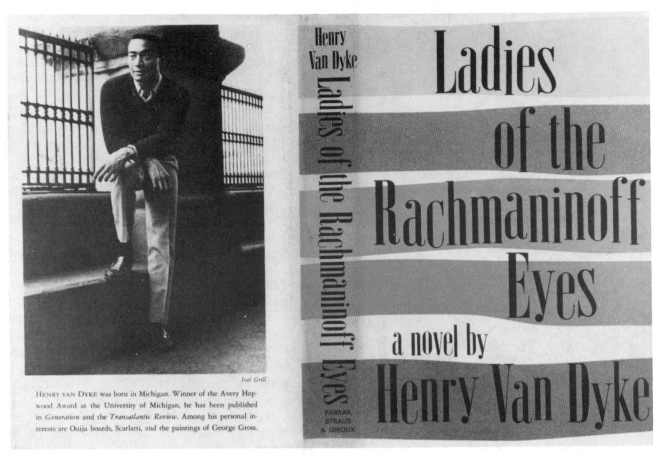

Joel Grill

HENRY VAN DYKE was born in Michigan. Winner of the Avery Hopwood Award at the University of Michigan, he has been published in *Generation* and the *Transatlantic Review*. Among his personal interests are Ouija boards, Scarlatti, and the paintings of George Grosz.

Dust jacket for Van Dyke's first novel, written at night while he held an editorial job at Basic Books

Oliver a "toy to keep her mind off Sargeant." Della Mae, the black cook, earthy and anxious to escape the Jewish-black kitchen, has once tried unsuccessfully to have sex with Oliver. Before she decamps for Chicago, she tells Oliver several times that Mrs. Klein is trying to ruin him by making him into a white boy. Patricia Jo also informs Oliver that as long as her Jewish mother-in-law "has this Sargeant ghost hanging about, Jerome will never be her son. Never.... Don't you see that? Nobody escapes. Even you. In fact—she's practically training *you* to be Sargeant." Anxious to communicate with Sargeant, Etta and Harriet invite Maurice LeFleur, a self-proclaimed "warlock" (in reality a thief and confidence man), to visit. When he states that Sargeant will speak only with Mrs. Klein, Aunt Harriet betrays the promise she had given to Sargeant that she would never tell the truth about his suicide. A closet homosexual, he had told Harriet everything about himself, especially his ill-fated love for Ray Flynn, a "stupid oaf" whom he had picked up in Harlem and had remade, only to have Ray totally

reject him and go off with a Londoner. At the end of this recital that dreadfully shocks Jerome, Etta lashes out and calls Harriet "an evil, evil, evil woman! A vicious old woman! You're a—a demented old, old—old evil nigger woman!" The novel is replete with love-friendship complications and conflicts between whites and blacks as well as between blacks and blacks. If in part Oliver turns Della Mae down because she is a cook and ill-educated, Oliver is in turn sexually rejected by an older white neighbor, Belle Thompson, who has had a brief fling with Jerome: "I've never bestowed any favors on a colored man—boy before." With the deaths of his Aunt and, a short time later, Etta, his departure for Cornell at the end of that summer marks the end of Oliver's innocence. He is faced with evaluating how white or black he is, whether he is himself or whether he has actually been converted into Sargeant Klein—who in her last days of madness Etta actually thinks he is. How black is really black; how much black is white; how much gentile is really Jewish? All of the characters are faced with problems of self-identity. At the end of the novel Oliver has survived being a white matriarch's pet, but he is still not sure just who he is. The reader is left to trust that Oliver, with his sharp insights into the truths and nuances of others, will discover himself.

Ladies was dedicated to Carl Van Vechten, celebrated for his novels and photographs, many of black artists; Louis Bromfield observed that Van Vechten "is not ponderous in his books, but he comes much nearer to depicting the American scene than many a laborious corn-fed realist." The same evaluation is true for all three of Van Dyke's published novels. Oliver, "intelligent and debonair," remains the narrator of *Blood of Strawberries* (1968), but in no sense is this novel a sequel to *Ladies*. During the spring of his junior year at Cornell, Oliver has gone to Greenwich Village to be the guest of Max and Tanja Rhodes, his patrons after the death of Etta, Tanja's sister. Although not a pure roman à clef, clearly there are similarities between the Rhodes and Carl and Fania Marinoff Van Vechten.

The novel is full of literary intrigues, bickerings, and rivalries. Much of the activity occurs in the Rhodes's large apartment in the Chelsea Hotel, separated by a hallway from that of Orson Valentine, Max's enemy-friend since the 1920s. Another center of interest is Gertrude Stein. Oliver plans to write his senior paper about her prose, especially her uses of repetition, a stylistic device that Van Dyke also uses. Max, an octogenarian, had known Stein in France. This spring a new production of one of her plays is to be presented. Both Max and Orson are involved, as well as Margot and Clive Tibberton, and Desdemona (Rita) Schwartz. Oliver's sexual partner, Desdemona is to have the leading role. Also involved in the madcap machinations are two servants, Willa, who works for the Rhodes, and Willette, for Orson.

Stylistically the novel has many affinities with literary works from the 1920s, 1930s, and earlier. Rather than Capote-like characters, as one critic found, the scintillating dialogues and Oliver's comments and summations have a much greater affinity with the novels of Ronald Firbank and Ada Leverson and the plays of Oscar Wilde and Noel Coward. If there are any echoes, Van Dyke has totally transformed them.

The novel has been rightly described as being

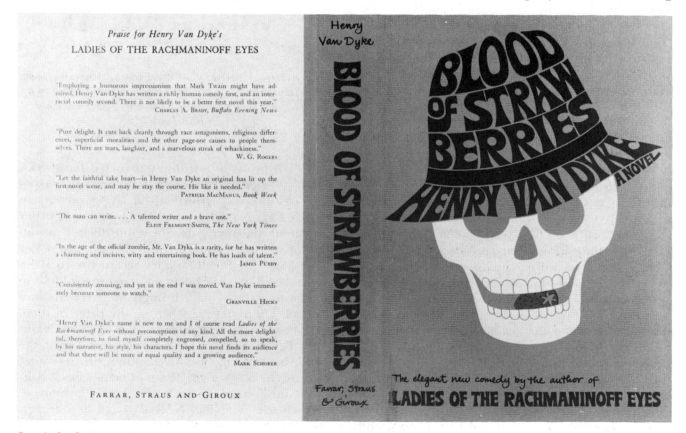

Dust jacket for Van Dyke's second novel, in which the narrator, Oliver, enjoys the patronage of a Greenwich Village couple based loosely on Carl and Fania Van Vechten. Van Dyke's first novel, also narrated by Oliver, was dedicated to Van Vechten.

"sprightly" and "a highly literate and vastly entertaining suspense-comedy." In spite of a wide variety of efforts to destroy the production, will the play ever reach the stage? Will Desdemona be up to the difficulty of her part? Was Tanja murdered? Why does Orson have wigs and dresses similar to Stein's in his closet? How sane is Max? Who tried to kill Oliver and Clive at the steambath? What is the sinister connection between the servants, also sisters? In this "last act of a Lost Generation cabal," was it Max or Orson who had really known Stein? Is Oliver Desdemona's Othello? Is Oliver really a slave to an octogenarian celebrity? On one level the novel can be read as being "a slightly macabre farce," presenting as it does a manic, Mack Sennett view of the artistic world. But Van Dyke is also concerned with presenting the problems of the aged, portraits of marriages, the sexual relationship between a young Jewess and a black, the conflicts between black cultures, and the control that servants can have over their "masters." Debonair, compassionate, and sometimes a rather smug manipulator, Oliver is still faced with finding the truth about himself and others.

Awareness of one's self and one's true needs is one of the major themes of *Dead Piano* (1971). Except for a coda which takes place six months later, the five major characters of this novel are involved in a violent confrontation that lasts a little more than two hours on 8 September 1968. Living in the affluent suburb of St. Albans, New York, much to the disgust of some whites, the Blakes appear to themselves to have made all of the correct moves. Olga Blake, light-skinned, is in a state of bad nerves, apparently most worried about the wrinkles in her neck. Dr. Finley Blake, much darker, a successful gynecologist in the city, reads a newspaper in their tastefully decorated living room. Sophie, their seventeen-year-old daughter, who plays Chopin on the spinet, will soon be a freshman at Bennington. However, they have been receiving letters from "The Committee" informing them something drastic would happen on this evening. Crank mail or real threats? Nerves taut, the three react in very personal ways to what may happen. Sharply at ten the bell rings, and the reader and the Blakes see Fargo Hurn, wearing a gold earring and sporting a "violent" Afro, and his girl friend, Miss Hedda Brewster. Armed with a switchblade and a rifle, these two threaten the Blakes with destruction of their correctly acquired artifacts and very possibly their lives, as well as a demand for ten thousand dollars.

Dust jacket for Van Dyke's third novel, which describes the violent confrontation between an affluent black family living in a predominantly white suburb and angry black militants from Harlem

By means of artfully constructed flashbacks, the omniscient narrator reveals hidden truths from the past. Having grown up in abject poverty in north Alabama, Olga worked as a servant in order to attend Alabama State. She is inordinately proud of her spacious house, her worldly possessions, her clubs, and the family's rather recent rise to affluence. Dr. Blake had taken on many menial jobs in order to pay his way through Meharry Medical School. Up to ten years before, the three of them had been poor when they lived in Harlem. Naturally Fargo has no idea what lies behind the large teddy bear that has its own chair in the living room; instead, he accuses the Blakes of being "black-half-white bushwa smug . . . throwing a few peanuts to that Uncle Tom-ing NAACP. . . . *You* our *first* enemy, baby. You been keepin' us down more'n whitey ever kept us down."

Against the violence and threats of Fargo and Hedda, the mother and daughter show the most courage. As a result of these two hours of terror and the revelation of truths, the characters go through metamorphoses. Once the teddy bear and the piano are destroyed, mother and daughter, rather than being full of hatred and jealousy, have reached a rapprochement. Dr. Blake regains what had been his lost manhood, and Fargo rejects his role as a

hired thug. In the framework of the eventually revealed mysteries, all of these major changes seem natural and right.

In addition to these three published novels, Van Dyke has at least four unpublished novels to his credit. Because almost all of his critics have justly found much to admire and praise in his works, one can only trust that these three novels give a promise of the riches yet to be revealed.

Mary Elizabeth Vroman
(circa 1924-29 April 1967)

Edith Blicksilver
Georgia Institute of Technology

BOOKS: *Esther* (New York: Bantam, 1963; London: Muller, 1965);
Shaped to Its Purpose: Delta Sigma Theta, The First Fifty Years (New York: Random House, 1965);
Harlem Summer (New York: Putnam's, 1967).

SCREENPLAY: *Bright Road*, M-G-M, 1953.

Mary Elizabeth Vroman was born in Buffalo, New York, grew up in the West Indies, and graduated from Alabama State Teachers College. Following in the footsteps of three generations of women on her mother's side of the family who became educators, she taught for twenty years in the public schools of Alabama, Chicago, and New York. She was married to Oliver M. Harper, a dentist, and her untimely death occurred at the age of forty-two because of complications following surgery.

Vroman's first published story, "See How They Run," depicted her experiences as a new teacher in a third-grade Alabama classroom. She adapted the story to a motion picture entitled *Bright Road* and became the first black woman member of the Screen Writers Guild.

"See How They Run," published when Vroman was twenty-seven, describes the challenges faced by an idealistic young black teacher in the rural South. The story in the June 1951 issue of the *Ladies' Home Journal* elicited 500 enthusiastic letters from readers. "See How They Run" was selected to win the Christopher Award for inspirational

magazine writing because of its "humanitarian quality."

Acclaimed as the "finest story to come out of the South since *Green Pastures*," "See How They Run" details the interaction of teacher Jane Richards with a class of forty-three black children and her influence on a poor, proud, and antagonistic eleven-year-old student named C. T. Young. As the result of Miss Richards's concerned devotion, C. T. is motivated to become an achiever. Skillfully using the stream-of-consciousness technique, Vroman reveals the sensitivities of the teacher as she tries to cope with children forced to walk two miles from home daily to attend class and who are too poor to purchase a nutritious school lunch or to afford a doctor when they are ill. The teacher's struggles to get a new piano and science equipment for the school and her patience in encouraging the children to develop their writing skills provide insights into the difficulties of educating black children in the rural South. A recurring symbol in the work is blind mice whose tails have been cut off by a farmer's wife. The mice are compared to Miss Richards's impoverished students whom she is determined to help, as the story title indicates, by urging them to run away from the restrictions of their environment. Vroman did not write the story to condemn the segregated educational system that existed then. "I just wanted people to love my children," she explained. "We've had lots of angry stories by angry writers. But it didn't change any-

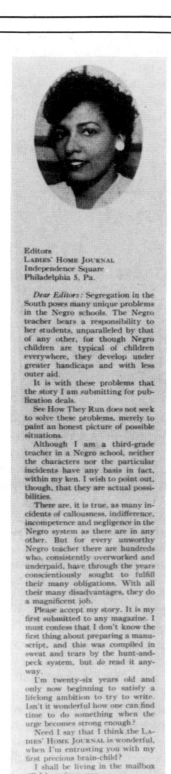

Editors
LADIES' HOME JOURNAL
Independence Square
Philadelphia 5, Pa.

Dear Editors: Segregation in the South poses many unique problems in the Negro schools. The Negro teacher bears a responsibility to her students, unparalleled by that of any other, for though Negro children are typical of children everywhere, they develop under greater handicaps and with less outer aid.

It is with these problems that the story I am submitting for publication deals.

See How They Run does not seek to solve these problems, merely to paint an honest picture of possible situations.

Although I am a third-grade teacher in a Negro school, neither the characters nor the particular incidents have any basis in fact, within my ken. I wish to point out, though, that they are actual possibilities.

There are, it is true, as many incidents of callousness, indifference, incompetence and negligence in the Negro system as there are in any other. But for every unworthy Negro teacher there are hundreds who, consistently overworked and underpaid, have through the years conscientiously sought to fulfill their many obligations. With all their many disadvantages, they do a magnificent job.

Please accept my story. It is my first submitted to any magazine. I must confess that I don't know the first thing about preparing a manuscript, and this was compiled in sweat and tears by the hunt-and-peck system, but do read it anyway.

I'm twenty-six years old and only now beginning to satisfy a lifelong ambition to try to write. Isn't it wonderful how one can find time to do something when the urge becomes strong enough?

Need I say that I think the LADIES' HOME JOURNAL is wonderful, when I'm entrusting you with my first precious brain-child?

I shall be living in the mailbox till I hear from you.

Yours hopefully and sincerely,
MARY ELIZABETH VROMAN.

Mary Elizabeth Vroman's letter of submission to Ladies' Home Journal *explaining why she wrote "See How They Run," her first short story. The letter was published in the June 1951 issue of the magazine, along with Vroman's story.*

thing, getting so angry. I just thought about how much I loved them [the children] and tried to put it down on paper. . . ."

Vroman's first full-length book, *Esther* (1963), describes life in a small rural Southern town, focusing on a dignified grandmother named Lydia Jones who saves her money as a midwife to purchase some land and uses her savings to encourage her granddaughter, Esther Kennedy, to pursue a nursing career. Lydia is realistic about the struggle involved when she admits that "folks don't give a colored woman no glory, nor much respect. You got to fight for it all the way." Using folklore remedies handed down from her own slave grandmother, Lydia is respected in the community; and she is distressed when Esther becomes a domestic worker. After being assaulted by her employer's son, Esther has a baby and is forced to postpone her professional goals.

Taking advantage of her grandmother's inheritance, Esther overcomes many hardships to become a nurse in a segregated hospital, where she tries to improve crowded patient conditions and replace the secondhand equipment. Through hard work and determination, Esther becomes a supervisor at the hospital, is voted the woman of the year by a local club, and marries her childhood sweetheart, who has become a prominent doctor in the town. The story ends on a note of optimistic brotherhood as both the black and white medical personnel cooperate together to aid the victims of ptomaine. Vroman has used Lydia Jones as her spokesperson, having her say "we are all together on this here earth and we can't one of us make it alone. We got to go down that road feeling for each other."

Vroman's second book, *Shaped to Its Purpose* (1965), is a history of the first fifty years of Delta Sigma Theta, a sorority of 40,000 college-trained professional black women, to which the author belonged.

Her third book, *Harlem Summer* (1967), was intended for teenage readers. John, sixteen, from Montgomery, Alabama, has come to spend the summer living with relatives and working in Harlem. He obtains a job in a grocery store owned by a white man and becomes friends with the other employee at the store, Mark. The incidents in John's Harlem summer expose him to ghetto living as he enjoys diversified entertainment at the Apollo Theatre, observes storefront religion, and seeks his own identity. John has been objective about white people even though his father was permanently disabled because of an incident on a segregated bus. His parents are strong, courageous, and loving; and

Harry Belafonte and Dorothy Dandridge in a scene from the movie Bright Road, *for which Vroman wrote the script (Culver Pictures)*

he has been happy in his rural home. Mark, an orphan growing up in Harlem, is bitter about conditions in his neighborhood. He is angry that white men control most of the businesses, and he is determined to save his money and own the store where he now works.

In Harlem, John is exposed to situations different from those of his own Montgomery community, and he meets a variety of people—the violent, the complacent, the defeated, the ambitious. John learns the meaning of black unity when Mark's uncle Paul tells him about Marcus Garvey and his movement to encourage blacks to develop ethnic pride: "he helped black people to respect themselves." He decides to become a lawyer, because he realizes that though the law can't change people's hearts, it can change the way they act. He has to help his fellow men to break the poverty cycle. He knows that poor blacks commit more crimes, drink, and take dope because they have no hope of changing their lives.

Mary Elizabeth Vroman honestly portrayed black life-styles without becoming cynical. In spite of adversities, her characters are proud and resilient: they retain their sense of humanity and they find joy in their lives. The words of John's father in *Harlem Summer* reveal the message central to Mary Elizabeth Vroman's works: "You're supposed to ask yourself *why* about everything. . . . Life isn't easy for any of us. Especially it ain't easy when you don't know who you are. That's what matters and I have wanted most . . . for you to know who you are and like who you are."

References:

Saul Bachner, "Black Literature: The Junior Novel in the Classroom—*Harlem Summer*," *Negro*

American Literature Forum, 7 (Spring 1973): 26-27;

Bachner, "Writing School Marm: Alabama Teacher Finds Literary Movie Success with First Short Story," *Ebony* (July 1952): 23-28;

Edith Blicksilver, "See How They Run," in *The Ethnic American Woman: Problems, Protests, Lifestyle* (Dubuque, Iowa: Kendall/Hunt, 1978), pp. 125-143.

Alice Walker
(9 February 1944-   )

Barbara T. Christian
University of California, Berkeley

See also the Walker entry in *DLB 6, American Novelists Since World War II, Second Series.*

BOOKS: *Once: Poems* (New York: Harcourt, Brace & World, 1968);

The Third Life of Grange Copeland (New York: Harcourt Brace Jovanovich, 1970);

Five Poems (Detroit: Broadside Press, 1972);

In Love and Trouble: Stories of Black Women (New York: Harcourt Brace Jovanovich, 1973);

Revolutionary Petunias & Other Poems (New York: Harcourt Brace Jovanovich, 1973);

Langston Hughes, American Poet (New York: Harper & Row, 1974);

Meridian (New York: Harcourt Brace Jovanovich, 1976);

Good Night Willie Lee, I'll See You in the Morning (New York: Dial, 1979);

You Can't Keep A Good Woman Down: Stories (New York: Harcourt Brace Jovanovich, 1981; London: Women's Press, 1982);

The Color Purple (New York: Harcourt Brace Jovanovich, 1982; London: Women's Press, 1983);

In Search of Our Mothers' Gardens: Womanist Prose (New York: Harcourt Brace Jovanovich, 1983).

OTHER: *I Love Myself When I Am Laughing: A Zora Neale Hurston Reader,* edited by Walker (Old Westbury, N. Y.: Feminist Press, 1979);

"*One* Child of One's Own: A Meaningful Digression Within the Work[s]," in *The Writer on Her Work,* edited by Janet Sternburg (New York: Norton, 1980), pp. 121-140.

SELECTED PERIODICAL PUBLICATIONS: "In Search of Our Mothers' Gardens," *Ms.,* 2 (May 1974): 64-70;

"In Search of Zora Neale Hurston," *Ms.,* 3 (March 1975): 74-79, 85-89;

"Lulls—A Native Daughter Returns to the South," *Ms.,* 5 (January 1977): 58-61, 89-90;

"Secrets of the New Cuba," *Ms.,* 5 (September 1977): 71-99;

"Embracing the Dark and the Light," *Essence,* 13 (July 1982): 67, 114-121.

Since 1968 when *Once,* her first work, was published, Alice Walker has sought to bring closer that day for which her maternal ancestors waited—"a day when the unknown thing that was in them would be known." In four collections of poetry, two volumes of short stories, three novels, and many essays, she has expressed with graceful and devastating clarity the relationship between the degree of freedom black women have within and without their communities and the "survival whole" of black people. Her particular angle of vision is sharpened by her use of the history of black people in this country, and therefore of the South, where they were most brutally enslaved. A Southerner, she also presents that land as the place from which their specific characteristics of survival and creativity have sprung. Her works confront the pain and struggle of black people's history, which for her has resulted in a deeply spiritual tradition. And in articulating that tradition, she has found that the creativity of black women, the extent to which they are permitted to exercise it, is a measure of the health of the entire society.

Alice Walker (photo © by Thomas Victor)

A writer who admits to "a rage to defy/the order of the stars/despite their pretty patterns," Walker consistently approaches the "forbidden" in society as a route to the truth. Perhaps the most controversial of her subjects is her insistence on investigating the relationships between black women and men, black parents and children, with unwavering honesty. A womanist (her term for a black feminist), Walker has, more than any contemporary writer in America, exposed the "twin afflictions" that beset black women, the sexism and racism that historically and presently restrict their lives. Walker develops literary forms (for example her concept of quilting, her use of folk language) that are based on the creative legacy left her by her ancestors. But that heritage is not only a source of her forms. Most important for Walker is its essence: that spirituality is the basis of the valuable and therefore of art. Unlike the stereotype of the socially conscious writer, she asserts "the importance of diving through politics and social forces to dig into the essential spirituality of individual persons."

Her work then, though clearly political in its thrust, expands that quality to mean personal inner change as a crucial aspect of radical social change. Stylistically her work is based on the idea that "a people's dreams, imaginings, rituals, legends . . . are known to contain the accumulated collective reality of the people themselves." In spite of the problems her works expose, she is essentially optimistic. Her work proceeds from Walker's belief in the human potential and desire for change.

Her belief in the relationship between personal and social change, her awareness that struggle and spirituality are primary characteristics of black Southern folk tradition, and her sense of that unknown thing in her ancestors that yearns to be articulated are not solely intellectual concepts for Alice Walker. They are part of her own personal history.

She was born 9 February 1944, the eighth and last child of Willie Lee and Minnie Lou Grant Walker, Eatonton, Georgia, sharecroppers. She grew up in that small Southern town at a time when many blacks, like her parents, worked in the fields for a pittance and when whites exerted control over practically every aspect of black life. Her childhood was filled with stories of past lynchings, and like other Southern black children she found "at 12 that the same little white girls who had been her playmates were suddenly to be called 'miss.'" The young Walker was certainly affected by the pervasiveness of the violent racist system of the South, especially the impact it had on black families. In an interview in *Library Journal* (15 June 1970) she explained how this relationship affected her first novel, *The Third Life of Grange Copeland* (1970): "I was curious to know why people in families (specifically black families) are often cruel to each other and how much of this cruelty is caused by outside forces such as various social injustices, segregation, unemployment, etc."

Perhaps Walker was particularly attuned to the relationship between social forces and personal development because at a young age she lived through the feeling of being an outcast. At eight she lost the sight of one eye when one of her older brothers shot her with a BB gun. Her eye was cov-

ered by a scar until she was fourteen, when a relatively simple operation corrected the disfigurement, which made her feel ugly; and for years she feared she would lose the sight of the other eye. This experience caused her really to notice relationships. For that reason, she also began to keep a notebook, in which she wrote poems, often in the fields where she had some privacy. Her writings seem indelibly marked by these years, for she focuses sharply on relationships, not only between people but also between human beings and nature. And her sense of her difference probably contributed to her tendency to tread forbidden paths. Ironically, Walker was awarded a "rehabilitation scholarship" from Georgia, a state which systematically oppressed black people. That, along with the fact that she was valedictorian of her senior class, enabled her to go to Spelman College.

Although, to some extent, the child Walker felt separate, she was also a part of a community which nurtured her. In spite of the oppressiveness of the racist Southern system, she had many excellent teachers. They saved her from "feeling alone; from worrying that the world she was stretching to

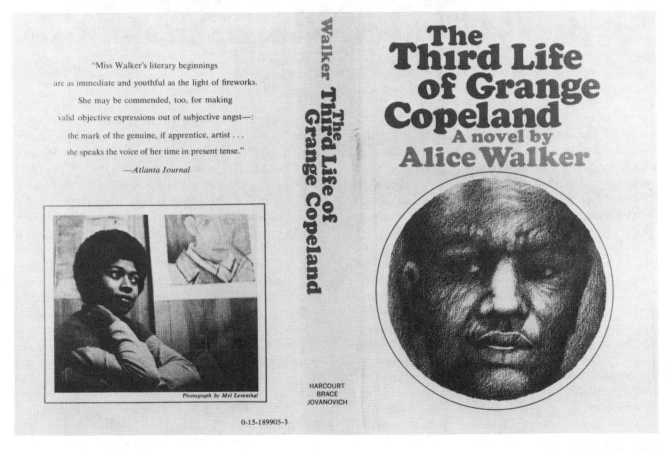

Dust jacket for Walker's first novel, which grew from her curiosity about "why people in families (specifically black families) are often cruel to each other"

find might not exist." And they lent her books, for her a necessary element in her development: "Books became my world because the world I was in was very hard." Her community, as well as her teachers, knew the importance of education. The men of Eatonton built what the schools needed, and parents raised money to keep them going.

At an early age, Walker saw black people working together to accomplish goals necessary to their survival and development. Despite the limits imposed upon them, they felt responsible for each other. In one of her essays she recalls that growing up in the South, a black might be afraid of whites but not of blacks. As a little girl, she walked and played with black convicts who were accused of murder. This sense of "One Life" that black people share, their belief that they are a community with a functional history and culture is, for Walker, one reason for the persistence of struggle characteristic of black Southern tradition. It is not so much the grand sweep of history or the artifacts created as it is the relations of people to each other, young to old, parent to child, man to woman, that make up that heritage—a theme that Walker has treated persistently in her works.

As influential as her community was, the person that seems to have shaped her the most was her mother. Walker has often said that the stories she now tells are her mother's stories and that she has absorbed something of the urgency of her mother that her story be told. Walker's writings are an example of what her mother and others like her might have created if they were not the "mules of the world" and had the opportunity to write, paint, or carve their own expressions. Yet, although these women did not have access to art forms, they did create in whatever forms were allowed them. In her essay "In Search of Our Mothers' Gardens," Walker illuminates this legacy of creativity as one of the spiritual bases of her own art:

> I notice that it is only when my mother is working in her flowers that she is radiant, almost to the point of being invisible—except as Creator: hand and eye. She is involved in work her soul must have. Ordering the universe in the image of her personal concept of Beauty.

> Her face, as she prepares the Art that is her gift, is a legacy of respect she leaves to me, for all that illuminates and cherishes life. She has handed down respect for the possibilities—and the will to grasp them.

Like the character Mem in *The Third Life of Grange Copeland,* Walker's mother created art as part of her daily life, against the pressures of working in the fields or as a maid and raising eight children. Although their society denied them the access to most of the means of creation and legislated that only a few cultivated souls could produce art, these women used quilting, gardening, cooking, sewing to order their universe in the image of their personal concept of beauty. Such a legacy has given Walker insight not only into the lives of black women but into the essential nature of art as a human process of illuminating and cherishing life. Walker was later to say that "if art doesn't make us better, then what on earth is it for?"

The mother also passed on to the daughter another quality that marks her art. Her mother and her aunts were the most independent people the child knew. Like the character Aunt Jimmy in Toni Morrison's *The Bluest Eye,* these women fished, hunted, worked like any man, and dressed as fine as any woman. Their sense of their own completeness certainly helped to instill the quality of assurance in the young Walker that she would need in order to be a black woman writer in America: "Unlike many women who were told throughout their adolescence they must marry, I was never told by my mother or anyone of her sisters it was something I need even think about. It is because of them, I know women can do anything and that one's sexuality is not affected by one's work."

Many critics have commented on Alice Walker's apparently natural quality of authority as a writer, her assurance with words. Walker possesses this quality because of the experience of her maternal ancestors. Because they were not seen as women in American society with the characteristics that that definition designated, they had to do everything—and therefore knew they could do everything. Walker uses a variation on this theme in her second novel, *Meridian* (1976), by speculating as to what black women will decide to do when they have a choice.

Walker left Eatonton to go to college, first at Spelman in Atlanta, then at Sarah Lawrence in New York. What she learned at these two very different institutions is indicative of her character and would influence her work. At that time Spelman was, in many ways, dedicated to turning Negro girls into ladies. However, during Walker's years there, the atmosphere of the school was strongly affected by the civil rights movement, what Walker calls "the Southern Revolution." She grew to worship the young leaders of SNCC, John Lewis, Ruby Davis

Robinson, and Julian Bond, and participated in civil rights demonstrations. She says of this period: "Everyone was beautiful, because everyone was conquering fear by holding the hands of the person next to them." Her experience, so strongly felt, is distilled in many of the poems of *Once*, her first published book of poetry, in short stories like "The Welcome Table," and most emphatically in *Meridian*. Throughout the novel the Sojourner tree is a striking symbol of struggle, apparent death, and rejuvenation. Years before she wrote *Meridian*, Walker evoked this memory of her years at Spelman: "Then, of course, the cherry trees—cut down now I think—that were always blooming away while we—young and bursting with fear and determination to change our world—thought beyond our fervid singing, of death."

The cherry trees, as the symbol of nature's constant thriving, the analysis of the relationship between violence and revolution, the paradox of life-giving death, the probing of the concept of womanhood as it was viewed by the college in the novel—all these are derived from Walker's years at Spelman. And the archives at the oldest college for black women would be the source for her portrayal of Nettie, the Southern black woman in her novel *The Color Purple* (1982) who went to Africa as a missionary. Spelman's tradition, then, represents for Walker both positive and negative aspects of the definition of Southern black women and their role in society.

White and wealthy Sarah Lawrence College is a school for women in Bronxville, New York. Walker's years there were a culmination of previous preoccupations, as well as the beginning of her public writing career. In attempting to understand the recurrent dreams of suicide that she had had since she was eight, she studied the philosophers' positions on suicide, "because by that time it did not seem frightening or even odd—but only inevitable." An experience she had during her senior year put the conclusion to a test and resulted in the writing of her first book, *Once*.

During the summer before, she had become pregnant and had traveled to Africa. She found that "I felt at the mercy of everything, including my body, which I had learned to accept as a kind of casing over which I considered my real self," and "began to understand how alone woman is, because of her body." She decided that if she failed to find an abortionist she would kill herself. A decision of such finality caused her to review her relationship with her mother, father, sisters, and community. She realized that her family would be hurt to hear of her death while they would be ashamed if they discovered she was pregnant. During the time while she anxiously waited for her friends to find an abortionist, she began writing *Once*. After she was "saved," she wrote without stopping, stuffing each completed poem under the door of Muriel Rukseyer, because "someone had to read them." Her first published poems, which are about love, death, Africa, and the civil rights movement, and her first published story, "To Hell With Dying," which is appropriately about an old man saved from death many times by the love of his neighbor's children, grew out of her gladness that she was alive. Walker has often said that all her poems result from her emergence out of a period of despair: "Writing poems is my way of celebrating with the world that I have not committed suicide the night before."

Walker's peculiar point of view on specific social issues in her large body of works can be traced to pivotal experiences she had in her college years that heightened her awareness of the position of blacks and women in the society. At Spelman, she confronted the concept of the "lady," which clashed with her experience of her mother's and aunts' lives. She was also absorbed in the civil rights movement, in which black women and men risked death. Meaningful struggle for more life was necessarily connected to death. It was also clear to her that if black women were to participate effectively in that movement, as indeed they did, they could not be restricted by a definition of woman that denied them their full potential. Black people's struggle to be free then could not be separated from the necessity for black women to be free enough to struggle—a theme that Walker probes in her second novel, *Meridian*.

At Sarah Lawrence, she discovered, in her pregnancy, the aloneness of woman in her body, the extreme result of which could also be death. In this crisis, she was saved by other women who knew that they too could be in her place. And she recognized, as have so many other women, the different standards of acceptance for women and men within her own family as well as the outer society. Such recognition of the social definition of woman meant her experience was not just a private one—thus her public acknowledgement of her pregnancy and abortion as the impetus for her first published book, *Once*. Like other women in the 1970s, this and other peculiarly female experiences would result in Walker's recognition that she had to unite with other women to raise society's consciousness. As her first works of fiction, *The Third Life of Grange Copeland* (1970) and *In Love and Trouble* (1973), illustrate,

Walker was one of the first contemporary black women writers to insist that sexism existed in the black community and was not only an issue for white women. She did this at a time when most black leaders focused only on racism and considered her position to be practically heresy. At the same time, she also dramatized in her works the nature of racism and the relationship between sexism and racism as modes of oppression that restricted the lives of all women and men in this country. Her experiences at Spelman and at Sarah Lawrence deepened her understanding of the interconnectedness of pivotal struggles for freedom in America.

As important, at the core of her perception of these two experiences is the risk of death that one takes in the society just to be oneself if that self is not the norm. This sense of the danger involved in being the "other" seems to be connected to her childhood accident and the recurrent dreams of suicide that followed it. In all these instances, Walker's response was the desire for death, then anger, followed by introspection and finally the insistence on being all of one's self, no matter what the cost. Thus the confrontation with death led to a struggle for a more genuine and free life, a paradox that Walker explores profoundly in many of her works.

During her college years, Walker deepened her knowledge of other writers. Books continued to be, as they were in her childhood, an integral part of her life. Her response to other writers has been extremely important to her literary development, as illustrated by the epigraphs for her books — excerpts from the Russian woman poet Akhmatova; the African poet Okotp'tek; the native American seer Black Elk; and the German poet Rilke. And her essays — "In Search of Our Mothers' Gardens," "One Child of One's Own," and "In Search of Zora Neale Hurston" — use the insights of writers Zora Neale Hurston, Virginia Woolf, and Phillis Wheatley as a means of illuminating the creativity of black women. Walker sees herself as part of an international community of writers from whom she learns and to whom she continually responds. This quality of hers is worth noting since white American society often views the Afro-American writer as separate from American literature, and therefore from all other literature — despite the reciprocal impact Afro-American writers have had with other writers of the world. Like Richard Wright, Walker claims insights of the entire world of writers as connected to her own.

The writers that have influenced Walker are indicators of her own preoccupations. In her sophomore year she read every Russian writer that she could get her hands on, for it seemed to her that "Russia must have something floating about in the air that writers breathe from the time they are born." What most impressed her was the ability of Tolstoy, Dostoevski, Turgenev, Gorki, and Gogol to render the tone of their entire society while penetrating the essential spirit of individual persons. The result is both scope and depth and the sounding of the genuine which is the universal in all people. This configuration of qualities certainly marks Walker's fiction, for there is always an interrelation between the lives of the black women she portrays, the values of the entire society, and essential spiritual questions that are asked in every human society.

Walker is also drawn to writers who are not afraid of fantasy, myth, and mystery, qualities that inspired her in the works of African writers Okotp'tek (who has written her favorite modern poem, "Song of Lowino"); Elechi Amadi, whose Concubine she calls a perfect story; Camara Laye and Bessie Head. Like Black Elk, whose vision permeates Meridian, and Gabriel García Márquez, the South American novelist, these writers seem to Walker to be "like musicians: at one with their cultures and their historical subconscious."

Though not in concert with their own cultures, the German writers Rilke and Hesse insisted on loving "those questions like locked rooms/full of treasures/to which [their] blind/and groping key/does not yet fit." Like them, Walker believes that the artist "must be free to explore, otherwise she or he will never discover what is needed (by everyone) to be known." She has successfully applied their questions to the nature of black women as they struggle in America.

The quality of mystery is especially evident in the poetry that has nurtured Walker: the Japanese haiku poets; e.e. cummings, Emily Dickinson, and William Carlos Williams; Ovid and Catallus; Okotp'tek; Gwendolyn Brooks, Arna Bontemps, and Jean Toomer. Though they come from vastly different cultures and periods in history, they all are passionate in their perception of the many, sometimes contradictory, meanings of experience, and in the way language can evoke the complexity of life. Most of these poets share another quality. They are economical yet sensual in their style. Walker clearly has a preference for this approach to language. The process of stripping off layers and honing down to the core is apparent in her fiction as well as her poetry.

Two other groups of writers, whose works are

often marked by these qualities, are of enormous importance to Walker: Afro-American writers, especially women, and women writers of other cultures. For these writers often have a view of the world that not only illuminates and records aspects of experience unknown to or interpreted differently by men and/or whites, they often write against great social barriers, sometimes internalized as their own psychological conflicts. Walker has been influenced by Virginia Woolf (especially *A Room of One's Own*) the Brontës, the South African writer Doris Lessing, and by the white American writer Kate Chopin, because "their characters can always envision a solution, an evolution to higher consciousness on the part of society, even when society itself cannot." Perhaps that belief in the possibility of change is related to retention of their own humanity despite the impact of oppressive forces. The same belief that human beings can evolve is central to Walker's two favorite books by Afro-American writers, Jean Toomer's *Cane* and Zora Neale Hurston's *Their Eyes Were Watching God*. Although Walker has been critical of Toomer's attempt to be "just an American," she emphasizes in these two writers their expression of an essential quality she believes Afro-Americans have retained from their African heritage—that of animism, "a belief that makes it possible to view all creation as living, as being inhabited by spirit." As a result these books are infused with the historical unconscious of black people in this country. But because of these writers' radical exploration of society, their expression of a belief contrary to the American world view, they were criticized, worse, ignored by their own communities.

But Walker not only claims these writers as nurturers of her own creativity, she is an activist in restoring their works to the reading public. In particular, her sense of the precarious position of the Afro-American woman writer in a racist, male-dominated society is dramatized in her successful attempt to rescue Zora Neale Hurston's works from oblivion. Walker did not discover this writer until she was in her twenties and was working on the short story "The Revenge of Hannah Kemhuff." She was appalled that in her many years of education, no one had told her about this literary ancestor of hers. She also recognized the incredible loss, particularly to black women, that the silence about Hurston's works represented.

In an interview in the early 1970s, Walker makes the connection between the fate of past Afro-American women writers and the attitudes that she herself had begun to encounter: "There are two reasons why the black woman writer is not taken as seriously as the black male writer. One is that she is a woman. Critics seem unusually ill-equipped to intelligently discuss and analyze the works of black women. Generally they do not even make the attempt; they prefer, rather, to talk about the lives of black women writers, not about what they write. And since black women writers are not, it would seem, very likeable (until recently they were the least willing worshippers of male supremacy) comments about them tend to be cruel."

In pursuit of her own literary sources, Walker saw that Afro-American women writers have, as part of their tradition, explored the relationship between sexism and racism, and therefore were a threat to established literary norms in both black and white society. As a result, many were maligned or ignored—a fate that could strike Walker as well. By placing a tombstone on Hurston's unmarked grave and writing about it in "In Search of Zora Neale Hurston" (1975), by teaching courses on black women writers—a result of which was the essay "In Search of Our Mothers' Gardens" (1974), and by editing *I Love Myself When I Am Laughing* (1979), an anthology of Hurston's works, Walker was not only thanking her literary ancestor, she was also acknowledging the tradition of Afro-American women writers and insisting that black women themselves would have to safeguard their own creative legacy. Her example would help to encourage and support a generation of black feminist writers.

After Walker finished college, she spent a brief time in New York's Lower East Side, an experience which formed the basis for certain sections of *Meridian* and her controversial story about interracial rape, "Advancing Luna—and Ida B. Wells." Because of her commitment to the Southern revolution, however, it was not long before she returned to the South. From the late 1960s to the middle 1970s, she worked in Mississippi in voter registration and welfare rights. During that time she married Mel Leventhal, a white civil rights lawyer. For many years, critics, particularly black male critics, had a tendency to focus on her marriage rather than on her work. Walker points out that these critics were "themselves frequently interracially married who moreover hung on every word from Richard Wright, Jean Toomer, Langston Hughes, James Baldwin, John A. Williams and LeRoi Jones, to name a few; all of whom were at some time in their lives interracially connected. . . . I, a black woman, had dared to exercise the same prerogative as they."

During her years in Mississippi, Walker collected folklore from ordinary black women and re-

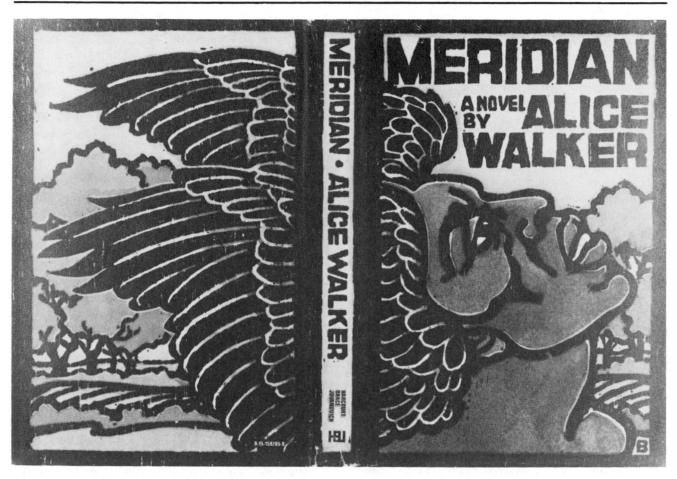

Dust jacket for Walker's second novel, based on the theme that before black people can win the struggle for freedom, black women must be free to join the struggle

corded the details of their everyday lives. Doubtless this activity deepened the knowledge she had acquired in her childhood of the character of Southern black women, how they saw themselves and their community, and how they contended with the vortex of conventions that limited their lives. In her essays during these years she articulated the cycle of works which she would complete in the next decade. In "In Search of Our Mothers' Gardens," she speaks about three types of black women: the physically and psychologically abused black woman; the exceptional black woman torn by "contrary instincts," who, in order to try to fulfill her creativity, is forced to repress the sources from which it comes; and the new black woman who can freely recreate herself out of the legacy of her maternal ancestors. Throughout each of her fictional works, Walker presents glimpses of all types, although one phase of the cycle is intensely focused on. For example, her characterization of Mem and Margaret Copeland in *The Third Life of Grange Copeland* as physically

and psychologically abused black women led her to the characterization of Ruth Copeland as a black woman who may be able to recreate herself whole. Walker insists that an understanding of the "herstory" of black women and the lives they are actually living is critical to growth and transformation.

Her first collection of short stories, *In Love and Trouble* (1973), demonstrates this two-pronged commitment, from Roselily, the poor mother of illegitimate children whose marriage to a Black Muslim is seen by most as a triumphant deliverance from her backward condition but who knows that she will still be confined, to Maggie in "Everyday Use" who is not knowledgeable about the new "blackness" but truly understands heritage, because through her quilting she loves the people who have passed unto her a tradition of caring. Most of the protagonists in this volume are Southern black women who, often against their own conscious wills in the face of pain, abuse, even death, challenge the conventions of sex, race, and age that attempt to restrict them. As a result, *In Love and Trouble* seemed heretical to some black male critics, for it clearly proclaimed the violent effects of sexism and racism as evils against which black women must struggle within black society.

The title poem of Walker's second book of poetry, *Revolutionary Petunias* (1973), is also indicative of her preoccupations during her Mississippi years. Its central character, Sammy Lou, is the image of the typical black Southern woman of whom "revolutionaries" are often contemptuous. Sammy Lou prays to the Lord, is against violence, names her children after presidents, even loves flowers, a misdirected use of time and energy according to the political figures of the day. Yet she insists on righteousness, on justice even to the point of dangerous action, for she kills the white man who has killed her husband—a rebellious act that inspires the folk to write songs about her. Walker sees the Sammy Lous—for there are many—as part of an ongoing revolution: "Any black revolution, instead of calling her incorrect will have to honor her single act of rebellion."

Revolutionary Petunias is also about the apparent decline of the Southern revolution, about that time when the external activism of the movement could not be sustained, when it became necessary for those who continued to struggle to look within as well as without and clarify for themselves the difference between rhetoric and principle. Walker says of this volume that "in a way the whole book is a celebration of people who will not cram themselves into any ideological or racial mold. . . . They are aware that the visions that created them were all towards a future when all people—and flowers too—can bloom. They require that in the midst of the bloodiest battles or revolution this thought not be forgotten." A black woman married to a white man and living in Mississippi; a writer committed to exposing the violence caused by sexism, racism, and the exploitation of the poor; a thinker who refuses to accept unquestioningly that violence is essential to revolution and who focuses on the importance of beauty in the lives of everyone; a political activist who insists that the history of ordinary, seemingly backward, folk is the underpinnings of the contemporary movement for social change—Alice Walker continued to walk forbidden paths.

Her inquiry into the lives of Southern black women affected Walker's craft as well as her subject matter. During this period she paid careful attention to the "low" media—quilting, gardening, cooking—that were the only forms through which most black women were allowed to express their creativity. Her fiction of this period has, at the core of its craft, the technique of quilting—the use of recurring economical patterns to create a synthesis of the bits and pieces of life into a work of functional beauty. Her second novel, *Meridian*, is such a work. Walker demonstrates the relationship between the history of ordinary black folk, particularly women, and the philosophical character Meridian, whose question—when is it necessary, when is it right, to kill?—provides the central theme of the novel. This relationship is made clear for the reader through Walker's quilting of intersecting and recurring motifs that stress, on the one hand, the fragmentation of life caused by the unnatural ideologies of sexism and racism and, on the other, the natural unity of life as expressed in nature itself, in music, in the love of human beings for each other.

Meridian is also an indication of how important the subject of motherhood is to Walker. Since black women are primarily glorified as mothers in their own communities and debased as mammies in white society, it is almost impossible to explore their lives, in the past or in the present, without examining the many ramifications that that role has meant for them.

In her first novel, *The Third Life of Grange Copeland*, Walker shows how the racist fabric of the American South affects the black family. Because the Copeland men are thwarted by the society in their drive for control of their lives—the American definition of manhood—they vent their frustrations by inflicting violence on their wives. Because the Copeland women, too, are thwarted in their desire to be "women" in the society—that is, to be taken care of—one finally kills herself and the other is killed by her husband when she tries to take care of their family. In each case, the children are not so much a source of the mother's strength as they are victims. Mothers, then, are not always respected in black society, nor are they always victorious.

In *Meridian,* Walker goes a step further, for Meridian's quest for wholeness is initiated by her feelings of inadequacy in living up to the myth of black motherhood. Again, Walker challenges a prevalent myth. She presents a major character who gives up her son (an act no black woman is supposed to do willingly) and has her tubes tied after a painful abortion, because she is so in awe of the state of motherhood she does not think she can fulfill it. In presenting this controversial series of actions, Walker heightens the restrictiveness of the role. For, while society deifies motherhood, it places little value on children, especially black children, or on mothers, especially black mothers. It often, in fact, punishes mothers for being mothers by restricting their development. Walker also broadens the definition of mother as more than a biological state. Meridian attains the state of motherhood because she believes so profoundly in the sacredness of all life that she takes responsibility for the life of all the people. Her aborted motherhood yields a perspective on life—that of "expanding her mind with action."

While Walker challenges the monumental myth of black motherhood in *Meridian,* she also maintains the importance of the perspective and culture that that historical role has given women. In her essay *"One* Child of One's Own" (1980), she questions the idea that some white American feminists were proposing—that motherhood is in and of itself an evil for women. The essay has as its central theme the writer as mother, a crucial question of the 1970s when many women protested, through books like Tillie Olsen's *Silences,* that women have traditionally had to choose between being mothers and being creative in the arts. Walker had a daughter, Rebecca, three days after she finished her first novel in 1969. Her child's birth awakened in her fears about the changes it might make in her life: "Well, I wondered, with great fear, where is the split in me now? What is the damage. . . . Was I, as a writer, done for?"

Walker makes clear in this essay that her fear and the fears of other women like her are not based on primal truth but on a social definition of woman. And that without those social and psychological limits, knowledge, rather than damage, could come from being a mother: "My child's birth was the incomparable gift of seeing the world at quite a different angle than before and judging it by standards far beyond my natural life." That different angle has strengthened Walker's commitment to an international women's movement that works for all women, all children, and against all injustice. And the two major injustices that affect her life and the lives of other black women are sexist and racist behavior—even from their most natural allies, black men and other women, whatever their race. Walker concludes that it is not her child who restricts her but the social system within which she lives: "It is not my child who tells me I have no femaleness white women must affirm; not my child who says I have no rights black men or women must respect."

"One Child of One's Own" was written while Alice Walker was living in New York City. For the latter half of the 1970s she taught at various colleges and universities in the North as a means of earning a living and of communicating to others the long tradition of black women writers. It was during these years when the women's movement in the Northeast was so visible that she encountered resistance among some white feminists to recognize black women as women and as a vital part of the history of American feminism. She also encountered the same resistance among black women to see themselves not only as black but also as women with all of the responsibility worldwide that such a conscious assertion would entail. In *"One* Child of One's Own," one of her most important essays, Walker clarifies for black women the long tradition of Afro-American feminism that is often conveniently forgotten and confronts white women with the racism with which they are poisoning the women's movement. Her analysis leads her to a principle that she, as well as others, can use in this complicated society:

> What was required of women of color, was to learn to distinguish between who was the real feminist and who was not, and to exert energy in feminist collaborations only when there is little risk of wasting it. The rigors of this discernment will inevitably keep throwing women of color back upon themselves, where there is, indeed, so much work, of a feminist nature, to be done. . . . To the extent that black women disassociate themselves from the women's movement, they abandon their responsibilities to women throughout the world. This is a serious abdication from and misuse of radical black herstorical tradition: Harriet Tubman, Sojourner, Ida B. Wells and Fannie Lou Hamer would not have liked it. Nor do I.

Along with a vocal movement of other women of color, Walker has raised questions about the relationship of woman to her world that would have been unasked only a few decades before. What these writers are demonstrating in their works is that the relationships between persons are politically critical, and might, in fact, be a major determinant of the relationship of the people to the state. Walker's third work of poetry, *Good Night Willie Lee, I'll See You in the Morning* (1979) is permeated by that concern. Like *Revolutionary Petunias,* it is about the vital connection between love and lasting change, though now the emphasis is on the changing of love relationships between women and men as the foundation for a radical and irreversible transformation in society.

In this succinct volume of poetry, Walker presents her inner process of demystifying love, especially for women, as a disease or a total giving up of self. Without going through this process, the poet at her deepest level will be trapped by these pervasive societal definitions. Walker constructs a more healthy definition of love, based on cherishing self, for it is only through self-love that the self who can love is preserved. Yet she maintains the need to give herself without giving up self, as part of the true interconnectedness of all.

The movement of *Good Night Willie Lee, I'll See You in the Morning* is instructive for an understanding of Walker's process in all her work. The title refers to the last farewell her mother gave her father at his funeral. Her parents' love, though it might have been a troubled one, was Walker's first experience of love between woman and man. Using that frame, Walker moves through a five-part journey from a night of loss to a morning of hope based on a deeper understanding of love. The poet begins with the pain of a love that has declined into disease ("Did This Happen to Your Mother? Did Your Sister Throw Up a Lot?"). She takes a stand on the inviolability of her self ("On Stripping Bark From Myself"), which allows her to ask questions about her commitment to a wider love, a radical change in society, in "Facing the Way." In becoming able to act because she loves, she analyzes those historical losses and scars in "Early Losses" that may impede love, and is able to forgive herself and others in the final section, "Forgiveness." It is through this process that she is able to love and insist on being loved without possessiveness or fear. Particularly striking about this volume is that black women, their history and their understanding of love are Walker's primary guides.

Published a year later, Walker's second collection of short stories complements *Good Night Willie Lee*. *You Can't Keep A Good Woman Down* (1981) was seen by critics who favored the work as her most blatant womanist book to date and by critics who disliked it as too polemical. In this volume Walker delved into issues raised by feminists in the 1970s—abortion, sadomasochism, pornography, interracial rape—issues often considered too topical for fiction. And she analyzed these issues from the perspective that intimate relationships are not only personal, they are political.

For example, "Porn" is a story about the sexual connection between a black man who prides himself on his sexual technique and a black woman who is

Dust jacket for Walker's second collection of stories, demonstrating her growing commitment to political feminism

"liberated," makes her own money, lives separately from her lover, and values her women friends. Walker focuses on the man's use of pornographic fantasies and the woman's reaction to them. She explores the way his fantasies underline his inability to make love to this woman with whatever flaws might result, because of his need to prove his superiority through his sexuality. His fantasies, as perceived by the woman, degrade her, him, and other people they know, for his porn collection uses stereotypes of black and white men and women. Her awareness of the insidiousness of his collection destroys the sexual pleasure she had believed they were sharing. Like "Porn," many of the stories in this volume show the connection between racist and sexist stereotypes, particularly in the area of sexuality, and reveal how it affects the quality of black women's lives.

You Can't Keep A Good Woman Down attempts a womanist technique as well as subject matter. Many of the stories are not classic in form—that is, they are not presented as finished, objective products. Rather, the author's subjective positions are obvious and the stories are presented as in process. Feminist thinkers of the 1970s asserted a link between process (the unraveling of thought and feeling) and the way women perceive the world. Walker experiments with this technique as a more honest and vital rendering of the truth. Her technique is especially evident in "Advancing Luna—and Ida B. Wells," a story about a young Southern black woman's growing understanding of the complexity of interracial rape. Because of the historical connection between rape and lynching, sex and race, that continues even today, the author cannot end her story conclusively. There are two endings, "After Thoughts" and "Discarded Notes and Postscripts," as Walker discloses her own thought processes.

Although *You Can't Keep A Good Woman Down* is clearly different in subject matter and style from Walker's previous works, it shares with them her fundamental values. Like her first collection of short stories, this book proves the extent to which black women are free to pursue their own selfhood in a society permeated by sexism and racism. But while the protagonists of *In Love and Trouble* wage their struggle in spite of themselves, the heroines of *You Can't Keep A Good Woman Down* consciously challenge conventions. Published eight years apart, these two collections are rooted in the same perspective yet demonstrate a clear progression of theme. And though the stories of *You Can't Keep A Good Woman Down* are contemporary in subject matter, they proceed, like *Meridian,* from the deeply felt history of black women.

Walker's third novel, *The Color Purple* (1982), exemplifies her belief that history is a necessary element of depth, that nothing is a product of the immediate present. Walker finished the novel after she and her husband divorced in 1977, and she moved to San Francisco. But she started writing it in New York City, where she tells us her major character, a rural early twentieth-century Southern black woman, seemed to elude her. It was not until she got a place in the country outside San Francisco that her characters' spirit, their language came rushing out. Whatever else critics may have said about this latest of Walker's works, they all agree that the black folk speech in which most of it is written is superb and resonates with a history of feeling and experience that is specifically Afro-American.

As is true of Walker's other two novels, this work spans generations of one poor black family in the context of rural Southern history. Again, the image of quilting is central to its concept. Yet this novel is also a further development in Walker's womanist process. It is written as a series of letters, reminding us that letters, along with diaries, were the dominant mode of expression allowed women in the West. In using the epistolary style, Walker is able to combine the subjective and the objective. As Celie, the main character, records the details of her life, she does so in images and in language that express the impact of oppression on her spirit as well as her resistance to it. Walker's subject matter is also emphatically womanist, for the emphases in *The Color Purple* are on the oppression black women experience in their relationship with black men and the sisterhood they must share with each other in order to liberate themselves. As a vehicle for these themes, two sisters' letters—Celie's to God, Nettie's to Celie and finally Celie's to Nettie—provide the novel's form. Form and content, then, are inseparable.

Walker continues to explore "forbidden" sex-

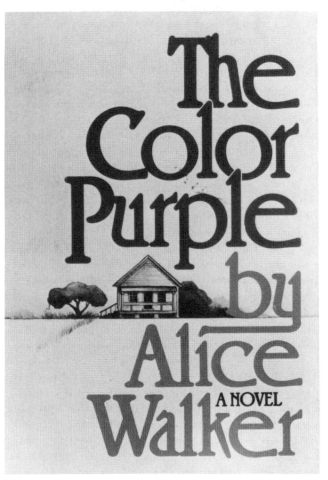

Dust jacket for Walker's third novel based on the story of her great-grandmother, who was raped at the age of twelve

ual themes, as she did in *You Can't Keep A Good Woman Down*. In *The Color Purple* she focuses on incest in a black family and portrays a lesbian relationship as natural and freeing. And like many of the protagonists in her short stories, the heroines of her third novel triumph despite the tremendous odds against them. In an interview in *California Living*, Walker reveals that Celie was based on the story of her great-grandmother who at twelve was raped and abused. Yet though the story ends happily, Walker does not flinch from presenting the sexual abuse, the wife-beatings, and the violence that Celie undergoes in a society that demeans her as a woman. As in all of her works, violence is a result of the unnatural ideologies of sexism and racism. And though many readers and critics would prefer to ignore it, Walker has always insisted on exposing the violence inflicted upon black women's bodies and spirits.

In *The Color Purple* Walker adds another dimension to the sexism black women experience. Through Nettie, Celie's sister, who escapes her condition in the South to become a missionary, Walker describes the subordination of women to men in Africa. She therefore suggests that sexism for black women does not derive from racism, though it is qualitatively affected by it. "We're going to have to debunk the myth that Africa is a haven for black people—especially black women. We've been the mule of the world there and the mule of the world here." Nettie's letters also provide other dimensions of history. They graphically demonstrate Afro-Americans' knowledge of their ancestral link to Africa, which, contrary to American myth, predates the black power movement of the 1960s; and they emphasize concrete ways in which colonization disrupts African life and values.

The Color Purple is remarkable in language, radical themes, and technique. Perhaps even more than Walker's other works, it especially affirms that the most abused of the abused can transform herself. It completes the cycle Walker announced a decade ago: the survival and liberation of black women through the strength and wisdom of others.

Alice Walker now lives in San Francisco. In 1981 she was the keynote speaker at a dinner honoring Rosa Parks on the twenty-fifth anniversary of the civil rights movement. In 1982 she appeared with Tillie Olsen at a benefit held by the Women's Party for Survival against nuclear weapons. Her message was as devastating as her written works. Reading an ancient curse that Zora Neale Hurston discovered in the South and that Walker used in the story "The Revenge of Hannah Kemhuff," a curse

Dust jacket for Walker's 1983 collection of "Womanist" essays

that sounds alarmingly like a nuclear holocaust, Walker warned the audience that "only justice can stop a curse."

Mostly, Alice Walker writes. She continues to observe and listen to black women wherever they are, as her San Francisco stories "A Letter" and "Source" indicate. And she has recently completed a collection of essays entitled *In Search of Our Mothers' Gardens: Womanist Prose*, published in 1983. Walker writes that "Guided by my heritage of a love of beauty and a respect for strength—in search of my mother's garden, I found my own."

Interviews:

John O'Brien, *Interviews With Black Writers* (New York: Liveright, 1973), pp. 186-221;

Jessica Harris, "Interview with Alice Walker," *Essence*, 7 (July 1976);

Gloria Steinem, "Do You Know This Woman? She Knows You—A Profile of Alice Walker," *Ms.*, 10 (June 1982): 35-37, 89-94;

Mary Helen Washington, "Her Mother's Gifts,"
Ms., 10 (June 1982): 38;

Pam Abramson, "Alice Walker Makes the Big Time
with Black Folk Talk," *California Living* (15
August 1982): 16-20;

Claudia Tate, "Alice Walker," in *Black Women Writers at Work,* edited by Tate (New York: Continuum, 1983), pp. 175-187.

References:

Barbara Christian, "The Black Woman Writer as
Wayward," *Black Women Writers, 1950-1980,*
edited by Mari Evans (Garden City: Doubleday, 1984), pp. 457-477;

Christian, "The Contrary Black Women of Alice
Walker: A Study of Female Protagonists in *In
Love and Trouble," Black Scholar,* 12 (March,
April 1981): 21-30, 70-71;

Christian, "Novels for Everyday Use," in *Black
Women Novelists* (Westport, Conn.: Greenwood Press, 1980), pp. 180-238;

Peter Erickson, "Cast Out Alone/To Heal/and
Re-Create/Ourselves: Family Based Identity
in the Work of Alice Walker," *CLA Journal,* 23
(September 1979): 71-94;

Karen C. Gaston, "Women in the Lives of Grange
Copeland," *CLA Journal,* 24 (March 1981):
276-286;

Trudier Harris, "Folklore in the Fiction of Alice
Walker: A Perpetuation of Historical and
Literary Traditions," *Black American Literature
Forum,* 2 (Spring 1977): 3-8;

Harris, "Violence in *The Third Life of Grange Copeland," CLA Journal,* 19 (December 1975): 238-247;

Deborah McDowell, "The Self in Bloom: Alice
Walker's *Meridian," CLA Journal,* 24 (March
1981): 262-275;

Bettye J. Parker-Smith, "Alice Walker's Women: In
Search of Some Peace of Mind," in *Black
Women Writers, 1950-1980,* edited by Mari
Evans (Garden City: Doubleday, 1984), pp.
478-493;

Mary Helen Washington, "An Essay on Alice
Walker," in *Sturdy Black Bridges,* edited by
Roseann P. Bell, Bettye J. Parker, and Beverly
Guy-Sheftall (New York: Anchor Books,
1979), pp. 133-149.

John Edgar Wideman

(14 June 1941-   )

Wilfred D. Samuels
University of Colorado, Boulder

BOOKS: *A Glance Away* (New York: Harcourt,
Brace & World, 1967);

Hurry Home (New York: Harcourt, Brace & World,
1969);

The Lynchers (New York: Harcourt Brace
Jovanovich, 1973);

Hiding Place (New York: Avon, 1981);

Damballah (New York: Avon, 1981);

Sent for You Yesterday (New York: Avon, 1983);

Brothers and Keepers (New York: Holt, Rinehart &
Winston, 1984).

PERIODICAL PUBLICATIONS:

Fiction:

"Shoes," *Ideas & Patterns in Literature,* 3 (1970);

"Orion," *Dark Waters* (1978);

"Bobby," *Tri-Quarterly* (Fall 1979);

"Mr. Thomas," *Callaloo* (Fall 1979);

"Across the Wide Missouri," *Seattle Review* (Fall
1979);

"Go To Hear a Poet," *Voyages* (November 1979);

"The Chinaman," *North American Review* (Winter
1979);

"Daddy Garbage," *North American Review* (Winter
1979);

"Freeda," *Callaloo* (Fall 1980).

Nonfiction:

"Charles W. Chesnutt: *The Marrow of Tradition,"
American Scholar,* 42 (Winter 1972-73);

"Frame and Dialect: The Evolution of the Black
Voice in Fiction," *American Poetry Review,* 5, no.
5 (1976);

"Defining the Black Voice in Fiction," *Black Ameri-
    can Literature Forum*, 2 (Fall 1977);

"*Of Love and Dust:* A Reconsideration," *Callaloo*, 1
    (May 1978);

" 'Stompin' the Blues' Ritual in Black Music and
    Speech," *American Poetry Review*, 4 (July/
    August 1978).

During the 1960s, the architects of the black
arts movement—Imamu Baraka (LeRoi Jones),
Larry Neal, Haki R. Madhubuti (Don L. Lee), Addison Gayle, and others—demanded that black writers use their talents and works for the betterment of
the black community and black life, for "the liberation of black people." Arguing that the black arts
movement was the "aesthetic and spiritual sister of
the black power concept," for example, Neal admonished black artists to speak directly to the needs
and aspirations of black Americans. Simultaneously, the black arts prophets called for a rejection
of Western ethics and aesthetics and for the establishment of a black value system based on an African
concept of art which would be used to evaluate the
creative works of Americans of African descent.

Although it had some impact, the black arts
movement did little to alter the fundamental direction of the Afro-American literary tradition, which
remained firmly in the grips of those writers with a
more conventional view of art. Led by writers such
as Ralph Ellison and James Baldwin, who were
more interested in craftsmanship than politics, this
tradition moved closer toward the mainstream
rather than away from its salient values.

Although he was among the cadre of young
black writers that emerged during the 1960s, John
Edgar Wideman did not align himself with the
politically oriented black arts movement. Instead,
from the beginning, he demonstrated an interest in
an art that carefully and logically resulted from the
creativity, expertise, and ability of the artist, rather
than one that sought to announce the political convictions of its creator. His intricate style, which includes experimentation with form, the use of surrealism and stream of consciousness, and multiple
allusions to literary masterpieces—coupled with
the absence of a focus on racial or cultural
experience—brought him immediate attention
from critics who felt he had successfully established
himself in a vein of contemporary American, rather
than Afro-American, fiction. In 1978, Robert Bone,
the author of *The Negro Novel in America,* declared
that Wideman was "perhaps the most gifted black
novelist of his generation."

John Edgar Wideman was born on 14 June
1941, in Washington, D.C., to Edgar and Betty
French Wideman. Almost a year after his birth,
young Wideman survived a near-fatal crash while
en route to Pittsburgh, Pennsylvania, where his
family has deep roots. Wideman spent the first ten
years of his life in Homewood, but later moved with
his parents to Shadyside, a predominantly white,
upper-middle-class district in Pittsburgh, where he
completed primary and secondary education at
Liberty School and Shadyside High School.
Nevertheless, Wideman remembers fondly his early
years in Homewood School, and he remembers well
the summer days spent at his grandmother's home
in Homewood. His mobility in both worlds—one
that was predominantly black, the other white—
was facilitated in part by his interest in sports, particularly basketball.

Because of his athletic and scholastic achievements, Wideman won a Benjamin Franklin Scholarship to the University of Pennsylvania in Philadelphia, where he majored first in psychology and then
in English, and became a basketball star. Graduating Phi Beta Kappa, Wideman, in 1963, won a
Rhodes Scholarship, bringing him international
attention, as Alain Locke had been the only Afro-
American to do so some fifty-five years earlier.
Wideman went to Oxford University, where he
spent three years pursuing an academic degree in
eighteenth-century studies and wrote a thesis on
four eighteenth-century novels. He played on Oxford's basketball team, including one that won the
amateur championship of England. Wideman, who
served as captain and coach, was voted the most
valuable player.

Leaving Oxford with a bachelor of philosophy
degree in 1966, Wideman, who had married Judith
Ann Goldman of Virginia in 1965, returned to the
United States and as a Kent Fellow attended the
Creative Writing Workshop at the University of
Iowa from 1966 to 1967. He left Iowa to begin a
six-year stint at the University of Pennsylvania as a
lecturer and later professor of English. While there,
he was responsible for initiating Penn's first Afro-
American studies program, which he chaired from
1972-1973, although he had no interest in administrative work. It was during his first years as a
member of Penn's faculty that Wideman, at
twenty-six, published his first novel, *A Glance Away*
(1967).

Primarily concerned with the main characters'
search for self, *A Glance Away* focuses on one day in
the life of Eddie Lawson, a thirty-one-year-old re-

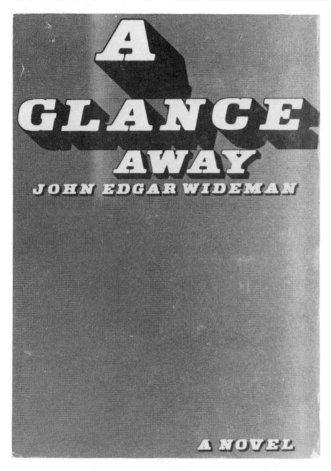

Dust jacket for Wideman's first novel, which recounts one day in the life of two men: a rehabilitated drug addict struggling to avoid drugs; and a homosexual English professor who feels unfulfilled in a world he regards as ephemeral

habilitated drug addict and former postal clerk who struggles to remain clean, and Robert Thurley, an English professor whose personal conflicts result in part from his homosexuality. The day of Eddie's homecoming, Easter Sunday, symbolizes his resurrection and rebirth, as it marks his return after a year's stay in a narcotic rehabilitation center, as well as his reassociation with his mother and sister, Bette; his sometime lover, Alice; and his best friend, Brother Small. Although convinced of his ability to find new meaning and desirous of making sense out of his life, Eddie discovers a Camus-like world, one that is ephemeral and unpredictable—one that is absurd. The fulfillment that he expects does not materialize because his world remains unsympathetic. He finds that his paraplegic mother continues to expect him to take the place of his dead brother, Eugene; his sister remains locked in a silent

and meaningless world that is controlled by their mother, who detests her; and his lover, psychologically damaged by Eddie's affair with her white girl friend, wallows in unforgiveness and refuses his love. For him, the only tangible element that remains in his former environment is his friendship with Brother Small (Alice's brother), an albino and addict, who supports his habit in part through his homosexual relationship with Thurley.

Thurley, too, finds that he leads an unfulfilled life in an ephemeral world. His memory is riddled by a past that includes a dominating mother, a failed marriage, and homosexual activities with black youths. He is able to find satisfaction only when he frequents a bar in the black section of town that is patronized by social pariahs like himself. It is through Brother that Eddie meets Thurley, who sees himself as "an aesthetic Catholic, in politics a passive communist." At the end of the novel, Eddie has decided to return to drugs as an escape from his meaningless existence. But rather than let him commit suicide through drugs, Thurley successfully engages Eddie in a dialogue, allowing him to become victorious over his hopeless fate—at least for one day.

In his first novel, Wideman reveals a concern with themes which continue to dominate his work: the significance of history, both personal and collective; the presence of a working imagination; the isolation of twentieth-century man; the sacredness of family and culture; and the importance of friendship, especially the fraternal relationship between men. For example, sensing alienation in their struggles for meaning, both Lawson and Thurley probe their pasts to find who and what they are. It is their reflections and assessments of their pasts that reveal logical minds trying to comprehend the meaning of existence in a world that seems unsympathetic and chaotic.

A Glance Away was greeted enthusiastically by critics. Declaring in the *New York Times Book Review* that Wideman had "written a powerfully inventive novel," Harry Roskolenko wrote that Wideman "has all sorts of literary gifts, including a poet's flair for taut, meaningful, emotional language." Stephen Caldwell wrote in *Saturday Review*: "What moves us is Wideman's artistry, his one-and-two paragraph evocations of joy and sorrow that first appear in his fine prologue and are echoed and revised time and again through the course of the book." And Kurt Vonnegut, Jr., wrote to Wideman, "You have written an American book. . . . The language is handsome."

Appearing two years after *A Glance Away,* *Hurry Home* (1969), Wideman's second novel, depicts the main character's search for identity and meaning. At thirty-one, Cecil Otis Braithwaite remains cradled in a sense of absence. Although he has a law degree, he works as a janitor and later as a hairdresser. Supported by Esther while he is in law school, Cecil, out of a sense of obligation, marries her on his graduation day; but aware that he does not love her and haunted by the memory of their stillborn son, Simon, he walks out on their wedding night. He meets Webb, who, seeking to compensate for his failure to acknowledge the son he had fathered with his black mistress, takes him to Europe. While there, Cecil seeks to come to grips with the strife that results from his suspension between two worlds; he seeks to transcend what W. E. B. Du Bois calls "double consciousness," an identity that is rooted in two cultures—one that is European (American) and the other which is African. Although Cecil's search finally leads him to Africa, he is unable to accept wholeheartedly his African self or heritage. After three years, he returns to his ghetto apartment in Washington, to a wife whose life remained unchanged for the most part, and to menial employment outside of his profession.

In *Hurry Home,* Wideman is again concerned with history, with the past. By frequenting the museums and galleries of France, Italy, and Spain, Cecil seeks cultural roots and meaning in a white, European world—a world in which, as a lawyer, he is expected to be mobile. Failing to do so, he travels to Africa to gain a sense of past and meaning for his present, but he remains on the threshold. Similarly Webb is haunted by his past, and the guilt which he suffers because he has failed to acknowledge his black offspring controls his every thought and reflection, rendering his effort as a writer totally useless.

By focusing as he does on both Braithwaite's and Webb's consciousness, Wideman again highlights in *Hurry Home* the working imagination, extensively utilizing surrealistic techniques. The inner workings of the characters' minds are revealed through thoughts, letters, journals, and diaries. Again, the friendship that Webb is able to establish with Braithwaite, and the companionship that he shares with Albert, gives him the only real sense of fulfillment that he has. Like Eddie, who finds meaning through his friendship with Brother, Webb grows to depend on Cecil and Albert, who are the only tangible sources of life in his immediate environment.

Dust jacket for Wideman's second novel in which a black lawyer seeks to discover his cultural identity

Critics welcomed *Hurry Home* and showered Wideman with accolades. Writing in the *Philadelphia Bulletin,* M. L. Stone concluded that it firmly established Wideman "in the front rank . . . of contemporary black literature." Stating in his *New York Times Book Review* that Wideman's second novel reveals a "formidable command of the techniques of fiction," Joseph Goodman described the work as a "dazzling display": "we can have nothing but admiration for Mr. Wideman's talent." Describing *Hurry Home* as a "rich and complicated novel," John Leonard, like other critics, compared Wideman to James Joyce and T. S. Eliot, finding similarity between Eliot's Prufrock and Wideman's Webb.

It would not be farfetched to say that both *A Glance Away* and *Hurry Home* are not black novels, for although written by a black author and developed around characters who are of African descent, neither novel is specifically or solely concerned with race, racial issues, or unique aspects of the black experience. For the most part, Eddie Lawson's and Cecil Braithwaite's conflicts do not emerge solely from the fact that they are Afro-American and know oppression as a result. Although both men are ghetto dwellers, their lives, unlike Bigger Thomas's of Richard Wright's *Native Son,* are not controlled by socioeconomic conditions that render them powerless. When Eddie reflects on his childhood experiences in an integrated middle-class neighborhood, there is not the sense of distinction and separation of races that the young Wright was forced to acknowledge and accept in *Black Boy.* Cecil does not seem irreversibly bound by his ghetto community and becomes a lawyer in spite of his economic status. Both Eddie's and Cecil's sense of absence results to a great degree from weaknesses in their own personalities. Cecil becomes an exile as much from his desire to escape a loveless marriage as from his desire as a professional to find meaning in a world that remains fragmented.

Equally significant is the presence of major white characters in both *A Glance Away* and *Hurry Home.* Unlike Frank Yerby, Willard Motley, and Ann Petry, who sought to demonstrate to the mainstream their competence by writing novels peopled mostly by white characters and centered around themes which, for the most part, were not related to the black experience, Wideman blends the two racial experiences, reducing them in the process to one basic human experience. Consequently, there is parallel development in Wideman's treatment of Eddie and Thurley in *A Glance Away* and Cecil and Webb in *Hurry Home.* What is true of the black characters is also true of the white ones: they, too, suffer from a sense of absence and alienation, which is due mostly to choices and decisions made by them early in life. Together, Eddie, Thurley, Cecil, and Webb are individuals who seek to understand and assess their past in order to best resolve, if possible, the conflicts that they presently face. Race remains secondary to their problems.

Beginning with the third novel, *The Lynchers* (1973), Wideman's emphasis shifts, and race, though it does not supersede his interest in form, language, and experimental techniques, becomes more important to his fundamental theme. Set in Philadelphia, *The Lynchers* develops around the main characters' desire to change the life of urban dwellers. Intended as a "fulcrum turning history," their planned lynching of a white policeman is conceived by Willie Hall ("Littleman"), a crippled social activist who views the lives of black Philadelphians as a process of slow death. Walking down South Street, he says, "This street means they're killing us,

whittling away day by day a man, woman, a baby at a time. And most of us just sitting on our asses wasting our time." Supported by Wilkerson (who becomes morally disturbed by his impending participation), Saunders, and Rice, the executioners of his plan, Littleman masterminds the murder not only of the white officer but also of his black prostitute concubine. The scheme is aborted, however, when, considering himself used and abused by the other lynchers, Rice kills Wilkerson.

In *The Lynchers*, setting becomes an important theme for the first time in Wideman's fiction. With its street vendors who remain aloof and unfriendly, schoolchildren who are more interested in their street lives than in books, filthy streets and roach-infested ghetto buildings within the sight of the more fashionable Lombard Street and Society Hill, where the wealthy climb marble steps to find refuge in the history left as legacy by the Age of Reason, Philadelphia emerges as a character in the novel. It renders its black inhabitants helpless in a life of meaninglessness and brutality. Equally important in this novel is the fraternal relationship between male characters. Most notable is the deep friendship that is shared by Orin Wilkerson and his father, Thomas, alias "Sweetman." Although the younger Wilkerson reveals a deep love and attachment for his mother, he also exhibits a sincere understanding of his alcoholic father. When Sweetman accidentally kills his best friend, his schoolteacher son is the first to visit him in jail. From behind bars, the father pours out, for the first time, his innermost feelings and fears: "I wanted to hide in him. I wanted all that was still alive in me to fall off my shoulders and give him back his life. I wanted to be dying in his arms, but all I could do was cry like a baby."

Although history remains important in *The Lynchers,* Wideman employs the aggregate history of blacks rather than the personal history of an individual. He begins his novel by chronicling lynching in the United States, listing over one hundred accounts that span more than three hundred years—a way of juxtaposing fact and fiction. Wideman isn't successful, as some critics noted, at showing the relevance of the lengthy chronicle to the rest of the novel. *The Lynchers* was not widely acclaimed. Richard P. Brickner wrote in the *New York Times Book Review* that although it was done "with enormous care and intelligence," *The Lynchers* "is often frustrated in a manner related to the frustration it concerns . . . it has trouble acting." Yet, the noted black critic Saunders Redding declared: "I think *The Lynchers* is far and away the truest, the most moving, and the most brilliantly

Dust jacket for Wideman's third novel, in which a group of Philadelphia blacks decide to lynch a white policeman

crafted novel of Negro life in almost a quarter of a century—that is, since Ellison's *Invisible Man,* which in some ways it surpasses."

After an eight-year silence in which Wideman and his wife, Judith, and children (Danny, Jacob, and Jamilla) exchanged Philadelphia for the open prairie of Wyoming, where he took a position as professor of English at the University of Wyoming at Laramie, Wideman, who spent some of that time steeping himself in his personal culture and history, published two more works. *Hiding Place* and *Damballah* (a collection of short stories) were both published in October 1981 by Avon Books. Each reveals a crystallization of Wideman's concern with history, culture, and heritage; but now he is concerned with the culture and heritage of Sybela Owens, his maternal great-great-great-grandmother.

In *Hiding Place* and *Damballah,* Wideman returns to Homewood, the Pittsburgh community that nurtured him through early childhood. Amid its landscape and cityscape, he weaves his tales around the fascinating offspring of Sybela Owens, who more than a hundred years ago helped to settle Homewood with her husband, Charles Bell, her master's son whose love led him to steal her before she could be sold by his father.

In *Hiding Place,* Tommy, Sybela's great-great-great-grandson, fails in his attempt to rob a local merchant and is wanted for the murder of his partner in crime. Though innocent, he flees Homewood and as a fugitive seeks sanctuary in Brunston Hill, where Mother Bess, the family's matriarch, who had known Sybela, has lived as a recluse since the deaths of her husband and son. At first Bess rejects Tommy, but she takes him in. When boredom drives Tommy back to Homewood, he is discovered and pursued. He returns to Bess while in flight, but he is captured and killed before she can offer him a hiding place.

In many ways, *Hiding Place* represents the zenith of the concern with the basic themes that have dominated Wideman's work. History, the sacredness of family, and culture, all present in his earlier novels, merge in this novel. They are powerfully presented through Mother Bess, who as a griot, in the traditional African sense, knows and recites the family's history. She knows *who* Tommy is: "You Lizabeth's son, Thomas. Your grandmother was my sister's girl. You wasn't even close to born when my sister Gert died. Freeda was her oldest. And some say the prettiest in her quiet way. John French your granddaddy. Strutting around in that big brown hat like he owned Homewood. . . . You a Lawson now. You and your three brothers and your sister in the middle."

With Tommy, Wideman reaches the peak of his treatment of his black male characters. As he did with Eddie and Cecil, Wideman burrows beneath the surface of Tommy's external and internal conflicts. Most intense and sensitive is his examination of Tommy's efforts to come to grips with his desire to be a husband to Sarah and a father to Clyde, and at the same time know a certain degree of freedom. He tells Sarah, "Loved you and loved that boy more than anything. But I wouldn't do right. Just couldn't do right to save my soul. Love him [his father] and love you and here I sit like some goddamn stranger drinking coffee at your table. He [his father] had to die to get us in the same room. Now what kind of sense that make?" Speaking about his son, Tommy says:

> Sonny's upstairs, woman. Wasn't for me he wouldn't be here. Ain't much but it's something. Say what you want about me. I'm still his daddy. I was a wrong nigger. Sometimes I knew I was fucking up and sometimes I didn't know. Sometimes I cared about fucking up and sometimes I didn't give a damn. Now that's a wrong nigger. That's me and I'm dealing with that. Got to deal with it. Look back sometimes and I want to cry. But I ain't crying. No time to cry. Don't do no good no way.

Wideman's treatment of Tommy reveals a continued interest with the physical alienation of twentieth-century man who seeks meaning and fulfillment.

Wideman reveals in these two works that he remains interested in a work that is experimental in form. In fact, he is not at all interested in conventional narration. He says, "Form for me, is a kind of adventure. Any writing is a kind of adventure, a form of play, very serious play, but something that I just like to do." In *Hiding Place* he fuses his interest in experimental form with his unending interest in the working imagination. The result is a novel dominated by stream of consciousness and interior monologues. Wideman's Clement demonstrates

that the inarticulate's world is more complex than it appears on the surface.

Form is also important to Wideman's *Damballah,* for each story, as his narrator tells us, is a letter. Addressed to Robby, whose incarceration forces him to lose touch with family, heritage, and culture, Wideman's stories/letters, like *Hiding Place,* focus on the people of Homewood who are Sybela Owens's relatives, giving Robby an intimate understanding of his legacy and family. As he does in *Hiding Place,* Wideman begins *Damballah* with Sybela's family tree.

Perhaps the most important story in the collection is the last one, "The Beginning of Homewood," in which the foundation of the family's history is unraveled by Aunt May and Mother Bess. "This woman, this Sybela Owens our ancestor, bore the surname of her first owner and the Christian name, Sybela, which was probably a corruption of Sybil, a priestess pledged to Apollo." In other stories which provide his kaleidoscopic view of Homewood and Sybela's progeny, Wideman spotlights Elizabeth, whose weekly visits to her imprisoned son, Tommy, cause her to lose, for a brief moment, her faith in God ("Solitary"). But also sensitively drawn are the grandmother, Freeda, whose premonition about death comes true ("The Chinaman"), and the father, Mr. Lawson, who though a waiter is a very proud and loving man ("Across the Wide Missouri").

Sybela Owens was born twenty years after David Walker admonished the black readers of his "The Appeal" to strike a blow against slavery, eleven years after Nat Turner and his men rebelled in Southampton County, Virginia, and ten years before William Wells Brown's *Clotel* first appeared, in which the heroine chooses death over slavery. One hundred and one years later, John Edgar Wideman was born, and forty years after his birth he found in his work a voice to celebrate her life and legacy.

For his most recent novel, *Sent for You Yesterday* (1983), which is once again set in Homewood, Wideman received the P.E.N./Faulkner Award. The jury for this major literary award chose this novel as the best volume of fiction published in 1983 over books by better-known writers such as Bernard Malamud, Cynthia Ozick, and William Kennedy. Scheduled for publication in autumn 1984 is Wideman's first nonfiction book, *Brothers and Keepers,* which he calls "a personal essay about my brother and myself." Wideman is said to hope that the book will lead to parole for his brother, who is in prison.

Holt, Rinehart & Winston ad, Publishers Weekly, *15 June 1984*

What Wideman brings to Afro-American literature and culture is a validation and celebration of Afro-American life. He continues to work to master the techniques of the novel. Additionally in part by having his three most-recent books published as paperback originals, he seeks a wider (black) audience than he has reached. His receiving the P.E.N./Faulkner Award may well enhance his visibility. More important, Wideman has a desire to utilize in his daily life the message his grandfather gave him: "Give them the benefit of the doubt." To Wideman, this means always taking a longer, slower look at people and situations before acting or speaking or writing.

Reference:

John O'Brien, ed., *Interviews with Black Writers* (New York: Liveright, 1973), pp. 213-223.

John A. Williams

(5 December 1925-   )

James L. de Jongh
City College of New York

SELECTED BOOKS: *The Angry Ones* (New York: Ace, 1960); republished as *One for New York* (Chatham, N.J.: Chatham Bookseller, 1975);

Night Song (New York: Farrar, Straus & Cudahy, 1961; London: Collins, 1962);

Africa: Her History, Lands and People (New York: Cooper Square, 1963);

Sissie (New York: Farrar, Straus & Cudahy, 1963); republished as *Journey Out of Anger* (London: Eyre & Spottiswoode, 1965);

The Protectors: Our Battle against the Crime Gangs, by Williams, as J. Dennis Gregory, and Harry Angslinger (New York: Farrar, Straus, 1964);

This Is My Country Too (New York: New American Library/World, 1965; London: New English Library, 1966);

The Man Who Cried I Am (Boston: Little, Brown, 1967; London: Eyre & Spottiswoode, 1968);

Sons of Darkness, Sons of Light: A Novel of Some Probability (Boston: Little, Brown, 1969; London: Eyre & Spottiswoode, 1970);

The Most Native of Sons: A Biography of Richard Wright, by Williams and Dorothy Sterling (Garden City: Doubleday, 1970);

The King God Didn't Save (New York: Coward, McCann, 1970; London: Eyre & Spottiswoode, 1971);

Captain Blackman (Garden City: Doubleday, 1972);

Flashbacks: A Twenty-Year Diary of Article Writing (Garden City: Anchor/Doubleday, 1973);

Mothersill and the Foxes (Garden City: Doubleday, 1975);

Minorities in the City (New York: Harper & Row, 1975);

The Junior Bachelor Society (Garden City: Doubleday, 1976);

!Click Song (New York: Houghton Mifflin, 1982);

Last Flight from Ambo Ber (Highland Park, Ill.: American Association of Ethiopian Jews, 1984).

SCREENPLAY: *Sweet Love, Bitter,* Film 2 Associates, 1967.

TELEVISION: *The Sophisticated Gents,* NBC, 1981.

John A. Williams (photo by Layle Silbert)

OTHER: *The Angry Black,* edited by Williams (New York: Lancer, 1962); republished with new material as *Beyond the Angry Black* (New York: Cooper Square, 1966);

Amistad I, edited by Williams and Charles F. Harris (New York: Knopf, 1970);

Amistad II, edited by Williams and Harris (New York: Knopf, 1971);

Yardbird No. 1, edited by Williams (Berkeley, Cal.: Reed & Young, 1979);

Introduction to Literature, edited by Williams (New York: McGraw-Hill, 1984).

John A. Williams, arguably the finest Afro-American novelist of his generation, is certainly among the most prolific. His fiction is characterized by complex and inventive narrative structures which often employ impending death as the occasion for moving fluidly through time and memory in unexpected ways to reveal a significant human story. Williams's novels are distinguished also by a synthesis of the historical discipline of the biographer with the imaginative freedom of the novelist in order to document with authority and insight the lives of black Americans. Although Williams focuses on the experience of American blacks, he composes on a broad geographic, social, and temporal scale, for he believes that the largely untold experiences of ordinary black men and women are intrinsic to the American experience. John A. Williams, above all, is blunt and uncompromising about the truth as he sees it.

Born in Jackson, Mississippi, in 1925 and raised in Syracuse, New York, John A. Williams joined the navy in 1943. There he felt the scourge of American racism, saw the war in the Pacific fought along racial lines with race riots in Guam, and was confined to the brig for failing to respect the navy's racial protocols. After the war, Williams returned to Syracuse, where he completed high school, married Carolyn Clopton in 1947, and fathered two sons. With the receipt of his B.A. in journalism and English from Syracuse University in 1950 and the dissolution of his marriage in 1952, he turned to writing. After a discouraging series of jobs, first in public relations, then in radio and TV, which took him to Hollywood, Williams moved to New York City, where he worked in publishing as publicity director for Comet Press, a vanity publisher, during 1955 and 1956, and as assistant to the publisher at Abelard-Schuman in 1957 and 1958. In this period, he completed two novels, "One for New York" in 1955 and "The Cool Ones" in 1958. "The Cool Ones," which traces the lives of three black schoolmates in military service during the Korean War, remains unpublished, but "One for New York," retitled *The Angry Ones,* was his first published novel. In the late 1950s and early 1960s, Williams traveled extensively throughout Europe and Africa as a correspondent for *Ebony, Jet, Holiday, Newsweek,* and other magazines.

In 1962, after the publication of *Night Song,* Williams was informed by the American Academy of Arts and Letters of his selection to receive the Prix de Rome, which included a cash award and a year in Rome; but after an interview with the director of the Academy in Rome, he was told without explanation that the award had been disapproved. The reason, Williams felt, was that he was about to marry a white woman. What Williams has called "a vast silence" descended over the whole affair in spite of the efforts of his publisher; but Alan Dugan, who was granted the Prix de Rome, exposed the entire affair in his acceptance remarks at the award ceremony, and, as a consequence of the scandal, the American Academy discontinued its prize for literature. In 1965, Williams married Lorrain Isaac; they have a son named Adam. In 1968, Williams was an interviewer for the "Newsfront" program on National Educational Television; and he began a series of teaching positions at the City College of New York (1968), at the College of the Virgin Islands (summer 1968), at the University of California at Santa Barbara (1972), at Sarah Lawrence College, where he was guest writer (1972), at LaGuardia Community College (1973-1974), at the University of Hawaii (summer 1974), and at Boston University (1978-1979). Since 1979 Williams has been professor of English at Rutgers University.

Williams's nine novels are often grouped in three phases: an initial cautious optimism about the black struggle is followed by a darker vision of racial apocalypse and by a subsequent consciousness of an emerging black unity. The first phase, comprising *The Angry Ones, Night Song,* and *Sissie,* is informed by a muted sense of hope as black protagonists struggle to survive and progress against formidable obstacles. *The Angry Ones* (1960), Williams's first published work, documents the hard knocks of Stephen Hill, an ambitious young black male trying to make a place for himself in New York City in the 1950s after almost succumbing to suicide in Los Angeles. Steve's frustrating attempts to find suitable work across the color line give the novel its context, and his tenure at Rocket, a vanity publisher, is the major focus of the narrative. Racial prejudice is detailed and protested through unconventional but perceptive characters, such as Rollie Culver, the homosexual editor at Rocket who hires Stephen when others will not in order to exploit his vulnerable racial status, and Hadrian Crispus, the would-be Southern writer who tries, albeit ineptly, to win fame and fortune with plantation-school portrayals of Negro stereotypes. For Stephen Hill, the reality of professional and personal failure is ever present. The deterioration of Obie Robertson, his drinking buddy on the staff of a black newspaper, is an object lesson in the despair that results from the segregated job market of New York City. Similarly, the disintegrating marriage of Stephen's white friends, Lint and Bobby, is a foil to the mutual exploitation of Stephen's affair with Lois, who is Jewish. In a drunken stupor, Lint mistakes Lois for Bobby in Stephen's apartment and behaves like a sad parody of a lynch mob. Lint's and Bobby's marital failure underscores the ambiguous potential of marriage to Stephen's childhood lover, Grace, who is now his widowed sister-in-law. Nevertheless, the novel ends on a muted note of hope as a new job materializes for Stephen, and he returns to Grace and the promise of a new generation.

Williams's characteristic narrative procedures are already present in *The Angry Ones.* The fictional events of the story are rooted in biography, in this instance Williams's autobiography; and two suicidal acts—Stephen's aborted attempt, which prompts him to leave Los Angeles for New York, and the fatal gesture of Obie Robertson—frame the novel, anticipating Williams's use of impending death in later works as the sustaining structure for extended journeys through time and memory. Also, in *The Angry Ones* Williams anticipates many of his major themes—guilt, black-Jewish interrelationships, black male and black female tensions, blacks in the military, the institutionalization of racism, and the mutual exploitation of interracial sex—to which he will return in a more sustained form.

Night Song (1961) may have evolved from a biography of Charlie Parker that Williams began with Robert George Reisner and then abandoned, but it is much more than a fictional rendering of the death of a great jazz artist. Williams's second novel begins with an immediacy that represents considerable growth in his narrative power. David Hillary, a failed English professor from an old white American family, is drowning his sorrow and guilt in alcohol on New York City's skid row when he encounters Richie Stokes, a legendary jazz musician known as Eagle. Eagle and the ailing Hillary set out together on an alcoholic binge. They are rescued by Keel Robinson, Eagle's self-appointed protector who has found a kind of personal refuge operating a musician's hangout and coffeehouse in Greenwich Village. With Keel's reluctant cooperation, Eagle nurses Hillary back to health; and Hillary later returns the favor by devising an impromptu ice bath which shocks Eagle back to life after a drug overdose in the flat of a white jazz groupie. Having won acceptance as "The Prof" in the black night world of music and drugs by saving Eagle's life, the white sojourner is guided towards spiritual rebirth and a return to his teaching post by Keel and Eagle. However, a fatally missed encounter between Eagle and Hillary in the professor's college town and Hillary's subsequent silent betrayal of Eagle set the musician

careening toward death by a mysterious overdose. But Keel—and his white girl friend Della, who made love to Hillary without loving him—commit themselves to their conflictive relationship, thus modulating the novel's conclusion with a note of personal illumination. In *Night Song,* the lives of Keel, Hillary, and Eagle intertwine eloquently as they probe the complex anguish of each other's past. Williams's descriptive evocations of the jazz world of black musicians are rich and lucid, and the symbolic and allegorical resonances of the white world of day and the black underworld of night are precise and expressive without seeming obtrusive.

Sissie (1963), Williams's third published novel, explores the lives of Sissie's surviving children, Iris and Ralph, as they reunite in New York City and travel to be with their dying mother, whose struggle to survive has shaped their destinies. While Sissie feels she had done her best, given the racial circumstances of her era, and turns to her children for affirmation, her legacy to her living children seems to be the lesson that love is a weakness in the struggle to survive. Iris has achieved a luxurious career as a Josephine Baker-like expatriate jazz singer, but her need to prove herself with wealth and as a celebrity has cost her Time, the bandleader who left her because she was afraid to let him love her. Ralph, with the therapeutic balm of success on Broadway and a good marriage, has only just come to terms with Sissie's abuse and abandonment of him as a child; but he still worries about the flaw that makes him suspect his happiness. Living in Los Angeles with the man who replaced her husband, Sissie has enjoyed her final years in relative comfort and is proud of her children's success. But she is holding on to life until her children can release her from her guilt. More from compassion than conviction Ralph concedes that he thinks Sissie did her best for them, but Iris refuses even to pretend to forgive. *Sissie*'s three sections are separate memories recalled from each of the three protagonists' point of view, but they amount to a portrait of a black family whose members have found refuge in success yet continue to be driven by the memory of earlier times. Williams provides compelling support for each of their views of the struggle to survive the debilitations of race in America, but he balances them with the memory of Robbie, Sissie's third offspring to survive childhood. Robbie was Sissie's youngest child and her favorite, the bright one who got good grades and wanted to be a doctor, whose eyes shone with a bold, bright, limitless faith in himself. Iris, Ralph, and Sissie all imply that he alone among Sissie's children had an unimpaired capacity for love; but he was killed, ironically, in combat in Korea.

The Man Who Cried I Am; Sons of Darkness, Sons of Light; and *Captain Blackman* reflect Williams's apocalyptic vision of black revolutionary impulses and reactionary white conspiracies in the late 1960s and early 1970s. *The Man Who Cried I Am* (1967), which brought Williams national and international recognition, is set in the fall of 1963, when the Afro-American journalist and novelist Max Reddick comes full circle in his career during the pause between the civil rights march on Washington and the ghetto uprisings. Dying painfully of colon cancer in Amsterdam, Reddick reviews the course of his career as he encounters the biggest story of his life. His worst fears as a writer and a black American are embodied in a contingency plan, code named King Alfred (from Williams's middle name), for moving the minority population of the United States into concentration camps within eight hours of a declared "Minority Emergency." King Alfred symbolizes the racist dynamics Reddick has encountered as a novelist, as a journalist, and as a speech writer for a president who closely resembles John F. Kennedy; and the poisonous racial forces of the body politic crystallized in King Alfred are a macrocosmic reflection of the cancer breaking down Reddick's physical system. Significantly, the biopsy of Max's physical malignancy and his identification of the cancerous racial politics of a reputedly idealistic president—the two points at which the poison of American racism are exposed at the personal and at the historic level—are occasions for the emergence of "the Saminone" (i.e., the Sam in one), an ironic black-talking inner voice which rebuts Reddick's cry "I am." Later, as his cancer and the CIA together fail to keep Reddick from exposing King Alfred to a Malcolm X-like character named Minister Q, the voice of "the Saminone" arises again. "*All you want to do is remind me that I am black. But, goddamn it, I also am,*" Reddick says; but the Saminone is undeniable, "*Whut you done done was a black act. No white man'd ever do that.*" Thus, Reddick's dual responsibility to be an individual artist (to say "*I am*") but also to express the group experience that makes him a writer in the first place (to say "*I am black*") is completed by his publication of the King Alfred plot, an ironic victory denied his mentor and rival Harry Ames, a fictional portrait of Richard Wright.

Sons of Darkness, Sons of Light (1969) is a parable of racial intrigue set in motion when Eugene Browning, a former college professor and second in command of a civil rights organization called the Institute for Racial Justice, makes the uncharacteristic decision to hire a professional killer to murder Carrigan, a policeman who killed an unarmed black boy. Browning wants a surgically precise revenge to instill fear and respect in the oppressors of blacks and forestall the ghetto uprisings which hurt the innocent along with the guilty. The hit is arranged easily enough by an aging crime don who was once denied permission to marry a black woman by the mob; but, because of a series of fascinating plot complications, the effect of Carrigan's assassination is ironic. A would-be revolutionary martyr named Green takes credit for the hit, fifteen cops are murdered by blacks nationwide in a two-week period, and gangs of policemen make reprisals in the ghetto. Furthermore, the head of the Institute for Racial Justice sees "selective assassination" as a professional threat and tries desperately to find the assassin in order to protect his own job security. Carrigan's murder also strikes a curious note in the heart of Itzak Hod, the Israeli who executed the hit. As Hod learns the political implications of his mercenary act, he senses a parallel to his own history as an Irgun terrorist. When Morris Green takes credit for Carrigan's death, Hod decides to execute the unpunished murderer of three black coeds and blame Green. The novel concludes as a band of militants launch a plot to wire the bridges of New York City with explosives and blackmail the Congress of the United States into paying reparations and resigning en masse. The outcome of the militant plot is never learned, but Browning, who has been troubled by professional and domestic problems as well as by the hit, succeeds in putting his life back in order. He abandons the ineffective Institute for Racial Justice, reclaims his wife, makes peace with his daughter and her white boyfriend, and prepares to see his family through the coming race war. *Sons of Darkness, Sons of Light* is an intriguing account of the despair about the American racial situation felt by many in the late 1960s. The novel challenges the commitment to working within the system as futile and debilitating, while expressing skepticism about the militants' desperate and improbable strategy. A decent man, the novel seems to say, can only order his own household and prepare to face the inevitable holocaust resolutely.

Captain Blackman (1972) explores the problematical status of the black soldier in the American military, a recurrent interest of Williams's touched upon in "The Cool Ones" and in an unfinished novel titled "Moody's Squad." In 1970, after petitioning the State Department for permission to visit black troops stationed in Southeast Asia and being denied access, Williams began his most developed fictional treatment of the subject. Abraham Blackman, a career soldier on a scouting mission in Vietnam, is cut down by snipers and experiences a series of hallucinations based on the black military history classes he has been conducting for the members of Charlie Company. In his delirium, Blackman and his comrades in arms in Vietnam become participants in outstanding moments of black military history, from action in the Battle of Bunker Hill in the Revolutionary War and the Battle of New Orleans in the War of 1812 to combat in the Fighting 369th in World War I and the Abraham Lincoln Brigade in the Spanish Civil War. The historic sweep of such episodes asserts the ubiquity and the heroism of the black military in America's wars, but the ironies of this participation are also emphasized. Blackman's rape of a white woman in full view of a helpless white Union soldier demonstrates that the brutalizing consequences of war ignore racial categories, and a haunting meeting with two Indians shows the collaboration of the black "buffalo soldiers" in the genocidal policy of the white generals. Abraham Blackman's progress through black military history modulates from hallucination into memory as Blackman regains consciousness and reviews his own military career since his enlistment during World War II. The systematic elimination of deserting black troops at Tombolo by American soldiers under the command of Lieutenant Whittman witnessed by Blackman places the talented black and the incompetent white officer on separate but unequal tracks, a fact demonstrated again in Korea and Vietnam. *Captain Blackman* concludes somewhat unconvincingly when a light-skinned mulatto from Blackman's Charlie Company becomes one of a large group of such "white" soldiers who manage to take over the nuclear defense system and, thus, control of the country. Whittman, now a general at the Strategic Air Command, goes berserk when he realizes that his racial nemesis has thwarted the racist policies of the military once again.

Mothersill and the Foxes, The Junior Bachelor Society, and *!Click Song* are distinguished by a consciousness of growing black unity and emerging group values which offer a foundation for future

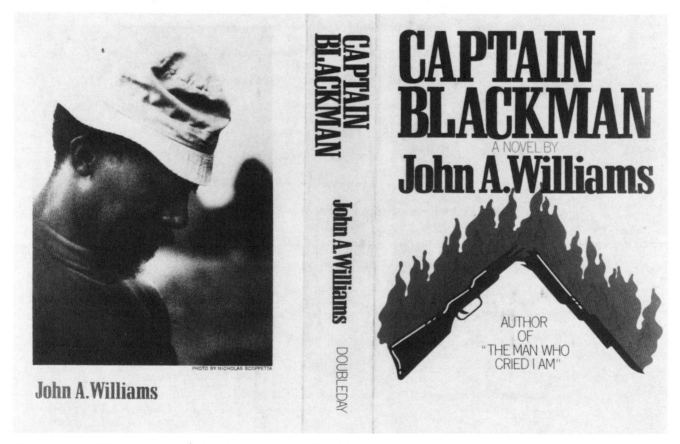

Dust jacket for Williams's 1972 novel, which explores the difficulties black soldiers face in American military service, a recurring theme in Williams's works

-121-

Yes, there was something about being in dress blues. Briskly now
he strode toward his place on the parade grounds, knowing that each
man behind him was skip-hopping into step.

It pleased him to be standing before the regiment, or what was
here of it on the fine May day. The colors whipped and skipped in
the hot Texas wind, and the line of troopers in full dress, sat stiffly
on their well-controlled, handsomely groomed horses, the detachments
told their companies by the colors of their animals, bay, sorrel, black
and calico.

Sweetly to Grierson came the the drumtaps and bugle calls; the
commands from the captains, lieutenants, sergeants; they echoed down
the line of black, brown, ginger and high-yellow men. The Colonel
felt then, as he always did at dress parades, when the flag whipped
and the lines moved evenly, that the Army was a special thing for
special men. There was honor here, he thought, and courage, and
devotion to duty, and enough glory for every man in an Army uniform,
regardless of his color. And Grierson was confident then, so much so,
that for seconds at a time his eyes grew wet, that the Army would
one day soon sing of these black men and their bravery, and take them
to its bosom without reservation for, even excluding the Civil War in
which they'd done well, they'd been outstanding in this No-Man's-Land.
He had the faith that his Army would make up for its past deeds.

Now Alvord with his heavy-butted walk, came over the grass to
within five precise paces of Grierson, threw a salute and bellowed:

"All present or accounted for, Sir."

Grierson returned the salute, wheeled, and squared and walked
to the reviewing position, his aides at his heels. Once again the

Page from the typescript for Captain Blackman

progress. *Mothersill and the Foxes* (1975) is the odyssey of Odell Mothersill: social services worker, adoption agency supervisor, Peace Corps administrator, OEO administrator, and college professor. His career takes him from New York City to Africa and the Caribbean, but the essential character of his odyssey is sexual. Well over a dozen different affairs, from prepubescent encounters with his sister and her twelve-year-old babysitter to fleeting escapades in a broom closet, are described; but these episodes, ranging from comic and farcical to perverse and bizarre, are only the highlights of an extravagant love life taking Odell past mass murder, suicide, and madness to the brink of incest. What seems to be a picaresque narrative comes full circle unexpectedly as Odell finds serenity in his daughter Candace Cone, the love child of a hilarious sexual bout with Mrs. Cohen, a prim and proper black housewife from St. Albans. Odell's social service odyssey and his sexual adventurism are revealed as an unconscious search for the fleeting home life which existed only when his father, a sleeping car porter, came home between runs and, also, for Belle, an abandoned child Odell's parents rescued but had to give up. The novel concludes when Odell's odyssey finally takes him back, as any proper odyssey should, to domestic tranquility with a faithful, loving wife, beautiful children, and even a herdsman (a dairyman named Gomes) to round out the Homeric motif.

The Junior Bachelor Society (1976) describes the reunion of the Junior Bachelor Society to celebrate the seventieth birthday of their high school coach and spiritual father Chappie Davis in Central City, the fictional town first described in *Sissie*. One by one the lives of the various teammates are reviewed as the testimonial celebration approaches. By and large those who moved away have been outstanding successes. Ralph Joplin, Sissie's son, is a renowned Broadway playwright. D'Artagnan Foxx is a singer in the tradition of Paul Robeson, and Clarie Henderson is an English professor at a West Coast university. The Bachelors who remained in Central City have also made respectable places for themselves. Bubbles and Cudjo are prosperous blue-collar workers in a local factory. Snake is a city commissioner. Shurley owns a successful bar, and Ezzard Jackson is the senior editor of a black photojournal. One Bachelor is bisexual and a drunk, another beats his wife, and a third is chafing under the thumb of a black tycoon who enjoys oppressing his employees; but thanks to the influence of Chappie Davis and the JBS, these Bachelors have not turned out too badly. The one exception is

Moon, a pimp in Los Angeles who has killed a corrupt cop and is on the run. Moon's possible arrival at the reunion attracts Swoop, who was always excluded from the Bachelors and still is shunned because he has become an unscrupulous policeman. Swoop plans to advance his own career by arresting Moon and, at the same time, humiliating the Bachelors. In spite of their fears and respective human failings, the Bachelors confront the threat to Moon together and reaffirm the communal values of their youth. But while Moon can trust in the Bachelors' silence, he has seen enough of the other side of human nature to be fairly certain that Swoop will betray him. So while the others reaffirm their fraternity over coffee, Moon murders Swoop in cold blood. Thus the Bachelors' sentimentality is counterposed by Moon's cynicism, and the reader is left to strike his own balance between them. Although the structure of *The Junior Bachelor Society* is commonplace and predictable, the crisp, knowing vignettes of the Bachelors constitute a rare, composite portrait of middle-class Afro-American society and its transition in less than a generation from the debilitating poverty depicted in *Sissie*.

!Click Song (1982) is the black novelist William Cato Douglass's journey through the past in the aftermath of the suicide of his friend, a white novelist named Paul Cummings. Douglass and Cummings begin together as writing students on the GI Bill and proceed in tandem as intimate friends for a time. Cummings wins enormous wealth and celebrity by writing about his return to his Jewish roots in works of ever declining quality, while Douglass's commitment to the truth of his blackness leads him to write better and better books which receive ever diminishing rewards and recognition. The intertwined careers of Cummings and Douglass offer a harsh and compelling indictment of what Williams sees as the greed, venality, and indifference to good writing of the publishing industry. But writing itself is affirmed by Douglass as one of the few genuine instrumentalities of hope and human possibility, because it has given meaning and satisfaction to his life despite the anguish of his struggles. For much of the novel, Douglass seems to be facing death. Its presence is sensed and perhaps even invited, but even as it is occurring, his actual dying eludes him except through analogies and dreams. Douglass's "strangely sharp and wonderfully sweet" gasp of breath, which ends the novel, may either be his last instant of awareness as he dies or his affirmation of life's worth and his willingness to go on, or both.

The title of *!Click Song* alludes to songs in the

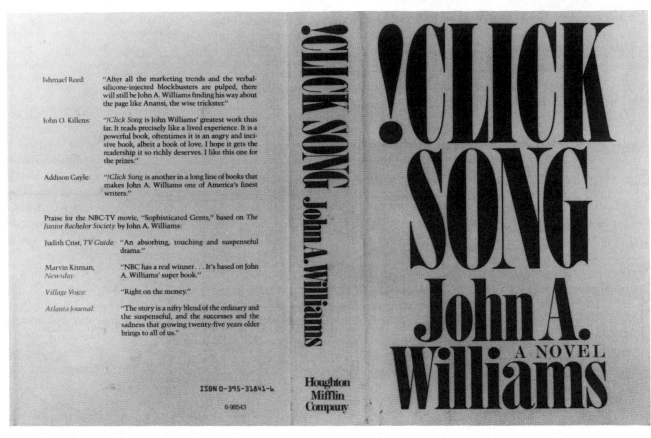

Dust jacket for Williams's 1982 novel, the title of which refers to the clicking sounds in some African tribal languages

tribal languages of black South Africans, for like them, this novel communicates with clicking sounds: the numberless instances of individual realization that sound within oneself or the occurrences of mutual recognition that pass between oneself and others, friends and enemies alike; the infantile sucking sounds of a first son in his crib; the defiant tongue clicks of black museum security guards who conspire with Douglass to subvert the museum's Eurocentrism; the number-crunching clatter of Book, the computer that reduces an author's work to digital codes and sales statistics; and the click of the empty and jammed guns which punctuate Douglass's final dream about his death. *!Click Song* is at least the equal of Williams's other masterpiece, *The Man Who Cried I Am*. The emotional power, the fluid structuring of time, the resonant synthesis of fiction and history are similar. But the novelist's mastery is greater, for Williams's technique here is seamless and invisible. The illusion of a fully experienced human life seems even more compelling, because the familiar issues of Williams's other novels are present, not as subjects

for thematic elaboration but as ineluctable elements of daily human activity.

The novels of John A. Williams treat a variety of social or political issues but are unified, beyond protest and apology, by the effort to correct history and dispel common myths and misunderstandings about black Americans. Williams uses biographical and historical data to lead the reader away from prejudice and misperception to fuller understanding. His black protagonists are professionals, separated by education from other blacks and by their skin color from full participation in American society, but they have the courage to battle themselves and their ambiguous status. The novels of John A. Williams are unified also by involvement in the tensions and possibilities of love, for love in its various forms is the human capacity offering hope and possibility which Williams affirms in the face of the personal anguish and social difficulties he feels compelled to explore in his novels.

Williams's nonfiction recapitulates the interests and concerns of his novels. *Africa: Her History, Lands and People* (1963) confronts myths and historical distortions to demonstrate that blacks have an ancient heritage. *The Protectors: Our Battle against the Crime Gangs* (1964) by Harry J. Angslinger, former U.S. Commissioner of Narcotics, with J. Dennis Gregory (a pseudonym Williams constructed from the initial for his first name plus the first names of his two oldest sons) depicts FBI tactics which are important elements in *The Man Who Cried I Am* and includes an intriguing chapter about the demise of black entertainers like Charlie Parker and Billie Holiday. *This Is My Country Too* (1965), the journal of Williams's odyssey across America commissioned by *Holiday* magazine to be a kind of black version of John Steinbeck's *My Travels with Charley*, includes interviews with blacks on a base in North Dakota reflecting Williams's concern with black soldiers in the American military. *The King God Didn't Save* (1970), a much-criticized profile of Martin Luther King, Jr., specifies Williams's reservations about Dr. King's philosophy of nonviolence and indicts his failure to perceive the general manipulation of black leaders by the institutional arms of white power. *The Most Native of Sons* (1970), portrays Richard Wright, unlike King, as being constantly vigilant against the institutionalized racism of America because of his firsthand knowledge of poverty and deprivation, his self-education, his skepticism about his own instant celebrity, and his sympathy with the black masses and their espousal of black power. *Flashbacks: A Twenty-Year Diary of Article Writing* (1973), Williams's retrospective miscellany of short nonfiction, includes "We Regret to Inform You," which describes the Prix de Rome experience he had replayed in fictional terms in *The Man Who Cried I Am*. *Minorities in the City* (1975) updates Williams's sense of the status of the black experience in America. And *Last Flight from Ambo Ber*, (1984), a drama first produced in Boston in 1981, describes the struggle for recognition of the Falashas, the Ethiopian Jews, from the efforts of Jacques Faitlovich in Paris in the 1900s through the creation of the state of Israel.

John A. Williams's earliest novels were hailed as auguries of a major literary talent, and his later efforts have confirmed that early promise. *The Man Who Cried I Am,* universally acclaimed as a powerful and innovative literary masterpiece, has earned Williams a place among the first rank of American writers, and *!Click Song*, thought by many critics to be an even greater achievement, has reaffirmed his critical standing. John A. Williams's mastery of the novel as "a political and historical document as well as a literary one" has been celebrated by Addison

Gayle, among others; and C. Lynn Munro praises Williams for his steadfast attempt "to demythologize black history, to rupture the stereotypes which thwart real understanding and to impress upon the reader—black and white—the need to understand the past and its effect upon the present and the future." Williams's integrity remains uncompromised, and the truth of his provocative analysis of the status of black America has never been challenged effectively. In spite of this, or perhaps because of it, John A. Williams can still be called "probably the most important—and least recognized—Negro writer in America today," as he was by the *New York Times Book Review* in 1969, for Williams has been denied the full degree of support and acceptance some critics think his work deserves. "John A. Williams can write circles around those permanent token writers who are so beloved by the critical and academic bureaucracy...," Ishmael Reed states in his *San Francisco Chronicle* review of *!Click Song,* "But Williams will never become a permanent token, for not only does he write well, he tells the truth in a society which prefers that its permanent slaves lie to it." No definitive assessment of such an active and prolific author as John A. Williams is possible at this time, but one may expect him to remain "faithful to his committed task—to bridge the racial gap by telling the truth about both sides." Williams's next projects are a short novel, "The Berhama Account," and a book on the life and work of Richard Pryor.

References:

David Boroff, "Blue Note for Bigotry," *Saturday Review,* 46 (30 March 1963): 49;

W. Frances Browne, "The Black Artist in New York: An Interview with John A. Williams," *Centerpoint,* 1, 3 (1975): 71-76;

Jerry H. Bryant, "John A. Williams: The Political Use of the Novel," *Critique,* 16, 3 (1975): 81-100;

William M. Burke, "The Resistance of John A. Williams: *The Man Who Cried I Am,*" *Critique,* 15, 3 (1973): 5-14;

Earl Cash, *John A. Williams: The Evolution of a Black Writer* (New York: Third Press, 1974);

Addison Gayle, Jr., *The Way of the New World* (Garden City: Doubleday, 1975), pp. 277-288;

David Henderson, "*The Man Who Cried I Am:* a Critique," in *Black Expression,* edited by Addison Gayle, Jr. (New York: Weybright & Talley, 1969), pp. 365-371;

Wolfgang Karrer, "Multiperspective and the

Hazards of Integration: John Williams' *Night Song* (1961)," in *The Afro-American Novel Since 1960* (Amsterdam: Grüner, 1982), pp. 75-101;

Clarence Major, *The Dark and the Feeling* (New York: Joseph Opaku, 1974), pp. 85-94;

C. Lynn Munro, "Culture and Quest in the Fiction of John A. Williams," *College Language Association Journal*, 22 (1970): 71-100;

John O'Brien, "Seeking a Humanist Level: Interview with John A. Williams," *Arts in Society*, 10 (1973): 94-99;

John M. Reilly, "The Reconstruction of Genre as Entry into Conscious History," *Black American Literature Forum*, 13 (1979): 3-6;

Noel Schraufnagel, *From Apology to Protest: The Black American Novel* (De Land, Fla.: Everett/ Edwards, 1973), pp. 147-151, 189-193;

Anneliese H. Smith, "A Pain in the Ass: Metaphor in John A. Williams' *The Man Who Cried I Am*," *Studies in Black Literature*, 3, 3 (1972): 25-27;

Ronald Walcott, "*The Man Who Cried I Am*: Crying in the Dark," *Studies in Black Literature*, 3, 1 (1972): 24-32.

Papers:

The manuscripts of John A. Williams are held by the Syracuse University Library, the Yale University Library, and the author.

Charles Stevenson Wright
(4 June 1932-   )

Joe Weixlmann
Indiana State University

BOOKS: *The Messenger* (New York: Farrar, Straus, 1963; London: Souvenir Press, 1964);
The Wig (New York: Farrar, Straus & Giroux, 1966; London: Souvenir Press, 1967);
Absolutely Nothing to Get Alarmed About (New York: Farrar, Straus & Giroux, 1973).

Charles Stevenson Wright's passionately idiosyncratic books have led to his being variously labeled by critics and reviewers attempting to harness his bountiful literary imagination in a phrase. He has, with some justification, been called a satirist, a black humorist, a surrealist, an experimentalist—even a phenomenologist. By virtue of the probing examinations of contemporary America which can be found in his slender, quasi-autobiographical novel *The Messenger* (1963); his devastating fantasy *The Wig* (1966); and the overtly autobiographical *Absolutely Nothing to Get Alarmed About* (1973), Wright has earned an intense literary following. With Amiri Baraka's *The System of Dante's Hell*, Barry Beckham's *Runner Mack*, and Ishmael Reed's *The Free-Lance Pallbearers*, Wright's work adds tragic clarity to the nightmare of contemporary Afro-American existence.

Charles Stevenson Wright was born on 4 June 1932 and raised about twenty-five miles west of

Columbia, Missouri, in New Franklin, whose approximately two hundred blacks comprised about one-quarter of the town's population. His parents were Stevenson, a laborer, and Dorothy Hughes Wright. In Wright's early childhood, his mother separated from her husband, a handsome, athletic man. After her death, when Wright was four, he was brought up by his maternal grandparents. The couple's only grandchild, young Wright commanded a copious amount of attention, and he would, in time, acquire his grandfather's passion for reading, eventually becoming a "newspaper fanatic." Wright remembers examining an issue of *Life* magazine in his early teens and being startled to see a feature on Richard Wright's *Black Boy;* the coincidence of the name, coupled with the notion that a black author could gain recognition, registered deeply in him. But books were not readily available to the black inhabitants of what Charles Wright describes as the "loosely segregated" community in which he was raised. The white school in New Franklin had books, whereas the one-room facility in which he was educated, until withdrawing from school during his sophomore year of high school, didn't even have a lavatory.

Having left school, Wright hitchhiked to California and, upon his return to Missouri, mostly "hung out" before being drafted into the army in 1952, although he did spend several summers in eastern Illinois at the Lowney Handy Writers Colony in Marshall, whose first and most renowned student was James Jones. Wright views the two years he spent in the military rather positively. He subsequently learned to deal effectively with people, developed a heightened degree of shrewdness and toughness, became a cook, and was able to travel to Asia. Upon being released from the army in 1954, Wright settled for several years in St. Louis, his living expenses paid in part by a twenty-six-week armed forces stipend; the remainder of his income came from his work as a stockboy. He subsequently returned to the Handy Writers Colony, where he composed what he now regards as a "very bad," very realistic Korean War novel that Putnam's rejected—and for which he never attempted to find another publisher.

Wright was drawn to New York City in the late 1950s, where he held a variety of jobs, most notably that of messenger, while continuing to write. His second novel, "No Regrets," a first-person account of an affair between a black beatnik from the East Village and an upper-class white girl whom he had impregnated, was rejected by several publishers. Both Wright's copy of the manuscript and another in Norman Mailer's possession are now lost. Finally, with the idea for *The Messenger* in mind, Wright had a salable commodity. Within a week of his presenting the concept to Farrar, Straus—the last publisher to consider "No Regrets"—he was given a contract for *The Messenger,* which he wrote between May and August 1962. The book was published in the summer of 1963, its dust jacket sporting endorsements from such luminaries as James Baldwin and Kay Boyle.

The Messenger was warmly received by reviewers, sold quite well, and developed a following for Wright. Presumably James Baldwin's reaction to the novel was typical of the response many readers had to the candid view of big-city life in *The Messenger:* "No matter what the city fathers may say, this *is* New York; this is the way we live here now." Others found the book's loose, episodic structure and Wright's skillful manipulation of language attractive as well.

The novel's protagonist, Charles Stevenson,

James Baldwin says: "I read *The Messenger* in one sitting—when I should, of course, have been doing something else. It's a very beautiful job, and reads with an urgency which is all the more painful for being, in the main, so quiet and so taut. It sometimes seems to be scarcely a book at all, but a *happening:* it seemed to me that I could hear the music, smell the smells, knew all those streets and all those people, and was attacked again by that wonder which attacks us so incessantly in life. He's caught the New York laconicism behind which so much anguish growls, and almost the exact shade of that awful half-light in which so many people are struggling to live. And he doesn't judge them; he accepts them; perhaps it's for this reason that the distance between ourselves and the people in this book seems so minimal. And, no matter what the city fathers may say, this is New York; this is the way we live here now. Charles Wright is a terrific writer, and I hope he goes the distance and lives to be 110."

Lucy Freeman says: "A poignant portrait of a young man without a country or even a city, Charles Wright's story is a sad, tragic tale, full of sound and fury but signifying much. The writer mirrors what countless other young men and women, white as well as Negro, feel today as they try to fill the emptiness of their lives with a constant search for pleasure in pads, seeking insensibility through liquor, and drugs, and sex. There is one difference, however, between Charles Wright and most of the others—*he* is a fine writer."

Kay Boyle says: "For some time now, a new and ruthlessly honest literature has been emerging from the lonely horror of the junkie and homosexual world of New York. Charles Wright's *The Messenger* is the most recent and in many ways the most moving of these statements from our contemporary lower depths. These lower depths are not to be ignored. Wright's book, which tells with young cynicism and bravado of the corruption of the hearts and bodies of men, is important as fresh, unencumbered writing and important as social comment as well. It is not just one more book about perversion, and about the Negro's place in the society of outcasts. It is a courageous and heartbreaking document in which even the most transient figure takes on and retains a terrifying life."

The Messenger

Charles Wright

Farrar, Straus and Company

T h e M e s s e n g e r
a work of fiction by Charles Wright

"And, no matter what the city fathers may say, this is New York; this is the way we live here now."
—James Baldwin

Dust jacket for Wright's autobiographical first novel

exhibits more than a nominal similarity to the author of *The Messenger*. In writing the book Wright drew so extensively on his childhood in central Missouri, his military service in Korea, and his life as a writer and messenger in New York that the points at which fact ceases and fiction begins are virtually impossible to determine. Through Wright's first-person, often present-tense narration, the reader is allowed inside the psyche of a twenty-nine-year-old, fair-skinned black Manhattanite who individualizes issues of general, not just personal, significance—most saliently, the isolation and alienation produced in persons who fall prey to America's social, economic, and racial caste systems.

The presence of the gay men, drug addicts, transvestites, male and female prostitutes, alcoholics, and con artists who provide the background against which the action of *The Messenger* is played out is not gratuitous, nor is Wright's inclusion of them an act of sensationalism. Many such persons populate our cities, as do the phonies, the gigolos, the matronly coquettes, the stockbrokers, the sexually unfulfilled women, the impotent men, the college students, the wife beaters, and the lovable, precocious children Wright also depicts. Stevenson comments: "I have always liked to believe that I am not too far removed from the heart of America (I have a twenty-five dollar U.S. Savings Bond) and I am proud of almost everything American. Yet I'm drowning in this green cornfield. . . . This country has split open my head with a golden eagle's beak."

Working for a messenger service in Rockefeller Center, the protagonist often finds himself on the edges of power: He carries scripts to wealthy actors; he stands beside nose-picking stockbrokers on Wall Street and watches huge sums of money change hands. Yet his wages are meager. His boss, waving an expensive cigar, schools him in the American Dream, and Stevenson concludes that "the sin is believing, hoping."

Then, too, his mulatto complexion makes him a racial outcast—or, to be more precise, doubly a racial outcast. He is neither black nor white, but "beige . . . a minority within a minority . . . the result of generations of bastard Anglo-saxon, African, Black-creek, and Choctaw Indian blood." Increasingly Stevenson comes to view his future dimly, indulging the consciously Faulknerian awareness that he is "the last of the Negro, southwestern, Missouri Stevensons" with "nothing to look forward to but my death."

The naturalistic city of New York, which "accept[s] victory or defeat with the same marvelous indifference," only serves to amplify his despondency, and he knows that he must escape it if he is to retain his sanity. Yet the city is also a part of him; it possesses an offbeat vitality which he does not wish to forfeit. And that is where Wright leaves his protagonist—caught between conflicting pulls. Although Stevenson is determined to take a bus out of New York in an attempt to leave "the fears, confusion, and pain of being alive" behind, the reader cannot help wondering how such an action would truly ameliorate the protagonist's condition. He had, after all, previously escaped *to* New York from Missouri because *its* realities failed to complement his longings. If, as critics have argued, *Invisible Man* opened up new intellectual space for the Afro-American novel by countering the negation implicit in Richard Wright's "The Man Who Lived Underground," then *The Messenger* might be seen as providing a critique of Ellison which narrows that space back down.

The direction open to Afro-American writing in the 1960s and beyond depends less on prescribed forms, an awareness Wright demonstrates ample understanding of in his second published novel, *The Wig*, in which realism yields to fantasy as the book's principal dramatic mode. Heartened by the reception of *The Messenger*, Wright combined travel abroad with writing, eventually producing a draft, written in the third person, of what was to become *The Wig*. Back in New York in February and March of 1965, Wright spent twenty-nine intense days during which he provided the novel with its first-person point of view and otherwise extensively revised the manuscript. "That was the happiest period of my life," Wright told interviewer John O'Brien. Even today, Wright feels as though he tapped the deepest and truest—indeed, the most prophetic—sources of his being in creating *The Wig*. Wright's publisher, Farrar, Straus and Giroux, like Wright, anticipated that the book would be greeted by raves when it appeared in February of 1966. But not only were most of the reviews that *The Wig* received mixed, many influential periodicals, most notably *Publishers Weekly*, failed to review the novel.

Whatever disputes might arise over *The Wig*, there is no denying that it is atypical of the American fiction of the mid-1960s and *most* atypical of the Afro-American fiction of that era. Wright's use of hyperbole and fantasy, while affording a metaphoric vision of reality as it is frequently perceived, effects a radical displacement of reality as it is commonly portrayed. *The Wig* encapsulates a familiar theme within an unaccustomed covering, an easily decodable message within an unusual form. While this is, undeniably, the principal reason for the novel's being so well regarded today, one can imagine that the book might have produced no small amount of consternation among those introduced to it in 1966.

Set "in an America of tomorrow," *The Wig* tells the story of a twenty-one-year-old black Harlemite named Lester Jefferson who Silky Smooths his hair in the illusive hope that his pomaded "wig" will have the power to purchase him a ticket on the American Success Express. A real American with a famous surname and a hyperbolically humble past ("My father had learned to read and write extremely well at the age of thirty-six. He died while printing the letter Z for me"), "a true believer in The Great Society" of Lyndon B. Johnson, Lester is determined to work his way to the top in the manner of Americans before him: "I'd turn the other cheek, cheat, steal, take the fifth amendment, walk bareassed up Mr. Jones's ladder, and state firmly that I was too human." But none of his efforts reach fruition. Lester first teams with Little Jimmie Wishbone, whose cinematic Uncle Tomming had for a time brought him immense wealth, to perform for Paradise Records. But the duo proves to be "a disgrace to your colored brethren *and* to this great republic! Why, you poor slobs can't even carry a tune."

Undaunted, and desirous of winning the affections of The Deb, a mercenary black prostitute who is unsettled by Lester's hair being "better" than hers and whom Lester idealizes as his "all-American girl," he takes a relatively high-paying, but patently demeaning, job as a "chicken man." Crawling around Manhattan on his hands and knees in a chicken suit with electrified feathers, ten hours a day, five and a half days a week, he advertises a Southern-fried chicken restaurant, crying, "*Eat me. Eat me. All over town*"—only to learn from his "sponsor," Mr. Fishback, that The Deb has died in a traffic accident and that Lester's self-debasement has been pointless. Utterly despondent, Lester allows Fishback to render him impotent. If *The Messenger* offers a critique of Ellisonian optimism, *The Wig* says No! in thunder. Buying the promises of America, Wright wishes his readers to realize, is too expensive for the black male. To do so, he must sacrifice his identity and, ultimately, his manhood—and both in vain.

Conrad Knickerbocker, whose reviews Wright had long respected and one of those to whom *Absolutely Nothing to Get Alarmed About* is dedicated, wrote in the *New York Times* that *The Wig* was "a brutal, exciting, and necessary book." Ishmael Reed called

The Wig "one of the most underrated novels written by a black person in this century" and credits the book with influencing his prose technique. And critics have, in retrospect, tended to regard *The Wig* as Wright's most significant accomplishment. Yet despite all this, one senses that the extreme elation which Wright experienced following the book's completion, coupled with the general ambivalence with which most reviewers responded to the novel, so depleted the author's spirit that he has yet to recover fully. "I was destroyed by *The Wig*," Wright recently remarked. "That was my retarded child," he told O'Brien. "I had to get away."

When not "hiding out" in New York, get away he did—to Paris, Morocco, Veracruz, and other foreign and domestic locales. But despite all his physical wandering, Wright's literary psyche remained firmly planted in New York City. It is unsurprising that the nonfictional pieces that flowed from his pen in the years immediately following the appearance of *The Wig* found their way into the *Village Voice,* in his "Wright's World" column. Collected, amended, and supplemented, these works came to comprise the book he called "Black Studies: A Journal," a title which the publicity department at Farrar, Straus and Giroux objected to so strenuously that, at the suggestion of Wright's editor, it was changed to *Absolutely Nothing to Get Alarmed About.* "The salesmen," Wright has wryly noted, "thought that it would get put on the wrong bookshelves."

Most reviews of *Absolutely Nothing to Get Alarmed About* were lukewarm, although it did receive good notices in the *New Yorker* and, especially, the *New York Times Book Review,* in which David Freeman commented cogently on the novelistic quality of Wright's journal. Rooted in fact, fertilized by a fictive intelligence, *Absolutely Nothing to Get Alarmed About* bristles with the same sort of scenes that one finds in Wright's novels. There are clear linkages of setting and theme that bind the three books together.

"*F. Scott Fitzgerald's sunny philosophy had always appealed to me,*" Wright observes in the opening section of his journal. "*I believed in the future of the country. At fourteen, I had written: 'I am the future.' Twenty-six years later – all I want to do is excrete the past and share with you a few Black Studies.*" Manhattan's drug users, its male and female prostitutes, its hyperforceful policemen and underinquisitive detectives, its murderers, its frequenters of VD clinics, even the dogs whose excrement litter its parks and sidewalks—these, plus America's unstinting racism, have rid Charles Stevenson Wright of his illu-

Dust jacket for Wright's 1973 collection of essays. At the suggestion of the publishers' sales manager, the title was changed from "Black Studies: A Journal."

ing jobs, in New York City and the Catskills, which keep him financially solvent. And writing of (and to) the then recently deceased Langston Hughes, Wright observes that "he did not sell out to whitey with his simple tales. He did not sell out to himself. . . . He created something that was real. . . . he had to eat and buy shoes. And none of it was easy. And it seems to me, Langston, that you knew what your literary black sons haven't learned: it's a closed game played on a one-way street."

Asked what's wrong, at the end of *The Messenger,* Charles Stevenson lies: " 'Nothing,' I said. 'Absolutely nothing.' " Having just been emasculated with a red hot poker at the close of *The Wig,* Lester Jefferson is asked how he feels, and he sardonically responds, "I'm beginning to feel better already." Charles Stevenson Wright concludes *Absolutely Nothing to Get Alarmed About* with a letter to Nathanael West, First Comfort Station, Purgatorial Heights: "Now Absurdity and Truth pave the parquet of my mind. The pain is akin to raw alcohol on the testicles. But I'm not complaining."

There is plenty to get alarmed about in Charles Wright's literary world. On the one hand, it records, in excruciating detail, the result of deferred and destroyed black dreams. On the other hand, it warns of the consequences that await the destroyers: "Did Frankenstein's monster kill his master?," Wright asks an old friend near the middle of *Absolutely Nothing to Get Alarmed About.* Receiving an affirmative answer, Wright said, "Yes, oh my God, yes! what a nice ending for a story."

Since the appearance of *Absolutely Nothing to Get Alarmed About,* Wright's literary profile has remained low. He has completed "Erotic Landslide," a short-story collection; has written an unpublished, unproduced play entitled "Madam Is on the Veranda"; and plans to do a novel based on the life of Jean Rhys. But there has been no major published work from him in over ten years. Yet if Wright's critical reputation were to rest on his output to date, he would be remembered.

sions as surely as Mr. Fishback rids Lester Jefferson of his masculinity at the end of *The Wig.* Add to these personal experiences the assassinations of John and Robert Kennedy, Malcolm X, Martin Luther King, and George Jackson, plus the horror of Vietnam and the failure of the Great Society program, what the once-optimistic Wright is left with is a pessimistic observation which both illuminates his state of mind and explains his choice of subject matter: "It seems somehow appropriate to mention human excrement and cannibalism as mankind prepares not to scale the summits but to take the downward path into the great valley of the void."

Never quite despairing, but constantly stoned—on booze, pot, pills—Wright dramatizes the pain of being black in America. Dedicated to three dead littcrateurs, *Absolutely Nothing to Get Alarmed About* also highlights the plight of the black author. Wright alludes repeatedly to the dishwash-

References:

Frances S. Foster, "Charles Wright: Black Black Humorist," *CLA Journal,* 15 (1971): 44-53;

Jerome Klinkowitz, *Literary Disruptions: The Making of a Post-Contemporary American Fiction* (Urbana: University of Illinois Press, 1975), pp. 177-183;

Eberhard Kreutzer, "Dark Ghetto Fantasy and the Great Society: Charles Wright's *The Wig,*" in *The Afro-American Novel Since 1960,* edited by Peter Bruck and Wolfgang Kaarer (Amsterdam: Grüner, 1982), pp. 145-166;

A. Robert Lee, "Making New: Styles of Innovation in the Contemporary Black American Novel," in *Black Fiction: New Studies in the Afro-American Novel Since 1945,* edited by A. Robert Lee (London: Vision Press, 1980), pp. 222-250;

John O'Brien, "Charles Wright," in *Interviews with Black Writers* (New York: Liveright, 1973), pp. 245-257;

Max F. Schulz, "The Aesthetics of Anxiety; and, The Conformist Heroes of Bruce Jay Friedman and Charles Wright," in *Black Humor Fiction of the Sixties: A Pluralistic Definition of Man and His World* (Athens: Ohio University Press, 1973), pp. 91-123;

Robert P. Sedlack, "Jousting with Rats: Charles Wright's *The Wig,*" *Satire Newsletter,* 7, no. 1 (1969): 37-39.

Sarah Elizabeth Wright
(9 December 1928-   )

Virginia B. Guilford
Bowie State College

BOOKS: *Give Me A Child,* by Wright and Lucy Smith (Philadelphia: Kraft, 1955);

This Child's Gonna Live (New York: Delacorte, 1969).

OTHER: "Roadblocks to the Development of the Negro Writer," in *The American Negro Writer and His Roots,* selected papers from The First Conference of American Negro Writers (New York: American Society of African Culture, 1960), pp. 71-73;

"Urgency" and "Window Pictures," in *Beyond the Blues,* edited by Rosey E. Pool (Detroit, Mich.: Broadside Press, 1971), pp. 184-185.

PERIODICAL PUBLICATIONS: "I Have Known Death," *Tomorrow,* 10 (3 November 1950): 46;

"Until They Have Stopped," *Freedomways,* 5, no. 3 (1965): 378-379;

"The Negro Woman in American Literature," *Freedomways,* 6 (Winter 1966): 8-10;

"Lament of a Harlem Mother," *American Pen,* 4 (Spring 1972): 23-27;

"Black Writers' Views of America," *Freedomways,* 19, no. 3 (1979): 161-162.

Sarah E. Wright has not been a prolific writer, but she is a significant one. Poet, novelist, perennial student of the arts, teacher of writing, lecturer, social activist, mother of two children, and wife, she has "paid her dues" in the last thirty-three years of her combat with the forces that would deny her the opportunity to tell it "like it damn sure is." Sarah E. Wright is a fighter who bubbles with life: she is committed not only to her personal mission of "ex-

tracting from life that which is illuminating," but to extending herself unselfishly to others in their endeavor to articulate the "truths" paramount to human survival and being. Her intense sense of life and artistic integrity have, in some ways, limited her own creative output, but she is leaving her mark in other ways. "What is very special about Ms. Wright is that she is not only a gifted artist, but she also has the unique ability to transmit her craftsmanship and artistry to others. . . . Hers is a talent that instructs and inspires," notes John Oliver Killens. Other such commendations from universities, colleges, libraries, and community organizations at which she has spoken, conducted writing workshops, or served as writer-in-residence affirm Killens's insight into the wholeness of Wright as a creative writer, a writer who believes that one of the artist's responsibilities is to look wide, deep, high, and low in order to see the whole and viably render the significant, however painful it might be to shatter facades and recognize others' humanity.

Sarah Elizabeth was born on 9 December 1928 to Willis Charles and Mary Amelia Moore Wright in Wetipquin, Maryland. She is the third of nine children—six boys, one of whom is deceased, and three girls. Her father—who died in March 1982—was an oysterman, barber, farmer, pianist, and organist; and Mrs. Wright, always homemaker and mother, contributed to the family's income as barber and farm and factory worker. For sixty years, the Wrights confronted the adversities of life, rearing their children during one of the most repressive periods for blacks in America and providing a model of fortitude that colors Wright's depiction of the laborers of the world.

Notable is Wright's almost sermonic articulation of the impact her parents' philosophy of life, sense of humanity, and endurance had on her. Her father radiated an aura of peace and serenity which stemmed from his Christian wholeness and love of the beautiful, the latter symbolized by his devotion to sacred music. Paralleling the personality of Jacob Upshur in *This Child's Gonna Live,* he was uncomplaining no matter the adversity and believed in the "nobility of labor." When Wright recalls her father's "integrity, selflessness, gentility, and steadfastness in devotion and performance of duty," she becomes enraged by the Moynihan report on the black family and other social and literary works which demean the black man, provide half-truths and fail to render the complexity of black life in America. Consequently, Wright frequently presents her father as a symbol of the roots to which the black youth must return, and she is currently writing a poetic essay on his "sense of being." Two of Mrs. Wright's greatest gifts to her daughter might have been a view of the female as a social bulwark and her indignation at injustice of any kind, the latter being one of the unifying themes of Wright's poetry and novel. Additionally, Wright has written: "One of my continuing occupations is that of housekeeper in my own home. . . . This job . . . should be classified and emphasized as socially useful work of a most exacting nature, for it is one of the most critically pronounced activities given to the sustaining and enhancement of human life. . . ." To her father and mother, Wright attributes her ability to endure the painful writing of her novel, because they taught her that "no matter how much the hurting, one must keep on going."

From 1934-1945, Wright attended the Wetipquin Elementary School and then the Salisbury Colored High School. It was in the third grade that she began writing rhyming lines, which she sheepishly labels "childish compositions," but Mr. Brown, her fourth grade teacher, told her she was a poet and encouraged her to continue writing verses. Later, her high school librarian and Latin teacher Ms. Brown, not related to her elementary teacher, recognizing this same creative gift introduced her to Sterling Brown's poetry and influenced her to attend Howard University to study under Brown. Mrs. Carrie Bailey, one of the first schoolteachers assigned to the Wetipquin Elementary School, told Wright some years ago that "she as head of a committee collected [Wright's] childhood verses, had

Sarah Elizabeth Wright (photo by Robert Desverny)

them printed, and sold them to raise money for a new school building."

Inspired but poor, Wright entered Howard University in 1945, when she was sixteen years old. Possessing a work ethic fostered in her as a small child, she worked throughout her college years in the "typical Booker T. Washington tradition," receiving "loving but small help" from her parents. It was at Howard that Wright's innately rebellious spirit, search for truth, and concern for her fellowman were nourished. In addition to being nurtured by Sterling Brown, and later Owen Dodson, she became a part of a group of young artists. Additionally, she worked with the Howard Players, served as editor of the *49er* and as feature editor of the *Hilltop,* contributed to the *Stylus,* and was frequently commissioned to write occasional poems. But one of Wright's singular experiences at Howard was her acquaintance with Langston Hughes and his work:

> I first met him and was profoundly moved by his reading of his own poems when he visited the campus. Although he was not a member of the Harlem Writers' Guild, but did accept

honorary membership at one point, he continued until his death a personal interest in my work and career, which interest began when I was still living in Philadelphia. One of my treasured gifts is one of his now widely published poems endorsed by Langston Hughes: "Especially 'for Sarah' at Christmastime," the title of which is "The Backlash Blues." He sent this poem to me the Christmas season before his death.

At Howard, too, Wright groped with her own identity and departed in 1949 as a symbolic precursor of the later more internationally recognized "Black Is Beautiful Movement" of the 1960s. Ironically, her "throwing away the hair straightening comb" shortly after leaving Howard initially subjected her to ostracism by her own people, a pain which she chose to endure, however, because she would not/could not compromise her own sense of personal worth: "I wanted my own self—I did not want to have to imitate some other group's standard of beauty to be accepted." Years later when she met the black and proud Odetta, she felt affirmed and not so isolated in her stand. Later in the mid-1960s, there were other black female artists in the New York black cultural community such as Aminata Moseka (Abbey Lincoln), Rosa Guy, and Maya Angelou who felt as strongly as Wright about self-worth, so they joined forces and organized the Cultural Association for Women of African Heritage, focused specifically to help black women see themselves as having personal and human worth.

After leaving Howard and until 1957, Wright sojourned in the Philadelphia area, developing marketable skills by acquiring teaching credits at Cheyney State Teachers College, enhancing her craftsmanship through participation in a poetry workshop at the University of Pennsylvania, and organizing against oppressive social forces. As she walked the streets in search of work, she experienced the discrimination which limited blacks to traditionally prescribed occupations—teaching being one. The gods temporarily smiled on Wright, however, for she was directed to the Jewish Employment Service which was "concerned about the plight of blacks," and through which she was introduced to the "culturally and historically knowledgeable" Kraft family. For a few years thereafter, she was "a one woman office" for the Kraft's small printing and publishing firm, being allowed and encouraged to learn firsthand about the printing and publishing industry. One of her dreams was

"to reproduce my own work as Walt Whitman had done, feeling that all of the arts had a common language." Consequently, she felt that "the design of a letter—a page—a volume should be compatible with the verbal message." During this period, Wright also assisted in the founding of the Philadelphia Writers' Workshop, of which Lucy Smith was a member and for which Arthur Huff Fauset, brother of novelist Jessie Fauset, served as mentor. She and Lucy Smith later helped to sustain the loosely structured organization: artists, scientists, and professionals engaged in effecting political change and ameliorating repressive social and economic conditions.

After the publication of *Give Me A Child* in 1955, Wright was lured toward New York by the work of the Harlem Writers' Guild and John Oliver Killens, in particular. But she did not move to New York and join the thirty-odd members of the Guild until 1957, at which time there were only a few published writers in the Guild: Killens, John Henrik Clarke, Alice Childress, Paule Marshall, and Irving Burgess. However, according to Wright, "these were writers learning from the 'guts' how to do it, reading writers from all cultures and classes, sharing observations, and criticizing each others' works-in-progress in order to articulate *our* people's experiences with authority and artistry." Wright's union with this group of writers made her "a serious student of fiction." During her active participation in the Guild (1957-1972), Wright helped to organize the First National Conference of Black Writers (1959), the Second National Conference of Black Writers (1965), and the Congress of American Writers (1971). Even now as an alumna of the Harlem Writers' Guild, Wright is most laudatory of its nourishment of her and other writers such as Rosa Guy, Lonnie Elder III, Ossie Davis, Julian Mayfield, Charles Russell, Jean Carey Bond, Loyle Hairston, and Maya Angelou, to name a few.

Although Wright's twenty-four-year residency in New York has been wrought by the normal anguish of a noncompromising artist, it has also been personally, professionally, and socially productive and stimulating. In New York, she met her husband, composer Joseph Kaye, of whom she has written: "It was he who worked and encouraged and anguished for me at all hours of the day or night, in all seasons of the years" during the writing of her novel. She has always engaged in multifarious activities simultaneously, some of the most taxing of which took place during the writing of *This Child's Gonna Live*. From 1958-1976, she enrolled in almost every creative writing and filmmaking workshop offered by the New School for Social Research. In 1960, at the invitation of the Casa de las Americas—House of the Americas—she attended the celebration of the Secondary Anniversary of the Revolution in Cuba. Artists worldwide were invited, but only a few from the States were in attendance; nevertheless, Wright attended because she had "nothing to lose but ignorance." In between serving as writer-in-residence, appearing on television and radio talk shows, speaking at various colleges and universities and community group meetings, conducting creative writing workshops, lecturing and reading poetry, she has found time to serve consecutive terms on the Council of the Authors Guild, and from 1980-1982 to become a trained poetry therapist, interning in various community institutions. She has won two consecutive MacDowell Colony Fellowships for Creative Writing (1972 and 1973); a New York State Creative Artists Public Service Award for Fiction in 1976, serving as a fiction consultant before that; and Howard University's 1976 Institute for the Arts and Humanities' Second National Conference of Afro-American Writers' Novelist-Poet Award. In addition to writing a sequel and a screenplay for *This Child's Gonna Live,* Wright is currently serving as chairwoman of the board of directors of Writers For Our Time, a nonprofit intercommunity creative writers' workshop which purports to "help fashion . . . a world that will hold 'all the faces, all the Adams and Eves and their countless generations.' " Wright's impact on this group is reflected in the lines above from "For My People" by Margaret Walker, one of her idols. As Dana Thomas, noted biographer and a founding member of Writers For Our Time, avers, "Sarah, as a writer, is very close to her roots, even now, but she has developed along international/cosmopolitan lines; she reaches out beyond the roots to all people."

Wright's *Give Me A Child,* coauthored with Lucy Smith, was published two years before she moved to New York. She and Lucy Smith, already friends and common participators in black artistic organizations/movements in Philadelphia and readers of their poetry in black churches and other community centers, had been meeting over lunch for a period of two years discussing their individual works and all people's need for the poetry in their lives to be made accessible to them. They decided to coauthor a work which would appeal to people generally. Wright asserts: "We were dismayed by poetry being hidden away on seldomly disturbed library shelves and by it being taught in schools in such a

manner as to make it appear something unnatural and unnecessary to human survival. We wanted to move it onto the living room coffee table." With the assistance of Charles Smith, painter, graphic artist, and brother of Lucy Smith, they became somewhat pioneers in their thematic fusion of art forms: art, photography, and poetry.

Thematically, *Give Me A Child* is divided into six parts, beginning with "No Greater Love" and ending with "Toward a Making of a Spring." Each division is unevenly developed by the seventeen poems of the volume. The title poem was written by Lucy Smith, and it captures the hopes of the black culture and of mankind via one woman's trauma as her husband prepares to leave for war and she whispers a plea for a conception which will enable her to endure:

> give me a child to wear close to my heart
> during the long winter
> when you are gone;
> A child that will grow as freedom grows—
>   a child born as freedom is born—
>   conceived in hope and born out of struggle.
>   Give me a child!

Wright contributed seven poems to the collection: "To Some Millions Who Survive Joseph Mander, Sr.," "Conversation With My Son About Flowers," "Conversation With My Daughter About a Star," "Urgency," "Play on a Witch," "Black and Lilac," and "Window Pictures." Stylistically, these poems are visceral, conversational, dramatic, ironic, metaphorical, passionate, and understated. The forms and imagery are individual, emerging from the experience of the poems themselves and punctuating Wright's concept of the highest achievement of the artist: "When his/her content leads to the discovery of form." Although she was initially intimidated by the academic evaluation of her craft, she is no longer mindful of poetic forms which she knows will not accommodate the way black people, or any people, verbalize themselves. She feels that content should dictate form.

The poems in *Give Me A Child* were written by a humanist who provides a spectrum of the human condition: the negation of life-sustaining brotherhood, the denial of the human spirit, man's emotional divorcement from life, individual loneliness and ostracism, and yet the "tired feet" that keep on responding to the "green light" and the ability of youth to rejuvenate, to rekindle belief. One of the most celebrated of the poems is "To Some Millions Who Survive . . . ," based on the actual tragedy in

Philadelphia of Joseph E. Mander Sr.'s drowning while trying to save the life of a white youth. Although Wright was ill at the time of Mander's tragedy, she felt compelled to immortalize this man, and in her poem, his fate becomes the irony of ironies: A black man denied life gives up his life for, symbolically, his "life-denier." But the poem is not a bitter recanting of the state of black oppression but rather a controlled yet fervent appeal to the American conscience via a depiction of the "invisible" but self-nurturing humanity, which the "peculiar institution" of slavery, Jim Crowism, and racism should have inevitably annihilated: "Trying to wash away brotherhood—/And Yet/It lives." The poet would have Mander's tragedy be transforming; she desires no stone monuments, no one-day tributes, no distanced "final-ended payment," but a recognition of the black man's humanity—an intrinsic step in the fashioning of a world of love, modeled after Mander's own "love-directed body." Essentially, the poet seeks a change of the human heart:

> Will you turn those fingers that point to say
>   "That's where a hero died"
>   back to yourselves—
>   point to your hearts
>   saying,
>   "But this is where he lives!"

"To Some Millions Who Survive . . ." became part of a movement in Philadelphia, and Wright was called upon to recite it throughout the city. The poem helped spur the major Philadelphia newspaper to spearhead an education trust fund drive for the Mander children and to purchase a home for the family, and the Philadelphia City Council ultimately had a playground erected in tribute to Mander, although in spite of the Mander Committee's petitioning the Council, the last verse of Wright's poem was never inscribed at the entrance.

Two other poems in the volume which merit individual note are "Play on a Witch" and "Urgency." "Play on a Witch" is an experimental poem, a three-act drama in verse whose supporting rhythm, idiom, and imagery derive from the folk culture. Although on one level a psychological study of the effects of war, the poem is more directly the dramatization of a community's insentience to an old woman's loss and the agony of her struggle to cope with the "gone" which persists. It is allegedly the bizarre behavior and occult brews of Julia's, dubbed Julio the neighborhood witch, which account for the strange birthmarks, suicides, clawing cats in the night, smell of death, etc., in the

neighborhood. Overall, the poem is an effectively balanced orchestration of the poet's insight into an old woman's crumbling psychological props—her "substitutes" for the son whose life has been taken in the war—and the superstitious mumbo jumbo of an oral folk tradition: "Julio-o'll get you if you don't nappy nap/Tie you up forever in her big black sack./Take you inside of her big black door,/With so many locks she can't add one more."

"Urgency" reflects Wright's ability to discern the truths of the common man. The terse experience of the poem is, on its surface, that of a daily streetcar rider whose grinding existence is momentarily relieved by the bus's "time-bitten punctuation of a pause." The ride is really one through life ("Go," "Stop," "Decide," "Ride."), and the coloring of that life is implied in the parenthetical allusion to racial discrimination ("he's white—he can get another job!"). The singular personal pronoun of the poem alternates throughout with the "we" of the bus, but the "we" become the unequivocal, exigent, dark-hued "riders"

> I must:
>   We must
>   Make it————————Now!

"Urgency" is a fusion of realism ("Let no throat, scorched by hasty coffee/Pantingly declare, 'I can make that car' "), and underplayed metaphors ("Thank God for red lights"). The poem can be viewed more as an allegory, but one borrowed, not created, from life as it is actually lived. This poem confirms Wright's assertion that she "tends to go off into the ramifications of the idea to get involved in tone colors/contours/sound."

"I Have Known Death," "Until They Have Stopped," and "Lament of a Harlem Mother" are the other most accessible of Wright's published poems not included in *Give Me A Child.* "I Have Known Death" is a cryptic eleven-line statement of the pain at "the death of love." "Until They Have Stopped" is a tribute to Paul Robeson; and although like "Some Millions Who Survive . . ." it is a more strident call for brotherhood. It lacks some of the subtleties of the Mander poem; the poetic voice is a sustained "No!" to the catalogue of crimes which America has perpetrated on "the working people of this earth." The imagery is earthy, virile, and caustic: "Until they have stopped slitting my throat like the defenseless animals'/in the near-Christmas time killing for the Christmas feast." "Fairy tales for food" and "television and radio" are only two of the numerous allusions to the means by which America sickens the human psyche. Unlike some of the revolutionary poetry of the 1960s, however, there is an intangible quality in Wright's poem which makes it a simply human cry against the pain of others and especially of the female's "hurting": "Full of determination and broken fingernails—/Hurting to the quick from digging and groveling. . . ." In contrast to those who would use the word "protest" in the limiting sense to describe her poems of this nature, Wright contends that her poetry affirms "our right to life—saying yes to life and no to that which is destroying."

This yessing to life is most evident in "Lament of a Harlem Mother," a poem which provides in capsule the urban counterpart to the sensibility of *This Child's Gonna Live*. This poem describes the female persona's open display of heartrending anxiety over her missed menstrual period, as she recalls that "moment of forgetfulness"—forgetting the closing-in world and allowing herself a respite of love with her husband as in their "first-in-love years": "Honey, Yes./Honey, Yes!" The Harlem

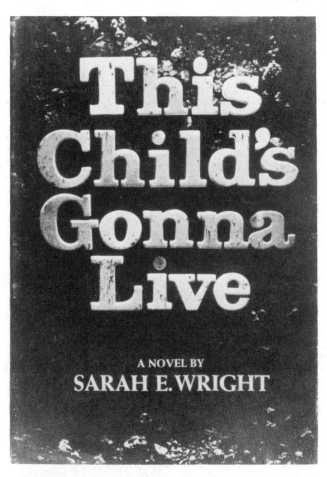

Dust jacket for Wright's only novel, a widely acclaimed feminist love story

mother's is a world of broken promises and dead dreams, a world in which another child would push her farther into the mire, but also a world in which she must get herself together and look "permanently permanent to the boss." Through an ironic flashback, the persona shares the "overkilling" route of her "aching" quest to become "a woman grown free." The first section of the poem is a powerful capturing of the speaker's dilemma in her own idiom, but the poet gradually overshadows her in the more generalized treatment of the female and human plight, resulting from the "Greedy wars fought to get to the moons of/perpetual plenty."

Thematically, Wright's poetry denotes that the extended treatment of the "working people" in *This Child's Gonna Live* (1969) was always the unifying stimulus of her creativity. She had begun fragments of what was to become her prizewinning novel before she moved to New York, but for a number of years, she did nothing to give form to the fragmentary ideas. However, she continued to live consciously with half-formed people who kept whispering to her that they "deserved to have someone articulate their being in the world." It was John Oliver Killens and Joseph Kaye who gave her the most sustained encouragement and convinced her that she owed it to the world and people to tell her story. Wright was even more inspired by the Icelandic writer Halldór Laxness and Russian writers in general: Sholokhov, Chekhov, Gorki, Tolstoy, Dostoevski, and Gogol and the African and Haitian writers in particular. These writers' fidelity to their land, their roots, their culture, and the authenticity of their depiction of the peasant "affirmed something" for Wright. They, in a sense, contributed to her artistic liberation; Wright began to think: "If I am to write about the 'Shore,' the Eastern Shore of Maryland, then the land there and the people have their personality and validity. My job as a chronicler is to reveal this faithfully." In essence, Wright had encountered free and compassionate writers whose humanity reaffirmed her own, but whose style she did not emulate: "Actually, I don't have a style nor do I believe in that artificiality. I submit myself to the material and allow the subject to emerge—to fight its way through. . . . I make myself the instrument through which the message flows." For ten years, then, she lived with the pain of birthing her characters and of faithfully rendering their unique existence. She shut out the world with music: musicians like Mahalia Jackson, Nina Simone, and Ray Charles kept her linked with the world of the "Shore," and Beethoven, Wagner, Tchaikovsky, and Shostakovich kept the heroic nature of her people and their battle for life focused.

This Child's Gonna Live is a prose poem, and Wright concedes that she "is inescapably addicted to seeing life as poetic." This bleak novel is set in a provincial poverty-stricken, God-fearing, self-supporting oystering and farming community called Tangierneck during the Depression. It delineates approximately two of the turbulent years in Mariah's and Jacob's crisis-ridden and seemingly hopeless struggle to keep their family alive, but flashbacks and stream of consciousness are used to develop comprehensive portraits. The novel begins in the winter with a dubious "sun" image, which is transformed immediately into a dream of death, and ends in the spring, which is indicative of life and hope. Death, however, is the dominant image—metaphoric and literal: Rabbit, Mariah's poetic son; Aunt Cora Lou and Vyella, Mariah's only real empathizers; and Thomas and Levi, Mariah's elusive symbols of hope.

Ostensibly, the novel is Mariah's lament (the beautiful but aged twenty-three-year-old mother of four children: one dead because of the alleged carelessness of a midwife; three living but being consumed by malnutrition and worms; and a possibly illegitimate one on the way), as she fights to find any way out of the spirit-killing "slowing-up roads" of Tangierneck: "All my children, all-you-all gonna live and be something besides ignorant scrubs like me." Mariah's battle is fourfold: She must struggle against her male supremacist husband; the self-glorifying, religious, and hypocritical community; social and economic oppression; and, at times, even herself. Periodically, Mariah succumbs to her guilt-ridden conscience and the only identity allowed her—whore—but her self-reinforcing refrain is: "I is so something else. I is so!" Wright herself asserts: "What is fascinating about Mariah is [her] struggle for her sense of personal worth, . . . a level which has nothing to do with Jacob, with race; this has to do with her personal worth as a woman."

But *This Child's Gonna Live* is more than a feminist novel. Although Mariah, as Joseph Kaye keenly observes, "looms larger than life," Jacob, too, possesses a quiet strength, dignity (his quest to repossess his family's stolen land—to have roots), and a coarse tenderness. Wright adds that even though "Mariah does raise the question of the woman's subjugation to the male, this is part of the whole structure—part of how *men* in our social/economic structure are oriented, part of the [prevailing] Judeo-Christian mystique." The novel's complexity derives from the complexity of the human condi-

tion. The black males' hypocrisy, self-righteousness, and brutal suppression of the black females of Tangierneck are presented in the total context of the larger forces which have emasculated them. Jacob acknowledges that he "Ain't master over nothing." This paradox of the victim/oppressor permeates the whole of the annihilating relationships in this black community. Moreover, one can not overlook the effect of the duality of a religion which, like James Baldwin, Wright views as both sustaining and emasculating. In this respect, Joseph Kaye avers that Wright's accomplishment comes in that she attacks male chauvinism and narrowness, but she does it out of love for that male.

More important, the novel is one of the most lyrical and excruciating love stories ever written. It is a studied portrait of the interpersonal effect of social and economic oppression and the regeneration that takes place when Jacob the "Sparrow" is transformed into Jacob the "windbeaten, life-beaten going nowhere man." Mariah has only dim memories of being able to fly on that spring day when Jacob "Gave me all of his tenderest life. Gave it all to me in my thighs and my back and my heart." Undeniably, they both hurt; they both contain their pain by lashing out, killing their love.

The "light" of this unrelieved novel of despair comes from hope and from the telling of their heroic story. The life of Tangierneck is captured impressionistically, and the people's consciousness is masterfully disclosed through the idiom of their own experience. Wright agonized over having her characters verbalize "their own being in the world," and she succeeded. Of the layers of Biblical allusions, analogies, and similes in the novel, Wright states: "The idiom instead of being Biblical was influenced by the Bible only in that their entire life was influenced by Western Christianity. Whatever they lived is what creates the idiom—the very fabric of their life." There is a proverbial quality to Wright's analogies and metaphors: "You can't run your way through the brambles and bushes of life. You got to chop down those vines and creepers first before you go headlong through them." And her gutsy, sensuous, graphic language is imbued with what Killens called the "sounds and smells and blood and sweat and love and hate and sugar and shit and poverty and heartache" of life.

These qualities of the novel contributed to its notable reception. *This Child's Gonna Live* was selected by the *New York Times* as one of the most important books of 1969, and the *Baltimore Sun* chose it for its 1969 Readability Award. It also received a litany of rave reviews: Wright was compared to James Joyce, John Steinbeck, Gorki, Dostoevski, and the Greek tragedians, suggestive of the so-called universality of the novel. However, Wright rejects the notion that her novel is significant because it is about "every man"; she vehemently argues that her novel is universal because her story is black:

> Blacks' suffering and their joys are immense; if anything, they have a larger human universality because of the wide range of intellectual and emotional responses and survival tactics they're forced to employ.... There is perhaps a huger universality in the Black Experience than is possible to discern in some of the white experiences because in the latter the intensity and frequency of encounters with crises of every sort is not there. We see the more-or-less comfortable white middle class, although experiencing conflict, drama, pain, and suffering, which has not been called upon to exercise its "emotional muscles" quite as strenuously, as often.

The reviewers' laudatory acknowledgment of the craft of her novel might best be reflected by the observations of Franklin Dunlap (*Chicago Sun Times*): "Her Negro jargon of narration is like the hand on the wedding guest, maintaining our knowledge of where we are and whom we are with — mankind. This is not pure English, it is pure People. And beautiful, beautiful, beautiful."

Sarah E. Wright is a writer to be reckoned with. She is not a part of a limited movement; she is a part of a human movement. She has not sought to create a new idiom, a new black aesthetic, but rather has consciously sought the means by which to articulate her own truth of "her people . . . herself in response to the world." She embraces her roots, but she does not reject values from other cultures. She has sought inspiration, humanity, and nobility from wherever they existed, but what she captures is her own black experience.

References:

Anne Z. Mickelson, "Winging Upward: Black Women: Sarah E. Wright, Toni Morrison, Alice Walker," in *Reaching Out: Sensitivity and Order in Recent American Fiction by Women* (Metuchen, N. J.: Scarecrow Press, 1979), pp. 112-124;

Eugene Redmond, *Drumvoices: The Mission of Afro-American Poetry* (Garden City: Doubleday, 1976), pp. 335-336;

Noel Schraufnagel, *From Apology to Protest: The Black American Novel* (De Land, Fla.: Everett/Edwards, 1973), pp. 170-171;

Roger Whitlow, "Sarah E. Wright," in *Black American Literature: A Critical History* (Chicago: Nelson Hall, 1973), pp. 162-165.

Al Young
(31 May 1939-　)

William J. Harris
State University of New York at Stony Brook

BOOKS: *Dancing: Poems* (New York: Corinth Books, 1969);

Snakes (New York: Holt, Rinehart & Winston, 1970; London: Sidgwick & Jackson, 1971);

The Song Turning Back Into Itself (New York: Holt, Rinehart & Winston, 1971);

Who Is Angelina? (New York: Holt, Rinehart & Winston, 1975; London: Sidgwick & Jackson, 1978);

Geography of the Near Past (New York: Holt, Rinehart & Winston, 1976);

Sitting Pretty (New York: Holt, Rinehart & Winston, 1976);

Ask Me Now (New York: McGraw-Hill, 1980; London: Sidgwick & Jackson, 1980);

Bodies & Soul (Berkeley: Creative Arts Book Company, 1981);

The Blues Don't Change: New and Selected Poems (Baton Rouge: Louisiana State University Press, 1982).

OTHER: *Yardbird Lives!*, edited by Young and

Ishmael Reed (New York: Grove, 1978);
Calafia, with Young as contributing editor (Berkeley, Cal.: Y'bird, 1979).

Al Young is his own man, refusing to go along with anybody's trend or latest survey: he is a black American in the American tradition of the singular individual. His art is dedicated to the destruction of glib stereotypes of black Americans. Not surprisingly, his work illustrates the complexity and richness of contemporary Afro-American life through a cast of highly individualized black characters. Since he is a gifted stylist and a keen observer of the human comedy, he manages to be both a serious and an entertaining author.

Albert James Young was born on 31 May 1939 in Ocean Springs, Mississippi, on the Gulf Coast near Biloxi and New Orleans. His parents were Albert James, a musician and auto worker, and Mary Campbell Young. He lived in various parts of rural Mississippi, including a small town called Pachuta, where he stayed with his grandparents in a house without running water or electricity. Wagons and mules—not cars—were the main form of transportation in that hamlet. Even though he and his parents moved to Detroit, Michigan, in 1946, he spent time, mostly summers, in Mississippi over the next several years. Hence, he grew up in both the urban Midwest and the rural South. He attended the University of Michigan at Ann Arbor between 1957 and 1961. After college, he held a variety of occupations, including professional musician, janitor, singer, and disc jockey. In the spring of 1961 he moved to the San Francisco Bay Area, where he still lives. He gained a sense of freedom moving to the West Coast; he felt that California "could accommodate inventiveness." His writing reflects the areas he has lived in, especially the Midwest and California. He married Arlin Belck in 1963; they have a son, Michael James.

Although the genre Young has exploited the most effectively and the most extensively is the novel, he has published four volumes of poetry: *Dancing* (1969), *The Song Turning Back Into Itself* (1971), *Geography of the Near Past* (1976), and *The Blues Don't Change* (1982). Young's poetry has been concerned with universal themes, such as joy, love, religion, family, and friendship, rather than specifically racial ones. Dancing and music figure as central metaphors in his poetry. He declares: "Poetry should be a music of love: song, a dance, the joyously heartbreaking flight of the human spirit through inner and outer space in search of itself." In particular, his work is dominated by the celebra-

Al Young (photo by Lee Marsullo)

tion of love in the mundane world: "I love you / I need you / you in the laundromat / among the telltale result / of the ubiquitous garment industry." Al Young's poetry celebrates the joys of being human.

Young's first novel, *Snakes* (1970), is beautifully written, rich in black language and characterization, and rich in black love. With his first novel he proved himself a writer of genuine and impressive accomplishment. Even though the book was not a best-seller, it was critically well received and reprinted in paperback. *Snakes* introduced most of the themes that preoccupied Young for the next decade: the beauty of black music and speech, the importance of family love, the dignity and romance of vocation, the quest for identity and the need to come to terms with one's life. Other themes he developed later were the centrality of the religious / mystical experience and the need for adult love and responsibility. Even though Young's novels mostly deal with black characters, he does not want to be ghettoized. For instance, although it is important that MC, the narrator and main character of *Snakes,* is undeniably black, it is equally important that he is young and trying to come to terms with who he is, trying to anchor himself in the world. Like all of Young's protagonists, MC faces the creative insecurity which forces him to ask questions about himself and the world.

In *Snakes* music becomes MC's avenue to self-definition. The novel is a celebration of black music, as is Young's entire canon. MC begins the book by declaring: "But one of the few things that's never let me down is music—not musicians, not promoters, certainly not club owners, recording companies, critics or reviewers—Music!" The story revolves around "a modest success, a single called *Snakes* that caught on for a few weeks in my hometown [Detroit]." This novel initiates Young's continuing concern with modest but dignified successes. Like MC, Young learned about jazz and popular music while growing up in the Motor City. Although MC characterizes himself as "a nice kid who played music instead of the dozens—and with records and books instead of with girls," he is the only character in the book who has the initiative to leave home and, like most black protagonists, seek freedom. Through working in a band he discovers that he has talent as a musician, a discovery which gives him a sense of self-worth and the courage to go to New York. As he leaves home he says: "For the first time in my life I don't feel trapped & I'm going to try & make this feeling last as long as I can." MC, like all of Young's characters, has a realistic sense of the limits of his freedom.

Champ, an older but disreputable high school buddy of MC's, is one of Young's wise men figures. He teaches MC the meaning of music, explaining to MC: "Yall got your instruments down under control but now you got to get on down inside yourself. That's where it's at, if you can dig it." Champ teaches MC that music is more than craft; it is also self-expression. Music has shaped Champ's life, his style. Yet while Champ loves music as much as MC, he cannot play an instrument and this might account for his drifting: Champ is an artist without an art. He is deeply involved with drugs because he does not have the talent or will to be a jazz musician. Champ confides to MC: "You into this music thing heavy and you take it real serious which is nice, which is what I shoulda done. . . . I stays kinda half high most of the time but it aint nothin else to do."

Young finds working hard at one's art a form of salvation. In his short story "Chicken Hawk's Dream," the protagonist, Chicken Hawk, only daydreams about becoming a musician, an artist—and consequently never becomes one. Conversely, in "What a dream," from *Bodies & Soul* (1981), Young recounts a tale of a young man who becomes a

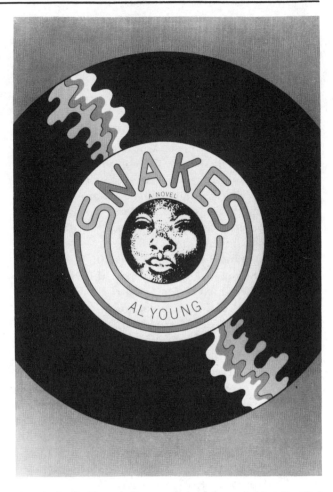

Dust jacket for Young's first novel about the modest but dignified success of a black musician. The title is from the main character's best known record.

musician through an act of pure will: "It would be wonderful to be able to go on and tell about how Mike [Frimkas, the hero of the story] eventually made a name for himself in the music world. He didn't. He went back to sculpting and, although I've heard second-hand that he hasn't done badly at it, the fact that I care about is that our lives intersected at a vital point where I was able to learn something from him. And what was that? Just this: it's possible to flower at anything you really want to do well simply by planting yourself in it and becoming a fanatic, totally, completely. That's what I started doing after I watched him do it, or rather, heard him."

Snakes is a celebration of black language as well as black music: the novel luxuriates in the beauty, individuality, and complexity of the black vernacular. In fact, through his career Young revels in the nuances of black language, illustrating Stephen

Henderson's point that black speech is a continuum extending from Black English to "Standard English." Further, in *Snakes* each character speaks in an individual style, expressing himself in a highly personalized idiom. Young observes: "I found out early that speech is characterization." MC speaks standard English; Champ speaks inner city argot; Shakes—short for Shakespeare—speaks poetry. Shakes, who is a high school buddy and member of the same band as MC, has a photographic memory and loves Shakespeare and extravagant speech. His own speech is a combination of black street argot and Elizabethan. His retelling of Cyrano de Bergerac's verbal courtship of Roxanne is a brilliant tour de force: "I just wanna knock out chicks and show these other dudes they aint hittin on doodleysquat when it come to talkin trash. I got it down, jim! You hip to Cyrano de Bergerac? I musta seen that flick fifteen-twenty times. Talk about a joker could talk some trash! Cyrano got everybody told! Didnt nobody be messin with Cyrano, ugly as he was. Some silly stud get to cappin on Cyrano's nose and he dont flinch an inch. He get right up in the stud's face and vaporize him with several choice pronouncements, then he go and waste the cat in a suhword fight."

Like Nikki Giovanni, Young knows that "Black love is Black wealth." Claude, MC's grandmother and guardian, embodies black love. She is tough but good-humored, respectable even though she plays the numbers. She doesn't want her grandson to go into the music business because she doesn't want him to become a drug addict. Nevertheless, she understands her grandson's need for freedom and, through a slight ruse, makes it easier for him to try his luck at his art without excess familial guilt.

Snakes did not fit the 1960s' stereotype of black ghetto art. One editor said to Young: "A little too sweet for a ghetto novel," and it was rejected by several publishers before it was finally accepted by Holt, Rinehart and Winston. From the beginning of Young's career he wanted to transcend simpleminded stereotypes of black people whether they emanated from blacks or whites. In the poem "A Dance for Militant Dilettantes," published in *Dancing,* he attacks black racial chic stereotyping of blackness:

> No one's going to read
> or take you seriously,
> a hip friend advises,
> until you start coming down on them
> like the black poet you truly are
> & ink in lots of black in your poems

> soul is not enough
> you need real color
> shining out of real skin
> nappy snaggly afro hair
> baby grow up & dig on *that!*

In 1972, while teaching creative writing at Stanford University, Young, along with fellow black novelist Ishmael Reed, originated the multicultural magazine *Yardbird Reader,* dedicated to the publication of writers from a variety of ethnic backgrounds. Despite the fact that most of Young's own books have been published by major New York publishers, he has been committed to the little magazine revolution.

In 1972 Young also began writing for Hollywood, adapting Dick Gregory's *Nigger* for the screen; but it was never produced. Young's career in Hollywood has not been entirely happy; he has been commissioned to write several screenplays but has never received screen credit. Young calls himself "an uncredited, backroom writer in Hollywood."

In 1974 he was awarded a Guggenheim Fellowship, and after rewriting *Who Is Angelina?*—the original version was destroyed in a fire—he published the new version of the novel in 1975. With *Who Is Angelina?* Young's settings for his novels shift to California; the novel is set in Berkeley and the protagonist is a twenty-six-year-old black woman whose full name is Angelina Green. She is another of Young's confused characters, seeking her identity and finding the contemporary world "this chaos called now." Young observes: "I really was trying to write about a young woman and options in the 1970's in America." Before the story begins Angelina has broken up with her boyfriend Larry. She comments: "He split and I flipped." She is on the edge and suicidal. Not only has Larry left her but her whole life seems out of control. She has overdosed on wine, drugs, and sex, and consequently has "grown sick of time and the world." To "clear her head" Angelina decides to go to Mexico for a vacation. In Mexico she meets an exciting black man named Watusi, a mysterious, romantic, and prosperous adventurer. Watusi is one of Young's many characters who demonstrates both the complexity of Afro-American speech and character: he is "agrammatical" but also very sophisticated; his speech does not stereotype him.

In the midst of her romantic involvement with Watusi, Angelina is called to grim Detroit: her father is seriously ill. Her father is an individual who thinks for himself, a postal supervisor whose custom is to "stay outta style, just a little bit." Young has declared that the father is a portrait of one of those unsung blacks who work two jobs to support his family. While at home Angelina reacquaints herself with her father. One of Young's wise men, he tries to help her come to terms with her life. She discovers that he is a religious man. In church with her father and other relatives Angelina has a mystical experience which gives her an "indescribable sense of belonging—if only for an instant—to something that was vaster and deeper than herself." She does not come home to "roots" but a rootedness in the universe. Young has referred to *Angelina* as a religious book and has said that his displaced protagonists are always seeking to be part of a meaningful whole. Young himself is responsive to the religious experience and it has influenced his work. He recounts having in April 1964 "the first of a remarkable and continuing series of (non-drug-induced) mystical experiences that I consider, thus far, to be the high points of my life. . . . since the mid-sixties I have been nourished by these intense and blissful interludes and, hence, have drawn much of my inspiration to write and many of my personal notions about poetics from what could be termed religious sources. I am not, of course, referring to church religion. Sometimes there is a vastness I feel growing within me that I could explore and delight in forever. No mere church could contain it. I cannot help but believe that all men have sensed this beautiful endlessness about themselves at one time or another. It is what I call soul. Occasionally it flowers from me gratuitously in the form of a poem."

Despite the fact that the father is somewhat bitter about his own life, he instructs Angelina to live her own life, to return to California: "You don't have to explain anything to me." After returning to California, she perceives that she has come into closer contact with her real self by simplifying her life, giving up the excesses of earlier times. She has escaped the external chaos by gaining control over her internal chaos. Angelina knows there will be no sudden, melodramatic change in her life; she will have to settle for whatever "momentary stay against confusion" she can manage.

Angelina is a remarkably sensitive portrait of a young woman attempting to achieve a sense of freedom, a sense of belonging, and a sense of self. At first she seems to define herself in terms of men; and, unlike Young's male protagonists, she doesn't define herself in terms of a career. Early in the story Angelina defines herself as a loner and thinks of marriage as "a sell-out." She wants to come into a

serious relationship with another human being but fears being trapped. Even though she wants a lasting relationship, she refuses to enter into one before she can be sure that she can provide a good answer to the question: *Who is Angelina?*

Sitting Pretty (1976) presents another one of Al Young's characters who are disoriented in the world—Sidney J. Prettymon, nicknamed Sitting Pretty or just Sit. The protagonist is fifty-five, has somehow lost twenty years of his life, and has a drinking problem. He lives in Palo Alto, California, in a rundown hotel called the Blue Jay and would be considered a loser by conventional standards. Yet Sit is a multifaceted Afro-American and like all of Young's main characters cannot be easily classified. This novel is another instance of Young's skill at showing the complexity of black characters without preaching. Sit—when he works—is a janitor; however, he is a philosophical janitor who has informed opinions on a wide variety of subjects. Like Langston Hughes, Young can create a character who shows his complexity instead of his simplicity through his dialect. Even though Sit does not speak standard English, he is consciously building his vocabulary and knows a little Latin—black speech is multifarious. Explaining his preoccupation with words, Sit tells the reader: "See, moon in Latin is *luna*, you know, same as in Spanish so that's where we get the word *lunatic* from. I dont think I need to go into it any deeper than that. I studies these things. The Professor gimme this big dictionary for a present a coupla years back. I be steady readin round in it to enhance my word power."

Like Young's other protagonists, Sit is a seeker; yet though he asks a lot of questions, he finds few answers. Sit had left his wife and children twenty years before the narrative begins: "I left a good job and a good family, lookin for that something else." Sit drifts until he happens onto a small success—not unlike MC's—which gives a focus to his life: he becomes a local celebrity by making a few television commercials to promote a radio talk show he regularly calls to let off steam. The ads provide a focus for Sit's talents, an opportunity for Sit's personality and ideas to cohere. That is, Sit becomes an artist of sorts, expressing himself through a popular medium. Young raises the possibility that this small success may change Sit's life, giving him a future in television commercials. Unwilling to commit himself, however, Sit closes his narrative without deciding what he is going to do.

The future is uncertain for all of Young's protagonists. The most one can hope for is "might." MC might have a future in New York playing music;

Angelina might be able to make something out of her new life. In the last section of *Sitting Pretty*, entitled "Spring," the traditional time of new beginnings, Sit gently confronts his new life. Sit, like Young's other heroes, faces the hard and chaotic world, but since he and they are realistic characters—people trying to grow up—he can only take "a little at a time and do the best" he can.

Ask Me Now (1980), a *New York Times* Outstanding Book of the Year, is another of Young's novels which depicts a modest but dignified success. Durwood "Woody" Knight is the biggest star in Young's galaxy thus far: he is a professional basketball player who is known all over the San Francisco Bay Area. However, Woody's position on the team is not a glamorous one: he is a guard whose genuine skill is not immediately obvious. Yet at thirty-nine Woody is in the midst of losing even this limited stardom. He has retired from pro ball and now must learn to live with his family, who have become strangers to him since he has spent much of the last several years on the road.

Ask Me Now is a novel of family relationships: between a father and a daughter, between a father and a son, between a husband and a wife. Woody is concerned about his fifteen-year-old daughter, Celia. Her supposed kidnapping creates the central action of the story. Even though it is Celia's idea to disappear for a few days, she chooses the wrong people for the job. Unbeknownst to Woody, he has in possession the pretend kidnappers' cache of narcotics; therefore, they turn into the real thing to regain their illegal goods. After Celia is safely returned home, her brother Leon explains her seemingly bizarre behavior. Both Leon and Celia have suffered from Woody's stardom; Celia's running away was her way of communicating her need for her father's love. Leon had had the same need when he was Celia's age; however, like MC he had his music to substitute for his absent parent. Leon says: "What it boils down to is Celia's gotten a taste of what it's like to have a father who's around, physically anyway, but who isn't available to her." After an emotional scene in which Celia confesses her collusion in the kidnapping, Woody tells her: "I might've been away from you guys for a long, long time, but you can bet your little bottom that I'm back now." Woody understands he must become a responsible father—and realizes that it might prove to be a harder job than being a superstar.

Woody's problems are not restricted to his children. Woody and his wife, Dixie, are having problems communicating "peaceably"; they have been married long enough to perfect the art of

Dust jacket for Young's 1980 novel about a black family united by the self-fabricated kidnapping of a fifteen-year-old girl

getting on each other's nerves. Even at a dinner commemorating Dixie's thirty-fifth birthday they cannot stop bickering; even after good sex they cannot stop fighting. Dixie fears some other woman has him "steamed up." The problem is that they have been married too long and need a little break from each other. Dixie goes to Reno for a few days and Woody, alone, has the chance to sow his wild oats. However, when he has the opportunity for an easy tryst, he opts for fidelity. He needs the temptation of infidelity to realize he is happy in his marriage.

The novel closes with father and son coming together by playing basketball. For Young physical activity is a source of release from the tensions of a highly industrialized and sedentary society. Yet it is more than this: when Woody was a professional athlete, basketball separated him from his family; now in his retirement, it brings him together with his son. Woody has come home to his family and likes being there.

In the past twelve years Young has produced a significant body of work in an unusually broad variety of genres: novels, poems, short stories, and recently, a musical memoir—*Bodies & Soul*. He has created an impressive gallery of well-rounded and three-dimensional realistic protagonists who belie ethnic stereotyping. In sum, Al Young has captured much of the beauty and complexity of black life and black speech in his impressive and extensive oeuvre.

Interviews:

"Al Young," in *Interviews with Black Writers*, edited by John O'Brien (New York: Liveright, 1973), pp. 259-269;

Nathaniel Mackey, "Interview with Al Young," *MELUS*, 5 (Winter 1978): 32-51;

Katharine Ogden, "Interview with Al Young," *San Francisco Review of Books*, 6 (August 1979): 9-12;

William J. Harris, "Interview with Al Young," *Greenfield Review* 10 (Summer/Fall 1982): 1-19.

References:

Alan Cheuse, "Woody's Comeback: *Ask Me Now*," *New York Times Book Review*, 6 July 1980, pp. 9, 20;

Neil Schmitz, "Snakes: Words to the Music," *Paunch*, 35 (February 1972): 44;

Mel Watkins, "Lookin for that something else: *Sitting Pretty*," *New York Times Book Review*, 23 May 1976, pp. 3-9.

Appendix

Afro-American Literary Critics:
An Introduction

Darwin T. Turner

Each year, increasing numbers of American readers are becoming familiar with and often enthusiastic about black creative writers. White scholars, critics, and students fret anxiously about the probable date of Ellison's next novel. They debate the value of Gwendolyn Brooks's latest style. They choose sides to support or attack Eldridge Cleaver's repudiation of James Baldwin. Without hesitation, reasonably knowledgeable readers could rattle off names of black writers who have earned national attention and acclaim in various literary genres and fields. If, however, one wanted to silence the chatter, he would need merely to ask for the names of black literary critics; for, even in this decade of discovery of black culture, Afro-American critics remain blackly invisible. Few are known among the general reading public; and perhaps only one—Nathan Scott, Jr.—is judged to be both eminent and influential.

Even when their subject has been literature by Afro-American writers, black critics have failed to make America see them, to say nothing of reading or hearing their words. The best-known critics of Afro-American literature are white. White Vernon Loggins, author of *The Negro Author* (1931); Robert Bone, author of *The Negro Novel in America* (1952, 1965); and Herbert Hill, editor of *Soon, One Morning* (1963) and *Anger and Beyond* (1966), are better known than black Hugh Gloster or Saunders Redding. The fact is ironic and regrettable, since black American critics can offer insights into the language, styles, and meanings intended by black writers, insights frequently denied to those who have not shared the experience of living as black people in the United States of America.

The irony cannot be overemphasized. Many Americans today read black writers with the hope of learning who black people are, what they think, and what they propose to be. These readers, however, seem not to comprehend that they will never understand blacks as long as they seek such understanding *solely* in judgments, evaluations, and interpretations made by others who are equally distant from the black experience. The individual who wishes to understand the literature of black people must know the ablest interpreters of that literature.

Many superficial explanations for the apparent dearth of eminent black critics have been whispered at one time or another: Afro-Americans do not write well; or they cannot write objectively about the work of other blacks; or they cannot think abstractly and formulate critical theories. Since these explanations are illogical and easily disproved, let us consider some of the actual reasons before turning to a history of the Afro-American critics themselves.

An established critic in a field is not necessarily the individual who has written the best work on a particular subject; instead, he is the individual who is most widely known for writing on that subject. This one fact, more than any other, has segregated black critics into the basement of the club of literary criticism: the masses of literate Americans do not read the publications of black critics and, consequently, do not know them.

Where does one look for a literary critic? He reads respected newsstand periodicals: *The Saturday Review, The New York Review of Books,* the New York *Times;* or, in years past, *Dial, The Atlantic,* or *The Nation.* He looks in the nationally known "little" magazines, such as *Poetry* or *The Kenyon Review.* He studies the anthologies of literary criticism, and he notes the names of editors of anthologies of literature. He scrutinizes the journals of the professional associations—*PMLA, American Literature, Shakespeare Quarterly,* for example. He attends lectures at the large universities and at the annual meetings of academic societies. In such arenas as these, one would expect to discover more literary critics than he could read or listen to in a lifetime.

But, except for rare individuals, the critics in these sources are white. Few anthologies include criticism by blacks: *The New Negro* (Alain Locke, 1925), *The Negro Caravan* (Sterling Brown *et al.,* 1941), *Soon, One Morning* (Herbert Hill, 1963), *Anger and Beyond* (Hill, 1966), *Images of the Negro in America* (Darwin T. Turner and Jean Bright, 1965), *Black Voices* (Abraham Chapman, 1968), *Images of the Negro in American Literature* (Seymour Gross and John Hardy, 1966), *Black Fire* (LeRoi Jones and

Larry Neal, 1968), *Black Expression* (Addison Gayle, Jr., 1969), *Black American Literature: Essays* (Turner, 1969). Most of these anthologies have been published within the past five years; and, significantly, of the eight anthologies during that half decade, four have been edited by white men. Few blacks have been hired into the white world of professional journalism as critics or columnists (the William Stanley Braithwaites and Carl Rowans are rare), and few white readers have searched the back pages of black newspapers for critical reviews. In general, the blacks who are invited to review for nationally known periodicals are those who have distinguished themselves as creative writers rather than as critics. They are such men as Langston Hughes, Ralph Ellison, James Baldwin, and Arna Bontemps. Until recently, few black scholars were hired on the staffs of large universities even as visiting lecturers—the Hugh Glosters, Sterling Browns, and Alain Lockes of previous decades were conspicuous. From 1949 to 1965, no more than two or three black scholars read papers at the annual meeting of the Modern Language Association, and only a few more appeared on programs of the National Council of Teachers of English. In fact, as recently as 1939, black scholars felt that they had so little opportunity to present papers at the regional or national Modern Language Association meetings that they formed an organization for black teachers of language and literature—the College Language Association. In short, black critics have been denied opportunity to present their works in the most respected media—or at least they have not been encouraged to contribute.

These facts, however, do not entirely absolve blacks of the responsibility for failing to produce more critics. Afro-American professional journalism has failed to develop and promote a literary market. *Negro Digest,* now called *The Black World,* (1942-51, 1961 to date) has been the most enduring among the commercial magazines that devote significant space to literature, but the Johnson Publishing Company has not given the *Digest* support equal to that for *Ebony* and *Jet.* Black commercial publishers have alleged that they would waste money if they attempted to promote literary culture among the disinterested black masses. (One wonders how these publishers explain the fact that, with little advertising and limited distribution, Broadside Press has managed, in two years, to sell fifty-six thousand copies of the poetry of Don Lee.)

Many white commercial publishers have similar reservations about the cultural interests of Americans, even though their potential market is eight times as large. Among whites, however, a substantial amount of literary criticism is published within the academic world. Here, too, black Americans have failed to promote literary scholarship as effectively as might be expected. Most major universities sponsor publishing companies which promote the university's reputation within the academic community and simultaneously provide platforms for the university's scholars. In contrast, although many predominantly Negro colleges have offered courses and even majors in printing and journalism, very few have attempted to publish anything more scholarly than a catalogue and a schedule of classes. Even though any one of these colleges may complain that high costs and a limited market militate against establishing an individual publishing company, it seems feasible for several black colleges to pool their resources to form a combined press.

Equally significant is the failure of black institutions to promote journals. Relatively small white universities have sponsored journals that have gained respect; but, at black colleges, such journals—when attempted—have rarely endured for more than an issue or two: the *Journal of Negro Education* at Howard University, *Phylon* at Atlanta University, and the *Journal of Human Relations* at Central State College in Ohio are perhaps the most successful. And the College Language Association is the only professional association for blacks to give attention primarily to literature. Furthermore, no enduring journal has concentrated on the study and promotion of Afro-American contributions in the arts. *Phylon* probably has achieved more toward this end than any other journal, but *Phylon* has reflected the social-science orientation that might be expected from a periodical established by W. E. B. Du Bois.

Finally, black scholars know how the fifteen-hour teaching schedule has buried research under mounds of freshman composition and how the small pay checks have driven potential critics into administrative positions merely to gain reasonable compensation for their drudgery.

After this pessimistic review of the problems of Afro-American literary critics, it may seem amazing that any have existed. And in limited space, I can do little more than name a few of the more prolific and to consider their practices briefly. I wish to give special attention to the Afro-American critics who have written about literature by blacks, and I shall include both literary historians and critics under the rubric of "critic." For convenience of discussion, I shall oversimplify by categorizing the historians and critics in six groups: (1) Afro-Americans who have become identified primarily with the "mainstream" of American criticism because of their research in the work of white authors; (2) black historians who have described literary achievements merely as a part of their broader study of Afro-American culture; (3) those individuals who have attracted attention because of their pronouncements about one particular black writer or one group of writers; (4) the creative writers, whose fame rests upon their own work rather than upon their criticism; (5) the academic critics, and (6) the new black critics, who argue for a Black Aesthetic. This survey is not definitive but suggestive: it is an introduction to a study that needs to be made.

i.

Some Afro-Americans have earned recognition primarily by writing about literature by whites. Probably the first such successful critic was William Stanley Braithwaite, a Bostonian black man of West Indian ancestry. A professional journalist, Braithwaite from 1913 to 1929 edited an annual anthology of magazine verse. In introductions to these volumes, Braithwaite directed attention to young white poets who had not yet been recognized by American critics. One should not look to Braithwaite for objective criticism, however. Generally, he assumed the role of a sociable master of ceremonies, introducing his protégés, rejoicing in their virtues, and abstaining from caustic condemnation. Although he published only one volume of criticism, *The Poetic Year,* a collection of essays about the poetry of 1916, he wrote a biography of the Brontë sisters, and he edited anthologies of Elizabethan, Georgian, and Restoration verse.

A second critic who published before World War I was Benjamin Brawley. Although his principal reputation today is based on his studies of black cultural history, Brawley, a professor at Morehouse College, Shaw University, and Howard University, also wrote *A Short History of English Literature,* designed for use in college classes. In taste, Brawley was a Victorian, in the conservative and genteel sense in which that term is understood. He preferred writers who wrote of beauty rather than squalor; and in his own biographical work he ignored those activities of his subjects that he could not commend. Although he must be mentioned at this point, Brawley will be considered more fully in a later section of this paper.

Some more-recent scholars have earned wider recognition for their publications about white authors than for their studies of blacks. For example, although Philip Butcher, a professor at Morgan State College, has written articles about young black novelists, he is better known for his two biographies of George Washington Cable, a nineteenth-century white novelist. Similarly, Esther Merle Jackson, recently a Fulbright professor at the University of Berlin and currently a professor at the University of Wisconsin, is better known as the author of a brilliant book-length study of Tennessee Williams than as a critic of black literature.

The contemporary black critic who is most firmly anchored in the mainstream is Nathan A. Scott, professor of theology at the University of Chicago, whose race is unknown to many of his ardent admirers. Scott occasionally has written about Afro-American literature, a field in which he is very knowledgeable. His best piece in black literary criticism is "The Dark and Haunted Tower of Richard Wright" (1964), one of the few articles commending Richard Wright as an existentialist. Nathan Scott's reputation, however, is based on such books as *Rehearsals of Discomposure* (1952) and *Modern Literature and the Religious Frontier* (1958), excellent works in which he examined philosophical and psychological dilemmas as they are revealed in the fiction of such writers as Kafka, Silone, Lawrence, and Eliot.

As was stated earlier, however, most of the attention in this paper will be focused on those black literary historians and critics who have been especially concerned with studies of black literature.

ii.

Criticism of black writers as a group is a relatively new venture. It was necessary, first, for black writers to produce a considerable body of literature and, second, for black and white critics to develop awareness that that work could be examined as literature rather than merely as sociology. As early as 1863, William Wells Brown included Phillis Wheatley among the black heroes whose lives he recorded in *The Black Man: His Antecedents, His Genius, and His Achievements.* Almost one half century later, Benjamin Brawley produced a pioneer work, *The Negro in Literature and Art* (1910). Like Brown, Brawley offered more biography than critical evaluation. Perceiving America's ignorance about black writers, Brawley chiefly assumed the responsibility of familiarizing readers with them; hence, he remained more historian than critic.

By the middle of the 1920s, the two requisite forces—an ample volume of work by black writers,

and readers' respect for that work as literature—
had coalesced. Therefore, most significant criticism
of Afro-American literature dates from that time.

Prominent among the black scholars since
1925 who have earned reputations for knowledge
of black literature, have been several whose major
interests lay in other disciplines. The first of these
was W. E. B. Du Bois, who earned his doctorate
from Harvard in history. Although he did not publish any books of criticism, Du Bois, as the first
editor of *The Crisis,* regularly commented on the
work of black writers. Unfortunately, during the
1920s, one of the most exciting periods in the annals
of Afro-American literature, Du Bois proved incapable of shedding the ideals of an earlier generation. Like most black intellectuals of the last decade
of the nineteenth century, Du Bois sought to earn
equality for black Americans by educating white
Americans to awareness of their virtues and their
sensitivity to oppression. A talented writer who
judged creative literature to be a major vehicle for
such education, Du Bois was appalled by some black
writers of the twenties who seemed to sully the black
man's image by revealing the squalid aspects of
Afro-American life and character.

Few men, if any, have had greater success than
Alain Locke in familiarizing America with the culture of black people. Although he earned a doctorate from Harvard in philosophy, served for
many years as chairman of the Philosophy Department at Howard University, and published studies
in philosophy, Locke used his compendious knowledge and his aesthetic sensitivity to art, music, and
literature as a basis for many articles and books
about black culture. In 1925, he edited *The New
Negro,* an anthology that is still respected as the best
introduction to the temper and art of the early years
of the Negro Awakening. He was the first to edit an
anthology of Afro-American drama, *Plays of Negro
Life* (1927). He edited one of the earliest critical
anthologies of poetry, *Four Negro Poets* (1927). For
more than twenty years, he annually reviewed literature of black Americans—first in *Opportunity,* then
in *Phylon.* Like Braithwaite, he applauded more
than he appraised; for his purpose was to record
literary achievement and to encourage additional
activity.

More recent historians of Afro-American literature are John Hope Franklin, Margaret Just
Butcher, and Ernest Kaiser. In *From Slavery to Freedom* (1948, 1956), Franklin, professor of history at
the University of Chicago, commented on Afro-
American writers as part of the cultural history of
black America. Margaret Butcher, a professor at

Federal City College, included appraisals of literary
works in *The Negro in American Culture* (1956), which
she developed from notes and materials that Alain
Locke had compiled. Ernest Kaiser, librarian at the
Schomburg Collection in New York City, is best
known as the author of brilliant essays on black
scholarship in history. In addition, Kaiser, who is
incredibly knowledgeable about literature by and
about Afro-Americans, has written perceptively
about current black writers. His work is frequently
published in *Negro Digest* and in *Freedomways,* for
which he regularly reviews recent books by and
about blacks.

All these cultural historians have played important roles by familiarizing Americans with the
names and works of black writers; but, because of
their training and their purpose, they had no desire
to provide for individual works or individual authors the kind of in-depth examination that is essential to literary criticism.

iii.

A few essayists have become known as critics
chiefly because of their evaluation of one writer or
one group. It may be unfair to place Harold Cruse
in this category, for *The Crisis of the Negro Intellectual*
(1967) is now judged on its own merits. Nevertheless, when the book was first published, the criticism
Cruse had written for magazines was not known
widely; consequently, his name was less familiar
than were the names of black writers he attacked
and black scholars whose critical theories he de-
nounced. It is probable, therefore, that much of the
early reaction to the book was stimulated by general
interest in Cruse's assault on such writers as Lorraine Hansberry and John Killens. Similarly, the
first international recognition of James Baldwin as a
critic came in response to "Everybody's Protest
Novel," which seemed to question the artistic competence of Richard Wright, who was then the most
famed and respected among Afro-American
novelists. As the wheel turns and attacker becomes
the attacked, it is fashionable today to quote Eldridge Cleaver's denunciation of Baldwin in *Soul on
Ice* (1968).

What is startling about these few instances is
the apparent eagerness of the reading public to
accept instantly the scathing pronouncements of an
individual who had no previous reputation as a
critic or who at least lacked a literary reputation
comparable to that of the writer he rejected. The
reason for this phenomenon, I believe, is that, despite fifty years of criticism of Afro-American liter-

ature, criteria for that criticism have not been established. Consequently, some readers judge literature by Afro-Americans according to its moral value, a few for its aesthetic value, most by its social value, and too many according to their responses to the personalities of the black authors. As long as this confusion continues, many readers, lacking confidence in their own ability to distinguish the worthwhile black literature from the inept, echo the most recent voice they hear.

iv.

When a white publisher has wanted a black man to write about Afro-American literature, the publisher generally has turned to a famous creative writer. The reason is obvious. White publishers and readers have not been, and are not, familiar with the names and work of black scholars—the academic critics. Therefore, publishers have called upon the only blacks they have known—the famous writers.

Since all the best-known black writers and many of the less well-known have been asked or permitted to serve as historian, critic, or polemicist, only a minimal summary of their work is possible in a paper as brief as this.

In 1922, novelist and poet James Weldon Johnson edited an anthology, *The Book of American Negro Poetry* (revised in 1931), for which he wrote an excellent critical introduction to black poets. From 1926 to 1928, Countee Cullen, best-known Afro-American poet of his day, wrote randomly about literary topics in "The Black Tower," published monthly in *Opportunity.* In 1927, he, too, prepared an anthology of poetry, *Caroling Dusk,* for which he provided an introduction and headnotes. Both Johnson and Cullen, however, are suspect as critics. Like many other authors, they sometimes devised theory to defend their personal practices. Nevertheless, both gave more attention to aesthetic theory than was common among Afro-American critics.

During the twenties, novelist Wallace Thurman received frequent invitations to write articles about fiction. From the thirties until his death in the sixties, Langston Hughes probably received more requests to write about Afro-American authors than any other black writer prior to James Baldwin. Most often, Hughes described personalities rather than works, or he recited the problems of black writers. It is difficult to determine whether Hughes chose to restrict his writing in this manner, or, more probably, whether these were the subjects of prime interest to the soliciting editors. In the forties, Richard Wright was the one whom editors called for

articles; and, when he chose, he produced as effectively in literary history as in fiction. One of the most perceptive analyses by an Afro-American writer is Wright's long essay on black poets, "The Literature of the Negro in the United States," published first in a French journal and later included in Wright's *White Man! Listen* (1957). In the essay, Wright describes the poets since Phillis Wheatley, and scrutinizes their relationships to American society.

The two best-known writer-critics are James Baldwin and Ralph Ellison, who come closer than any others to being the professional critics among black writers. A professional critic, as I use the term, is a man who earns his living primarily by writing about literature; for example, Brooks Atkinson, for years drama critic for the New York *Times,* or Edmund Wilson or George Jean Nathan. To survive, a professional critic normally must be associated with a newspaper or magazine; a free-lance critic risks starvation. (And, as I have said earlier, few blacks have been hired on the staffs of periodicals or dailies.) Nevertheless, Baldwin, in his early years in Paris, gambled at being a free-lance writer on literary subjects even before he became famous as a novelist. He included many of his better essays in *Notes of a Native Son* (1955) and *Nobody Knows My Name* (1961). Ralph Ellison also distinguished himself as a free-lance writer on literary and musical topics. Some of his more significant essays are included in his collection *Shadow and Act* (1964).

A writer-critic in great demand at the moment is Arna Bontemps, one of the last of the talented writers of the Harlem Renaissance. By preference and by invitation, Bontemps most frequently writes nostalgically and illuminatingly about the twenties and thirties. Although he has published many novels and anthologies, Bontemps has published no books of literary history, an oversight one hopes he will correct.

v.

The most significant group of black literary critics should be the academic critics, for these are the individuals trained to study and evaluate literature. They have the breadth of information to facilitate comparison of American writers with foreign ones and comparison of current writers with those of previous centuries. Unfortunately, because they have published most often for small printing houses or in professional journals (often those read by few whites), the academic critics are the least well-known of black critics.

The first major academic critic was Benjamin

Brawley, whose early efforts were designed to promote appreciation rather than evaluation. For example, in his critical biography of Paul Laurence Dunbar (1936), Brawley deliberately ignored personal failings of the man, and minimized many of Dunbar's weaknesses as a writer. When the writers of the twenties appeared, Brawley, like Du Bois, revealed himself unable to adapt to the tastes of a new generation: He continued to echo the precepts of Matthew Arnold. Complaining about what he believed to be the young writers' unnecessary interest in the ugliness of life, he argued that they lacked the high moral purpose essential to great literature. Perhaps the most accurate measure of Brawley's literary taste is the fact that he selected as Dunbar's best story a highly sentimental one in which a husband decides to remain with his wife because he is thrilled by the tenderness with which their newly born child clutches his hand.

Despite his deficiencies in criticism, Brawley was the first significant academic critic-historian of Afro-American literature. The next was Sterling Brown, younger than Brawley but his contemporary as a teacher at Howard University. Brown is the dean of black academic critics. No other black critic has inspired as much admiration and respect from his students and his successors in the field. In every stream of creative black literature, Sterling Brown is the source to which critics return. His first published critical books were *The Negro in American Fiction* (1937), a detailed examination of the Afro-American as a character, and *The Negro in Poetry and Drama* (1937). An almost unknown classic is his unpublished study of Afro-American drama, which he undertook as part of the Myrdal-Carnegie research project. Brown was the senior editor of *The Negro Caravan* (1941), the most comprehensive anthology of Afro-American letters that has been published. Unlike Brawley, Brown understood the need to evaluate the image of the black man as character and the achievement of the black man as writer. Brown has published no books since 1941, although he continued until recently to publish infrequent articles on folk tales, folklore, and folk speech. As a critic, Brown benefited from catholic taste and sensitivity, which enabled him to appreciate and applaud the realistic as well as the genteel, the folk as well as the sophisticated.

The best single volume of criticism by a black, I believe, is Saunders Redding's *To Make a Poet Black* (1939). A brilliant writer, the author of history, an autobiography, a novel, and a collection of essays, Redding, now a professor at Georgetown University, studied writers from Jupiter Hammon through

those of the twenties. His insights are striking, and his style is admirable. This is a book to read; it is regrettable that Redding has not revised the book to bring it up to the present.

In the 1930s and the 1940s, two other academic critics—Nick Ford and Hugh Gloster—published book-length studies of Afro-American literature. Ford examined twentieth-century fiction in *The Contemporary Negro Novel* (1936). Gloster's *Negro Voices in American Fiction* (1948)—the more detailed of the two—focuses on the Afro-American writers' depiction of the relationship of their black characters to the American scene. Gloster, however, was concerned more with sociological import than with aesthetic quality.

The forties and fifties spawned numerous Afro-American critics who published in *Phylon*, the *College Language Association Journal*, and other professional periodicals. Among the most productive of these were John Lash, Blyden Jackson, and Nick Ford. All three, at various times, prepared the annual review of Negro literature for *Phylon*, but also published frequently in other journals. All three concentrated on fiction. Criticism of poetry is surprisingly sparse during the period, and criticism of drama is almost non-existent.

A characteristic common to all these critics—and one that Harold Cruse denounces—is the tendency to evaluate literature by black writers according to the criteria established and approved for white American writers. In one sense, this standard is justifiable, for most of the black writers, in their effort to earn respect, initiated the styles supposedly approved. But this insistence encouraged excessively enthusiastic praise of writers working within tradition, and suspicion of the few who broke away from tradition.

vi.

For a decade, there was a hiatus in criticism by the academicians. Many of the black scholars drifted into administrative positions to secure financial rewards commensurate with their ability. Others abandoned Afro-American literature because they believed that black writers had finally become part of the mainstream of American literature. During this period—roughly, 1954 to 1965—significant social changes occurred. The Supreme Court desegregation decision of 1954 at first seemed to assure Afro-Americans the equality they had desired. Consequently, many black educators considered it deplorable and un-American to study Negro identity apart from

American identity. However, by 1960, only six years later, it was evident that school integration had not produced the anticipated amalgamation. Meanwhile, intensifying insistence from black Americans persuaded blacks and whites to want to learn more about Afro-American culture and history.

This impulse has produced two developments. The first is the emergence of a new generation of academic critics and a return of many who had discontinued their studies about Afro-American literature: James Emanuel, W. Edward Farrison, Addison Gayle, Stephen Henderson, and George Kent are among the currently productive writers. Richard Long, Helen Johnson, and Richard Barksdale are perfecting studies intended for publication. Of these, only Emanuel and Farrison have written books of criticism—Emanuel, a biography of Langston Hughes (1967), and Farrison, a biography of William Wells Brown (1969). Gayle, however, has published two anthologies of criticism by Afro-Americans—*Black Expression* (1969) and this volume on the Black Aesthetic and a collection of essays *The Black Situation* (1970).

The second development is perhaps more significant. A new group of black critics has developed. These reject the standards previously applied to works by Afro-Americans, and are demanding that that literature be judged according to an aesthetic grounded in Afro-American culture. Many of these critics that insist, to have value, black literature must contribute to the revolutionary cause of black liberation, not merely in polemics against white oppression but also in reinterpretation of the black experience. All the new critics agree that the literature should not be judged good or bad according to its imitation of the styles and tastes of Europeans, but according to its presentation of the styles and traditions stemming from African and Afro-American culture. For example, they point out the foolishness of expecting iambic meter in work of a poet who moves instead to the rhythms of jazz or be-bop, and they argue that it is supercilious or even racist to complain that literature does not conform to the patterns and tastes of the white literary world if it does suit and meet the needs of black people.

None of these critics has yet produced a book; they were given platforms originally by Hoyt Fuller of *Negro Digest* and John Henrik Clarke of *Freedomways*. More recently, they have been publishing in newer magazines. The best-known are LeRoi Jones and Larry Neal, who coedited *Black Fire* (1968). Jones is known as a writer of the new literature; Neal has been more productive as an exponent of the theories of the new literature. Others of signifi-

cance are Clarence Major, editor of *New Black Poetry* (1969); Carolyn Rodgers, whose "Black Poetry—Where It's At" (*Negro Digest,* 1969) is the best essay on the work of new black poets; Sarah Fabio; Cecil Brown, author of a recent novel, *The Life and Loves of Mr. Jive-Ass Nigger;* and Ed Bullins, the leading interpreter of current black theater.

It is important that these new critics are explaining theory rather than merely commenting on practice. Previously, as I have said, most Afro-American critics assumed that the desirable standards were necessarily those currently favored by the American literary establishment. This attitude inevitably restricted black writers to imitation rather than innovation: the "good" writer was expected to use the forms and styles that appealed to white readers. And he dared not aspire to the avant-garde, because he needed assurance that the style was approved. In a sense, then, he continued to permit himself to be defined by the white American. Today, however, black critics are postulating theories about what literature is or should be for black people, according to a Black Aesthetic, as was explained in a recent issue of *Negro Digest.*

The writings of these theorists and critics are not hammering at the consciousness of the American literary masses, because most new critics are not attempting to publish in the journals subscribed to predominantly by whites. Most are publishing in *Negro Digest, Journal of Black Poetry, Critique, The Black Scholar, Black Theater,* and other popular publications aimed at a black market. One who wishes to learn what the new black critics are doing and saying must read such journals as these.

At present, the major weakness of the Black Aesthetic critics are their tendencies to denigrate older black writers while lauding the newest. They are further handicapped by the necessity of devising theory prior to the creation of works. That is, Aristotle actually did little more than examine works he and other Greeks admired. He distinguished the elements these works shared. Then he stipulated that great literature must include such elements. Arnold, too, deduced his theories from literature already created. Many new black critics, however, are structuring theories while calling for writers to create the works that are needed to demonstrate the excellence of the theories. It is not accidental, therefore, that most of the new critics are writers. And because their social theories are as revolutionary as their literary theories, few are permanently connected with the well-established academic institutions.

It is always dangerous to predict the future for

any group of writers; nevertheless, a few guesses can be made about future directions of black critics. First, as increasing numbers of predominantly white institutions hire black instructors, and as additional money is given to black institutions, black scholars will find the time, the motivation, and the connections for publishing. This means that they will be producing increasing numbers of books about both white and black writers. As their publications increase, more black critics will become recognized and respected.

Second, as some of the present ferment subsides, the new black critics will look more closely at the current black writers. They will begin to evaluate more carefully on aesthetic bases, as Carolyn Rodgers is now doing. Perhaps by that time, or soon afterwards, they will have expanded American critical theory to a degree at which Americans can more fully appreciate poetry that depends on oral presentation and can appreciate drama that involves less physical action than has been the custom in the Anglo-American theatre. In short, the new black critics may develop theory that may become influential in the evaluation of all American literature.

I would like to conclude on this note of optimism. But I cannot. The chances are great that unless America changes drastically within the next few years, most American readers will continue to look at literature through the eyes of the white critics rather than the black. Full awareness of black critics will develop only when publishers make greater effort to look beyond the prestige colleges for authors of scholarly books, and when the literary public learns to look beyond the prestige journals for literary scholarship. And full appreciation of the criticism of Afro-American literature will develop only when all readers perceive that a thorough knowledge and understanding of the Afro-American experience, culture, and literary history is a prerequisite for an individual who wishes to be a critic of that literature.

Reprinted from *The Black Aesthetic,* edited by Addison Gayle, Jr. (Garden City: Doubleday, 1971).

Books for Further Reading

The American Negro Writer and His Roots. Selected papers from The First Conference of American Negro Writers, March 1959. New York: American Society of African Culture, 1960.

Baker, Houston A., Jr. *The Journey Back: Issues in Black Literature and Criticism.* Chicago: University of Chicago Press, 1980.

Baker. *Singers of Daybreak: Studies in Black American Literature.* Washington, D.C.: Howard University Press, 1974.

Baker, ed. *Black Literature in America.* New York: McGraw-Hill, 1971.

Baker, ed. *Reading Black: Essays in the Criticism of African, Caribbean, and Black American Literature.* Ithaca: Cornell University Africana Studies and Research Center, 1976.

Barthold, Bonnie J. *Black Time: Fiction of Africa, the Caribbean, and the United States.* New Haven, Conn.: Yale University Press, 1981.

Bell, Roseann P., Bettye J. Parker, and Beverly Guy-Sheftall, eds. *Sturdy Black Bridges: Visions of Black Women in Literature.* New York: Doubleday, 1979.

Bigsby, C. W. E. *The Second Black Renaissance: Essays in Black Literature.* Westport, Conn.: Greenwood, 1980.

Bigsby, ed. *The Black American Writer: Volume 1 – Fiction.* De Land, Fla: Everett/Edwards, 1969.

Bone, Robert A. *The Negro Novel in America,* revised edition. New Haven: Yale University Press, 1965.

Brown, Lloyd W., ed. *The Black Writer in Africa and the Americas.* Los Angeles: Hennessey & Ingalls, 1973.

Bruck, Peter, and Wolfgang Karrer, eds. *The Afro-American Novel since 1960.* Amsterdam: Grüner, 1982.

Chapman, Abraham. *The Negro in American Literature and A Bibliography of American Literature By and About Negro Americans.* Stevens Point: Wisconsin State University, 1966.

Christian, Barbara. *Black Women Novelists: The Development of a Tradition, 1892-1976.* Westport, Conn.: Greenwood, 1980.

Cooke, M. G., ed. *Modern Black Novelists: A Collection of Critical Essays.* Englewood Cliffs, N.J.: Prentice-Hall, 1971.

Davis, Arthur P. *From the Dark Tower: Afro-American Writers 1900 to 1960.* Washington, D. C.: Howard University Press, 1974.

Davis, Charles T. *Black is the Color of the Cosmos: Essays on Afro-American Literature and Culture, 1942-1981.* Edited by Henry Louis Gates, Jr. New York: Garland, 1982.

Deodene, Frank, and William P. French. *Black American Fiction Since 1952; A Preliminary Checklist.* Chatham, N.J.: Chatham Bookseller, 1970.

Dickstein, Morris. "Black Writing and Black Nationalism: Four Generations." In his *Gates of Eden: American Culture in the Sixties*. New York: Basic Books, 1977.

Evans, Mari, ed. *Black Women Writers, 1950-1980: A Critical Evaluation*. Garden City: Doubleday, 1984.

Exum, Pat C., ed. *Keeping the Faith: Writings by Contemporary Black American Women*. Greenwich, Conn.: Fawcett, 1974.

Fisher, Dexter, and Robert B. Stepto, eds. *Afro-American Literature: The Reconstruction of Instruction*. New York: Modern Language Association, 1979.

Gayle, Addison, Jr. *The Black Aesthetic*. Garden City: Doubleday, 1971.

Gayle. *The Way of the New World: The Black Novel in America*. Garden City: Anchor Press, Doubleday, 1975.

Gayle, ed. *Black Expression: Essays By and About Black Americans in the Creative Arts*. New York: Weybright and Talley, 1969.

Gibson, Donald B. *The Politics of Literary Expression: A Study of Major Black Writers*. Westport, Conn.: Greenwood, 1981.

Gross, Seymour L., and John Edward Hardy, eds. *Images of the Negro in American Literature*. Chicago: University of Chicago Press, 1966.

Harper, Michael S., and Robert B. Stepto, eds. *Chant of Saints: A Gathering of Afro-American Literature, Art, and Scholarship*. Urbana: University of Illinois Press, 1979.

Harris, Trudier. *From Mammies to Militants: Domestics in American Literature*. Philadelphia: Temple University Press, 1982.

Hemenway, Robert, ed. *The Black Novelist*. Columbus, Ohio: Charles E. Merrill, 1970.

Hill, Herbert, ed. *Anger, and Beyond: The Negro Writer in the United States*. New York: Harper & Row, 1966.

Houston, Helen Ruth. *The Afro-American Novel, 1965-1975: A Descriptive Bibliography of Primary and Secondary Material*. Troy, N.Y.: Whitston, 1977.

Jackson, Blyden. *The Waiting Years: Essays on American Negro Literature*. Baton Rouge: Louisiana State University Press, 1976.

Jahn, Janheinz. *Neo-African Literature: A History of Black Writing*. New York: Grove Press, 1969.

King, Bruce, and Kolawole Ogungbesan, eds. *A Celebration of Black and African Writing*. Zaria: Ahmadu Bello University Press, 1975; Oxford: Oxford University Press, 1975.

Klotman, Phyllis R. *Another Man Gone: The Black Runner in Contemporary Afro-American Literature*. Port Washington, N.Y.: Kennikat, 1976.

Lee, A. Robert, ed. *Black Fiction: New Studies in the Afro-American Novel Since 1945*. New York: Barnes & Noble, 1980.

Littlejohn, David. *Black on White: A Critical Survey of Writing By American Negroes*. New York: Grossman, 1966.

Margolies, Edward, and David Bakish. *Afro-American Fiction, 1853-1976*. Detroit: Gale, 1979.

Margolies. *Native Sons: A Critical Study of Twentieth-Century Negro American Authors.* Philadelphia & New York: J. B. Lippincott, 1968.

McPherson, James M., et al. *Blacks in America: Bibliographical Essays.* Garden City: Doubleday, 1971.

Miller, Elizabeth W. *The Negro in America: A Bibliography,* second revised edition. Cambridge, Mass.: Harvard University Press, 1970.

Miller, R. Baxter, ed. *Black American Literature and Humanism.* Lexington: University Press of Kentucky, 1981.

O'Brien, John, ed. *Interviews with Black Writers.* New York: Liveright, 1973.

Ostendorf, Berndt. *Black Literature in White America.* New York: Barnes & Noble, 1982.

Page, James A., comp. *Selected Black American Authors: An Illustrated Bio-Bibliography.* Boston: G. K. Hall, 1977.

Payne, Ladell. *Black Novelists and the Southern Literary Tradition.* Athens: University of Georgia Press, 1981.

Peavy, Charles D. *Afro-American Literature and Culture Since World War II: A Guide to Information Sources.* Detroit: Gale, 1979.

Popkin, Michael, ed. *Modern Black Writers.* New York: Ungar, 1978.

Porter, Dorothy B. *The Negro in the United States: A Selected Bibliography.* Washington, D.C.: Library of Congress, 1970.

Schraufnagel, Noel. *From Apology to Protest: The Black American Novel.* De Land, Fla.: Everett/Edwards, 1973.

Spradling, Mary Mace, ed. *In Black and White: Afro-Americans in Print.* Kalamazoo, Mich.: Kalamazoo Library System, 1971.

Stepto, Robert B. *From Behind the Veil: A Study of Afro-American Narrative.* Urbana: University of Illinois Press, 1979.

Studies in the Novel, special issue on American black novelists, 3 (Summer 1971).

Tate, Claudia, ed. *Black Women Writers at Work.* New York: Continuum, 1983.

Werner, Craig Hansen. *Paradoxical Resolutions: American Fiction Since James Joyce.* Urbana: University of Illinois Press, 1982.

Whitlow, Roger. *Black American Literature: A Critical History.* Chicago: Nelson Hall, 1973.

Williams, Sherley Anne. *Give Birth to Brightness: A Thematic Study in Neo-Black Literature.* New York: Dial, 1972.

Contributors

Valerie M. Babb	*Georgetown University*
Jane Ball	*Wilberforce University*
Susan L. Blake	*Lafayette College*
Edith Blicksilver	*Georgia Institute of Technology*
Jean M. Bright	*North Carolina A & T State University*
Mary Hughes Brookhart	*University of North Carolina at Chapel Hill*
Keith E. Byerman	*University of Texas*
Barbara T. Christian	*University of California, Berkeley*
Rita B. Dandridge	*Norfolk State University*
James L. de Jongh	*City College of New York*
Frances Smith Foster	*San Diego State University*
Henry Louis Gates	*Yale University*
Greg Goode	*University of Rochester*
Sandra Y. Govan	*University of North Carolina at Charlotte*
Maryemma Graham	*University of Mississippi*
Johnanna L. Grimes	*Tennessee State University*
Virginia B. Guilford	*Bowie State College*
William J. Harris	*State University of New York at Stony Brook*
Australia Henderson	*GMI Engineering and Management Institute*
Helen R. Houston	*Tennessee State University*
Leota S. Lawrence	*Washington, D.C.*
Carol P. Marsh	*Georgia State University*
Edward G. McGehee	*Montgomery, Alabama*
R. Baxter Miller	*University of Tennessee*
Frank E. Moorer	*University of Iowa*
Margaret Anne O'Connor	*University of North Carolina at Chapel Hill*
Sondra O'Neale	*Emory University*
Margaret Perry	*Valparaiso University*
Marilyn Richardson	*Massachusetts Institute of Technology*
John W. Roberts	*University of Pennsylvania*
Wilfred D. Samuels	*University of Colorado, Boulder*
Valerie Smith	*Princeton University*
Carmen Subryan	*Howard University*
Estelle W. Taylor	*Howard University*
Charles P. Toombs	*Purdue University*
Ronald Walcott	*City University of New York, Kingsborough Community College*
Joe Weixlmann	*Indiana State University*
William H. Wiggins, Jr.	*Indiana University*
Hammett Worthington-Smith	*Albright College*
Richard Yarborough	*University of California, Los Angeles*

REF REF 809 DICT

Afro-American fiction
writers after 1955

$160.00

WITHDRAWN

MUNSTER HIGH SCHOOL
LIBRARY MEDIA CENTER
8808 Columbia Avenue
Munster, Indiana 46321

DEMCO

ISBN 0-8103-1711-7
90000

9 780810 317116